Lecture Notes in Computer Science 2939
Edited by G. Goos, J. Hartmanis, and J. van Leeuwen

AF619533

Dear MyCopy Customer,

This Springer book is a monochrome print version of the eBook to which your library gives you access via SpringerLink. It is available to you at a subsidized price since your library subscribes to at least one Springer eBook subject collection.

Please note that MyCopy books are only offered to library patrons with access to at least one Springer eBook subject collection. MyCopy books are strictly for individual use only.

You may cite this book by referencing the bibliographic data and/or the DOI (Digital Object Identifier) found in the front matter. This book is an exact but monochrome copy of the print version of the eBook on SpringerLink.

Springer-Verlag Berlin Heidelberg GmbH

Ton Kalker Ingemar J. Cox
Yong Man Ro (Eds.)

Digital Watermarking

Second International Workshop, IWDW 2003
Seoul, Korea, October 20-22, 2003
Revised Papers

Series Editors

Gerhard Goos, Karlsruhe University, Germany
Juris Hartmanis, Cornell University, NY, USA
Jan van Leeuwen, Utrecht University, The Netherlands

Volume Editors

Ton Kalker
Philips Research/Technical University Eindhoven
Prof. Holstlaan 4, 5656AA Eindhoven, The Netherlands
E-mail: Ton.Kalker@ieee.org

Ingemar J. Cox
University College London
Department of Computer Science and
Department of Electronic and Electrical Engineering
Torrington Place, London WC1E 7JE, UK
E-mail: ingemar@ee.ucl.ac.uk

Yong Man Ro
Information and Communications University (ICU)
103 - 6 Moonji Dong Yuseong, Daejeon, 305-714, Korea
E-mail: yro@icu.ac.kr

Cataloging-in-Publication Data applied for

A catalog record for this book is available from the Library of Congress.

Bibliographic information published by Die Deutsche Bibliothek
Die Deutsche Bibliothek lists this publication in the Deutsche Nationalbibliografie; detailed bibliographic data is available in the Internet at <http://dnb.ddb.de>.

CR Subject Classification (1998): K.4.1, K.6.5, H.5.1, D.4.6, E.3, E.4, F.2.2, H.3, I.4

ISSN 0302-9743
DOI 10.1007/978-3-540-24624-4

This work is subject to copyright. All rights are reserved, whether the whole or part of the material is concerned, specifically the rights of translation, reprinting, re-use of illustrations, recitation, broadcasting, reproduction on microfilms or in any other way, and storage in data banks. Duplication of this publication or parts thereof is permitted only under the provisions of the German Copyright Law of September 9, 1965, in its current version, and permission for use must always be obtained from Springer-Verlag. Violations are liable for prosecution under the German Copyright Law.

Springer-Verlag is a part of Springer Science+Business Media

springeronline.com

© Springer-Verlag Berlin Heidelberg 2004

MyCopy version of the original edition 2004

Typesetting: Camera-ready by author, data conversion by PTP-Berlin, Protago-TeX-Production GmbH
Printed on acid-free paper SPIN: 10987353 06/3142 5 4 3 2 1 0
www.springer.com/mycopy

Preface

We are happy to present to you the proceedings of the 2nd International Workshop on Digital Watermarking, IWDW 2003. Since its modern re-appearance in the academic community in the early 1990s, great progress has been made in understanding both the capabilities and the weaknesses of digital watermarking.

On the theoretical side, we all are now well aware of the fact that digital watermarking is best viewed as a form of communication using side information. In the case of digital watermarking the side information in question is the document to be watermarked. This insight has led to a better understanding of the limits of the capacity and robustness of digital watermarking algorithms. It has also led to new and improved watermarking algorithms, both in terms of capacity and imperceptibility. Similarly, the role of human perception, and models thereof, has been greatly enhanced in the study and design of digital watermarking algorithms and systems.

On the practical side, applications of watermarking are not yet abundant. The original euphoria on the role of digital watermarking in copy protection and copyright protection has not resulted in widespread usage in practical systems. With hindsight, a number of reasons can be given for this lack of practical applications.

First and foremost, we now know that watermark imperceptibility cannot be equated to watermark security. An information signal that cannot be perceived by the human sensory system is not necessarily undetectable to well-designed software and hardware systems. The existence of watermark readers bears proof of this observation. Designing watermarking methods that are robust to intentional and targeted attacks has turned out to be an extremely difficult task. Improved watermarking methods face more intelligent attacks. More intelligent attacks face improved watermarking methods. This cycle of improved attacks and counterattacks is still ongoing, and it is not foreseen that it will end soon.

Secondly, watermarking methods for copy(right) protection do not operate in an isolated environment, but are in general part of an ambient Digital Rights Management (DRM) system. The integration of digital watermarking into a complete DRM system is still very much a research topic. In particular, a watermarking system need not be stronger than the weakest link of the DRM system into which it is embedded. The identification of that weakest link, and its implications for the design and implementation of digital watermarking methods are not very well understood yet.

It was the goal of IWDW 2003 to update the scientific and content owner community on the state of the art in digital watermarking. To that end, more than 90 submissions to IWDW 2003 were carefully reviewed. Emphasizing high quality and the state of the art, a little over 50% of the submitted papers were selected for oral or poster presentation. The topics that are addressed in the accepted papers cover all the relevant aspects of digital watermarking: theoretical modeling, robustness, capacity, imperceptibility and the human perceptual system, security and attacks, watermarking systems, and implementations and integration into DRM systems. Every effort was made to give the authors the best possible podium to present their finding, be it in an oral or poster presentation.

We hope that you find these proceedings to be a catalyst for your future research.

October, 2003

Ton Kalker
Ingemar Cox
Yong Man Ro

Committee Listings

General Chair

Se Hun Kim (KAIST, Korea)

Advisory Committee

Chieteuk Ahn (ETRI, Korea)
Myung Joon Kim (ETRI, Korea)
Soo Ngee Koh (NTU, Singapore)
Sang Uk Lee (Seoul National University, Korea)
Won Geun Oh (ETRI, Korea)
Paul Seo (KETI, Korea)

Program Committee Chair

Ton Kalker (Philips, The Netherlands)
Ingemar Cox (UCL, UK))

Program Committee Co-chair

Yong Man Ro (ICU, Korea)

Program Committee

Jean-Luc Dugelay (Institute Eurecom, France)
Touradj Ebrahimi (EPFL, Switzerland)
Jessica Fridrich (SUNY Binghamton, USA)
Jinwoo Hong (ETRI, Korea)
Jiwu Huang (Zhongshan Univ., China)
Keiichi Iwamura (Canon, Japan)
Byeungwoo Jeon (Sungkyunkwan University, Korea)
Mohan Kankanhalli (NUS, Singapore)
Eiji Kawaguchi (Kyushu Institute of Technology, Japan)
Hae Yong Kim (Universidade de Sao Paulo, Brazil)
Hyoung Joong Kim (Kangwon National University, Korea)
Reginald L. Lagendijk (TU Delft, The Netherlands)
Deepa Kudur (Texas A&M, USA)
Heung Gyu Lee (KAIST, Korea)
Hong-Yung Mark Liao (Academia Sinica, Taiwan)
Pierre Moulin (University of Illinois at Urbana Champaign, USA)
Ji-Hwan Park (Pukyong National University, Korea)
Soo-Chang Pei (National Taiwan University, Taiwan)
Fernando Perez-Gonzalez (University of Vigo, Spain)

Fabien A.P. Petitcolas (Microsoft Research, UK)
Ioannis Pitas (University of Thessaloniki, Greece)
Alessandro Piva (Universita di Firenze, Italy)
Rei Safavi-Naini (University of Wollongong, Australia)
Kouichi Sakurai (Kyushu University, Japan)
Shan Suthaharan (North Carolina University, USA)
Min Wu (University of Maryland, USA)

Organizing Committee Chair

Chee Sun Won (Dongguk University, Korea)

Table of Contents

Invited Talks

I: DRM I

II: Theory

III: Non-St+Stego

IV: Systems

V: Estimation

VI: Perception+Audio

VII: DRM II

Posters

The Importance of Aliasing in Structured Quantization Index Modulation Data Hiding*

Fernando Pérez-González

Dept. Teoría de la Señal y Comunicaciones, ETSI Telecom.,
Universidad de Vigo, 36200 Vigo, Spain
fperez@tsc.uvigo.es

Abstract. The informed embedding data hiding problem with structured lattice codes is analyzed and the use of aliased probability density functions is proposed for analytical purposes. A formula for the capacity of distortion-compensated quantization index modulation with lattice partitioning is given for the case of equiprobable symbols. The scalar case is analyzed in detail and a novel approximation to the optimal distortion compensation parameter is provided. This approximation has its roots in a Fourier series expansion of the aliased pdf's that is introduced here. Finally, the case of general additive attacks is studied, showing that for the scalar case with equiprobable (and possibly infinite) symbols, Gaussian noise does not minimize capacity.

1 Introduction and Problem Formulation

The Data Hiding field has blossomed out in the last few years, due to the contributions from experts in areas such as Signal Processing, Digital Communications, Statistics and Information Theory. In particular, it can be said that Digital Communications furnished the theoretical background that was necessary in the late 90's for the development of watermarking as a discipline. However, despite the fact that some of these concepts are now routinely used, it is somehow perceived that with the advent of informed embedding methods [1], [2], new analytical tools not originally developed for digital communications must be sought. Certainly, while ideas such as that of distortion compensation [3] have proven to be crucial for quantization-based schemes, structured embedding closely resembles the so-called *precoding* problem, long known to digital communications researchers [4] and from where some useful analytical ideas, that will be perused in this paper can be drawn [5]. The main purpose of this paper is to show how the use of structured quantizers for informed data hiding gives raise to the concept of "aliased" probability density functions, and to provide some novel consequences with theoretical value.

Next, we will introduce some quantities and notation that will be used throughout the paper. Let $\mathbf{x}$ be a vector containing the N samples of the host

* Work partially funded by *Xunta de Galicia* under grants PGIDT01 PX132204PM and PGIDT02 PXIC32205PN; CYCIT, AMULET project, reference TIC2001-3697-C03-01; and FIS, IM3 Research Network, reference FIS-G03/185 .

T. Kalker et al. (Eds.): IWDW 2003, LNCS 2939, pp. 1–17, 2004.
© Springer-Verlag Berlin Heidelberg 2004

signal that will convey the hidden information; these vector samples are taken in a certain domain of interest that in the case of images may be the spatial, discrete cosine transform (DCT), discrete wavelet transform (DWT), etc. We make the hypothesis that the samples of vector $\mathbf{x}$ are independent and identically distributed (i.i.d.) random variables with zero-mean and variance $\frac{1}{N}E\{\mathbf{x}^T\mathbf{x}\} = \sigma_x^2$.

Typically, the watermark vector $\mathbf{w}$ is obtained using a cryptographic key known to the embedder and the decoder. Although in modern data hiding methods the characteristics of the Human Visual System are exploited when generating $\mathbf{w}$ aiming at guaranteeing transparency, here we will consider the embedding strength constant along the available coefficients with the sole purpose of making the exposition clear. In data hiding applications, $\mathbf{w}$ is a function of the desired information message m. Also, without loss of generality we will write the watermarked signal as the addition $\mathbf{y} = \mathbf{x} + \mathbf{w}$.

One way of measuring the amount of energy devoted to the watermark is to use a Mean-Squared Error (MSE) distortion, denoted by D_w, and which can be defined as $D_w \triangleq \frac{1}{N}E\{\mathbf{w}^T\mathbf{w}\}$, where it has been considered that $\mathbf{w}$ is a random vector representing the watermark. Although the MSE has been sometimes criticized as a good distortion measure, for it cannot be well related to the characteristics of the HVS, we will use this criterion throughout this paper due its manageability and the fact that it has been employed in most of the relevant literature. See [6] for a more in-depth discussion.

Let us introduce the ratio of the host signal variance and the embedding distortion, i.e. $\lambda \triangleq \sigma_x^2/D_w$, that allows us to define the *document-to-watermark ratio* as $\text{DWR} = 10\log_{10}\lambda$. We will also assume that before any attempt to decode the hidden information, the watermarked object undergoes an probabilistic channel with additive noise $\mathbf{n}$ independent of $\mathbf{x}$ and $\mathbf{w}$, yielding a received signal $\mathbf{z} = \mathbf{y} + \mathbf{n}$. This channel models certain attacking operations, that may be unintentional, as it occurs with noise introduced in the print and scan process, or intentional, due to the presence of an active attacker that aims at avoiding that the hidden information be reliably decoded. Obviously, the attacker is also limited in the amount of distortion he/she can introduce so as not to reduce too much the value of the resulting data.

As before, in order to keep the discussion simple, we will assume that the noise $\mathbf{n}$ samples are i.i.d. with zero mean and variance σ_n^2. As we will see, it is necessary to measure the amount of *attacking distortion*, which is defined similarly to the embedding distortion, that is, $D_c \triangleq \frac{1}{N}E\{\mathbf{n}^T\mathbf{n}\} = \sigma_n^2$. With regard to the distribution of this noise, the Gaussian probability density function (pdf) has been most commonly used in previous analysis as a test bench for measuring system performance. For this reason, we will deal here mainly with Gaussian attacks, although we will also address the question of other additive attacks. As with the DWR, it will be useful to introduce the following ratio $\xi \triangleq D_w/D_c$, that relates the power of embedding and channel distortions. In addition, we will call *watermark-to-noise ratio* to $\text{WNR} = 10\log_{10}\xi$.

2 Fundamentals of Lattices

Let $\{\mathbf{x}_1, \mathbf{x}_2, \cdots, \mathbf{x}_L\}$ be a set of linearly independent vectors, then the set of points in an N-dimensional Euclidean space having the form

$$\mathbf{x} = \sum_{i=1}^{L} k_i \mathbf{x}_i \tag{1}$$

for any integers k_i, $i = 1, \cdots, L$, defines a *lattice.* A lattice is nothing but a regularly spaced set of points. The number of points is countably infinite. An important observation to be made from (1) is that any lattice must always include the origin, denoted as $\mathbf{0}$.

Lattices are advantageous in source and channel coding applications because 1) they have a fixed minimum distance, 2) they are generated by a vector of integers, being desirable for fixed-point implementations, and 3) algebraically they constitute a group, and this structure can be exploited for both implementation and analysis purposes.

For communications applications, lattices can not be used as such, because the distance of their members to the origin is unbounded. Note that the average transmitted power is proportional to the average distance to the origin. A simple idea is to bound the lattice by means of a finite *shaping region* S, so the set of points actually used for conveying information (i.e., the *constellation*) has the form $\Omega_A = (\Lambda + \mathbf{a}) \cap S$, where Λ is the lattice, and $\mathbf{a}$ is an offset vector that allows to shift the constellation so as to achieve a certain property. For instance, in communications, it is possible to show that from a power consumption point of view, the optimal value of $\mathbf{a}$ is such that the center of masses for the constellation Ω_A lies at the origin.

Associated with a lattice Λ is the nearest-neighbor quantizer $Q_\Lambda(\cdot)$ defined as

$$Q_\Lambda(\mathbf{x}) = \mathbf{c} \in \Lambda, \quad \text{such that } ||\mathbf{x} - \mathbf{c}|| \le ||\mathbf{x} - \mathbf{c}'||, \quad \text{for any } \mathbf{c}' \in \Lambda \tag{2}$$

Essentially, lattice properties depend on two fundamental parameters: the *minimum distance* $d_{min}(\Lambda)$ between points in the lattice, and the *fundamental volume* $V(\Lambda)$, which is the volume of the decision region associated with a particular lattice point. The fundamental volume can be regarded to as the inverse of the number of points per unit volume. We will also let $\Phi(\Lambda)$ denote the *Voronoi region* associated with the zero centroid for the lattice Λ, i.e., $\Phi(\Lambda) = \{\mathbf{x} : Q_\Lambda(\mathbf{x}) = \mathbf{0}\}$.

An idea with important implications for quantization-based data hiding is that of *lattice partitioning.* Given a lattice Λ, a *sublattice* Λ' is a subset of the points in the lattice which is itself a lattice. Related to this concept, given a sublattice Λ' of Λ, one may construct a so-called coset of Λ' as the set

$$\{\lambda' + \mathbf{c} : \lambda' \in \Lambda'\} \tag{3}$$

for some vector $\mathbf{c} \in \Lambda$, which is called *coset representative.* The set of all cosets of Λ' in Λ is called a *partition* of Λ induced by Λ' and is denoted as Λ/Λ'. The *order of the partition* is the number of different cosets and is written as $|\Lambda/\Lambda'| \triangleq D$. It can be shown that $D = V(\Lambda')/V(\Lambda)$. Although partitioning can be carried along further in order to construct a so-called chain of partitions, we will restrict our discussion to the case of a single partition.

3 Quantization Index Modulation with Lattice Partitioning

In this section, we will illustrate how lattices can be used to hide information in an image $\mathbf{x}$ in vector form. Suppose we have an index set $\mathcal{M} \triangleq \{1, \cdots, M\}$. We first select a lattice Λ which can be used as a reasonably good channel code (i.e., in the sphere-packing sense), and partition it by means of a lattice Λ' which gives a reasonably good source code (i.e., in the sphere-covering sense) [7] seeking that $|\Lambda/\Lambda'| = M$. An example with hexagonal lattices is shown in Fig. 1. See [5] and [8] for more details on code construction and asymptotic properties.

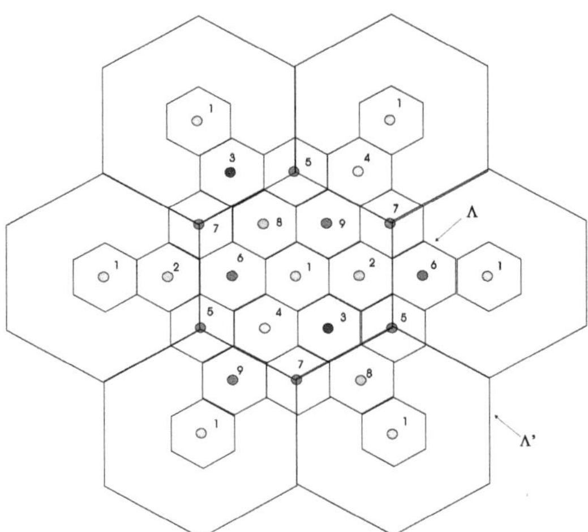

Fig. 1. Hexagonal lattices for QIM. Numbers indicate the coset index associated with the channel code.

Now, in order to send a message $m \in \mathcal{M}$, we select the appropriate coset representative $\mathbf{c}_m \in \Lambda$ and compute $\mathbf{x} - \mathbf{c}_m$. Then, we use the quantizer for Λ' to yield $Q_{\Lambda'}(\mathbf{x} - \mathbf{c}_m)$ and then restore the original coset offset:

$$\mathbf{y} = Q_{\Lambda'}(\mathbf{x} - \mathbf{c}_m) + \mathbf{c}_m \tag{4}$$

The size of the quantizer, and thus the volume of the decision region, depends on the desired average watermarking distortion. Equivalently, a fixed quantizer may be used by properly scaling the input signal.

However, instead of working with a fixed quantizer located at the origin, it is much simpler to think of the set of quantizers, $Q_{\Lambda',\mathbf{c}_i}(\cdot) \triangleq Q_{\Lambda'+\mathbf{c}_i}(\cdot)$, $i = 1, \cdots, M$, so the idea is, given the message $m \in \mathcal{M}$, to simply generate the watermarked image vector $\mathbf{y}$ as

$$\mathbf{y} = Q_{\Lambda',\mathbf{c}_m}(\mathbf{x}) \tag{5}$$

Henceforth we will assume without loss of generality that the coset representative located at the origin is assigned to the first message, i.e., $\mathbf{c}_1 = \mathbf{0}$.

In decoding, given the received vector $\mathbf{z}$, we simply decide the message $\hat{m}$ such that $Q_\Lambda(\mathbf{z}) \in \Lambda' + \mathbf{c}_{\hat{m}}$. This amounts to a minimum distance decoder which is not necessarily optimal in the mimum probability of error sense. Due to the space limitation, here we will not discuss the general form of the optimal decision regions.

From the way the information is embedded, one can see why this scheme is given the name of *quantization index modulation* (QIM): information is sent by just using a particular quantizer. Notice, however, that no actual modulation takes place, so a more proper term would be *quantization index keying.* QIM was proposed by Chen and Wornell in 1999 [1] who rediscovered a forgotten paper by M. Costa [3] which already contains most of the ingredients of present quantization-based methods. For instance, the basic QIM method described here can be largely improved by making use of the concept of *distortion compensation* which was proven by Costa to be indispensable for achieving capacity. Instead of changing $\mathbf{x}$ to the nearest centroid in $Q_{\Lambda',\mathbf{c}_m}(\cdot)$, distortion compensation uses the quantizer to compute an *error vector* that is scaled by a distortion compensating parameter $\nu \in [0, 1]$ which allows to trade off the amount of embedding distortion and the robustness against channel attacks.

The watermarked image vector $\mathbf{y}$ now becomes

$$\mathbf{y} = \mathbf{x} + \nu\left(Q_{\Lambda',\mathbf{c}_m}(\mathbf{x}) - \mathbf{x}\right) \tag{6}$$

so the watermark $\mathbf{w} = \nu(Q_{\Lambda',\mathbf{c}_m}(\mathbf{x}) - \mathbf{x})$ is a fraction of the quantization error.

Equivalently, we can write

$$\mathbf{y} = Q_{\Lambda',\mathbf{c}_m}(\mathbf{x}) + (1-\nu)\left(\mathbf{x} - Q_{\Lambda',\mathbf{c}_m}(\mathbf{x})\right) \triangleq Q_{\Lambda',\mathbf{c}_m}(\mathbf{x}) + \mathbf{s}$$

so the watermarked can be seen as being generated by adding a fraction of the quantization error back to the desired centroid. The term $\mathbf{s}$, can be regarded to as *self-noise*, because it has the effect of moving the watermarked image off the centroid.

Note that if $\mathbf{x}$ were uniformly distributed within the quantization region, the term $\mathbf{s} = (1-\nu)(\mathbf{x} - Q_{\Lambda',\mathbf{c}_m}(\mathbf{x}))$ would be also uniformly distributed inside an identical region scaled by $(1-\nu)$. A consequence of this is that if $(1-\nu)$ is very large, we will no longer obtain zero probability of error in the absence of attacking distortions, because the uniform region will "invade" the neighboring decision regions under $Q_{\Lambda'}(\cdot)$.

If we consider the quantization error, this always lies in this fundamental region

$$\mathbf{e} \triangleq (Q_{\Lambda',\mathbf{c}_m}(\mathbf{x}) - \mathbf{x}) \in \Phi(\Lambda') \tag{7}$$

Equivalently, the following modulo notation can be used

$$\mathbf{e} = (\mathbf{x} - \mathbf{c}_m) \mod \Lambda' \tag{8}$$

One fundamental assumption will ease the derivation of most results that will be presented later on. This assumption states that the host image variance is large when compared to the equivalent side of the fundamental volume for the "coarse" lattice Λ':

$$V^{2/N}(\Lambda') << \sigma_x^2 \tag{9}$$

This assumption is closely related to the requirement of a large DWR which occurs in practice due to the imperceptibility constraint. Two important consequences follow from this fundamental assumption:

- The host image $\mathbf{x}$ may be considered uniform within the quantization cells for Λ', and obviously, for Λ.
- Considering the set of typical values of $\mathbf{x}$, for any coset $\mathbf{c}_i + \Lambda'$ the number of associated centroids occurring with non negligible probabilities is large. Moreover, it may be safely assumed that those centroids occur with identical probabilities.

Once we have defined the basic embedding scheme, refined by means of distortion compensation, and after our fundamental assumption, we can write the embedding distortion as

$$D_w = E\{\nu^2 \mathbf{e}^T \mathbf{e}\} = \frac{\nu^2}{V(\Lambda')} \int_{\Phi(\Lambda')} ||\mathbf{e}||^2 d\mathbf{e} \tag{10}$$

4 Probability of Error

Here we analyze the probability of error that results when the decoder based on the fine lattice is used and messages $m \in \mathcal{M}$ are chosen with identical probabilities. Then, due also to our fundamental assumption, we may assume without loss of generality that message $m = i$ is sent, and that the host signal vector is such that $\mathbf{x} \in \Phi(\Lambda')$. Therefore, $\mathbf{y} = \mathbf{c}_i$. In the sequel, and for the sake of compactness, we will drop the conditioning on the feasible values of $\mathbf{x}$.

An error is made whenever the decoded message $\hat{m} \neq i$. The symbol error probability (SER), P_e, is then

$$P_e = Pr\{\hat{m} \neq i\} = 1 - Pr\{\hat{m} = i\} \tag{11}$$

But now it is important to see that the probability of correct decision is not the probability that the received vector $\mathbf{z}$ lies just outside $\mathbf{c}_i + \Phi(\Lambda)$ (this would rather produce a lower bound), because an infinite number of replicas of the correct centroid will exist. For large watermark to noise ratios we can neglect those replicas, but in robust data hiding negative WNR's are quite possible, so they *must* be taken into account for an accurate analysis.

Thus, the probability of correct decision P_c must be obtained by integrating over all the replicas:

$$P_c = \sum_{\mathbf{v} \in \mathbf{c}_i + \Lambda'} \int_{\mathbf{v}+\Phi(\Lambda)} f_{\mathbf{z}}(\mathbf{z}|m=i) d\mathbf{z} \tag{12}$$

Let us assume an additive attack, so that $\mathbf{z} = \mathbf{y} + \mathbf{n}$, with noise $\mathbf{n}$ independent of the host image and with pdf $f_{\mathbf{n}}(\mathbf{n})$. On the other hand, let $f_{\mathbf{s}}(\mathbf{s})$ denote the pdf of the self-noise term (see (7)). In the given setup, $\mathbf{s}$ is uniform in $(1-\nu)\Phi(\Lambda')$. Finally, if we introduce the *total noise* random variable $\mathbf{t}$ as $\mathbf{t} = \mathbf{n} + \mathbf{s}$, it is clear that its pdf $f_{\mathbf{t}}(\mathbf{t})$ can be written as $f_{\mathbf{t}}(\mathbf{t}) = f_{\mathbf{n}}(\mathbf{t}) * f_{\mathbf{s}}(\mathbf{t})$, where the operator $*$ stands for convolution. With all these considerations, and our preliminary assumptions, $f_{\mathbf{z}}(\mathbf{z}|m=i) = f_{\mathbf{t}}(\mathbf{z} - \mathbf{c}_i)$, and therefore the probability of correct decision (12) can be rewritten as

$$P_c = \sum_{\mathbf{v} \in \mathbf{c}_i + \Lambda'} \int_{\mathbf{v}+\Phi(\Lambda)} f_{\mathbf{t}}(\mathbf{z} - \mathbf{c}_i) d\mathbf{z} = \int_{\Phi(\Lambda)} \sum_{\mathbf{v} \in \Lambda'} f_{\mathbf{t}}(\mathbf{z} - \mathbf{v}) d\mathbf{z} = \int_{\Phi(\Lambda)} \tilde{f}_{\mathbf{t}}(\mathbf{z}) d\mathbf{z} \tag{13}$$

where

$$\tilde{f}_{\mathbf{t}}(\mathbf{t}) \triangleq \begin{cases} \sum_{\mathbf{v} \in \Lambda'} f_{\mathbf{t}}(\mathbf{t} - \mathbf{v}) & \text{if } \mathbf{t} \in \Phi(\Lambda') \\ 0 & \text{otherwise} \end{cases} \tag{14}$$

The resulting probability of correct decision is then independent of the message that was sent, this being a consequence of both the fundamental assumption and the uniformity with which the messages are chosen.

It is not difficult to show that the function $\tilde{f}_{\mathbf{t}}(\mathbf{t})$ constructed in (14) is in fact a pdf which corresponds to the random variable $\tilde{\mathbf{t}} \triangleq \mathbf{t} \mod \Lambda'$. Then, $\tilde{f}_t(\mathbf{t}) \equiv f_{\tilde{\mathbf{t}}}(\tilde{\mathbf{t}})$, although we will prefer the first form to stress the fact that this pdf is constructed by adding up all the replicas of $f_t(\mathbf{t})$ obtained after translating it by any vector in Λ'.

Some additional insight is afforded by noticing that the operation in (14) closely resembles the "aliasing" phenomenon well-known from Signal Processing theory. The main difference is that instead of Fourier transforms one must add here pdf's; throughout this paper we will make extensive use of the existing similarities. For instance, one must note that it is impossible to recover the original pdf from the aliased one, i.e. aliasing here is in general non invertible. Equivalently, there are infinite pdf's yielding the same aliased version. Given, $\tilde{f}_{\mathbf{t}}(\mathbf{t})$, we construct the set $\mathcal{F}$, defined as

$$\mathcal{F} = \left\{ f_{\mathbf{t}}(\mathbf{t}) : \sum_{\mathbf{v} \in \Lambda'} f_{\mathbf{t}}(\mathbf{t} - \mathbf{v}) = \tilde{f}_{\mathbf{t}}(\mathbf{t}), \quad \mathbf{t} \in \Phi(\Lambda') \right\} \tag{15}$$

where $f_{\mathbf{t}}(\mathbf{t})$ is a valid pdf. Let $\sigma^2(f_{\mathbf{t}})$ denote the variance of the (zero-mean) r.v. whose pdf is $f_{\mathbf{t}}(\mathbf{t})$, then we can state the following lemma

Lemma 1.

$$\sigma^2(\tilde{f}_{\mathbf{t}}) = \min_{f_{\mathbf{t}} \in \mathcal{F}} \sigma^2(f_{\mathbf{t}})$$

A corollary is that the Gaussian pdf cannot be the worst attack for data hiding with lattice quantizers, except for limiting cases.

5 The Capacity of Data Hiding with Lattice-Based QIM

Capacity gives a measure of the maximum achievable information rate that can be exchanged over a communication channel modeled in probabilistic form. Communications engineers are familiar with Shannon's capacity, which sets the ultimate limits for practical communications schemes. During some time, it was thought that by considering the host image as noise, Shannon's formula would be also applicable to the data hiding problem. After the rediscovery of Costa's results [1], [3], a more appropriate channel description for the data hiding problem emerged. In this new model some variable known as "channel state" was made available to the transmitter but not to the receiver and additional Gaussian noise (unknown to both ends) was put by the channel. Since then, results having their roots in Costa's paper have populated the literature. Costa's result basically states that the data hiding channel capacity is the same as if the receiver would also know the host image, and so the capacity in bits per sample is

$$C = \frac{1}{2} \log_2 \left(1 + \frac{D_w}{D_c}\right) = \frac{1}{2} \log_2 (1 + \xi) \tag{16}$$

where D_w and D_c are the embedding and attacking distortion, respectively, and ξ is the WNR in natural units. Note that formula (16) is independent of the host image and that for no attacks, i.e. $D_c = 0$, we get infinite capacity.

Costa's proof also demands a distortion compensation parameter ν used in the same way as it was discussed above. This parameter must be optimized for each WNR; otherwise (16) is not achieved. Although Costa and Shannon's capacities have the same form, this need of choosing a WNR-dependent parameter at the *embedder* makes an important difference with classical communications, where no parameter at all is required. Costa showed this optimal value to be

$$\nu_C = \frac{D_w}{D_w + D_c} = \frac{1}{1 + \xi^{-1}} \tag{17}$$

Costa's paper uses random coding arguments to achieve capacity. Unfortunately, random codes have very little practical utility. Interestingly, very recently Erez and Zamir [9] have shown that Costa's capacity can be achieved by using nested lattices, although their proof requires the existence of good source and channel lattices, which again are not amenable to practical implementations.

For a certain lattice-based scheme, the capacity is defined as the maximum of the mutual information $I(\mathbf{z}; m)$ between the channel output and the input message. The maximum is taken over the range of possible distortion compensating parameters ν. Moreover, from the fundamental assumption, it can be shown that $I(\mathbf{z}; m) = I(\mathbf{z}; m|\mathbf{z} \in \Phi(\Lambda'))$. This is intuitively not surprising, since knowing the centroid in Λ' to which $\mathbf{z}$ is quantized does not provide any information on m.

A particularly interesting case for computing the mutual information, for practical reasons, is that of equiprobable symbols, for which $Pr\{m = i\} = 1/M$. For a fixed given ν we can write the following identities, where conditioning to $\mathbf{z} \in \Phi(\Lambda')$ is dropped for the sake of compactness in notation, and $h(\mathbf{z})$ denotes the differential entropy of the r.v. $\mathbf{z}$,

$$I(\mathbf{z}; m) = h(\mathbf{z}) - h(\mathbf{z}|m) = h(\mathbf{z}) - h(\mathbf{z}|m = 1)$$

which after some manipulations can be shown to be

$$I(\mathbf{z}; m) = D\left(\tilde{f}_{\mathbf{z}}(\mathbf{z}|m = 1)||\frac{1}{M}\sum_{i=1}^{M}\tilde{f}_{\mathbf{z}}(\mathbf{z}|m = i)\right)$$

where $D(f||g)$ denotes the Kullback-Leibler distance (KLD) between the pdf's f and g, and

$$\tilde{f}_{\mathbf{z}}(\mathbf{z}|m = i) \triangleq \begin{cases} \sum_{\mathbf{v}\in\Lambda'} f_{\mathbf{z}}(\mathbf{z} - \mathbf{v}|m = i) & \text{if } \mathbf{z} \in \Phi(\Lambda') \\ 0 & \text{otherwise} \end{cases} \tag{18}$$

Note that the mutual information given here depends on the parameter ν through $f_{\mathbf{z}}(\mathbf{z})$, so the capacity of a certain scheme would be defined as the maximum over ν of this mutual information. Also, note that zero-information is achieved iff the KLD is zero, that is, iff $\tilde{f}_{\mathbf{z}}(\mathbf{z}|m = 1) = (\sum_{i=1}^{M}\tilde{f}_{\mathbf{z}}(\mathbf{z}|m = i))/M$. Bearing in mind that $\tilde{f}_{\mathbf{z}}(\mathbf{z}|m = 1) = \tilde{f}_{\mathbf{t}}(\mathbf{z})$, a sufficient condition is then that $\tilde{f}_{\mathbf{t}}(\mathbf{t})$ be constant within $\Phi(\Lambda')$. But $\tilde{f}_{\mathbf{t}}(\mathbf{t})$ is equivalent to one period of the convolution between $f_{\mathbf{t}}(\mathbf{t})$ and a generalized impulse train $\sum_{\mathbf{v}\in\Lambda'}\delta(\mathbf{t}-\mathbf{v})$, so this sufficient condition very closely resembles Nyquist criterion for zero intersymbol interference (ISI).

Nyquist criterion has a nice interpretation in the dual domain: the sampled response becomes a Dirac's delta. The Fourier transform of the impulse train $\sum_{\mathbf{v}\in\Lambda'}\delta(\mathbf{t} - \mathbf{v})$ is itself an impulse train in the dual lattice of Λ', that we will denote by $\Lambda^{\perp}$. If $\mathbf{f}$ denotes the frequency variable, this impulse train has the form

$$\frac{1}{V(\Lambda')}\sum_{\mathbf{v}\in\Lambda^{\perp}}\delta(\mathbf{f} - \mathbf{v}) \tag{19}$$

Then, the sufficient condition in the dual domain for a zero-information attack is that the multivariate characteristic function of $f_{\mathbf{t}}(\mathbf{t})$, denoted as $F_{\mathbf{t}}(\mathbf{f})$, is zero at

$\Lambda^{\perp}$, except for the origin. Moreover, since for distortion compensation we have $F_{\mathbf{t}}(\mathbf{f}) = F_{\mathbf{n}}(\mathbf{f}) \cdot F_{\mathbf{s}}(\mathbf{f})$, this *zero forcing* condition extends to the characteristic function of the noise.

For M very large it is possible to resort to the so-called *continuous approximation* in order to calculate the mutual information since

$$\lim_{M\to\infty} \int_{\mathbf{z}\in\Phi(\Lambda')} \log_2 \left(\frac{1}{M} \sum_{i=1}^{M} \tilde{f}_{\mathbf{z}}(\mathbf{z}|m=i) \right) d\mathbf{z} = - \int_{\mathbf{z}\in\Phi(\Lambda')} \tilde{f}_{\mathbf{t}}(\mathbf{z}) \log_2 V(\Lambda') d\mathbf{z}$$
$$= -\log_2 V(\Lambda')$$

so, in the limit, the capacity of a lattice Λ'-based QIM scheme with equiprobable symbols becomes

$$C_{\Lambda',\mathrm{QIM}} = \max_{\nu} \int_{\mathbf{t}\in\Phi(\Lambda')} \tilde{f}_{\mathbf{t}}(\mathbf{t}) \log_2 \tilde{f}_{\mathbf{t}}(\mathbf{t}) d\mathbf{t} + \log_2 \left(V(\Lambda')\right) \quad (20)$$

The second term is fixed for a certain lattice, thus it is possible to find $f_{\mathbf{n}}(\mathbf{n})$ such that the first term in (20) is minimized. This would constitute a worst-case attack in terms of capacity. The problem can be solved by means of constrained nonlinear optimization techniques.

6 A Frequency-Domain Approach

Since $\tilde{f}_{\mathbf{t}}(\mathbf{t}|m=1)$ is equivalent to one period of the convolution between $f_{\mathbf{t}}(\mathbf{t})$ and $\sum_{\mathbf{v}\in\Lambda'} \delta(\mathbf{t}-\mathbf{v})$ it is worth to compute the characteristic function of this convolution which, as we stated, is an impulse train in the dual lattice $\Lambda^{\perp}$.

As Forney et al. have recently shown [5], it is possible to distinguish two cases:

- **High WNR**. Here, most of the pdf of $f_{\mathbf{t}}(\mathbf{t})$ is already contained in $\Phi(\Lambda')$, so $\tilde{f}_{\mathbf{t}}(\mathbf{t}|m=1) \approx f_{\mathbf{t}}(\mathbf{t})$. This condition holds when $V^{2/N}(\Lambda') >> \sigma_n^2$, with σ_n^2 the variance of the attacking noise.
- **Low WNR**. In this case $\tilde{f}_{\mathbf{t}}(\mathbf{t}|m=1)$ becomes nearly constant, so it is adequate to approximate it by the DC-term (i.e., $\mathbf{f}=\mathbf{0}$) and the "fundamental frequency terms" in the dual lattice, for which $||\mathbf{f}||^2 = d_{min}^2(\Lambda^{\perp})$.

In addition, the frequency domain approach can be used for computational purposes. Recall that for determining $\tilde{f}_{\mathbf{t}}(\mathbf{t}|m=1)$ we need to reduce $f_{\mathbf{t}}(\mathbf{t})$ modulo Λ'. But since $f_{\mathbf{t}}(\mathbf{t}) = f_{\mathbf{s}}(\mathbf{t}) * f_{\mathbf{n}}(\mathbf{n})$, from frequency domain considerations it is possible to show that $\tilde{f}_{\mathbf{t}}(\mathbf{t}) = \tilde{f}_{\mathbf{s}}(\mathbf{t}) \circledast \tilde{f}_{\mathbf{n}}(\mathbf{n})$, where $\tilde{f}_{\mathbf{s}}(\mathbf{t})$ and $\tilde{f}_{\mathbf{n}}(\mathbf{t})$ are respectively generated from $f_{\mathbf{s}}(\mathbf{t})$ and $f_{\mathbf{n}}(\mathbf{t})$ in an identical fashion as the procedure given in (14) to produce $\tilde{f}_{\mathbf{t}}(\mathbf{t})$ from $f_{\mathbf{t}}(\mathbf{t})$, and $\circledast$ is the modular convolution operator working over the domain $\Phi(\Lambda')$. An interesting consequence of this result is that $\tilde{f}_{\mathbf{n}}(\mathbf{t})$ can be computed by means of a multidimensional DFT.

7 The Scalar Case

The scalar case has been the most extensively studied in the watermarking literature, since it constitutes the simpler lattice-based data hiding scheme available. And yet, some issues such as the selection of the optimal distortion compensating parameter ν remain open. In the scalar case, the quantities involved, e.g. the host image, the watermark and the attack are all real numbers. For mathematical convenience and without loss of generality we will assume that the coarse lattice Λ' is chosen in such a way that its fundamental volume is one, i.e., $V(\Lambda') = 1$. Then, it is easy to see that $\Lambda' = \mathbb{Z}$, and the associated fundamental region is $\Phi(\Lambda') = (-1/2, 1/2]$.

Now, suppose that our message may take one out of M possible values, with M even, so we construct the following coset representatives

$$c_i = \begin{cases} \frac{i-1}{M}, & i = 1, \cdots, \frac{M}{2}+1 \\ \frac{i-M-1}{M}, & i = \frac{M}{2}+2, \cdots, M \end{cases} \tag{21}$$

which as it can be readily seen define a multilevel constellation with M symbols. With the representatives given by (21) it is obvious that the "fine" lattice is $\Lambda = M^{-1}\mathbb{Z}$ whose fundamental volume is M^{-1} and Voronoi region $(-1/2M, 1/2M]$. Thus, the order of the partition becomes $|\Lambda/\Lambda'| = M$.

With the representatives introduced in (21) we define the following minimum distance quantizers:

$$Q_{\Lambda',c_i}(z) = c_i + k, \text{ if } z - c_i \in (k - 1/2, k + 1/2] \tag{22}$$

$$Q_{\Lambda}(z) = c_i + k, \text{ if } z - c_i \in (k - 1/2M, k + 1/2M] \tag{23}$$

Now, in order to send a message $m \in \mathcal{M}$ hidden in the host image coefficient x, we compute the watermarked image as $y = Q_{\Lambda',c_m}(x) + (1-\nu)(Q_{\Lambda',c_m} - x)$. This image coefficient is passed through an attacking channel that generates a noise sample n that is added to y to produce an attacked image coefficient z, given by $z = y + n$. The decoder decides a message $\hat{m}$ after observing z. The decoding rule is based on (23), that is,

$$\hat{m} = i, \text{ if } Q_{\Lambda}(z) \in \Lambda' + c_i \tag{24}$$

If the fundamental assumption holds, the watermark is uniformly distributed in $(-1/2, 1/2]$ and therefore the embedding distortion D_w in (10) becomes $D_w = \nu^2/3$. Moreover, the self-noise term s will also follow a uniform distribution, i.e., $s \sim U(-(1-\nu)/2, (1-\nu)/2]$.

Consider next that the attack sample n is drawn from a Gaussian random variable with variance σ_n^2. Obviously, the attacking distortion D_c will be simply $D_c = \sigma_n^2$. Noting that the total noise pdf $f_t(t)$ corresponding to $t = n + s$ satisfies $f_t(t) = f_n(t) * f_s(t)$, it is possible to write

$$f_t(t) = \frac{1}{(1-\nu)} \left(\mathcal{Q}\left(\frac{t - (1-\nu)/2}{\sigma_n} \right) - \mathcal{Q}\left(\frac{t + (1-\nu)/2}{\sigma_n} \right) \right) \tag{25}$$

where $\mathcal{Q}(x) \triangleq \frac{1}{\sqrt{2\pi}} \int_x^\infty e^{-\frac{\tau^2}{2}} d\tau$. From (25) it is possible to construct the modular pdf $\tilde{f}_t(t)$ by simply adding the shifted versions of $f_t(t)$. Then, $\tilde{f}_t(t)$ is such that $\tilde{f}_t(t) = \sum_{k\in\mathbb{Z}} f(t-k)$, for $t \in (-1/2, 1/2)$, and is zero elsewhere.

An evident problem arises when trying to use the resulting $\tilde{f}_t(t)$ to determine quantities such as the entropy of $\tilde{t}$, since it is not possible to obtain closed-form expressions. Even some of the approximations given in Section 6 have limited utility. Next, we will discuss these and other alternatives.

High WNR. In this case, it is reasonable to write $\tilde{f}_t(t) \approx f_t(t)$, but unfortunately working with the random variable t whose pdf is given in (25) does not lead to analytical expressions either. However, if the attacking noise variance is large compared to the self-noise variance, $f_t(t)$ will be well-approximated by a Gaussian distribution with zero mean and variance $\sigma_n^2 + (1-\nu)^2/12$. Noting that $\sigma_n^2 = \nu^2/12\xi$, the total variance can be rewritten in terms of the WNR as

$$\sigma_t^2 = \frac{\nu^2 + (1-\nu)^2\xi}{12\xi} \tag{26}$$

Low WNR. In this case, the overlap between the shifted pdf's $f(t-k)$, $k \in \mathbb{Z}$, will be non negligible, and thus it is not possible to resort to any of the approximations in the previous paragraph. Then, a Fourier series expansion as in Section 6 is more useful. According to Fourier series theory, under some mild conditions, an even $\tilde{f}_t(t)$ can be written as

$$\tilde{f}_t(t) = \begin{cases} 1 + \sum_{k=1}^{\infty} a_k \cos(2\pi k t) & , \ t \in (-1/2, 1/2] \\ 0 & , \ \text{elsewhere} \end{cases} \tag{27}$$

In our case we can show that

$$a_k = 2\exp\left(-\frac{\nu^2\pi^2k^2}{6\xi}\right) \cdot \frac{\sin(\pi(1-\nu)k)}{\pi(1-\nu)k} \tag{28}$$

When the attacking noise variance is large compared to the self-noise variance it is possible to show that a good approximation for $\tilde{f}_t(t)$ follows by retaining the first two terms in (27). In this case, we write $\tilde{f}_t(t) = 1 + a_1\cos(2\pi t)$, $t \in (-1/2, 1/2]$.

7.1 Capacity in the Scalar Case

Considering the transmission of equiprobable symbols, it is possible to specialize (20) for the scalar case, noting that $V(\Lambda') = 1$, so

$$C_{\mathbb{Z},\mathrm{QIM}} = \max_{\nu} \int_{-0.5}^{0.5} \tilde{f}_t(t) \log_2 \tilde{f}_t(t) dt = \max_{\nu} -h(\tilde{f}_t) \tag{29}$$

with $h(\cdot)$ the differential entropy of the r.v. whose pdf is $f_t(t)$. This case has been studied by Eggers, who termed this data hiding method as *Scalar Costa Scheme* (SCS) and gave empirical estimates of the capacity, already taking into account the aliasing on the derivation of $\tilde{f}_t(t)$ [2]. Eggers also correctly discovered that the value of ν that optimizes (29) differs from that obtained by Costa, especially for negative WNR's. Since explicit determination of the optimal ν value for the problem in (29) is not possible, Eggers [2] has obtained experimentally this value for WNR's in the range of -20 to 20 dB and then performed some curve-fitting to give the following approximation, that we will denote by ν_E,

$$\nu_E = \frac{1}{\sqrt{1 + 2.71\xi^{-1}}} \tag{30}$$

Unfortunately, Eggers' results give little insight into the "how" and "why" of the behavior of distortion compensated mechanisms. Here, we will use the results in the preceding section to take a step in the direction of finding the optimal values of ν. For large WNR's $\tilde{f}_t(t)$ can be approximated by a Gaussian pdf, with variance given in (26), so its entropy is $0.5 \log_2 2\pi e \sigma_t^2$. Maximizing the capacity in (29) is equivalent to minimizing the entropy, so the optimal ν can be found by minimizing σ_t^2. Differentiating (26) and setting to zero yields exactly the same ν as in (17), which is nothing but the value determined by Costa.

However, for low WNR's the Gaussian approximation is not valid, and this is the reason why Costa's value differs significantly from that found by Eggers. In this case, making use of the approximation with two Fourier series terms is more reasonable. Let us introduce the following set of pdf's parameterized by $a \in \mathbb{R}$

$$\tilde{f}_x(x, a) = 1 + a \cos(2\pi x), \quad x \in (-1/2, 1/2] \tag{31}$$

where $0 \leq a_1^- \leq a \leq a_1^+ \leq 1$. The following lemma helps to understand how a good value of ν can be found.

Lemma 2. *$h(\tilde{f}_x(x, a)) \geq h(\tilde{f}_x(x, a_1^+))$, with equality if and only if $a = a_1^+$.*

This suggests choosing ν to maximize a_1 as given by (28). Although this value cannot be given in explicit form, it can be readily shown to be the unique solution in $(0, 1)$ to the equation

$$(1 - b\nu(1 - \nu)) \sin(\pi\nu) + \pi(1 - \nu) \cos(\pi\nu) = 0 \tag{32}$$

where $b = \pi^2/3\xi$. The validity of the solution to (32) seems to be restricted to those values of ν for which the coefficient a_1 is greater than -1; otherwise the two-term approximation to $\tilde{f}_t(t)$ would take negative values and could no longer be interpreted as a pdf. However, it is easy to show that

$$\left| \frac{\sin(\pi x)}{\pi x} \right| > \left| \frac{\sin(\pi k x)}{\pi k x} \right| \tag{33}$$

for any $x \in \mathbb{R}$, any $\nu \in (0, 1)$ and any integer $k > 1$. In turn, this can be used to show that $|a_1| > |a_k|$ for $k > 1$ in (28) so, the DC term excluded, the fundamental frequency term produces the largest contribution for any ν and any WNR. Therefore, in view of Lemma 2 it seems reasonable to maximize a_1 in hope of finding the optimal ν value using (32). In Fig. 2 we plot the corresponding value, labeled as ν_F, together with ν_C, ν_E and the actual optimal value obtained through numerical search. Note the very good agreement of our value of ν with the true one. Much more important than being able to produce a tight approximate value of ν with no need of numerical integration is the fact that maximization of a_1 is indeed a good criterion for achieving capacity, and this property is expected to hold for many other pdf's as long as the fundamental frequency term is larger than the remaining AC terms. Furthermore, it is possible to derive some approximate forms to (32) and show that for large values of ν and large WNR's the solution is in fact given by Costa's distortion compensating parameter. This can be readily confirmed from Fig. 2, where it can be also checked that Costa's optimal ν value significantly differs from the true one for small WNR's.

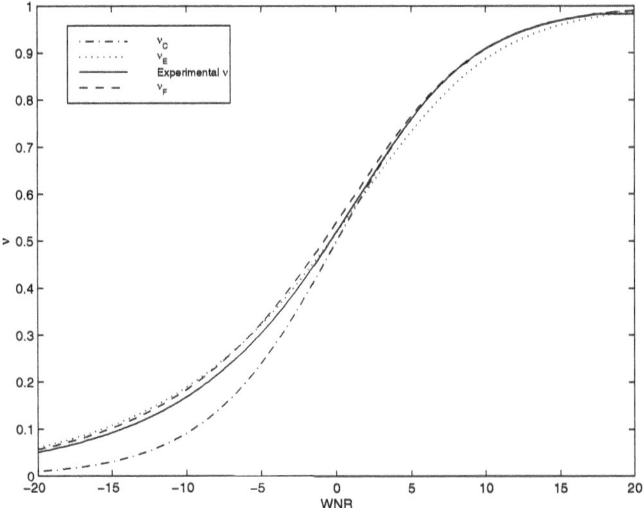

Fig. 2. Distortion compensation parameter vs. WNR, for Costa's problem (ν_C), Eggers' approximation (ν_E), the value proposed in this paper (ν_F), and the empirically obtained one.

In Figure 3 we represent Costa's capacity as a function of the WNR (from formula (16)) together with $C_{\mathbb{Z},\mathrm{QIM}}$ as obtained from (20) through both numerical integration (to obtain h) and numerical optimization. It can be shown that the difference between the two curves asymptotically amounts to $10\log_{10}(\pi e/6) \approx 1.53$ dB. This loss from the theoretical capacity, is a consequence of not using a continuous Gaussian pdf at the channel input, as required by Costa's proof [3].

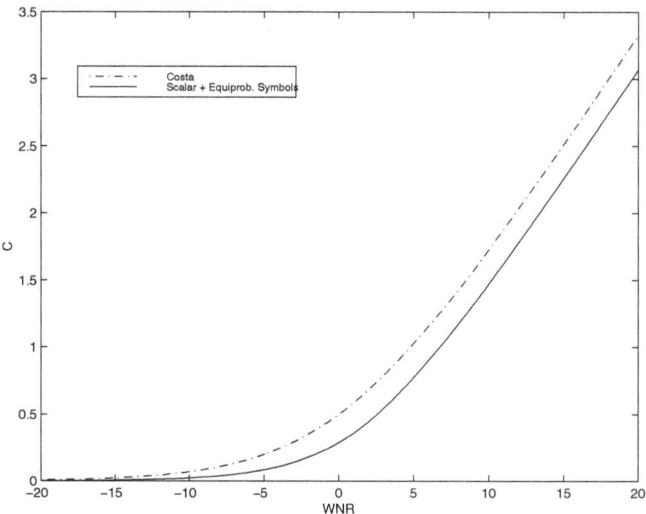

Fig. 3. Costa's capacity and capacity attained in the scalar case when $M \to \infty$.

We must note here that this loss can be progressively compensated for by using larger-dimensional constellations, which provide the so-called *shaping gain* [4].

So far it has been considered that the attack $\mathbf{n}$ consists in a Gaussian vector with i.i.d. components, but is interesting to tackle the problem of a more general pdf for the attack, without abandoning the additive and i.i.d. constraints. Suppose that the attacker knows the distortion compensation parameter ν; after all, this is used in embedding, that is, prior to sending the watermarked image through the channel, so the attacker could devise a method to estimate ν.

We will consider that the attacker is interested in minimizing the mutual information in (5) either for both cases of finite and infinite number of symbols. Then, for a given WNR and a given structured QIM scheme, the attacker's strategy would seek $f_{\mathbf{n}}(\mathbf{n})$ such that this mutual information is minimized. We will follow the notation $I_S(A, \nu)$, where S is the data hiding scheme that has been used, A denotes the attack (which maps into a certain noise pdf), ν is the parameter used by the embedder (who plays first in the game) and the WNR is assumed to be fixed.

As we have remarked, it is reasonable for the embedder to assume that the attacker knows ν, so we will write $A(\nu)$ to stress this dependence. Let $\mathcal{A}$ denote the feasible set of attacks for the given WNR. Then, the attacker's strategy will be to choose $A^*(\nu) \in \mathcal{A}$ such that $A^*(\nu) = \arg\min_{A \in \mathcal{A}} I_S(A(\nu), \nu)$, and the embedder's optimal strategy for the game would be to select ν^* such that $\nu^* = \arg\max_{\nu \in (0,1)} I_S(A^*(\nu), \nu)$.

When the number of equiprobable symbols M used by data hiding scheme S is such that $M \to \infty$, then we *redefine* the capacity of S as

$$C_S \triangleq I_S(A^*(\nu^*), \nu^*) \tag{34}$$

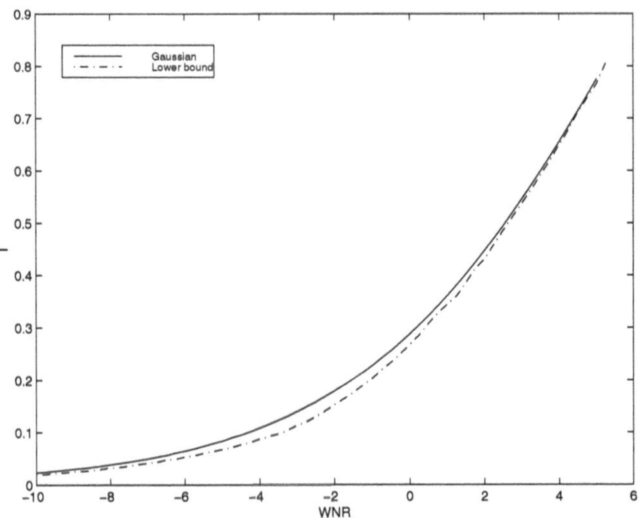

Fig. 4. Maximum Mutual Information for a Gaussian attack and lower bound.

In Fig. 4, we plot the mutual information for an infinite number of symbols of the scalar scheme (i.e., $\Lambda = \mathbb{Z}$), both for the Gaussian attack, and a lower bound to capacity obtained through numerical optimization techniques. The true capacity given in (34) lies between the two curves. An important consequence is that the Gaussian attack is not the worst one for scalar QIM with equiprobable symbols. This is in contrast with the results given by Cohen and Lapidoth [10] who proved that Gaussian noise is the worst additive attack for a certain capacity achieving scheme.

8 Conclusions

In this paper we have shown how lattice partitioning can be used for supporting informed embedding mechanisms. Due to space restrictions, we have deliberately avoided considering other forms of coding (e.g., convolutional) that can be combined with the channel fine lattice Λ to improve overall performance. The main consequence of using lattices is the appearance of *aliasing* in the noise pdf. For low WNR's this *aliasing* must be considered for an accurate estimate of the symbol error probability. Although we have not delved into this issue here, it can be shown that even for Gaussian attacks and no distortion compensation the optimal (in the maximum likelihood sense) decision regions are not necessarily limited by hyperplanes or, put in other words, that the Euclidean distance is not necessarily optimal, this again being a consequence of aliasing. Finally, we have considered the scalar case and provided a novel approximation to the optimal distortion compensation parameter that can be analytically justified, and we have studied the case of general additive attacks, where we have shown a loss of capacity against that afforded by Gaussian noise.

Acknowledgments. Thanks are due to P. Comesaña for contributing with several optimization programs and to Profs. V. Santalla and S. Voloshynovskiy for some enlightening discussions.

References

1. B. Chen and G. W. Wornell, "Quantization index modulation: A class of provably good methods for digital watermarking and information embedding," *IEEE Trans. on Information Theory*, vol. 47, pp. 1423–1443, May 2001.
2. J. Eggers, R. Bauml, R. Tzschoppe, and B. Girod, "Scalar costa scheme for information embedding," *IEEE Transactions on Signal Processing*, vol. 51, pp. 1003–1019, April 2003.
3. M. H. Costa, "Writing on dirty paper," *IEEE Trans. on Information Theory*, vol. 29, pp. 439–441, May 1983.
4. R. Fischer, *Precoding and Signal Shaping for Digital Transmission.* John Wiley and Sons, 2002.
5. G. Forney, M. Trott, and S. Chung, "Sphere-bound-achieving coset codes and multilevel coset codes," *IEEE Transactions on Information Theory*, vol. 46, pp. 820–850, May 2000.
6. F. Pérez-González, F. Balado, and J. Hernandez, "Performance analysis of existing and new methods for data-hiding with known-host information in additive channels," *IEEE Transactions on Signal Processing*, vol. 51, pp. 960–980, April 2003.
7. J. Conway and N. Sloane, *Sphere Packings, Lattices and Groups*, vol. 290 of *Comprehensive Studies in Mathematics.* Springer, 3rd ed., 1999.
8. R. Zamir, S. Shamai, and U. Erez, "Nested linear/lattice codes for structured multiterminal binning," *IEEE Transactions on Information Theory*, vol. 48, pp. 1250–1276, June 2002.
9. U. Erez and R. Zamir, "Lattice decoding can achieve $\frac{1}{2}\log(1+SNR)$ on the AWGN channel using nested codes." submitted to IEEE Trans. on Information Theory, May 2001.
10. A. S. Cohen and A. Lapidoth, "The Gaussian watermarking game," *IEEE Transactions on Information Theory*, vol. 48, pp. 1639–1667, June 2002.

Watermark Embedding for Black-Box Channels

Matt L. Miller

NEC Labs America, Princeton NJ 08540, USA,

Abstract. The problem examined here is that of tailoring watermarks to survive given communications channels, where the channels are described by procedural simulations. To maximize generality, the embedder is not allowed to know anything about how the simulations work, so they are referred to as "black-box channel models". The detector is assumed to have no knowledge of either the original cover work or the channel model.
A simple, iterative embedding algorithm is presented that addresses the problem. The algorithm repeatedly applies a black-box channel model to a work, modifying it slightly each time that the watermark does not survive. When the watermark survives 100 times in a row, the algorithm terminates. This algorithm is shown experimentally to produce good results with three different channel models.

1 Introduction

In many watermarking applications, marks must survive some expected set of distortions. For example, a video watermark intended to be detected by a television receiver must survive television broadcast. The expected distortions in this case would probably include some digital filtering, lossy compression, analog blurring, addition of random noise, ghosting, and so on. Such distortions form a communication channel across which the watermark must carry information.

While it is possible to design watermarks that are robust to a wide variety of distortions, robustness to each distortion must necessarily come at some cost in payload and fidelity. Thus, depending on the application, we might want less robustness against some unlikely distortions, in exchange for more embedded information or better fidelity. If we want a single watermarking system that can be used in a wide variety of applications, then we want a system that can be somehow tailored to each given channel. This raises the interesting challenge of building a system that, given any description of a channel, can approach an optimal tradeoff between robustness, payload, and fidelity.

To meet this challenge, we must first come up with a way to describe the channel. One possibility is to implement a simulation of the channel as a stochastic procedure. For example, for the above television monitoring application, we can write a procedure that takes a video stream as input, compresses it with random compression parameters, applies various randomly-chosen filters, and adds noise, to produce a video stream that might be received after broadcasting. This procedure, or model, can then be employed within a watermark embedder and/or detector. To ensure maximal flexibility, we'll insist that the model

T. Kalker et al. (Eds.): IWDW 2003, LNCS 2939, pp. 18–34, 2004.
© Springer-Verlag Berlin Heidelberg 2004

is treated as a "black-box" – the watermarking system must not employ any knowledge of how the model works.

Such black-box channel models have been employed for watermarking at least once before, by Liang and Rodriguez in [1]. In their image watermarking system, the watermark embedder repeatedly applies the channel model to a cover image, and measures the effects on the image's DCT coefficients. It then embeds the watermark in the n coefficients that proved to be most robust. The detector must be told which coefficients were used, so the system requires informed (non-blind) detection.

The present paper examines the problem of using a black-box channel model for image watermarking with a blind detector. The detector is assumed to know nothing of the original cover work or the channel model. Given a cover image, a desired message, and a channel model, the embedder's task is to produce an image that is a) perceptually close to the cover image, and b) likely to make the detector output the desired message, even after the image is distorted by the modeled channel.

The new embedding method is presented within the framework of Costa's dirty-paper channel, which is introduced briefly in Section 2. Section 3 then focuses on the piece of Costa's formulation, the "embedding function", which can be tailored to specific channels when the detector knows nothing of them. An algorithm for doing this is proposed in Section 4. Section 5 describes some experiments performed with this algorithm and Section 6 reports their results. Finally, Section 7 reviews some strengths and weaknesses of the proposed method, and introduces related problems for future study.

2 Costa's Dirty-Paper Channel

In [2], Costa studied the channel shown in Figure 1. Much recent watermarking research has been based on his analysis, for example [3,4,5,6,7].

The channel Costa studied consists of two additive white Gaussian noise (AWGN) sources. The transmitter must encode a message, m, with a signal, $\mathbf{x}$, according to a power limit

$$\sum_i \mathbf{x}_i^2 \leq P. \quad (1)$$

Before it selects $\mathbf{x}$, however, the transmitter is informed of the noise, $\mathbf{s}$, that will be added by the first AWGN noise source. This type of channel is referred to as a "dirty-paper channel", because this first noise source can be likened to a sheet of dirty paper, which we get to examine before trying to write a message upon it. The analogy between this channel and watermarking is as follows: $\mathbf{s}$ is analogous to the cover work, the power constraint is analogous to a fidelity constraint, $\mathbf{s}+\mathbf{x}$ (labeled $\mathbf{s_u}$ in Figure 1) is analogous to the watermarked work, and the second noise source is analogous to the channel that the watermark must survive.

Costa proved the rather surprising result that the capacity of his dirty-paper channel is independent of the first noise source. That is: no matter how dirty the paper, we can always transmit the same amount of information. This result

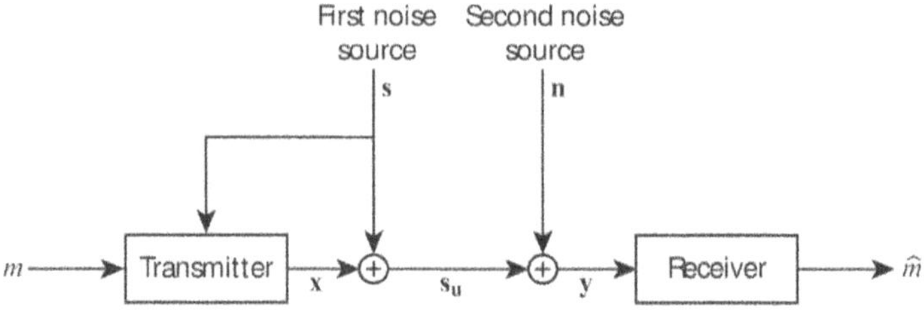

Fig. 1. Costa's dirty-paper channel.

was later extended, in [8] and [9], to cases where **s** is drawn from an arbitrary distribution. This implies that, in the absence of such real-world problems as clipping and round-off errors, the capacity of watermarks that must survive AWGN channels should be independent of the distribution of cover works.

Costa's proof consists of a prescription for generating and using random codes that (with high likelihood) achieve capacity. The codes have the property that each message is represented by a variety of different signals. We refer to such codes as *dirty-paper codes*. The transmitter begins by finding the set of code signals that represent the desired message, and then identifying the member of that set, **u**, that is (in some sense) closest to **s**. Then, based on **u** and **s**, it chooses the signal to transmit, **x**.

The way in which **x** is chosen is of critical importance. The straightforward idea would be to simply let $\mathbf{x} = \mathbf{u} - \mathbf{s}$. This would ensure that $\mathbf{s_u} = \mathbf{u}$, so the code signal would be uncorrupted by **s**. However, this approach can run afoul of the power constraint, and fails to achieve capacity. Instead, Costa lets $\mathbf{x} = \mathbf{u} - \alpha\mathbf{s}$, where α is a carefully-selected scalar constant. Thus

$$\mathbf{s_u} = \mathbf{u} + (1 - \alpha)\mathbf{s}. \tag{2}$$

Costa shows that, with the right code and choice of α, this formulation achieves capacity.

Watermarking systems that follow Costa's formulation, then, comprise two parts: a *watermark code*, which maps each message (m) to a watermark pattern ($\mathbf{u}$), according to the cover work in which it is to be embedded ($\mathbf{s}$), and an *embedding function*, which yields a watermarked work ($\mathbf{s_u}$) from a cover work and a watermark pattern. In Costa's case, the embedding function is essentially a weighted average of the cover work and watermark pattern[1], as given in Equation 2.

[1] Strictly speaking, Equation 2 is not a weighted average, because **u** is not scaled by α. However, as α is constant, and **u** is drawn from a predefined set, we can just divide all the **u**'s by α beforehand, and rewrite Equation 2 as $\mathbf{s_u} = \alpha\mathbf{u} + (1 - \alpha)\mathbf{s}$.

3 Tailoring Embedding Functions

Costa's system is designed specifically for channels in which the second noise source is additive white Gaussian. However, we are interested in making a system that can be tailored for any arbitrary channel. Clearly, the optimal codes and embedding functions for different channels will be different from one another. In principle, then, tailoring a watermarking system to a given channel should entail changing both the code and the embedding function.

Unfortunately, we have no opportunity to modify the watermark code, because any change in the code would have to be told to the detector, and this would violate the stipulation that the detector should be completely uninformed. Thus, the code is fixed by the detector, and must be as general as possible, designed for robustness against all conceivable distortions.

This leaves us with the possibility of tailoring only the embedding function to the given channel. It may seem that the embedding function, by itself, is not as important as the code. But varying the embedding function can be surprisingly powerful.

The power of varied embedding functions is illustrated in Figure 2. This figure should be interpreted as follows:

- Each portion of the figure, (a), (b), (c), and (d), shows a two-dimensional media space (each point in the space corresponds to a single work).
- The polygon drawn with dashed lines in each portion represents the detection region for a single, target watermark pattern. That is, all the works within the polygon will be detected as containing this pattern.
- Within each polygon, a "robustness region" is shown with a ragged contour. Each of the four figures shows the robustness region for a different channel. If any work within one of these robustness regions is distorted by the corresponding channel, the resulting distorted work has a high probability of lying inside the detection region – that is, the watermark is likely to survive the distortion.
- Around the outside of each figure is a set of open dots, representing several unwatermarked cover works.
- Each unwatermarked cover work is connected by a line to a star, representing the optimal result of an embedding function applied to that cover work and the target watermark pattern. Ideally, we'd like the embedding function to find the point closest to the cover work in the robustness region.

The important point to note in Figure 2 is that the ideal watermarked work for a given cover work is highly dependent on the channel (corresponding open dots in the four portions of the figure move to different locations within the detection region). This implies that, by making the embedding function dependent on the channel, we can obtain significantly improved results.

4 Proposed Embedding Algorithm

Finding the optimal watermarked works indicated in Figure 2 is difficult, especially when we only have a black-box channel model to work with. However,

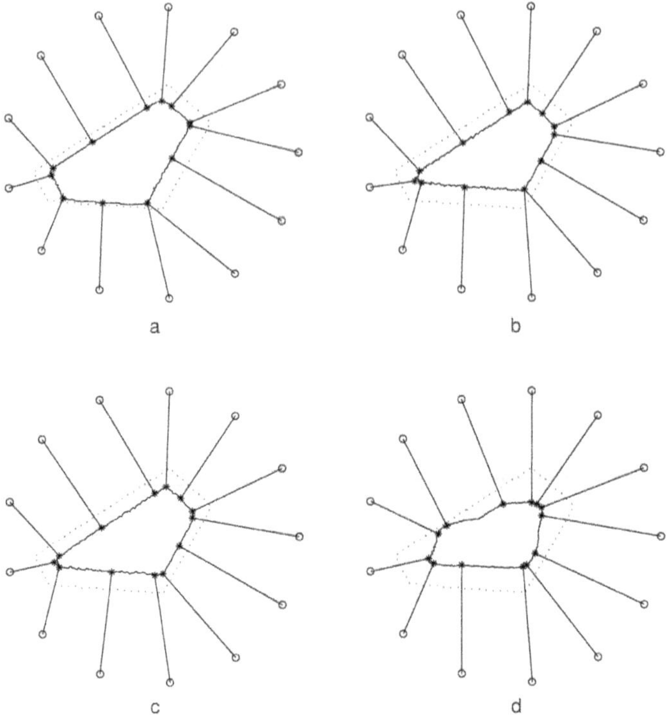

Fig. 2. Optimal embedding functions for four different channel models: (a), (b), and (c) are colored Gaussian noise channels with different covariances, and (d) is a channel that quantizes by a random step size.

a simple, iterative algorithm can be used to obtain an approximate solution, which yields significantly better results than more conventional approaches. The algorithm proceeds as follows:

1. Given an unwatermarked cover work, $\mathbf{s}$, a watermark pattern, $\mathbf{u}$, and a channel model, $C(\cdot)$, begin by initializing an initial guess at a watermarked work, $\mathbf{s_u}$, to $\mathbf{s_u} \leftarrow \mathbf{s}$. Also initialize a counter, $j \leftarrow 0$.
2. Apply the channel model to the current guess at a watermarked work, to obtain a corrupted work, $\mathbf{s}'_\mathbf{u} \leftarrow C(\mathbf{s_u})$.
3. Identify the watermark pattern, $\mathbf{u}'$, that is closest to $\mathbf{s}'_\mathbf{u}$.
4. If $\mathbf{u}' \neq \mathbf{u}$, then the watermark failed to survive this distortion. Let

$$j \leftarrow 0 \tag{3}$$

$$\mathbf{s_u} \leftarrow \mathbf{s_u} + \delta \frac{\mathbf{u}' - \mathbf{u}}{|\mathbf{u}' - \mathbf{u}|} \tag{4}$$

where δ is a small constant scalar, and go back to Step 2.

5. If $\mathbf{u}' = \mathbf{u}$, then the watermark survived the distortion in this iteration. Let $j \leftarrow j + 1$. If $j < T$, where T is a constant integer, then go back to Step 2. Otherwise, terminate.

The idea behind this algorithm is that we test the robustness of the watermark in each iteration. If the watermark does not survive the channel, then we find the error that was introduced, and update the watermarked work to reduce the chance of that particular error happening again. Once the watermark survives the channel in T consecutive iterations, we determine that the watermark is robustly embedded, and terminate.

More abstractly, the algorithm can be viewed as crude form of gradient ascent. The detection region and the channel model together define a (usually) smooth "robustness" function of marking space, whose value at each work is the probability that a distorted version of the work will lie inside the detection region. The assumption is that the gradient of this function is generally perpendicular to the boundaries of the detection region. Thus, by finding a nearby boundary of the detection region (the boundary between the detection regions for $\mathbf{u}$ and $\mathbf{u}'$), and taking a small step toward it, we tend to climb the gradient toward the closest point where the function is above some threshold (implicitly defined by T).

Figure 3 shows the effect of running this algorithm on the problems illustrated in Figure 2. Here, the straight lines connecting the unwatermarked works to their watermarked counterparts are replaced by lines that trace the paths followed during the course of the algorithm (note that these paths are stochastic – what is illustrated is the result of one run of the algorithm, other runs would likely produce slightly different paths). This figure shows that, for the three additive-noise channels, the algorithm yields near-optimal results. For the quantization channel, however, the result is sometimes far from optimal. The reason for this is that, in this channel, the gradient is sometimes far from perpendicular to the detection boundary, so the algorithm climbs in the wrong direction. Nevertheless, as will be seen below, the algorithm produces good results when used with quantization channels on real images.

It should be noted that the algorithm presented here is very similar to the one presented in [7]. That algorithm, too, iteratively modified a work based on the watermarks found in distorted versions of it. The differences are that a) in that algorithm, the addition of noise followed by watermark detection was an approximation to a search for the closest incorrect watermark pattern, rather than a direct test of robustness, and b) the method by which the work was updated in each iteration was based on a numerical estimate of its robustness to additive white noise. There was no mechanism for tailoring the watermark to different channel models. The present algorithm is simpler, more flexible, and usually closer to optimal than the earlier one.

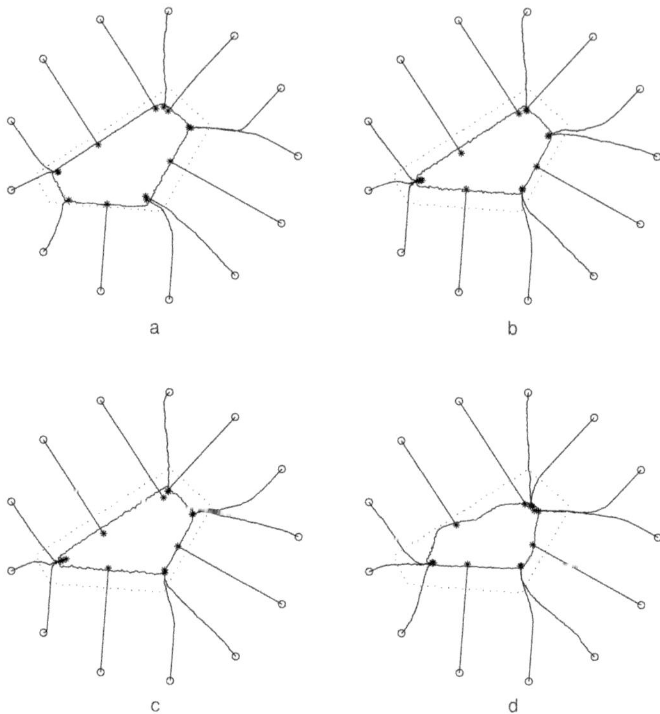

Fig. 3. Behavior of the proposed algorithm with the same channel models as in Figure 2.

5 Experiments

To test the proposed algorithm, an image watermarking system was built with the following details:

- The system operates on 8-bit grey-scale images.
- Watermark signals are extracted from images in a similar manner as in [7]. Each image is transformed into the block-DCT domain, and 14 low-frequency AC coefficients are arranged into the signal in a key-dependent, pseudo-random order.
- The code used is a dirty-paper trellis code, as described in [7]. It has 64 states, each with 64 arcs.
- The embedder extracts a signal from the cover image, uses the dirty-paper trellis code to obtain a watermark pattern, embeds the watermark pattern in the extracted signal according to the proposed embedding algorithm, and inverts the extraction process to obtain the watermarked image.
- The detector extracts a signal from the cover image and decodes it according to the dirty-paper trellis code.

For comparison, a second watermark embedder was created, identical to the first except that, in step 4 of the proposed algorithm, it does not subtract $\mathbf{u}'$ from $\mathbf{u}$. That is, it lets

$$\mathbf{s_u} \leftarrow \mathbf{s_u} + \delta \frac{\mathbf{u}}{|\mathbf{u}|}. \tag{5}$$

Thus, this embedder iteratively adds more and more of the watermark pattern, without regard to the patterns the detector is detecting, until the watermark survives the channel model. This can be viewed as a simulation of a user gradually cranking up the watermark strength in a conventional embedder, until a desired level of robustness is reached.

To differentiate between the two embedders in the following text, the first one (the full-blown implementation of the proposed algorithm) can be referred to as the "relative" embedder, because it updates $\mathbf{s_u}$ relative to $\mathbf{u}'$. The second one (the simulation of a user cranking up embedding strength) can be referred to as the "absolute" embedder, because each iteration increases the absolute strength of the watermark.

Both embedders were applied to each of 100 images, randomly-selected from the Corel database [10]. The images had a resolution of 256 × 384 pixels. In each image, a random, 512-bit watermark was embedded. In both embedders, the value of δ was set to 1, and the value of T was 100.

Four different channel models were used:

AWGN adds a random value to each pixel, drawn independently from a Gaussian distribution with a standard deviation of 4.5.

DCTQ converts the image into the block-DCT domain, quantizes the coefficients by the JPEG quantization matrix multiplied by a value chosen uniformly between 0 and 2 (one multiplier is chosen for the whole image), and converts back to the spatial domain.

LPF applies a Gaussian, low-pass filter with a width (sigma) chosen uniformly between 0 and 0.55.

COMBO chooses one of the above three channels at random and applies it to the image.

The maximum multiplier for the DCTQ channel (2) was selected to correspond to JPEG compression with a quality factor of about 25%. The constants in the AWGN and LPF channels (4.5 and 0.55, respectively) were chosen to yield similar signal-to-noise ratios as that produced by the DCTQ channel.

Each of the 800 watermarked images (100 images × 2 embedders × four channels) was then tested for robustness against various levels of additive white noise, DCT quantization, and low-pass filtering. The severity of these distortions ranged from 0 (no distortion) to levels beyond the most severe distortions applied in the channel models during embedding. After each distortion of each image, the watermark detector was applied and the resulting bit sequence was compared against the embedded bit sequence. If even one bit had been corrupted, the watermark was considered as having failed to survive.

At least three main results can be expected from this experiment:

First, as neither of the two embedders terminates before the watermark survives 100 applications of the channel model, all the watermarks should be virtually guaranteed to survive distortions up to the level employed in that model. For example, watermarks embedded using the DCTQ model are expected to survive DCT quantization up to a multiplier of 2. Watermarks embedded with the COMBO model should survive all three forms of distortion: additive noise up to a standard deviation of 4.5, DCT quantization up to a multiplier of 2, and low-pass filtering up to a filter width of 0.55.

Second, the two embedders should differ in the fidelity of the watermarked images. In terms of Figures 2 and 3, both these algorithms find points inside the robustness region for the given channel, but the relative algorithm should find a point that is closer to the original than the one found by the absolute algorithm.

Finally, the improvement in fidelity will most likely come at the expense of robustness against distortions not included in the channel model – either distortions of different kinds, or distortions of greater severity. Thus, for example, watermarks embedded with the DCTQ model will likely have poor robustness against low-pass filtering, and those embedded with the LPF model will have poor robustness against DCT quantization. Furthermore, error rates should increase rapidly as the severity of a distortions increases beyond the maximum severity implemented in the model. Thus, while watermarks embedded with the DCTQ model should survive DCT quantization with a multiplier of 2, they should nearly always fail when the multiplier is much more than 2. These are actually desirable properties of the proposed system, as the objective is to embed the least visible watermark that will survive the channel – any robustness to distortions beyond those implemented in the channel implies that we could have achieved the required robustness with a weaker, and less visible, watermark.

6 Results

The first result to be reported pertains to the second expectation: that the relative algorithm should yield better fidelity than the absolute algorithm. The reason for looking at this result first is that it will allow a quick dismissal of the absolute algorithm. Figure 4 shows histograms of the signal to noise ratios[2] (SNR's, expressed in dB) of the watermarks embedded by the two algorithms. Each of the graphs in the figure corresponds to one of the four channel models. The dashed line in each graph shows the distribution of SNR's that resulted from the absolute algorithm. The solid line shows the distribution that resulted from the relative algorithm. As expected, the relative algorithm yielded substantially better results (higher SNR's).

Figure 5 illustrates the perceptual impact of the two algorithms using the COMBO channel model. The SNR for this image was close to the average in

[2] The "signal" here is the original image, and the "noise" is the watermark.

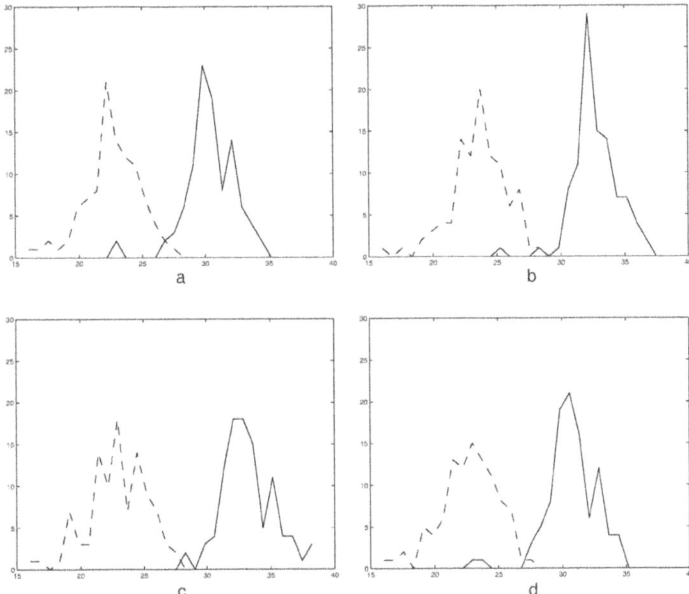

Fig. 4. Histograms of signal-to-noise ratios (SNR's) obtained by embedding with various channel models. The x axis in each graph is SNR in dB. The y axis is the number of images out of 100. The dashed lines show the results from the absolute embedder. The solid lines show the results from the relative embedder. The channel models are (a) AWGN, (b) DCTQ, (c) LPF, and (d) COMBO.

both cases. Clearly[3], the fidelity of the absolute method, for this number of bits and level of robustness, is very poor. The fidelity of the relative method, however, is quite good. Figure 6 indicates that the good fidelity shown for the relative method in Figure 5 extends beyond the average case. This figure shows the watermarked images that had the lowest and second-lowest SNR's of all those embedded using the relative algorithm.

Tests on the robustness of watermarks embedded with the absolute method indicated that, as expected, they are highly robust to the modeled distortions. However, it is not worth examining these results in detail, because the watermarks have such poor fidelity that their robustness is of only academic interest. Instead, the rest of this section discusses the detailed results for the relative method.

Figures 7, 8, and 9 show the robustness of the watermarked images against additive Gaussian noise, DCT quantization, and low-pass filtering, respectively. In each graph, the x axis indicates severity of the distortion, with 0 meaning no

[3] This should be clear assuming that the copy of this paper you are reading is high enough quality to show the distortion present in Figure 5a. If not, you'll have to take my word for it.

a

b

Fig. 5. Typical perceptual fidelity of (a) the absolute embedder and (b) the relative embedder, when the watermark was embedded using the COMBO model. The SNR for (a) is 23dB. The SNR for (b) is 31dB.

distortion at all. The vertical dotted line marks the maximum severity implemented in the channel model. The y axis indicates the fraction of watermarks that failed to survive the distortion. Each graph has four data lines, giving the results for watermarks embedded with each of the four channel models. The lines for watermarks that are expected to survive the distortion (at least at lower severities) are solid, while the lines for other watermarks are dashed. In

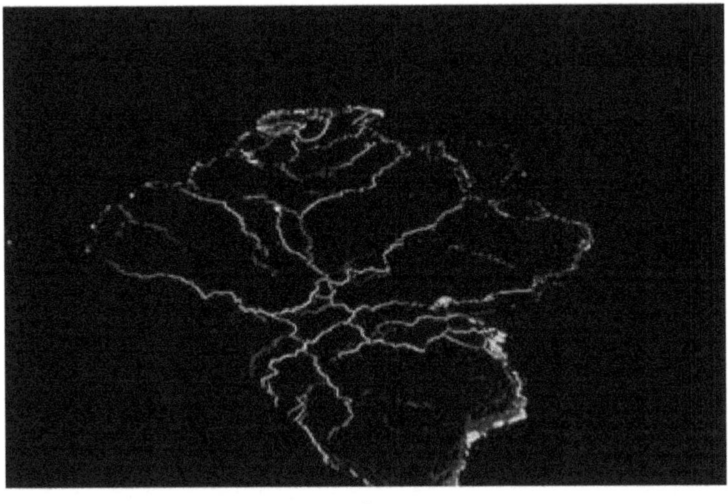

a

b

Fig. 6. (a) Worst, and (b) second-worst SNR images obtained using the relative embedder with the COMBO model. The SNR for (a) is 23dB. The SNR for (b) is 23.5dB. Presumably, the reason for the low SNR in (a) is simply that this image has a very small signal (it is an image of a lava flow at night).

each case, the line for watermarks embedded with the COMBO model is solid, because these should survive all three types of distortion.

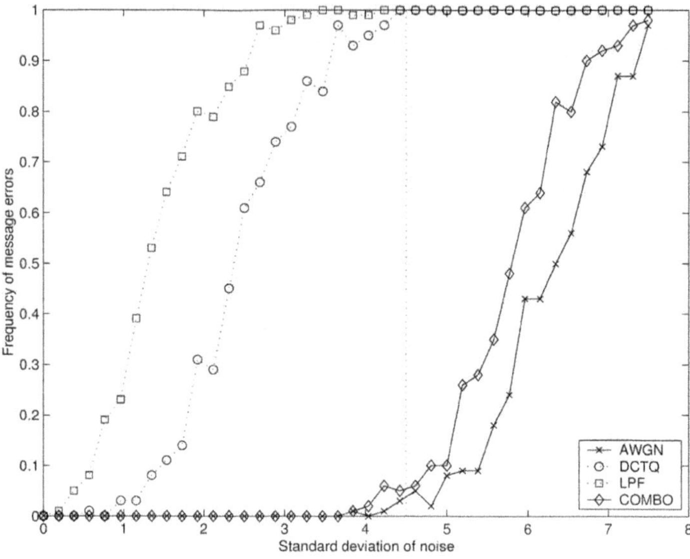

Fig. 7. Robustness against additive, white Gaussian noise.

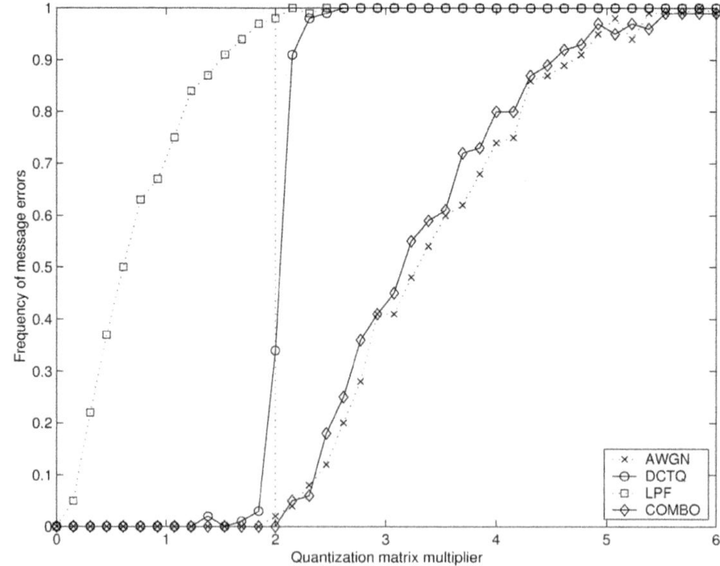

Fig. 8. Robustness against DCT quantization.

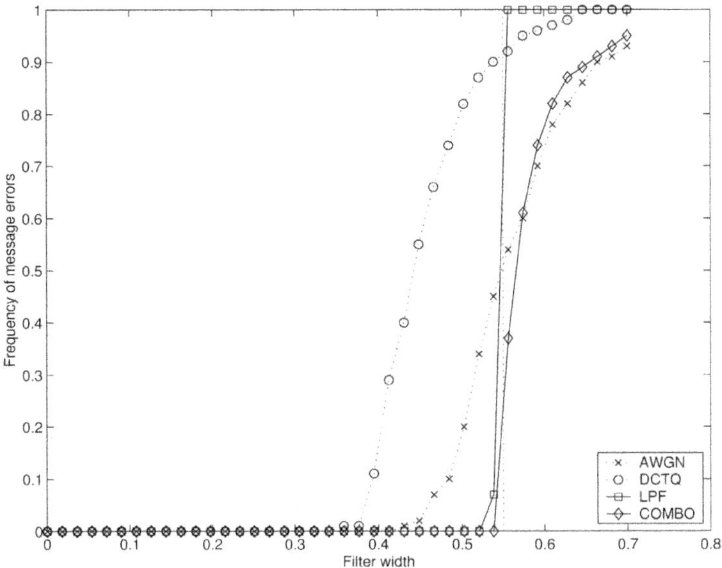

Fig. 9. Robustness against Gaussian low-pass filtering.

In all three tests, watermarks that were embedded with models that matched the distortions had very low error rates. Thus, nearly all watermarks embedded with the AWGN model survived additive Gaussian noise up to a standard deviation of 4.5; nearly all watermarks embedded with the DCTQ model survived DCT quantization up to a multiplier of 2; and nearly all watermarks embedded with the LPF model survived low-pass filtering up to a width of 0.55. The COMBO watermarks survived all three types of distortion up to the expected severity levels.

Beyond the levels of severity anticipated by the models, the error rates rose very fast, as expected. In the cases of DCT quantization and low-pass filtering, the error rates rise almost immediately to 100%. In the case of additive Gaussian noise, the rates rose more slowly. This can be understood by noting that, unlike DCT quantization and low-pass filtering, the additive Gaussian noise distortion is stochastic even after a severity level is specified. Thus, no matter how severe the distortion, there's always some chance that a watermark will survive additive Gaussian noise.

While the COMBO watermarks were the only ones that exhibited near ideal behavior in all three tests, the robustness of the AWGN watermarks was not terrible. That is, watermarks embedded with the AWGN channel model were moderately robust to both DCT quantization and low-pass filtering. This provides some further evidence for the assertion we've made in the past [11,12] that making a watermark robust against additive Gaussian noise tends to make it robust to other things.

On the other hand, the DCTQ and LPF watermarks exhibited poor robustness against distortions for which they were not designed. This implies that it may be wrong to assume that, because it often quantizes high frequencies to zero, JPEG quantization is similar to low-pass filtering.

Finally, Figure 10 shows an example of something that happened quite frequently. The two images shown here were watermarked with the same message, using the same key, and virtually the same SNR's – yet the image on the top is more robust to DCT quantization than the image on the bottom, while the image on the bottom is more robust to low-pass filtering. That this can happen is not surprising given the above discussion. However, this result might be intriguing to those of us who were accustomed to thinking of watermark robustness, within the context of a given detection algorithm, as a one-dimensional, scalar value.

7 Directions for Further Research

This paper has focused on the problem of tailoring watermarks for arbitrary channels, specified by black-box procedural models, when the detector is blind, knowing nothing of the original cover work or the channel model. The stipulation that the detector should have no knowledge of the channel model means that we cannot tailor the watermark code to the model. Thus, the only step in the embedding process that can be tailored is the embedding function. A simple, iterative algorithm for channel-specific embedding has been presented, and shown to yield good results for three different types of channel.

The main advantage of the proposed method is that it does not sacrifice fidelity for robustness against distortions that do not occur in the channel model. It thus yields a watermarked image closer to the original than other methods would, while still providing the desired level of robustness to expected distortions. Another good point about this method is that it is very simple.

While the proposed method produced the desired results in tests, there are several areas for further research:

- The proposed method is sub-optimal in at least some cases. Specifically, in the 2D illustrations shown in Figure 3, the method often failed to find the closest watermarked work that will survive the quantization channel. It is therefore interesting to look for more sophisticated solutions to the problem chosen here. The task of finding the closest robust work might be approached as a learning problem, and might succumb to some variation on existing learning methods.
- The system described here relies on designing a watermarking code that is robust to a wide range of distortions. If the code is not robust to some distortion present in the channel model (for example, the code tested here is not robust to geometric distortions), the iterative embedding method will fail (in fact, it will never terminate). It is thus interesting to remove the stipulation that the detector knows nothing of the channel, and ask how codes might be tailored to black-box channel models.

a

b

Fig. 10. A case in which two copies of an image, both watermarked with the same message, same key, and essentially the same fidelity, but each watermarked using a different channel model, yield qualitatively different robustness. Copy (a) was marked with the DCTQ model, and has an SNR of 33.04dB. Copy (b) was marked with the LPF model, and has an SNR of 33.06dB. Copy (a) is more robust to DCT quantization than copy (b) ((a) is robust up to a quantization multiplier of 2.3, while (b) is only robust to a multiplier of 1.1). However, copy (a) is *less* robust to low-pass filtering than copy (b) ((b) is robust up to a filter width of 0.56, but (a) is only robust only to a width of 0.41).

- The results in Section 6 show that the system is sometimes quite sensitive to differences between the channel model used during embedding and the distortions applied before detection. This raises the possibility of using systems like this for semi-fragile or telltale watermarks. Can we explicitly tailor watermarks to be robust against one black-box model, but fragile against another?
- Finally, the type of embedding function proposed here might have theoretical implications for channel capacity. Cohen and Lapidoth [9] conjecture that, when using the embedding function of Equation 2, Costa's main result – the irrelevance of the first noise source to channel capacity – can only be obtained if the second noise source is additive Gaussian. This conjecture says nothing about what results can be obtained when using other embedding functions. It may be that, using iterative embedding functions like the one presented here, Costa's result can be extended to a wider range of channels.

References

1. Liang, T., Rodriguez, J. J.: Robust watermarking using robust coefficients. *Security and Watermarking of Multimedia Contents II*, SPIE0-3971:326–335, (2000)
2. Costa, M.: Writing on dirty paper. *IEEE Transactions on Information Theory*, 29:439–441, (1983)
3. Chen, B., Wornell, G. W.: An information-theoretic approach to the design of robust digital watermarking systems. *IEEE Transactions on Acoustics, Speech, and Signal Processing* (1999)
4. Chou, J., Pradhan, S. S., Ramchandran, K.: On the duality between distributed source coding and data hiding. *Thirty-third Asilomar Conference on Signals, Systems, and Computers* 2 (1999) 1503–1507
5. Ramkumar, M.: *Data Hiding in Multimedia: Theory and Applications.* PhD thesis, New Jersey Institute of Technology (1999)
6. Eggers, J. J., Su, J. K., Girod, B.: A blind watermarking scheme based on structured codebooks. *IEE Seminar on Secure Images and Image Authentication* (2000) 4/1–4/21
7. Miller, M. L., Doërr, G. J., Cox, I. J.: Applying informed coding and embedding to design a robust, high capacity watermark. *IEEE Transactions on Image Processing* (to appear)
8. Erez, U., Shamai, S., Zamir, R.: Capacity and lattice-strategies for canceling known interference. *Proc. of the Cornell Summer Workshop on Information Theory* (2000)
9. Cohen, A. S., Lapidoth, A.: Generalized writing on dirty paper. *International Symposium on Information Theory (ISIT)* (2002)
10. Corel Stock Photo Library 3. Corel Corporation, Ontario, Canada
11. Cox, I. J., Miller, M. L., McKellips, A.: Watermarking as communications with side information. *Proceedings of the IEEE* 87(7) (1999) 1127–1141
12. Cox, I. J., Miller, M. L., Bloom, J. A.: *Digital Watermarking.* Morgan Kaufmann (2001)

Image Steganography and Steganalysis: Concepts and Practice

Rajarathnam Chandramouli[1], Mehdi Kharrazi[2], and Nasir Memon[3]

[1] Department of Electrical and Computer Engineering
Stevens Institute of Technology, Hoboken, NJ 12345,USA
mouli@stevens-tech.edu

[2] Department of Electrical and Computer Engineering
Polytechnic University, Brooklyn, NY 11201, USA
mehdi@isis.poly.edu

[3] Department of Computer and Information Science
Polytechnic University, Brooklyn, NY 11201, USA
memon@poly.edu

Abstract. In the last few years, we have seen many new and powerful steganography and steganalysis techniques reported in the literature. In the following paper we go over some general concepts and ideas that apply to steganography and steganalysis. Specifically we establish a framework and define notion of security for a steganographic system. We show how conventional definitions do not really adequately cover image steganography and an provide alternate definition. We also review some of the more recent image steganography and steganalysis techniques.

1 Introduction

Steganography refers to the science of "invisible" communication. Unlike cryptography, where the goal is to secure communications from an eavesdropper, steganographic techniques strive to hide the very presence of the message itself from an observer. Although steganography is an ancient subject, the modern formulation of it is often given in terms of the *prisoner's problem* [1] where Alice and Bob are two inmates who wish to communicate in order to hatch an escape plan. However, all communication between them is examined by the warden, Wendy, who will put them in solitary confinement at the slightest suspicion of covert communication. Specifically, in the general model for steganography, illustrated in Figure 1, we have Alice wishing to send a secret message m to Bob. In order to do so, she "embeds" m into a *cover-object* c, to obtain the *stego-object* s. The stego-object s is then sent through the public channel. In a *pure steganography* framework, the technique for embedding the message is unknown to Wendy and shared as a secret between Alice and Bob. However, it is generally not considered as good practice to rely on the secrecy of the algorithm itself. In *private key steganography* Alice and Bob share a secret key which is used to embed the message. The secret key, for example, can be a password used to seed a pseudo-random number generator to select pixel locations in an image

T. Kalker et al. (Eds.): IWDW 2003, LNCS 2939, pp. 35–49, 2004.
© Springer-Verlag Berlin Heidelberg 2004

cover-object for embedding the secret message (possibly encrypted). Wendy has no knowledge about the secret key that Alice and Bob share, although she is aware of the algorithm that they could be employing for embedding messages. In *public key steganography*, Alice and Bob have private-public key pairs and know each other's public key. In this paper we restrict our attention to private key steganography.

The warden Wendy who is free to examine all messages exchanged between Alice and Bob can be passive or active. A *passive* warden simply examines the message and tries to determine if it potentially contains a hidden message. If it appears that it does, she suppresses the message and/or takes appropriate action, else she lets the message through without any action. An *active* warden, on the other hand, can alter messages deliberately, even though she does not see any trace of a hidden message, in order to foil any secret communication that can nevertheless be occurring between Alice and Bob. The amount of change the warden is allowed to make depends on the model being used and the cover-objects being employed. For example, with images, it would make sense that the warden is allowed to make changes as long as she does not alter significantly the subjective visual quality of a suspected stego-image. In this paper we restrict our attention to the passive warden case and assume that no changes are made to the stego-object by the warden Wendy.

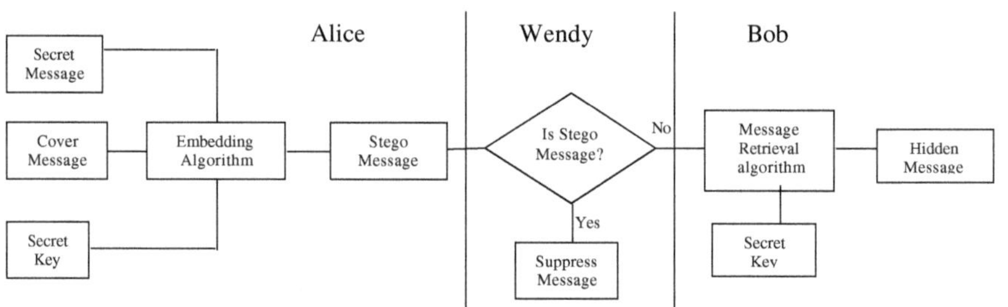

Fig. 1. Framework for Secret Key Passive Warden Steganography. Alice embeds secret message in cover image (left). Wendy the warden checks if Alice's image is a stego-image (center). If she cannot determine it to be so, she passes it on to Bob who retrieves the hidden message based on secret key (right) he shares with Alice.

It should be noted that the general idea of hiding some information in digital content has a wider class of applications that go beyond steganography. The techniques involved in such applications are collectively referred to as *information hiding*. For example, an image printed on a document could be annotated by metadata that could lead a user to its high resolution version. In general, metadata provides additional information about an image. Although metadata can also be stored in the file header of a digital image, this approach has many limitations. Usually, when a file is transformed to another format (e.g., from

TIFF to JPEG or to bmp), the metadata is lost. Similarly, cropping or any other form of image manipulation destroys the metadata. Finally, metadata can only be attached to an image as long as the image exists in the digital form and is lost once the image is printed. Information hiding allows the metadata to travel with the image regardless of the file format and image state (digital or analog).

A special case of information hiding is *digital watermarking.* Digital watermarking is the process of embedding information into digital multimedia content such that the information (the watermark) can later be extracted or detected for a variety of purposes including copy prevention and control. Digital watermarking has become an active and important area of research, and development and commercialization of watermarking techniques is being deemed essential to help address some of the challenges faced by the rapid proliferation of digital content. The key difference between information hiding and watermarking is the absence of an active adversary. In watermarking applications like copyright protection and authentication, there is an active adversary that would attempt to remove, invalidate or forge watermarks. In information hiding there is no such active adversary as there is no value associated with the act of removing the information hidden in the content. Nevertheless, information hiding techniques need to be robust against accidental distortions.

Unlike information hiding and digital watermarking, the main goal of steganography is to communicate securely in a completely undetectable manner. That is, Wendy should not be able to distinguish in any sense between cover-objects (objects not containing any secret message) and stego-objects (objects containing a secret message). In this context, *steganalysis* refers to the body of techniques that aid Wendy in distinguishing between cover-objects and stego-objects. It should be noted that Wendy has to make this distinction without any knowledge of the secret key which Alice and Bob may be sharing and sometimes even without any knowledge of the specific algorithm that they might be using for embedding the secret message. Hence steganalysis is inherently a difficult problem. However, it should also be noted that Wendy does not have to glean anything about the contents of the secret message m. Just determining the existence of a hidden message is enough. This fact makes her job a bit easier.

Given the proliferation of digital images, and given the high degree of redundancy present in a digital representation of an image (despite compression), there has been an increased interest in using digital images as cover-objects for the purpose of steganography. For a good survey of image steganography techniques, the reader is referred to [2]. The development of techniques for image steganography and the wide-spread availability of tools for the same have led to an increased interest in steganalysis techniques for image data. The last two years, for example, have seen many new and powerful steganalysis techniques reported in the literature. Many of such techniques are specific to different embedding methods and indeed have shown to be quite effective in this regard. However, our intention here is not to present a comprehensive survey of different embedding techniques and possible ways to detect them. Instead we focus on some general concepts and ideas that apply across different techniques and cover-media. The rest of this paper is organized as follows: in section 2 we first establish a formal framework and define the notion of security for a steganographic system. We point out how conventional definitions do not really adequately cover image steganography (or steganography using any multimedia object for that matter) and provide alternate definitions. In section 3, we go over the more recent steganography and steganalysis techniques and in section 4 we conclude.

2 Steganographic Security

In this section we explore the topic of steganographic security. Some of the earlier work on this topic was done in [3,4,5]. Here, a steganographic system is considered to be insecure if the warden Wendy is able to prove the existence of a secret message. In other words, if she can distinguish between cover-objects and stego-objects, assuming she has unlimited computing power. Let P_C denote the probability distribution of cover-objects and P_S denote the probability distribution of stego-objects. Cachin [3] defines a steganographic algorithm to be ϵ-secure ($\epsilon \geq 0$) if the relative entropy between the cover-object and the stego-object probability distributions (P_C and P_S, respectively) is at most ϵ, i.e.,

$$D(P_C||P_S) = \int P_C \cdot log \frac{P_C}{P_S} \leq \epsilon \tag{1}$$

From this equation we note that $D(.)$ increases with the ratio $\frac{P_C}{P_S}$ which in turn means that the reliability of steganalysis detection will also increase. A steganographic technique is said to be *perfectly secure* if $\epsilon = 0$ (i.e. $P_C = P_S$). In this case the probability distributions of the cover and stego-objects are indistinguishable. Perfectly secure steganography algorithms (although impractical) are known to exist [3].

We observe that there are several shortcomings in the ϵ-secure definition presented in Eq. (1). Some of these are listed below.

- The ϵ-secure notion as presented in [3] assumes that the cover and stego-objects are vectors of independent, identically distributed (i.i.d.) random variables. This is not true for many real-life cover signals such as images. One approach to rectify this problem is to put a constraint that the relative entropy computed using the n-th order joint probability distributions must be less than, say, ϵ_n and then force the embedding technique to preserve this constraint. But, it may then be possible, at least in theory, to use $(n+1)$st order statistics for successful steganalysis. This line of thought clearly poses several interesting issues:
  - Practicality of preserving nth order joint probability distribution during embedding for medium to large values of n.
  - Behavior of the sequence $\{\epsilon_n\}$ depends on the cover message as well as the embedding algorithm. If this sequence exhibits a smooth variation then, for a desired target value, say, $\epsilon = \epsilon^*$, it may be possible to precompute a value of $n = n^*$ that achieves this target.

Of course, even if these nth order distributions are preserved, there is no guarantee that embedding induced perceptual distortion will be acceptable. If this distortion is significant, then it is not even necessary to use a statistical detector for steganalysis!

- While the ϵ-secure definition may work for random bit streams (with no inherent statistical structure), for real-life cover-objects such as audio, image, and video, it seems to fail. This is because, real-life cover-objects have a rich statistical structure in terms of correlation, higher-order dependence, etc. By exploiting this structure, it is possible to design good steganalysis detectors even if the first order probability distribution is preserved (i.e., $\epsilon = 0$) during message embedding. If we approximate the probability distribution functions using histograms, then, examples such as [6] show that it is possible to design good steganalysis detectors even if the histograms of cover and stego are the same.
- Consider the following embedding example. Let X and Y be two binary random variables such that $P(X = 0) = P(Y = 0) = 1/2$ and let them represent the host and covert message, respectively. Let the embedding function be given by the following:

$$Z = X + Y \mod 2. \tag{2}$$

We then observe that $D(P_Z||P_X) = 0$ but $E(X - Z)^2 = 1$. Therefore the non-zero mean squared error value may give away enough information to a steganalysis detector even though $D(.) = 0$.

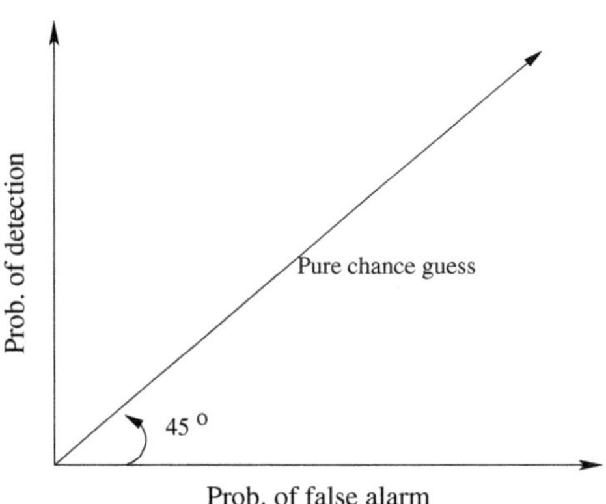

Fig. 2. Detector ROC plane.

Given these arguments, is there an alternative measure for stego security that is perhaps more fundamental to steganalysis? In the rest of this section we present an alternate definition of steganographic security. In our new definition, the *false alarm probability* (α=P(detect message present|message absent)) and the *detection probability* (β=P(detect message present| message present) play an important role. A steganalysis detector's receiver operating characteristic (ROC) is a plot of α versus β. Points on the ROC curve represent the achievable performance of the steganalysis detector. The average error probability of steganalysis detection is given by,

$$P_e = (1-\beta)P(\text{message embedded}) + \alpha P(\text{message not embedded}). \quad (3)$$

If we assume $P(\text{message embedded}) = P(\text{message not embedded})$ then, from Eq. (3),

$$P_e = \frac{1}{2}\left[(1-\beta)+\alpha\right] \quad (4)$$

Note that, α and β are detector dependent values. For example, for a chosen value of α, β can be maximized by using a Neyman-Pearson statistical detector [7] or, both α and β can be fixed and traded-off with the number of observations required for detection by using Wald's sequential probability ratio test [8]. Observe from Eq. (4) that, if $\alpha = \beta$ then $P_e = 1/2$ as shown in Fig. 2. That is, the detector makes purely random guesses when it operates or forced to operate on the 45 degree line in the ROC plane. This means that the detector does not have sufficient information to make an intelligent decision. Therefore, if the embedder forces the detector to operate on the 45 degree ROC line by employing appropriate algorithms and/or parameters, then we say that the stego message is secure and obtain the following definitions.

Definition 1 *A stego embedding algorithm is said to be $\gamma_{\mathcal{D}}$-secure w.r.t. a steganalysis detector $\mathcal{D}$ if $|\beta_{\mathcal{D}} - \alpha_{\mathcal{D}}| \leq \gamma_{\mathcal{D}}$, where $0 \leq \gamma_{\mathcal{D}} \leq 1$.*

Definition 2 *A stego embedding algorithm is said to be perfectly secure w.r.t. a steganalysis detector $\mathcal{D}$ if $\gamma_{\mathcal{D}} = 0$.*

Clearly, from these definitions we can think of embedding and steganalysis as a zero sum game where the embedder attempts to minimize $|\beta - \alpha|$ while the steganalyst attempts to maximize it.

3 Steganalysis

There are two approaches to the problem of steganalysis, one is to come up with a steganalysis method specific to a particular steganographic algorithm. The other is developing techniques which are independent of the steganographic algorithm to be analyzed. Each of the two approaches has it's own advantages and disadvantages. A steganalysis technique specific to an embedding method would give very good results when tested only on that embedding method, and might fail on all other steganographic algorithms. On the other hand, a steganalysis method which is independent of the embedding algorithm might preform less accurately overall but still provide acceptable results on new embedding algorithms. These two approaches will be discussed below and we will go over a few of the proposed techniques for each approach.

Before we proceed, one should note that steganalysis algorithms in essence are called successful if they can detect the presence of a message. The message itself does not have to be decoded. Indeed, the latter can be very hard if the message is encrypted using strong cryptography. However, recently there have been methods proposed in the literature which in addition to detecting the presence of a message are also able to estimate the size of the embedded message with great accuracy. We consider these aspects to be extraneous and only focus on the ability to detect the presence of a message.

3.1 Embedding Algorithm Specific Steganalysis Techniques

We first look at steganalysis techniques that are designed with a particular steganographic embedding algorithm in mind. Steganographic algorithms could be divided into 3 categories based on the type of the image used as the cover medium, i.e. Raw images (for example bmp format), Palette based images (for example GIF images), and finally JPEG images.

Raw Images are widely used with the simple LSB embedding method, where the message is embedded in a subset of the LSB (least significant bit) plane of the image, possibly after encryption. It is well known that an image is generally not visually affected when its least significant bit plane is changed. Popular steganographic tools based on LSB like embedding [9,10,11], vary in their approach for hiding information. Some algorithms change LSB of pixels visited in a random walk, others modify pixels in certain areas of images, or instead of just changing the last bit they increment or decrement the pixel value.

An early approach to LSB steganalysis was presented in [12] by Westfeld and Pfitzmann. They note that LSB embedding induces a partitioning of image pixels into Pairs of Values (PoV's) that get mapped to one another. For example the value 2 gets mapped to 3 on LSB flipping and likewise 3 gets mapped to 2. So (2, 3) forms a PoV. Now LSB embedding causes the frequency of individual elements of a PoV to flatten out with respect to one another. So for example if an image has 50 pixels that have a value 2 and 100 pixels that have a value 3, then after LSB embedding of the entire LSB plane the expected frequencies of 2 and 3 are 75 and 75 respectively. This of course is when the entire LSB plane is modified. However, as long as the embedded message is large enough, there will be a statistically discernible flattening of PoV distributions and this fact is exploited by their steganalysis technique. The length constraint, on the other hand, turns out to be the main limitation of their technique. LSB embedding can only be reliably detected when the message length becomes comparable with the number of pixels in the image. In the case where message placement is known, shorter messages can be detected. But requiring knowledge of message placement is too strong an assumption as one of the key factors playing in the favor of Alice and Bob is the fact that the secret message is hidden in a location unknown to Wendy.

A more direct approach for LSB steganalysis that analytically estimates the length of an LSB embedded message in an image was proposed by Dumitrescu et. al. [13]. Their technique is based on an important statistical identity related to certain sets of pixels in an image. This identity is very sensitive to LSB embedding, and the change in the identity can quantify the length of the embedded message. This technique is described in detail below, where our description is adopted from [13].

Consider the partition of an image into pairs of horizontally adjacent pixels. Let $\mathcal{P}$ be the set of all these pixel pairs. Define the subsets X, Y and Z of $\mathcal{P}$ as follows:

- X is the set of pairs $(u, v) \in \mathcal{P}$ such that v is even and $u < v$, or v is odd and $u > v$.
- Y is the set of pairs $(u, v) \in \mathcal{P}$ such that v is even and $u > v$, or v is odd and $u < v$.
- Z is the subset of pairs $(u, v) \in \mathcal{P}$ such that $u = v$.

After having made the above definitions, the authors make the assumption that statistically we will have

$$|X| = |Y|. \tag{5}$$

This assumption is true for natural images as the gradient of intensity function in any direction is equally likely to be positive or negative.

Furthermore, they partition the set Y into two subsets W and V, with W being the set of pairs in $\mathcal{P}$ of the form $(2k, 2k+1)$ or $(2k+1, 2k)$, and $V = Y - W$. Then $\mathcal{P} = X \cup W \cup V \cup Z$. They call sets X, V, W and Z as *primary sets*.

When LSB embedding is done pixel values get modified and so does the membership of pixel pairs in the primary sets. More specifically, given a pixel pair (u, v), they identify the following four situations:

00) both values u and v remain unmodified;
01) only v is modified;
10) only u is modified;
11) both u and v are modified.

The corresponding change of membership in the primary sets is shown in Figure 3.

By some simple algebraic manipulations, the authors finally arrive at the equation

$$0.5\gamma p^2 + (2|X'| - |\mathcal{P}|)p + |Y'| - |X'| = 0. \tag{6}$$

where $\gamma = |W| + |Z| = |W'| + |Z'|$. The above equation allows one to estimate p, i.e the length of the embedded message, based on X', Y', W', Z' which can all be measured from the image being examined for possible steganography. Of course it should be noted that we cannot have $\gamma = 0$, the probability of which for natural images is very small.

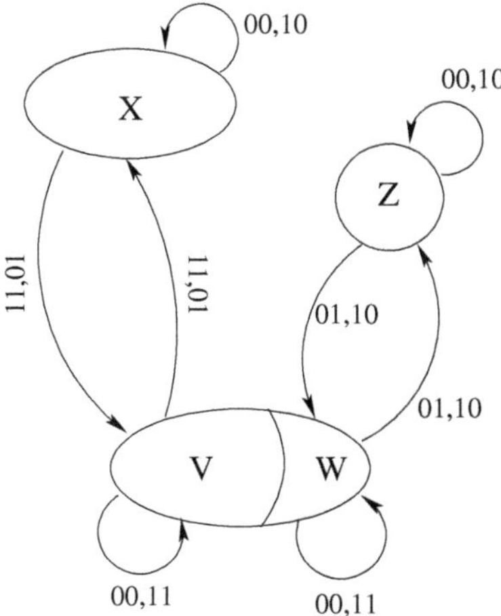

Fig. 3. State transition diagram for sets X, V, W, Z under LSB flipping.

In fact, the pairs based steganalysis described above was inspired by an effectively identical technique, although from a very different approach, called RS-Steganalysis by Fridrich et. al. in [14] that had first provided remarkable detection accuracy and message length estimation even for short messages. However, RS-Steganalysis does not offer a direct analytical explanation that can account for its success. It is based more on empirical observations and their modelling. It is interesting to see that the Pair's based steganalysis technique essentially ends up with exactly the same steganalyzer as RS-Steganalysis.

Although the above techniques are for gray scale images, they are applicable to color images by considering each color plane as a gray scale image. A steganalysis technique that directly analyzes color images for LSB embedding and yields high detection rates even for short messages was proposed by Fridrich, Du and Long [15]. They define pixels that are "close" in color intensity to be pixels that have a difference of not more than one count in any of the three color planes. They then show that the ratio of "close" colors to the total number of unique colors increases significantly when a new message of a selected length is embedded in a cover image as opposed to when the same message is embedded in a stego-image (that is an image already carrying a LSB encoded message). It is this difference that enables them to distinguish cover-images from stego-images for the case of LSB steganography.

In contrast to the simple LSB method discussed above, Hide [11] increments or decrements the sample value in order to change the LSB value. Thus the techniques previously discussed for LSB embedding with bit flipping do not detect Hide. In order to detect embedded messages by Hide, Westfeld [16] proposes a similar steganalysis attack as Fridrich, Du and Long [15] were it is argued that since the values are incremented or decremented, 26 neighboring colors for each color value could be created, were as in a natural image there are 4 to 5 neighboring colors on average. Thus by looking at the neighborhood histogram representing the number of neighbors in one axis and the frequency in the other one would be able to say if the image carries a message. This is clearly seen in Fig. 4.

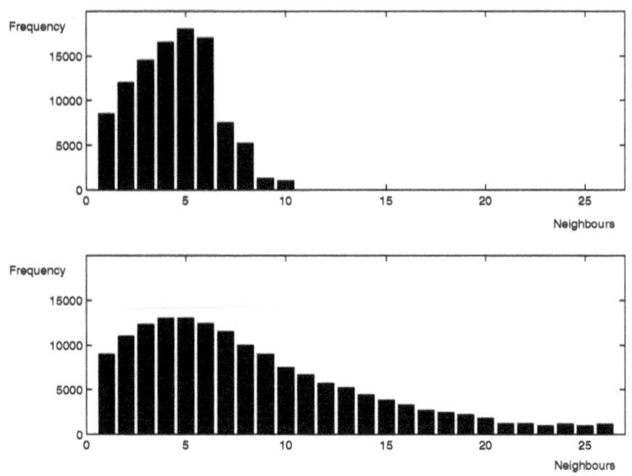

Fig. 4. Neighborhood histogram of a cover image (top) and stego image with 40 KB message embedded (bottom)[16]

Palette Based Images like GIF images, are another popular class of images for which there have been a number of steganography methods proposed [17,18, 19]. Perhaps some of the earliest steganalysis work in this regard was reported by Johnson and Jajodia [20]. They mainly look at palette tables in GIF images and anomalies caused therein by common stego-tools that perform LSB embedding in GIF images. Since pixel values in a palette image are represented by indices into a color look-up table which contains the actual color RGB value, even minor modifications to these indices can result in annoying artifacts. Visual inspection or simple statistics from such stego-images can yield enough tell-tale evidence to discriminate between stego and cover-images.

In order to minimize the distortion caused by embedding, EzStego [17] first sorts the color pallet so that the color differences between consecutive colors is minimized. It then embeds the message bits in the LSB of the color indices in the sorted pallet. Since pixels which can modified due to the embedding process get mapped neighboring colors in the palette, which are now similar, visual artifacts are minimal and hard to notice. To detect EzStego, Fridrich [6] argues that a vector consisting of color pairs, obtained after sorting the pallet, has considerable structure due to the fact there a small number of colors in pallet images. But the embedding process will disturb this structure, thus after the embedding the entropy of the color pair vector will increase. The entropy would be maximal when the maximum length message is embedded in to the GIF image. Another steganalysis techniques for EzStego were proposed by Westfeld [12], but the technique discussed above provides a much higher detection rate and a more accurate estimate of the message lengths.

JPEG Images are the the third category of images which are used routinely as cover medium. Many steganalysis attacks have been proposed for steganography algorithms [21,22,23] which employ this category of images. Fridrich [6] has proposed attacks on the F5 and Outguess algorithms, both of which work on jpeg images. F5 [23] embeds bits in the DCT coefficients using matrix embedding so that for a given message the number of changes made to the cover image is minimized. But F5 does alter the histogram of DCT coefficients. Fridrich proposes a simple technique to estimate the original histogram so that the number of changes and length of the embedded message could be estimated. The original histogram is simply estimated by cropping the jpeg image by 4 columns and then re-compressing the image using the same quantization table as used before. As is evident in Fig 5, the resulting DCT coefficient histogram would be a very good estimate of the original histogram. Although no analytical proof is given for the estimation method, steganalysis based on this simple technique preforms very well.

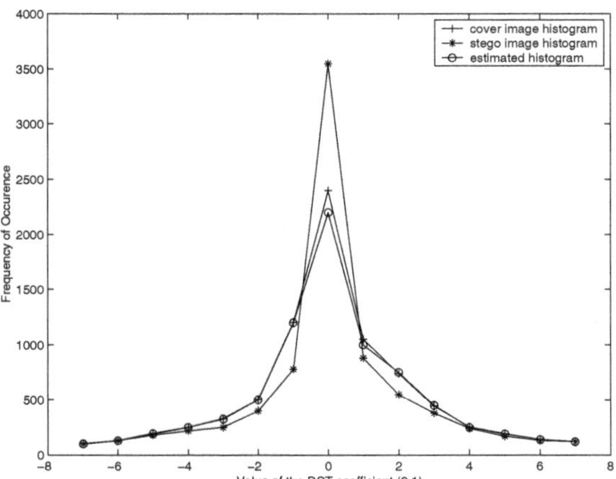

Fig. 5. The effect of F5 embedding on the histogram of the DCT coefficient (2,1).[6]

A second technique proposed by Fridrich [6] deals with the Outguess [21] embedding program. Outguess first embeds information in LSB of the DCT coefficients by making a random walk, leaving some coefficients unchanged. Then it adjusts the remaining coefficient in order to preserve the original histogram of DCT coefficients. Thus the previous steganalysis method where the original histogram is estimated will not be effective. On the other hand when embedding messages in a clean image, noise is introduced in the DCT coefficient, therefore increasing the spatial discontinuities along the 8x8 jpeg blocks. Given a stego image if a message is embedded in the image again there is partial cancellation of changes made to the LSB of DCT coefficients, thus the increase in discontinuities will be smaller. This increase or lack of increase in the discontinuities is used to estimate the message size which is being carried by a stego image.

3.2 Universal Steganalysis Techniques

The steganalysis techniques described above were all specific to a particular embedding algorithm. A more general class of steganalysis techniques pioneered independently by Avcibas et. al. [24,25,26] and Farid [27], are designed to work with any steganographic embedding algorithm, even an unknown algorithm. Such techniques have subsequently been called *Universal Steganalysis* techniques or *Blind Steganalysis Techniques.* Such techniques essentially design a classifier based on a training set of cover-objects and stego-objects arrived at from a variety of different algorithms. Classification is done based on some inherent "features" of typical natural images which can get violated when an image undergoes some embedding process. Hence, designing a feature classification based universal steganalysis technique consists of tackling two independent problems. The first is to find and calculate features which are able to capture statistical changes introduced in the image after the embedding process. The second is coming up with a strong classification algorithm which is able to maximize the distinction captured by the features and achieve high classification accuracy.

Typically, a good feature should be accurate, consistent and monotonic in capturing statistical signatures left by the embedding process. Prediction accuracy can be interpreted as the ability of the measure to detect the presence of a hidden message with minimum error on average. Similarly, prediction monotonicity signifies that the features should ideally be monotonic in their relationship to the embedded message size. Finally, prediction consistency relates to the feature's ability to provide consistently accurate predictions for a large set of steganography techniques and image types. This implies that the feature should be independent on the type and variety of images supplied to it.

In [26] Avcibas et. al. develop a discriminator for cover images and stego images, using an appropriate set of Image Quality Metrics (IQM's). Objective image quality measures have been utilized in coding artifact evaluation, performance prediction of vision algorithms, quality loss due to sensor inadequacy etc. In [26] they are used not as predictors of subjective image quality or algorithmic performance, but specifically as a steganalysis tool, that is, as features used in distinguishing cover-objects from stego-objects.

To select quality metrics to be used for steganalysis, the authors use Analysis of Variance (ANOVA) techniques. They arrive at a ranking of IQM's based on their F-scores in the ANOVA tests to identify the ones that responded most consistently and strongly to message embedding. The idea is to seek IQM's that

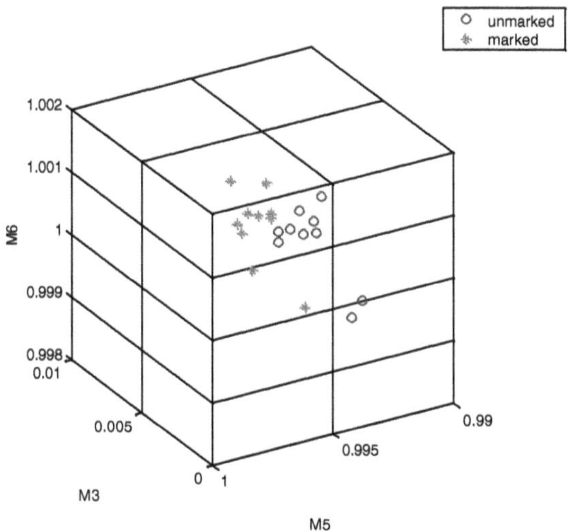

Fig. 6. Scatter plot of 3 image quality measures showing separation of marked and unmarked images.

are sensitive specifically to steganography effects, that is, those measures for which the variability in score data can be explained better because of some treatment rather then as random variations due to the image set. The rationale of using several quality measures is that different measures respond with differing sensitivities to artifacts and distortions. For example, measures like mean-square-error respond more to additive noise, whereas others such as spectral phase or mean square HVS-weighted (Human Visual System) error are more sensitive to pure blur; while the gradient measure reacts to distortions concentrated around edges and textures. Similarly embedding techniques affect different aspects of images. Fig.6 shows separation in the feature plane between stego images and cover images, for 3 example quality metrics.

A second technique proposed by Avcibas et. al. [24] looks at seventh and eight bit planes of an image and calculates several binary similarity measures. The approach is based on the fact that correlation between contiguous bit-planes is effected after a message is embedded in the image. The authors conjecture that correlation between the contiguous bit planes decreases after a message is embedded in the image. In order to capture the effect made by different embedding algorithms several features are calculated. Using the obtained features a MMSE linear predictor is obtained which is used to classify a given image as either as a cover image or an image containing hidden messages.

A different approach is taken by Farid et. al[27] for feature extraction from images. The authors argue that most of the specific steganalysis techniques concentrate on first order statistics, i.e. histogram of DCT coefficients, but simple counter measure could keep the first order statistics intact thus making the steganalysis technique useless. So they propose building a model for natural images by using higher order statistics and then show that images with messages embedded in them deviate form this model. Quadratic mirror filters (QMF) are used to decompose the image, after which higher order statistics such as mean, variance, kurtosis, and skewness are calculated for each subband. Also the error obtained from an optimal linear predictor of coefficient magnitudes of each subband is used as a second set of features.

In all of the above methods, the calculated features are used to train a classifier, which in turn is used to classify clean and stego images. Different classifiers have been employed by different authors, Avcibas et. al. uses a MMSE Linear predictor, where as Farid et. al[27] uses a Fisher linear discriminant [28] and also a Support Vector Machine (SVM) [29] classifier. SVM classifiers seem to have much better performance in terms of classification accuracy compared to linear classifiers since they are able to classify non-linearly separable features. All of the above authors have reported good accuracy results in classifying images as clean or containing hidden messages after training with a classifier. Although, direct comparison might be hard as is in many classification problems, due to the fact that the way experiments are setup or conducted could be very different and thus could effect the overall results.

4 Conclusions

The past few years have seen an increasing interest in using images as cover media for steganographic communication. There have been a multitude of public domain tools, albeit many being ad-hoc and naive, available for image based steganography. Given this fact, detection of covert communications that utilize images has become an important issue. There have been several techniques for detecting stego-images that have been developed in the past few years. In this paper we have reviewed some fundamental notions related to steganography using image media, including security. We also described in detail a number of steganalysis techniques techniques that are representative of the different approaches that have been taken.

References

1. G. Simmons, "The prisoners problem and the subliminal channel," *CRYPTO*, pp. 51–67, 1983.
2. N. F. Johnson and S. Katzenbeisser, "A survay of steganographic techniques," *in S. Katzenbeisser and F. Petitcolas (Eds.): Information Hiding, pp 43–78. Artech House, Norwood, MA.*, 2000.
3. C. Cachin, "An information-theoretic model for steganography," *2nd International Workshop Information Hiding*, vol. LNCS 1525, pp. 306–318, 1998.
4. J. Zollner, H. Federrath, H. Klimant, A. Pfitzman, R. Piotraschke, A. Westfeld, G. Wicke, and G. Wolf, "Modeling the security of steganographic systems," *2nd Information Hiding Workshop*, pp. 345–355, April 1998.

5. R. Chandramouli and N. Memon, "Steganography capacity: A steganalysis perspective," *To appear in SPIE Security and Watermarking of Multimedia Contents V*, vol. 5020, 2003.
6. J. Fridrich, M. Goljan, D. Hogea, and D. Soukal, "Quantitive steganalysis of digital images: Estimating the secret message lenght," *ACM Multimedia Systems Journal, Special issue on Multimedia Security*, 2003.
7. R. Chandramouli and N. Memon, "Analysis of lsb image steganography techniques," *IEEE Intnl. Conf. on Image Processing*, vol. 3, pp. 1019–1022, 2001.
8. ——, "On sequential watermark detection," *IEEE Transactions on Signal Processing*, vol. 51, no. 4, pp. 1034–1044, April 2003.
9. F. Collin, "Encryptpic," *http://www.winsite.com/bin/Info?500000033023.*
10. G. Pulcini, "Stegotif," *http://www.geocities.com/SiliconValley/9210/gfree.html.*
11. T. Sharp, "Hide 2.1, 2001," *http://www.sharpthoughts.org.*
12. A. Westfeld and A. Pfitzmann, "Attacks on steganographic systems," *Information Hiding. 3rd International Workshop*, p. 61–76, 1999.
13. S. Dumitrescu, X. Wu, and N. Memon, "On steganalysis of random lsb embedding in continuous-tone images," *IEEE International Conference on Image Processing, ROchester, New York.*, September 2002.
14. J. Fridrich, M. Goljan, and R. Du, "Detecting lsb steganography in color and gray-scale images," *IEEE Multimedia Special Issue on Security*, pp. 22–28, October-November 2001.
15. J. Fridrich, R. Du, and L. Meng, "Steganalysis of lsb encoding in color images," *ICME 2000, New York, NY, USA.*
16. A. Westfeld, "Detecting low embedding rates," *Information Hiding. 5th International Workshop*, p. 324–339, 2002.
17. R. Machado, "Ezstego," *http://www.stego.com*, 2001.
18. M. Kwan, "Gifshuffle," *http://www.darkside.com.au/gifshuffle/.*
19. C. Moroney, "Hide and seek," *http://www.rugeley.demon.co.uk/security/hdsk50.zip.*
20. N. F. Johnson and S. Jajodia, "Steganalysis of images created using current steganography software," *in David Aucsmith (Eds.): Information Hiding, LNCS 1525, Springer-Verlag Berlin Heidelberg.*, pp. 32–47, 1998.
21. N. Provos, "Defending against statistical steganalysis," *10th USENIX Security Symposium*, 2001.
22. D. Upham, "Jpeg-jsteg," *ftp://ftp.funet.fi/pub/crypt/steganography/jpeg-jsteg-v4.diff.gz.*
23. A. Westfeld, "F5—a steganographic algorithm: High capacity despite better steganalysis," *Information Hiding. 4th International Workshop*, p. 289–302, 2001.
24. I. Avcibas, N. Memon, and B. sankur, "Steganalysis using image quality metrics." *Security and Watermarking of Multimedia Contents, San Jose, Ca.*, Feruary 2001.
25. ——, "Image steganalysis with binary similarity measures." *IEEE International Conference on Image Processing, ROchester, New York.*, September 2002.
26. ——, "Steganalysis using image quality metrics." *IEEE transactions on Image Processing*, January 2003.
27. H. Farid and S. Lyu, "Detecting hidden messages using higher-order statistics and support vector machines," *5th International Workshop on Information Hiding.*, 2002.
28. R. Duda and P. Hart, "Pattern classification and scene analysis," *John Wiley and Sons.*, 1973.
29. C. Burges, "A tutorial on support vector machines for pattern recognition," *Data Mining and Knowledge Discovery.*, pp. 2:121–167, 1998.

On the Integration of Watermarks and Cryptography

Stefan Katzenbeisser*

Institute for Informatics
Technische Universität München
Boltzmannstrasse 3/I7
D–85748 Garching, Germany
skatzenbeisser@acm.org

Abstract. Applications that involve watermarking schemes are typically composed of both watermarks and cryptographic primitives. The entire application is required to meet specific application-dependant security properties, which critically depend on both the properties of the watermarking scheme and the security of cryptographic primitives. Although the design of secure cryptographic protocols is more or less well-understood, the combination of watermarks and cryptographic primitives poses new problems. This paper reviews some of the fallacies and pitfalls that occur during the design of secure watermarking applications, and provides some practical guidelines for secure watermarking protocols.

1 Introduction

Digital watermarking schemes were introduced in the early 1990's in order to find a digital analogue for paper watermarks that were used for centuries to mark origin and quality of paper. A digital watermarking scheme allows to insert additional information (called *watermark*) imperceptibly into a digital object. Primarily designed to counteract copyright infringements, watermarking schemes are now used in different application scenarios ranging from copy protection and dispute resolving to labeling of digital goods. Although a large number of papers on watermarks were written in the last few years, surprisingly little attention is paid to the combination of watermarks and cryptography. However, the design of secure systems requires to carefully assess the security and applicability of watermarking schemes in various application scenarios.

In many applications, watermarking schemes are typically combined with cryptographic primitives in one communication protocol. The resulting protocol is required to meet specific security properties that differ from application to application. For example, in a dispute resolving scheme one naturally requires that ownership disputes over a digital work are always resolved in favor of the

* This work was performed while the author was visiting the Otto-von-Guericke Universität Magdeburg, Germany.

T. Kalker et al. (Eds.): IWDW 2003, LNCS 2939, pp. 50–60, 2004.
© Springer-Verlag Berlin Heidelberg 2004

true author. Similarly, in fingerprinting applications one expects that only people who committed copyright infringements are identified as traitors, but never innocent customers.

Whereas the design principles for secure cryptographic protocols are now well-understood (see for example the recent book by Ross Anderson [7]), watermark applications are still designed in an ad-hoc manner, lacking clear guidelines. History of watermarking has shown that such ad-hoc designs can result in severe security problems. For example, a simple watermark-based dispute resolving scheme (introduced in Section 5) was considered "secure" until the discovery of protocol attacks.

This paper informally summarizes some of the fallacies and pitfalls one may encounter during the design of watermarking applications; furthermore, it tries to establish some general design principles one should follow when designing new watermarking protocols. I am fully aware of the fact that this work is necessarily incomplete and that it gives a "snapshot" of the problems of watermark protocol design that are known today. However, I think that the problems mentioned in the following sections need to be addressed before a watermarking application can be considered secure.

2 Trust Assumptions

A fundamental part of every protocol design is the careful analysis of trust assumptions. In many cases, the design of the protocol implicitly assumes that certain protocol participants are more trustworthy than others. For example, in electronic commerce applications it was traditionally assumed that the seller is (more or less) trustworthy, whereas the customer is not; that is, an attack against the system is mounted only from the customer side. If these trust assumptions do not match the reality, communication protocols may fail miserably. *It is therefore necessary to thoroughly analyze the assumptions about trust and to critically compare them with reality.*

For example, consider the following scenario, called "Mafia Online Store". This store, that is owned by the mafia, sells digital videos and music clips to its customers, who possess special media players that implement copy protection mechanisms. One part of its sales is official, but the other part is not. In order to avoid being caught because of tax evasion, no records of inofficial sales are kept. However, the design of the systems requires the multimedia objects to contain fingerprinting information, otherwise the media player of the customers will refuse to play back the media they have bought from the Mafia Online Store. Now, as no sales records can be produced, no valid fingerprinting information can be embedded in the digital objects. Thus, the mafia shop is required to forge this information. The simplest way to do this is to take the identity of another customer whose sales records exist and use his identity to forge the fingerprint. Consequently, this innocent customer will be blamed for all copyright infringements of objects sold by the mafia without records. This problem, first reported by Qiao and Nahrstedt [17] and subsequently by Memon and Wong [15], is now known as "customers rights problem".

A careful analysis clearly indicates that the problem stems from false trust assumptions of the fingerprinting protocol. Assuming that the seller is completely trustworthy might be acceptable in a small environment where the trustworthiness can be established by traditional means (e.g., by checking the trade license). However, it is completely unrealistic in the current e-business scenario. Consequently, the fix presented in [15] relies on the reduction of trust. Specifically, a protocol is designed in a way so that the fingerprinted content is not available to the seller, implying that he cannot distribute objects containing invalid fingerprints. Fingerprinting schemes that satisfy this property are called asymmetric [16] and can be constructed out of cryptographic primitives.

A similar problem arises in dispute resolving schemes or ownership proofs. Such protocols normally require a registration authority for digital objects [4]. Alternatively, they rely on the presence of a trusted judge, who decides the ownership status of an object. Typically, this party gets to know any information needed to verify a watermark (i.e., the watermark payload together with the key). As noted by Craver [9], this information suffices in most cases to eliminate the watermark and thus undermine the security of the watermarking protocol "in the future". Although a judge might seem trustworthy at a first glance, it is always possible that some sensitive information leaks through by error (e.g., this happened during a trial on the DVD protection scheme, when apparently secret business information appeared in the official court proceedings).

As a general design principle, *watermarking protocols should be designed with as little trust assumptions as possible.* A trusted party should be avoided entirely, if possible. If a trusted party is necessary, the amount of information stored by this party should be limited. Ideally, this party should have no "history" of previous transactions; specifically, no secret information of the previous transactions should be kept.

Another serious problem that is naturally coupled with trust assumptions is the possibility of colluding parties. Even if a protocol meets its design goals in normal operation, there may be the possibility of an attack in case one or more protocol participants collude in order to reach a joint goal. In an ownership proof scenario, for example, an attacker colluding with an apparently trusted party can subvert the system. As a general design principle, we note that *the security of an application should be analyzed for the possibility of colluding parties.*

3 Asymmetric and Zero-Knowledge Watermarking

Sometimes a trusted party cannot be avoided in watermarking protocols, since security-critical information (which should not be available to an attacker that observes the communication) must be disclosed during the execution of the protocol. As indicated above, one attempts to make as little assumptions on trust as possible. One way to reduce the trust assumptions is to use asymmetric or zero-knowledge watermarking schemes. In both approaches, no security-critical information about the watermark must be disclosed during the watermark detection process. For example, [6] constructed a dispute resolving scheme where the dispute resolver does not get to know embedded watermarks.

Asymmetric watermarking schemes can be roughly compared to digital signature schemes; they use one key for watermark embedding (private key) and one for watermark detection (public key). In such schemes, the public detection key can be disclosed freely and any party is able to verify the presence of a watermark with it. Besides other requirements (for an overview see [10]), the public key must not enable an attacker to remove a watermark. Specifically, it should not be possible to derive information about security-critical parameters (like the watermark payload and private key) from the public key in reasonable time. Furthermore, no public key should enable an attacker to insert watermarks in digital objects, as otherwise watermarks could be forged.

Asymmetric watermarking schemes draw their asymmetry directly from the construction. For example, proposed schemes use properties of Legendre sequences [18], "one-way signal processing" techniques [12] or eigenvectors of linear transforms [14]. Unfortunately, none of these schemes is sufficiently robust against malicious attacks; for an overview of possible attacks see [13].

Specifically problematic attacks against asymmetric watermarking schemes are oracle attacks [8]. It was noted early that the presence of a watermark detection device (even if an attacker has only black-box access to this device) makes attacks against the robustness of watermarking schemes easier (see Section 6). An attacker can use the oracle to remove most watermark information while retaining the perceptual quality of the object. Clearly, the use of asymmetric watermarking techniques gives the attacker unlimited access to a detection oracle (by publishing the public key). It is thus necessary that oracle attacks are prevented by an appropriate design of the asymmetric watermarking scheme.

A different approach, called zero-knowledge watermark detection, uses traditional symmetric watermarking schemes and wraps a cryptographic protocol around the detection process. For an overview of such systems see [2]. Security is obtained by employing cryptographic zero-knowledge proofs in the watermark detection process. Informally, a zero-knowledge proof allows one party (called prover) to prove a fact to another party (called verifier) without actually disclosing the fact. In our case, the secret knowledge is the watermark payload and the detection key. The zero-knowledge property assures that this information is not (even partially) released to the detecting party.

In general, zero-knowledge watermarking schemes operate in the following manner. The prover *encodes* the watermarked object, watermark and reference data (like a watermarking key or the original, unmarked object) such that the verifier cannot easily invert this encoding. Then, he uses the zero-knowledge watermark detector to prove to the verifier that the encoded watermark is present in the encoded watermarked object, relative to the encoded key, without actually removing the encoding. The zero-knowledge property of the detector assures that the watermark stays as secure as if the watermark detection had not been performed at all.

Crucial to the security of the overall scheme is the secrecy of the encoding. Ideally, this encoding is done with a cryptographic commitment, as in the approach of [5]. Other approaches used weaker encodings, such as a permutation of the watermark and the watermarked object [10]. It is important to note that a secure encoding mechanism is necessary for the operation of zero-knowledge watermark detection. If the encoding already leaks some information about the watermark or key, there is no need in concealing them in a cryptographic protocol. For example, in the scheme that used a permutation as encoding [10], an attacker gains a good estimate of the statistical properties of the watermark (like the minimum/maximum coefficient, or their average).

Sometimes there is confusion about the meaning of "zero-knowledge". Basically, a protocol is zero-knowledge, if it leaks no information *besides* the input to the protocol and all information that can be computed in polynomial time from it. In other words, every information obtained by an attacker (during a run of the zero-knowledge protocol) can readily be computed by him from seeing the inputs alone, without execution of the protocol. This property assures that no information about the encoded watermark and key is leaked during the detection phase. Furthermore, this is another reason why a strong encoding mechanism is necessary. If (in an extreme case) the encoding would be omitted, then every watermark detection scheme would trivially be zero-knowledge, because a successful watermark detection operation does not reveal any information that is not yet present in the inputs to the protocol.

However, the need for a secure encoding has a strong disadvantage. Technically, a zero-knowledge proof enables the prover to prove to the verifier that one specific encoded watermark is detectable in the object (this property is called *completeness* of the proof); it is not possible for the verifier to inspect the watermark in order to verify its payload, as this would violate the zero-knowledge property. Traditionally, watermarks contained an identity string of a party or some other verifiable information. With zero-knowledge watermarking, it is not possible any more to access the inner structure of the watermark. Although the completeness of the proof procedure assures that an attacker cannot produce a random encoded watermark and falsely claim that the encoded mark is detectable, he cannot easily prove that the mark contained in the encoding is *his* mark or that he actually inserted the mark previously. However, we will see that the latter problem is very general and exists also with traditional symmetric watermarking schemes (see Section 4).

Unfortunately, zero-knowledge proofs make countermeasures against such *protocol attacks* much more difficult. One possible approach is to use additional zero-knowledge proofs to prove the legality of the mark, but this increases the complexity of the overall solution [2].

4 Protocol Attacks

This brings us to another watermark protocol design principle: if a watermark is detectable in a certain object, *this is no proof that this mark was inserted by some party.* Indeed, as the watermark detection relies on statistical methods, a small probability of false alarms (i.e., a watermark detector incorrectly reports a watermark to be present although it was never inserted) cannot be eliminated. It is one of the central design criteria for watermark detectors to keep this probability to a minimum. Unfortunately, this criterion conflicts with the robustness requirement.

False alarms give rise to a protocol attack against the watermarking scheme, called ambiguity attack. In such an attack, a person engineers a watermark, a key (and possibly a fake original object), such that this watermark is detectable in a given object, although it was never embedded there. A trivial (brute-force) attack is to generate a huge number of statistically independent watermarks $W_1, \ldots, W_n$ and check whether one of these marks is present in the object in question. If the attacker finds such a mark, he has successfully performed an ambiguity attack.

If the probability of false alarms is quite high, this naive attack can be efficient (e.g., if the probability of false alarms is about 10^{-6}, then about 10^6 trials suffice on the average). Of course, if the structure of the watermarking scheme is known to an attacker, more efficient ways to find a detectable mark are possible. For example, in a system where the watermark detector responds on the correlation between an object and the watermark, a detectable watermark can be engineered from an object by appropriate filtering.

This problem stimulated research on watermarking schemes that are not susceptible to protocol attacks like the ambiguity attack. The construction should reduce the false positives or—ideally—should provide a low false positives rate independent of the underlying detection mechanism. The main idea was to incorporate some sort of cryptographic primitive in the watermark embedding process. Basically, a watermark is constructed from a human-readable text, like an identity string, by use of cryptography. In this setup, the human-readable text is piped through a cryptographic primitive and the output is actually embedded as a watermark. The hope was that this primitive reduced the possibility of protocol attacks; several authors made such attempts (see e.g. [11],[17] or [19]).

The implicit assumption of these constructions was that the attacker uses a two-way procedure to forge a mark. First, he tries to find any detectable mark, independent of its internal structure. In a second step, he tries to invert the cryptographic primitives in order to obtain the "human-readable" watermark payload; specifically, given the mark W he finds some value X such that $W = H(X)$, where H denotes the cryptographic primitive in use. This is of corse hard, even if one assumes very liberal security properties for H.

But this is another example of a fallacy, as an attacker will likely *not* behave as expected. In general, *one cannot make any assumptions about the behaviour of an attacker.* Specifically, there is no reason to assume that an attacker will conform to the two-step attack presented above. In fact, he can continue the naive attack. Instead of choosing random watermarks, he chooses a large number of values X_i, applies the cryptographic primitive to them, hereby obtaining $W_i = H(X_i)$, and checks whether one of the resulting marks W_i is detectable. Again, the success of this procedure is limited by the false positives probability and so the construction does not meet its goals (for details, see [1]). This is a very general result, applicable to many proposed solutions that use cryptographic "preprocessing" in order to prevent protocol attacks. Currently the only solution (besides relying on a trusted third party as advocated in [3]) is to use only watermarking schemes that have a very low false alarm probability.

These problems can be studied in the context of dispute-resolving schemes, which were considered as one of the first applications for watermarks. They are also a nice example for the fallacies of watermark protocol design.

5 Dispute Resolving and Ownership Proofs

Suppose two parties A and B dispute over the copyright of an object O. Early attempts tried to solve this problem by simply using watermarks containing the identity of the owner. Assume that A owns the object O. Now, A watermarks O with his watermark W_A to obtain a watermarked object O' and continues to distribute O', but keeps the original, unmarked media O locked away. Once an illegal copy O''—apparently derived from O'—is found, A can prove that his watermark W_A is detectable in the pirated copy. The robustness of the watermarking scheme guarantees that W_A is still detectable in the modified work O'', as long as the modifications do not impair the object quality.

How can this system be attacked? Clearly, a different party B could have inserted his own watermark in the object O'' previously. Now, also B can claim that he is the "true" owner of the object. To resolve the situation, some mechanism must be present that "orders" the claims of A and B. Some authors tried to provide such a mechanism by testing whether W_A or W_B has been "inserted" previously. Traditionally, this question is answered by the inspection of the objects both A and B claim to be their originals. Specifically, if B inserted his mark after A, then A's original cannot contain W_B; similarly, if A inserted his mark after B, then B's original cannot contain W_A. Thus, early approaches for dispute resolving just checked the presence of watermarks in the objects claimed to be "originals" by the participants.

However, [11] showed that this reasoning is flawed. More precisely, they constructed a protocol attack (called inversion attack) that allows B to engineer a mark that is not only detectable in the disputed object, but also in the original A kept locked away. Now, A's original contains W_B and B's original contains W_A. So the above reasoning is obviously false. Why did the simple dispute-resolving protocol fail so miserably?

One possible explanation is that during the design of the protocol both principles discussed in the last section were violated. First, one made a concrete assumption on the behaviour of an attacker, i.e. that he uses the watermark insertion device to *insert* his own watermark. It was assumed that this is the only reasonable way to engineer a detectable mark. Although the possibility of removing the mark was also discussed (this can be coped with by using a robust watermarking scheme), one did not think of alternative attacks. We have seen earlier that this is a major design problem, as the attacker is free to choose *any* strategy that works in favor of his goals. In this specific situation, he is free to engineer W_B in an arbitrary way (which does not necessarily involve the watermark embedder). A protocol can only be seen secure, once *every* possible attacker strategy fails. Unfortunately, this fact is hard to prove (in general, one will have to reduce any attack to a well-known hard problem). Second, the implicit assumption of the protocol is that both W_A and W_B are "legal" watermarks, inserted by the insertion device. Again, this assumption is not realistic given the possibility of a protocol attack.

Another problem arises when more than two people dispute over the copyright of a single object. Suppose that we have three parties A, B and C; furthermore assume that A is the true owner of an object, implying that both B and C "stole" the object. Theoretically, such n-party disputes can always be broken down to two-party disputes by running a two-party dispute resolving scheme on each pair of disputants. The dispute is resolved in favor of the party who won all disputes; if no such party exists, the protocol fails (in this case the "true" author is not present among the n parties or an attack succeeded). Unfortunately, there are subtle problems that arise in n-party dispute resolving schemes.

In theory, there are three possible ways for the distribution of the object: either both B and C got the object from A independently or one cheater forwarded the object to the other one. Both cheaters B and C could dispute over the copyright of the object, although both are not the legitimate owner. Now, which result should a dispute resolving protocol give? The traditional way is to pose no restrictions on the outcome of the resolving process in this case, i.e. if only cheaters participate in the resolving process, any answer can be obtained (apparently it does not make sense to favor one cheater to another). In other words, the protocol only guarantees that the copyright owner is found in case he participates in the protocol. *This restriction has been commonly neglected in the past.*

From a theoretical perspective, this restriction makes sense, but for the practice it poses a difficult problem. If the dispute resolving process can make a "random" decision if the true author is not present, can the system really be used to resolve the copyright situation? Consider the following two scenarios; in the first scenario the true author A and cheater B dispute over the copyright. Clearly, A wins this dispute. In the second scenario, both cheaters B and C dispute. In the latter scenario, either B or C will be identified as owners. Now, how should a judge be able to distinguish between these two scenarios? In both cases, he receives the answer that one of the participants is the alleged copyright holder. But he cannot distinguish these two scenarios; specifically, he cannot distinguish whether the winner of the dispute resolving scheme is the "true" owner or again a cheater (just because the true owner did not participate). A traitor can use this fact by claiming that the "winning" party is also a cheater. Although this does not support his own ownership claims, he can hinder the resolving process by plausibly denying A's authorship rights. This problem was termed "conclusiveness problem" in [6].

The problem stems from another fallacy, namely the *assumption that a dispute resolving scheme can be used to decide the authorship* of a digital work. As seen in the previous example, dispute resolving schemes can only try to "order" the claims of some disputants, but they may fail in case the true author is not present. For providing ownership proofs, it is necessary to define a formal model of "authorship". One such model can be found in [4]. In this scheme, an object O is courtesy of a specific person A if A registered his work at a central registration authority at time t and there existed no "similar" work O', registered at a time $t' < t$. In such a model, secure authorship proofs can indeed be given [4,6].

In general, *the existence of the conclusiveness problem questions the applicability of watermark-based dispute resolving schemes in practice.*

6 Information Leakage and Previous Knowledge

As mentioned in Section 3, a serious problem with watermarking schemes that allow public watermark detection are oracle attacks. Although an attacker will normally not know the specific nature of a watermark embedded in a digital object, he sometimes possesses an "oracle" that tests the presence of a specific watermark. Consider the following example: in a copy-protection environment, a compliant player refuses to play back a digital object containing a detectable watermark. In order to be able to play the object in his compliant device, an attacker can try to remove the mark in several steps. He creates a slightly modified work (thereby trying to maintain the visible or audible quality of the work) and tries to play this work in the player. If the player refuses to play the modified work, he knows that the mark is still detectable; in this case, he iterates this process until he obtains a work that will be played in the compliant device. This attack works, since a *mis-used detector can leak security critical information.*

In general, a party which issues intentionally modified works in a watermarking protocol can subvert the security of the general system. Therefore, in a security analysis, one has to take the presence of intentionally modified documents into account.

A common fallacy is the assumption that oracle attacks target only keyless or asymmetric watermarking schemes, as the attacker has no access to the key otherwise. This assumption is wrong in general, since an attacker may be able to launch an oracle attack also on keyed watermarking schemes, in case the key is "embedded" in the oracle (as the above example shows, this assumption is generally valid for consumer-electronic products).

Another problem pops up if the attacker possesses previous knowledge obtained from participation in previous watermarking protocol runs. As it is unrealistic to assume that an attacker gets to see only one run of the protocol, a necessary requirement for secure watermarking applications is that *the information obtained in one protocol run does not impair the security of the system "in the future"*. Furthermore, *the information gained in several rounds of the protocol should not be sufficient to derive secret information usable to subvert the system.* We have already seen that some watermarking applications do not fulfill this requirement, as sensitive information needs to be disclosed during watermark detection. Again, a possible countermeasure is to reduce the trust in the protocol participants or to use zero-knowledge watermark detection.

7 Conclusion

We have seen that there are several ways to attack watermarking-based applications besides the "traditional" robustness attack. Attackers might violate the trust assumption of the application scenario by colluding with apparently trustworthy parties, they might produce detectable watermarks by protocol attacks and they behave in a manner that is not predictable to the watermark protocol designer. It is important to note that a protocol can only be considered "secure", if *any* possible attack scenario fails.

Watermarking protocols differ from traditional cryptographic protocols in several ways. The most important difference is that a watermark can be seen as a very weak cryptographic primitive, whose security cannot be guaranteed by the watermark embedder itself. In general, the security of the overall system can only be guaranteed by strong cryptographic mechanisms, thereby seeing the watermark just as a channel for information transfer. However, combining cryptography and watermarks in a naive manner does normally not solve the problem (see Section 4).

The establishment of reliable design principles for watermarking applications is just rising from its infancy. This paper surveyed some of the most important problems that pop up when using watermarks in different application scenarios.

Acknowledgements. The author thanks André Adelsbach, Jana Dittmann, Ahmad Reza-Sadeghi and Helmut Veith for fruitful discussions on this topic. The visit to the Otto-von-Guericke Universität Magdeburg was funded by the Vienna University of Technology.

References

1. A. Adelsbach, S. Katzenbeisser, and A.-R. Sadeghi. On the insecurity of non-invertible watermarking schemes for dispute resolving. In *International Workshop on Digital Watermarking (IWDW'03)*, 2003.
2. A. Adelsbach, S. Katzenbeisser, and A.-R. Sadeghi. Watermark detection with zero-knowledge disclosure. *ACM Multimedia Systems Journal*, 2003. to appear.
3. A. Adelsbach, S. Katzenbeisser, and H. Veith. Watermarking schemes provably secure against copy and ambiguity attacks. In *Digital Rights Management (DRM'2003)*, 2003.
4. A. Adelsbach, B. Pfitzmann, and A. Sadeghi. Proving ownership of digital content. In *Proceedings of the Third International Workshop on Information Hiding*, volume 1768 of *Lecture Notes in Computer Science*, pages 117–133. Springer, 2000.
5. A. Adelsbach and A.-R. Sadeghi. Zero-knowledge watermark detection and proof of ownership. In *Proceedings of the Fourth International Workshop on Information Hiding*, volume 2137 of *Lecture Notes in Computer Science*, pages 273–188. Springer Verlag, 2001.

6. A. Adelsbach and A.-R. Sadeghi. Advanced techniques for dispute resolving and authorship proofs on digital works. In *Proceedings of the SPIE vol. 5020, Security and Watermarking of Multimedia Contents V, to appear*, pages 677–688, 2003.
7. R. Anderson. *Security Engineering.* Wiley, 2001.
8. I. Cox and J.-P. Linnartz. Some general methods for tampering with watermarks. *IEEE Journal on Selected Areas in Communications*, 16(4):587–593, 1998.
9. S. Craver. Zero knowledge watermark detection. In *Proceedings of the Third International Workshop on Information Hiding*, volume 1768 of *Lecture Notes in Computer Science*, pages 101–116. Springer, 2000.
10. S. Craver and S. Katzenbeisser. Copyright protection protocols based on asymmetric watermarking. In *Communications and Multimedia Security Issues of the New Century*, pages 159–170. Kluwer, 2001.
11. S. Craver, N. Memon, B. L. Yeo, and M. M. Yeung. Resolving rightful ownerships with invisible watermarking techniques: Limitations, attacks and implications. *IEEE Journal on Selected Areas in Communications*, 16(4):573–586, 1998.
12. P. Duhamel and T. Furon. An asymmetric public detection watermarking technique. In *Proceedings of the Third International Workshop on Information Hiding*, volume 1768 of *Lecture Notes in Computer Science*, pages 89–100. Springer, 1999.
13. J. J. Eggers, J. K. Su, and B. Girod. Asymmetric watermarking schemes. In *Sicherheit in Netzen und Medienströmen*, pages 124–133. Springer, 2000.
14. J. J. Eggers, J. K. Su, and B. Girod. Public key watermarking by eigenvectors of linear transforms. In *Proceedings of the European Signal Processing Conference*, 2000.
15. N. Memon and P. W. Wong. Buyer-seller watermarking protocol based on amplitude modulation and the El Gamal public key crypto system. In *Proceedings of the SPIE 3657, Security and Watermarking of Multimedia Contents*, pages 189–294, 1999.
16. B. Pfitzmann and M. Schunter. Asymmetric fingerprinting. In *Advances in Cryptology—EUROCRYPT'96*, volume 1070 of *Lecture Notes in Computer Science*, pages 84–95. Springer, 1996.
17. L. Qiao and K. Nahrstedt. Watermarking schemes and protocols for protecting rightful ownerships and customer's rights. *Journal of Visual Communication and Image Representation*, 9(3):194–210, 1998.
18. R. G. van Schyndel, A. Z. Tirkel, and I. D. Svalbe. Key independent watermark detection. In *Proceedings of the IEEE International Conference on Multimedia Computing and Systems*, volume 1, pages 580–585, 1999.
19. W. Zeng and B. Liu. On resolving ownerships of digital images by invisible watermarks. In *IEEE Int. Conf. on Image Processing*, volume I, pages 552–555, 1997.

Content-Dependent Anti-disclosure Image Watermark

Chun-Shien Lu* and Chao-Yong Hsu

Institute of Information Science, Academia Sinica,
Taipei, Taiwan 115, Republic of China
{lcs, cyhsu}@iis.sinica.edu.tw

Abstract. Watermarking methods usually claim a certain degree of robustness against those attacks that aim to destroy the hidden watermark at the expense of degrading the quality of media data. However, there exist watermark-estimation attacks (WEAs), such as the collusion attack and copy attack that are clever at disclosing the hidden watermark for unauthorized purposes while maintaining media's quality. The aim of this study was to deal with the WEA problem. We begin by gaining insight into WEA, leading to formal definitions of optimal watermark estimation and perfect cover data recovery. Subject to these definitions, the content-dependent watermark (CDW) is proposed to resist watermark-estimation attacks. The key is to introduce a media hash as a constituent component of the CDW. Mathematical analyses and experiment results consistently verify the effectiveness of the content-dependent watermarking scheme. To our knowledge, this anti-disclosure watermarking is the first work that takes resistance to both collusion and copy attacks into consideration.

1 Introduction

Digital watermarking is the technology of embedding a piece of information into the cover media data to carry out a specific mission. However, no matter what kinds of missions are considered, robustness is the critical issue affecting the practicability of a watermarking system. Robustness refers to the capability of resistance to attacks that are used to destroy, remove, or disable watermark detection. As previously discussed in [15], attacks can be classified into four categories: (1) removal attacks; (2) geometrical attacks; (3) cryptographic attacks; and (4) protocol attacks. The robustness of current watermarking methods has been examined with respect to either removal attacks or geometrical attacks or both. In particular, removal attacks contain operations, including filtering, compression, and noise adding, that will more or less degrade the quality of media data. Even though the employed removal attack cannot guarantee successful removal of the hidden watermarks, the media quality will inevitably be reduced. However, there indeed exists a kind of attacks that can defeat a watermarking

* Corresponding author

T. Kalker et al. (Eds.): IWDW 2003, LNCS 2939, pp. 61–76, 2004.
© Springer-Verlag Berlin Heidelberg 2004

system without certainly sacrificing media quality. Among currently known attacks [15], the collusion attack [10,11], which is a removal attack, and the copy attack [6], which is a protocol attack, are typical examples of attacks that can achieve the aforementioned goal. The common step used to realize a collusion or copy attack is watermark estimation. Consequently, we call both the collusion and copy attacks watermark-estimation attacks (WEAs).

The aim of the collusion attack is to collect and analyze a set of watermarked media data[1] so that unwatermarked copies can be constructed to create the false negative problem. A collusion attack naturally occurs in video watermarking because a video is composed of many frames, and one way of watermarking a video is to embed the same watermark into all the frames. This scenario was first addressed in [11]. However, we argue that the collusion attack is not exclusively applied to video watermarking. In the literature, image watermarking with resistance to geometrical attacks has received much attention because even a slight geometrical modification may disorder the hidden watermark bits and disable watermark detection. In view of this, some researches [1,12,16] inserted multiple redundant watermarks into an image in the hope that robustness can be maintained as long as at least one watermark exists. Commonly, various kinds of image units, such as blocks [16], meshes [1], or disks [12], are extracted as carriers for embedding. With this unique characteristic, we propose to treat each image unit in an image like a frame in a video; in this way, collusion attacks can be equally applied to those image watermarking methods that employ a multiple redundant watermark embedding strategy.

In contrast to the collusion attack, the copy attack [6] has been developed to create the false positive problem; i.e., one can successfully detect a watermark from an unwatermarked image. Compared with the collusion atatck, the copy attack can be executed on only one media data; thus, it is more flexible. We will also show that the copy attack is rather easier to carry out than the denoising attack (a special case of the collusion attack). Based on the aforementioned reasons, the copy attack must be taken into consideration when the robustness of a watermarking system is to be evaluated.

In this paper, we propose a new scheme to cope with the watermark-estimation attacks (WEAs). After introducing a general watermarking framework in Sec. 2, the WEA will be thoroughly explored in Sec. 3. We will begin by investigating the achievable performance of the denoising attack and the copy attack to show that the copy attack is, in fact, easier to carry out. Then, we analyze to know that both accurate estimation of a watermark's sign and complete subtraction of a watermark's energy are indispensable for achieving effective watermark removal. On the other hand, they also serve as clues to breaking WEA. In order to withstand WEA, we propose the concept of content-dependent watermark (CDW), which is composed of an informative watermark that carries

[1] This set of watermarked media data in fingerprinting [13] is generated from the same cover data but individually embedded with different watermarks, while in watermarking it is generated from visually similar/dissimilar image blocks or video frames embedded with the same watermark.

information about an owner and a media hash that represents the cover carrier. The design of the media hash will be addressed in Sec. 4. Based on the presented media hash, in Sec. 5, CDW will be constructed and its properties examined. Furthermore, the validity of resistance to a collusion attack or copy attack using CDW will be analyzed. Finally, experiments and concluding remarks will be summarized in Sec. 6 and Sec. 7, respectively.

2 Basic Framework of Digital Watermarking

A general digital watermarking scheme is described as follow. In the embedding process, a watermark is a message (author key) that is first converted into a binary sequence and then encoded as $\mathbf{S}$ using an error correction code (ECC) to enhance error correction. Before embedding, the ECC encoded sequence $\mathbf{S}$ are mapped from $\{0\ \ 1\}$ to $\{-1\ \ 1\}$ such that $\mathbf{S}$ is a Gaussian distribution with zero mean and unit variance. $\mathbf{S}$ is also shuffled by means of a secret key K known by the owner only. Finally, the resultant sequence $\mathbf{S}$ will be magnified under the constraint of perceptual masking $\mathbf{M_I}$ and embedded into a cover image $\mathbf{I}$ to produce a corresponding watermarked (or stego) image $\mathbf{I^s}$ by

$$I^s(i) = I(i) + S(i)M_I(i)\ \forall i \in [1\ \ L],$$

where L denotes the length of $\mathbf{S}$ and $\mathbf{M_I}$ stands for the masking matrix derived from $\mathbf{I}$. We call the finally embedded sequence $\mathbf{S} \cdot \mathbf{M_I}$ as the watermark $\mathbf{W}$. The watermark $\mathbf{W}$ is assumed to be a Gaussian sequence with zero mean and variance ρ^2. Notice that the variance ρ^2 from $\mathbf{M_I}$ determines the watermark's energy. In addition, $\mathbf{S}$ determines the watermark's sign and is secured by the secret key K.

In the detection process, a watermark $\mathbf{W^e}$ is first extracted and decoded into a bipolar sequence $\mathbf{S^e}$ by

$$\mathbf{S}^e(i) = sgn(\mathbf{W}^e(i)), \tag{1}$$

where the sign function, $sgn(\cdot)$, is defined as

$$sgn(t) = \begin{cases} +1, & \text{if } t \geq 0, \\ -1, & \text{if } t < 0. \end{cases}$$

Due to the high-frequency property of a watermark signal, denoising is naturally an efficient way of achieving blind watermark extraction [5,6,14]. It is said that a watermark exists provided that the normalized correlation δ_{nc} between $\mathbf{S}$ and $\mathbf{S^e}$ (with equal energy $\sqrt{L}$) is larger than a threshold T, where

$$\delta_{nc}(\mathbf{S}, \mathbf{S^e}) = \frac{1}{L} \sum S(i)S^e(i) \tag{2}$$

and $\delta_{nc}(\cdot,\cdot) \in [-1\ \ 1]$. In fact, Eq. (2) is also equal to $1 - 2P_e$, where P_e stands for the bit error rate (BER).

3 Watermark Estimation Attack

Basically, removal attacks try to vanish the hidden watermark by manipulating a stego image $\mathbf{I}^{\mathbf{s}}$ so that the quality of the attacked image $\mathbf{I}^{\mathbf{a}}$ is further destroyed. Specifically, $PSNR(\mathbf{I}, \mathbf{I}^{\mathbf{s}}) \geq PSNR(\mathbf{I}, \mathbf{I}^{\mathbf{a}})$ always holds. However, a more clever removal attack can achieve $PSNR(\mathbf{I}, \mathbf{I}^{\mathbf{s}}) \leq PSNR(\mathbf{I}, \mathbf{I}^{\mathbf{a}})$. The collusion attack is a typical example of an attack that follows the above scenario. Usually, a collusion attack is applied to video watermarking by averaging of a set of estimated watermarks to obtain the hidden watermark. As for image watermarking, some recent works have been proposed embedding multiple redundant watermarks into local areas [1,12,16] so that global/local geometrical distortions can be resisted. Provided we treat a local region in an image similar to a video frame in a video, then collusion attack can also be applied to region-based image watermarking to create the false negative problem. It should be noted that the conventional denoising-based removal attack [14], which is only applied to a single image, is a special case of the collusion attack.

On the other hand, an estimated watermark can be inserted into unwatermarked media data to produce a counterfeit stego data. This is the so-called copy attack [6], which has been developed to create the false positive problem; i.e., one can successfully detect a watermark from an unwatermarked data. As classified in [15], copy attack belongs to a type of protocol attacks. The copy attack is operated as follows: (i) a watermark is first predicted from a stego image; (ii) the predicted watermark is added into a target image to create a counterfeit stego image; and (iii) from the counterfeit image, a watermark can be detected that wrongly claims rightful ownership.

To our knowledge, the collusion attack and the copy attack have not been simultaneously taken into consideration when investigating the robustness issue. Owing to watermark estimation is the first step in both attacks, these are called, watermark-estimation attacks (WEAs).

3.1 Analysis of the Achievable Performance of the Denoising Attack and Copy Attack

Two typical examples of watermark-estimation attacks, i.e., the denoising attack [14] (recall that it is a special case of the collusion attack) and the copy attack [6], will be discussed. Without loss of generality, suppose the decision on a watermark's existence will be based on the linear correlation, as defined in Eq. (2). Let $\mathbf{X}$, $\mathbf{X}^{\mathbf{s}}$, $\mathbf{Z}$, and $\mathbf{Z}^{\mathbf{s}}$ represent the original image, watermarked image, faked original image, and faked watermarked image, respectively. Among them, $\mathbf{X}^{\mathbf{s}}$ is generated from $\mathbf{X}$ through an embedding process, and $\mathbf{Z}^{\mathbf{s}}$ is generated from the combination of $\mathbf{Z}$ and a watermark estimated from $\mathbf{X}^{\mathbf{s}}$.

Let $\mathbf{W}$ be a watermark to be hidden in $\mathbf{X}$, and let $\mathbf{W}^{\mathbf{e}}$ be an estimated watermark obtained by denoising $\mathbf{X}^{\mathbf{s}}$. For the purpose of watermark removal, $\mathbf{W}^{\mathbf{e}}$ will be subtracted from $\mathbf{X}^{\mathbf{s}}$ to produce an attacked image $\mathbf{X}^{\mathbf{a}}$, i.e.,

$$\mathbf{X}^{\mathbf{a}} = \mathbf{X}^{\mathbf{s}} - \mathbf{W}^{\mathbf{e}}.$$

In the watermark detection process, a watermark, $\mathbf{W^a}$, is extracted from $\mathbf{X^a}$ and correlated with $\mathbf{W}$. If denoising-based watermark removal is expected to succeed, then $\delta_{nc}(sgn(\mathbf{W}), sgn(\mathbf{W^a})) < T$ must hold. This result indicates that the ratios of the correctly (C_w) and wrongly (NC_w) decoded watermark bits should, respectively, satisfy

$$C_w \leq \frac{1+T}{2} \quad \text{and} \quad NC_w \geq \frac{1-T}{2}, \tag{3}$$

where $C_w + NC_w = 1$ and NC_w corresponds to the bit error rate (BER). Based on the false analyses of normalized correlation (pp. 186 of [2]), if we would like to have a false positive probability at the level of 10^{-8} when $|\mathbf{W}| = 1024$, then we should set the threshold T to be 0.12. As a consequence, it is evident from the above analyses that an efficient watermark removal attack should be able to vanish *most* watermark bits since T is usually small. In fact, the actual number of bits required to be destroyed has been specified in Eq. (3).

As for the copy attack, the estimated watermark $\mathbf{W^e}$ is added to the target image $\mathbf{Z}$ to form a counterfeit image $\mathbf{Z^s}$, i.e.,

$$\mathbf{Z^s} = \mathbf{Z} + \mathbf{W^e}. \tag{4}$$

In the watermark detection process, a watermark, $\mathbf{W^z}$, is extracted from $\mathbf{Z^s}$ and correlated with $\mathbf{W}$. The copy attack is claimed to succeed if $\delta_{nc}(sgn(\mathbf{W}), sgn(\mathbf{W^z})) \geq T$ holds. This implies that C_w only needs to be at least increased from $\frac{1}{2}$ (due to the randomness of an arbitrary image, $\mathbf{Z}$) to $\frac{1+T}{2}$. Actually, the amount of increase, ξ^{copy}, only needs to satisfy

$$\xi^{copy} \geq \frac{1+T}{2} - \frac{1}{2} = \frac{T}{2}. \tag{5}$$

Comparing Eqs. (3) and (5), we can conclude that a copy attack is easier to perform successfully than a denoising attack because $\frac{1-T}{2}$ is quite a bit larger than $\frac{T}{2}$ based on the fact that T is usually small. However, if the denoised results (i.e., more than one estimated watermark) are collected and colluded to generate an estimation that is closer to its original, then the collusion attack will exhibit more powerful performance than the denoising attack, as evidenced in [10,11].

3.2 Optimal Watermark Estimation and Perfect Cover Data Recovery

Mathematical Definition. From an attacker's perspective, the energy of each watermark bit must be accurately predicted so that the previously added watermark energy can be completely subtracted to accomplish effective watermark removal. Especially, correction estimation of watermark's energy is closely related to the accuracy of removal attack. Several scenarios are shown in Fig. 1, which illustrates the variations of (a) an original watermark; (b) an estimated watermark (in gray-scale); and (c) a residual watermark generated by subtracting the estimated watermark from the original watermark. From Fig. 1, we can

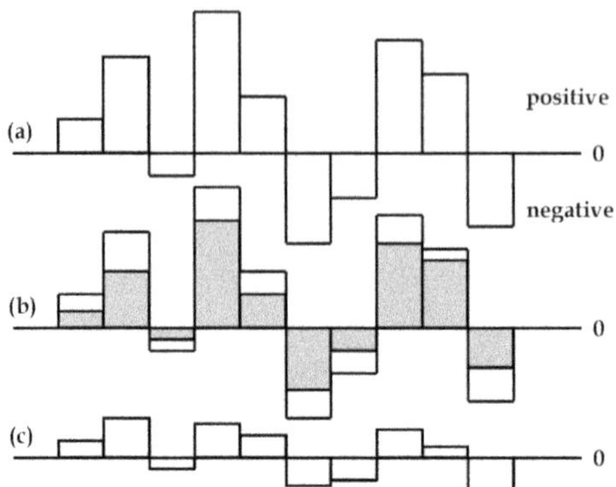

Fig. 1. Watermark estimation/removal illustrated by energy variations: (a) original embedded watermark with each white bar indicating the energy of each watermark bit; (b) gray bars show the energies of an estimated watermark; (c) the residual watermark obtained after removing the estimated watermark. A sufficiently large correlation (Eq. (2)) between (a) and (c) exists to indicate the presence of a watermark.

realize that if the energy of a hidden watermark cannot be completely removed, the residual watermark still suffices to reveal the encoded message according to Eq. (1). Furthermore, if the sign of an estimated watermark bit is different from its original one (i.e., $sgn(W(i)) \neq sgn(W^e(i))$), then any additional energy subtraction will not helpful in improving removal efficiency. On the contrary, watermark removal by energy subtraction operated in the opposite polarity will severely damage the media data's fidelity. Actually, this corresponds to adding a watermark with higher energy into cover data without satisfying the masking constraint. The importance of polarities of watermark bits has been previously emphasized in [8] by embedding two complementary watermarks that are modulated in different ways to resist different sets of attacks. With this understanding, we shall define "optimal watermark estimation" and "perfect cover data recovery," respectively, as follows for use in further analyses.

Definition 1 (Optimal Watermark Estimation): Given an original embedded watermark $\mathbf{W}$ and its approximate version $\mathbf{W^e}$ estimated from $\mathbf{I^s}$ using either a watermark removal attack or a collusion attack, the necessary condition for optimal estimation of $\mathbf{W}$ as $\mathbf{W}^e$ is defined as

$$\delta_{nc}(sgn(\mathbf{W}), sgn(\mathbf{W^e})) = 1, \tag{6}$$

where $sgn(\mathbf{v}) = \{sgn(v_1), sgn(v_2), ..., sgn(v_L)\}$ represents the signs of elements in a vector $\mathbf{v} = \{v_1, v_2, ..., v_L\}$. This is the first step, where a watermark may be undetected by an owner if more than $\frac{L(1+T)}{2}$ sign bits of the watermark can be obtained by attackers. Beyond this, however, to avoid leaving a residual watermark (as illustrated in Fig. 1(c)) that can reveal the hidden watermark, accurate estimation of the energy of $\mathbf{W^e}$ is absolutely indispensable. In addition to Eq. (6), watermark removal can be achieved only if the watermark energy to be subtracted is larger than or equal to the added energy, i.e., $mag(W^e(i)) \geq$

$mag(W(i))$, where $mag(t)$ denotes the magnitude $|t|$ of t. Therefore, the sufficient and necessary condition for complete watermark removal can be defined $\forall i$ as

$$mag(W^e(i)) \geq mag(W(i)), |mag(W^e(i)) - mag(W(i))| < JND(i), sgn(W^e(i)) = sgn(W(i)), \tag{7}$$

where $JND(i)$ denotes a masking threshold. After the optimal watermark estimation scheme defined in Eq. (7) is employed, the extracted watermark would behave like a random signal so that no trace of the watermark can be observed.

Definition 2 (Perfect Cover Data Recovery): Under the prerequisite that Definition 1 is satisfied, it is said that $\mathbf{I}^{\mathbf{r}}$ is an perfect recovery of $\mathbf{I}$ if

$$PSNR(\mathbf{I}, \mathbf{I}^{\mathbf{r}}) \approx \infty, \tag{8}$$

where $\mathbf{I}^{\mathbf{r}} = \mathbf{I} - sgn(\mathbf{W}^{\mathbf{e}})mag(\mathbf{W}^{\mathbf{e}})$ and $mag(\mathbf{v}) = \{mag(v_1), mag(v_2), ..., mag(v_L)\}$ represents the magnitudes of elements in a vector $\mathbf{v} = \{v_1, v_2, ..., v_L\}$. Of course, it is best to get $mag(W^e(i))$ as the upper bound of $mag(W(i))$; otherwise, even if watermarks have been completely removed, the quality of the attacked images will be poor. Typically, evaluation of $mag(\mathbf{W}^{\mathbf{e}})$ can be achieved either by means of averaging [11] or remodulation [14].

In summary, under the condition of sufficiently large $\delta_{nc}(sgn(\mathbf{W}), sgn(\mathbf{W}^{\mathbf{e}}))$, $PSNR(\mathbf{I}, \mathbf{I}^{\mathbf{s}}) \leq PSNR(\mathbf{I}, \mathbf{I}^{\mathbf{r}})$ will undoubtedly hold. Unlike other watermark removal attacks that reduce the quality of the media data, the collusion attack may improve the quality of colluded data.

4 Image Hash

From the analyses of watermark-estimation attack (WEA) described in Sec. 3, we have found that the success of WEA mainly depends on the fact that the hidden watermark totally behaves like a noise, and can be easily and reliably obtained by means of a denoising process. In order to disguise this prior knowledge and hide it from attackers, a watermark must be designed to carry information relevant to the cover image itself. Meanwhile, the content-dependent information must be secured[2] by a secret key and be robust to digital processing [9] in order not to affect watermark detection. To this end, we shall introduce the concept of the image hash as a kind of content-dependent information used to create the so-called content-dependent watermark (CDW).

The image hash [3], also known as the "digital signature" [9] or "media fingerprint" [4], has been used in many applications, including content authentication, copy detection, and media recognition. In this paper, the proposed image hash extraction procedure is operated in the 8×8 block-DCT domain. For each block,

[2] This is because either an owner or an attacker can freely derive content-dependent information. Hence, a secret key is required for shuffling. How to combine shuffled content-dependent information and watermark will be discussed in Sec. 5.

a piece of representative but robust information is created. It is defined as the magnitude relationship between two AC coefficients:

$$r(i) = \begin{cases} +1, & \text{if } |f_i(p_1)| - |f_i(p_2)| \geq 0, \\ -1, & \text{otherwise,} \end{cases}$$

where $r(i)$ is a robust feature value in a sequence $\mathbf{r}$, and $f_i(p_1)$ and $f_i(p_2)$ are two AC coefficients at positions p_1 and p_2 in block i. The length of $\mathbf{r}$, $|\mathbf{r}|$, is equal to the number of blocks. The DC coefficient will not be selected because it is positive and, thus, not random. In addition, the two selected AC coefficients should be at lower frequencies because high-frequency coefficients are vulnerable to attacks. In this paper, p_1 and p_2 are selected to be the first two largest AC coefficients from the 64 available frequency subbands. We call this feature value $r(\cdot)$ robust because this magnitude relationship between $f_i(p_1)$ and $f_i(p_2)$ can be mostly preserved under incidental modifications. Please refer to [9] for similar robustness analyses. It should be noted that depending on different watermarking algorithms the proposed media hash extraction method can be adjusted correspondingly.

In practice, each media hash must be constructed within the range where one watermark is embedded so that resistance to geometrical distortions can still be preserved. Under this constraint, when the sequence $\mathbf{r}$ is extracted, it is repaired to form an image hash with $|\mathbf{r}| = L$. If $|\mathbf{r}| > |\mathbf{W}|$, then the extra elements at the tail of $\mathbf{r}$ are deleted; otherwise, $\mathbf{r}$ is cyclically appended. We call the finally created sequence media hash $\mathbf{MH}$, which is a bipolar sequence. Next, media hash $\mathbf{MH}$ of an image is mixed with the watermark, $\mathbf{W}$, to generate the content-dependent watermark ($\mathbf{CDW}$) as

$$\mathbf{CDW} = S(\mathbf{W}, \mathbf{MH}), \tag{9}$$

where $S(\cdot, \cdot)$ is a mixing function, which is basically application-dependent and will be used to control the combination of $\mathbf{W}$ and $\mathbf{MH}$. The sequence $\mathbf{CDW}$ is what we will embed into a cover image.

5 Image-Dependent Watermark

The properties of the image-dependent watermark will be discussed first. Then, its resistance to WEA will be analyzed based on block-based image watermarking.

5.1 Properties

Let an image $\mathbf{I}$ be expressed as $\oplus_{i \in \Omega} \mathbf{B}_i$, where all blocks $\mathbf{B}_i$ are concatenated to form $\mathbf{I}$ and Ω denotes the set of block indices. As far as the block-based image watermarking scheme [1,12,16] is concerned, each image block $\mathbf{B}_i$ will be embedded with a content-dependent watermark $\mathbf{CDW}_i$ to form a stego image $\mathbf{I}^{\mathbf{s}}$, i.e.,

$$\mathbf{B^s}_i = \mathbf{B}_i + \mathbf{CDW}_i, \qquad \mathbf{I^s} = \oplus_{i \in \Omega} \mathbf{B^s}_i, \tag{10}$$

where $\mathbf{B^s}_i$ is a stego block and $\mathbf{CDW}_i$, similar to Eq. (9), is defined as the mixture of a fixed informative watermark $\mathbf{W}$ and a block-based hash $\mathbf{MH_{B_i}}$, i.e.,

$$\mathbf{CDW}_i = S(\mathbf{W}, \mathbf{MH_{B_i}}). \tag{11}$$

In Eq. (11), the mixing function $S(\cdot,\cdot)$ will be designed as a procedure of permuting the media hash $\mathbf{MH_{B_i}}$ using the same secret key K, followed by shuffling the watermark to enhance security. Specifically, it is expressed as

$$S(\mathbf{W}, \mathbf{MH_{B_i}})(k) = W(k)PT(\mathbf{MH_{B_i}}, K)(k),$$

where PT denotes a permutation function controlled by the secret key K with the aim of achieving uncorrelated crosscorrelation,

$$\delta_{nc}(PT(\mathbf{MH_{B_i}}, K), \mathbf{MH_{B_i}}) = 0,$$

and autocorrelation:

$$\delta_{nc}(\mathbf{MH_{B_i}}, \mathbf{MH_{B_j}}) = \delta_{nc}(PT(\mathbf{MH_{B_i}}, K), PT(\mathbf{MH_{B_j}}, K)).$$

The proposed content-dependent watermark possesses the characteristics described as follows. They are useful for proving resistance to WEA.

Definition 3 Given two image blocks $\mathbf{B}_i$ and $\mathbf{B}_j$, their degree of similarity depends on the correlation between $\mathbf{MH_{B_i}}$ and $\mathbf{MH_{B_j}}$, i.e.,

$$\delta_{nc}(\mathbf{B}_i, \mathbf{B}_j) = \delta_{nc}(\mathbf{MH_{B_i}}, \mathbf{MH_{B_j}}). \tag{12}$$

Accordingly, we have two extreme cases: (i) if $\mathbf{B}_i = \mathbf{B}_j$, then $\delta_{nc}(\mathbf{B}_i, \mathbf{B}_j) = 1$; (ii) if $\mathbf{B}_i$ and $\mathbf{B}_j$ look visually dissimilar, then $\delta_{nc}(\mathbf{B}_i, \mathbf{B}_j) \approx 0$.

Proposition 1 Given two image blocks $\mathbf{B}_i$ and $\mathbf{B}_j$, $\delta_{nc}(\mathbf{B}_i, \mathbf{B}_j)$, and their respectively embedded content-dependent watermarks $\mathbf{CDW}_i$ and $\mathbf{CDW}_j$ that are assumed to be i.i.d. with Gaussian distributions $\mathcal{N}(0, \rho^2)$, the following properties can be established: (i) $\delta_{nc}(\mathbf{CDW}_i, \mathbf{CDW}_j)$ is linearly proportional to $\delta_{nc}(\mathbf{B}_i, \mathbf{B}_j)$; (ii) $\delta_{nc}(\mathbf{CDW}_i, \mathbf{CDW}_j) \leq \delta_{nc}(\mathbf{W}^2)$; (iii) $\delta_{nc}(\mathbf{n}, \mathbf{CDW}) = 0$ ($\mathbf{n}$ is generally a Gaussian noise with zero mean). Due to limits of space, proofs of Proposition 1 by exploiting the above properties will not be shown here.

5.2 Resistance to Collusion Attacks

By means of a collusion attack, the averaging operation is performed on stego blocks $\mathbf{B^s}_i$'s of a stego image $\mathbf{I^s}$. From an attacker's perspective, each hidden watermark has to be estimated by means of a denoising operation (e.g., Wiener filtering), so deviations of estimation will inevitably occur. Let $\mathbf{W^e}_i$ be an estimated watermark from $\mathbf{B^s}_i$. Without loss of generality, it is assumed to have zero mean. In fact, $\mathbf{W^e}_i$ can be modeled as a partial hidden watermark plus a noise component, i.e.,

$$\mathbf{W^e}_i = \alpha_i \mathbf{CDW}_i + \mathbf{n}_i, \tag{13}$$

where $\mathbf{n}_i$ represents an image block-dependent Gaussian noise with zero mean, α_i denotes the weight that the watermark has been extracted, and $\mathbf{W^e}_i \sim \mathcal{N}(0, \rho^2)$ is enforced to ensure that the estimated watermark and the hidden watermark have the same energy. Under these circumstances, $1 \geq \alpha_i = \delta_{nc}(\mathbf{W^e}_i, \mathbf{CDW}_i) > T$ always holds based on the fact that a watermark is a high-frequency signal and can be efficiently estimated by means of denoising [5,6,14]. This factor α_i plays a crucial role in two ways: (i) on one hand, from an attacker's viewpoint, α_i should be adjusted in a pixel/coefficient-wise manner so that perceptual fidelity can be maintained [14]; (ii) on the other hand, from an owner's viewpoint, a watermarking system should be able to allow large α_i in order that strong attacks can be tolerated. Let $\mathcal{C}$ ($\subset \Omega$) denote the set of blocks used for collusion. By employing the Central Limit Theorem the average of all the estimated watermarks can be expressed as

$$\bar{\mathbf{W}}^{\mathbf{e}} = \frac{\sqrt{|\mathcal{C}|}}{|\mathcal{C}|} \sum_{i \in \mathcal{C}} \mathbf{W^e}_i = \frac{1}{\sqrt{|\mathcal{C}|}} \sum_{i \in \mathcal{C}} (\alpha_i \mathbf{CDW}_i + \mathbf{n}_i) \tag{14}$$

because $\mathbf{W^e}_i$'s are obtained from (nearly) visually dissimilar image blocks, which can be regarded as i.i.d. approximately.

Proposition 2 In a collusion atatck, an attacker first estimates $\bar{\mathbf{W}}^{\mathbf{e}}$ from a set $\mathcal{C}$ of image blocks. Then, a counterfeit unwatermarked image $\mathbf{I^u}$ is generated from a watermarked image $\mathbf{I^s} = \oplus_{i \in \Omega} \mathbf{B^s}_i$ by

$$\mathbf{B^u}_i = \mathbf{B^s}_i - \bar{\mathbf{W}}^{\mathbf{e}}, \qquad \mathbf{I^u} = \oplus_{i \in \Omega} \mathbf{B^u}_i. \tag{15}$$

It is said that the collusion attack fails in an image block $\mathbf{B^u}_k, k \in \Omega$, i.e., $\delta_{nc}(\mathbf{B^u}_k, \mathbf{CDW}_k) > T$, if and only if $\delta_{nc}(\bar{\mathbf{W}}^e, \mathbf{CDW}_k) = \frac{\alpha_k}{\sqrt{|\mathcal{C}|}} < 1 - T$.

Proof: By making use of Eq. (14) and Proposition 1, we get:

$$\begin{aligned} \delta_{nc}(\bar{\mathbf{W}}^{\mathbf{e}}, \mathbf{CDW}_k) &= \frac{\sqrt{|\mathcal{C}|}}{|\mathcal{C}|} \delta_{nc}(\sum_{i \in \mathcal{C}} (\alpha_i \mathbf{CDW}_i + \mathbf{n}_i), \mathbf{CDW}_k) \\ &= \frac{1}{\sqrt{|\mathcal{C}|}} \sum_{i \in \mathcal{C}} \alpha_i \delta_{nc}(\mathbf{CDW}_i, \mathbf{CDW}_k) + \frac{1}{\sqrt{|\mathcal{C}|}} \sum_{i \in \mathcal{C}} \delta_{nc}(\mathbf{n}_i, \mathbf{CDW}_k) \\ &= \frac{\alpha_k}{\sqrt{|\mathcal{C}|}}, \end{aligned} \tag{16}$$

where $\mathbf{CDW}_k$ represents the content-dependent watermark embedded in $\mathbf{B}_k$. According to Eq. (16), our derivations are further explained as follows: the first row is resulted from Eq. (14) while the second term of the second row is zero by employing the independence of $\mathbf{n}_i$ from $\mathbf{CDW}_k$. Consequently, given property 2 of Proposition 1 and Eqs. (15) and (16), we get:

$$\begin{aligned} \delta_{nc}(\mathbf{B^u}_k, \mathbf{CDW}_k) > T \text{ iff } & \delta_{nc}(\mathbf{B}_k + \mathbf{CDW}_k - \bar{\mathbf{W}}^{\mathbf{e}}, \mathbf{CDW}_k) > T \\ \text{iff } & \delta_{nc}(\mathbf{CDW}_k, \mathbf{CDW}_k) - \delta_{nc}(\bar{\mathbf{W}}^{\mathbf{e}}, \mathbf{CDW}_k) > T \\ \text{iff } & \delta_{nc}(\bar{\mathbf{W}}^{\mathbf{e}}, \mathbf{CDW}_k) = \frac{\alpha_k}{\sqrt{|\mathcal{C}|}} < 1 - T. \end{aligned} \tag{17}$$

Remarks (Further interpretation of $|\mathcal{C}|$): If $|\mathcal{C}| = 1$ (we mean that the collusion attack is only applied to one block), then the collusion attack degenerates into a denoising-based removal attack. Under this circumstance, the success of the collusion attack depends on the accuracy of estimation or the factor α_k (as pointed out previously, this factor plays a trade-off role between fidelity and robustness). By substituting $|\mathcal{C}| = 1$ into Eq. (17) and using $T < \alpha_k$, we get $T < 0.5$. In other words, α_k must be larger than or equal to 0.5 to guarantee success of the collusion attack when $|\mathcal{C}| = 1$. This result totally depends on the effectiveness of denoising in estimating an added signal. Provided that $|\mathcal{C}|$ becomes infinite, i.e., $|\mathcal{C}| = |\Omega| \to \infty$, $\delta_{nc}(\bar{\mathbf{W}}^{\mathbf{e}}, \mathbf{CDW}_k) \to 0$ is obtained such that T can be an arbitrarily small but positive value, which means that the incorrectly estimated watermarks dominate the correctly estimated ones. On the other hand, the proposed content-dependent watermarking scheme is unfavorable to the collusion attack, which is by definition applied to more than one image block. It is interesting to note that this result contradicts the expected characteristic of a collusion attack. In particular, the performance degradation of the proposed method can be interpreted as being lower bounded by the denoising-based watermark removal attack (e.g., for $|\mathcal{C}| = 1$), as proved in Proposition 2 and later verified in experiments.

5.3 Resistance to Copy Attack

Next, we will proceed to show why the presented content-dependent watermark can be immune to a copy attack. Let $\mathbf{MH_X}$ and $\mathbf{MH_Z}$ denote the hash sequences generated from two different image blocks, $\mathbf{X}$ and $\mathbf{Z}$, respectively. In addition, let $\mathbf{CDW_X}$ denote the content-dependent watermark to be hidden into the cover image block $\mathbf{X}$. As has been stated previously, let the watermark estimated from $\mathbf{X^s}$ be $\mathbf{W^x}$, which will contain partial information from $\mathbf{CDW_X}$. By directing the copy attack at the target block $\mathbf{Z}$, we can get the counterfeit watermarked block $\mathbf{Z^s}$ as defined in Eq. (4). Later, in the detection process, the content-dependent watermark, $\mathbf{W^z}$, estimated from block $\mathbf{Z^s}$ will be

$$\mathbf{W^z} = (\alpha \times \mathbf{CDW_X} + \mathbf{n}), \tag{18}$$

according to Eq. (13), where $\mathbf{n}$ indicates the noise sequence (which is irrelevant to watermarks) generated by means of denoising $\mathbf{Z^s}$. Based on the evidence that denoising is an efficient way to estimate watermarks [6,14,16], $||\alpha\mathbf{CDW_X}||_2 > ||\mathbf{n}||_2$ can undoubtedly hold, with $||\cdot||_2$ being the energy. Given Eqs. (11) and (18), Proposition 1, and Definition 3, normalized correlation between $\mathbf{CDW_Z}$ and $\mathbf{W^z}$ can be derived as follows based on blocks $\mathbf{X}$ and $\mathbf{Z}$ that are dissimilar:

$$\begin{aligned}\delta_{nc}(\mathbf{CDW_Z}, \mathbf{W^z}) &= \frac{1}{|\mathbf{W}|\rho^2}\sum_{i=1}^{|\mathbf{W}|} CDW_Z(i)W^z(i) \\ &\approx \frac{\alpha}{|\mathbf{W}|\rho^2}\sum_{i=1}^{|\mathbf{W}|} CDW_Z(i)CDW_X(i) \approx 0.\end{aligned} \tag{19}$$

6 Experimental Results

In our experiments, ten varieties of gray-scale cover images of size 512 × 512, as shown in Fig. 2, were used for watermarking. In this study, Voloshynovskiy *et al.*'s block-based image watermarking approach [16] was chosen as the benchmark, denoted as Method I, due to its strong robustness and computational simplicity. Each image block is of size 32 × 32 so that the watermark's length was 1024 and the number of blocks was $|\Omega| = 256$. The combination of our CDW and Voloshynovskiy *et al.*'s scheme is denoted as Method II. We would like to manifest the advantage of using CDW by comparing the results obtained using Methods I and II when WEA is imposed. However, we would like to particularly emphasize that the proposed CDW can be readily applied to other watermarking algorithms. On the other hand, Lee's Wiener filter [7] was used to perform denoising-based blind watermark extraction.

Fig. 2. Cover images.

6.1 CDW Resistance to Collusion Attack

The collusion attack (operated by colluding $|\mathcal{C}| = |\Omega| = 256$ blocks) was applied to Method I and Method II, respectively, on ten cover images. The impacts of collusion attack and CDW will be examined with respect to the three scenarios: (s1) the BER of the estimated watermark's sign bits from an owner's perspective; (s2) the quality of a colluded image; and (s3) watermark detection after collusion. For (s3), there are 256 correlations resulted in an image. Only the minimum and the maximum correlations are plotted for each image. All the numerical results are depicts in Figs. 3∼5, respectively. Some colluded images are illustrated in Fig. 6 for visual inspection. In summary, as long as an image hash is involved in constructing a watermark, the quality of the colluded images will be degraded,

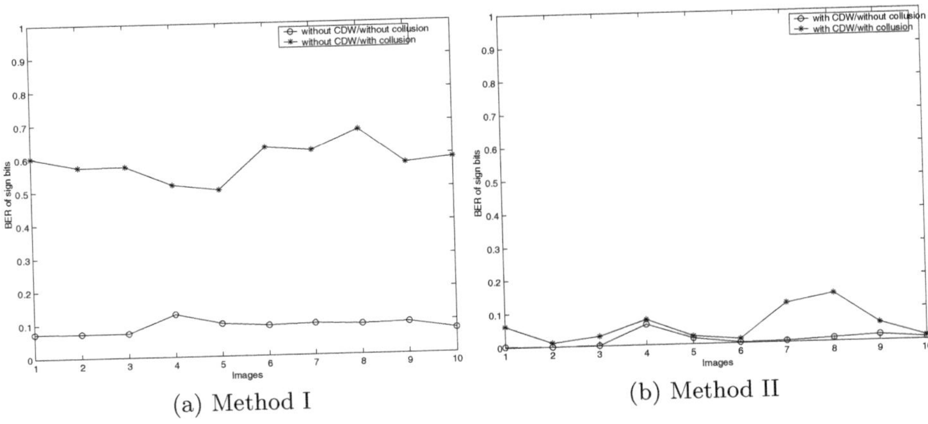

(a) Method I (b) Method II

Fig. 3. Scenario 1 (BER of the estimated watermark's sign bits): (a) most of the watermark's sign bits are correctly estimated by a collusion attack; (b) when CDW is introduced, the watermark's sign bits mostly remain unchanged. This experiment confirms that CDW is efficient in randomizing watermarks in order to disable collusion.

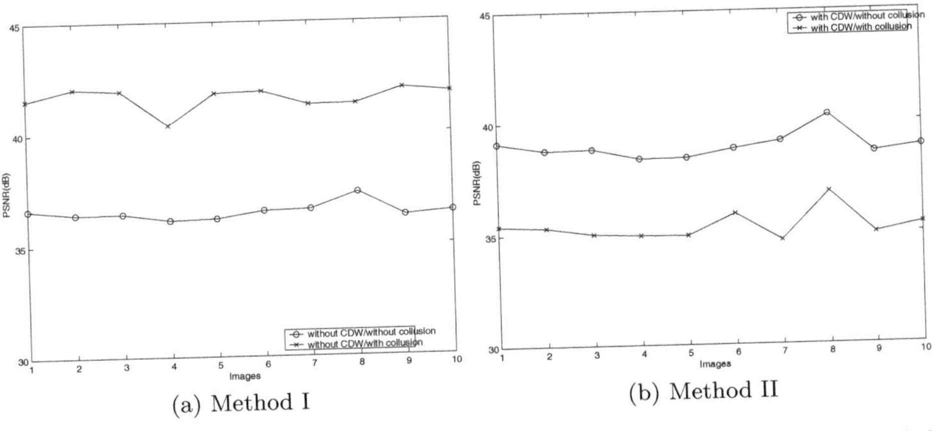

(a) Method I (b) Method II

Fig. 4. Scenario 2 (quality of a colluded image): (a) the PSNR values of the colluded images are higher than those of the stego images; (b) when CDW is applied, the PSNR values of the colluded images are lower than those of the stego images. This experiment reveals that a collusion attack will fail to improve the fidelity of a colluded image when CDW is involved.

but it will still be possible for the watermarks to be extracted. Therefore, the merits of CDW in resisting collusion have been thoroughly demonstrated.

6.2 CDW Resistance to the Copy Attack

The copy attack was applied to Method I and Method II to compare their capability of resistance. One of the ten images was watermarked, estimated, and copied to the other nine unwatermarked images to form nine counterfeit stego

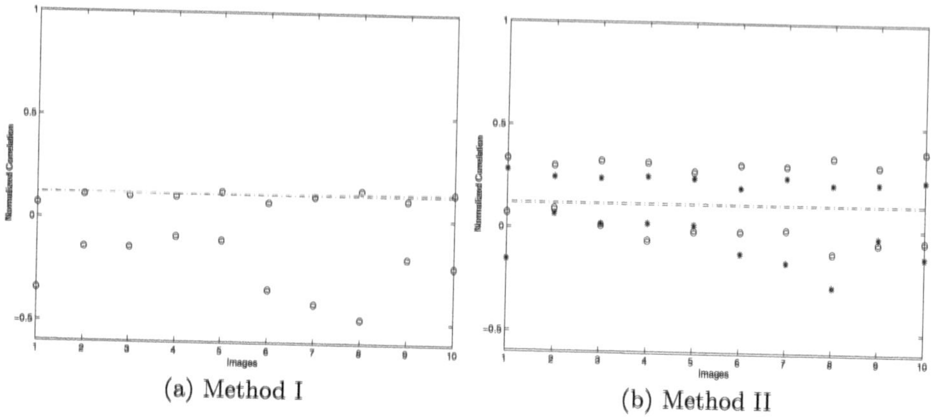

(a) Method I (b) Method II

Fig. 5. Scenario 3 (watermark detection after collusion): (a) without using CDW, normalized correlations show the almost complete absence of hidden watermarks; (b) using CDW, normalized correlations mostly show the presence of hidden watermarks. In (b), 'o' denotes the results obtained by colluding all blocks ($|\mathcal{C}| = 256 = |\Omega|$), while '*' denotes those obtained by colluding only one block ($|\mathcal{C}| = 1$). The dashdot line indicates the threshold $T = 0.12$. Definitely, the result of (b) verifies Proposition 2. Furthermore, when the watermarks extracted from all the image blocks are integrated (a kind of collusion estimation) to obtain the final watermark, Method II produces normalized correlations as high as 0.9, while Method I produces normalized correlations close to 0.

images. By repeating the above procedure, a total of 90 counterfeit stego images were obtained. The PSNR values of the 90 attacked images were in the range of $26 \sim 36$dB (no masking was used). The 90 correlation values obtained by applying the copy attack to Method I fell within the interval $[0.474 \;\; 0.740]$ (all were sufficiently larger than $T = 0.12$), which indicates the presence of watermarks. However, when CDW was introduced, these correlations decreased significantly to $[-0.090 \;\; 0.064]$, which indicates the absence of watermarks. The experimental results are consistent with the analytic result, derived in Eq. (19). Obviously, the proposed CDW is able to deter the detection of copied watermarks.

7 Concluding Remarks

Although multiple watermarks can be embedded into an image to withstand geometrical distortions, they are vulnerable to be colluded or copied, and the desired functionality is lost. To cope with this problem, an anti-disclosure watermark with resistance to watermark-estimation attack (WEA) has been investigated in this paper. We have pointed out that both accurate estimation of a watermark's sign and complete subtraction of a watermark's energy constitute the sufficient and necessary conditions to achieve complete watermark removal. We have introduced the concept of the media hash and combined it with hidden information to create the so-called content-dependent watermark (CDW).

(a) colluded Lenna (Method I) (b) colluded Lenna (Method II)

(c) colluded Sailboat (Method I) (d) colluded Sailboat (Method II)

Fig. 6. Perceptual illustrations of colluded images obtained using Method I (without using CDW) and Method II (using CDW). By comparing these two examples, it can be found that when a collusion attack is encountered, CDW is able to make the colluded image perceptually noisy.

The characteristics of CDW have been analyzed to justify its resistance to WEA. The experimental results have confirmed our mathematical analyses of WEA and CDW. Extensions of our content-dependent watermark to other multiple watermark embedding techniques or other media watermarking are straightforward. To our knowledge, the proposed content-dependent anti-disclosure watermark is the first to enable both resistance to the collusion and the copy attacks. Media hash with geometric-invariance is a worthy direction for further studying.

Acknowledgment. This paper was supported by the National Science Council under NSC grants 91-2213-E-001-037 and 92-2422-H-001-004.

References

1. P. Bas, J. M. Chassery, and B. Macq, "Geometrically Invariant Watermarking Using Feature Points," *IEEE Trans. on Image Processing*, Vol. 11, pp. 1014–1028, 2002.
2. I. J. Cox, M. L. Miller, and J. A. Bloom, "Digital Watermarking," *Morgan Kaufmann*, 2002.
3. J. Fridrich, "Visual Hash for Oblivious Watermarking," *Proc. SPIE: Security and Watermarking of Multimedia Contents II*, Vol. 3971, 2000.
4. IEEE Int. Workshop on Multimedia Signal Processing (MMSP), special session on Media Recognition, Virgin Islands, USA, 2002.
5. T. Kalker, G. Depovere, J. Haitsma, and M. Maes, "A Video Watermarking System for Broadcast Monitoring," *Proc. of the SPIE*, Vol. 3657, pp. 103–112, 1999.
6. M. Kutter, S. Voloshynovskiy, and A. Herrigel, "The Watermark Copy Attack", *Proc. SPIE: Security and Watermarking of Multimedia Contents II*, Vol. 3971, 2000.
7. J. S. Lee, "Digital Image Enhancement and Noise Filtering by Use of Local Statistics", *IEEE Trans. on Pattern Anal. and Machine Intell.*, Vol. 2, pp. 165–168, 1980.
8. C. S. Lu, S. K. Huang, C. J. Sze, and H. Y. Mark Liao, "Cocktail Watermarking for Digital Image Protection", *IEEE Trans. on Multimedia*, Vol. 2, pp. 209–224, 2000.
9. C. S. Lu and H. Y. Mark Liao, "Structural Digital Signature for Image Authentication: An Incidental Distortion Resistant Scheme", *IEEE Trans. on Multimedia*, Vol. 5, No. 2, pp. 161–173, 2003.
10. K. Su, D. Kundur, D. Hatzinakos, "A Content-Dependent Spatially Localized Video Watermark for Resistance to Collusion and Interpolation Attacks," *Proc. IEEE Int. Conf. on Image Processing*, 2001.
11. M. D. Swanson, B. Zhu, and A. H. Tewfik, "Multiresolution Scene-Based Video Watermarking Using Perceptual Models," *IEEE Journal on Selected Areas in Communications*, Vol. 16, No. 4, pp. 540–550, 1998.
12. C. W. Tang and H. M. Hang, "A Feature-based Robust Digital Watermarking Scheme," *IEEE Trans. on Signal Processing*, Vol. 51, No. 4, pp. 950–959, 2003.
13. W. Trappe, M. Wu, J. Wang, and K. J. Ray Liu, "Anti-collusion Fingerprinting for Multimedia", *IEEE Trans. on Signal Processing*, Vol. 51, pp. 1069–1087, 2003.
14. S. Voloshynovskiy, S. Pereira, A. Herrigel, N. Baumgartner, and T. Pun, "Generalized Watermarking Attack Based on Watermark Estimation and Perceptual Remodulation", *Proc. SPIE: Security and Watermarking of Multimedia Contents II*, Vol. 3971, San Jose, CA, USA, 2000.
15. S. Voloshynovskiy, S. Pereira, V. Iquise, and T. Pun, "Attack Modelling: Towards a Second Generation Watermarking Benchmark," *Signal Processing*, Vol. 81, No. 6, pp. 1177–1214, 2001.
16. S. Voloshynovskiy, F. Deguillaume, and T. Pun, "Multibit Digital Watermarking Robust against Local Nonlinear Geometrical Distortions," *Proc. IEEE Int. Conf. on Image Processing*, pp. 999–1002, 2001.

Performance Measurement of Watermark Embedding Patterns

Robert Scealy, Reihaneh Safavi-Naini, and Nicholas Paul Sheppard

School of Information Technology and Computer Science
The University of Wollongong NSW 2522
Australia
{rcs07,rei,nps}@uow.edu.au

Abstract. Segmented watermarking is an approach to multiple watermarking that can be used to acknowledge the contribution of multiple authors or to embed a fingerprint code word, but is susceptible to cropping attacks that discard portions of the watermarked media. Careful selection of the watermark embedding pattern can increase the resilience of a segmented watermark in the presence of cropping attacks. In this paper, we consider performance measures for embedding patterns and compare the performance of several proposed embedding patterns using these measures.

1 Introduction

In a segmented watermarking scheme [6], the object to be watermarked is divided into a series of segments, and each segment is watermarked independently. In this way, the ownership of multiple owners can be represented by embedding each of the owners' watermarks into a different segment, or a fingerprint code word can be encoded by embedding one code letter into each segment.

This method is obviously subject to a cropping attack, in which an attacker may discard some of the segments of no interest to him or her, possibly eliminating one or more watermarks or code letters from the object. Since, in general, there may be more segments than watermarks or code letters, and each watermark or code letter may be embedded multiple times, we can expect the segmented watermark to have at least some resilience against this kind of attack.

The *embedding pattern* chosen for mapping watermarks or letters to segments will affect the resilience of the overall watermark to these kinds of attacks. A good embedding pattern should allocate watermarks and letters to segments in such a way as to minimise the possibility of a watermark being eliminated or a code word being lost.

In applications where each segment represents a fingerprint code letter, we consider the case where the mark in each segment encodes both the letter itself and its position in the code word, that is, it encodes (i, c_i) for position i and letter c_i. In another approach, the letter's position in the code word might be implied only by the location of the segment in the original object. However, this

T. Kalker et al. (Eds.): IWDW 2003, LNCS 2939, pp. 77–85, 2004.
© Springer-Verlag Berlin Heidelberg 2004

location information is likely to be lost in any significant cropping attack. The measure of resilience of the former kind of encoding is the same as in the case where each segment represents an owner: after a cropping attack, we would like to have at least one segment corresponding to each $i \in \{1, \ldots, m\}$ for a set of m owners or code words of length m.

In this paper, we consider segmented watermarking of still images by dividing them into rectangular blocks, and an attacker who selects a rectangular sub-image from the original image. We propose average-case metrics for measuring the resilience of embedding patterns in the presence of cropping attacks based on the idea of a *minimal cropping region*, and give the values of these metrics for various embedding patterns.

2 Related Work

Our problem is similar to the problem of multi-dimensional data de-clustering, used in databases to reduce latency when retrieving data from multiple disks using parallel I/O. In this problem, the time required to process a query is proportional to the greatest amount of data retrieved from a single disk.

A *range query* is a query formed by taking all of the data points that lie between a given maximum and minimum value in each dimension, i.e. a kind of "cropping" of the data set. To minimise the time required to satisfy such a query, we want the segments of data in the range query to be distributed as homogeneously as possible over all disks. If we think of the disks as watermarks, the similarity between this problem and ours becomes apparent.

The two problems are not quite identical, however. In the de-clustering problem, we wish to minimise the number of segments in any region that lie on a single disk. In our waterkmarking problem, we wish to maximise the number of different watermarks in any region. Nonetheless, an allocation that is good for one seems likely to be a good choice for the other one.

Prabhakar, et al. [5] give a survey of de-clustering methods and propose a general paradigm (the *cyclic* paradigm) for de-clustering that generalises many previously-existing schemes. They compare them by computing the average cost of a query over all possible range queries. Obviously this approach becomes impractical for large data sets, and they later resort to using a randomly-chosen subset of all possible queries. In this paper, we propose a deterministic method of choosing the subset of cropping regions to be tested such that the set chosen gives a good representation of the performance of the embedding pattern against an arbitrary attack.

Atallah and Frikken [2] define an area as *complete* if it contains at least one copy of all watermarks (equivalently, uses all disks), and *full* if it does not contain any duplicate watermarks (or disks). They then define two metrics called the *maximum non-complete area* (MNCA) and *minimum non-full area* (MNFA). They show that the optimal values for the MNCA and MNFA can be achieved only for a number of watermarks $m = 1$, 2, 3 or 5, in the sense that an "optimal" pattern is one in which any rectangle of area at least m contains all watermarks.

They furthermore show how to construct embedding patterns that have a non-optimal MNCA of $O(m)$ and a non-optimal MNFA of $\Omega(m)$. They also give an experimental evaluation of both metrics for a number of different embedding patterns taken from work in database de-clustering.

The notion of a complete area seems more applicable to the watermarking problem than the notion of a full one, since in this case we are only interested in whether or not watermarks are present and not so much in whether or not they are duplicated (the latter is more of an issue in the data de-clusterig problem). The MNCA is a measure of the worst-case performance of an embedding pattern in the presence of cropping attacks. In this paper, we will introduce metrics that measure the average-case performance of embedding patterns in terms of the completeness of cropped regions.

3 Embedding Patterns

For the purposes of this study, an embedding pattern is a map $\phi : \mathcal{N} \times \mathcal{N} \rightarrow \mathcal{A}$ from a two-dimensional space to an m-element data set $\mathcal{A} = \{0, \ldots, m-1\}$, where m is the number of watermarks to be embedded. The segment at position (x, y) in the segmentation grid will receive watermark $\phi(x, y)$.

3.1 Cyclic Methods

Many of the methods currently used for data de-clustering can be categorised as *cyclic* methods [5]. In these methods, we set

$$\phi(x, y) = (xH + yJ) \bmod m \tag{1}$$

for some integers H and J. For example, the "disk modulo" method [3] is a cyclic method with $H = J = 1$ and the "optimal" method [1] is a cyclic method with $H = \lfloor \frac{m}{2} \rfloor$ and $J = 1$. The latter method is optimal for a few special values of m in the sense that no range query of size T requires more than $\lceil \frac{T}{m} \rceil$ disks.

If we choose H and J to be relatively prime to m, we will guarantee that every element of $\mathcal{A}$ will appear in the pattern (assuming that the range of x and y is large enough). In this paper, we will always choose $J = 1$ but allow H to vary, as in [5].

3.2 Fieldwise Exclusive Method

The *fieldwise exclusive* (FX) method [4] was introduced for the case when m is a power of two, however, its definition is also valid for arbitrary m. In this method, we set

$$\phi(x, y) = x \oplus y \bmod m\text{‘}, \tag{2}$$

where '$\oplus$' denotes the bit-wise exclusive-OR function.

3.3 Tile Rotation Method

It is possible for an embedding pattern to have an unbounded MNCA if it contains incomplete rows or columns, that is, an $a \in \mathcal{A}$ such that $\phi(x, y) \neq a$ for any x with fixed y, or any y with fixed x. To avoid this, we would like to ensure that every row and column of the pattern contains every watermark. We can achieve this by forming a large pattern from rotations of a basic complete pattern, which we will call the *tile rotation* method.

Let $m' = a \times b$ be the smallest composite number at least as large as m. Consider an $a \times b$ tile L consisting of all the elements of $\mathcal{A}$ in an arbitrary arrangement (note there will be empty positions if $m' > m$). Let $\mathrm{rotr}(L, i)$ denote and i-column rotation of the rows of L, and $\mathrm{rotc}(L, i)$ denote rotation of the columns similarly. Then we can define an embedding pattern by dividing the segmentation grid into $a \times b$ blocks and assigning $\mathrm{rotr}(\mathrm{rotc}(L, j), i)$ to the block at (i, j). That is, set

$$\begin{aligned} \phi(x, y) &= \mathrm{rotr}(\mathrm{rotc}(L, \lfloor \frac{y}{b} \rfloor), \lfloor \frac{x}{a} \rfloor)(x \bmod a, y \bmod b) \\ &= \mathrm{rotc}(L, \lfloor \frac{y}{b} \rfloor)(x + \lfloor \frac{x}{a} \rfloor \bmod a, y \bmod b) \\ &= L(x + \lfloor \frac{x}{a} \rfloor \bmod a, y + \lfloor \frac{y}{b} \rfloor \bmod b) \end{aligned} \tag{3}$$

4 Measurement Methods

For the purposes of watermark detection, a segment can be considered to have been completely eliminated if there is an insufficient part of it remaining to reliably detect the watermark after cropping, and to be wholly intact otherwise. Hence we can consider all cropping to take place along the segment boundaries.

In principle, an attacker may crop an image to some arbitrary rectilinear polygon. However, non-rectangular images are of limited value and, furthermore, could not reasonably be accepted as a proof of ownership since they have obviously been tampered with. Our metrics will consider only rectangular regions to be interesting.

In general, no rectangle of the original image is any more valuable to the attacker than any other. We therefore model a cropping attack as the random selection of a rectangular area of the segmentation grid.

4.1 Minimal Cropping Regions

Ideally, we would like every area of size m or greater to contain the complete set of watermarks. However, Atallah and Frikken have shown that this is possible only for a very limited choice of m. One method of measuring the performance of an embedding pattern, then, might be to test all regions of size m, and count the number of attacks that would succeed, that is, count the number of points at which the embedding pattern fails to be optimal.

However, this can give misleading results if m has few factors since there will not be many rectangles with area exactly m and this selection of rectangles may not be very representative of the collection of possible cropping attacks. In particular, if m is prime, only $1 \times m$ and $m \times 1$ rectangles will be tested, completely ignoring attacks that take square or near-square regions.

On the other hand, an obvious way of measuring the performance of an embedding pattern would be to test all possible cropped regions, and count the number of attacks that succeed, similar to the experiments performed in [5]. However, this leads to testing many very large areas that will never fail under any reasonable embedding pattern, and very small areas that cannot possibly contain all watermarks.

We define a *minimal cropping region* for area T to be an $a \times b$ sub-image C of B such that

- if $a \leq b$ and $a \leq \sqrt{T}$, then $b = \lceil \frac{T}{a} \rceil$; and
- if $a > b$ and $b \leq \sqrt{T}$, then $a = \lceil \frac{T}{b} \rceil$.

Intuitively, the set of all minimal cropping regions for an area T is the set of all rectangles with area at least T and minimal in each dimension. For example, the minimal cropping regions for $T = 5$ are of size 5×1, 3×2, 2×3 and 1×5.

An embedding pattern ϕ is *periodic* if $\phi(x + \delta x, y + \delta y) = \phi(x, y)$ for some periods δx and δy; all of the patterns considered in this paper are periodic. Our measurements consist of placing every possible minimal cropping region at every possible position over one period of the pattern, and counting the number of incomplete regions found. This reduces the number of tests required by a linear factor compared to testing all regions, since the number of minimal cropping regions is $O(m)$ but the number of all possible regions is $O(\delta x \delta y)$ and all of the embedding patterns used in this study have $\delta x, \delta y \geq m$.

4.2 Proposed Metrics

We propose two new average-case metrics based on the concept of a minimal cropping region, and two variations of Atallah and Frikken's worst-case metrics.

The All-Exclusion (AE) Metric. We define the *all-exclusion metric* as the number of complete minimal cropping regions, divided by the the total number of minimal cropping regions. This metric gives an indication of the general robustness of the embedding pattern.

The Single-Exclusion (SE) Metric. We define the *single-exclusion* metric as the probability that a minimal cropping region will contain any given watermark. Let c_n be the proportion of minimal cropping regions that exclude n watermarks. Then we can compute the SE metric as

$$\mathrm{SE} = 1 - \sum_{n=1}^{m} \frac{c_n n}{m}. \tag{4}$$

This metric favours cropping regions that are closer to being complete (i.e. do not exclude many watermarks) and gives an indication of how evenly distributed the watermarks are.

The (modified) Maximum Non-Complete Area (MaxNCA). For ease of computation, we modify Attallah and Frikken's notion of the maximum non-complete area to incorporate minimal cropping regions. Our modified maximum non-complete area is the maximum integer N such that there exists an incomplete minimal cropping region of size N. This metric gives an indication of the largest cropping attack that might succeed. As noted in Section 3.3, this value is unbounded if the pattern contains incomplete rows or columns (which would extend indefinitely through all periods of the pattern). In our tests, our program aborted with an error if it found an incomplete minimal cropping region of some large size chosen to control the programme's running time.

The Minimum Complete Area (MinCA). Similarly, we define the *minimum complete area* as the minimum integer N such that there exists a complete minimal cropping region of size N. This metric gives an indication of the smallest cropping attack that might fail.

5 Results

We computed the values of all of the metrics described in Section 4.2 for $2 \leq m \leq 10$ for each of the embedding patterns described in Section 3.

For the cyclic method, we performed two series of tests with different step sizes H. The first has $H = 1$, i.e. it is the "disk modulo" method.

Since the pattern for $H = m - a$ is symmetric to the pattern for $H = a$, we do not need to consider H's greater than half m. If H is not relatively prime to m, the pattern will not include all watermarks. Therefore we chose the second H to be the greatest number that is relatively prime to m but not greater than half m; this is equivalent to the "relatively prime HalfM" method of Prabakhar, et al. We conjectured that this would be the best choice for H since it maximises the difference between two adjacent rows, therefore minimising the number of repetitions within a rectangle covering two or more rows. Indeed, Prabakhar et al. show results indicating that this method is superior to all of the previously-existing methods for database de-clustering.

Figures 2 and 3 show our all-exclusion and single-exclusion metrics, respectively.

Figures 4 and 5 show the maximum non-complete area and minimum complete area, respectively. Note that the FX method with $m = 6$, 7, 9 and 10 has an unbounded MaxNCA.

6 Discussion

As we might have expected from the observations made in Section 2, our results are broadly similar to those obtained by Prabhakar, et al. for data de-clustering.

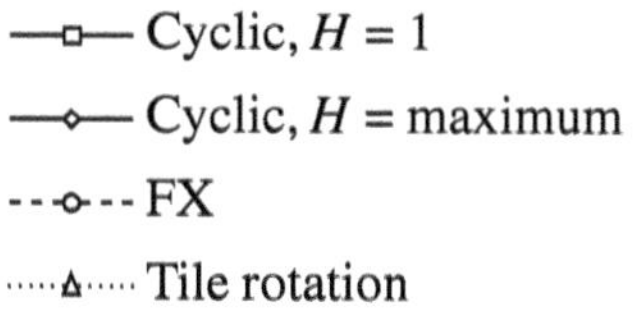

—□— Cyclic, $H = 1$
—◇— Cyclic, $H =$ maximum
- -○- - FX
·····△····· Tile rotation

Fig. 1. Graph legend

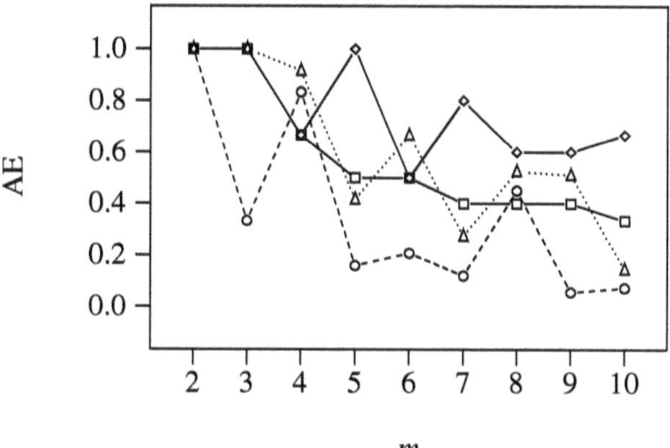

Fig. 2. All-exclusion metric

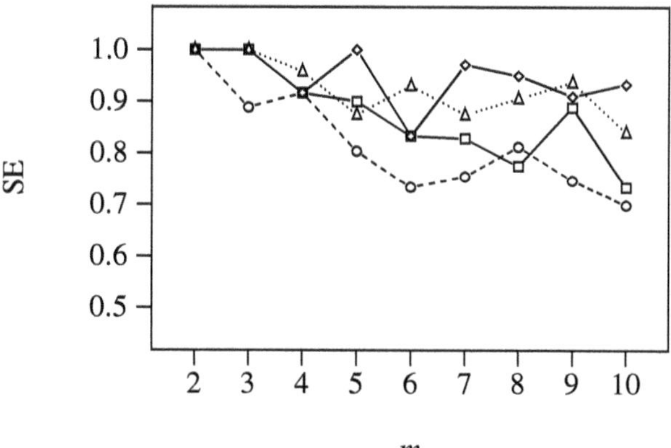

Fig. 3. Single-exclusion metric

The cyclic method with maximum step generally scores the best results, and always improves on the cyclic method with minimum step. The FX method scores reasonably well when m is a power of 2, but poorly for other values of m.

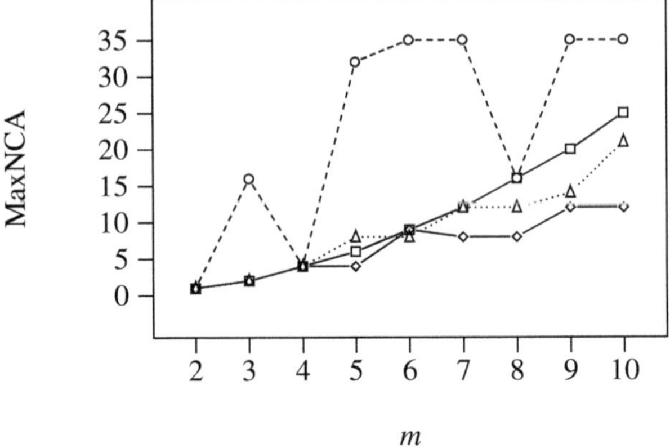

Fig. 4. (Modified) maximum non-complete area

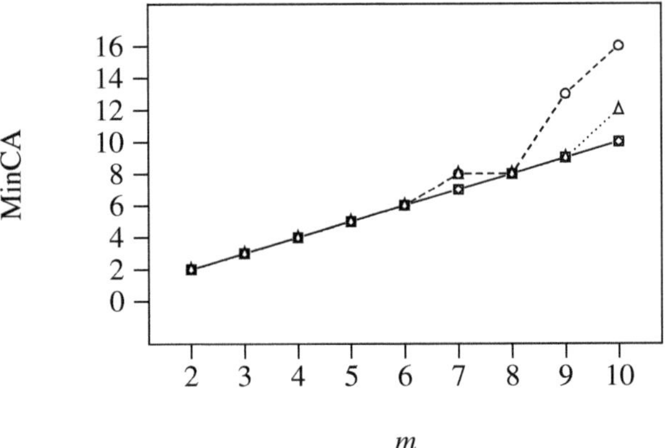

Fig. 5. Minimum complete area

The new tile rotation method generally scores a little worse than the maximum-step cyclic method, but scores better for $m = 4$ and 6. In these two cases, the highest relatively prime number less than half m is just 1, meaning that the maximum-step method is the same as the minimum-step method.

On the other hand, there are dips in the score for the tile rotation method at $m = 5$ and 7, which are prime numbers. This might be expected since the basic tile from which the pattern is constructed will have an empty position if m is prime (recalling that the tile must have composite area at least as great as m). The presence of empty positions obviously reduces the effectiveness of the pattern.

7 Conclusion

We have introduced two new metrics for measuring the average-case performance of embedding patterns for segmented watermark, based on the notion of a minimal cropping region. Using minimal cropping regions substantially reduces the number of tests required for testing the average-case performance of embedding patterns as compared to the brute force approach.

As in related work, our measurements favour embedding patterns based on the cyclic paradigm, and, in particular, cyclic methods with a large step size.

References

1. K. Abdel-Ghaffar and A. El Abbadi. Optimal allocation of two-dimensional data. In *International Conference on Database Theory*, pages 409–418, Delphi, Greece, 1997.
2. M. Atallah and K. Frikken. Cropping-resilient segmented multiple watermarking. In *Workshop on Algorithms and Discrete Structures*, 2003.
3. H. C. Du and J. S. Sobolewski. Disk allocation for cartesian product files on multiple-disk systems. *ACM Transactions on Database Systems*, 7:82–101, 1982.
4. M. H. Kim and S. Pramanik. Optimal file distribution for partial match retrieval. In *ACM International Conference on Management of Data*, pages 173–182, Chicago, USA, 1988.
5. S. Prabhakar, K. Abdel-Ghaffar, D. Agrawal, and A. El Abbadi. Efficient retrieval of multi-dimensional datasets through parallel I/O. In *ACM Symposium on Parallel Algorithms and Architectures*, pages 78–87, 1998.
6. N. P. Sheppard, R. Safavi-Naini, and P. Ogunbona. On multiple watermarking. In *Workshop on Security and Multimedia at ACM Multimedia*, pages 3–6, Ottawa, Canada, 2001.

Image Fusion Based Visible Watermarking Using Dual-Tree Complex Wavelet Transform

Yongjian Hu[1,2,3], Jiwu Huang[1], Sam Kwong[3], and Y.K. Chan[3]

[1] School of Information Science and Technology, Sun Yat-Sen University, Guangzhou 510275, PRC,
[2] Department of Automatic Control Engineering, South China University of Technology, Guangzhou 510641, PRC
eeyjhu@scut.edu.cn,
[3] Department of Computer Science, City University of Hong Kong, Kowloon, Hong Kong

Abstract. Digital watermarking has been researched extensively due to its potential use for data security and copyright protection. Much of the literature has focused on developing invisible watermarking algorithms. However, not much has been done on visible watermarking. A visible watermark is apparently needed for copyright notification. This work proposes a new framework of visible watermarking based on image fusion, a common technique used in combining images acquired from different modalities. To better protect the host features and increase the robustness of the watermark, the dual-tree complex wavelet transform (DT-CWT) is used. A new classification strategy is proposed to classify complex wavelet coefficients into 6 classes with different perceptual significance. The embedding decision can be made based on the classification information. Small watermark coefficients are prohibited from embedding. In the host edges, the insertion of watermark energy is controlled by using the inversely proportional embedding scheme to better preserve the sensitive region, while in other regions, the embedding strength becomes stronger as texture activity increases. This work also addresses the problem of low-pass subband watermark embedding, which is a special issue of visible watermarking. Experimental results show that the proposed algorithm yields significantly superior image quality than the current DCT-based method.

Keywords: visible watermark, image watermarking, image fusion, complex wavelet, adaptive watermarking.

1 Introduction

Marking can be visible, as on U.S. currency, or secrete (not easily seen without instruments). Currently, most efforts in the literature focus on the latter, i.e., invisible watermarking. However, one major application for digital watermarking is to identify the source of a document and convey visible ownership information to prevent misappropriating the material in the web, for example, in a digital

T. Kalker et al. (Eds.): IWDW 2003, LNCS 2939, pp. 86–100, 2004.
© Springer-Verlag Berlin Heidelberg 2004

library. Generally, a visible watermark is a secondary image which may be a line of text or a logo. It can be translucently overlaid onto a primary image without causing significant perceptual artifacts [1]. In real-world applications, a visible watermark can act as a restriction as well as an advertisement.

So far few works on visible watermarking can be found in the literature. The IBM digital library organization first proposed a visible watermarking technique and used it to mark the digitized pages of manuscript from the Vatican Library [2]. They scaled the strength of watermark image and embedded it to the luminance component of the original image. Based on this work, Meng and Chang proposed a compressed domain visible watermarking for video [3]. Local video features such as brightness and complexity are used to scale the watermark to achieve consistent perceptual visibility. Kankanhalli et al. proposed a block-DCT domain algorithm for images where the texture, edge and luminance information in each block is analyzed in order to find adaptive embedding factors [4]. Mohanty et al. furthered the work in [4] and adaptively exploited texture sensitivity of the human visual system (HVS) [5]. In typical visible watermarking algorithms such as [4] and [5], the researchers proposed to embed a relatively weaker watermark signal in edges and flat regions while embedding a stronger watermark signal in textures. The goal is to make the watermark look more consistent. But the underlying defects in block-DCT based algorithms may result in visual discontinuity.

One of the latest efforts can be found in [6] where visible watermarking is implemented in the discrete wavelet transform (DWT) domain. Since the outputs of the wavelet transform are localized in both space and frequency, better adaptivity is expected. Compared to [4] and [5], [6] used the inversely proportional embedding scheme and embedded more watermark energy in featureless regions and less watermark energy in edges and textures. This measure effectively avoids destroying the details of the host image, however, it suffers some lose of robustness since the watermark embedded in flat or textureless regions could be removed by using the averaging technique. A new type of attack against visible watermarks can also be found in [7].

In this paper, we improve the inversely proportional embedding scheme and increase visual consistency and robustness by enhancing the watermark energy in texture regions. More than that, we introduce a new framework of visible watermarking based on the principle of image fusion. Image fusion can be defined as the process by which several images, or some of their features, are combined together to form a single image [8]. We consider the features of both the host image and the watermark during the process of watermark insertion. In order to better retain image details in all directions, we implement the algorithm in the dual-tree complex wavelet transform domain.

This paper is organized as follows. Section 2 briefly describes the dual-tree complex wavelet transform. In section 3, the framework of the proposed algorithm is introduced. We discuss how to use the principle of image fusion. We also investigate the rules that we must obey to calculate the scaling and embedding factors. Section 4 describes the strategy for classification. We first classify all

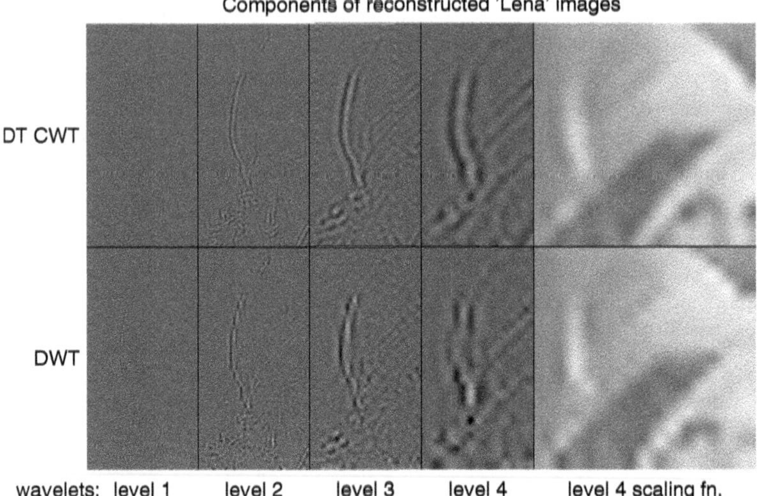

Fig. 1. Comparison between DT-CWT and DWT

complex wavelet coefficients into 6 different classes based on their energy, then finely regroup the classes based on local texture activity. In section 5, we discuss how to make the embedding decision according to the classification information. We also give the formulas to compute the scaling and embedding factors. Section 6 discusses the low-pass subband embedding, which is a special issue of visible watermarking. Experimental results and conclusions are presented in Sections 7 and 8.

2 The Dual-Tree Complex Wavelet Transform

The tree structure of the DWT is non-redundant as it produces the same number of output coefficients as input coefficients. This has a number of advantages including storage requirements and fast computation, and can be found its application in signal compression. However, in image processing other than compression, such as denoising, the use of DWT is less enthusiastic due to its lack of shift invariance and poor directional selectivity. The down-sampling introduces aliasing, so the results of inverse transform depends on the precise location of the origin for perfect reconstruction. Small shifts in the input signal can cause abrupt variations in the distribution of energy between wavelet coefficients at different scales. To overcome these problems, some other wavelet transforms have been studied recently. For example, overcomplete wavelet transforms, such as shift invariant discrete wavelet transform (SIDWT), discard all down-sampling in DWT to achieve shift invariance. Unfortunately, it incurs great computational load. Besides, the poor directional selectivity remains unsolved. In a conventional DWT, the wavelet filters are separately performed in the row and column directions. This way is the most efficient to perform 2-D filtering, but it causes

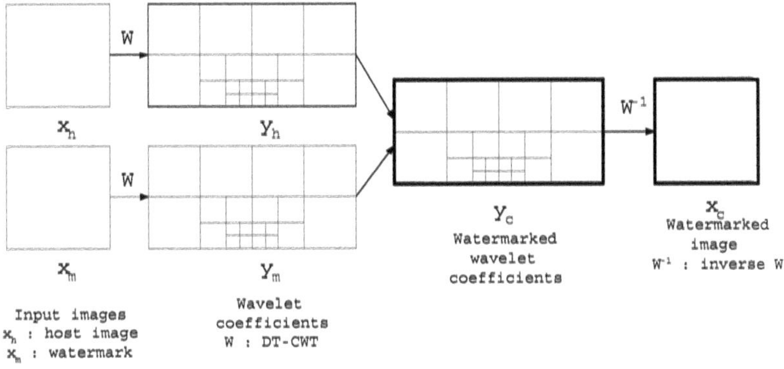

Fig. 2. DT-CWT domain visible watermarking

poor directional selectivity. DT-CWT has both approximate shift invariance and good directional selectivity [9]. It generates two parallel fully-decimated trees after first scale nondecimated filtering. These two trees produce real and imaginary parts of complex coefficients. Translations can cause large changes to the phase of the wavelet coefficients, but the magnitude is much more stable, and hence, the energy varies little. In other words, the transform is approximately shift invariant. As separable complex filtering is applied iteratively to images, the transform also has good directional selectivity. The horizontal and vertical subbands are divided into six distinct subbands at each scale with orientations $\pm 15°$, $\pm 45°$ and $\pm 75°$. We show the advantage of DT-CWT by comparing the performance of DT-CWT and DWT in Fig.1. The detailed information about the design of DT-CWT can be referred to [9] and [10].

3 Visible Watermarking in DT-CWT Domain

A multiresolution representation of the image in DT-CWT domain contains limited redundancy ($2^m : 1$ for m-dimensional signal). The complex wavelet decomposition can be expressed as

$$x^{(0)} = \{y^{(1)}, y^{(2)}, ..., y^{(K)}, x^{(K)}\} \tag{1}$$

where $x^{(K)}$ represents the low-pass image with the lowest resolution, $y^{(k)}(k = 1, 2, ..., K)$ the high-pass subbands at scale k. $x^{(0)}$ refers to the original image. $y^{(k)} = \{y^{(k)}(.|1), ..., y^{(k)}(.|6)\}$ corresponds to six high-pass subbands in the aforementioned six directions.

The process of the proposed visible watermarking algorithm is depicted in Fig.2. The watermark is embedded pixel by pixel into the host image in a way of

$$y_c^{(k)}(i,j|p) = C^{(k)}(y_h^{(k)}(i,j|p), y_m^{(k)}(i,j|p), \delta(i,j|p), v(i,j|p)) \tag{2}$$

where $y_c^{(k)}(i,j|p)$ denotes the watermarked coefficient. $y_h^{(k)}(i,j|p)$ and $y_m^{(k)}(i,j|p)$ denote the coefficients of the host image and the watermark at the same scale,

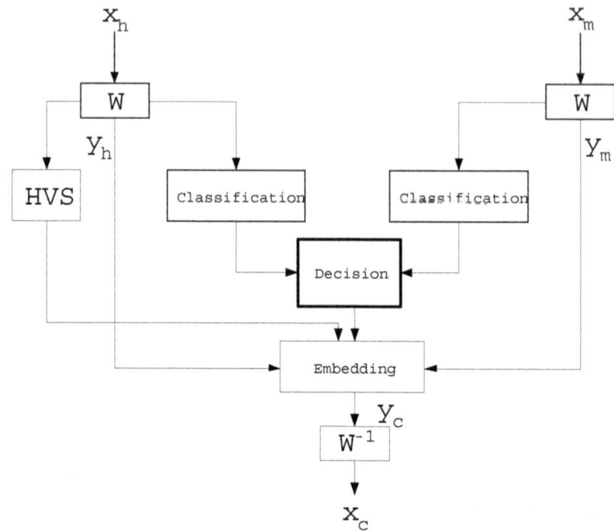

Fig. 3. The framework of visible watermarking

subband and position, respectively. $C^{(k)}$ is a combination function parameterized by the decision $\delta(i,j|p)$ and the local spatial characteristics $v(i,j|p)$. (i,j) refers to the coordinates and $p(=1,...,6)$ denotes one of the six directions. For simplicity of description, we will ignore indexes (k) and $(i,j|p)$ below.

Applying the principle of image fusion to visible watermarking, we recognize two things. First, we have to discard parts of perceptually unimportant image pixels. Second, we should consider the relation between the host image and the watermark in the process of watermark embedding. The use of these two principles makes our algorithm different from any previous one in the literature. The difference between image fusion and visible watermarking lies in the process of image combination. In the former, all source images are equally important and treated symmetrically; however, in the latter, the host image is much more important than the watermark. The pixels to be discarded only belong to the watermark. The implementation of the principles can be expressed as

$$C(y_h, y_m, \delta, v) = w_h(\delta, v)y_h + w_m(\delta, v)y_m \tag{3}$$

where $w_h(\delta, v)$ and $w_m(\delta, v)$ represent the scaling and embedding factors, respectively. Their value depends on the decision δ and the host feature v. The framework of the proposed algorithm is illustrated in Fig.3.

4 Classification

In this paper, the decision is made based on the analysis of classification information of the host image and the watermark. Classification can make a global

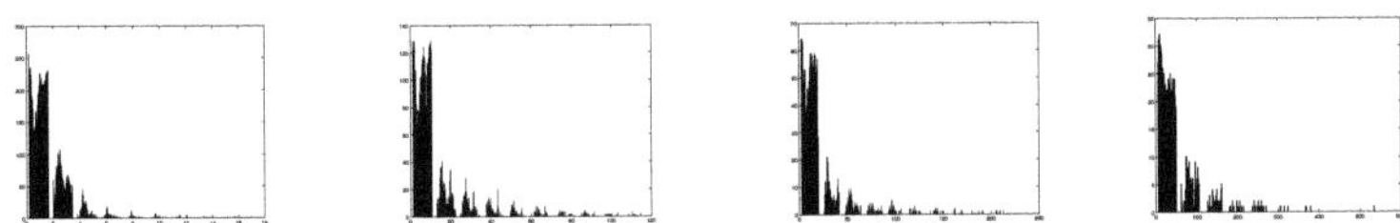

Fig. 4. The distribution of the magnitude of complex wavelet coefficients. From left to right, histograms of the magnitude of complex wavelet coefficients in subbands $(k = 1, p = 5)$, $(k = 2, p = 3)$, $(k = 3, p = 2)$ and $(k = 4, p = 1)$, respectively. The test image is *Lena*. The horizontal axis is the magnitude axis, and the vertical axis is the histogram count axis.

interpretation of the image content at an abstract level. Complex wavelets consist of real and imaginary parts. The magnitude of the complex coefficients is directly proportional to the energy. High energy areas correspond to signal features of sharp variation such as edges and textures; low energy areas correspond to smooth regions [11]. In order to differentiate their perceptual importance, complex wavelet coefficients in high-pass subbands can be classified based on energy. We use 6 perceptual classes in this paper. From $g^{(1)}$ to $g^{(6)}$, they are edge, very busy, busy, moderately busy, uniform with moderate intensity and uniform with either high or low intensity. The energy represented by these classes is in descending order.

Although it is difficult to exactly group these coefficients, the distribution of the magnitude of subband coefficients could help find a good way to achieve it. It can be observed, for example, in Fig.(4), that the pdf (probability density function) of the magnitude of complex coefficients approximately follows an exponential distribution, and the shape is sharp near the origin. This coincides with the fact that most of coefficients with small magnitude constitute large portions of uniform regions in the image, while edges and textures often with large magnitude only constitute small portions. Then we may adopt an energy-based classification strategy to separate them. We first choose a large magnitude as the initial threshold to pick out the edges, and then, use half of the initial threshold to obtain the very busy regions. The rest of coefficients are uniformly divided into four classes corresponding to busy, moderately busy, uniform with moderate intensity and uniform with either high or low intensity, respectively. The process can be further described as below.

Given a threshold set $\{T_1, T_2, ..., T_N\}(n = 1, 2, ..., 5)$. Let $T_1 = T_0/2$ and $T_2 = T_1/2$. T_3, T_4 and T_5 can be chosen as $3T_2/4, 2T_2/4$ and $T_2/4$ in order. Here T_0 is the subband-level maximum magnitude. By using these thresholds, all high-pass coefficients in a subband can be classified into 6 classes with different perceptual significance. The classification process repeats subband by subband in all directions across all scales. It is worth mentioning that we perform subband-level classification instead of scale-level as we expect to preserve the characteristics of a subband at different directions and scales.

As pointed out before, to make the watermark more perceptually uniform and robust, we will embed heavily in texture regions and slightly in edges and flat regions. Having the above classification information, we can take different measures to deal with the coefficients belonged to different classes. From knowledge of the HVS, we know that the human eye is most sensitive to noise in the regions represented by the coefficients in $g^{(1)}$. The noise sensitivity decreases from $g^{(5)}$, $g^{(6)}$, $g^{(4)}$, $g^{(3)}$ and $g^{(2)}$ in order [12]. So special attention should be paid to the coefficients in $g^{(1)}$ and $g^{(2)}$. However, there is a possibility that parts of coefficients originally classified as $g^{(1)}$ and $g^{(2)}$ are wrongly grouped resulting from adopting the energy-based strategy because their magnitude is very close. So we need to regroup those coefficients by using other classification standards. In this paper, a fine separation and reclassification scheme is proposed based on local texture activity.

Usually, edges or high textures, or even few uniform regions with high intensity, could have large intensity, i.e., large magnitude. But the spread of fluctuations of magnitude in the block neighboring the coefficient is different. For example, the standard deviation of a 3×3 block centered at the current coefficient would indicate whether it contains an edge or high texture, or just a flat region with high intensity. From analysis we know, in a highly textured block, the standard deviation would be low, while in a block with prominent edge, the standard deviation would be high; in a uniform region with high intensity, the standard deviation would approximate zero. This conclusion motivates us to take the local texture activity based classification strategy to refine the coefficients in $g^{(1)}$ and $g^{(2)}$. We first set two texture activity thresholds λ_1 and λ_2 ($\lambda_1 < \lambda_2$). If $\sigma' < \lambda_1$, the current coefficient is reallotted to $g^{(6)}$; if $\lambda_1 \leq \sigma' < \lambda_2$, the coefficient to $g^{(2)}$; if $\sigma' > \lambda_2$, the coefficient to $g^{(1)}$. Here σ' is the standard deviation of the block which is normalized with the maximum standard deviation value at that subband. Using this strategy, we can regroup the coefficients accordingly.

5 The Embedding Decision

Applying the classification strategy to the host image and the watermark separately, we are able to classify high frequency coefficients into 6 different classes. Based on the perceptual significance represented by these classes, we can make the embedding decision. We first decide whether a watermark coefficient is to be embedded, and then, determine the strength of a chosen watermark coefficient and its corresponding host coefficient. For the sake of description, we first give the formulas to calculate the pixel-wise scaling factor w_h and embedding factor w_m.

$$w_h = L_h^{'}\sigma' \tag{4}$$

$$w_m = (1 - L_h^{'})/\sigma' \tag{5}$$

where $L_h^{'}$ denotes luminance masking that we will discuss in the next section. σ' is the normalized standard deviation mentioned in section 4, which is scaled to the range [0.9,1] when used in Eq.(4) and Eq.(5). Here $L_h^{'}$ and σ' are used to represent the host feature v. Obviously, Eq.(4) and Eq.(5) reflect the inversely proportional embedding scheme in [6]. Although this scheme can effectively protect the host features, it has some defects, for example, it can be observed that the watermark signal is not strong enough in texture regions. So we try to improve the scheme in this paper. The goal is to improve the visibility of the watermark and increase robustness. The above formulas can be modified according to the noise sensitivity of the HVS as follows:

$$w_h = L_h^{'}\sigma' + t \tag{6}$$

$$w_m = (1 - L_h^{'})/\sigma' + t \tag{7}$$

where t introduces our consideration of texture activity. As will be discussed later in this section, t depends on both the classification information and σ' of the host coefficient.

Having classification information and these formulas, the decision δ can be described as follows:
if $y_m^{(k)}(i,j|p) \in g_m^{(6)}$,
Keeping the host coefficient unchanged;
elseif $y_h^{(k)}(i,j|p) \in g_h^{(1)}$ & $(y_m^{(k)}(i,j|p) \in g_m^{(1)} \mid y_m^{(k)}(i,j|p) \in g_m^{(2)} \mid y_m^{(k)}(i,j|p) \in g_m^{(3)} \mid y_m^{(k)}(i,j|p) \in g_m^{(4)} \mid y_m^{(k)}(i,j|p) \in g_m^{(5)})$,
Using Eqs.(4) and (5) to embed the watermark;
else
Using Eqs.(6) and (7) to embed the watermark.

where $\mid$ and & refer to logical operations OR and AND, respectively. $y^{(k)}(i,j|p) \in g^{(n)}$ represents that a coefficient at position (i,j) with direction p and scale k belongs to the class $g^{(n)}$.

As stated earlier, a watermark coefficient $y_m^{(k)}(i,j|p)$ which is classified into $g_m^{(6)}$ has small magnitude and represents a featureless region, so its contribution to perception is trivial. To avoid destroying the host details, we discard this coefficient while embedding. The rationale behind this selection is logically sound because it is impossible, and even unnecessary, to reveal every detail of the watermark for visible watermarking purpose. On the other hand, it also decreases the cost of computation. We let the corresponding host coefficient unchanged in this case.

When a watermark coefficient belongs to other class $g_m^{(n)}$ $(n = 1, 2, ..., 5)$, it has the perceptual significance defined by its corresponding class. Under this circumstance, we will embed the watermark coefficient according to the importance of its host counterpart. If the host coefficient $y_h^{(k)}(i,j|p)$ belongs to $g_h^{(1)}$, it means that the host counterpart is located in edges. To avoid reducing the salient contrast in the watermarked image, we use the inversely proportional embedding scheme, i.e. Eqs.(4) and (5), to control the input of watermark energy. If the host counterpart is in the other class, such as $g_h^{(n)}(n = 2, 3, ..., 6)$, we use Eqs.(6) and (7). Since the human eye is less sensitive to noise in textured regions, we could use the proportional embedding scheme and embed more watermark energy as the texture increases. So t is designed according to the noise sensitivity of the human eye to different regions.

$$t = K_c(8 - n)\sigma' \tag{8}$$

where K_c is a constant and empirically set to 0.01. Due to the use of subband-level classification strategy, t also carries some global information.

6 Low-Pass Subband Embedding

Low-pass subband addition is a special issue of visible watermarking. As in image fusion, the combination of low-pass coefficients of the host image and the watermark contributes much to make the composite image look natural. However, the technique used in visible watermarking is more complex than the simple average of the two approximation subimages in image fusion. We have to insert the watermark energy while keeping the low resolution representation of the host image not severely distorted because each pixel in this subband corresponds to manifold pixels in the original image and small addition error will be magnified in the reconstruction.

The low-pass coefficients can be used to provide values of background luminance [13]. Therefore, the watermark insertion in this subband is mainly related to variations in luminance. To embed enough watermark energy, it is natural to use luminance masking. Masking can reduce the visibility of the watermark component in the presence of the host signal. As a matter of fact, a watermark signal with proper strength is also helpful for robustness because most content-preserving image processing has low-pass nature. Unfortunately, there are not many visual models in the literature which are easy to be used in this subband. In this paper, we only design a primitive luminance masking model based on knowledge of the HVS.

It can be measured with a simple psychovisual experiment that the curve of the JND (just noticeable difference) has the form of a parabola [14]. The eye is most sensitive to noise against middle gray background and less sensitive to noise for brighter or darker background. Based on this observation, we use truncated Gaussian function to model the effect of luminance masking.

$$L(i,j) = exp(-(x_h^{(K)}(i,j) - x_{mean}^{(K)})^2) \tag{9}$$

where $L(i,j)$ denotes luminance masking. $x_h^{(K)}(i,j)$ and $x_{mean}^{(K)}$ represent the low-pass coefficients of the host image and their mean, respectively. Both $x_h^{(K)}(i,j)$ and $x_{mean}^{(K)}$ are normalized prior to calculation. Since there are two low-pass subbands in DT-CWT decomposition, one for orientation 15°, 45° and 75°, the other for −15°, −45° and −75°, this computation will be performed in each low-pass subband, respectively.

The scaling and embedding factors for the low-pass subband addition can be calculated as follows:

$$w_h(i,j) = L'(i,j) \tag{10}$$

$$w_m(i,j) = 1 - L'(i,j) \tag{11}$$

where L' is the scaled L. To better approximate the noise sensitivity of the HVS, and at the same time, to avoid dramatically changing the host coefficients, we scale L into a narrow range [0.9,0.95]. It can be seen that, in a region with middle gray value, $w_h(i,j)$ achieves its largest, while $w_m(i,j)$ gets its smallest. The smallest value of $w_m(i,j)$ is 0.05. The reason of this arrangement is for visibility. With regard to robustness, it depends more upon adaptive embedding.

Table 1. The number of coefficients in each class in the first scale of DT-CWT decomposition of *Lena*. *ori* means original class and *new* the corrected one.

Position	$g^{((1)}$	$g^{(2)}$	$g^{(3)}$	$g^{(4)}$	$g^{(5)}$	$g^{(6)}$
ori(p=1)	136	1779	1602	3521	14164	44334
new(p=1)	210	1674	1602	3521	14164	44365
ori(p=2)	137	1154	1439	4313	19373	39120
new(p=2)	246	1039	1439	4313	19373	39126
ori(p=3)	172	1568	1458	2870	8093	51375
new(p=3)	242	1497	1458	2870	8093	51376
ori(p=4)	154	1424	1277	2518	7795	52368
new(p=4)	335	1243	1277	2518	7795	52368
ori(p=5)	155	1486	2136	6821	23762	31176
new(p=5)	227	1412	2136	6821	23762	31178
ori(p=6)	104	1070	1195	3403	15811	43953
new(p=6)	223	951	1195	3403	15811	43953

The effect of luminance masking in high-pass subbands, which has been used in Eqs.(4)-(7), can be calculated in a way of

$$L_h^{'}(i,j) = L'(i/2^{K-k}, j/2^{K-k}) \tag{12}$$

where K and k represent the decomposition scales and the current scale,respectively.

Fig. 5. Original logos.

7 Experiments

The standard images *Lena*, *Baboon*, *Peppers* and *Lake*, of size $512 \times 512 \times 8bits$, are used as test images. We perform 4-scale DT-CWT decomposition. Three logos are used (Fig.5). Before embedding, the logo is resized to the dimensions of the host image so that the pixel-to-pixel correspondence is established. The

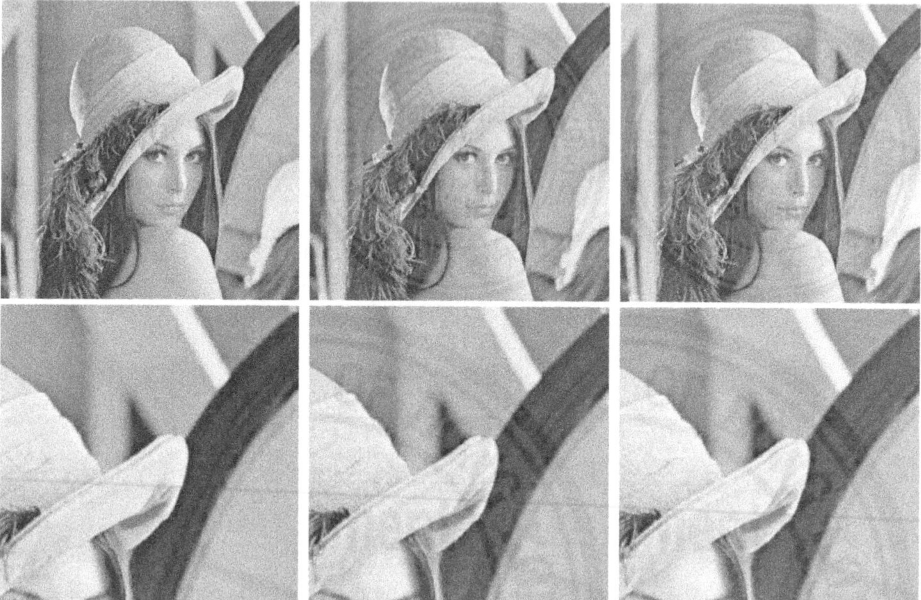

Fig. 6. From left to right, original Lena, watermarked Lena, and watermarked Lena with Mohanty's method.

gray value of the watermark image is scaled into the range of the host image to avoid causing much intensity deviation.

To show the effectiveness of the classification strategy, we give in Table 1 the number of coefficients in each class in the first scale of DT-CWT decomposition. It can be observed that some coefficients in $g^{(1)}$ and $g^{(2)}$ are wrongly classified when only the energy-based strategy is used. The texture activity based strategy successfully separate and reclassify those edges with moderate energy. Some coefficients in flat regions with high intensity are also picked out. Since the number of corrected coefficients is large, it can be expected that the effect is great on preserving host details. Furthermore, compared to DWT decomposition, DT-CWT has six directions, so that subbands in three more directions are considered. $\lambda_1 = 0.1$ and $\lambda_2 = 0.5$ are used in this paper.

We compare our algorithm with that in [5], which is a typical DCT-based one. The results from the method in [5] clearly show some defects. First, the watermarked images look brighter than the original host ones. This is because the authors of [5] inserted larger watermark energy to enhance the visibility. The sum of the scaling factor and its corresponding embedding factor is always larger than 1. Although sharp pictures with high contrasts seem more attractive to the human eye, the intensity increase may result in the loss of host details. For example, there are bright artifacts in the regions near the nose in *Baboon*. In contrast, the results from our method look more natural since we keep the sum of scaling factor and its corresponding embedding factor close to 1 in most cases

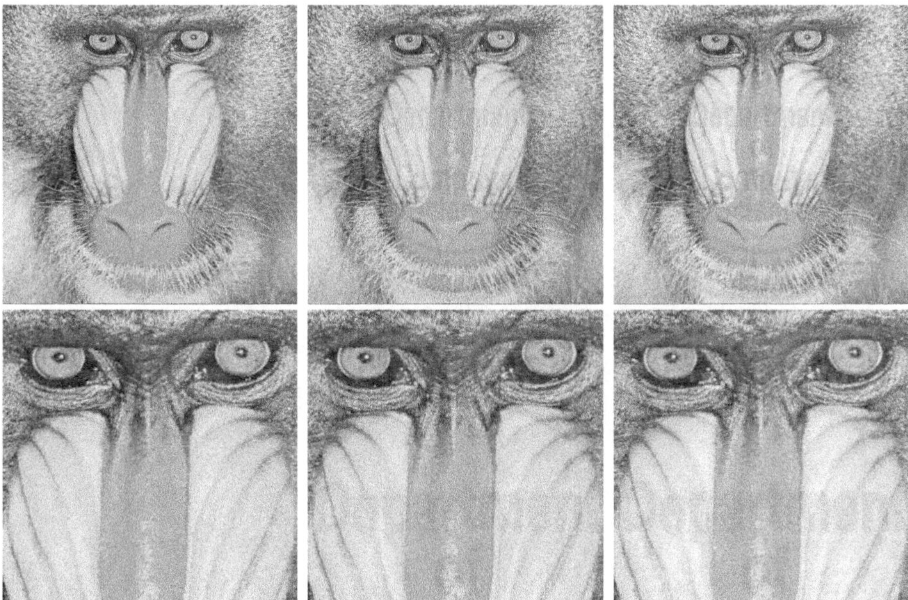

Fig. 7. From left to right, original Baboon, watermarked Baboon, and watermarked Baboon with Mohanty's method.

except in highly textured regions. Second, block-based scaling and embedding usually can not protect as much edge information as wavelet-based algorithms do. It can be observed that the edges of the watermark is blurred in the resulting images from [5]. For example, the letter N in the close-up of *Lena* from [5] has poor edge. Contrarily, due to the use of DT-CWT, the letter N from our method has clear outline. It demonstrates that wavelet-based algorithms usually have an advantage over DCT-based ones in protecting local edge information. In particular, it shows that DT-CWT has good directional selectivity and can well protect edges in more directions. Third, embedding small coefficients of the watermark in [5] weakens the richness of the host image. This phenomenon appears more apparent in middle gray regions, e.g., in the close-up of *Peppers*. However, there is no apparent loss of host richness in the results from our method. On the other hand, one can not perceive any loss of watermark features in the resulting image from our method. It validates that rejecting small watermark coefficients during insertion is possible as well as necessary.

To further demonstrate the good quality of the proposed algorithm, we give more experimental results in Fig.(9) where two other types of logos are used. It can be seen that our method can well adapt to different logos and obtain high quality watermarked images. On the contrary, the method in [5] is not suited to different logos and host images. In Fig.(9), it can be observed that apparent block artifacts are produced in the mid-gray regions with slowly changing intensity, for example, in the clouds on *Lake*. The edges of the watermark are also not very

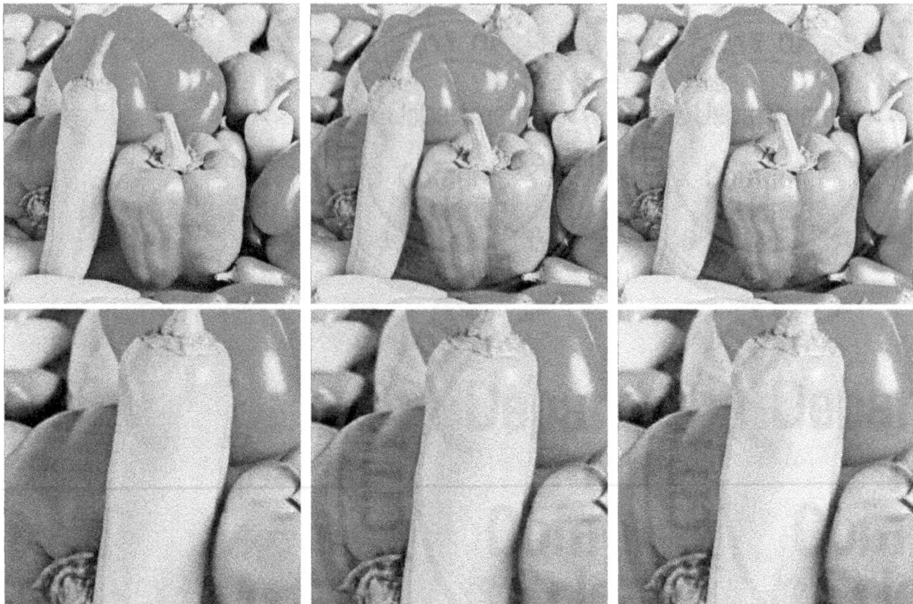

Fig. 8. From left to right, original Peppers, watermarked Peppers, and watermarked Peppers with Mohanty's method.

clear because of block-based watermark scaling. Generally, the above problems would also be met in other block-based algorithms.

8 Conclusions

The issue of visible watermarking has rarely been addressed in the literature. As shown in this paper, we have proposed an effective visible watermarking algorithm. The framework of watermark embedding is based on the principle of image fusion, which enables pixel-wise addition of the host image and the watermark. The use of DT-CWT allows us to examine image details in six directions and perform multiresolution embedding operations. Based on energy as well as texture activity, the classification strategy can well group complex wavelet coefficients into 6 classes, and thus, provide useful information for making the embedding decision. In the process of embedding, a large number of small watermark coefficients are deliberately discarded to avoid destroying the host image quality. The experiments verify that this manipulation has little effect on the watermark appearance in the watermarked image. When performing insertion in the host edges, the inversely proportional embedding scheme is used to protect the salient image features, while in other regions, the improved embedding scheme is applied, which ensures the embedding strength variable according to the noise sensitivity of the HVS. In addition to addressing the problem of high-pass subband embedding, we also investigate the way of low-pass subband addition. We

Fig. 9. In the upper row, from left to right, original Lena, watermarked Lena, and watermarked Lena with Mohanty's method. In the lower row, from left to right, original Lake, watermarked Lake, and watermarked Lake with Mohanty's method.

pointed out that a proper low-pass watermark signal is the requirement of visibility as well as robustness. The results of the proposed algorithm have shown substantial improvement over the current DCT-based method in visual quality of both the host image and the watermark.

Acknowledgement. This work is supported by City University Strategic Grant 7001488, NSFC (69975011, 60172067, 60133020), "863" Program (2002AA144060), NSF of Guangdong (013164), and Funding of China National Education Ministry. The first author would like to thank Nick Kingsbury for providing complex wavelet transform codes of his work.

References

1. Yeung, M.M., Mintzer, F.C., Braudaway, G.W., and Rao, A.R. : Digital watermarking for high-quality imaging. Proc. IEEE First Workshop on Multimedia Signal Processing. pp. 357–362, Jun. 1997.
2. Braudaway, G.W., Margerlein, K.A., and Mintzer, F.C. : Protecting public-available images with a visible image watermark. Proc. SPIE Conf. on Optical Security and Counterfeit Deterrence Techniques. vol. SPIE 2659, pp. 126–132, Feb. 1996.

3. Meng, J., and Chang, S.F. : Embedding visible video watermarks in the compressed domain. IEEE Int. Conf. on Image Processing. vol. 1, pp. 474–477, Oct. 1998.
4. Kankanhalli, M.S., Rajmohan, and Ramakrishnan, K.R. : Adaptive visible watermarking of images. IEEE Int. Conf. on Multimedia Computing and Systems. vol.1, pp. 568–573. Jul. 1999.
5. Mohanty, S.P., Ramakrishnan, K.R., and Kankanhalli, M.S. : A DCT domain visible watermarking technique for images. IEEE Int. Conf. on Multimedia and Expo. vol.2, pp. 1029–1032, 2000.
6. Hu, Y., and Kwong, S. : Wavelet domain adaptive visible watermarking. Electronics Letters. vol. 37, pp. 1219–1220, Sep. 2001.
7. Huang, C.H., and Wu, J.L. : Inpainting attacks against visible watermarking schemes. Proc. SPIE Conf. on Security And Watermarking Of Multimedia Contents. vol. SPIE 4314, pp. 376–384, 2001.
8. Nikolov, S., Hill, P., Bull, D., and Canagarajah, N. : Wavelets for image fusion. A.A. Petrosian and F.G. Meyer (eds.) : Wavelets in signal and image analysis. 2001 Kluwer Academic Publishers. Netherlands.
9. Kingsbury, N. : A dual-tree complex wavelet transform with improved orthogonality and symmetry properties. IEEE Int. Conf. on Image Processing. vol.2, pp. 375–378, Sep. 2000.
10. Kingsbury, N. : The dual-tree complex wavelet transform: a new efficient tool for image restoration and enhancement. Procs. EUSIPCO 98, pp. 319–322, Sep. 1998.
11. Chang, S.G., Yu, B. and Vetterli, M. : Spatially adaptive wavelet thresholding with context modeling for image denoising. IEEE Trans. Image Processing. vol. 9, pp. 1522–1531, Sep. 2000.
12. Tao, B., and Dickinson, B. : Adaptive watermarking in the DCT domain. IEEE Int. Conf. on Acoustics, Speech, and Signal Processing. Vol. 4 , pp. 2985–2988, Apr. 1997.
13. Lewis, A.S., and Knowles, G. : Image compression using the 2-D wavelet transform. IEEE Trans. on Image Processing. Vol. 1, pp. 244–250, April 1992.
14. Nadenau, M. : Integration of human color vision models into high quality image compression. Ph.D. dissertation, Swiss Federal Institute of Technology, Lausanne, Swiss, 2000.

Optimal Data-Hiding Strategies for Games with BER Payoffs

Pedro Comesaña, Fernando Pérez-González, and Félix Balado

Dept. Tecnologías de las Comunicaciones. ETSI Telecom., Universidad de Vigo, 36200 Vigo, Spain
pcomesan@gts.tsc.uvigo.es, {fperez,fiz}@tsc.uvigo.es,

Abstract. We analyze three different data hiding methods from a game-theoretic point of view, using the probability of bit error as the payoff. Those data hiding schemes can be regarded to as representatives of three families of methods: spread-spectrum, informed-embedding and hybrid. In all cases, we have obtained theoretical expressions for the BER which are then optimized to derive the strategies for both the attacker and the decoder, assuming that the embedder simply follows point-by-point constraints given by the perceptual mask. Experimental results supporting our analyses are also shown, with examples of watermarking in the spatial domain as well as the DCT domain.

1 Introduction

Some researchers have dealt with game-theoretic aspects of data hiding capacities [1], [2]. However payoffs other than channel capacity are also possible in the data hiding game, as already suggested in [3] and developed in [4]. Here, we build on this idea to determine optimal playing strategies by considering that the bit error rate (BER) for the hidden information defines the payoff in the game.

The main purpose of this paper will be to obtain those optimal strategies for the three main classes of data hiding methods, namely, spread-spectrum, quantization-based and hybrid schemes. We have chosen a representative algorithm of each kind and developed closed-form expressions for the bit error probability which are then used as cost functions for deriving optimal or near-optimal tactics for the decoder and the attacker. To the authors' knowledge, the closest works to ours are those of Eggers and Girod in [2] and Moulin and Ivanovic in [4], compared to which the two main differences are: 1) the game payoff, which is channel capacity in [2] (although specifically optimized for each method) and probability of correct detection (zero-rate spread-spectrum scheme) in [4]; and 2) the agents involved, that are the embedder and the attacker in both mentioned works, whereas here we consider them to be the attacker and the decoder for reasons which will be explained later.[1] Note that while in a data hiding game involving only an embedder and an attacker, the latter has the final word, this is

[1] The exception is Quantized Projection data hiding, for which both the embedding and decoding strategies are chosen simultaneously (see Section 5.)

T. Kalker et al. (Eds.): IWDW 2003, LNCS 2939, pp. 101–116, 2004.
© Springer-Verlag Berlin Heidelberg 2004

clearly not the case if we consider that there is optimization at the final decoding stage.

As we have said, three agents generally play the data hiding game: embedder, attacker and decoder, as depicted in Figure 1. Each one has different objectives and constraints which frequently lead to colliding interests. First of all, the embedder is responsible for hiding the information in the host image in a secret way, trying to hinder the estimation of the watermark by the attacker. In most applications, the embedder faces very strict perceptual constraints so as to guarantee that there is no loss of value in the watermarked image.

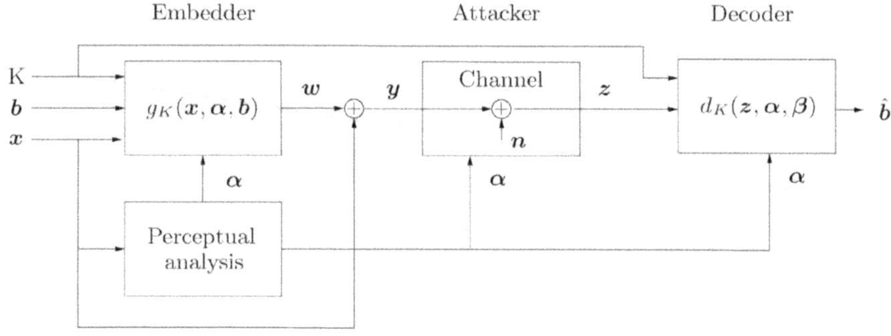

Fig. 1. Data hiding model.

Second, the watermark is manipulated by the attacker. The attacker can play an active role by frustrating or at least making it difficult the decoding process. Needless to say, the attacker's strategy will also be constrained by a distortion measure with some perceptual meaning. In this paper we will consider only additive noise attacks.

Finally, the decoder is in charge of retrieving the information in a reliable way. He/she could have information about the attacker's strategy (this is more likely in unintentional attacks), and in this case, he/she could use this information to improve the performance of the system. Note that the converse could also be true, but we must note once again that the decoder does have the final word.

The paper is structured as follows: Section 2 is devoted to defining the problem and discussing several ways of measuring distortions; optimal strategies are presented in Sect. 3 for spread-spectrum systems, in Sect. 4 for binary dither modulation schemes, and in Sect. 5 for quantized projection methods. Experimental results are shown in Section 6 while Section 7 contains our conclusions and discusses future lines of research.

2 Problem Statement

For notational simplicity, we will assume that host signal samples in any domain given are arranged following a vector, denoted by bold characters. The same notation will be used for matrices.

We will consider here only additive data hiding, that is, given the *host image* $\boldsymbol{x}$ and the watermark $\boldsymbol{w}$, the resulting watermarked image can be written as

$$\boldsymbol{y} = \boldsymbol{x} + \boldsymbol{w} \tag{1}$$

We will also follow the customary scheme [5], [6] for embedding a particular information bit b_i by using a tile $\mathcal{S}_i \triangleq \{k_1, \cdots, k_{|\mathcal{S}_i|}\}$ of pseudorandomly chosen indices, selecting $L_i = |\mathcal{S}_i|$ samples from $\boldsymbol{x}$ depending on a cryptographic key K, so that this tile will be known to the decoder, but not to the attacker. Also we will assume that tiles $\mathcal{S}_i$ and $\mathcal{S}_j$, for all $i \neq j$ do not overlap. Each one of the possible partitions of the host signal in this way will be denoted as $\mathcal{T}$, and $\mathcal{U}$ will the set containing them. If N bits are going to be hidden, we will define $\mathcal{S} = \bigcup_{i=1}^{N} \mathcal{S}_i$. Throughout this paper we will not elaborate on the possibility of adding an upper coding layer.

At the embedder's side, a perceptual mask vector $\boldsymbol{\alpha}$ is computed from the host signal $\boldsymbol{x}$. For practical effects, we will consider that $\boldsymbol{x}$ is an image in the spatial or the DCT domain. This vector $\boldsymbol{\alpha}$ indicates the maximum allowed watermark energy that produces the least noticeable modification of the corresponding sample of $\boldsymbol{x}$.

Consequently, we will regard the watermark $\boldsymbol{w}$ as being produced from the desired information vector $\boldsymbol{b}$ by using a certain function, $\boldsymbol{w} = g_K(\boldsymbol{x}, \boldsymbol{\alpha}, \boldsymbol{b})$, where K is a secret key. For notational simplicity we will assume that $b_i \in \{\pm 1\}$, $i = 1, \cdots, N$. It must be also taken into account that the function $g_K(\cdot)$ depends on the specific watermarking scheme, as we will later confirm.

We will assume an additive probabilistic noise channel for modeling attacks. Therefore, the image at the decoder's input $\boldsymbol{z}$ can be written as $\boldsymbol{z} = \boldsymbol{y} + \boldsymbol{n} = \boldsymbol{x} + \boldsymbol{w} + \boldsymbol{n}$, where $\boldsymbol{n}$ is noise independent of $\boldsymbol{x}$. Therefore we are not considering all the possible range of attacks (think of *JPEG* as an example). By virtue of the pseudorandom choice of the indices in $\mathcal{S}$ we may assume that the samples in $\boldsymbol{n}$ are also mutually independent, with zero mean and variances $\sigma_{n_i}^2$, $i \in \mathcal{S}$.

The decoder uses a certain decoding function $\hat{\mathbf{b}} = d_K(\mathbf{z}, \boldsymbol{\alpha}, \boldsymbol{\beta})$, where $\boldsymbol{\beta}$ are some weights used to improve the decoding process. Then, the BER for the i-th bit is just $P_e(i) = P\{\hat{b_i} \neq b_i\}$, and the game consists in the maximization/minimization of $P_e = \sum_k P_e(i)/N$ by respectively the attacker and the decoder, .i.e.

$$\min_{\boldsymbol{\beta}} \max_{\boldsymbol{\sigma}_n} P_e, \quad \max_{\boldsymbol{\sigma}_n} \min_{\boldsymbol{\beta}} P_e. \tag{2}$$

The game has a pure (deterministic) equilibrium if the minimax solution equals the maximin one at a given BER value (called the value of the game) for some deterministic optimal values $\boldsymbol{\sigma}_n^*$ and $\boldsymbol{\beta}^*$. Then, the payoff function is said to have a saddle-point at $(\boldsymbol{\sigma}_n^*, \boldsymbol{\beta}^*)$. If this happens, the order in which the agents play the game is indifferent as neither the attacker nor the decoder want to deviate from the most conservative option marked by the saddle-point. Nevertheless, the order is relevant if there does not exist at least one saddle-point.

A crucial issue in our development are the constraints the embedder and the attacker must verify. A certain trade-off between the mathematical suitability of the Mean Square Error (MSE), that it is arguably inadequate for data hiding [6], and perceptual adequateness is achieved by an MSE-like condition imposed on each set of coefficients devoted to a particular information bit. For instance, the attacker constraints would read as

$$\frac{1}{L_i}\sum_{j\in\mathcal{S}_i} E\{|z_j - y_j|^2\} = \frac{1}{L_i}\sum_{j\in\mathcal{S}_i}\sigma_{n_j}^2 \leq D_c(i),\ \text{for all } i\in\{1,\cdots,N\} \tag{3}$$

for some specified positive quantities $D_c(i)$, $i = 1,\cdots,N$. The problem with this constraint is that the attacker is supposed to know which coefficients are devoted to the same bit, what depends on the cryptographic key K.

Also, the perceptual masks can be directly mapped into a set of point-by-point constraints

$$E\{|y_i - x_i|^2\} = E\{w_i^2\} \leq \alpha_i^2,\ \text{for all } i\in\mathcal{S}. \tag{4}$$

Even though it is a less flexible strategy than the previous one, it will be used to restrict the embedding power.

Finally, it is useful, mainly for comparison purposes, to define the *watermark-to-noise ratio* (WNR) as the ratio (in decibels) between the total energy devoted to the watermark and that devoted to the distortion, that is,

$$\text{WNR} \triangleq 10\log_{10}\left(\frac{\sum_{k\in\mathcal{S}}\text{E}\{w_k^2\}}{\sum_{k\in\mathcal{S}}\sigma_{n_k}^2}\right) \tag{5}$$

3 Spread-Spectrum

Given the assumptions of Section 2, spread-spectrum methods compute the watermark to be embedded as

$$w_j = g_K(x_j,\alpha_j,b_k) = b_k\alpha_j s_j,\ \text{for all } j\in\mathcal{S}_k, k\in\{1,\cdots,N\} \tag{6}$$

where s_k is a pseudorandom sequence generated using a pseudonoise generator initialized to a state which depends on the value of K, with $E\{s_k\} = 0$ and $E\{s_k^2\} = 1$, so that (4) is satisfied. Here, we will assume the simplest distribution of this kind, that is, $s_k \in \{\pm 1\}$.

Before decoding, a transformation is applied to the received signal. The more widespread of these transformations is a simple linear projection onto one dimension:

$$r_i = \sum_{j\in\mathcal{S}_i}\beta_j s_j z_j,\ i\in\{1,\cdots,N\} \tag{7}$$

which is similar to the correlation receiver applied in spread-spectrum communications, but replacing $\boldsymbol{\alpha}$ with a more general weighting vector $\boldsymbol{\beta}$. It can be shown that, under some practical assumptions, the optimal decoder is equivalent to a bit-by-bit hard-decision maker with the threshold located at the origin [5]. Then, the output of the decoder, known the partition $\mathcal{T}$, is

$$\hat{b_i} = \text{sign}\,(r_i|\,\mathcal{T}), i \in \{1, \cdots, N\} \tag{8}$$

In the spatial domain case the watermarked image $\boldsymbol{y}$ could undergo a linear filtering operation as a way of reducing the host-interference power at the decoder. This can be represented by means of a spatial-varying and noise independent filtering. Wiener filtering [7] is included in this category, since the host signal power usually is much greater than the noise power (at least if the attacked signal is to remain valuable), so Wiener filter's coefficients are not going to be modified in a significant way by the addition of noise. We can represent this situation by a $M \times M$ matrix that will be denoted by $\boldsymbol{H}$, so that the filtered host image would become $\boldsymbol{x}_f \triangleq \boldsymbol{Hx}$. As it was shown in [7], the observation vector $\boldsymbol{r}$ when $\mathcal{T}$ is known can be modeled as the output of an additive white Gaussian noise (AWGN) channel, $r_{i|\mathcal{T}} = a_{i|\mathcal{T}} b_i + u_{i|\mathcal{T}}$, $i \in \{1, \cdots, N\}$, where

$$a_{i|\mathcal{T}} = \sum_{k \in \mathcal{S}_i|\mathcal{T}} \beta_k h_{k,k} \alpha_k, \;\; i = 1, \cdots, N \tag{9}$$

and $u_{1|\mathcal{T}}, \cdots, u_{N|\mathcal{T}}$ are samples of an i.i.d. zero-mean Gaussian random process with variance

$$\sigma^2_{u_{i|\mathcal{T}}} = \sum_{k \in \mathcal{S}_i|\mathcal{T}} \beta_k^2 \left[x^2_{f_k} + \sum_{l=1}^{M} h^2_{k,l} \left(\alpha_l^2 + \sigma^2_{n_l} \right) - h^2_{k,k} \alpha_k^2 \right], \quad i = 1, \cdots, N \tag{10}$$

being M the length of the host signal. Since $\mathcal{T}$ is generated by K, we will assume the attacker does not know it. So he/she will try to maximize the probability of error considering the averaged channel, whose statistics for the case of uniform partitions are

$$a = \sum_{\forall \mathcal{T} \in \mathcal{U}} \mathrm{E}(r_i|\mathcal{T}) \Pr(\mathcal{T}) = \frac{1}{N} \sum_{k=2}^{M} \beta_k h_{k,k} \alpha_k \tag{11}$$

$$\begin{aligned} \sigma_u^2 &= \sum_{\forall \mathcal{T} \in \mathcal{U}} \mathrm{Var}(r_i|\mathcal{T}) \Pr(\mathcal{T}) + \sum_{\forall \mathcal{T} \in \mathcal{U}} \mathrm{E}^2(r_i|\mathcal{T}) \Pr(\mathcal{T}) - \left(\sum_{\forall \mathcal{T} \in \mathcal{U}} \mathrm{E}(r_i|\mathcal{T}) \Pr(\mathcal{T}) \right)^2 \\ &= \frac{1}{N} \sum_{k=1}^{M} \beta_k^2 \left[x^2_{f_k} + \sum_{l=1}^{M} h^2_{k,l} \left(\alpha_l^2 + \sigma^2_{n_l} \right) - h^2_{k,k} \alpha_k^2 \right] \\ &+ \frac{N-1}{N^2} \sum_{k=1}^{M} \beta_k^2 h^2_{k,k} \alpha_k^2 \end{aligned} \tag{12}$$

and since N typically will be large, $(N-1)/N^2$ can be substituted by $1/N$.

From (8), and recalling we are taking into account the averaged channel

$$\overline{P_e} = Q\left(\frac{a}{\sigma_u}\right) \tag{13}$$

with $Q(x) \triangleq \frac{1}{\sqrt{2\pi}} \int_x^{\infty} e^{-\frac{\tau^2}{2}} d\tau$, so from the attacking point of view, the objective will be to maximize the partition-averaged signal to noise ratio given by

$$\overline{\mathrm{SNR}} \triangleq \frac{a}{\sigma_u} \tag{14}$$

while from the decoding point of view, the objective will be to maximize the per-pulse signal to noise ratio given to be

$$\mathrm{SNR}_i \triangleq \frac{a_{i|\mathcal{T}}}{\sigma_{u_{i|\mathcal{T}}}} \tag{15}$$

for all $i \in \{1, \cdots, N\}$, since the decoder knows the partition which is being used, so he/she knows the probability of error for this partition is

$$P_e = \frac{1}{N} \sum_{i=1}^{N} Q\left(\frac{a_{i|\mathcal{T}}}{\sigma_{u_{i|\mathcal{T}}}}\right) \tag{16}$$

Optimal Decoding Weights for a Known Attack Distribution. First, we will consider the case in which the attacking-noise distribution is known and determine the optimal decoding weights vector $\boldsymbol{\beta}^*$ that minimizes the BER in (16). Substituting (9-10) into (15) and inverting the result, we obtain the noise-to-signal ratio that the decoder should *minimize*:

$$\mathrm{NSR}_i = \frac{\sum_{j \in \mathcal{S}_i} \beta_j^2 \left[x_{f_j}^2 + \sum_{l=1}^{M} h_{j,l}^2 \left(\alpha_l^2 + \sigma_{n_l}^2\right) - h_{j,j}^2 \alpha_j^2\right]}{\left(\sum_{j \in \mathcal{S}_i} \beta_j h_{j,j} \alpha_j\right)^2}, \ \forall\, i = 1, \cdots, N \tag{17}$$

The problem can be solved in a general form to yield the following optimal weights

$$\beta_i^* = \frac{K h_{i,i} \alpha_i}{x_{f_i}^2 + \sum_{l=1}^{M} h_{i,l}^2 \left(\alpha_l^2 + \sigma_{n_l}^2\right) - h_{i,i}^2 \alpha_i^2}, \ i \in \mathcal{S} \tag{18}$$

with K any positive constant.

Optimal Attack for Known Decoding Weights. In the case that the attacker knows the decoding weights vector $\boldsymbol{\beta}$, his/her problem becomes that of maximizing the $\overline{\mathrm{NSR}}$ in (14) subject to an imperceptibility constraint. It can be proven that for a MSE distortion constraint the optimal attack would imply concentrating all the distortion in those coefficients with the largest values of $\tau_j = \sum_{k=1}^{M} \beta_k^2 h_{k,j}^2$. Note that this strategy will likely produce visible results (see Section 6) and clearly shows that constraining just the MSE may lead to impractical attacks.

Optimal Attack When the Decoder Follows the Optimum Strategy. Now, suppose that the decoder knows which distribution the attacker is using, so that he/she employs the optimal strategy as derived in Sect. 3. In this case, the best an attacker can do is to minimize (14) after replacing β_i with (18), while satisfying a certain distortion constraint. Therefore, making the assignments $p_j^2 = x_{f_j}^2 + \sum_{l=1}^M h_{j,l}^2 \left(\alpha_l^2 + \sigma_{n_l}^2\right) - h_{j,j}^2 \alpha_j^2$, $q_j = h_{j,j}\alpha_j$ and $t_j = 0$ the attacker has to minimize

$$\overline{\mathrm{SNR}} = \frac{\left(\sum_{k=1}^M \beta_k q_k\right)^2}{N\left[\sum_{k=1}^M \beta_k^2 p_k^2 + \beta_k^2 q_k^2\right]} = \frac{\left(\sum_{k=1}^M \frac{q_k^2}{p_k^2}\right)^2}{N\left[\sum_{k=1}^M \frac{q_k^2}{p_k^2} + \frac{q_k^4}{p_k^4}\right]}. \tag{19}$$

Since $p_j^2 \gg q_j^2$ we may neglect the second term in the denominator, so we can reformulate the problem as the minimization of

$$\varphi = \sum_{k=1}^M \frac{q_k^2}{p_k^2} = \sum_{k=1}^M \frac{h_{k,k}^2 \alpha_k^2}{m_k^2 + \sum_{l=1}^M h_{k,l}^2 \sigma_{n_l}^2}, \tag{20}$$

where $m_k = x_{f_k}^2 + \sum_{l=1}^M h_{k,l}^2 \alpha_l^2 - h_{k,k}^2 \alpha_k^2$. Unfortunately, a close look at (20) reveals that each particular noise sample exerts influence on several terms of the sum, thus making it difficult the interpretation of the solution. Aiming at producing meaningful results, for the remaining of this section we will make the simplification $\boldsymbol{H} = \mathrm{diag}(h_{1,1}, \cdots, h_{M,M})$ which is reasonable in many practical situations: as an example we have closely studied Wiener filtering and made the whole numerical optimization taking into account all the values of $h_{k,l}$ [8], [9]. The results are virtually the same as those we obtained with the proposed simplification. The explanation is based on the fact that the central element of the filter is much larger than the others, so the influence of the latter on the optimization is very small. So (20) becomes $\varphi = \sum_{k=1}^M \frac{\alpha_k^2}{\frac{x_{f_k}^2}{h_{k,k}^2} + \sigma_{n_k}^2}$ and (18) simplifies to $\beta_i = \frac{k\alpha_i h_{i,i}}{x_{f_i}^2 + h_{i,i}^2 \sigma_{n_i}^2}$. As in the previous section, the attack is constrained to meet a condition for the maximum allowed distortion introduced in the image, that is $D_c = \frac{1}{M}\sum_{j=1}^M \sigma_{n_j}^2$ and also it must verify $\sigma_{n_j}^2 \leq L \cdot D_c$. This last condition tries to avoid the effect of assigning all the power to a few coefficients. One host image coefficient should not be assigned more power than the averaged power dedicated to each bit. In this case it can be shown that the optimal attacking distribution is

$$\sigma_{n_i}^{*\,2} = \min\left[\frac{D_c}{N}, \left(\xi\alpha_i - \frac{x_i^2}{h_{i,i}^2}\right)^+\right], \text{ for all } 1 \leq i \leq M \tag{21}$$

where $(x)^+ \triangleq \max\{x, 0\}$, and ξ is a suitably chosen parameter so that

$$\frac{1}{M}\sum_{i=1}^M \min\left[L \cdot D_c, \left(\xi\alpha_i - \frac{x_i^2}{h_{i,i}^2}\right)^+\right] = D_c \tag{22}$$

Although the analyzed problem is very different, this is quite similar to the expression obtained in [4] in which after getting the diagonalization by the KLT, the eigenvalues of the covariance matrix of the noise, and therefore the elements of this matrix, are

$$\sigma_{n_i}^{*\ 2} = \left(\xi_2 \alpha_i - \sigma_{x_i}^2\right)^+ \tag{23}$$

where $\sigma_{x_i}^2$ is the variance of x_i and ξ_2 a constant such that

$$\frac{1}{M}\sum_{i=1}^{M} \left(\xi_2 \alpha_i - \sigma_{x_i}^2\right)^+ = D_c \tag{24}$$

4 Distortion-Compensated Dither Modulation

Informed embedding watermarking or, equivalently, quantization-based methods, are based on hiding information by constructing a set of vector quantizers $\boldsymbol{Q_b}(\cdot)$, each representing a different codeword $\boldsymbol{b}$. So, given a host vector $\boldsymbol{x}$ and an information codeword $\boldsymbol{b}$, the embedder constructs the watermarked vector $\boldsymbol{y}$ by simply quantizing $\boldsymbol{x}$ with $\boldsymbol{Q_b}(\cdot)$, i.e. $\boldsymbol{y} = \boldsymbol{Q_b}(\boldsymbol{x})$ [10]. We will only consider here one of the simplest implementations of quantization-based schemes, carried out by means of uniform dithered quantizers, which has been named Distortion-Compensated Dither Modulation (DC-DM).

In binary DC-DM the watermark is obtained as

$$w_j = g_K(x_j, \alpha_j, b_k) = \nu_k e_j, \text{ for all } j \in \mathcal{S}_k, k \in \{1, \cdots, N\} \tag{25}$$

i.e. the L_i-dimensional quantization error $\boldsymbol{e}_i \triangleq \boldsymbol{Q}_b(\boldsymbol{x}_i) - \boldsymbol{x}_i$ weighted by an optimizable constant ν_i, $0 < \nu_i \leq 1$, with $i = 1, \cdots, N$. Consequently, we will have

$$\boldsymbol{y}_i = \boldsymbol{Q}_b(\boldsymbol{x}_i) - (1 - \nu_i)\boldsymbol{e}_i, \ i = 1, \cdots, N \tag{26}$$

When $\nu_i = 1$, we have the uncompensated (i.e., pure DM) case.

The uniform quantizers $\boldsymbol{Q}_{-1}(\cdot)$ and $\boldsymbol{Q}_1(\cdot)$ are such that the corresponding centroids are the points in the lattices

$$\Lambda_{-1} = 2(\Delta_1 \mathbb{Z}, \cdots, \Delta_L \mathbb{Z})^T + \boldsymbol{d}_i \tag{27}$$
$$\Lambda_1 = 2(\Delta_1 \mathbb{Z}, \cdots, \Delta_L \mathbb{Z})^T + \boldsymbol{d}_i + (\Delta_1, \cdots, \Delta_L)^T \tag{28}$$

where $\boldsymbol{d}_i$ is an arbitrary (possibly key-dependent) vector. Since the presence of a known offset $\boldsymbol{d}_i$ in the lattices will not modify the results, we will suppose that $\boldsymbol{d}_i = \boldsymbol{0} \triangleq (0, \cdots, 0)^T$.

If the quantization step in each dimension is small enough, we can consider that the quantization error $\boldsymbol{e}_i$ in each dimension will be uniformly distributed in $[-\Delta_k, \Delta_k]$, being $2\Delta_k$ the quantization step. From (25), this in turn implies that the watermark is also uniformly distributed in a hyperrectangle. Thus, the embedding distortion in each dimension will be $D_{w_k} = \nu_i^2 \Delta_k^2/3$, for all $k \in \mathcal{S}_i$.

Decoding is implemented as

$$\hat{b}_i = \arg\min_{-1,1} \left\{ \left(\boldsymbol{z}_j - \boldsymbol{Q}_{b_j}(\boldsymbol{z}_j) \right)^T \boldsymbol{B}_j \left(\boldsymbol{z}_j - \boldsymbol{Q}_{b_j}(\boldsymbol{z}_h) \right) \right\}, \ i = 1, \cdots, N \quad (29)$$

where $\boldsymbol{B}_j \triangleq \text{diag}\left(\beta_{j1}/\Delta_{j1}^2, \cdots, \beta_{jL_j}/\Delta_{jL_j}^2\right)$ being the β_i some weights the decoder will use to improve decoding. Following the discussion on the decision regions made in [11], we can assume without loss of generality that a symbol $b_i = -1$ is sent, and that $\boldsymbol{x}_i$ is such that $Q_{-1}(\boldsymbol{x}_i) = \boldsymbol{0}$. Let $P_e(i)$ denote the bit error probability conditioned to the transmission of the i-th bit, $i = 1, \cdots, N$. Then, assuming that all the bits sent are equiprobable, we can write

$$P_e = \frac{1}{N} \sum_{i=1}^{N} P_e(i) \quad (30)$$

so we will be interested in computing the bit error probability for the i-th bit. However, for the remaining of this section and for the sake of notational simplicity we will drop the subindex i whenever there is no possible confusion.

Let $\boldsymbol{u} \triangleq \boldsymbol{n} - (1-\nu)\boldsymbol{e}$, then $\boldsymbol{z} = \boldsymbol{u}$. Recalling that $\boldsymbol{e}$ has independent components, $e_k \sim U(-\Delta_k, \Delta_k)$, it follows that the random vector $\boldsymbol{u}$ will also have independent components, each having pdf

$$f_{u_k}(u_k) = \begin{cases} f_{n_k}(u_k) * \frac{1}{(1-\nu)} f_{e_k}(u_k/(1-\nu)), 0 < \nu < 1 \\ f_{n_k}(u_k), \qquad \nu = 1 \end{cases} \quad (31)$$

being $f_{n_k}(\cdot)$ and $f_{e_k}(\cdot)$ the marginal pdf's of respectively the noise and the quantization error components of each dimension. We will find useful to define an auxiliary variable $v_j \triangleq u_j/\Delta_j$

4.1 Approximate Computation of the Bit Error Probability

If the noise pdf is symmetric with respect to the coordinate planes, then both $\boldsymbol{u}$ and $\boldsymbol{v}$ will inherit this symmetry. In that case, we can concentrate our analysis in the positive orthant $\mathcal{O}$, so we can upperbound $P_e(i)$ as [11]

$$\begin{aligned} P_e(i) \le P_s(i) &\triangleq P\left\{\boldsymbol{v}_i^T \boldsymbol{B}_i \boldsymbol{v}_i > (\boldsymbol{v}_i - (1,\cdots,1)^T)^T \boldsymbol{B}_i (\boldsymbol{v}_i - (1,\cdots,1)^T) | \boldsymbol{v}_i \in \mathcal{O}\right\} \\ &= P\left\{ \sum_{k \in \mathcal{S}_i} \beta_k v'_k > \frac{1}{2} \sum_{k \in \mathcal{S}_i} \beta_k \right\} \end{aligned} \quad (32)$$

being $v'_k \triangleq |v_k|$ (since we are considering only $\mathcal{O}$), with pdf given by

$$f_{v'_k}(v'_k) \triangleq \begin{cases} 2\Delta_k f_{u_k}(v'_k \Delta_k), \ u'_k > 0 \\ 0, \qquad \text{otherwise} \end{cases}, \ k \in \mathcal{S}_i \quad (33)$$

If we define

$$t_i = \sum_{k \in \mathcal{S}_i} \beta_k v'_k, \ i = 1, \cdots, N \quad (34)$$

then the pdf of the random variable t_i will be the convolution of L independent random variables with pdf $f_{v'_k}(v'_k/\beta_k)/\beta_k$, for all $k \in \mathcal{S}_i$, and from (32) $P_s(i)$ can be obtained by integrating its tail from $\sum_{k\in\mathcal{S}_i} \beta_k/2$. Moreover, by virtue of the central limit theorem (CLT), as $L \to \infty$, $f_{t_i}(t_i)$ will tend to a normal distribution. Then, for very large L, t_i can be approximated by a Gaussian, so

$$P_s(i) \approx Q\left(\frac{\sum_{k\in\mathcal{S}_i} \beta_k/2 - \sum_{k\in\mathcal{S}_i} \beta_k \mathrm{E}\{v'_k\}}{\sqrt{\sum_{k\in\mathcal{S}_i} \beta_k^2 \mathrm{Var}\{v'_k\}}}\right) \tag{35}$$

for all $i = 1, \cdots, N$. As discussed in [6], the CLT-based approximation applied to highly-skewed pdf's results in a very slow convergence. In any case, it may be reasonable to use (35) as the functional to be maximized (minimized) by the attacker (decoder). The exact value of P_e can be obtained [12], but it leads to a cumbersome expression that hinders the solution.

Optimal Decoding Weights for a Known Attack Distribution. Recalling that the $Q(\cdot)$ function is monotonically decreasing, it follows that $P_s(i)$ is minimized when its argument—that is, the signal to noise ratio SNR_i— is maximized. Then, the optimal weights can be found by differentiating

$$\begin{aligned}\frac{\partial \mathrm{SNR}_i}{\partial \beta_j} &= \left(\frac{1}{2} - \mathrm{E}\{v'_j\}\right)\left(\sqrt{\sum_{k\in\mathcal{S}} \beta_k^2 \mathrm{Var}\{v'_k\}}\right) \\ &- \left(\frac{1}{2}\sum_{k\in\mathcal{S}} \beta_k - \sum_{k\in\mathcal{S}} \beta_k \mathrm{E}\{v'_k\}\right)(\beta_j \ \mathrm{Var}\{v'_j\})\left(\sum_k \beta_k^2 \mathrm{Var}\{v'_k\}\right)^{-1/2}\end{aligned} \tag{36}$$

and setting to zero, which yields

$$\beta_j^* = \frac{\left(\frac{1}{2} - \mathrm{E}\{v'_j\}\right)}{\mathrm{Var}\{v'_j\}} \cdot \frac{\left(\sum_{k\in\mathcal{S}_i} \beta_k^2 \mathrm{Var}\{v'_k\}\right)}{\left(\sum_{k\in\mathcal{S}_i} \beta_k \left(\frac{1}{2} - \mathrm{E}\{v'_k\}\right)\right)}, \ j \in \mathcal{S}_i \tag{37}$$

The second factor in (37) is an irrelevant constant, since $\boldsymbol{\beta}^*$ can be scaled without any impact on performance. It is worth mentioning that β_j^* in (37) can take negative values, which are due to large noise values in certain dimensions. The result here obtained implies that for those dimensions it is profitable to *subtract* the corresponding square distance terms in (29). This is reasonable if one thinks, for instance, of a noise pdf uniform in $[-3\Delta_j/2, 3\Delta_j/2]$. When the modular transformation is applied and the absolute value is taken, the resulting pdf has a mean with value 1.75/3. If this held for all dimensions and the decoder were not using β^*, he/she would get $P_e > 0.5$.

Optimal Attack for Known Decoding Weights. In this case, it is easy to verify that the procedure of building the Lagrangian and equating its derivatives to zero leads to a system of nonlinear equations, which requires numerical methods for solving it. Since this does not shed any light on the strategy that the attacker should follow, we will not develop it here.

Optimal Attack When the Decoder Follows the Optimal Strategy. Now, the question is to decide what is the optimal attack when the decoder is using the optimum $\boldsymbol{\beta}$. This problem is quite difficult to solve even in the simplest cases. In fact, we will concentrate on the case where the attacker knows $\mathcal{T}$, the attack consists on uniform noise in each dimension with distribution $[-\eta_k \Delta_k, \eta_k \Delta_k]$ ($[-\eta_k, \eta_k]$ once it has been normalized by Δ_k) for all $k \in \mathcal{S}$, and there is no distortion compensation (pure DM case). So, replacing $\boldsymbol{\beta}$ by its optimal value in the argument of (35), the attacker has to minimize

$$\mathrm{SNR}_i = \sum_{k \in \mathcal{S}_i} \frac{\left(\frac{1}{2} - \mathrm{E}\{v'_k\}\right)^2}{\mathrm{Var}\{v'_k\}} = \sum_{k \in \mathcal{S}_i} \frac{3\,(1-\eta_k)^2}{\eta_k^2}, \ i = 1, \cdots, N \tag{38}$$

constrained to $\sum_{k \in \mathcal{S}_i} \frac{\Delta_k^2 \eta_k^2}{3} \leq D_c(i)$, $i = 1, \cdots, N$.

Using the Lagrange multipliers technique, we may proceed to differentiate the unconstrained functional with respect to η_i and equate to zero to get

$$\frac{(\eta_i - 1)\,\eta_i^2 - (\eta_i - 1)^2\,\eta_i}{\eta_i^4} + \lambda_k \eta_i \Delta_i^2 = 0, \ \text{ for all } i \in \mathcal{S}_k, \quad k = 1, \cdots, N \tag{39}$$

So even in this simple case, the following fourth order equation has to be solved for every η_i, $i \in \mathcal{S}_k$,

$$\lambda_k \eta_i^4 \Delta_i^2 + \eta_i - 1 = 0 \tag{40}$$

Equation (40) gives a hint on the complexity of the problem for DC-DM, because in such case the noise due to distortion compensation is combined with the additive noise from the attacker.

5 Quantized Projection

In the Quantized Projection method [6], the set of samples $\mathcal{S}_i$ assigned to one bit b_i, is projected onto one dimension obtaining the variable r_{x_i}, which is later quantized with a uniform scalar quantizer with step $2\Delta_i$. Hence, centroids of the decision cells associated to $\hat{b}_i = 1$ and $\hat{b}_i = -1$ are respectively given by the unidimensional lattices Λ_{-1} and Λ_1 in (27-28), with $d_i = -\Delta_i/2$ due to symmetry considerations on the pdf of the host signal projection. The projection of $\boldsymbol{y}_i$ is written as

$$r_{y_i} = \sum_{k \in \mathcal{S}_i} y_k s_k \beta_k, \quad i \in \{1, \cdots, N\} \tag{41}$$

where $\boldsymbol{s}$ is a key-dependent pseudorandom vector verifying $E\{s_k\} = 0$ and $E\{s_k^2\} = 1$, and r_{y_i} must be a centroid belonging to one of the two former lattices depending on the transmitted bit.

Following the procedure in [6] it is straightforward to show that $P_e(i)$ that can be approximated by

$$P_e(i) \approx 2Q\left(\frac{\Delta_i}{2\sigma_{r_{n_i}}}\right) = 2Q\left(\frac{\tau_i\left(\sum_{j\in\mathcal{S}_i}\alpha_j\beta_j\right)}{2\sqrt{\sum_{j\in\mathcal{S}_i}\sigma_{n_j}^2\beta_j^2}}\right), \quad i\in\{1,\cdots,N\} \tag{42}$$

where $\tau_i \in [\sqrt{3}, 2]$ is a function that depends on the ratio $\frac{\sigma_{r_{x_i}}}{\Delta_i}$, and consequently also on $\boldsymbol{\beta}$, although in a weaker way. Therefore, as $Q(\cdot)$ is monotonic, we have to maximize (minimize) the argument of this function in (42).

Optimal Decoding Weights for a Known Attack Distribution. If we assume that τ_i does not depend on $\boldsymbol{\beta}$ (in fact, there is only a weak dependence), it can be proven that the optimal weights becomes

$$\beta_j^* = \frac{K\alpha_j}{\sigma_{n_j}^2}, \text{ for all } j\in\mathcal{S}_i, \quad i\in\{1,\cdots,N\} \tag{43}$$

being K any constant.

Optimal Attack for Known Decoding Weights. In this case, we are in the same situation as in Section 3, so all the considerations made there are perfectly valid here. All the attacking power will be concentrated in those coefficients with the largest values of β_k^2.

Optimal Attack When the Decoder Follows the Optimum Strategy. If we follow a strategy similar to the one described in Section 3, assuming the attacker does not know the actual partition, we will have a expression like (19), but now with $p_j = \sigma_{n_j}$, $q_j = \alpha_j$, $t_j = 0$. In this case it is not so clear that $p_j \gg q_j$. In fact, for WNR>0, $q_j > p_j$. Therefore the same simplification cannot be done and the problem requires to be solved by numerical optimization. To show empirical results, we have studied also the case when the attacker knows the partition, and the solution is $\sigma_{n_j}^2 = \xi_i\alpha_j$, for all $j\in\mathcal{S}_i, i\in\{1,\cdots,N\}$, where $\xi_i = L\cdot D_c(i)/\left(\sum_{j\in\mathcal{S}_i}\alpha_j\right), i\in\{1,\cdots,N\}$.

6 Experimental Results

We show next the results of applying the strategies derived along previous sections to real data. In the figures that follow, symbols refer to empirical (MonteCarlo) simulations, while lines show theoretical results. Empirical data come from the gray-scale *Lena* image (256×256), for which the spatial perceptual mask $\boldsymbol{\alpha}$ has been computed using the method detailed in [7], except for the DC-DM scheme where, for illustrative purposes, we have chosen to work in the DCT domain, with a perceptual mask that has been obtained as in [13].

First, in Figure 2 the P_e's resulting when different strategies are considered for spread-spectrum (Section 3) are shown. Watermarking has been performed in the spatial domain with Wiener filtering prior to decoding and 50 pixels per bit ($L = 50$) have been used. Three cases are analyzed: first, the noise variance $\sigma^2_{n_j}$ at each sample is made proportional to α_j^2 and $\boldsymbol{\beta} = C\boldsymbol{\alpha}$, with C any positive constant; second, the attack is the same as in the previous case but the optimal decoding weights β^* are employed; finally, the plot labeled as "worst attack" refers to the case where the attacker follows his/her optimal strategy knowing that the decoder also uses the optimal decoding weights. In all cases, the theoretical results lie close to the empirical ones, although for those where the optimal $\boldsymbol{\beta}^*$ is used the difference is larger.

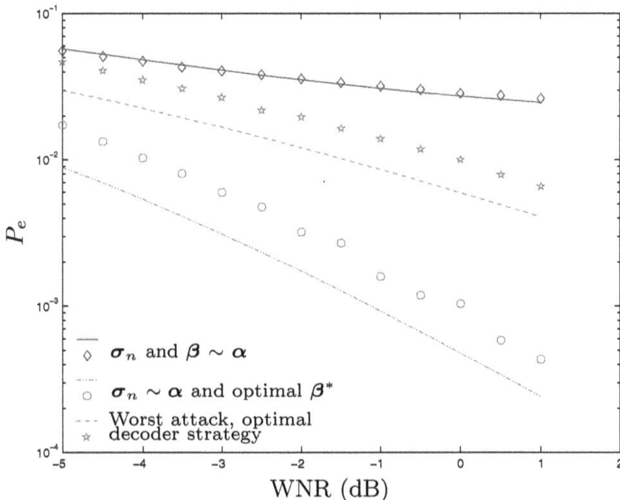

Fig. 2. BER versus WNR for spread-spectrum (L=50) showing three different attacking/decoding strategies.

The cases depicted in Figures 3 correspond to the binary DC-DM method where, as mentioned, watermarking is done in the DCT domain. The distortion compensating parameter ν is set to 0.7 (see Section 4). In order to establish a meaningful case for the experiments, we have selected uniform noise proportional to the quantization step that results when a JPEG quality factor of 80 is selected. For both Figures we have set $L = 10$ (notice that now less samples are needed when compared to spread-spectrum in order to achieve similar BER's for identical WNR's). Two scenarios are depicted in Figure 3: in the first case, each sample, say the j-th, is scaled by Δ_j at the decoder but no further weighting (i.e., $\beta_j = 1$) is considered; in the second plot, the optimal $\boldsymbol{\beta}^*$ that follows from applying the results from Section 4.1 is used. The fact that in this second case the empirical results lie above the theoretical ones may be surprising at first sight since the latter have been obtained with Eq. (35) which was said to be an upper bound to P_e. The explanation to this phenomenon is that in such case some β_j^* take negative values which affect the validity of the CLT approximation (see Section 4.1). Note that as we have less noise (i.e., the WNR increases), it becomes more unlikely to have negative values of $\boldsymbol{\beta}^*$ (since the average value of v_k' decreases), so the theoretical curve and the empirical results get much closer.

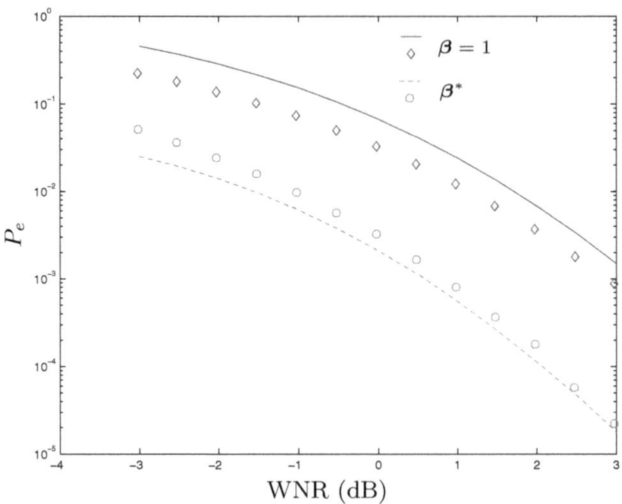

Fig. 3. BER versus WNR for DC-DM (L=10, $\nu = 0.7$) and JPEG noise when no weights are used, and for the optimal weighting.

Finally figure 4 shows a similar comparison for the case considered in Section 5. The decoding weights are set so that $\boldsymbol{\beta} = \boldsymbol{\alpha}$, and the optimal attack for this case is compared to an attack consisting in using noise variances $\sigma_{n_k}^2$ proportional to α_k.

7 Conclusions and Future Research

As a conclusion of this paper, one aspect that clearly requires further study is that of distortion constraints and their relationship with optimal strategies. For instance, as it can be checked in Sects. 3 and 5, the optimal attack will end up in a visible attacked image. Whether this image keeps some of its original value is a moot question that largely depends on the final application scenario.

Related to this, we can think of the problem where the embedder has an active role (as we have already done in QP), and does not just generate the watermarked image independently of the possible attacks. In any way, the distortion introduced by the embedder has to be extremely small; in that regard,

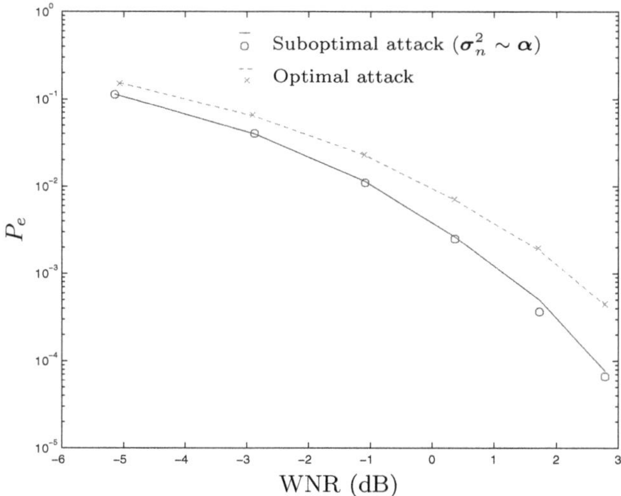

Fig. 4. BER versus WNR corresponding to the optimal and suboptimal attacks for QP when the attacker knows the decoder weights (L=10)

we can assume that the attacker has always more freedom to making it difficult the decoding process.

References

1. A. S. Cohen and A. Lapidoth, "The gaussian watermarking game," *IEEE Transactions on Information Theory*, vol. 48, pp. 1639–1667, June 2002.
2. J. J. Eggers and B. Girod, *Informed Watermarking*. Kluwer Academic Publishers, 2002.
3. P. Moulin and J. O'Sullivan, "Information-theoretic analysis of information hiding," *IEEE Trans. on Information Theory*, 2003.
4. P. Moulin and A. Ivanovic, "The zero-rate spread-spectrum watermarking game," *IEEE Trans. on Signal Processing*, 2003.
5. J. R. Hernández and F. Pérez-González, "Statistical analysis of watermarking schemes for copyright protection of images," *Proceedings of the IEEE*, vol. 87, pp. 1142–1166, July 1999. Special Issue on Identification and Protection of Multimedia Information.
6. F. Pérez-González, F. Balado, and J. R. Hernández, "Performance analysis of existing and new methods for data hiding with known-host information in additive channels," *IEEE Trans. on Signal Processing*, 2003. Special Issue "Signal Processing for Data Hiding in Digital Media & Secure Content Delivery".
7. J. R. Hernández, F. Pérez-González, J. M. Rodríguez, and G. Nieto, "Performance analysis of a 2D-multipulse amplitude modulation scheme for data hiding and watermarking of still images," *IEEE J. Select. Areas Commun.*, vol. 16, pp. 510–524, May 1998.

8. M. E. Vázquez-Méndez, *Análisis y control óptimo de problemas relacionados con la dispersión de contaminantes.* PhD thesis, Universidade de Santiago de Compostela, 1999.
9. J. Herskovits, "Feasible direction interior-point technique for nonlinear optimization," *Journal of optimization theory and applications*, 1998.
10. B. Chen and G. W. Wornell, "Quantization index modulation: A class of provably good methods for digital watermarking and information embedding," *IEEE Trans. on Information Theory*, vol. 47, pp. 1423–1443, May 2001.
11. F. Pérez-González and F. Balado, "Nothing but a kiss: A novel and accurate approach to assessing the performance of multidimensional distortion-compensated dither modulation," in *Proc. of the 5th International Workshop on Information Hiding*, Lecture Notes in Computer Science, (Noorwijkerhout, The Netherlands), Springer-Verlag, October 2002.
12. F. Pérez-González, P. Comesaña, and F. Balado, "Dither-modulation data hiding with distortion-compensation: Exact performance analysis and an improved detector for jpeg attacks," in *Proc. of the IEEE International Conference on Image Processing (ICIP)*, (Barcelona, Spain), September 2003.
13. J. R. Hernández, M. Amado, and F. Pérez-González, "DCT-domain watermarking techniques for still images: Detector performance analysis and a new structure," *IEEE Trans. on Image Processing*, vol. 9, pp. 55–68, January 2000.

Robust Wavelet-Based Information Hiding through Low-Density Parity-Check (LDPC) Codes

Yu Yi, Moon Ho Lee, Ji Hyun Kim, and Gi Yean Hwang

Institute of Information & Communication, Chonbuk National University,
664-14, Dukjin-dong, Jeonju, 561-756, South Korea
yuyi1020@hotmail.com, moonho@chonbuk.ac.kr
infoman@mail.chonbuk.ac.kr

Abstract. In this paper, in order to mitigate the channel conditions and improve the quality of the watermark, we proposed the application of LDPC codes on implementing a fairly robust image watermarking system. The implemented watermarking system operates in the spectrum domain where a subset of the discrete wavelet transform (DWT) coefficients is modified by the watermark without using the original image during watermark extraction. The quality of watermark is evaluated by taking into account the trade-off between the chip-rate and the rate of LDPC codes. Many simulation results are presented in this paper, these results indicate that the quality of the watermark is improved greatly and the proposed system based on LDPC codes is very robust to attacks.

1 Introduction

The fast development of multimedia applications on the internet, combined with the simplicity of duplication and distribution of digital data, has recently stimulated many research efforts towards the design and study of sophisticated digital media protection methodologies. A new emerging technology, digital watermarking [1], protects digital media by embedding or hiding a robust signal or some other distinguishing piece of information directly into the media, thus providing a promising way to protect the digital media from illicit copying and manipulation. Much work done in this field in the past decade have resulted in the advancement of robust, unperceivable, watermarking strategies [2] and many algorithms have been derived for watermarking images, and VRML models [3].

However, when the watermarked media is transmitted over the watermark channel modeled as the AWGN channel, the watermark information is often interfered by the channel noise and produces a large number of errors. So many error-correcting codes have been applied in the digital image watermarking system to protect the embedded message from the noise, such as BCH codes, Reed-Solomon (RS) codes and Turbo codes. LDPC codes were demonstrated as good correcting codes achieving Shannon limit performance and outperforming turbo codes with low decoding complexity. As we all know, in the communication system, LDPC encoder plays a role of adding parity bits to information data for the purpose of protecting information data. LDPC decoder plays a role of recovering information data after correcting errors occurred by the noisy channel from transmitted data including parity check bits. Digital

T. Kalker et al. (Eds.): IWDW 2003, LNCS 2939, pp. 117–128, 2004.
© Springer-Verlag Berlin Heidelberg 2004

watermarking is a distinguishing piece of information that is adhered to image for protecting rightful ownership of image. In this paper, in order to mitigate the channel conditions and improve the quality of watermark, we proposed the application of LDPC codes as channel codes on implementing a fairly robust digital image watermarking system because of their advantages. The implemented watermarking system operates in the spectrum domain where a subset of the DWT coefficients is modified by the watermark without using original image during watermark extraction. The quality of watermark is evaluated by taking into account the trade-off between the chip-rate and the rate of LDPC codes. Many simulation results are presented in this paper, these results indicate that the quality of watermark is improved greatly and the proposed system based on LDPC codes is very robust to attacks.

This paper is organized as follows: section 2 introduces the proposed digital image watermarking system used in this paper, which includes watermark generation, watermark embedding and watermark extraction. In section 3, LDPC codes and the iterative decoding algorithm are described in detail. Various simulation results are presented in section 4. Finally, section 5 gives conclusion.

2 Digital Image Watermarking System

An abstract block diagram of digital image watermarking system model used in this paper is shown in Fig. 1.

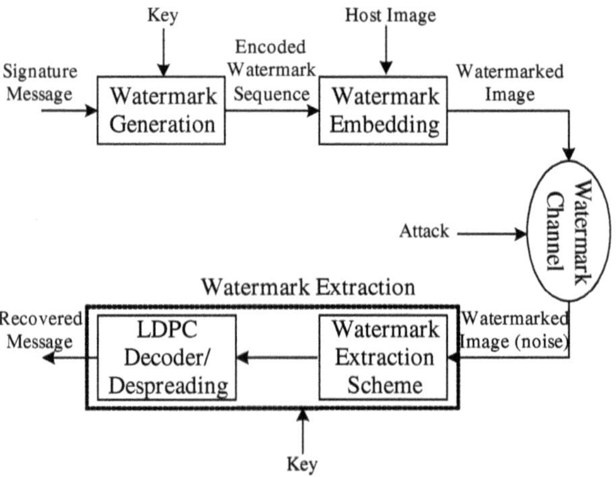

Fig. 1. An block diagram of watermarking system based on LDPC codes

As indicated in Fig. 1, there are three main stages in the design of the proposed digital image watermarking system: watermark generation, watermark embedding and watermark extraction.

Watermark generation is the generation of the watermark sequence to be embedded in the host or cover image. Besides signature message (watermark), the watermark sequence also depends on secret keys. As we all know, the secret keys involved in the generation of the watermark not only provide the security, but also can be used as a method of distinguishing different data owners from each other. In our work we use the watermarking scheme that is similar to spread-spectrum (SS) communication at the watermark generation stage. Two ways generating the spread watermark sequence can be chosen, one is based on the pseudo-random sequence and the other is based on the pseudo-noise sequence. We use the second approach that is the signature message consists of a number of bits, which are modulated by pseudo-noise sequence in this paper to generate the watermark sequence. However, when the watermarked host image is transmitted over the noisy channel, we can find out the spread watermark sequence embedded in the host image is interfered by channel noise and produces a large number of errors. So we apply the LDPC codes technique in this proposed system to correct the errors in the embedded watermark sequence. Especially, LDPC encoder is used in watermark generation. The spread watermark sequence is transformed to the encoded watermark sequence by LDPC encoder. According to the above description, in our watermarking system, the watermark generation consists of spread spectrum watermark function and LDPC encoder.

Watermark embedding is a method of inserting the encoded watermark sequence from the watermark generation into the host image to get the watermarked image. Based on the scheme of embedding, digital watermark embedding can be classified as: spatial domain watermarking and spectrum domain watermarking [4]. In spatial domain watermarking schemes, the watermark is embedded by modifying the pixel value of an image directly. Though they are simple and don't need the original image to extract the watermark, spatial domain watermarking schemes are not robust to the signal processing operations, since the watermark doesn't spread all over the image and some common signal processing operations can easily erase the embedded watermark without affecting the quality of the watermarked image. On the contrary, spectrum domain watermarking schemes involve embedding the watermark by modifying the spectrum coefficients, after the image has been transformed to the spectrum domain, such as the Discrete Cosine Transform (DCT) domain, Discrete Fourier Transform (DFT) domain and Discrete Wavelet Transform (DWT) domain. Since these transforms de-correlate the spatial value of an image, most of the energy of the image is put on low frequency components in the spectrum domain. The watermark is usually inserted into the low frequency and middle frequency coefficients and the modifications will spread throughout the image. Because low and middle frequency coefficients are less likely to be affected during common signal processing than high frequency coefficients, the spectrum domain watermarking schemes are more robust than the spatial domain watermarking schemes. Because of the advantage of spectrum domain watermarking schemes, they are used in the watermark embedding and we can get the watermarked host image from the host image based on the DWT and encoded watermark sequence. Then it is transmitted over the watermark channel modeled as the AWGN channels and attacked by the channel noise.

Watermark extraction is the recovery of the signature message from the watermarked host image. Besides the watermarked host image, the presence of the secret keys involved in the watermark generation is required. In this paper, the signature message is extracted without the original cover image. So as mentioned in the watermark generation stage and the watermark embedding stage, we can know that the watermark extraction consists of watermark extraction function, LDPC decoder and the dispreading function. LDPC decoder is used to correct the errors in the recovered signature message from the watermark extraction function. Finally, we can get the recovered signature message from dispreading function.

2.1 Watermark Generation

In this section, watermark generation is described in detail. The generation of the watermark sequence is in many aspects similar to the spread-spectrum (SS) modulation scheme. In the spread spectrum communication, a narrow band signal is transmitted over a much larger bandwidth such that the signal energy present in any single frequency is undetectable [4]. The spreading is accomplished by methods of a spreading sequence. Also, the same sequence is used at the receiver side for dispreading and data recovery. Similarly the watermark bits are spread by a large factor called chip-rate so that it is imperceptible. The block diagram of watermark generation is shown in Fig. 2.

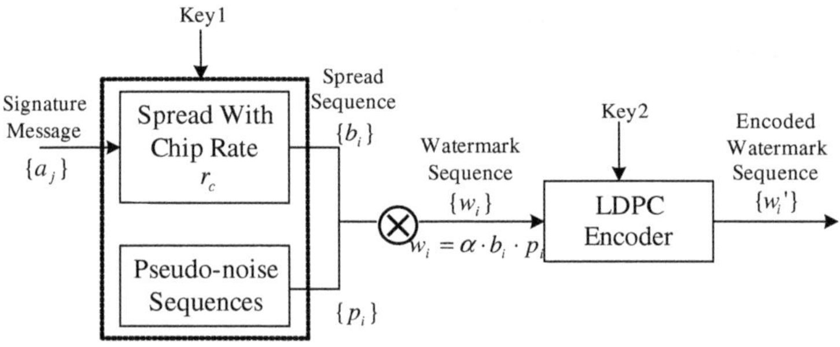

Fig. 2. A block diagram of watermark generation

According to the above Fig. 2, some notations are described as follows [6], let M be the total number of pixels in a cover image, a total of L signature message bits be embedded in the host image and r_c be the chip-rate used to spread the message bits.

$$r_c = M / l \quad (1)$$

The chip-rate is considered as a parameter to study watermark because it clearly affects watermark robustness and watermark capacity. For a fixed number M of modified coefficients, the number of L of embedded signature message bits, for instance, the watermark quality increases as the chip-rate decreases. However, a decrease in the chip-rate results in a lower energy of each message bit, and therefore leads to a loss in watermark robustness. After repeating each message bit r_c times, the resulting sequence of consecutive +1's and –1's is reordered in a random fashion. This reordering is done by the key that is the dependent random permutation and provides increased watermark security. Without the knowledge of the correct key, it is impossible to extract the hidden message, since one does not know where the corresponding bits are embedded. So in the proposed system the spread spectrum watermarking sequence is formed with key1 and LDPC encoder are applied with key2. Let $\{a_j\}$ be the sequence of signature message bits that has to be embedded into the cover image. Each data element a_j is either represented by +1 or −1. This discrete signal is spread by a large factor, that is the chip-rate r_c, to obtain the spread sequence $\{b_i\}$:

$$b_i = a_j, \text{ where } j \cdot r_c \le i \le (j+1) \cdot r_c \tag{2}$$

The purpose of spreading is to add redundancy by embedding one bit of information into r_c pixels of the image. The spread sequence $\{b_i\}$ is then modulated by a pseudo-noise sequence $\{p_i\}$, where $p_i \in \{-1,1\}$. $\{p_i\}$ serves for frequency spreading. The modulated signal is scaled with a factor α :

$$w_i = \alpha \cdot b_i \cdot p_i \tag{3}$$

Where w_i is the spread spectrum watermark sequence, which is arranged into a matrix with size equal to the image size. However, modern communication infrastructure supports the possibility of delivering quality signals. The different noises in channel of communication will interfere the hidden message, LDPC codes in our watermarking system to detect and correct the errors caused by the noise. The spread watermark sequence w_i is transformed by LDPC encoder to the encoded watermark w'_i to protect from the noise.

2.2 Watermark Embedding

In this paper, the spectrum domain watermarking is considered as the watermarking embedding scheme based on DWT to improve the robustness of watermark channels. The diagram of watermark embedding is shown in Fig. 3.

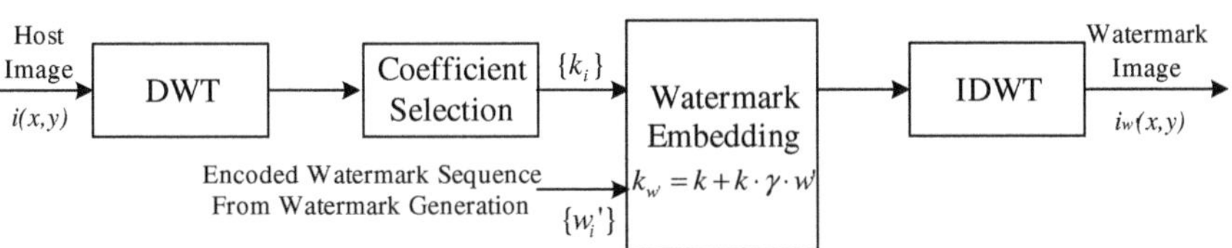

Fig. 3. A block diagram of watermark embedding

According to the Fig. 3, it is well known that the embedding in the low frequency band is more robust to manipulation such as enhancement and image compression. However, changes made to the low frequency components may result in visible artifacts. Modifying the data in a multiresolution framework, such as a wavelet transform, appears quite promising for obtaining good quality embedding with little perceptual distortion. The dyadic frequency decomposition of the wavelet transform resembles the signal processing of the HVS and thus permits to excite the different perceptual bands individually. Here, three levels DWT with a Daubechies filter are used. The selection of the coefficients that are manipulated in the embedding process is determined by the hiding technique and the application. The main distinction is between the approximation image *(LL)* which contains the low-frequency signal components and the detail sub-band (LH_j, HL_j, HH_j, j is the resolution level) that represent the high-frequency information in horizontal, vertical and diagonal orientation. In this work, the message or signature data are encoded by LDPC codes and are embedded by some coefficients in the detail sub-bands, which are above threshold selected according to the numbers of the encoded watermark sequence from the channel $(\{w'_i\})$. The magnitude values of the selected DWT coefficients are ordered into a sequence $\{k_i\}$ of length *M*. The watermark sequence $\{w'_i\}$ from the LDPC encoder also consists of *M* elements. Each coefficient k_i is modified proportional to magnitude, according to an additive-multiplicative embedding rule as proposed in [6]

$$k_{w',i} = k_i(1+\gamma \cdot w') \tag{4}$$

where γ controls watermark strength. Also, the parameter γ reflects a trade-off between watermark imperceptibility and watermark robustness. Small values of γ clearly improve watermark transparency, while diminishing the watermark power and making the embedded watermark more susceptible to attacks. Large values of γ, however, increase watermark robustness but also watermark visibility.

After the watermark embedding into the set of the selected coefficients, the watermarked image $i_{w'}(x, y)$ is obtained by taking the Inverse Discrete Wavelet Transform (IDWT). Ideally the difference between the host image $i(x, y)$ and the watermarked image $i_{w'}(x, y)$ should be as small as possible.

2.3 Watermark Extraction

The watermark extraction can create estimate of the embedded watermark signal. We can show the diagram of the watermark extraction in Fig. 4.

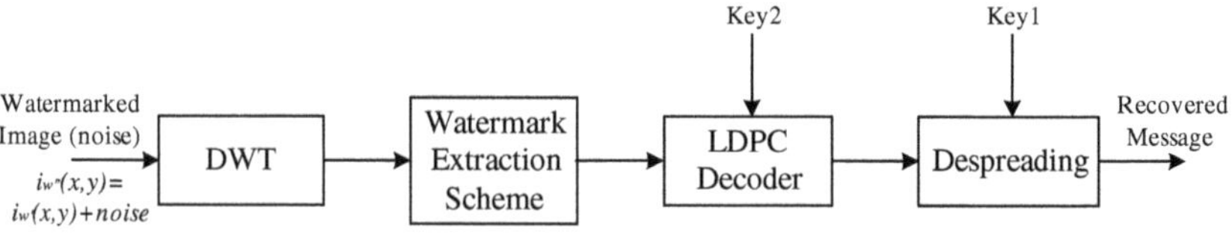

Fig. 4. A block diagram of watermark extraction

The watermark could be extracted without using the original image by the means of a correlation receiver. But the pseudo-noise sequence $\{p_i\}$ is needed for watermark extraction. The watermarked image is first high pass filtered to remove major components of the image itself. The second step is de-modulation, which is the multiplication of the filtered watermarked image with the same pseudo-noise sequence $\{p_i\}$ that was used for embedding. This is followed by summation over a window of length equal to the chip-rate, yielding the correlation sum s_j for the jth information bit.

The watermarked image, $k_{w',i} = k_i(1+\gamma \cdot w')$ where w' is from the LDPC encoder. At the receiver, we can get the watermark image disturbed by noise, $i_{w''}(x,y) = i_{w'}(x,y) + noise$. Then, LDPC decoder with key2 and dispreading with key1 are also applied to the extracted watermark message. The high pass filter removes major components of $k_{w',i}$. Therefore, we can get the recovered message in the following [4],

$$s_j = \sum_{i=jr_c}^{(j+1)r_c-1} p_i \cdot w_i = \sum_{i=jr_c}^{(j+1)r_c-1} p_i^2 \cdot \alpha \cdot b_i \tag{5}$$

$$s_j = a_j \cdot r_c \cdot \alpha \tag{6}$$

$$sign(s_j) = sign(a_j \cdot r_c \cdot \alpha) = sign(a_j) = a_j \tag{7}$$

This is because $r_c > 0, \alpha > 0, p_i^2 = 1$ and $a_j = \pm 1$. Thus the embedded bit can be retrieved without any loss. This means that the embedded information bit is 1 if the correlation is positive and –1 if it is negative. But since the image cannot be completely removed by the high pass filter, there may be errors in the extracted watermark bits.

3 Low-Density Parity-Check (LDPC) Codes

The LDPC code is a linear block code specified by a very sparse parity-check matrix [7]. In this paper, LDPC codes are defined by $M \times N$ parity-check matrix as (N, K, j, k) LDPC, where K=N-M is the original information bits, j is the column weight and k is the row weight. Note that the code rate is R=K/N. Also, LDPC codes can be represented by a Factor Graph, called as Tanner Graph, which can contains two types of nodes: the "bit nodes" and the "check nodes". Each bit node corresponds to a column of a parity-check matrix, which represents a parity-check equation. An edge between a bit node and a check node exists if and only if the bit participates in the parity-check equation represented by the check node. We can show an example of a parity-check matrix, H and its' corresponding bipartite graph in Fig. 5 and Fig. 6, respectively [8].

Parity Check Matrix

$$H=\begin{bmatrix} 1 & 0 & 0 & 1 & 0 & 0 & 1 & 0 & 0 \\ 0 & 1 & 0 & 0 & 1 & 0 & 0 & 1 & 0 \\ 0 & 0 & 1 & 0 & 0 & 1 & 0 & 0 & 1 \\ 1 & 0 & 0 & 0 & 1 & 0 & 0 & 0 & 1 \\ 0 & 1 & 0 & 0 & 0 & 1 & 1 & 0 & 0 \\ 0 & 0 & 1 & 1 & 0 & 0 & 0 & 1 & 0 \end{bmatrix}\begin{matrix} A_1 \\ A_2 \\ A_3 \\ A_4 \\ A_5 \\ A_6 \end{matrix}$$

(columns $x_1\ x_2\ x_3\ x_4\ x_5\ x_6\ x_7\ x_8\ x_9$)

Fig. 5. An example of the H matrix

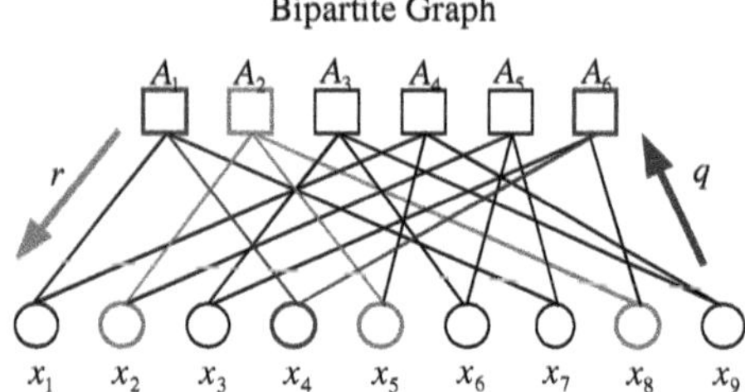

Fig. 6. The bipartite graph

In the family of LDPC codes, two kinds of LDPC codes are paid attention to, one is regular LDPC code and the other is irregular LDPC code. Regular LDPC codes are defined that degrees of all message nodes are equal, and the degrees of all check nodes are equal. This means that the parity-check matrix of the code described above contains the same number of ones in each row and the same number of ones in each column. However, irregular LDPC codes are defined that the degrees of the nodes on each side of the graph can vary widely. In terms of the parity-check matrix H, the weight per row and column is not uniform, but instead governed by an appropriately chosen distribution of weights. In this paper, regular binary LDPC codes are used to implement the proposed watermarking system.

4 Experiment Results

In this section, we present some results for proposed watermarking system.
The 59×177 signature image and 256×256 cover image shown in Fig. 7 are chosen for simulation. In this paper, we use LDPC codes as error-correcting scheme to protect the signature message and we lay emphasis on the analysis of the recovered watermark image quality improvement using LDPC codes, LDPC codes with different code rate and block size are applied The signature image is first spreaded and modulated by pseudo noise sequences, the output sequence is then coded by LDPC codes to generate watermark sequence. Fig. 8 shows the watermarked image and the difference between original image and the watermarked image is illustrated in Fig. 9.

To retrieve watermark with good quality, the embedding strength and chip-rate are both the most important factors that should be considered. Embedding strength reflects a trade-off between the watermark imperceptibility and the watermark robust-

sample

Fig. 7. Host image and signature image

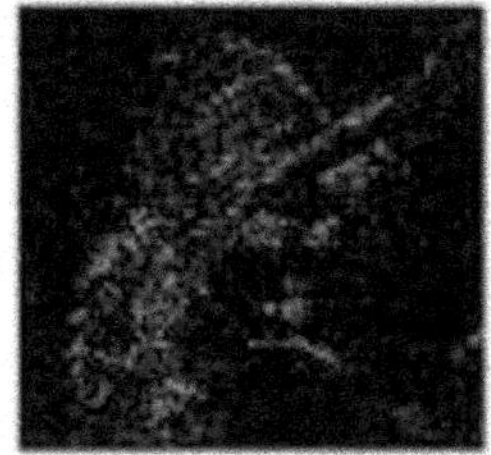

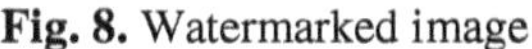

Fig. 8. Watermarked image

Fig. 9. The difference between the original image and watermarked image

ness. Chip-rate, which is decided by the lengths of signature message and the watermark sequence, can clearly affect watermark robustness and watermark capacity. In this paper, we analyze the probability of error as a function of the embedding strength and the chip-rate. Fig. 10 indicates the relationship between bit error rate and chip-rate under the condition of different embedding strength. From this figure, we can see that an increase in embedding strengths in lower error rates and higher capacity of watermarking channel.

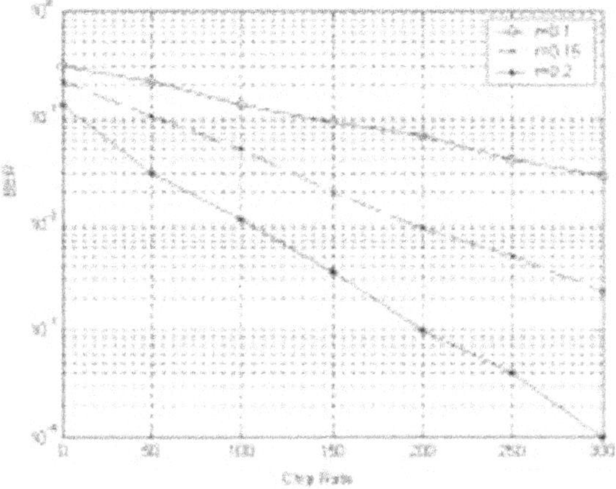

Fig. 10. BER versus Chip Rate with different embedding strength

Signature message is the most important information that should be protected. However, when the covered image embedded spread watermark sequence is transmitted over the noisy channel, it is easily to be attacked by noise and this often results in the quality decrease of recovered watermark information. To correct the errors in the embedded watermark sequence caused by noise, we apply LDPC codes to protect the important signature information. In this paper, we analyze the BER and PSNR performances of the watermarked images. Four cases are studied here; LDPC codes with code rate of 1/2, 1/3 and block size of 512bit and 1024bit are applied in the simulation. From Fig. 11 and Fig. 12, it can be proved that LDPC codes with lower code rate and bigger block size can tolerate higher noise levels.

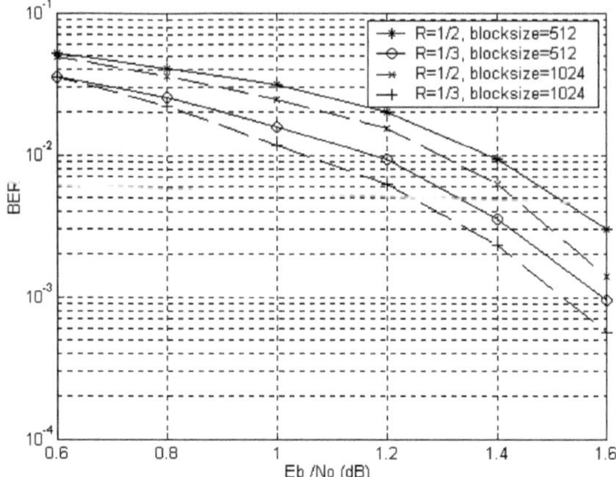

Fig. 11. BER performance of watermarked images

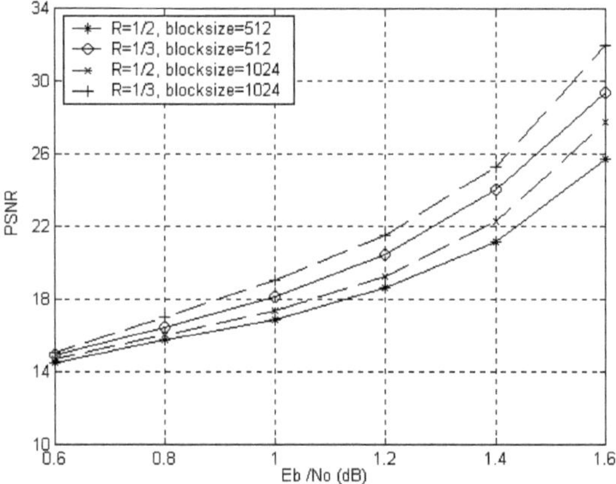

Fig. 12. PSNR performance of watermarked images

By implementing the proposed watermarking system, we can retrieve signature message with the good quality at a very lower signal to noise ratio. Fig. 13 denotes the reconstructed signature images. In this figure, (a) shows the recovered signature images protected by LDPC codes with code rate of 1/3 and block size of 1024, (b) demonstrates reconstructed images without error correcting. It is obvious that the recovered images protected by LDPC codes have much better quality even at a very low signal to noise ratio such as 1.7 and 1.5. The quality of retrieved signature images without error correction is totally unacceptable. Fig. 13 shows that signature information can be extracted successfully when signal to noise ratio is very low by using LDPC.

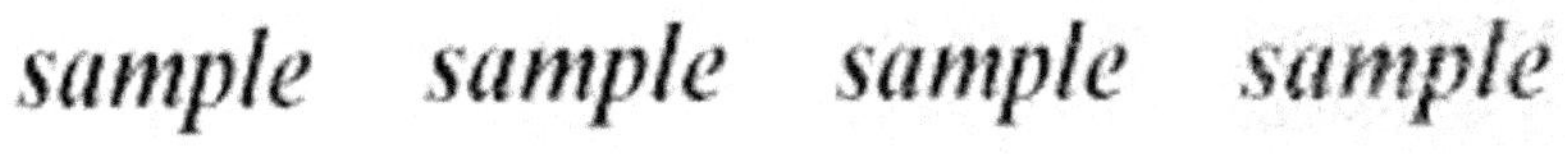

Eb / No=1.7	Eb / No=1.5	Eb / No=1.1	Eb / No=0.3
PSNR=35	PSNR=29.05	PSNR=20.15	PSNR=12

(a)

Eb / No=1.7	Eb / No=1.5	Eb / No=1.1	Eb / No=0.3
PSNR=11.82	PSNR=11.49	PSNR=11.39	PSNR=11.18

(b)

Fig. 13. Reconstructed signature images: (a) protected by LDPC codes with code rate of 1/3 and block size of 1024 (b) without error protection

5 Conclusion

In this paper, we propose the application of LDPC codes on implementing a fairly robust digital image watermarking system. As indicated in this paper, the performance of LDPC codes is the best in the family of error correcting codes. So LDPC codes can play an important role of correcting the errors of the embedded message caused by the disturbance of channel noise in the proposed system. At the same time, the spread spectrum technology and DWT are used to implement this system. Many simulation results and figures are presented in this paper, these results indicate the quality of the watermark is improved greatly and the proposed system based on the LDPC codes is very robust to attacks.

Acknowledgement. This work was partially supported by ITRC and KOSEF (No. 303-15-2).

References

1. R.B.Wolfgang and E. J. Delp, "Overview of image security techniques with applications in multimedia systems, " Proceedings of the SPIE International Conference on Multimedia Networks: Security, Displays, Terminals, and Gateways, November 4–5, 1997, Dallas, Texas, vol. 3228, pp. 297–308.
2. M. D. Swanson, M. Kobayashi, and A. H. Tewfik, "Multimedia data-embedding and watermarking technologies," Proceedings of the IEEE , 86, pp. 1064–1087, June 1998.
3. J. R. Smith and B. O. Comiskey, "Modulation and information hiding in images," in Proc. Of First Int. Workshop on Information Hiding, Lecture Notes in Computer Science, vol. 1174, pp. 207–226, 1996.

4. I. J. Cox, J.Kilian, F. T. Leighton, and T. Shammon. Secure Spread Spectrum Watermarking for multimedia. IEEE Transactions on Image Processing, 6:1673–1686, December 1997.
5. Mercy George, Jean-Yves Chouinard, and Nicolas Georganas, "Digital Watermarking of Images and Video using Direct Sequence Spread Spectrum Techniques," ICEIC, 1999.
6. Piva A., M. Barni, F. Bartolini, V.Cappellini and A. De Rosa, "Improving the Robustness of Non-additive Watermarks Through Optimum Detection Theory," Proceedings of SPIE, Vol. 3971, 2000.
7. R.G.Gallager, "Low Density Parity Check Codes," MIT Press, Cambridge, Mass., 1963.
8. D.J.C.Mackay, "Good error-correcting codes based on very sparse matrices," IEEE Transaction on Information Theory, vol. 45, pp. 399-431, Mar. 1999.

Natural Language Watermarking Using Semantic Substitution for Chinese Text

Yuei-Lin Chiang, Lu-Ping Chang, Wen-Tai Hsieh, and Wen-Chih Chen

Advanced e-Commerce Technology Lab., Institute for Information Industry, 17FL.-A, No.333, Sec.2, Duenhua S. Rd., Taipei, Taiwan, 106, R.O.C.
{ylchiang, clp, wentai, wjchen}@ iii.org.tw

Abstract. Numerous schemes have been designed for watermarking multimedia contents. Many of these schemes are vulnerable to watermark erasing attacks. Naturally, such methods are ineffective on text unless the text is represented as a bitmap image, but in that case, the watermark can be erased easily by using Optical Character Recognition (OCR) to change the representation of the text from a bitmap to ASCII or EBCDIC. This study attempts to develop a method for embedding watermark in the text that is as successful as the frequency-domain methods have been for image and audio. The novel method embeds the watermark in original text, creating ciphertext, which preserves the meaning of the original text via various semantic replacements.

1 Introduction

The Internet is a two-edged sword: While the Internet offers authors the chance to publish their works worldwide, it simultaneously creates the risks of unauthorized publishing and copying. Copyright is not lost when publishing via the Internet. However, the right alone generally is insufficient to protect intellectual property. The Internet is becoming more important than the traditional medium of CD-ROM. However, effective protection is required owing to inexpensive CD writers and the mass-production of pirated CDs overseas.

The principle of digital watermarking is widely applied in bank notes. Insignificant characteristics are sufficient to verify originality and identify counterfeits. Modern digital watermarks are a widespread method for making a published work unique and thus enabling its automatic identification. Digital watermarks enable author rights to be verified in the event of unauthorized publication or copying. Several methods exist for digitally watermarking images and music, all of which involve imprinting video- and audio-files with an innocuous mark. This mark of authorship simplifies identification, and enables pirates to be caught and sentenced easily and inexpensively.

Many techniques have been proposed for watermarking multimedia contents. However, many of these techniques are defective in that they are vulnerable to watermark erasing attacks. The most successful of these techniques operate in the frequency domain [1], [2], [6]. Naturally, such methods do not work on text unless the text is represented as a bitmap image (with, for instance manipulation of kerning and/or spacing to hide the watermark), but in that case the watermark easily can be erased by

T. Kalker et al. (Eds.): IWDW 2003, LNCS 2939, pp. 129–140, 2004.
© Springer-Verlag Berlin Heidelberg 2004

using OCR (Optical Character Recognition) to change the representation of the text from a bitmap to ASCII or EBCDIC. This study attempts to develop a method for embedding watermarks in the text that is as effective as the frequency-domain methods have been for image and audio. The proposed method embeds watermark in original text, creating a ciphertext, which preserves the meaning of the original text through various synonym replacements. The proposed is context based rather than format based. The proposed method thus can enhance the protection of text contexts.

The rest of the paper is organized as follows. Section 2 describes related works, then Section 3 provides a detailed description of our method for Chinese NLP Watermarking. Experimental results then are reported in Section 4, and future directions are given in Section 5.

2 Related Work

2.1 Natural Language Watermarking

Mikhail Atallah and Victor Raskin proposed a technique for information hiding in natural language text. Moreover,[7], [8] established the basic technique for embedding a resilient watermark in NL text by combining a number of information assurance and security techniques with the advanced methods and resources of natural language processing(NLP). A semantically based scheme significantly improves the information-hiding capacity of English text by modifying the granularity of meaning of individual terms/sentences. However, this scheme also suffered the limitations :

1. The NLP technique is suitable for English. However, for Chinese the NLP technique is differs from the English domain. The technique thus requires adapting to Chinese text contexts.
2. The technique was merely conceptual. The details of the technique were not clarified. Such details include how to select the candidate terms/sentences for embedding watermark bits in terms/sentences, the encoding/decoding algorithm, the synonymous change algorithm, and so on.
3. The technique was applicable to long text because it ensured the embedding of just one bit of the watermark bit string in each terms/sentences and required a marker sentence for each watermark-bearing sentence, thus effectively reducing the bandwidth to 0.5.

2.2 Quadratic Residue

This study uses a theorem - Euler's Quadratic Residue Theorem, to help embed watermark in the text. This theorem is important in determining whether the integer x is the square of an integer modulo p. If there is an integer x exists such that $x^2 \equiv q(\mathrm{mod}\, p)$, then q is said to be a quadratic residue (mod p). If not, q is said to be a quadratic non-residue (mod p). Hardy and Wright [4] use the shorthand notations $q\,\mathrm{R}\,p$ and $q\,\mathrm{N}\,p$, to indicate whether q is a quadratic or non-quadratic residue, respectively. For example, $4^2 \equiv 6 \pmod{10}$, so six is a quadratic residue (mod 10). The entire set of quadratic residues (mod 10) is given by 1, 4, 5, 6, and 9, making the numbers 2, 3, 7, and 8 the quadratic non-residues (mod 10). Figure 1 shows the entire set of quadratic residues (mod 10).

$$
\begin{array}{lll}
1^2 \equiv 1 \pmod{10} & 2^2 \equiv 4 \pmod{10} & 3^2 \equiv 9 \pmod{10} \\
4^2 \equiv 6 \pmod{10} & 5^2 \equiv 5 \pmod{10} & 6^2 \equiv 6 \pmod{10} \\
7^2 \equiv 9 \pmod{10} & 8^2 \equiv 4 \pmod{10} & 9^2 \equiv 1 \pmod{10}
\end{array}
$$

Fig. 1. Quadratic residues (mod 10)

3 System Architecture

Owing to the imperfect nature of human hearing and sight, watermarks can be used to hide information in texts. For example, when a green pixel is placed in the middle of a group of red pixels in a graph, human sight will not recognize the green pixel. Similarly, information can be hidden in music files using psychoacoustics. These flaws in OMIT human sensory organs cause redundancies in information hiding. These redundancies can be used to recognize the legality of the file modification, or whether the encrypted message is already hidden. However, this redundancy is smaller for natural language texts than for other texts. For example, the meaning may differ when some terms are modified or when term sequences in the text are changed. Therefore, this study proposes an approach for enabling the natural language based watermark. This approach can be used to embed a watermark, such as copyrights, in the text. The meaning of the text remains unchanged after encrypting, while the property right is protected.

This study uses the NLP watermarking definition described in [8]. The definition is :

NLP for Watermarking. Let T denote a natural language text, and let W be a string that is much shorter than T. This study attempts to generate natural language text T' such that:

1. T' has essentially the same meaning as T;
2. T' contains W as a secret watermark, and the presence of W can be demonstrated in a court of low (that is, W could say, "This is the Property of X, and was licensed to Y on date Z");
3. The watermark W is not readable from T' without knowledge of the secret key that was used to introduce W;
4. For someone who knows the secret key, W can be obtained from T' without knowledge of T;
5. Unless someone knows the secret key, W is impossible to remove from T' without significantly changing the meaning of T';
6. The process by which W is introduced into T to obtain T' is not secret, rather, it is the secret key that makes the scheme secure;

The following sections describe the above approach in detail.

3.1 Embedding Watermark

Watermark embedding involves five steps - term segmentation and tagging, secret key generation, candidate selection, semantic substitution and ciphertext generation. Figure 2 presents the process of watermark embedding.

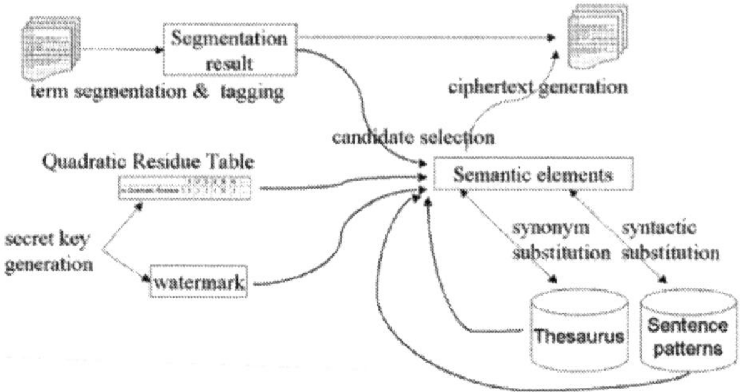

Fig. 2. Steps involved in watermark embedding

3.1.1 Term Segmentation and Tagging

Term segmentation and tagging are essential to semantic processing especially for the proposed approach. In this study, the terms are segmented and tagged using AutoTag - a segmentation and tagging tool for Chinese. AutoTag was developed by the Chinese Knowledge Information Processing group (CKIP), which is a Chinese term segmentation system designed by Academia Sinica. AutoTag has the richest lexical dictionary in Chinese.

3.1.2 Secret Key Generation

In this study, the secret key has two primary components - watermark and user quadratic residue key. First, the watermark is translated into a bit string to create the secret encoding key. Unicode, ASCII, ANSI or other techniques can be used to conduct this translation. This study uses Unicode. Assuming that the watermark is 『ACT』, and its bit string is like 『00101』, then the quadratic residue key is a prime candidate for producing a quadratic residue table. This table then can be used to identify which number is residue, or non-residue between 1 and the quadratic residue key. Here residue indicates 1, and non-residue indicates 0. Subsequently, this table is used to help in term selection, as mentioned later. Table 1 illustrates the quadratic residue table of the prime number 10007.

Table 1. Quadratic Residue Table of prime number 10007

	1	2	3	4	5	6	...	10007
Is Quadratic Residue ?	1	1	1	1	0	1	...	0

3.1.3 Candidate Selection

Candidate selection involves selecting candidate elements for syntactic or synonym substitution for watermark embedding. In syntactic substitution, the sentences matching the defined sentence patterns are selected. However, synonym substitution must consider additional factors. Not all terms in the text can be used for watermark embedding, and unsuitable terms should be filtered out. The filtering rules generalized here are illustrated in Fig. 3:

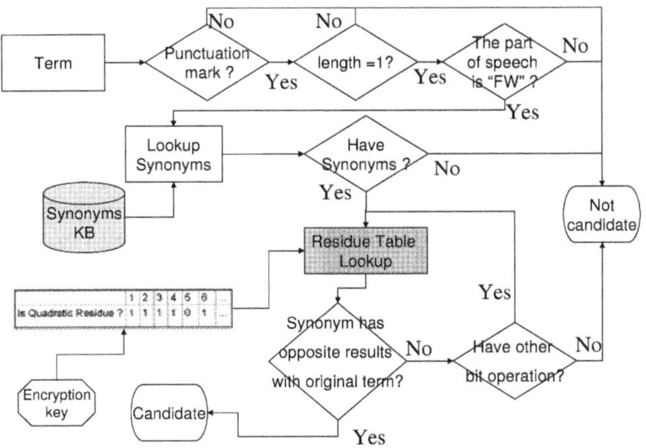

Fig. 3. Term selection flow

1. Punctuation mark: Punctuation marks in the text are fixed and difficult to tune. Punctuation marks thus are ignored for the present purposes.
2. The length of the term segmented is 1 :In AutoTag, terms with a length is 1 mostly comprise prepositions(介詞, P), DE(e.g. 的), or pronouns(代名詞, Nh). These terms are either difficult or impossible to substitute. Therefore, these terms also are skipped.
3. The part of speech is "FW" in AutoTag: In AutoTag, the part of speech of the term "FW" means foreign language, such as English, Japanese, that do not belong to Chinese. This study ignores the issue of how to treat such terms.
4. The term has no synonym: The approach proposed here uses synonym substitution to embed the watermark in the text. Consequently, if the term has no synonyms, it will not be embedded in the watermark. The term thus must be truncated.
5. Although the term does have synonyms, no opposite results appear by looking up the quadratic residue table after the following bit operations.

This approach uses bit matching to embed a watermark in the text. Therefore, the opposite result is needed. Synonyms exist which can be substituted when bit matching fails. This study uses the following bit operations： XOR, AND, OR, +, -, /. Assuming that a term in Chinese "分配"(dispatch), can be divided into two characters and their bit strings - 『分：10011』和『配：10101』. After performing the AND bit operation, "分配"(dispatch) is expressed by『10001』and the decimal number

『17』. Then, the quadratic residue key (e.g. 10007) is taken to modify this decimal number and the remainder are used to look up the quadratic residue table. This process obtains result 1. The quadratic residue table results of these three terms are listed in Table 2 below:

Table 2. Some quadratic residue table results of three terms

Term	Synonym	Residue：1	Non-Residue：0
分配(dispatch, Verb)	發給(send), 分發(deliver)	分配(dispatch), 發給(send)	分發(deliver)
賺取(earn, Verb)	創利(make), 贏利(profit), 盈利(gain), 創收(obtain)	盈利(gain), 創收(obtain)	賺取(earn), 贏利(profit), 創利(make)
情形(situation, Noun)	情況(circumstance), 狀況(status), 狀態(state), 條件(condition)	情形(situation), 狀況(status), 條件(condition)	情況(circumstance), 狀態(state)

3.1.4 Semantic Substitution

Semantic substitution involves two main operations --- syntactic substitution and synonym substitution. These operations can be used to embed the watermark in the text. First, this study performs embedding by syntactic substitution. The candidate sentences are selected based on the substitution rules gathered here. Tree structures then are used to express those sentences. Figure 4 is an example of the tree of sentence "月光和角落裡的貓"(Moonlight, and a cat in the corner).

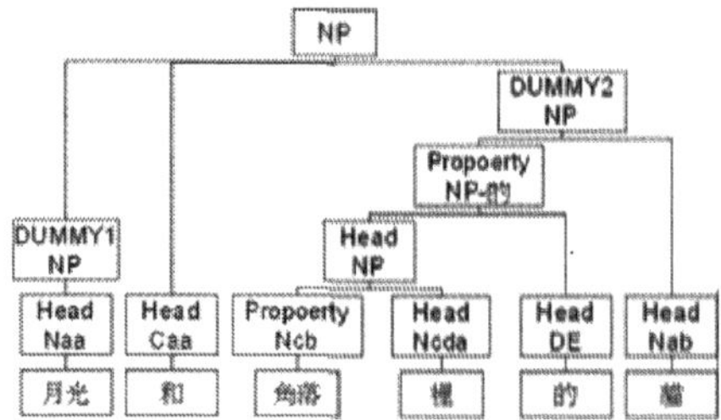

Fig. 4. Tree structure of a Chinese sentence

A Chinese Parser was used to construct the tree structure of a Chinese sentence. With the emergence of large treebanks, supervised statistical English parsers are achieving promising results. Penn Chinese Treebank [9] has an average sentence length of 30 words and presents a rich source of Chinese treebanks. Extraction of Probabilistic Context Free Grammar (PCFG) from a treebank is straightforward [5]. This study adopted the Chart parsing algorithm in[3], that depicts each symbol position as a unique role using CFG grammar rules, This study started to consider that when a category plays different roles, the different probability distributions of its expanding rules will embody the subtlety of phrasing preferences.

Every node in the tree structure represents a part of speech. Moreover, every part of speech is assigned a unique score for calculating the Depth First Search (DFS) and Breadth First Search (BFS) scores.

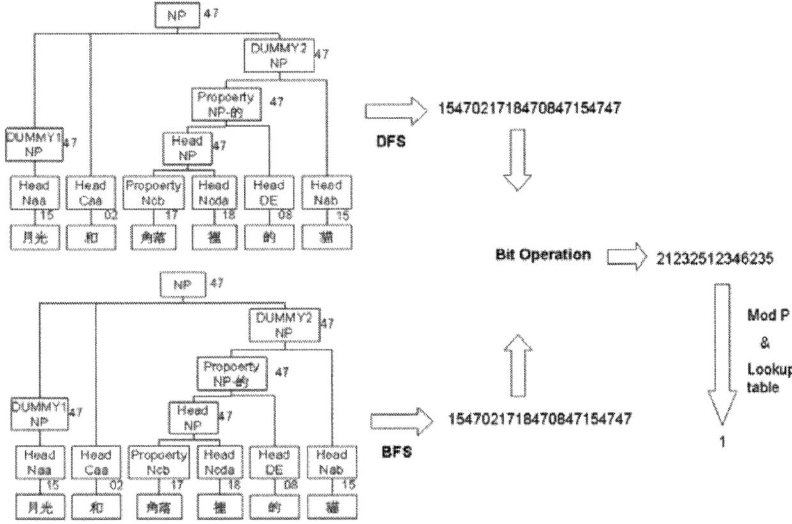

Fig. 5. Look up the residue value of the origin sentence

A residue value then can be obtained by a bit and mod operation. The quadratic residue key is used to perform the mod operation to look up quadratic residue table (see Fig. 5). Syntactic substitution is not performed when the residue values of the synonymous and origin sentences are the same. Otherwise, syntactic substitution is performed (see Fig. 6). After completing all syntactic substitutions, the watermark is embedded by synonym substitution.

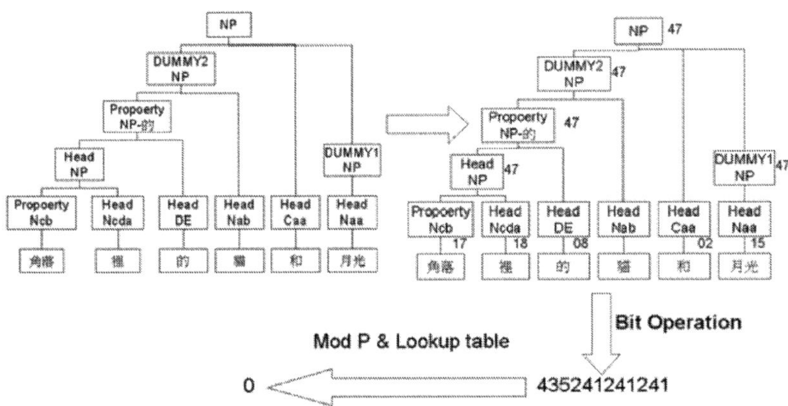

Fig. 6. Look up the residue value of the substitute sentence

In synonym substitution, the bit string of the watermark is taken to embed it in the text in order with one bit being embedded in each embedding. When 0 is embedded in the text, and the quadratic residue value in the current term is 1, then the substitution is performed. Otherwise, no substitution is required. Additionally, this study also considers semantics following substitution. Ciphertext should be similar to plaintext semantically. Thus, the embedding is said to be successful. The synonym selection rules in this study are as follows:

1. Opposite results in the quadratic residue table : A term may have numerous synonyms. If term substitution is required, then terms with opposite results need to be selected in the quadratic residue table.
2. The part of speech of the term should be exactly the same as the original term: A term may indicate numerous parts of speech in different scenarios. Therefore, the part of speech of the term should be considered in substitution.
3. Common usage: One or more synonyms with the same the part of speech. Thus, the corpuses should be used to select one synonym with higher common usage.

After selecting the synonyms through the above three rules, the appropriate synonym must be selected to preserve the same meaning, and can embed maxima watermark bits. All synonyms appear in the corpus, and thus can maintain their meaning unchanged. The Binary Tree based Synonyms Selection algorithm was proposed, which can select the synonym embed maxima watermark bits. The BTSS algorithm involves tree steps:

1. Translate all words in all synonyms to bit strings.
2. Construct the binary tree.
   (1) Group all synonyms together.
   (2) Divide all synonyms to two sub-groups by bit operation and Quadratic Residue Table lookup, as described in section 3.1.3. The bit operation is applied sequentially. Previously used bit operations cannot be reused.
   (3) Each sub-group should be divided into two sub-groups using step ii, until a sub-group has one synonym or no bit operations can be used.
3. Selecting the appropriate synonym embeds maxima watermark bits based on the watermark bit strings.

According to the above example, the term "賺取"(earn) has four synonyms {"創利"(make), "贏利"(profit), "盈利"(gain), "創收"(obtain)}. For the step1, all of the words in all synonyms, including the term "賺取", are translated to bit strings as listed in Table 3.

Table 3. Bit strings for each synonym

Term	Translated to bit strings for each words in term
賺取(earn)	『賺：10011』,『取：01001』
創利(make)	『創：11010』,『利：01101』
贏利(profit)	『贏：00111』,『利：01101』
盈利(gain)	『盈：10111』,『利：01101』
創收(obtain)	『創：11010』,『收：01110』

Step2 first used the bit operation OR to calculate each synonym and consult the Quadratic Residue Table. Table 4 lists the result.

Table 4. Quadratic Residue for each synonym

Term	Translated to bit strings for each words in term	Bit Operation OR	Quadratic Residue
賺取(earn)	『賺：10011』,『取：01001』	『賺取：11011』	0
創利(make)	『創：11010』,『利：01101』	『創利：11111』	0
贏利(profit)	『贏：00111』,『利：01101』	『贏利：01111』	0
盈利(gain)	『盈：00101』,『利：01101』	『盈利：01101』	1
創收(obtain)	『創：11010』,『收：01110』	『創收：11110』	1

Table 4 reveals that the terms "賺取"(earn), "創利"(make) and "贏利"(profit) are grouped together. Additionally, the terms "盈利"(gain) and "創收"(obtain) also are grouped together. The bit operation add(+) is used for the "盈利"(gain) and "創收"(obtain) group, and Table 5 shows the result.

Table 5. Quadratic Residue for each synonym in sub-group {盈利(gain), 創收(obtain)}

Term	Translated to bit strings for each words in Term	Bit Operation add	Quadratic Residue
盈利(gain)	『盈：00101』,『利：01101』	『盈利：10010』	1
創收(obtain)	『創：11010』,『收：01110』	『創收：01000』	0

From Table 5, the terms "盈利"(gain) and "創收"(obtain) are divided into two sub-groups. Figure 7 illustrates the Final Binary tree.

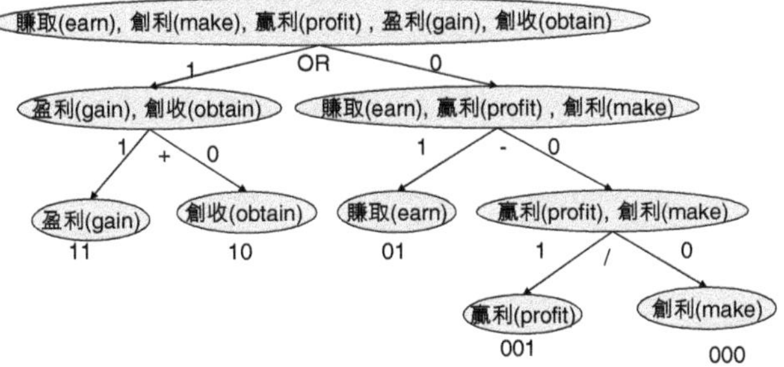

Fig. 7. The binary tree of synonyms

In step 3, the appropriate synonym embeds maxima watermark bits according to the watermark bit strings. If the watermark bit strings are 001, the term贏利(profit) is the appropriate synonym. Moreover, if the watermark bit strings are 11, then the term盈利(gain) is the appropriate synonym. The BTSS algorithm proposed here overcomes the drawback of one synonym only being able to encode one watermark bit. Because the BTSS algorithm is based on the binary tree, the average bits which can be embedded in synonyms are log N, where N denotes the number of synonyms.

3.1.5 Ciphertext Generation

The ciphertext is generated after the proceeding the above steps. Moreover, the author can spread the ciphertext in public. When unauthorized usage occurs the watermark can be extracted to demonstrate ownership. Section 3.2 describes how to extract the watermark from the text.

3.2 Watermark Extraction

The rapid development of a network multimedia environment has enabled digital data to be distributed faster and more easily than ever before. Duplicating digital data thus also has become easier than previously. The preceding section described how to embed the watermark in a text. Meanwhile, this section explains how to extract a watermark from a text when unauthorized usage is suspected. Except for the lack of synonym substitution, the other steps involved are similar. Figure 8 presents the process of watermark extraction.

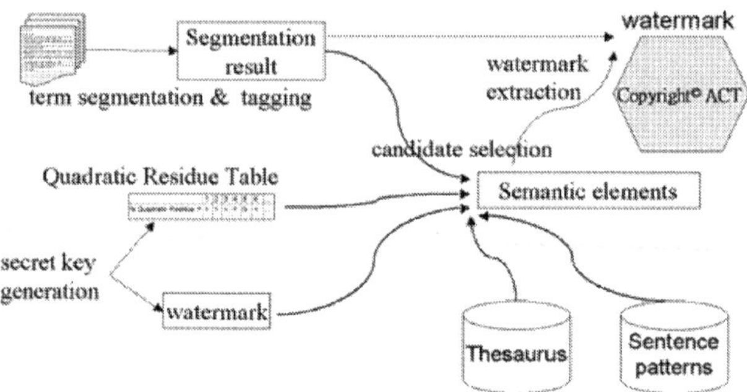

Fig. 8. Watermark extraction process

The first three steps, namely term segmentation and tagging, secret key generation and term selection, are the same as for watermark embedding. Following term selection, residue values can be looked up from the quadratic residue tale in the last step. Those residue values then can be assembled into a bit string. Finally, passed through transformation between the bit string and Unicode to exact the watermark.

4 Experiments

The training data are 200 related report documents dealing with the computer industry from III (Institute for Information Industry) and MIC (Market Intelligence Center). The average terms count of these documents is 1000. Moreover, the average sentences count of these documents is 150. Additionally, the average number of terms selected for hiding the watermark bit string is 120. Furthermore, the average number of sentences selected for hiding the watermark bit string is ten. Finally, the average number of synonyms for each term is three.

As described in section 3.1.4, the BTSS algorithm can enhance the numbers of watermark bits from one bit to log n bits per synonym. The watermark can be hidden in the text as often as possible. The numbers of times that watermark can be hidden depend on the length of the text. In the standard version, which does not use the BTSS algorithm, a relationship of ca. 1:10 exists between the encoded information and the protected text (e.g. for every ten terms of text one bit of watermark can be hidden). The version, which uses the BTSS algorithm, creates a relationship of ca. 1:6.6 between the encoded information and the protected text. Table 6 lists the experimental result.

Table 6. The experimental result

	Without BTSS	With BTSS
The average number of sentences	150	150
The average number of sentences selected for embedding watermark bit string	10	10
The average number of terms	1000	1000
The average number of terms selected for embedding watermark bit string	120	120
The average number of synonyms for one terms	3	3
Average bits hidden in one synonyms	1	1.5
Relationship of ca.	1:10	1:6.6

Two kinds of tests are conducted to measure the perceptual transparency. Blind test, where human subjects are presented with protected text without original text. Non-Blind test, where human subjects are presented with protected text with original text. The test data are fifty documents and ten people are invited to measure the perceptual transparency. The PSNR is used to measure the perceptual transparency. $PSNR = \frac{\sum U_i}{\sum S_i}$, where S_i is the total number of sentences for each document. And U_i is the total number of unsuitable sentences for each document. The PSNR in Blind test is 0.03 and in Non-Blind test is 0.0699. Table 6 lists the experimental result of transparency.

Table 7. The experimental result of transparency

	Blind test	Non-Blind test
The average number of sentences	150	150
The total number of sentences	75650	75650
The total number of unsuitable sentences	2270	5290
The average number of terms selected for embedding watermark bit string	0.0300	0.0699

5 Conclusions and Future Works

This study proposed a synonym-based watermarking algorithm, which is context rather than format based. The synonym-based watermarking is suitable for Chinese textual messages. The algorithm was designed to select appropriate candidate terms from textual messages for use in the embedding watermark. The binary tree encoding methodology of the synonym-based watermarking algorithm can select the suitable synonym, which embeds the maximum watermarking bits. The average watermarking lengths that can be encoded in one term are log n bits, where n denotes the total number of synonyms of the term. The encoding/decoding algorithm of the encryption key based watermark also is proposed, and enables higher watermark resilience. Besides extending the thesaurus to improve the reliability of synonym substitution, future efforts should explore the Syntactic and Semantic approaches that not only maintain consistent context semantics but also enable increased watermark resilience. In the Syntactic approach, watermark bits are hidden in the structure of sentences. The converting technology for the same meaningful sentence, including the co-reference, zero anaphora and grammar approaches, is used to deal with the problem of watermark encoding.

Acknowledgement. This research was supported by the III Innovative and Prospective Technologies Project of Institute for Information Industry and sponsored by MOEA, ROC

References

1. Brassil, J., Low, S., Maxemchuk, N., and O' Gorman, L., Electronic marking and identification techniques to discourage document copying. Proceedings of IEEE INFOCOM '94, 1994 3, pp. 1278–1287.
2. Brassil, J., Low, S., Maxemchuk, N., and O' Gorman, L. Hiding information in document images. Proceedings of the 29th Annual Conference on Information Sciences and Systems, 1995, pp. 482–489.
3. Charniak, E. 1997. Statistical parsing with a context-free grammar and word statistics. In Proceedings of NCAI-1997, pp 598–603.
4. Hardy, G. H. and Wright, E. M. "Quadratic Residues." §6.5 in An Introduction to the Theory of Numbers, 5th ed. Oxford, England: Clarendon Press, pp. 67–68, 1979.
5. Johnson, M. 1998. The effect of alternative tree representations on tree bank grammars. In Proceedings of the Joint Conference on New methods in Language Processing and Computational Natural Language Learning (NeMLaP3/CoNLL'98), pp 39–48.
6. Low, S., Maxemchuk, N., Brassil, J., and O' Gorman, L., Document marking and identification using both line and word shifting. Proceedings of IEEE INFOCOM '95, 1995.
7. M. Atallah, V. Raskin, C. F. Hempelmann, M. Karahan, R. Sion, K. E. Triezenberg, U. Topkara, "Natural Language Watermarking and Tamperproofing", Proc. of the Information Hiding Workshop IHW 2002, Lecture Notes in Computer Sciences, Springer Verlag (LNCS)
8. Mikhail J. Atallah, Victor Raskin, Michael Crogan, Christian Hempelmann, Florian Kerschbaum, Dina Mohamed, and Sanket Naik. "Natural Language Watermarking: Design, Analysis, and Proof-of-Concept Implementation" published in the Proceedings of the 4th International Information Hiding Workshop, Pittsburgh, Pennsylvania, April 25–27, 2001.
9. Xia, Fei; Palmer, Martha; Xue, Nianwen; Okurowski, Mary Ellen; Kovarik, John; Chiou, Fu-Dong; Kroch, Tony and Marcus, Mitch (2000) Developing Guidelines and Ensuring Consistency for Chinese Text Annotation in Second International Conference on Language Resources and Evaluation (LREC-2000) pp. 3–10.

Resilient Information Hiding for Abstract Semi-structures*

Radu Sion, Mikhail Atallah, and Sunil Prabhakar

Computer Sciences Department and
The Center for Education and Research in Information Assurance,
Purdue University, West Lafayette, IN, 47907, USA,
{sion,mja,sunil}@cs.purdue.edu

Abstract. Most work on watermarking has resulted in techniques for different types of data: image, audio, video, text/language, software, etc. In this paper we discuss the watermarking of abstract structured aggregates of multiple types of content, such as multi-type/media documents. These *semi-structures* can be usually represented as graphs and are characterized by value lying both in the structure *and* in the individual nodes. Example instances include XML documents, complex web content, workflow and planning descriptions, etc. We propose a scheme for watermarking abstract semi-structures and discuss its resilience with respect to attacks. While content specific watermarking deals with the issue of protecting the value in the structure's nodes, protecting the value pertaining to the structure itself is a new, distinct challenge. Nodes in semi-structures are value-carrying, thus a watermarking algorithm could make use of their encoding capacity by using traditional watermarking. For example if a node contains an image then image watermarking algorithms can be deployed for that node to encode parts of the global watermark. But, given the intrinsic value attached to it, the graph that "glues" these nodes together is in itself a central element of the watermarking process we propose. We show how our approach makes use of these two value facets, structural and node-content.

1 Introduction

Digital Watermarking, in the traditional sense [5] [6] can be summarized as a steganographic technique embedding un-detectable (un-perceivable) hidden information into media objects (i.e. images, audio, video, text) with the main purpose of protecting the data from unauthorized duplication and distribution by enabling provable ownership. More recent results take on various other data domains such as natural language processing [1], software [4] [10] and relational

* Portions of this work were supported by Grants EIA-9903545, IIS-0325345, IIS-0219560, IIS-0312357, IIS-9985019, IIS-9972883 and IIS-0242421 from the National Science Foundation, Contract N00014-02-1-0364 from the Office of Naval Research, by sponsors of the Center for Education and Research in Information Assurance and Security, and by Purdue Discovery Park's e-enterprise Center.

T. Kalker et al. (Eds.): IWDW 2003, LNCS 2939, pp. 141–153, 2004.
© Springer-Verlag Berlin Heidelberg 2004

data [13], [11]. Here we introduce an algorithm for watermarking abstract structured aggregates of multiple types of content that can be usually represented as graphs and are characterized by value lying both in the structure *and* in the individual nodes (e.g. XML documents, complex Web Content, workflow and planning descriptions).

Most media watermarking techniques make use of the inherent large noise-bandwidth associated with Works that are to be "consumed" by the human sensory system with its limitations. In the case of abstract semi-structures, watermarking bandwidth appears to be available from capacities associated to properties of both the graph and the composing nodes. This introduces a whole new set of challenges and associated trade-offs. The trade-off between a required level of mark resilience and the ability to maintain guaranteed error bounds, structural equivalence and higher level semantics needs to be explored. Our solution is based on a canonical labeling algorithm that self-adjusts to the specifics of the content. Labeling is tolerant to a significant number of graph attacks ("surgeries") and relies on a complex "training" phase at watermarking time in which it reaches an optimal stability point with respect to these attacks. We perform attack experiments on the introduced algorithms under different conditions.

The paper is structured as follows. Section 2 is dedicated to a more in depth presentation of generic issues associated with watermarking in the framework of semi-structures. We analyze associated challenges and discuss attacks. Section 3 introduces important building blocks and concepts for the presented semi-structure watermarking algorithm, such as *tolerant canonical labeling* and *tolerant content summaries*. It presents and analyzes the main algorithm. Section 4.2 discusses experimental results. The **wmx.*** package is introduced. Section 5 concludes.

2 Challenges

2.1 The Model

One fundamental difference between watermarking and generic data hiding resides in the main applicability and descriptions of the two domains. Data hiding in general and covert communication in particular, aims at enabling Alice and Bob to exchange messages in a manner as stealthy as possible, through a medium controlled by evil Mallory. On the other hand, digital watermarking (especially for rights assessment) is deployed by Alice to prove rights over a piece of data, to Jared the Judge, usually in the case when Mallory benefits from using/selling that very same piece of data or maliciously modified versions of it.

In digital watermarking, the actual value to be protected lies in the Works themselves whereas information hiding usually makes use of them as simple value "transporters". Rights assessment can be achieved by demonstrating that a particular Work exhibits a rare property (read "hidden message" or "watermark"), usually known only to Alice (with the aid of a "secret" - read "watermarking key"). For court convince-ability purposes this property needs to be so rare that if one considers any other random Work "similar enough" to the one in question, this property is "very improbable" to apply (i.e. bound on false-positives). There is a threshold determining Jared's convince-ability related to the "very improbable" assessment. This defines a main difference from steganography: from Jared's perspective, specifics of the property (e.g. watermark message) are irrelevant as long as Alice can prove "convincingly" it is she who embedded/induced it to the original (non-watermarked) Work.

It is to be stressed here this particularity of watermarking for rights assessment. In watermarking the emphasis is on "detection" rather than "extraction". Extraction of a watermark (or bits of it) is usually a part of the detection process but just complements the process up to the extent of increasing the ability to convince in court. If recovering the watermark data in itself becomes more important than detecting the actual existence of it (i.e. 'yes/no answer') then this is a drift toward covert communication and pure steganography.

2.2 Semi-structures

When dealing with graphs in general and semi-structures in particular, we are faced with the issue of uniquely identifying and referencing nodes [1]. In graph theory, this is summarized under the term *canonical labeling* [2] [3] [7] [9] and no solution has been provided with a high enough degree of generality.

Thus, before deploying any specific mark encoding techniques we have to ensure a resilient labeling scheme, able to survive minor modifications and attacks on the actual graph structure. We show how content specific watermarking techniques (for node content watermarking) coupled with a technique of content summarization provide a resilient labeling scheme, suited for our watermarking purposes. The value-carrying nodes are solving the labeling issue in quite a surprising manner.

2.3 Attacks

Given a certain value carrying watermarked semi-structure several attack options present themselves, including: elimination of value-"insignificant" nodes (A1), elimination of inter node relations (A2), value preserving graph partitioning into independent usable partitions (A3), modification of node content, within usability vicinity (A4), addition of value insignificant nodes aimed at destroying ulterior labeling attempts (A5). One has to keep in mind the ultimate goal of any attack, namely eliminating the watermark property, while preserving most of the attached value, within usability limits [2].

In order to prevent success for A5, we propose a preliminary step of **value pruning** in which all value-insignificant nodes are marked as to-be-ignored in

[1] Especially if required to maintain consistency *before* and *after* attacks (e.g. possible structural changes).

[2] Collusion attacks are not discussed in this paper as they are relevant when fingerprinting is deployed. Although we envision extensions of this work for fingerprinting, we are not considering these here.

the ulterior watermarking steps. Another approach deploys structural changes to bring the semi-structure to the limits of the usability space [12], increasing its fragility to further modifications and thus the failure likelihood of any ulterior attempts to attack by adding nodes. A4 mandates the ability of the labeling scheme to depend as little as possible on node content or to provide for a mechanism of detecting altered-content nodes at extraction time. Another possibility of defending against A4 would be to actually alter the main considered nodes toward their allowed fragility limit, such that any further un-knowledgeable changes will fail to provide a usable result. Attack A3 is one of the most powerful challenges. In order to survive it, meaning that the watermark has to be preserved (maybe in a weaker form) also in the resulting graph's partitions, the watermarking scheme has to consider some form of hierarchical embedding in such a way as to "touch" most of the potential partitions in the graph. The issue becomes more complex if the usability domains of all possible graph partitions are unknown, making it difficult to envision the attacker's "cut". Fortunately, in many cases (see Scenarios) the number of available partitioning schemes that make sense and the associated usability domains are limited. Cases A1 and A2 make it necessary to devise a node labeling scheme that tolerates node and edge elimination while preserving most of the other nodes' labels. This is a must because of the necessity to reference nodes at extraction time. Even if there would exist a working traditional canonical graph labeling algorithm it would need to be heavily modified in order to provide for edge and node removal tolerance. We used the term "heavily" to outline the fact that canonical labeling has always been linked to proofs of graph isomorphism, whereas in this case the trend is aimed exactly toward the opposite, namely preserving node labels in the context of admittedly slight graph changes.

3 Solution

3.1 Tolerant Canonical Labeling

The node labeling scheme is at the heart of watermarking semi-structures. The ability to identify and reference nodes within the to-be-watermarked structure is of paramount importance and the labeling scheme has to take into account the specifics of the case, in particular the requirement to be able to "recognize" all relevant nodes in an attacked version of the graph, based on labels issued on the original one.

Although canonical labeling for graphs was known for a long time to be a hard problem of graph theory, specific algorithms have been developed for some cases . In particular, reasonable solutions have been proposed for tree canonical labeling and apparently, many semi-structure watermarking applications (e.g. HTML) would fit the assumption of tree structuring. One can partition existing value-carrying semi-structures into a set of tree-shapes and remaining structural elements. Watermarking only those partitions might provide enough power and reduce the problem to tree shapes. Unfortunately the requirement of being able to label nodes consistently before and especially *after* attacks, renders useless existing tree canonical labeling algorithms due to their high fragility to any changes (e.g. attacks) made to the structure.

Fortunately, the dual nature of semi-structures enables a novel approach to labeling, the main idea being the use of a combination of structural and node content information.

On the one hand, content is combined in computing a node's label by using a special "tolerant" summary (i.e. a function of the content with specific properties, see Section 3.2) of its content. The assumption here is that content changes are small and that we are able to construct a function of the node content that will basically degrade gracefully with minor alterations to its input. On the other hand some node topology information is necessarily involved in the relative position of the node versus its neighbors and the entire graph. One simple solution that comes to mind is to use the neighbors' labels, which does capture the position of the current node in relationship to its neighbors, and through the entire labeling scheme, applied recursively, to the graph as a whole. Thus the primitive labeling algorithm can be summarized by the following iterative formula:

$$l(node) = \alpha * l(node) + \gamma * \sum_{nb \in neighbors(node)} l(nb)$$

Note: α determines the "weight" of the node content in the labeling scheme. If essential content changes are unlikely in an attack, α is to be increased so as to provide labeling stability. γ provides control over being able to more specifically localize the node with respect to the neighbors and also to the entire graph. If structural changes are highly unlikely in the course of an attack an increased γ provides for stability [3].

The algorithm starts with the initial labels as being the keyed tolerant content summary values $SUMMARY(key, content(node), key)$ (see section 3.2).

Step One. The first step performs a number of iterations i over the formula above (this number being kept as part of the watermark detection key and used later on in re-labeling the attacked graph), until the necessary labeling provisions are met. At this stage we are mainly concerned with a minimal number of identical labels [4].

Step Two. In order to provide resilience to a certain number of graph modifications ("surgery"), the next step is to artificially degrade the graph and re-perform step one again.

Intuitively (for experimental results see Section 4.2), removing and/or adding nodes and relations to the graph will result in changes in the initial labeling

[3] It might be interesting to note the fact that if γ is 0, this labeling scheme converges to a simple intuitive content-based addressing scheme.

[4] A number of iterations at least equal to the diameter of the graph are necessary in order to localize a given node with respect to the entire graph. But this is sometimes not desired nor required. The ability to set the number of performed iterations and make it part of the recovery key is another point of control over the labeling scheme.

performed on an un-modified graph. Control over those changes is enabled by specifying the α and γ values. Experiments show that, given a graph, for certain α and γ value bounds, labeling becomes controllable.

The result of step two, for each node, is a range of values for the corresponding label, depending also on the three main control factors (step-one iteration number, α, γ). The actual label of the node will be defined by the lower and upper bounds of the resulting labeling range. This basically ensures that, when labeling the attacked/modified version of the graph (i.e. by performing step one of this same algorithm later on, in court), the resulting labels will fall within the corresponding node's label interval with a high likelihood. For a given set of surgeries, performing the labeling algorithm in the space of (α, γ, i) results in a "bounded space of labeling points" (see Figure 1).

The next challenge is to identify an optimum in this "space", given a certain ability to compare two particular "points". Remember that a "point" corresponds to a labeled graph as a set of interval-labels for the graph's nodes, given the particular (α, γ, i) coordinates. Our initial comparison formula for two different graph interval-label sets aims at capturing optimality in terms of both minimal number of label overlaps within each set as well as minimal potential for future overlap. If the two considered "points" are the actual interval-label sets $A = \{(a_{11}, a_{12}), ..., (a_{n1}, a_{n2})\}$ and $B = \{(b_{11}, b_{12}), ..., (b_{n1}, b_{n2})\}$ (i.e. (a_{i1}, a_{i2}) is the label-interval corresponding to node i in the graph labeling A) then the comparison formula is

$$compare_1(A, B) = \text{overlaps(B)} \times \text{avg\_overlap(B)} - \text{overlaps(A)} \times \text{avg\_overlap(A)}$$
$$compare_2(A, B) = \text{closest\_inter\_label\_size(A)} - \text{closest\_inter\_label\_size(B)}$$
$$compare(A, B) = compare_1(A, B) + compare_2(A, B)$$

where *overlaps(X)* is the number of overlapping interval-labels in labeling X, *avg_overlap(X)* the average interval size of the overlapping portions and *closest_inter_label_size(X)* the size of the interval between the closest two interval-labels in X. Intuitively, $compare_1()$ models and compares the current optimality of both labelings and $compare_2()$ captures the potential for future overlap (i.e. because having very "close" interval-labels hints to possible issues in labeling the graph in an attacked version of it).

What happens if overlapping labeling intervals (i.e. "colliding composite labels") occur ?

- If nodes are in virtually identical/indistinguishable positions and with similar content then this is normal. The nodes are marked as such and treated identical throughout the watermarking process.
- If nodes differ in content but positions are similar, or content is close but positions are different, then variations in α, γ and the content summary key are performed in such a way as to differentiate labels
- If nodes differ in both content and position, changing also the iteration number in step one is required.
- If everything has been done and label intervals are still overlapping we can simply "melt" the labels together and treats the nodes as in case 1 (i.e. identical).

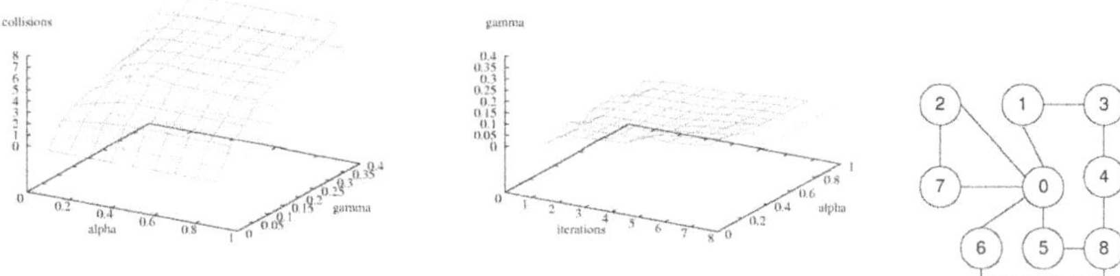

Fig. 1. (a) The surface defining the composite label collisions appearing after 4 stages of training (i.e. $i = 4$) with a random generated set of surgeries applied to the graph. It is to be noted that lower γ values seem to yield a lower number of composite label collisions but in turn results in a lower resistance to structural attacks (i.e. as labeling will not be as resilient to graph surgeries). (b) The zero-collision (for composite labels) surface in the (iterations,alpha,gamma) space corresponding to the same set of surgeries. Its existence proves the ability to label resiliently (to the considered surgeries) without colliding resulting composite labels. Computed using the **wmx.*** package. (c) The considered graph.

In summary, the labeling process (i) collects all relevant labeling data over a number of iterations in which all of (α, γ, numbers of step-one iterations (i), content summary key and number of performed surgeries) are varied, and then (ii) decides upon a certain point in this space (defined by α, γ, i, content summary key and number of performed surgeries) which minimizes the number of overlapping label intervals and the potential for future overlaps (in case of attacks). By adapting to the given structure (i.e. through adjusting of α, γ, etc), the labeling algorithm allows for control over the required trade-offs between label resilience and tolerated graph changes [5].

3.2 Tolerant Content Summaries

Finding an appropriate (set of) content summary function(s) that satisfy the requirements above is not trivial and strongly tied to the type of semi-structure node content and its associated transforms and envisioned attacks. The main requirements of the content summary functions considered are *the ability to be at the same time quite content specific while also degrading gracefully with minor changes in the content.* The idea is to capture and quantify certain global specific properties of the content that are still preserved in the watermarking/attack process. Research by Ari Juels et. al. [8] investigates a related notion, suggestively qualified as "fuzzy commitment".

[5] Special consideration needs to be offered to the case of an attack modifying all existing nodes' content in a similar fashion. Alteration to the labeling scheme can be prevented in this case by introducing an additional final step of globally normalizing the labels (label intervals).

```
label(graph G)
  foreach node n do label(n) = SUMMARY(key, n)
  for (α = 0.1; α < 0.9; α = α + 0.1)
    for (γ = 0.1; γ < 0.9; γ = γ + 0.1)
      foreach artificial graph "surgery" (i.e. expected attacks) do
        perform surgery (remove node/relation(s))
        for (iteration = 1; iteration < diameter(G); iteration + +)
          foreach node n do
            label(n) = α × label(n) + γ × Σ_neighbors(n) label(nb)
        foreach node n do store label(n)
      foreach node n do store clabel(n) = [min(label(n)), max(label(n))]
  choose (α, γ) minimizing the number of overlapping label intervals
```

Fig. 2. Labeling Algorithm.

In our implementation we used a simple content summary, a linear combination of the high order bits of the node content. The assumption here was that high order bits are reasonably stable to changes and attacks. Other applications require different consideration. In the case of JPEG content for example, frequency domain transforms like the DCT could be considered. The tolerant summary of a JPEG file would be a combination of the most significant bits of its significant DCT coefficients etc. Feature extraction algorithms (e.g. property histograms) should be also investigated for multimedia content as a means to provide a tolerant content summary.

3.3 Watermarking Algorithm

The main idea behind our algorithm is to use the structural resilience of the labeling scheme while leveraging content-specific one-bit watermarking methods for each node. In other words, each node in the semi-structure is considered to be a potential recipient of a one-bit watermark (using a traditional content-type specific marking method), while the actual instances of these encodings are going to be determined in a secret fashion by the node labels.

Let *clabels*() be the composite labeling intervals as computed above (see Section 3.1). Depending on the size of the intervals in *clabels*(), choose b as the maximal number of most significant bits that can be considered in the numbers of every interval such that $\forall (x,y)_j \in clabels(), msb(x,b) = msb(y,b)$, where $msb(x,b)$ are the most significant b bits of x. In other words we aim to discover an interval-specific invariant. For each node j and corresponding interval $(x,y)_j$ by notation, let $msb_j = msb(x,b)$.

Let k be a seed to a b-bit random number generator RND and $k_1, ..., k_n$ the first n b-bit random numbers produced by RND after a secret initial warm-up run. We say that node j is "fit" for encoding iff $(msb_j \oplus k_j) \bmod e = 0$, where e is a adjustable encoding parameter determining the percentage of considered nodes. In other words, a node is considered "fit" if its label satisfies a certain secret criteria. On the one hand this ensures the secrecy and resilience of our method, on the other hand, it effectively "modulates" the watermark encoding process according to the actual graph structure. This naturally provides a witness and rights "protector" for the structure itself.

```
embed(G, wm, k, e)
  clabels() = label(graph)
  b = {max(z)|∀(x,y)_j ∈ clabels(), msb(x,z) = msb(y,z)}
  initialize RND(k)
  i = 0
  sort clabels()
  foreach (x,y)_k ∈ clabels() do
    k_j = RND()
    if ((msb(x,b) ⊕ k_j) mod e = 0) then
      content_wm_node(k,(wm_i ⊕ lsb(k_j,1)),k_j)
      i = i + 1
```

```
detect(G, k, e, b)
  clabels() = label(graph)
  initialize RND(k)
  i = 0
  sort clabels()
  foreach (x,y)_k ∈ clabels() do
    k_j = RND()
    if ((msb(x,b) ⊕ k_j) mod e = 0) then
      wm_i = content_det_node(k,k_j)
      i = i + 1
```

Fig. 3. (a) Watermark Embedding Algorithm (b) Watermark Detection Algorithm

Each node considered fit is then watermarked with the one-bit watermark defined by the XOR between the least significant bit of its corresponding k_j and $wm_i, i \in (0, |wm|)$ the corresponding watermark bit. Because of the e factor we have an average guaranteed bandwidth of $\frac{n}{e}$. In case the watermark length $|wm|$ is less than $\frac{n}{e}$, we can choose for example, the watermark bit ($\frac{n}{e}$ mod $|wm|$), effectively deploying a majority voting scheme etc. The 1-bit watermark embedding uses traditional (node) content-watermarking techniques. Because these do not constitute the main contribution of this research, in our abstract watermarking suite we considered a simple place-holder, in which each node contains a large integer value. A "1" watermark bit is considered to be present when the value is odd, a "0" otherwise.

Note: The key used in the content-watermarking technique can be the same k_j or any other agreed upon secret. There might be some benefit associated with using the *same* single key for all nodes as this could defeat inter-node collusion attacks (in which the same node content is watermarked with different keys). It is also assumed that the content watermarking method deployed is respecting the maximum allowable distortion bounds associated with the given content. In particular, these node content-specific constraints are not impacting structural consistency. In other words, slight modifications to the actual node content (e.g. JPEG images or natural language text) do not alter global structural consistency constraints. This is subject to further research.

In the decoding phase, the *clabels*() set is re-computed. The result should be identical (in case no alterations occurred) or fairly close (because of the inherent labeling tolerance to alterations). We know $k_1, ..., k_n$, the secret node-selection keys and b. Based on these values and the composite labels, the algorithm performs node-selection and identifies a majority (or all in the case of some graph alterations occurring) of the initial nodes that were watermarked. Content-specific watermark detection is then applied to each node to retrieve each watermark bit.

In order to perform error correction, if enough bandwidth is available (e.g. n is large enough), the algorithm embeds multiple copies of the watermark (or any other error correction encoding). Upon detection, majority voting is deployed to increase the likelihood of accurate detection.

3.4 Discussion

What happens if we cannot discover a "nice enough" b ? That is, what happens if different label intervals in *clabels*() are behaving so "wildly" apart that b is going to be really small. In other words, what if there exists a node whose composite label interval has its endpoints very very far away such that the MSB common bits are just a few, or even none.

We would argue that this is a highly unlikely scenario and experiments confirm it. But if it is indeed the case then we have several options, one of which is simply ignoring the label(s) that are having far-away endpoints. Another option would be to introduce an initial normalizing step in which all the labels are normalized with respect to a common "average" value (e.g. means of means).

In order to fight false-positive claims in court we ask: What is the probability of a given watermark of length m to be detected in a random graph of size n. The assumption is of course that $m < \frac{n}{e}$. It is easy to prove that this probability is $(\frac{1}{2})^m$. In case multiple embeddings are used (e.g. majority voting) and all available bits are utilized, this probability decreases even more to $(\frac{1}{2})^{\frac{n}{e}}$. For example, in the case of a structure with 60 nodes and with $e = 3$, this probability reads *one in a million*, reasonably low.

In the absence of additional information, Mallory, faced with the issue of destroying the watermark while preserving the value of the data, has only one alternative available, namely a random attack. Two sub-types of attacks present themselves as outlined in Section 2.3: structural and node-content altering.

Structural attacks are handled by the tolerant nature of the labeling scheme and an experimental analysis is presented in Section 4.2. Here we are concerned with the node-content alteration attacks. We ask: what is the probability of success of such an attack ? In other words, if an attacker starts to randomly alter a total number of a nodes and succeeds in each case to flip the embedded watermark bit with a success rate p, what is the probability of success of altering at least $r, r < a$ watermark bits in the result, $P(r, a)$? It can be shown that $P(r, a) = \sum_{i=r}^{a} [aCi] \times p^a \times (1-p)^{a-i}$.

Now, remember that only every e-th node is watermarked, thus the attacker effectively attacks only an average of $\frac{a}{e}$ nodes actually watermarked. If $r > \frac{a}{e}$ then $P(r, a) = 0$. In the case of $r < \frac{a}{e}$ we have we have the corrected version

$$P(r,a) = \sum_{i=r}^{(\frac{a}{e})} [(\frac{a}{e})Ci] \times p^{(\frac{a}{e})} \times (1-p)^{(\frac{a}{e})-i}$$

If $r = 4$, $p = 10\%$, $a = 20$ (33% of the nodes are altered by the attacker !) and $e = 4$, we have $P(4,20) \approx 55 \times 10^{-6}$, again a reasonable figure, reading *fifty-five in a million*. Space constraints do not allow for a more in-depth analysis.

4 Implementation and Experiments

4.1 The wmx.* Package

wmx.* is our java software test-bed package for watermarking abstract semi-structures. We developed and implemented the algorithms presented and experimented with various semi-structured shapes. The package allows for dynamic generation and storing of graphs, graph surgeries and attacks, as well as for run-time customizable labeling and watermarking parameters (e.g. α, γ, *iterations*, *collision_bounds*). In the experiments, most of the nodes were defined as allowing for specific node content watermarking that encodes one bit per node.

Given the low probability of attack and false-positives discussed above in Section 3.4, one thing we believe needs to be analyzed in more detail is the actual feasibility and resilience of the labeling method. Given its importance to the overall algorithm, we implemented a test suite that allows experiments on abstract, dynamically redefine-able structures composed of a customizable number of nodes with associated random generated (or predefined) content. We then extended the package to allow for watermarking of abstract define-able semi-structures. We performed experiments on structures with varying number of nodes and levels of connectedness. The computations were conducted on a 500Mhz PC with 128MB RAM running Linux. Code was written in Java.

4.2 Experiments

One of our main concern was labeling collisions, i.e. composite label sets *clabels*() in which multiple labeling intervals are overlapping. These appear as a result of the training surgery phase, in which modifications are performed to the graph to produce the new label set. It is bad news as it creates potential ambiguity in the detection process. Surprisingly, in most cases, by adjusting the labeling training parameters $\alpha, \gamma, iterations$ we could obtain points that did feature zero collisions. In Figure 4 we show the zero-collision surfaces (in the α, γ space, with 3 training iterations) for two simple structures.

The considered set of training surgeries (i.e. the set of surgeries performed on the original graph before each individual labeling iteration) was randomly computer-generated from a set of global surgeries and included periferic node removals, edge additions and removals. (To be noted that this is consistent with the assumptions made in section 2.3 when discussing attack A5).

In Figure 4 (c) we show the watermark behavior in the case of a random artificially generated structure with 32 nodes and 64 edges. The embedded watermark

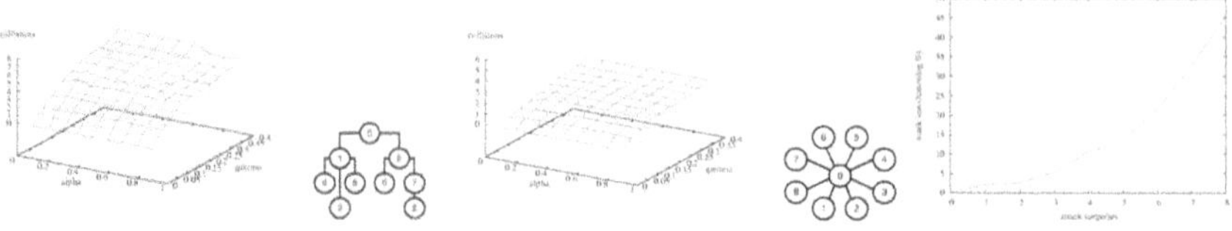

Fig. 4. Surfaces defining the composite label collisions appearing after 3 stages of training with a random generated set of surgeries. (a) Tree shaped graph. Much of the web content online is tree-shaped. Again, note that lower γ values seem to yield a lower number of composite label collisions, with drawbacks as presented in figure 1 (b). (b) Star shaped graph. Note the smoother shape and the lower collision bounds, compared to (a). The same nodes were used, differently interconnected. Computed using the **wmx.*** package. (c) Averaged watermark loss over 10 runs of an 8 bit watermark embedded into an arbitrary 32 node graph with 64 edges. Surgery attacks are applied randomly (node removals 60%, link addition 20%, link removal 20%). The labeling scheme was trained for 3 surgeries.

is 8 bits long. The labeling scheme was trained for 3 surgeries, also $e = 3$ (average bandwidth available is thus 10.6 bits, enough for the 8 bit watermark). It can be seen how composite labeling training results in highly resilient labels. As the number of attack surgeries increases, the watermark degrades slightly. The results are averaged over 10 runs on the same graph with different random attacks. When 8 attack surgeries are applied to the graph we can still recover 60-65% of the watermark. One has to consider also the fact that an attacker is bound not to modify the structure too much as it will eventually distort.

5 Conclusions

We introduced an algorithm for rights protection watermarking of semi-structured content. More specifically we are concerned with protecting the value inherent in the structure itself. Various new challenges are associated with this new domain. Benefiting from the dual nature of semi-structures, our algorithm makes use of both the available node content as well as of the value-carrying structure, through the processes of canonical labeling, node content summarization and content-specific mark encoding. The idea behind content-specific mark encoding is to use traditional known watermarking techniques, in encoding parts of the watermark in the node content. Providing a canonical labeling scheme, "trained" to tolerance for a set of graph modifications is essential in being able to later-on identify nodes selected in the 1-bit node mark content-specific encoding process. Our algorithm does not require the original un-watermarked object in order to perform mark detection. Further work is required in improving content summarization and tolerant labeling. Different application domains will require specific approaches. An alternative idea would be using bandwidth available in the specifications of inter-node relations.

References

1. M.J. Atallah, V. Raskin, C. F. Hempelmann, M. Karahan, R. Sion, K. E. Triezenberg, and U. Topkara. Natural language watermarking and tamperproofing. In *Lecture Notes in Computer Science, Proc. 5th International Information Hiding Workshop 2002*. Springer Verlag, 2002.
2. L. Babai and L. Kucera. Canonical labeling of graphs in linear average time. In *Proc. 20th IEEE Symposium on Foundations of Computer Science*, 39–46., 1979.
3. L. Babai and E. Luks. Canonical labeling of graphs. In *Fifteenth Annual ACM Symposium on Theory of Computing*, pages 171–183. ACM, 1983.
4. Christian Collberg and Clark Thomborson. Software watermarking: Models and dynamic embeddings. In *Principles of Programming Languages*, San Antonio, TX, January 1999.
5. Ingemar Cox, Jeffrey Bloom, and Matthew Miller. Digital watermarking. In *Digital Watermarking*. Morgan Kaufmann, 2001.
6. Stefan Katzenbeisser (editor) and Fabien Petitcolas (editor). Information hiding techniques for steganography and digital watermarking. In *Information Hiding Techniques for Steganography and Digital Watermarking*. Artech House, 2001.
7. Faulon J. Automorphism partitioning and canonical labeling can be solved in polynomial time for molecular graphs. In *J. Chem. Inf. Comput. Sci.* 38, 1998, 432–444., 1998.
8. Ari Juels and Martin Wattenberg. A fuzzy commitment scheme. In *ACM Conference on Computer and Communications Security*, pages 28–36, 1999.
9. Ludek Kucera. Canonical labeling of regular graphs in linear average time. In *IEEE Symposium on Foundations of Computer Science*, pages 271–279, 1987.
10. J. Palsberg, S. Krishnaswamy, M. Kwon, D. Ma, Q. Shao, and Y. Zhang. Experience with software watermarking. In *Proceedings of ACSAC, 16th Annual Computer Security Applications Conference*, pages 308–316, 2000.
11. Radu Sion. Proving ownership over categorical data. In *Proceedings of the IEEE International Conference on Data Engineering ICDE 2004*, 2004.
12. Radu Sion, Mikhail Atallah, and Sunil Prabhakar. Power: Metrics for evaluating watermarking algorithms. In *Proceedings of IEEE ITCC 2002, CERIAS TR 2001-55*. IEEE Computer Society Press, 2002.
13. Radu Sion, Mikhail Atallah, and Sunil Prabhakar. Rights protection for relational data. In *CERIAS-TR 2002-28, Proceedings of ACM SIGMOD*, 2003.

Model-Based Steganography

Phil Sallee

University of California, Davis
Davis, CA 95616, USA
sallee@cs.ucdavis.edu
http://redwood.ucdavis.edu/phil

Abstract. This paper presents an information-theoretic method for performing steganography and steganalysis using a statistical model of the cover medium. The methodology is general, and can be applied to virtually any type of media. It provides answers for some fundamental questions which have not been fully addressed by previous steganographic methods, such as how large a message can be hidden without risking detection by certain statistical methods, and how to achieve this maximum capacity. Current steganographic methods have been shown to be insecure against fairly simple statistical attacks. Using the model-based methodology, an example steganography method is proposed for JPEG images which achieves a higher embedding efficiency and message capacity than previous methods while remaining secure against first order statistical attacks.

1 Introduction

Steganography, derived from the Greek words for 'covered writing', is the science of hiding information so that it remains undetected except by its intended receiver. It is necessary when one wishes to communicate privately without arousing the suspicion that would be caused by sending an encrypted message in plain view. The secret communication is hidden inside a larger message, referred to as the *cover message*, which can be transmitted without arousing any suspicion. The resulting message which contains the hidden content is referred to as the *stego message* or *steganogram*. A number of methods have been proposed for hiding messages in digital media including JPEG images, and MP3 audio files[8, 12,9]. Current methods generally encode the messages in the least significant bits (LSBs) of the cover media coefficients. While such LSB encoding is often not detectable by visual inspection, it can alter the statistical properties of the coefficients in easily detectable ways [12,11]. This is because by altering the LSBs indiscriminately, the marginal statistics (histograms) of the coefficient values will be changed in ways that make steganographic tampering evident.

By reducing the size of the message, these kinds of statistical signatures can be made less evident. Obviously, however, one would prefer to use a steganography method that is secure despite having a large capacity, where capacity is defined as the ratio between the size of the message and the size of the cover

T. Kalker et al. (Eds.): IWDW 2003, LNCS 2939, pp. 154–167, 2004.
© Springer-Verlag Berlin Heidelberg 2004

data in which it is hidden [12]. Recently, some methods have been devised which offer reasonably high capacity steganography while attempting to preserve the marginal statistics of the cover coefficients. One such method for encoding messages inside JPEG images is F5 [12]. Rather than flipping LSBs to encode the message bits, F5 increments and decrements coefficient values in order to maintain coefficient histograms that appear unaltered. However, it has been shown that F5 still changes the histograms of the coefficients in a detectable way. By estimating the original histograms of the coefficients from a cropped and re-JPEG'd version of the image, differences between the steganogram's histograms and the estimated original histograms become evident [7]. Another method which preserves marginal statistics more successfully is the OutGuess algorithm[9]. OutGuess reserves around half of the available coefficients for the purpose of correcting the statistical deviations in the global coefficient histogram caused by changing LSBs in the other half. For example, if a coefficient's value was moved from histogram bin A to bin B during the encoding process, another coefficient has to be moved from bin B to bin A to correct this change. While this is effective at maintaining the global histogram of the coefficients, it reduces the capacity by about half.

This raises the following types of questions: Is it possible to avoid detection by attacks that rely on marginal statistics of the coefficients without sacrificing half of the message capacity? What is the maximum message size that can be embedded in a given cover medium without risking detection? How can we achieve this maximum capacity? For answers, we turn to a new methodology based on statistical modeling and information theory. This paper presents a general framework for performing steganography and steganalysis using a statistical model of the cover media. To demonstrate the value of the model-based approach, an example steganography method is proposed for JPEG images which achieves a higher message capacity than previous methods while remaining secure against first order statistical attacks.

2 General Methodology

2.1 Compression and Steganography

Before describing the details of the model-based approach, it is helpful to first discuss the relationship between compression and steganography. This relationship has been previously discussed in [1] but it is useful to review it here. Suppose we had a method for perfect compression of some cover media, such as images taken from the real world. Thus, we could feed our compressor random scenes from our world and it would return perfectly compressed, truly random bit sequences (containing no statistical regularities) for each image. This is only possible if our compressor has available to it a complete and perfect model of the statistical properties found in natural scenes. Every statistical redundancy, every predictable quality, must be taken into account in order to accomplish this task - edges, contours, surfaces, lighting, common objects, even the likelihood of finding objects in certain locations.

We could, of course, place these compressed bit sequences in the corresponding decompressor to get back our original images. But suppose we instead had the idea to put our own random bit sequences into the decompressor. Out would come sensible images of the real world, sampled from the machine's perfect statistical model. Nothing would prevent us from also putting compressed and encrypted messages of our own choosing through the decompressor and obtaining for each message an image which should arouse no suspicion whatsoever were we to send it to someone. Assuming that our encryption method produces messages that appear random without the proper key, and that our intended receiver has the same image compressor we do, we will have perfectly secure steganography. Steganography is considered perfectly secure if there is no statistical difference between the class of cover messages and the class of stego messages [3].

Granted, this is decidedly unhelpful in that we cannot hope to obtain such a compression machine. But let us now consider a different approach that uses the same concept of decompression for practical steganography without the necessity of having a perfect model of the cover media. Assume instead that we have a model which captures some, but not all, of the statistical properties of the cover media. We can use a similar paradigm to provide steganography that is undetectable by all except those that possess a superior model of the cover media, or more specifically, a model which captures statistical properties of the cover media that are not captured by our model. This is accomplished by applying this decompression paradigm with a parametric model to replace only a least significant portion of cover media that has been sampled from the real world. The security of this steganography system will depend on the ability of the assumed model to accurately represent the distribution over cover messages. Specifically, such steganography will be *ϵ-secure against passive adversaries*, as defined by Cachin[3], where ϵ is the relative entropy between the assumed model and the true distribution over cover messages. Thus, this model-based approach provides a principled means for obtaining steganography that is provably secure in the information theoretic sense, insofar as the statistical model upon which it is based captures the statistical properties of the cover media.

As long as it remains possible that someone possesses a better model of the cover media, we cannot be sure that such steganography is completely undetectable. But if we consider a steganographic algorithm to be reasonably secure if it is not detectable by a specific statistical model, we can start to make some definitive statements regarding the maximum message length that can be securely hidden with this model and give a working strategy for obtaining this capacity. This approach will hopefully shift the emphasis which has up to now been placed on embedding methods towards more principled steganography methods based on statistical models. That is, we can start asking how to best model our cover data rather than trying to anticipate specific attacks or invent clever ways to flip least significant bits. And we can ask whether a steganographic method embeds messages optimally given its assumed statistical model. This provides us with a unifying framework with which to view and improve steganography and steganalysis methods.

2.2 Method

Let x denote an instance of a class of potential cover media, such as JPEG compressed images transmitted via the internet. If we treat x as an instance of a random variable X, we can consider the probability distribution $P_X(x)$ over transmissions of this class of media. Thus, if we transmit signals drawn from P_X, we can be assured that they are indistinguishable from similar transmissions of the same class regardless of how many such signals we transmit. Since P_X represents data taken from the real world, we can draw a valid instance from P_X using a digital recording device. Given such a sample, x, we separate it into two distinct parts, x_α which remains unperturbed, and x_β which will be replaced with x'_β, our encoded message. For LSB encoding, x_α represents the most significant bits of the cover coefficients as well as any coefficients not selected to send the message, and x_β represents the least significant bits of the selected coefficients. We can consider these parts as instances of two dependent random variables X_α and X_β. Using our model distribution $\hat{P}_X$, we can then estimate the distribution over possible values for X_β conditioned on the current value for X_α: $\hat{P}_{X_\beta|X_\alpha}(X_\beta|X_\alpha = x_\alpha)$. Provided that we select x'_β so as to obey this conditional distribution, the resulting $x' = (x_\alpha, x'_\beta)$ will be correctly distributed according to our model $\hat{P}_X$.

Now, in truth, it would appear that we haven't gained anything from this since we cannot model $P_{X_\beta|X_\alpha}$ perfectly any more than we could perfectly model P_X. However, we have gained something quite important. If we make a careful choice as to how X_α and X_β are separated, we can ensure that our changes to x_β are difficult or impossible to detect using the most sophisticated model of P_X on the planet: the human perceptual system. For instance, if we generate random samples from current image models, the result at best looks like 1/f noise or texture. But while the human visual system is fantastic at modeling images, it lacks a certain degree of precision. This lack of precision is what LSB encoding methods exploit. However, even the simplest models, such as those that capture the marginal statistics of X_β, do not lack this precision, and thus can be used to detect when LSBs are modified by some other distribution.

The solution proposed here is to use a parametric model of P_X to estimate $P_{X_\beta|X_\alpha}$, and then use this conditional distribution to select x'_β so that it conveys our intended message and is also distributed according to our estimate of $P_{X_\beta|X_\alpha}$. We can accomplish this task using the decompression paradigm previously discussed. Given a message M that is assumed to be compressed and encrypted so that it appears random, decompress M according to the model distribution $\hat{P}_{X_\beta|X_\alpha}$ using an entropy decoder, where x_α is part of an instance x drawn from the true distribution P_X via a digital recording device. While this cannot guarantee perfect security unless our model of P_X is perfect, it prevents all attacks except for those that use a better model of $P_{X_\beta|X_\alpha}$ than ours. Unless an attacker models statistical properties of X that we do not, or models them more accurately, our steganogram x' will contain the same measured statistical properties as others drawn from the true distribution P_X.

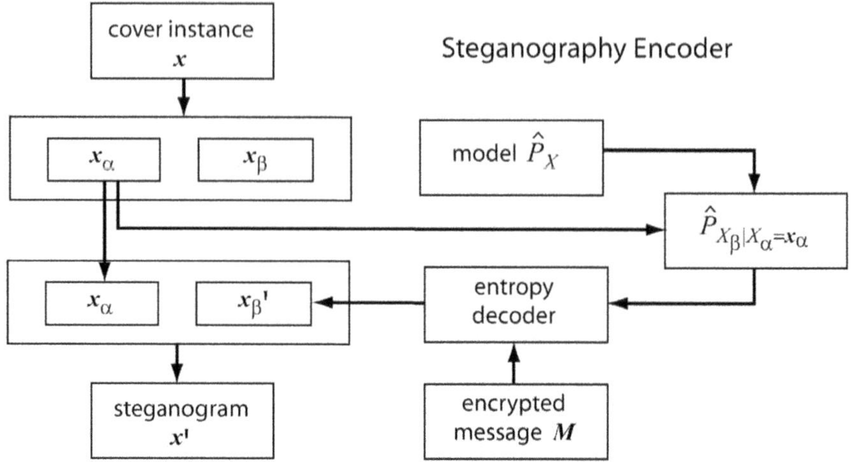

Fig. 1. Model-based steganography encoder: A cover x, such as an image, is split into two parts x_α (e.g. MSBs) and x_β (e.g. LSBs). A parametric model $\hat{P}_X$ over possible instances X is used to calculate the distribution over possible x_β instances given x_α. These probabilities are passed to an entropy decoder and used to decompress the encrypted message M, creating x'_β which is combined with x_α to create the steganogram.

Figure 1 illustrates the proposed model-based method for encoding steganography. First, an instance x of our class of cover media X is separated into x_α and x_β. x_α is fed to our model estimate of P_X which is used to compute the conditional probability distribution $P_{X_\beta|X_\alpha}$. The compressed and encrypted message M is given to an entropy decoder which uses $P_{X_\beta|X_\alpha}$ to decompress M resulting in a sample x'_β drawn from this distribution. The parts x_α and x'_β are then combined to form the steganogram x', distributed according to our model P_X which is transmitted to our receiver. Figure 2 illustrates the method used to recover the original message. Our steganogram x' is divided into x_α and x'_β. The x_α portion is fed into the model P_X which is again used to compute the condition distribution $P_{X_\beta|X_\alpha}$. Thus, the same model is given to the entropy encoder that was fed into the entropy decoder during the encoding stage. The entropy decoder returns the encrypted message. Assuming we have a key, we can decrypt the message and verify its contents. If on the other hand, we do not have the key, the encrypted message will appear random, which is the same result we would get from decoding an instance of X that does not contain steganography. Note that the encryption key does not necessarily need to be a private key. If we use a public key encryption method, we can just as easily obtain a method for public key steganography as suggested in [1].

2.3 Capacity

Determining how large a message can be hidden inside a cover message without becoming detectable has been a long unanswered question. If what we mean

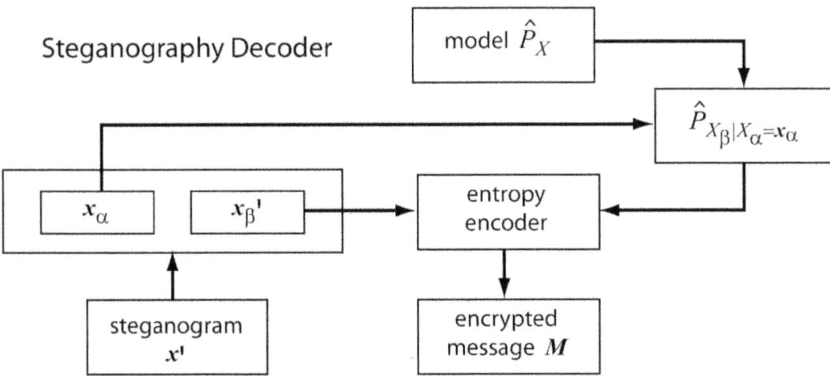

Fig. 2. Model-based steganography decoder: A steganogram x' is split into parts x_α and x'_β. A parametric model $\hat{P}_X$ is used to calculate the same probability distribution over possible x_β sequences that was used in the encoding process. x'_β is then fed into the entropy encoder which uses these probabilities to return the original message M.

by detectable is detectable by any method, this question remains unanswered as we would need to model P_X perfectly to ensure total security. However, we can estimate the average maximum message length that can be hidden without becoming detectable by our measured statistics of P_X. If we consider that X_β is being used as an information channel, we know from information theory that the maximum amount of information on average that can be transmitted through such a channel is equal to the entropy of the conditional distribution $\hat{P}_{X_\beta|X_\alpha}$:

$$H(X_\beta|X_\alpha = x_\alpha) = -\sum_{x_\beta} \hat{P}_{X_\beta|X_\alpha}(x_\beta|x_\alpha) \log_2 \hat{P}_{X_\beta|X_\alpha}(x_\beta|x_\alpha) \tag{1}$$

Using our model, this capacity limit can be measured for a given x_α. We can also see that our encoding method will be able to encode messages with this length on average, since an entropy encoder is designed to achieve this limit. Note that this limit is a function of x_α, and thus may vary depending on the content of our particular cover instance x.

2.4 Implicit Models Used by Current Methods

With this framework, we can gain a deeper understanding of current steganography methods. For instance, we can view current methods which encode messages in the coefficient LSBs at a rate of one bit per coefficient as equivalent to the model-based approach but using an implicit model that assumes the coefficients of their cover media are statistically independent, and that each coefficient is distributed according to a uniform distribution. Any other distribution would not have an equal probability of a 0 or 1 for every LSB. In this case x_β represents the LSBs of the coefficients, and the entropy decoder will simply copy bits of the message into the LSBs of the coefficients. Since coefficient histograms are definitely not uniform, one can easily see that encoding at such a rate must result in a significant change to the marginal statistics of the coefficients. While methods such as OutGuess attempt to compensate for this change by making compensatory changes to extra coefficients, we can see that this approach is not guaranteed to obtain maximum capacity, and is likely to reduce the capacity we could achieve if we incorporate the true marginal distributions of the coefficients into our model.

2.5 Steganalysis

We can also use this framework to perform steganalysis. If we have a target instance x, and we suspect that a steganographic system encoded a message into x_β using a weaker model of P_X than ours, we can measure the negative log likelihood of x_β given x_α under our model: $-\log_2 \hat{P}_{X_\beta|X_\alpha}(X_\beta = x_\beta|X_\alpha = x_\alpha)$, which has an expected value equal to the entropy $H(X_\beta|X_\alpha = x_\alpha)$, our expected message length. While this likelihood value can be computed directly, an equivalent method is to use the steganographic decoding process we have already described on x and measure the length of the resulting "message". It is easy to see why this works. If the statistics of x_β violate our expectation according to our model, we can expect a significantly longer message string. This is because the entropy coder assigns longer compressed bit sequences for x_β values which are less probable according to our model.

3 Applying the Methodology to JPEG

In order to demonstrate how the model-based methodology works in practice, we will now describe an example steganography system that is applied to compressed images stored in the file format defined by the Joint Photographic Experts Group (JPEG). Although JPEG is undoubtedly not the best compression format available, it is chosen for this demonstration because of its abundant use in email transmissions and on public internet sites. While the discussions from this point on will be aimed specifically at this JPEG implementation, the method used here can be easily applied to other file formats. In the JPEG compression standard, images are broken into 8x8 blocks. Each pixel block is passed through a 2-dimensional DCT (Discrete Cosine Transform) to produce 64 DCT coefficients for each block. Compression is accomplished by quantizing these DCT coefficients and then encoding them using a Huffman (or other entropy) encoder. The amount of compression is determined by the quantizer step size used before the entropy encoding, which is lossless.

The method described here is not intended to be secure against any known attack, but rather is primarily intended to demonstrate the methodology described in the previous section. We will use a fairly simple model which captures only the marginal statistics of the quantized DCT coefficients. Our total image model, then, assumes that images are generated by statistically independent

DCT coefficients. While this takes into account some correlations between image pixels, it is still a very limited image model as it does not describe higher order dependencies or even correlations across 8x8 blocks. It is expected that more complete image models which take into account joint statistics of the DCT coefficients would provide better steganographic security, and could also be used to attack this method. An example of such an attack is described by Farid and Lyu[5], who detect steganographic content by examining the marginal statistics of wavelet coefficients. Since the wavelet basis is much better than the DCT basis at describing the structure found in images, this would describe certain dependencies present between DCT coefficients. Taking into account joint statistics while encoding a message into DCT coefficients appears difficult, however, and so to some degree we are limited in our steganographic security by the image model imposed by our choice of cover media. If these methods were applied to a wavelet compression format such as JPEG 2000 instead of JPEG, however, it would provide resistance to attacks which use marginal statistics of wavelet coefficients.

3.1 Model

As with many steganographic methods, we will modify the least significant portions of the coefficients to encode our hidden information. Our model will consist of a parametric description of the marginal DCT coefficient densities. Because the DC coefficients (which represent the mean luminance within a block) are not well characterized by a parametric model, and because modifications to these coefficients are more likely to result in perceptible blocking artifacts, we will use only the AC coefficients during the encoding. Zero valued coefficients are also skipped for the encoding, because these often occur in featureless areas of the image where changes are most likely create visible artifacts. The remaining AC coefficients are modeled using the following parametric density function, which is a specific form of a Generalized Cauchy distribution:

$$P(u) = \frac{p-1}{2s}(|u/s|+1)^{-p} \tag{2}$$

where u is the coefficient value and $p > 1, s > 0$. The corresponding cumulative density function is

$$D(u) = \begin{cases} \frac{1}{2}(1+|u/s|)^{1-p} & \text{if } u \leq 0, \\ 1 - \frac{1}{2}(1+|u/s|)^{1-p} & \text{if } u \geq 0 \end{cases} \tag{3}$$

Other probability distributions, such as the generalized Laplacian distribution [10], have also been used to describe coefficient histograms that are peaked at zero. The distribution used here was chosen because it appeared to provide a better fit to the AC coefficient histograms, particularly in the tails of the distribution, and also because there is a closed form solution for its cumulative density function. This allows more precise fitting of the distribution to coefficient histograms and provides an efficient means of computing the probabilities for each histogram bin.

The first step in the embedding algorithm is to compute low precision histograms (with bin size > 1) of *each type* of AC coefficient for a cover image x. We will call the bin size of the low precision histogram the embedding step size. Each coefficient value is represented by a histogram bin index and a symbol which indicates its offset within the bin. If the embedding step size is 2, for instance, there will be two possible offsets within each nonzero bin. The zero bin is restricted to a width of 1 because we are skipping zero valued coefficients. The bin indices for all the coefficients comprise x_α, which will remain unchanged, and the bin offsets will comprise x_β which will be changed to encode our message.

For each image, the model parameters s and p are fit to these low precision histograms we have computed. The distributions are fit to only the most significant information in the coefficients because it is critical that both the encoder and the decoder compute the same estimated probabilities. The steganography decoder cannot know the least significant portions of the original coefficients as these may have been altered by the encoder. We fit the model parameters s and p to a histogram h of the coefficients by maximizing the likelihood $P(h|p, s)$ that the coefficients were generated from the model. During embedding, the coefficients are altered only within these low precision histogram bins (only the bin offsets are changed) so that the same estimates for p and s for each coefficient type may be obtained by the decoder. Figure 3 shows the histogram of the (2,2) DCT coefficients for a sample image measured in log probability and the model density after being fit to the histogram using the maximum likelihood approach.

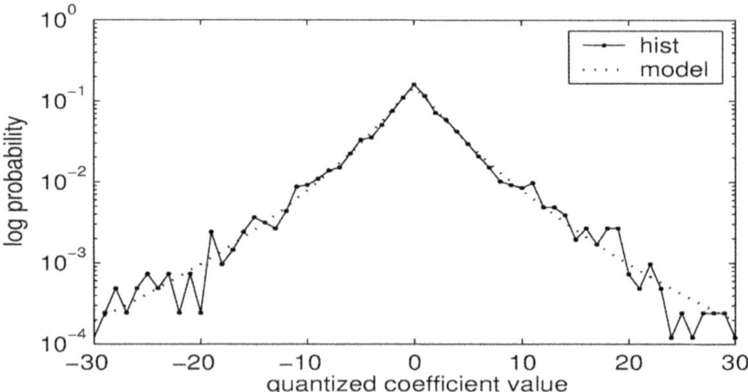

Fig. 3. Measured histogram (in log probability) of DCT coefficient (2,2) for the goldhill image, and the model pdf with parameters $s = 18.28$, $p = 6.92$.

3.2 Embedding Method

Once the model is fit to the histograms for an image, it is used to compute the probability of each possible offset symbol for a coefficient given its bin index. These offset symbols, and their respective probabilities are passed to a non-adaptive arithmetic entropy decoder [4] along with the message we wish to embed in the cover image. The offset symbols returned by the entropy decoder comprise x'_β which are combined with the bin indices to compute the coefficient values of the steganogram x'. To avoid visual attacks caused by changing coefficients only in part of the image, the order in which coefficients are used for encoding the message is determined by computing a pseudo-random permutation seeded by a key. This technique is known as permutative straddling [12]. If we run out of symbol probabilities before running out of message bits, we have reached our maximum message length for this image. In order to anticipate when this will happen, we can obtain the average maximum message length by computing the entropy of our symbol frequencies. If the message is shorter than the maximum message length, any remaining symbols are assigned according to the original coefficient offsets so that these coefficients remain unchanged.

A similar process is used to decode the message from the steganogram, except that the bin offset symbols x'_β in the steganogram are passed along with the symbol probabilities to an arithmetic encoder. Assuming the message length is encoded into the message, we can stop once the end of the message is reached. The algorithms for embedding and retrieving the message are outlined below:

Outline of the embedding algorithm

1. Given a cover image in JPEG format, and an encrypted message, generate low precision (bin size > 1) histograms of coefficient values. This information comprises x_α.
2. Fit the p and s parameters of our parametric model to each histogram by maximum likelihood.
3. Assign symbols to represent the offset of each coefficient within its respective histogram bin. These symbols comprise x_β. Compute the probability of each possible symbol for each coefficient using the model cdf.
4. Choose a pseudo-random permutation to determine the ordering of the coefficients.
5. Pass the message, and the symbol probabilities computed in step 3 in the order specified by step 4 to a non-adaptive arithmetic decoder in order to obtain symbols specifying the new bin offsets for each coefficient. The resulting symbols comprise x'_β.
6. Compute the new coefficients from the histogram bin indices (x_α) of the symbol offsets (x'_β).

Outline of the decoding algorithm

1-4. Same as embedding algorithm steps 1-4.

5. Pass the symbols and symbol frequencies obtained in steps 1-4 to the non-adaptive arithmetic encoder to obtain the original message.

Embedding step sizes. An embedding step size of 2 roughly corresponds to LSB encoding since each nonzero AC coefficient can take on one of two new values. Larger embedding step sizes will increase the message capacity (still without altering the marginal statistics) by sacrificing some image quality. If the cover media is not highly quantized, a higher embedding step size can be used before image quality becomes noticeably diminished. This provides a convenient means of increasing message capacity. However, transmitting images that are not very highly compressed may arouse suspicion in some situations.

Arithmetic encoding. The model-based approach described here requires an entropy codec. We used a non-adaptive arithmetic encoding method altered from the arithmetic encoding algorithm published in [13] to accept frequencies passed for each symbol rather than estimating them adaptively. For another example of non-adaptive entropy coding see [2], or refer to [4,13] for details on arithmetic encoding methods.

Embedding efficiency. One way to demonstrate the effectiveness of the model-based approach is to calculate the embedding efficiency. Embedding efficiency is the average number of message bits embedded per change to the coefficients [12]. It is generally assumed that the more changes that are made to the coefficients, the easier on average it will be to detect the steganography. Thus, we would like to minimize the number of these changes for a particular message length. In the model-based approach, the embedding efficiency will be determined by the entropy of the symbol distributions. Let us assume for now that we are using an embedding step size of 2, since that is most comparable to other steganography methods. We can show that the embedding efficiency of the model-based method described here will always achieve an embedding efficiency greater than or equal to 2, regardless of the message length.

Let k represent the probability of one of the two offset symbols for a given coefficient. The average number of bits we will encode, or the embedding rate, is equal to the entropy of the channel: $H = -(k \log_2 k + (1-k)\log_2(1-k))$. The probability that the value of the coefficient will be changed by encoding a different symbol than the original one, the rate of change, is $k(1-k)+(1-k)k = 2k(1-k)$. The expected embedding efficiency is the ratio of these two rates,

$$E[\texttt{efficiency}] = \frac{-(k \log_2 k + (1-k)\log_2(1-k))}{2k(1-k)} \tag{4}$$

which is never smaller than 2 for $0 < k < 1$. If $k = \frac{1}{2}$, the embedding efficiency will be exactly 2 because we will encode our message at a rate of 1 bit per coefficient and will be changing a coefficient from its original state half of the time. Otherwise, the embedding efficiency will always be greater than 2 and will be the largest (and the capacity the smallest) when the symbol probabilities are furthest apart. The F5 algorithm uses a technique known as matrix encoding to obtain an arbitrarily high embedding efficiency by reducing the message capacity.

However, for its maximum message capacity which is around 13%, the embedding efficiency is only 1.5 [12]. The OutGuess algorithm, since it must change about two coefficients on average for every other bit it embeds, has an embedding efficiency close to 1. In practice, we found that OutGuess provided an embedding efficiency of about 0.96 and a maximum message capacity of about 6.5%.

3.3 Results

Table 1 gives the results obtained from encoding maximal length messages in several grayscale test images using the proposed model-based method. While we tested our method on grayscale images, nothing prevents its application to color images. The images were first compressed to a JPEG quality factor of 80. This method does not double compress, which would leave a detectable signature on the coefficient histograms [6]. Instead the least significant bits of the coefficients are simply replaced, so the result steganogram maintains the same quantization tables as the original. The steganogram file size, message length and embedding efficiency for an embedding step size of 2 are shown for each image. Figure 4 shows the coefficient histograms of the DCT coefficient (2,2) before and after different steganography methods have been applied to the goldhill image. As can be seen, the F5 method greatly increases the number of zeros while the model-based method described here retains the shape of the original histogram. Note that they aren't expected to be identical to the original, since we are sampling from a model to select our coefficient values. The maximum allowable message length was used for each method during the comparison.

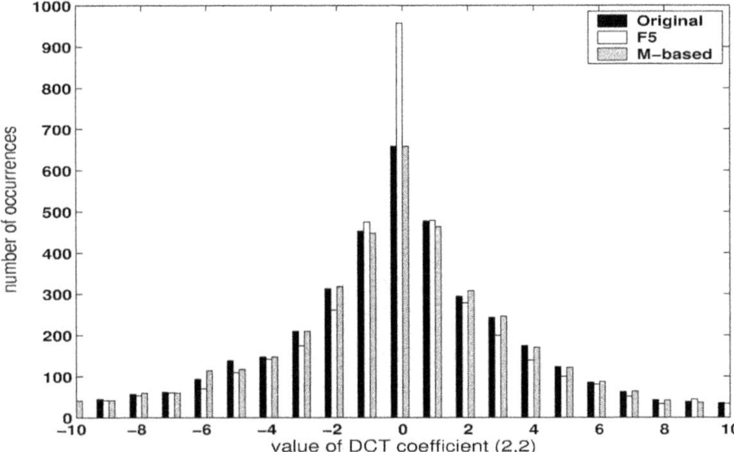

Fig. 4. A comparison of the coefficient histograms after different embedding methods. Each bar represents the number of occurrences for each value of the DCT coefficient (2,2). Shown are histograms for the original image, an image with 4984 bytes embedded using F5, and an image with 6544 bytes embedded using the model-based method.

Table 1. Results from embedding maximal length messages into several 512x512 grayscale JPEG images with an embedding step size of 2. Files were compressed using JPEG quality factor of 80 and optimized Huffman tables.

Image name	File size (bytes)	Message size (bytes)	Capacity	Embedding Efficiency
barb	48,459	6,573	13.56%	2.06
boat	41,192	5,185	12.59%	2.03
bridge	55,698	7,022	12.61%	2.07
goldhill	48,169	6,607	13.72%	2.11
lena	37,678	4,707	12.49%	2.16
mandrill	78,316	10,902	13.92%	2.07

4 Summary and Conclusions

We have presented a new model-based approach to steganography. This approach provides a unified framework for understanding steganography and steganalysis methods. We have shown that it is possible to determine the maximum length message that can be hidden without detection by a given model, and have described a general methodology by which this maximum message length may be obtained. It is hoped that this will encourage future research to focus on developing and applying advanced statistical models rather than on ad hoc embedding methods. As a proof of concept, we have demonstrated how to apply the model-based methodology to JPEG images using a model which captures marginal statistics of the DCT coefficients. The resulting algorithm achieves higher embedding efficiency than current methods while maximizing message capacity, and is resistant to first order statistical attacks. For example, it can embed twice as long a message as the OutGuess algorithm while changing fewer coefficients, and unlike OutGuess maintains not only global coefficient histograms but individual coefficient histograms as well.

5 Future Work

This line of investigation is open to a number of different directions. For instance, the algorithm described here for JPEG images can be readily applied to many other types of cover media such as MP3 audio files, video, or image formats other than JPEG. Primarily, however, we will focus on making the steganographic method more secure (and the steganalysis more powerful) by improving the statistical model to capture some joint statistical dependencies of the cover coefficients. For instance, we will consider a model conditioned on a local neighborhood of coefficients. Current steganography methods for JPEG images can be detected using attacks which measure increases in "blockiness" which occur during embedding [6]. We will investigate methods for defending against such attacks. A simple way to improve the underlying statistical model is to use a better representation for the cover media. It may be possible to extend this method in order to embed in the wavelet domain, even if the resulting image will be compressed using a different transform. However, this would require that the embedding method is robust against compression. The method presented here is particularly fragile because a change to even one coefficient will cause the arithmetic encoding process to produce a completely different message after that point. It may be possible, however, to use a different entropy encoding method to make the system more robust. One approach is to reset the encoding process at regular intervals and add redundancy to the message for error correction. This approach may also provide a method for defending against active attacks, in which the image may be altered by the adversary in order to prevent the hidden communication from reaching its intended receiver.

Acknowledgments. Supported by NIMH MH57921 (Bruno A. Olshausen) and MH60975 (E.G. Jones / B.A. Olshausen), and DOE-GAANN #P200A980307.

References

1. Anderson, R.J., Petitcolas, F.A.P.: On the Limits of Steganography. IEEE Journal of Selected Areas in Communications: Special Issue on Copyright and Privacy Protection), 16(4) (1998) 474–481
2. Buccigrossi, R.W., Simoncelli, E.P.: Progressive Wavelet Image Coding Based on a Conditional Probability Model *Proceedings ICASSP-97*, Munich Germany (1997)
3. Cachin, C.: An Information-Theoretic Model for Steganography *Proceedings of 2nd Workshop on Information Hiding*, LNCS, Springer (1998)
4. Cover, T., Thomas, J.: *Elements of Information Theory.* Wiley, New York, (1991)
5. Farid, H., Lyu, S.: Detecting Hidden Messages Using Higher-Order Statistics and Support Vector Machines. In: Petitcolas, F.A.P. (Ed.): *Inf. Hiding: 5th Intl. Workshop.* LNCS 2578. Springer-Verlag, Berlin Heidelberg (2003) 340–354
6. Fridrich, J., Goljan, M., Hogea, D.: Attacking the OutGuess. *Proc. ACM: Special Session on Multimedia Security and Watermarking*, Juan-les-Pins, France (2002)
7. Fridrich, J., Goljan, M., Hogea, D.: Steganalysis of JPEG Images: Breaking the F5 Algorithm. In: Petitcolas, F.A.P. (Ed.): Inf. Hiding: 5th Intl. Workshop. LNCS, 2578. Springer-Verlag, Berlin Heidelberg (2003) 310–323
8. Petitcolas, F.: MP3Stego (1998) `http://www.cl.cam.ac.uk/~fapp2/steganography/mp3stego`
9. Provos, N.: Defending Against Statistical Steganalysis. In: *Proc. 10th USENIX Security Symposium.* Washington, DC (2001)
10. Simoncelli, E.P., Adelson, E.H.: Noise Removal Via Bayesian Wavelet Coring. *3rd IEEE Int'l Conf Image Processing.* Lausanne, Switzerland (1996)
11. Westfeld, A., Pfitzmann, A.: Attacks on Steganographic Systems. In: Pfitzmann A. (Ed.): *Inf. Hiding: 3rd Intl. Workshop.* LNCS 1768. Springer-Verlag, Berlin Heidelberg (2000) 61–75
12. Westfeld, A.: High Capacity Despite Better Steganalysis (F5 - A Steganographic Algorithm). In: Moskowitz, I.S. (Ed.): *Inf. Hiding: 4th Intl. Workshop.* LNCS 2137. Springer-Verlag, Berlin Heidelberg (2001) 289–302
13. Witten, I. H., Neal, R. M., Cleary, J. G.: Arithmetic coding for data compression, *Communications of the ACM*, 30(6) (1987)

Authentication of 3-D Polygonal Meshes

Hsueh-Yi Lin[1], Hong-Yuan Mark Liao[2], Chun-Shien Lu[2], and Ja-Chen Lin[1]

[1] Department of Computer and Information Science,
National Chiao-Tung University,
1001 Ta Hsueh Rd.,
Hsinchu 300, Taiwan
{HYLin, JCLin}@CIS.NCTU.edu.tw

[2] Institute of Information Science,
Academia Sinica,
Nankang, Taipei 115, Taiwan
{Liao, LCS}@IIS.Sinica.edu.tw

Abstract. Designing a powerful fragile watermarking technique for authenticating 3-D polygonal meshes is a very difficult task. Yeo and Yeung [17] were first to propose a fragile watermarking method to perform authentication of 3-D polygonal meshes. Although their method can authenticate the integrity of 3-D polygonal meshes, it is unable to distinguish malicious attacks from incidental data processings. In this paper, we propose a new fragile watermarking method which not only is able to detect malicious attacks, but also is immune to incidental data processings. During the process of watermark embedding, mesh parameterization techniques are employed to perturb the coordinates of invalid vertices while cautiously maintaining the appearance of the original model. Since the proposed embedding method is independent of the order of vertices, the hidden watermark is immune to some attacks, such as vertex reordering. In addition, the proposed method can be used to perform region-based tampering detection. The experimental results have shown that the proposed fragile watermarking scheme is indeed powerful.

1 Introduction

Transferring digitized media via the Internet has become very popular in recent years. Content providers who present or sell their products through networks are, however, faced with the copyright protection problem. In order to properly protect the rights of a content owner, it is desirable to develop a robust protection scheme that can prevent digital contents from being stolen or illegally distributed. From a user's point of view, after receiving a piece of digital content, he/she usually needs to verify the integrity of the content. As a result, there should be an authentication mechanism that can be used to perform the verification task. With the rapid advance of watermarking technologies in recent years, many investigators have devoted themselves to conducting research in this fast growing area. According to the objectives that a watermarking technique may achieve, two main-stream digital watermarking categories are: robust watermarking and fragile watermarking. While the former aims to achieve intellectual

T. Kalker et al. (Eds.): IWDW 2003, LNCS 2939, pp. 168–183, 2004.
© Springer-Verlag Berlin Heidelberg 2004

property protection of digital contents, the latter attempts to authenticate the integrity of digital contents.

There are a great number of existing robust watermarking algorithms designed to protect 3-D graphic models [1,2,3], [8], [11,12,13], [16], [19]. Their common purpose is to provide a robust way to protect target contents when attacks are encountered. The existing fragile watermarking algorithms that are designed to authenticate 3-D graphic models are relatively few. In [5], Fornaro and Sanna proposed a public key approach to authenticating CSG models. In [17], Yeo and Yeung proposed a fragile watermarking algorithm for authenticating 3-D polygonal meshes. They embed a fragile watermark by iteratively perturbing vertex coordinates until a predefined hash function applied to each vertex matches the other predefined hash function applied to that vertex. Since their embedding algorithm relies heavily on the neighboring information of a vertex, it is unable to tolerate topological modifications, such as vertex reordering or polygonal simplification. In addition, particular attacks, such as floating-point truncation, applied to vertex coordinates might increase the false-alarm probability of tampering detection.

In this paper, we propose a new fragile watermarking algorithm for authenticating 3-D polygonal meshes. The proposed method not only is able to detect malicious attacks, but also is immune to the aforementioned unintentional data processings. In addition, the allowable range for alternating a vertex is explicitly defined so that the new scheme is able to tolerate reduction of floating-point precision. During the process of watermark embedding, the mesh parameterization technique is employed to perturb the coordinates of invalid vertices while cautiously maintaining the appearance of the original model. Since the proposed embedding method is independent of the order of vertices, the hidden watermark is immune to some vertex order-dependent attacks, such as vertex reordering.

The remainder of this paper is organized as follows. In Sec. 2, Yeo and Yeung's scheme for authenticating 3-D polygonal meshes is briefly reviewed. In Sec. 3, the proposed fragile watermarking method is described in detail. Experimental results are given in Sec. 4. Finally, conclusions are drawn in Sec. 5.

2 Yeo and Yeung's Approach and Its Drawbacks

In [17], Yeo and Yeung proposed a novel fragile watermarking algorithm which can be applied to authenticate 3-D polygonal meshes. In Yeo and Yeung's scheme [17], there are three major components, i.e., two predefined hash functions and an embedding process. For a given vertex, the vertex is identified as valid if and only if the values calculated by both hash functions are identical. Otherwise, the vertex is identified as invalid. During the authentication process, invalid vertices are considered as the set of vertices that has been tampered with. On the other hand, valid vertices indicate the set of vertices which has never been modified. In the embedding process, the coordinates of valid vertices are kept unchanged, but those of invalid vertices are iteratively perturbed until each of them becomes valid.

The first step in Yeo and Yeung's approach is to compute location indices. In this step, the first hash function is defined by a conversion function and associated with a given watermark pattern WM. The conversion function is used to convert a vertex coordinate $v = (v_x, v_y, v_z)$ into a location index $L = (L_x, L_y)$. The idea behind the conversion function is to map a three dimensional coordinate onto a two dimensional plane formed by a watermark pattern of dimension $WM\_X\_SIZE \times WM\_Y\_SIZE$. As a result, the location index L is used to point to a particular position in the watermark pattern. Then, the content of that particular position $WM(L)$ (either 0 or 1) is used for the purpose of comparison. Since the conversion function defined in [17] calculates the centroid of the neighboring vertices of a given vertex, the causality problem occurs. Furthermore, the traversal of vertices during the alternation of vertex coordinates must take causality into account so as to avoid error propagation.

The second step in Yeo and Yeung's approach is to compute value indices. In this step, the second hash function is related to a set of look-up tables, i.e., K_1, K_2, and K_3. These look-up tables, which are composed of sequences of bits, are generated and protected by an authentication key. Yeo and Yeung [17] proposed to convert each component of a vertex coordinate into an integer number so as to index into each of the look-up tables. The content of an indexed location is either 0 or 1. The three binary values derived from the three coordinates $p = (p_1, p_2, p_3)$ are then XOR processed to generate a final binary value. This binary value $K(p)$ is used as one of the components for deciding whether the current vertex is valid or not. If the vertex is not valid, then it is perturbed until it is valid. The amount of change that makes this vertex valid is the watermark embedded.

After establishing the above-mentioned two hash functions, the next step is to perturb the coordinates of all invalid vertices until they become valid. In [17], the authors proposed an iterative procedure which can gradually perturb an invalid vertex until both hash functions are matched. On the one hand, in order to maintain transparency, the embedding procedure must traverse in an orderly manner each vertex during the alteration of vertex coordinates. In addition, the ordering of vertices must be maintained during the watermark extraction process. Since the embedding process depends on the causality of the traversal of vertices, their method cannot tolerate an incidental modification, such as vertex reordering. This drawback to some extent limits the power of Yeo and Yeung's method. In this paper, we shall propose a new scheme that is more powerful than the existing fragile watermarking algorithms.

3 The Proposed Fragile Watermarking Method

In this section, we shall propose a new fragile watermarking scheme for authenticating 3-D polygonal meshes. In order to tackle the issues that were not handled by Yeo and Yeung [17], we employ the following concepts: (1) Each hash function can be designed so as to form a binary state space particularly helpful for defining the domain of allowable alternation for a given vertex. Accordingly, the domain of acceptable alternation for a given vertex can be defined as the intersection of the binary state spaces where the values of both hash functions match each other. (2) In order to resolve the causality problem, the conversion function used in the first hash function can be designed to simply perform the mapping from the 3-D space to a 2-D plane without considering the neighboring vertices of a vertex. Based on the above two concepts, we have designed a new scheme, which is shown in Fig. 1. With the new authentication scheme, malicious attacks applied to 3-D polygonal meshes can be easily distinguished from incidental ones. In what follows, we shall describe our authentication scheme in more detail.

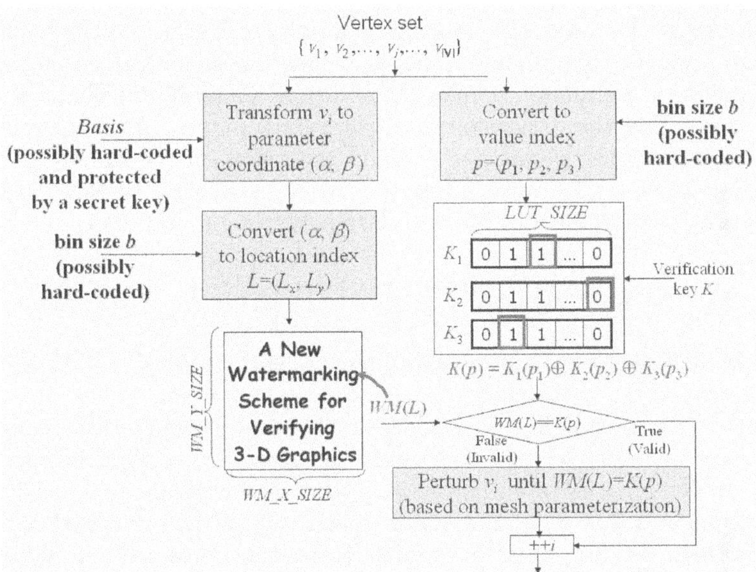

Fig. 1. The flowchart of the proposed authentication scheme for 3-D polygonal meshes.

3.1 Computing Location Indices

Since the conversion function used in the first hash function (the left hand side of Fig. 1) aims to calculate the location index that can be used to locate a particular bit in the watermark pattern, any functions that can transform a 3-D coordinate into a 2-D coordinate can serve this purpose. Therefore, it is possible to use some parameterization schemes to achieve the goal. As mentioned in the previous section, Yeo and Yeung did not use an analytical method to perturb invalid vertices. However, a systematic perturbation strategy is always preferable. Therefore, we propose to adopt the parameterization-based approach to make the vertex perturbation process analytic. For the purpose of clarity, we propose to split the location index computation process into two steps:

Step 1. Given a vertex coordinate v, the specified parameterization $S : R^3 \rightarrow R^2$ converts the vertex coordinate into a parameter coordinate. We propose to use so-called cylindrical parameterization [6] to perform the conversion task. The procedure involved in performing cylindrical parameterization is as follows [6]:

Given an oriented 3-D point, it is composed of a 3-D point m and its orientation n. A cylindrical parameterization process can be expressed as

$$S_{(m,n)}(v) \rightarrow (\alpha, \beta) = (\sqrt{\|v - m\|^2 - (n \cdot (v - m))^2}, n \cdot (v - m)), \tag{1}$$

where (α, β) is the coordinate in the parameter domain. The range for each dimension of the parameter domain is $\alpha \in [0, \infty)$ and $\beta \in (-\infty, \infty)$, respectively.

Step 2. Convert the parameter coordinate formed in Step 1 into the so-called bin coordinate, i.e., the location index (L_x, L_y). This conversion can be accomplished by quantizing the parameter domain. In addition, a modulus operator is required to map them onto the dimension of a watermark pattern. In what follows, we shall describe how the parameter domains are quantized. Assume that the size of a 2-dimensional watermark pattern is $WM\_X\_SIZE \times WM\_Y\_SIZE$, the quantization formula for a cylindrical parameterization domain is as follows:

$$L = (L_x, L_y) = (\left\lfloor \frac{\alpha}{b} \right\rfloor \% WM\_X\_SIZE, \left\lfloor \frac{\beta}{b} \right\rfloor \% WM\_Y\_SIZE), \tag{2}$$

where b is the quantization step for ordinary numeric values and % represents a modulus operator.

One thing to note is that the basis for cylindrical parameterization described in Step 1 can possibly be hard-coded into the algorithm so that detecting a watermark for the purpose of authentication can be realized as oblivious detection. A very important feature of the above design is that the quantized parameterization domain and the watermark pattern together form a binary state space. Such a state space is helpful for defining a legal domain of alternation for a given vertex. The state space corresponding to the cylindrical parameterization is illustrated in Fig. 2(a).

3.2 Computing Value Indices

Even though any functions for converting a floating-point number into an integer can be used to calculate value indices, the following conversion function was designed since it is able to form a binary state space. Assuming that the size of each look-up table is LUT_SIZE, the conversion function is formulated as

$$p = (p_1, p_2, p_3) = (\left\lfloor \frac{v_x}{b} \right\rfloor \% LUT\_SIZE, \left\lfloor \frac{v_y}{b} \right\rfloor \% LUT\_SIZE, \left\lfloor \frac{v_z}{b} \right\rfloor \% LUT\_SIZE), \tag{3}$$

where b is the same quantization step as used to compute location indices.

As we have already mentioned, the quantization step b can be hard-coded into the implementation process. In addition, Fig. 2 reveals that the domain of acceptable alternation for a given vertex can be defined as the intersection of the binary state spaces where the values of both hash functions applied to that vertex match each other. Ideally, the largest acceptable displacement of alternation for a valid vertex is close to $\sqrt{3b^2}$ when the oriented point is chosen as $m(0,0,0)$ and $n(1,0,0)$.

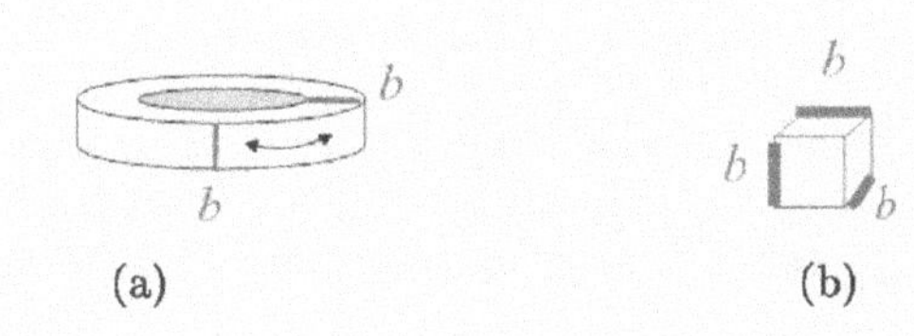

Fig. 2. The binary state space for a vertex: (a) the state space formed by cylindrical parameterization; (b) the state space formed by the conversion function for computing value indices.

3.3 Watermark Embedding

Since both hash functions have been well-designed to define the domain of acceptable alternation for a given vertex, the embedding procedure can focus on perturbing the coordinates of invalid vertices while maintaining transparency. In this paper, we apply a local mesh parameterization approach proposed in [10] for alternation of an invalid vertex. Our method is as follows: Given an invalid vertex v and its neighboring vertices in the counter-clockwise order $N(v) = \{v_1, v_2, \ldots, v_{|N(v)|}\}$, where $|N(v)|$ is the number of v's neighboring vertices, the proposed alternation procedure for an invalid vertex is divided into four steps, which can be explained with the help of Fig. 3. The details of the four steps are as follows:

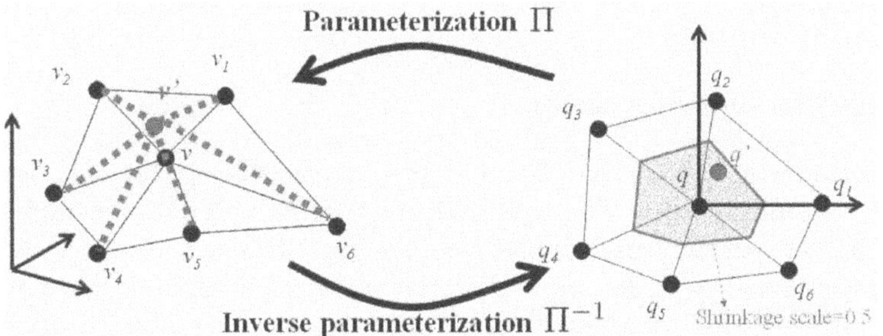

Fig. 3. The proposed alternation procedure for an invalid vertex.

Step 1. Transform the vertex coordinate v into the parameter coordinate q and its neighboring vertices $\{v_1, v_2, \ldots, v_{|N(v)|}\}$ to $\{q_1, q_2, \ldots, q_{|N(v)|}\}$, respectively, using arc-length parameterization [4]. Let $ang(a, b, c)$ be the angle formed by vectors $\overrightarrow{ba}$ and $\overrightarrow{bc}$. Then, the parameter coordinates are provided with the following properties:

$$\|q_k - q\| = \|v_k - v\|, \tag{4}$$

$$ang(q_k, q, q_{k+1}) = 2\pi \cdot ang(v_k, v, v_{k+1})/\theta, \tag{5}$$

where $\theta = \sum_{k=1}^{|N(v)|} ang(v_k, v, v_{k+1})$, $v_{|N(v)|+1} = v_1$, $q_{|N(v)|+1} = q_1$, and $k = 1, \ldots, |N(v)|$. If we set $q = (0, 0)$ and $q_1 = (\|v_k - v\|, 0)$, the parameter coordinates $q_2, q_3, \ldots, q_{|N(v)|}$ can be easily derived from Eqs. (4) and (5).

Step 2. Define an allowable region for alternating an invalid vertex in the parameter domain. Let the region be a shrunken ring whose origin is the parameter coordinate, q, and let the scale for shrinkage be 0.5. (Note that the reason for doing this is to avoid geometrical degeneracies, like triangle flipping, T-joints, etc.)

Step 3. Within the allowable region, find a new parameter coordinate q' satisfying the condition $WM(L(\Pi(q'))) = K(p(\Pi(q')))$. If there does not exist such a new parameter coordinate, alternation for the current invalid vertex is skipped, and $q' = q$ is assigned.

Step 4. Record the new vertex coordinate $v' = \Pi(q')$.

Note that after Step 1 is executed, the parameterization $\Pi : R^2 \rightarrow R^3$, also known as a bijective map [10], is established. In addition, Π^{-1} represents the inverse of the parameterization procedure. A bijective map can be realized by means of the well-known barycentric map [4]. Accordingly, the values of both hash functions applied to a parameter coordinate q' can be determined by $WM(L(\Pi(q')))$ and $K(p(\Pi(q')))$, respectively; on the other hand, the parameter coordinate q' can be transformed back into the vertex coordinate $v' = \Pi(q')$.

3.4 Analysis and Discussion

In this section, we shall conduct a thorough analysis of our authentication scheme for 3-D polygonal meshes. The watermarking parameters that can influence the quality of transparency and robustness are the shrinkage scale and bin size. On the other hand, we also know that the correlation value C can never reach 1. Therefore, we shall examine several crucial issues: (1) how to optimize the performance so that C can be very close to 1; (2) how to balance the competition between transparency and capacity using the shrinkage scale; and (3) how to guarantee the robustness of a hidden watermark. In what follows, we shall discuss these issues.

First of all, we aim to optimize the performance of our algorithm so that the watermark correlation value C can be very close to 1. In order to study this capacity issue, we make the following hypotheses: (1) the spacing between vertices will disable an invalid vertex from seeking a valid state; and (2) uniform parameterizations cannot tackle the irregularity of polygonal meshes, as illustrated in Fig. 4. In addition, the correlation of two watermarks is computed using Eq. (3) from [17]. To test the above two hypotheses, we picked five different models to generate analysis models with different mesh resolutions using a mesh resolution control algorithm described in [7]. Furthermore, for each model, we generated five analysis models corresponding to five different mesh resolutions. Fig. 5 shows the flat-shaded HIV model and its analysis models corresponding to five different mesh resolutions. In this analysis, we fixed the shrinkage scale as 0.5 and the bin size as 2. With varied mesh resolution levels, our fragile watermark was embedded into each model to test the effect of the mesh resolution on the watermark correlation value. In addition, we ran each test five times using different keys and reported the median value. Fig. 6(a) shows the effect of different mesh resolutions on the watermark correlation value. Note that the mesh resolution of zero in Fig. 6(a) indicates that the original models were not subjected to the mesh resolution control algorithm. Obviously, the curves shown in Fig. 6(a) confirm our two hypotheses. Furthermore, a polygonal mesh with higher mesh resolution would possess higher capacity for watermarking.

In order to investigate how the shrinkage scale can force a compromise between transparency and capacity, a suitable visual metric was needed to evaluate the difference between the original model and the watermarked model. In the literature [9], a Laplacian-based visual metric has frequently been used to capture human visual perceptibilities, such as smoothness. We, therefore, adopted this visual metric and measured the transparency as the Peak Signal to Noise Ratio $\text{PSNR} = 20\log_{10}(\text{peak}/diff)$, where peak means the longest edge of the object's bounding box and $diff$ is the Laplacian-based visual metric used in [9]. In this analysis, we picked five models that were at the fourth resolution. We chose the bin size and the shrinkage scale as 2 and 0.5, respectively. With various shrinkage scales, our fragile watermark was embedded into each model for transparency and capacity tests. In the same way, we ran each test five times using different keys and reported the median value. Figs. 6(c)-6(d) show the effects of different shrinkage scales on the watermark correlation value and PSNR value, respectively. From Figs. 6(c)-6(d), it is clear that the best choice of shrinkage scale is 0.5.

In order to demonstrate how robust our watermark is, we attacked the embedded watermark by means of randomization of vertex coordinates. To simulate such attacks, randomization of vertex coordinates was controlled by means of the noise strength, which is defined as the ratio of the largest displacement to the longest edge of the object's bounding box. In this analysis, we picked five models with the largest resolution level from the set of analysis models and fixed the shrinkage scale at 0.5. With various bin sizes, our watermark was embedded into each model and then attacked using different noise strengths in robustness tests.

In the same way, we ran each test five times using different keys and reported the median value. Fig. 6(b) shows the results of robustness tests using different bin sizes for the HIV-lv5 model. From these plots, it can be seen that a larger bin size can provide a hidden watermark with higher robustness. However, the drawback is that the false-alarm rate is increased as well.

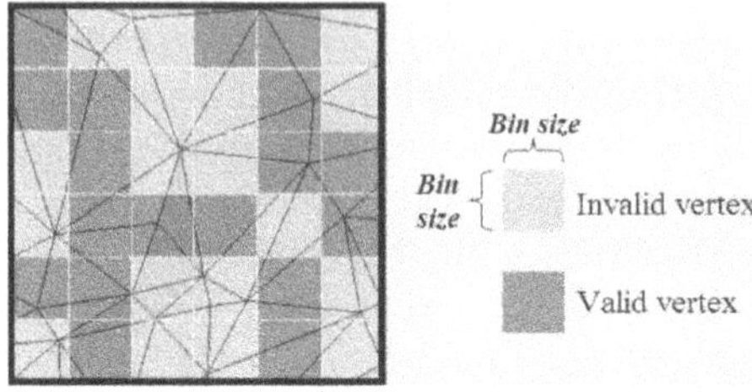

Fig. 4. Irregular polygonal mesh superimposed on uniform parameterization.

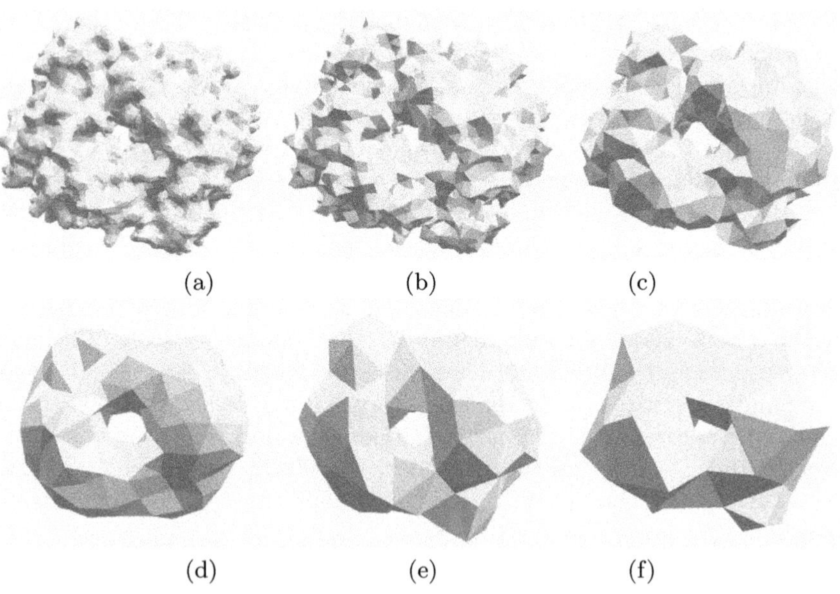

Fig. 5. Analysis models for the HIV protease surface model: (a) original HIV model; (b) HIV-lv1 model; (c) HIV-lv2 model; (d) HIV-lv3 model; (e) HIV-lv4 model; (f) HIV-lv5 model.

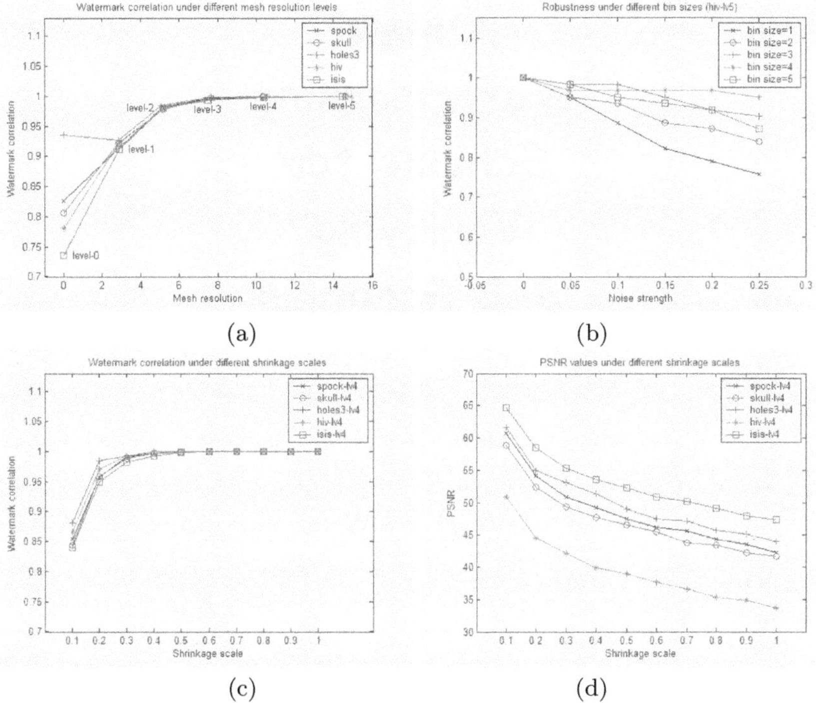

Fig. 6. Analysis on our authentication scheme for 3-D polygonal meshes: (a) effect of mesh resolution on the watermark correlation value; (b) robustness under different bin sizes for the HIV-lv5 model; (c) effect of shrinkage scale on the watermark correlation value; (d) effect of shrinkage scale on the trnsparency of our fragile watermark.

4 Experimental Results

A series of experiments were conducted to test the performance of the proposed fragile watermarking method. We shall start with parameter selection and then report quantitatively some experimental results. In addition, we shall present a set of visualization results that can demonstrate the power of the proposed method in distinguishing malicious attacks from incidental modifications.

4.1 Selecting Appropriate Parameters

We have reported in Sec. 3 that several parameters were needed during watermark embedding and detection. These parameters included a binary watermark pattern, a set of look-up tables, a basis for parameterization, and the degree of quantization. All of the parameters used in our experiments were set as follows. A binary watermark pattern with a size of 512×512 (as indicated in Fig. 7) was used in our experiments. That means, $WM\_X\_SIZE = WM\_Y\_SIZE = 512$. In addition, a set of look-up tables were generated and protected by one authentication key. The size of each table was 256. Therefore, $LUT\_SIZE = 256$.

Fig. 7. The binary watermark pattern used in our experiments.

Table 1. A list of five triangulated meshes used in our experiments and their watermark correlation values detected using the proposed method.

Model	Number of Vertices/Faces	Watermark Correlation Value
dolphins	855/1692	1
spock	16386/32768	0.953558
mannequin	711/1418	0.998594
holes3	5884/11776	0.985214
HIV	9988/20000	0.900681

As to the basis for parameterization, since the 3-D vertex space is periodically aggregated into binary state spaces, its selection is not crucial to the proposed method. Therefore, we fixed the basis as $m(0,0,0)$ and $n(1,0,0)$ in the experiments. As for appropriate quantization steps, we selected them empirically. We assigned the ordinary numeric value, $b = 1$, in all the experiments.

4.2 Experimental Results on Authentication

The data set used in our experiments was a set of triangulated meshes, listed in Table 1. Each of them was watermarked using our fragile watermarking method presented in Sec. 3. The last column in Table 1 shows the watermark correlation values for the five different models. From the experimental results, it is easy to see that at least 90 percent of the vertices became valid after the proposed embedding method was applied.

The five test models were watermarked and tested to evaluate the robustness against reduction of floating-point precision. The results of this experiment are shown in Fig. 8, where the precision of a floating-point number is specified by a nonnegative decimal integer preceded by a period (.) and succeeded by a character f. It is clearly shown in Fig. 8 that the proposed method is very robust against reduction of floating-point precision up to ten to the minus three.

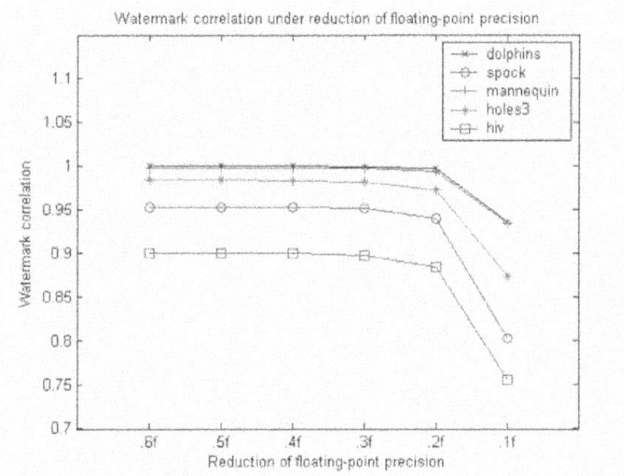

Fig. 8. Five test models were watermarked and tested to evaluate the robustness against reduction of floating-point precision.

4.3 Visualization of Authentication Results

Visualization is a good way to "see" whether the proposed watermarking method is valid or not. Fig. 9 shows that the original and the watermarked Spock models were rendered as either wireframe or flat-shaded models, respectively. It can be seen that the watermarked model maintained high correlation with the original model, whether in a wireframe format or in a flat-shaded format.

The results of experiments on detecting malicious attacks are shown in Figs. 10-11. Fig. 10(a) shows that the watermarked Spock model was tampered with by stretching out Spock's nose. Fig. 10(b) shows some detected potentially modified regions before the closing operator was applied. Note that approximately 50 percent of vertices on Spock's nose were identified as invalid vertices, as shown in Fig. 10(b). Therefore, in order to amplify the effect of the authentication results, the morphological operators described in [15] were adopted so that the parts being tampered with in a model could be detected and highlighted. Fig. 10(c) shows the authentication results of Fig. 10(b) after some morphological operations were applied. Fig. 11 shows another example of malicious tampering, which could possibly occur in the real world. In this case, it is not obvious that the two dolphins were tampered with. Nevertheless, the proposed method still succeeded in malicious tampering detection. As shown in Fig. 11(d), among the two dolphins that were tampered with, one was translated, and the other one stretched out. Both attacks were detected and highlighted.

5 Conclusion

A new fragile watermarking scheme which can be applied to authenticate 3-D polygonal meshes has been presented in this paper.Watermarks are embedded using a local mesh parameterization technique and can be blindly extracted for

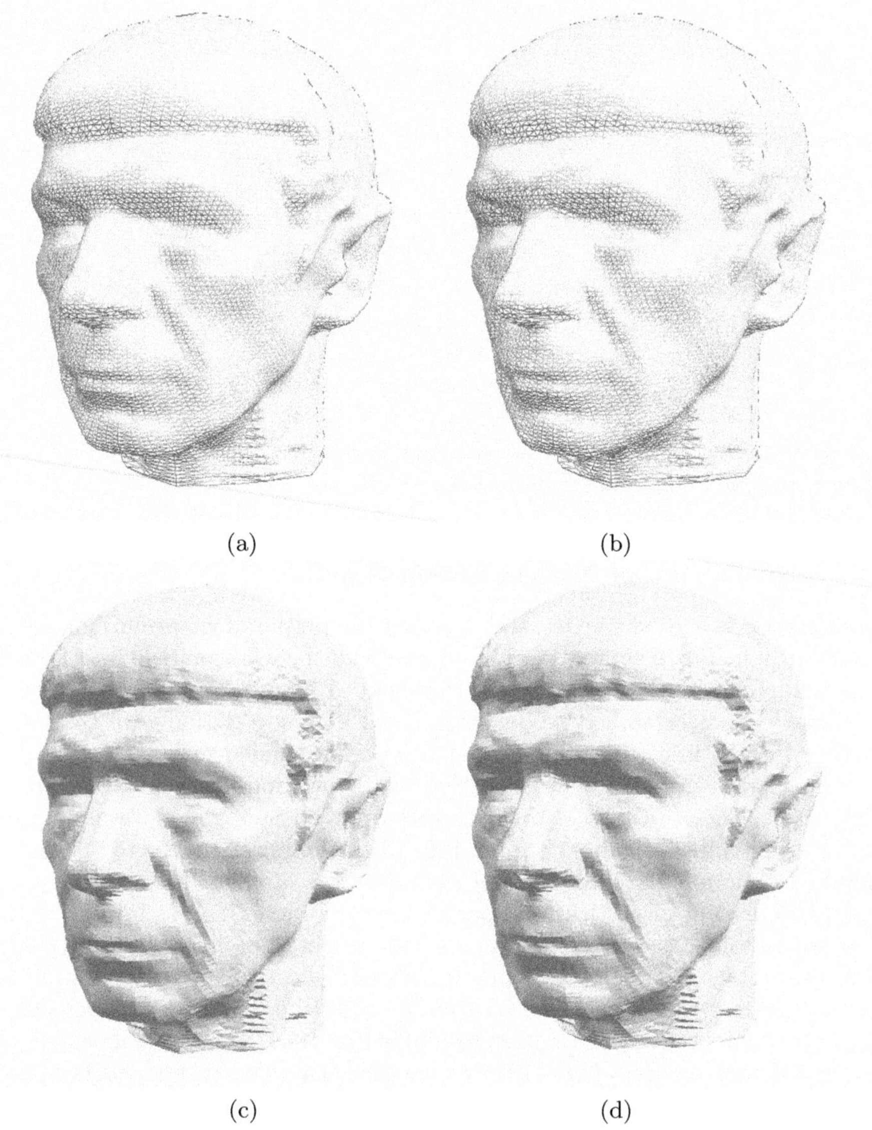

Fig. 9. Visualization of the transparency test: (a) the original Spock model rendered in a wireframe format; (b) the watermarked Spock model rendered in a wireframe format; (c) the original Spock model rendered in a flat-shaded form; (d) the watermarked Spock model rendered in a flat-shaded form.

authentication applications. The proposed scheme has three remarkable features: (1) the domain of allowable alternation for a vertex is explicitly defined by two well-designed hash functions; (2) region-based tampering detection is achieved by a vertex-order-independent embedding process; (3) fragile watermarking is

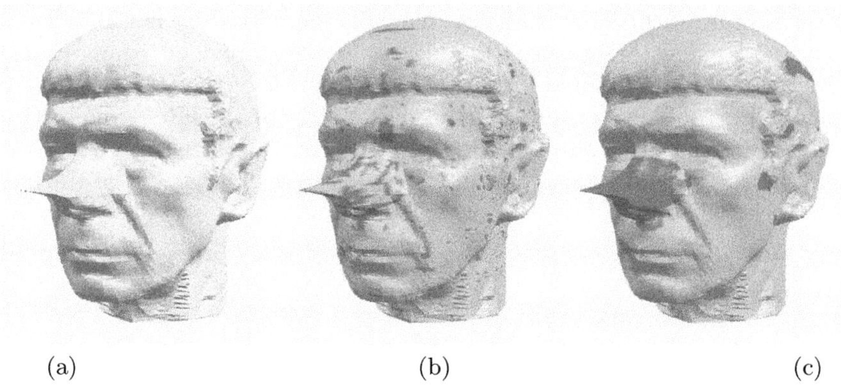

(a) (b) (c)

Fig. 10. Region-based tampering detection: (a) the watermarked Spock model was tampered with by stretching out its nose; (b) the detected potentially modified regions (before morphological operators were applied); (c) the detected modified regions after the morphological operators were applied.

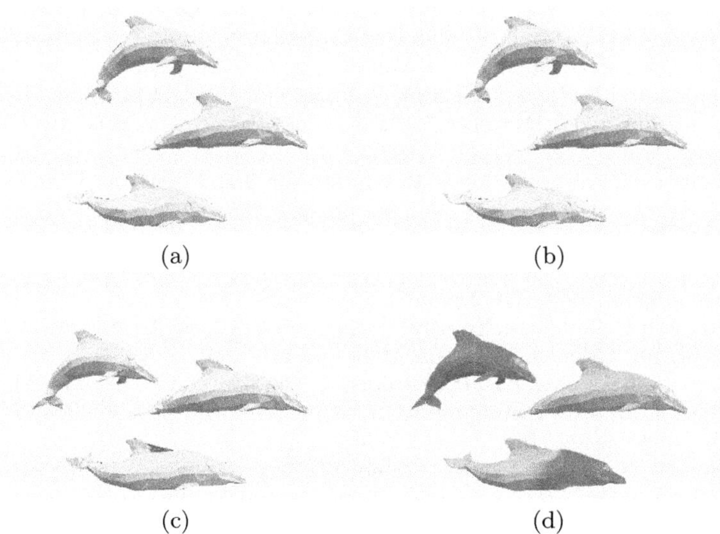

(a) (b)

(c) (d)

Fig. 11. Malicious tampering detection: (a) the original dolphins model; (b) the watermarked dolphins model; (c) a slightly modified dolphins model; (d) two out of the three dolphins have been tampered with. The maliciously modified dolphins were effectively detected.

achieved for the detection of malicious modification and tolerance of incidental manipulations. To the best of our knowledge, this is the first 3-D mesh authentication scheme that can detect malicious attacks involving incidental modifications.

Acknowledgements. This work was partially supported by DigiBits Interactive, Inc. Polygonal meshes used in this paper were provided courtesy of the University of Washington and Cyberware. For the use of the HIV protease surface model, we would like to thank Arthur Olson, The Scripps Research Institute. Part of our implementation used the triangle facet data structure and code of Henning Biermann and Denis Zorin at the Media Research Lab of the University of New York.

References

1. O. Benedens, Geometry-Based Watermarking of 3-D Models, *IEEE Computer Graphics and Applications*, Vol. 19, pp. 46–45, 1999.
2. F. Cayre and B. Macq, Data Hiding on 3-D Triangle Meshes, *IEEE. Trans. Image Processing*, Vol. 51, pp. 939–949, 2003.
3. F. Cayre, P. Rondao-Alface, F. Schmitt, B. Macq, and H. Maître, Application of Spectral Decomposition to Compression and Watermarking of 3-D Triangle Mesh Geometry, *Signal Processing: Image Communication*, Vol. 18, pp. 309–319, 2003.
4. M. S. Floater, Parameterization and Smooth Approximation of Surface Triangulations, *Computer Aided Geometric Design*, Vol. 14, pp. 231–250, 1997.
5. C. Fornaro and A. Sanna, Public Key Watermarking for Authentication of CSG Models, *Computer-Aided Design*, Vol. 32, pp. 727–735, 2000.
6. A. Johnson and M. Hebert, Using Spin-Images for Efficient Multiple Model Recognition in Cluttered 3-D Scenes," *IEEE Trans. Pattern Analysis and Machine Intelligence*, Vol. 21, pp. 433–449, 1999.
7. —, Control of Polygonal Mesh Resolution for 3-D Computer Vision, *Graphical Models and Image Processing*, Vol. 60, pp. 261–285, 1998.
8. S. Kanai, H. Date, and T. Kishinami, Digital Watermarking for 3-D Polygons Using Multiresolution Wavelet Decomposition, in *Proc. Sixth IFIP WG 5.2 GEO-6*, Tokyo, Japan, 1998, pp. 296–307.
9. Z. Karni and C. Gotsman, Spectral Compression of Mesh Geometry, in *Proc. SIGGRAPH*, New Orleans, Louisiana, 2000, pp. 279–286.
10. A. W. F. Lee, W. Sweldens, P. Schröder, L. Cowsar, and D. Dobkin, MAPS: Multiresolution Adaptive Parameterization of Surfaces, in *Proc. SIGGRAPH*, Orlando, Florida, 1998, pp. 95–104.
11. R. Ohbuchi, H. Masuda, and M. Aono, Watermarking Three-Dimensional Polygonal Models Through Geometric and Topological Modifications, *IEEE J. Select. Areas in Commun.*, Vol. 16, pp. 551–560, 1998.
12. R. Ohbuchi, S. Takahashi, and T. Miyazawa, Watermarking 3-D Polygonal Meshes in the Mesh Spectral Domain, in *Proc. Graphics Interface*, Ontario, Canada, 2001, pp. 9–17.
13. E. Praun, H. Hoppe, and A. Finkelstein, Robust Mesh Watermarking, in *Proc. SIGGRAPH*, Los Angeles, CA, 1999, pp. 154–166.
14. E. Praun, W. Sweldens, and P. Schröder, Consistent Mesh Parameterizations, in *Proc. SIGGRAPH*, Los Angeles, CA, 2001, pp. 179–184.
15. C. Rössl, L. Kobbelt, and H. P. Seidel, Extraction of Feature Lines on Triangulated Surfaces Using Morphological Operators, in *Symposium Smart Graphics*, Stanford University, 2000.
16. K. Yin, Z. Pan, S. Jiaoying, and D. Zhang, Robust Mesh Watermarking Based on Multiresolution Processing, *Computers and Graphics*, Vol. 25, pp. 409–420, 2001.

17. B. L. Yeo and M. M. Yeung, Watermarking 3-D Objects for Verification, *IEEE Computer Graphics and Application*, Vol. 19, pp. 36–45, 1999.
18. M. M. Yeung and B. L. Yeo, An Invisible Watermarking Technique for Image Verification, in *Proc. Into'l Conf. Image Processing*, Piscataway, N.J., 1997, Vol. 2, pp. 680–683.
19. M. G. Wagner, Robust Watermarking of Polygonal Meshes, in *Proc. Geometric Modeling and Processing*, Hong Kong, China, 2000, pp. 201–208.
20. W. Sweldens and P. Schröder, Course 50: Digital Geometry Processing, SIGGRAPH'2001 Course Note, 2001.

Use of Motion Estimation to Improve Video Watermarking for MPEG Encoders

Isao Echizen[1], Hiroshi Yoshiura[2], Yasuhiro Fujii[1], and Satoru Tezuka[1]

[1] Systems Development Laboratory, Hitachi, Ltd.,
890 Kashimada, Saiwai-ku, Kawasaki, 212-8567, Japan
{iechizen, fujii, tezuka}@sdl.hitachi.co.jp

[2] Faculty of Electro-Communication, the University of Electro-Communications,
1-5-1, Chofugaoka, Chofu, 182-8585, Japan
yoshiura@hc.uec.ac.jp

Abstract. Maintaining picture quality is an essential requirement for video watermarking, and this paper proposes a new method that uses motion estimation (block-matching techniques) to preferentially allocate watermarks to picture contents with motion based on our criterion for estimating watermark imperceptibility that takes motion into account. Experimental evaluations have shown that the new method significantly reduces degradation in picture quality and that, for the same picture quality after MPEG encoding and decoding, 30% more watermarks can be embedded than with the previous method. This new method would be most effective when implemented in MPEG encoders, which already have the necessary motion estimation functions.

1 Introduction

Digital watermarking can be used to embed copyright and copy control information in motion pictures and will therefore be used in DVD players and recorders as well as in digital broadcasting equipment such as set-top boxes. Because watermarking must not degrade picture quality, the properties of pictures have been taken into consideration when determining the allocation of watermarks [1,2,3,4]. However, even when watermarks are preferentially embedded in messy areas rather than plain areas where they are easier to perceive, picture quality is often degraded because the conventional watermarking methods consider only the properties of each frame (still picture) and neglect inter-frame properties (i.e., motion). The method described in this paper allocates watermarks by using motion estimation and would be most effective when used in MPEG encoders, since they already have the functions needed for this estimation.

2 Previous Methods for Maintaining Picture Quality

2.1 Typical Use of Video Watermarking

As shown in Fig. 1, watermarks (WMs) representing copyright information are embedded into video pictures, and the watermarked pictures are compressed

T. Kalker et al. (Eds.): IWDW 2003, LNCS 2939, pp. 184–199, 2004.
© Springer-Verlag Berlin Heidelberg 2004

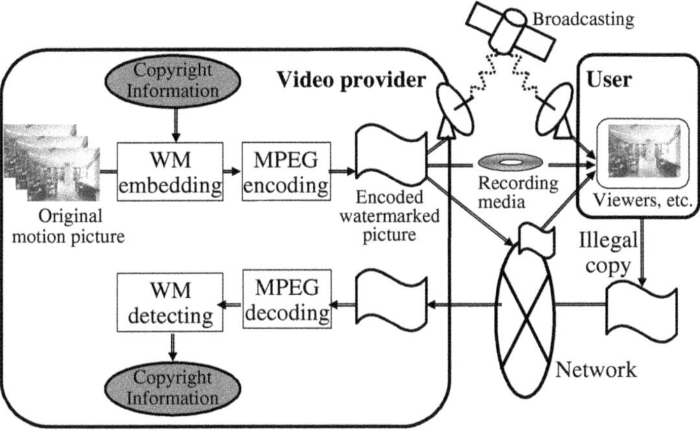

Fig. 1. One use of video watermarking.

using an MPEG encoder. The video provider broadcasts the encoded pictures or distributes them over a network or on recording media such a DVD-ROM. When the encoded watermarked pictures are received, they are decoded, and the user can watch them on a TV set or a personal computer. If the user illegally copies and redistributes the pictures (for example, by placing them on a web page), the illegal copying can be detected by detecting the copyright information embedded in the pictures. The video provider could even identify the illegal copier if the identifier of the user had been embedded in the pictures.

2.2 Requirements for Video Watermarking

Methods of video watermarking can be classified into two types: those changing the pixel values and those changing the frequency coefficients. This paper is concerned with the former type and focuses on representative methods of that type: those changing the luminance values.

Video watermarks should not degrade picture quality. That is, they should not interfere with the user's enjoyment. They should nonetheless be robust enough to be reliably detected after common image processing procedures such as MPEG, and they should never be found in unmarked pictures. We concern maintaining picture quality and describe problem with previous methods.

2.3 Definition of Terminology

We first define some terminology used in this paper.

Watermark Embedding: Changing pixel values in order to embed information into images. The luminance set of the t th frame, which consists of $n \times m$ pixels, is

$$\mathbf{Y}^{(t)} = \{Y_{i,j}^{(t)} \mid 1 \leq i \leq n \,, 1 \leq j \leq m\},$$

so embedding operation E giving luminance set $\mathbf{Y}'^{(t)}$ of a watermarked frame is

$$E : \mathbf{Y}^{(t)} \rightarrow \mathbf{Y}'^{(t)}.$$

Watermark Strength: Luminance change due to watermark embedding. Watermark strength $f_{i,j}^{(t)}$ of pixels (i, j) of the t th frame is described as follows:

$$f_{i,j}^{(t)} = |Y'^{(t)}_{i,j} - Y_{i,j}^{(t)}|.$$

Embedding Quantity: Total amount of luminance change distributed among pixels in a frame. The relation between the embedding quantity Q and the watermark strength is

$$Q = \sum_{ij} f_{i,j}^{(t)}.$$

2.4 Problem with Previous Methods for Maintaining Picture Quality

Previous methods for maintaining picture quality can be classified into two types:

(a) Those that reduce the quantity of WMs embedded in pictures by enabling even a small amount of WMs to be robust enough to be precisely detected [5,6,7,8,9].
(b) Those that embed WMs where they are less perceptible [1,2,3,4].

One example of type (a) is an improvement [9] in the patchwork algorithm reported by Bender and coworkers [10], which embeds WMs by giving a statistically meaningful difference between the average luminance of pixels (a_i, b_i), $1/N \sum_{i=1}^{N} Y_{a_i,b_i}^{(t)}$, and the average luminance of pixels (c_i, d_i), $1/N \sum_{i=1}^{N} Y_{c_i,d_i}^{(t)}$, where the locations of pixels (a_i, b_i) and (c_i, d_i) are randomly chosen in each frame without overlapping. Small luminance changes in those pixels were shown to result in a statistically meaningful difference if (a_i, b_i) and (c_i, d_i) were neighboring for each i [9]. The methods of type (a) reduce the luminance change while maintaining the robustness of the WMs and thus maintain picture quality.

The methods of type (b), on the other hand, maintain picture quality directly and are usually more effective. Most of them use "masking effects" found in the human eye system [1,2,3]. Because picture content masks WMs, these methods embed WMs strongly in messy areas of pictures and weakly in plain areas. The methods select as "messy areas" regions with large luminance differences and many high-frequency elements. The quality of motion pictures is still degraded, however, because these methods consider only the properties of each frame (still picture) and neglect inter-frame properties (i.e., motion) when selecting areas where WMs would be less perceptible.

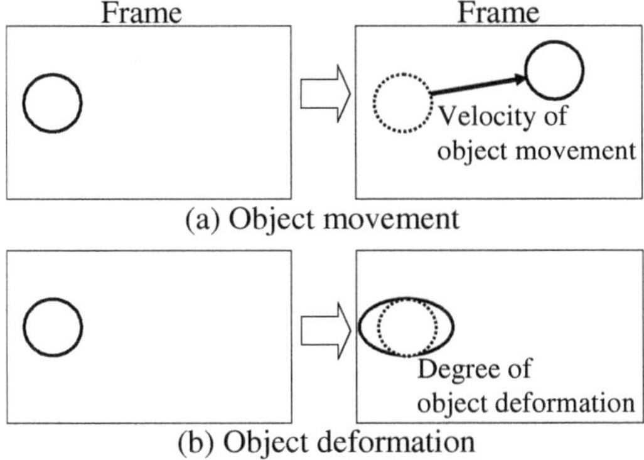

Fig. 2. Relation between WM imperceptibility and motion picture properties.

3 Improved Video Watermarking for MPEG Encoders

3.1 New Criterion for Measuring WM Imperceptibility

In our proposed method, the strength of embedded WMs is adjusted according to an "estimation of WM imperceptibility." That is, WMs are embedded more strongly in areas where they are estimated to be relatively imperceptible. This section describes our new criterion for estimating WM imperceptibility that takes motion into account.

Analysis of WM imperceptibility. Analyzing the relation between WM imperceptibility (WMIP) and motion picture properties, we observed the following:

- WMIP depends on the velocity of object movement between frames, as shown in Fig. 2(a), and the larger the velocity is, the less perceptible the WMs are.
- WMIP also depends on the degree of object deformation between frames as shown in Fig. 2(b), and the more the deformation is, the more imperceptible the WMs are.

These observations imply that WMIP depends not only on the properties of the still pictures making up the sequence of images constituting a motion picture, but also on the motions of the objects: their velocities and their degrees of deformation. In the following we describe the block-matching techniques widely used for motion estimation in MPEG encoders and present a new criterion for measuring WMIP that uses these techniques.

Block-matching techniques. Block-matching techniques [11] are based on between-frame matching of MPEG macro-blocks (16×16-pixel blocks) and determine one motion vector for each macro-block.

Step 1: The sum of absolute difference $D(k,l)$ between the macro-block of current frame $\mathbf{Y}^{(t)}$ and that of reference frame $\mathbf{Y}^{(t-1)}$, which is displaced by (k,l) from the block of $\mathbf{Y}^{(t)}$, is calculated using the following formula (see Fig. 3):

$$D(k,l) = \sum_{i,j=0}^{15} |Y^{(t)}_{b_x+i,b_y+j} - Y^{(t-1)}_{b_x+k+i,b_y+l+j}|,$$

where (b_x, b_y) is the pixel location representing the starting point of the macro-block.

Step 2: The $D(k,l)$s are calculated within search range k,l. A range of $-15 \le k,l \le 15$ is typically searched [11], and 31×31 $D(k,l)$s are generated.

Step 3: The motion vector $\mathbf{v}$ is identified as the vector (k_0, l_0) for the minimum of 31×31 $D(k,l)$s. That is, according to the formulas

$$d = D(k_0, l_0) = \min_{k,l} D(k,l),$$

where d is the inter-frame deformation of the object, and $\mathbf{v} = (k_0, l_0)$ is the motion vector representing the velocity of the movement of the object. If more than one (k_0, l_0) gives the same minimum value, $D(k_0, l_0)$, the shortest (k_0, l_0) vector is chosen as motion vector $\mathbf{v}$.

This procedure is carried out with all macro-blocks in a frame. For each macro-block, the computation of the motion vector $\mathbf{v}$ requires $31 \times 31 - 1$ comparisons to select the minimum of 31×31 $D(k,l)$s. The computation of each $D(k,l)$ also requires 16×16 subtractions, 16×16 absolute operations, and $16 \times 16 - 1$ additions. Though the block-matching techniques have an impact on the performance and computational complexity of the proposed criterion for measuring WMIP, we could reduce the impact by implementing WM embedding process using the proposed criterion in MPEG encoders that already have the motion estimation as described in Section 3.2.

Criterion using the motion information. We first define the following terminology.

WMIP $R_{i,j}$ of a pixel in a motion picture: A measure representing the degree of imperceptibility of a luminance change at a pixel (i,j). If, for example, the WMIP of pixel (1,0) is larger than that of pixel (2,0), a change in luminance at pixel (1,0) is less perceptible than a change at pixel (2,0).

As described in Section 3.1, the $R_{i,j}$ of a pixel in a motion picture depends on two kinds of motion information as well as on the still picture properties. Thus, $R_{i,j}$ is a function of d, $\mathbf{v}$, and $S_{i,j}$:

$$R_{i,j} = F(d, \mathbf{v}, S_{i,j}), \tag{1}$$

where $S_{i,j}$ is the pixel's WMIP based only on the still picture properties. We next explain how $S_{i,j}$ and function F are determined.

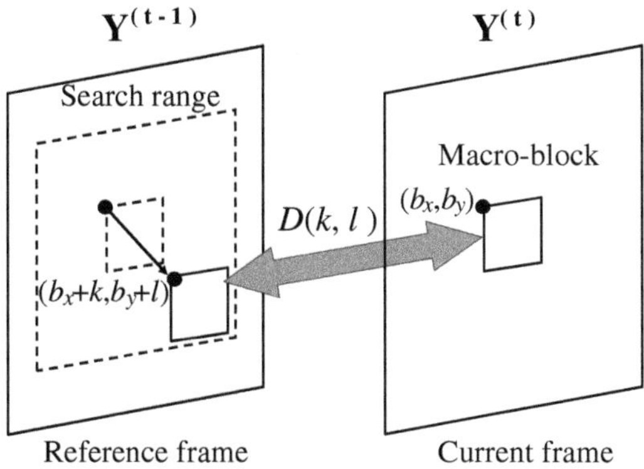

Fig. 3. Block-matching method.

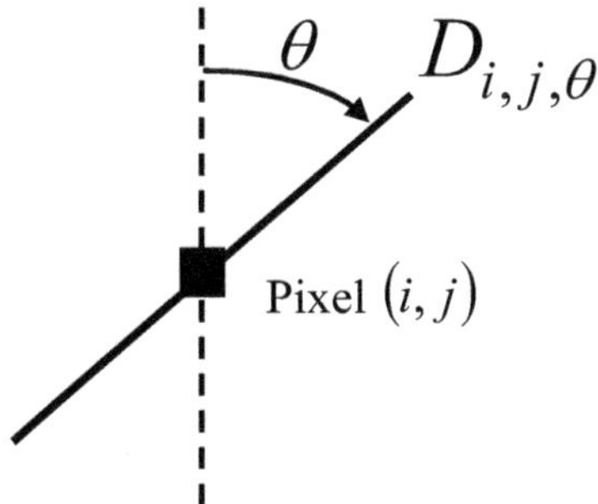

Fig. 4. Definition of $D_{i,j,\theta}$.

Determination of $S_{i,j}$. Various methods for determining $S_{i,j}$ have been proposed. We use the one reported by Echizen and coworkers [4]. This method uses luminance set $D_{i,j,\theta}$ on the line at angle θ centered on pixel (i, j), as shown in Fig. 4:

$$S_{i,j} = \min_{\theta} \sqrt{\sigma^2(D_{i,j,\theta})}, \tag{2}$$

where $\sigma^2(\bullet)$ is an operation that calculates the variance of elements in a set. They clarified the effect of the number of pixels in $D_{i,j,\theta}$ and the effect of the resolution of angular orientation θ.

- If the number of pixels in $D_{i,j,\theta}$ is too large (i.e., the line segment included in $D_{i,j,\theta}$ is too long), $S_{i,j}$ is affected by picture areas far from the target pixel (i, j) and thus does not adequately represent local imperceptibility at pixel (i, j). If, on the other hand, the number of pixels in $D_{i,j,\theta}$ is too small,

values of $S_{i,j}$ are always small because of the high correlation among neighboring luminance values, so $S_{i,j}$ does not adequately represent the degree of imperceptibility.
- The larger the resolution of angular orientation θ, the more precisely $S_{i,j}$ can be estimated.

Based on these analyses and experimental evaluations of image quality, they concluded that image quality is best when the number of pixels in $D_{i,j,\theta}$ is five and the angular orientation is eight, which corresponds to the finest angular resolution in the five-pixel case. We thus use these values here.

Determination of function F. There has been little research on the determination of F, so there is still no clue for determining F optimally. We therefore used as the simplest candidate a two-step function of motion vector $\mathbf{v}$ and deformation quantity d. The suitability of this function was demonstrated by the results of the experimental evaluations given in Section 4.

To establish the two-step function specifically, we classified the macro-blocks in each frame into two types based on the motion estimation:

Static areas: Macro blocks in which the length of motion vector $|\mathbf{v}|$ is less than threshold value $T_\mathbf{v}$ and deformation quantity d is less than threshold value T_d: $d < T_d$ and $|\mathbf{v}| < T_\mathbf{v}$. Objects in these areas are static.

Motion areas: Macro blocks in which $|\mathbf{v}|$ is not less than $T_\mathbf{v}$ or d is not less than T_d: i.e., $d \geq T_d$ or $|\mathbf{v}| \geq T_\mathbf{v}$. Objects in these areas are to be moving or deformed.

Based on the above classification, the WMIP $R_{i,j}$ is given by a two-step function:

$$R_{i,j} = F(d, \mathbf{v}, S_{i,j}) = \begin{cases} S_{i,j} & d < T_d, |\mathbf{v}| < T_\mathbf{v} \\ \alpha S_{i,j} & \text{otherwise} \end{cases}, \qquad (3)$$

where coefficient α is greater than 1. $R_{i,j}$ is small in static areas and large in motion areas. Thus, this criterion is consistent with the results of our preliminary analysis and can be considered appropriate.

Setting $T_\mathbf{v}$, T_d, and α. Threshold values $T_\mathbf{v}$, T_d and coefficient α in formula (3) are set as follows:

Step 1: The values of $T_\mathbf{v}$ and T_d are set according to the results of a subjective evaluation using standard video samples [12].

Step 2: The value of α is also set subjectively using the $T_\mathbf{v}$ and T_d values determined in Step 1.

Setting $T_\mathbf{v}$ and T_d: First, $T_\mathbf{v}$ is determined from the motion vectors measured, after MPEG compression, in areas where WMs are easier to perceive and in areas where they are harder to perceive (WM perceptibility is judged using standard pictures). Next, T_d is determined using a similar procedure.

Step 1: WMs are embedded by considering only the properties of the still pictures (embedding quantity Q is distributed among the pixels in each frame on the basis of only $S_{i,j}$, and the luminance of each pixel in each frame is changed based on the distributed quantity).

Step 2: The watermarked pictures are encoded using MPEG2 with four different bit rates (2, 4, 6, and 8 Mbps).

Step 3: After decoding, the pictures are evaluated subjectively to identify evaluators for discriminating areas in which WMs are easier to perceive from those in which they are harder to perceive.

Step 4: The motion vectors and the deformation quantities are measured in these areas to determine $T_{\mathbf{v}}$ and T_d.

Carrying out this procedure with five embedding quantities produced threshold values of $T_{\mathbf{v}} = 6$ and $T_d = 5000$. The threshold values were almost the same at the different MPEG bit rates because the areas subjectively discriminated in Step 3 were nearly same at the four different bit rates.

Setting α: The value of α also needs to be set appropriately because if α were too small there would be no difference between the previous and proposed methods and if it were too large, the picture quality would be degraded in motion areas. We therefore used several values of α when making a watermarked picture and evaluated the picture quality after MPEG2 compression using the following procedure:

Step 1: WMs are embedded into a standard video sample (Walk through the Square [12]) by using several values of α and the above threshold values of $T_{\mathbf{v}} = 6$ and $T_d = 5000$.

Step 2: These pictures watermarked with different values of α are encoded using MPEG2 at four different bit rates (2, 4, 6, and 8 Mbps).

Step 3: The decoded pictures are evaluated subjectively to identify evaluators for determining picture quality (details of the subjective evaluation procedure are described in Section 4.1).

Carrying out this procedure with five embedding quantity produced the values of α at the four different MPEG bit rates. The results for 8 Mbps are shown in Fig. 5; the horizontal axis represents the average embedding quantity per pixel, q, and the vertical axis represents the level of picture quality. Pictures watermarked with three different values of α ($\alpha = 1.5, 2.5, 3.5$) were evaluated, and the picture watermarked with $\alpha = 2.5$ was judged to have the best quality. We thus set the value of α for 8 Mbps to 2.5. The same evaluation was done at 2, 4, and 6 Mbps. The results, listed in Table 1, show that the value of α depends inversely on the bit rate. We used these values in the detailed evaluation reported in Section 4.

3.2 WM Embedding System

Overall structure. The proposed method would be most effective when implemented in MPEG encoders because they already have the necessary motion

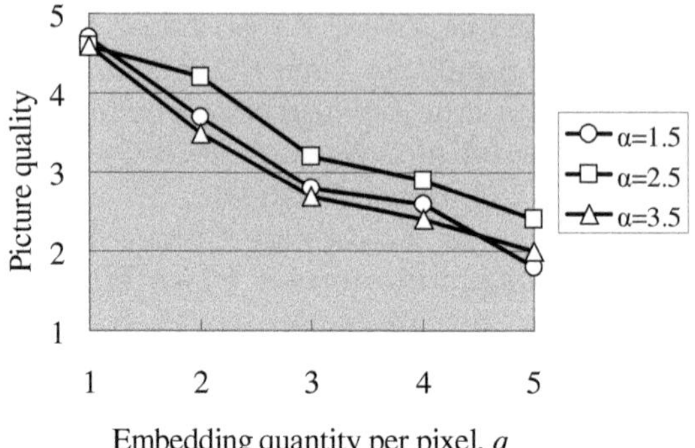

Fig. 5. Evaluated quality of watermarked pictures (8 Mbps).

Table 1. Values of α.

	2 Mbps	4 Mbps	6 Mbps	8 Mbps
α	3.5	3.0	2.8	2.5

estimation functions. Fig. 6 shows the overall system structure of the proposed method implemented in an MPEG encoder. As shown in Fig. 6(a), the watermarking process embeds copyright information into each frame by using the motion information from the motion estimation of the MPEG encoder. Then watermarked frames are encoded by the encoding process.

Fig. 6(b) shows the structure of the watermarking process, which consists of an embedding process and an embedding control process:

Embedding process: Embeds into each frame WMs representing the copyright information. The WM strength is determined using the $R_{i,j}$ calculated in the embedding control process.

Embedding control process: Calculates $R_{i,j}$ (WMIP of each pixel) of the original frames. This process consists of two subprocesses:

(a) **Intra-frame analysis:** Calculates $S_{i,j}$ for each frame by using formula (2).

(b) **$R_{i,j}$-operation:** Calculates $R_{i,j}$ from $S_{i,j}$, $\mathbf{v}$, and d.

The embedding control process can be used in various WM embedding systems because it is combined with the embedding processes only though $R_{i,j}$, which can be calculated independently of the embedding process.

Process flow. The process flow of the 1-bit-WM embedding is described below. Steps 2 and 3 represent the flow of the embedding control process and Steps 4 and 5 represent that of the embedding process. For multiple-bit embedding, each

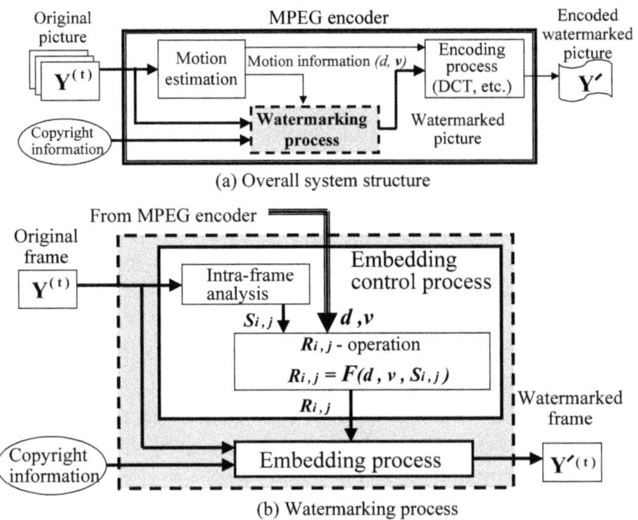

Fig. 6. Watermark embedding system using the proposed method.

frame is divided into regions, and the 1-bit embedding process is applied to each region. See appendix for the corresponding WM detection.

Step 1: Do the following steps over $t = 1, 2, \ldots$.
Step 2: Calculate $S_{i,j}$ from luminance set $\mathbf{Y}^{(t)}$ of the input frame.
Step 3: Calculate $R_{i,j}$ from $\mathbf{v}$, d (calculated by motion estimation of the encoder) and $S_{i,j}$.
Step 4: Determine WM strength $f_{i,j}^{(t)}$ at pixel (i, j) of frame $\mathbf{Y}^{(t)}$:

$$f_{i,j}^{(t)} = \frac{R_{i,j}}{\sum_{ij} R_{i,j}} Q, \tag{4}$$

where Q is the specific embedding quantity for frame $\mathbf{Y}^{(t)}$[1]. This means that the Q for a frame is distributed among its pixels in proportion to $R_{i,j}$.
Step 5: Generate watermarked frame $\mathbf{Y}'^{(t)}$ by adding WM pattern $\mathbf{M}$ ($= \{M_{i,j} \mid M_{i,j} \in \{-1, +1\}, 1 \leq i \leq n, 1 \leq j \leq m\}$ comprising a pseudo random array of ± 1s) to original frame $\mathbf{Y}^{(t)}$ depending on embedding bit b:

$$Y'^{(t)}_{i,j} = \begin{cases} Y_{i,j}^{(t)} + f_{i,j}^{(t)} M_{i,j} & \text{if } b = 1 \\ Y_{i,j}^{(t)} - f_{i,j}^{(t)} M_{i,j} & \text{if } b = 0 \end{cases}. \tag{5}$$

[1] Q is set by the system designer and controlled by the users in accordance with the intended use.

4 Experimental Evaluation

4.1 Subjective Evaluation of Watermarked Picture Quality

Procedure. To evaluate the MPEG quality, we used 30 standard motion pictures [12], each of which had 450 frames of 720 × 480 pixels. After the previous and proposed methods were used to embed WMs into luminance set $\mathbf{Y}^{(t)}$ of the motion picture, the visual qualities of these two watermarked pictures were compared by standard subjective evaluation [13] after MPEG2 encoding and decoding using a hardware codec.

Proposed method: WMs were embedded using the procedures described in Section 3.2 with embedding bit $b = 1$.

Previous method: The watermarking procedures were the same as those of the proposed method except that $S_{i,j}$ instead of $R_{i,j}$ was used in Step 4. The embedding quantity for each frame was set the same as that with the proposed method. The difference between $R_{i,j}$ and $S_{i,j}$ results in different distributions of WMs among the pixels.

The 30 sample pictures were categorized into five types according to the degree of object movement between frames and the degree of object deformation between frames (see Fig. 7).

(a) Walk

(b) Flamingos (c) Whale (d) Hall (e) Leaves

Fig. 7. Evaluated pictures.

(a) Walk through the Square (Walk): People walking in a town square: medium movement and medium deformation.

(b) Flamingos: Pan-scanned scene of flamingos: much movement and little deformation.

(c) Whale Show (Whale): Spraying whale with audience: little movement and much deformation.

Table 2. Level of disturbance and rating scale.

Disturbance	Points
Imperceptible	5
Perceptible but not annoying	4
Slightly annoying	3
Annoying	2
Very annoying	1

(d) **Entrance Hall (Hall):** Three people talking in an entrance hall: little movement and little deformation.

(e) **Rustling Leaves (Leaves):** Fluttering leaves: much movement and much deformation.

The pictures were subjectively evaluated using the procedure described in Recommendation ITU-R BT.500-7 [13]. The original and watermarked pictures after MPEG encoding and decoding were shown simultaneously to ten evaluators, who rated the picture quality according to the scale listed in Table 2. For each picture, the average of the ten scores was used as the quality level.

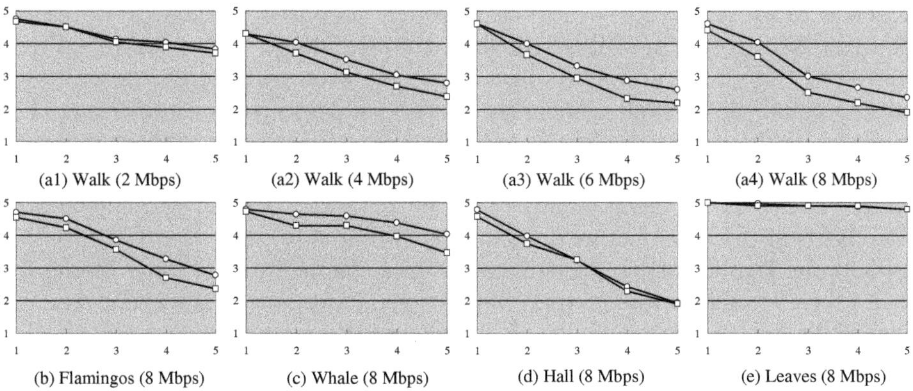

Fig. 8. Quality of watermarked pictures (circles and squares indicate proposed and previous methods).

Results. Evaluation results are shown in Fig. 8, in which the horizontal axis represents averaged embedding quantity per pixel, $q = Q/(720 \times 480)$, and the vertical axis represents the level of picture quality.

Figs. 8(a1)-(a4) show the results for Walk (the standard) at the four different bit rates. The degradation in picture quality was significantly reduced at 4,

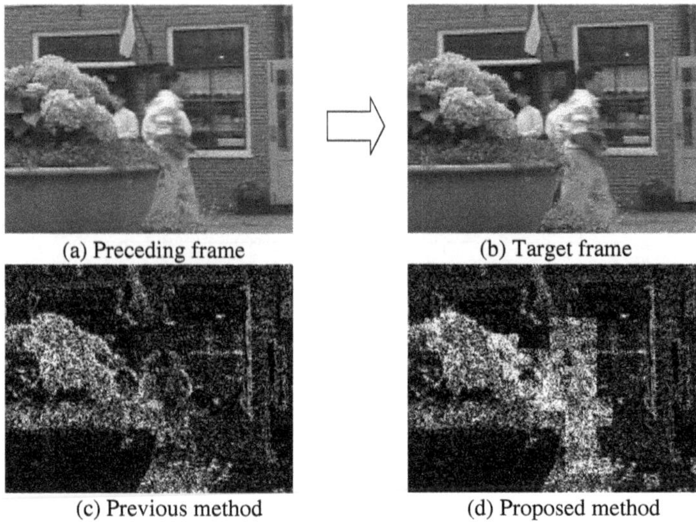

Fig. 9. Strength of watermarking (white indicates strong watermarking).

6, and 8 Mbps (Figs. 8(a2)-(a4)) because the proposed method preferentially allocates WMs to the moving areas where they should be less perceptible. Fig. 9 represents the strength of WMs in a frame. As shown in Fig. 9, the proposed method could preferentially allocates WMs to walking person in a frame. The proposed method was not effective at 2 Mbps (Fig. 8(a1)) because the noise with low-bit-rate MPEG dominates the WM noise, preventing the WM noise from being recognized. In the standard case, the proposed method can embed 30% more WMs at the same picture quality. Figs. 8(b) and (c) show that the proposed method also significantly reduces degradation in picture quality (only the results for 8 Mbps are shown due to space limitations). The proposed method was not as effective for the pictures in which there was little movement and deformation (Fig. 8(d)) and much movement and deformation (Fig. 8(e)) because most parts of the frames were static or moving, so it is difficult to preferentially allocate WMs to parts with motion.

For all the pictures evaluated, the quality of the proposed method is better than that of the previous method.

4.2 Estimation of WM Detection Rate

This section describes the results of evaluating the proposed method with respect to improvement in WM detection by comparing the WM detection ratios of the proposed method and the previous method. The ratios were measured at the same picture quality after MPEG encoding.

Table 3. Percentage of correct detection.

	2 Mbps	4 Mbps	6 Mbps	8 Mbps
Proposed	36.0	51.6	57.6	76.7
Previous	34.2	37.6	49.1	55.3

Procedure. We evaluated the detection rate using the standard picture (Walk).

Step 1: Select the level of picture quality, L, at which the evaluation is to be done (for example, $L = 4$, "Perceptible but not annoying"). Obtain average embedding quantity $q_{\text{prop}}^{(L)}$ for the proposed method that corresponds to L by referring to the relationship between q and picture quality shown in Fig. 8. Similarly obtain average embedding quantity $q_{\text{prev}}^{(L)}$ for the previous method. For instance, for Fig. 8(a4), $q_{\text{prop}}^{(4)}$ and $q_{\text{prev}}^{(4)}$ are, respectively, 2.0 and 1.5.
Step 2: Embed 64-bit information into each of the 450 frames of the picture using the proposed and previous methods so that the average embedding quantities are, respectively, $q_{\text{prop}}^{(4)}$ and $q_{\text{prev}}^{(4)}$ (resulting in two watermarked pictures with the same quality).
Step 3: Encode and decode the watermarked pictures using an MPEG2 hardware codec.
Step 4: Using a process based on WM detection described in the appendix, detect the 64-bit information in each frame of the two watermarked pictures [2]
Step 5: Count the number of frames in which the information was correctly detected.

This procedure was performed for the four different MPEG2 bit rates (i.e. 2, 4, 6, and 8 Mbps).

Results. Evaluation results are summarized in Table 3, which lists the percentages of the 450 frames from which information was detected correctly (correct detection rates). The percentages of incorrect detection stand for the false negative error rates. At all MPEG2 bit rates, the proposed method gave better detection ratios [3]. Thus the proposed method can improve the WM detection.

5 Conclusion

Maintaining picture quality is an essential requirement for video watermarking. This paper showed that watermarks are less perceptible where picture contents

[2] To clarify the improvement in WM detection of the proposed method, we set the threshold value of determining bit-value to zero ($T = 0$) so that the 64-bit information is always detectable.

[3] These detection ratios are too low for practical use but they can be improved sufficiently by using a better coding technique, such as redundant coding or error-correction coding.

are moving than where they are static. It then described a new watermarking method that uses motion detection to preferentially allocate watermarks to moving parts of pictures. Also described were a motion-based criterion for estimating watermark imperceptibility, a method for controlling watermark allocation, and an implementation of the proposed method in an MPEG2 encoder. Experimental evaluations demonstrated that degradation in picture quality was significantly reduced with the proposed method and that the proposed method can, for a given picture quality, embed 30% more watermarks than the previous method. The proposed method would be most effective when implemented in MPEG encoders because they already have the motion estimation functions needed. Future work will focus on improving the criterion for watermark imperceptibility and evaluate watermark survivability when image processing is other than MPEG2 (i.e., MPEG4, resizing, and filtering).

References

1. Swanson et al.: Multimedia data-embedding and watermarking technologies, *Proc. IEEE*, Vol. 86, No. 6, pp. 1064–1087 (1998).
2. Delaigle et al.: Watermarking algorithm based on a human visual model, *Signal Processing*, Vol. 66, pp. 319–335 (1998).
3. De Vleeschouwer et al.: Invisibility and application functionalities in perceptual watermarking–An overview, *Proc. IEEE*, Vol. 90, No. 1, pp. 64–77 (2002).
4. Echizen et al.: General quality maintenance module for motion picture watermarking, *IEEE Trans. Consumer Electronics*, Vol. 45, No. 4, pp. 1150–1158 (1999).
5. Echizen et al.: Estimating the Bit-error-rate in Digital Watermarking Using Inferential Statistics, *IPSJ Journal*, Vol. 42, No. 8, pp. 2006–2016 (2001).
6. Hartung et al.: Digital watermarking of raw and compressed video, *Proc. SPIE*, Vol. 2952, pp. 205–213 (1996).
7. Kundur et al.: Digital watermarking using multiresolution wavelet decomposition, *Intl. Conf. Acoustics, Speech and Signal Processing*, Vol. 5, pp. 2969–2972 (1998).
8. Sakai et al.: Evaluation of digital watermarking based on frequency transform, *Technical Report of IEICE*, ISEC 97–22, pp. 87–96 (1997).
9. Kobayashi et al.: DataHiding based on Neighbor Pixels Statistics, *Proc. IPSJ 56th Annual Conf.*, 1V–03 (1998).
10. Bender et al.: Techniques for data hiding, *Proc. SPIE*, Vol. 2020, pp. 2420–2440 (1995).
11. Dufaux et al.: Motion estimation techniques for digital TV: a review and new contribution, *Proc. IEEE*, Vol. 83, No. 6, pp. 858–876 (1998).
12. The Institute of Image Information and Television Engineers, Evaluation video sample (standard definition).
13. Rec. ITU-R BT.500-7, Methodology for the subjective assessment of the quality of television pictures (1995).

Appendix

The process flow of the 1-bit-WM detection associated with the WM embedding described in Section 3.2 comprises the following steps:

Step 1: Do the following steps over $t = 1, 2, \ldots$.

Step 2: Calculate bit-decision value v by correlating WM pattern $\mathbf{M}$ with watermarked image $\mathbf{Y}'^{(t)}$. That is,

$$\begin{aligned} v &= \frac{1}{mn} \sum_{ij} M_{i,j} {Y'}_{i,j}^{(t)} = \frac{1}{mn} \sum_{ij} M_{i,j} (Y_{i,j}^{(t)} \pm f_{i,j}^{(t)} M_{i,j}) \\ &= \frac{1}{mn} \sum_{ij} M_{i,j} Y_{i,j}^{(t)} \pm \frac{1}{mn} \sum_{ij} f_{i,j}^{(t)}, \end{aligned}$$

where $M_{i,j}$ are random arrays of ± 1. Thus, v is expressed by

$$v \simeq \pm \frac{1}{mn} \sum_{ij} f_{i,j}^{(t)}.$$

Step 3: Determine bit-value b by comparing v with threshold value $T (> 0)$:

$$b = \begin{cases} 1 & \text{if } v \geq T \\ 0 & \text{if } v \leq -T \\ \text{``not detected''} & \text{if } -T < v < T \end{cases}.$$

A Robust Printed Image Watermarking Based on Iterative Halftoning Method

In-Gook Chun and Sangho Ha

School of Information Technology Engineering, Soonchunhyang University, Asan-si, Choongchungnam-do, Republic of Korea
{chunik, hsh}@sch.ac.kr

Abstract. In this paper, we propose a noble watermark embedding and extraction method for printed images. Watermark bits are hidden at pseudo-random locations within a printed halftone image during halftoning process. To remove the artifacts and distortion due to the inserted watermark bits, iterative error minimizing technique is used. During each iteration the pattern which decreases the halftone error is selected as the next pattern where the halftone error is defined as the difference of HVS-filtered printed halftone image and grayscale image. The inserted watermarks are extracted from the scanned images after a series of image processing operation which is described in detail. In order to be robust to cropping and rotation, the watermark is inserted periodically in halftone images. Experiments using real scanned images show that the proposed method is feasible method to hide the large amount of data within a halftone image without noticeable distortion and the watermark is robust to cropping and rotation.

1 Introduction

Digital watermarking of image is a technique to protect the copyright of images by embedding of copyright information into the images. Watermark methods should enable a sufficient amount of embedded information introducing only minimal distortion to the image and its visual quality. There are a lot of watermarking methods. The common approaches of watermarking are to embed watermark in the spatial domain or frequency domain. But watermarking techniques previously developed mainly deal with on-line digital image. In this paper, we deal with watermarks for a special type of images, namely, printed image rather than on-line image. Printed image watermarking means that watermarks are inserted into hardcopy images generated by printers. Potential application might be secure printing, preventing forgery of printed tickets and authentication of picture ID cards. In the proposed method, watermarking is performed by exploiting the printing process itself i.e. halftoning. Halftoning is a process

This work is supported by the Korea Science and Engineering Foundation (KOSEF-R12-2002-052-04004-0) through the BIT Wireless Communication Devices Research Center at Soonchunhynag University.

T. Kalker et al. (Eds.): IWDW 2003, LNCS 2939, pp. 200–211, 2004.
© Springer-Verlag Berlin Heidelberg 2004

to convert continuous-tone images to two-tone images [1]. It is widely used in printing process because most printers have limited numbers of colors. Figure 1 shows the magnification of a printed image. Most previous watermarking methods were designed for grayscale images and they can not be applied directly to halftone images because halftone images have only two tones: black and white.

(a) (b)

Fig. 1. Most printers use halftoning techniques for printing grayscale images (a) a printed image scanned at 2400dpi (b) the magnified image of (a).

There are a lot of halftoning methods, but most popular methods are ordered dithering, error diffusion and iterative halftoning method [2]. Ordered dithering uses a threshold pattern and needs only simple computation. Error diffusion is a computationally complicated but its visual quality is fairly good. In error diffusion, the halftone error between the actual pixel intensity and halftone value is fed back to its neighboring pixels. There is another halftoning method called iterative halftoning method. Iterative halftoning method refines the initial halftone by iterative procedure. DBS(Direct Binary Search) is one of the iterative halftoning methods. It requires several passes to determine the final halftone image. It is computationally expensive method but its visual quality is quite good compared with other halftoning methods. And it is specially an attractive halftoning method for watermarking because the error-minimizing iteration of DBS makes the watermark not-detectable. In this paper, a iterative halftoning-based watermarking method for halftone images is proposed.

There are some researches on this field. There are two popular methods. The first method is to use two different halftone screens and switch the halftone screen according to the binary value of watermark bits [3], [4], [5]. The problem here is how to design an optimal halftone screen pair which allows minimal distortion and easy extraction of watermark bits. The second method is to change directly the pixel value of the halftone image according to the watermark information. Ming and Oscar have proposed a data hiding method for halftone image generated by error diffusion method [6], [7], [8], [9]. Data Hiding Error Diffusion (DHED) integrates the data hiding into the error diffusion operation. DHED hides data by forced complementary toggling at pseudo-random locations within a halftone image. But their method shows some artifacts due to the watermark insertion. The main reason is that the data hiding error is only compensated by the future pixel, that is, the next pixels in the scanning order.

In this paper, a robust watermarking method for printed image using iterative halftoning method is described. In order to make only minimal distortion to the image, we use the concept of halftone error and error-minimizing iteration. The proposed method can reduce the distortion by finding an optimal pixel arrangement using iterative search. The disadvantage of iterative halftoning is the computation overhead. But from our experiment, it is observed that after a few iterations, the proposed method quickly converged to its final halftone image. The watermark pattern is designed to be robust to cropping and geometric distortion. The watermark extraction algorithm consists of two major modules. The first module generates the binary halftone image from the scanned image using image processing operations. The second module extracts the watermark from the binary halftone image. If the printed image is scanned at higher resolution than printing resolution, watermark can be detected reliably. The proposed method is a true blind watermarking scheme which requires no information from the encoder except the seed of random number generator. Experiments are performed against real scanned images.

2 Watermarking Algorithm

2.1 Watermark Embedding

Because both of halftone image and watermark are binary, the pixel values of halftone images can carry the watermark information. So in the proposed method, random locations in the halftone image are generated by some seed value and the pixel values of these locations are set to be black or white dot according to the watermark bits as shown in Figure 2. If this seed value is sent to the watermark decoder, one can extract the watermark bits just by reading the value of these random locations generated by received seed value.

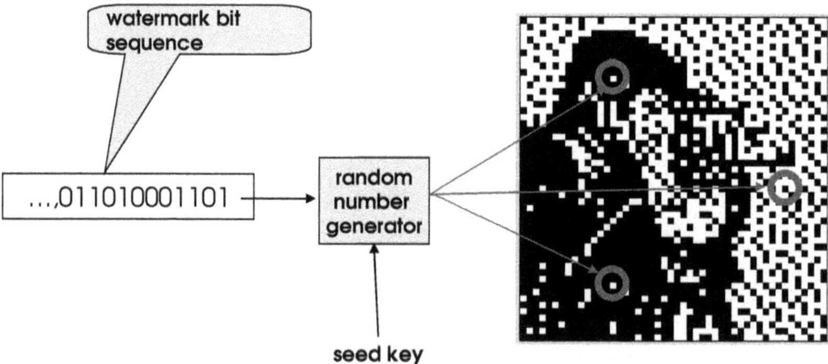

Fig. 2. The watermark bits are inserted into the random locations which are generated by random number generator seeded by some key.

The main problem is the distortion of a halftone image caused by the inserted watermark bits. If the amount of the watermark bits is not small, the distortion could be noticeable. In the proposed method, the distortion is minimized by finding optimal neighborhood pixel configuration through iterative search. Figure 3 is the detailed block diagram of the watermark embedding system. It consists of three stages, initial halftoning stage, watermark-inserting stage, error-minimizing stage. In the initial halftoning stage, the original grayscale image is halftoned with a predefined threshold matrix.

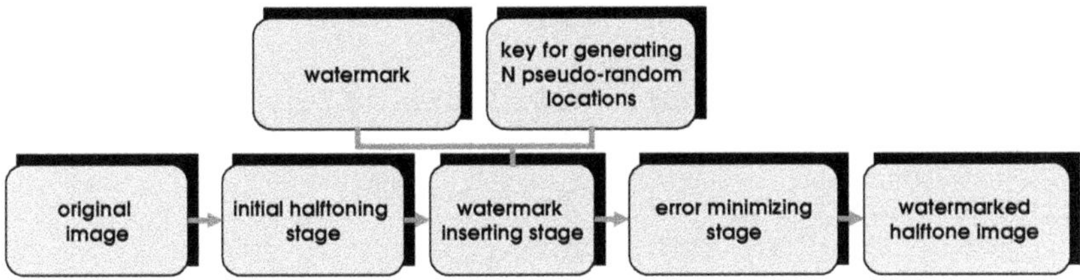

Fig. 3. The block diagram of watermark embedding system

In the watermark inserting stage, we use a symmetric key cryptography. N pseudo-random locations are generated by a secret key known to both encoder and decoder. Watermark data is hidden at these pseudo-random locations. Data can be any kinds of binary bit data, namely raw binary data or data with error correction codes. One bit of data is hidden at each of the N pseudo-random locations by forcing the pixel value at those locations to be zero or one according to the watermark data.

In the error-minimizing stage, the initial halftone image with watermark generated from the previous stage is enhanced by the iterative procedure [3]. The pixel value except the watermark pixels are toggled or swapped with neighbor pixels in the direction of decreasing the halftoning error between grayscale image and halftone image. The halftone error is defined as follows:

$$E = \sum_{m}\sum_{n} \left| h(m,n) ** g(m,n) - h(m,n) ** f(m,n) \right|^{2} \tag{1}$$

where *h(m,n)* represents the point spread function(PSF) of an inverse-halftoning filter, *f(m,n)* is the continuous-tone original image, which is assumed to lie between 0.0(white) and 1.0(black), *g(m,n)* is the halftone image and ** denotes 2D convolution. In the above equation, *h(m,n)*** *g(m,n)* is the inverse-halftoned image, and $|h(m,n)**g(m,n) - f(m,n)|$ means the halftoning error for a particular pixel. The simplest *h(x,y)* is the PSF of low-pass filter. In this paper, *h(x,y)* is assumed as any HVS(Human Visual System) filter. As the error is minimized, the inverse-halftoned image becomes closer to the original continuous-tone image.

The error-minimizing procedure is based on Direct Binary Search (DBS) halftoning method [3]. DBS uses the direct binary search like toggling or swapping to minimize the error. The whole halftone image is scanned one by one from left-top location to right-bottom. At the particular location, possible candidate patterns are generated by toggling and swapping. The error of each binary pattern is calculated and the minimum error pattern is chosen among them. The minimal error binary pattern replaces the original binary pattern. When no changes are accepted during a single iteration the algorithm has converged. DBS converges to a local minimum but it is observed that choosing different starting points has little effect on the final value of E and on the visual quality. The following code is the pseudo-code of this error-minimizing procedure.

```
generate an initial halftone image;
while(any pixel is changed) {
 for all pixel location (x,y) in halftone image {
  if (x,y) is one of pseudo-random locations
   continue;
  else {
   for all toggled and swapped patterns at (x,y)
    calculates the halftone error of that pattern;
   choose the minimum error pattern;
   replace the block by the minimum error pattern;
  }
 }
}
```

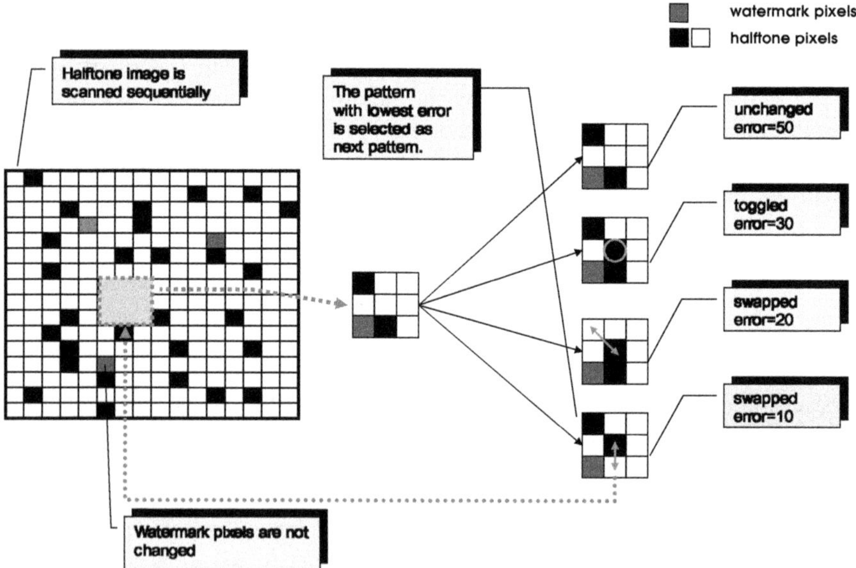

Fig. 4. Error minimizing procedure. Each pattern is generated by toggling or swapping.

Figure 4 shows the error-minimizing procedure where four candidates patterns are generated and the fourth one is selected as the next pattern.

In order to provide robustness to cropping and geometrical robustness, the same watermarks are inserted multiple times at periodic shifted locations. This redundancy can be used to identify the parameters of geometrical affine transformation [12]. Since the watermark has been embedded multiple times, the autocorrelation of watermarked image has multiple peaks. If the image has undergone a geometrical transformation, the peaks in the autocorrelation function will reflect the same transformation. Hence using these point pairs, we can compute the parameter of the geometrical transformation parameters. The Figure 5 shows that the same watermarks are embedded four times in four non-overlapping blocks. The first *P* bits of base watermark block are preset to known values. These preset bits act like a reference mark which can be used in order to compute the amount of translation. Note that the values of preset bits are known but the positions of preset bits are not preset. The positions are determined according to the secret key.

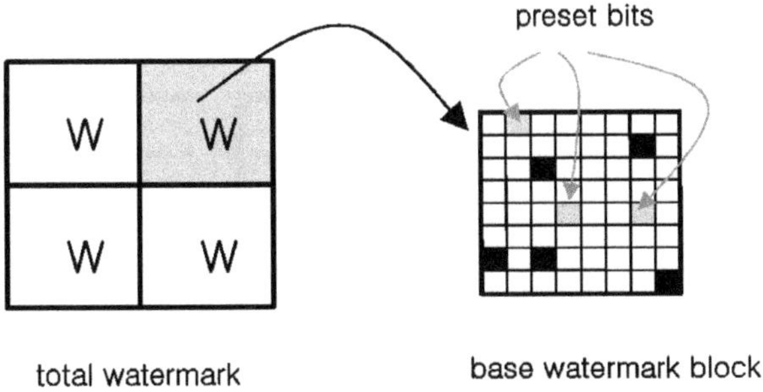

Fig. 5. Periodic watermark with preset bits

2.2 Watermark Extraction

We assume that the input is a scanned image which is obtained by scanning the printed halftone image containing watermark. The resolution of scanner is set to be higher than that of printer. Otherwise it is very difficult to recover the accurate pixel value because of scanner noise and alignment error. So we scan the printed image at much higher resolution and process the scanned image using image processing technology in order to get an original binary halftone image.

The watermark extraction algorithm consists of two major modules. The first module generates the binary halftone image from the scanned image. The second module extracts the watermark from the binary halftone image. Figure 6 shows the overall block diagram of watermark extraction system.

The first step is skew detection. Generally the scanned image can be skewed arbitrary. There are many ways to detect the skew angle but in this paper, simple Hough transform method is used. The horizontal edge pixels are identified and Hough transform computes the skew angle of these horizontal edges [13]. Using this skew angle information we can correct the skewed image. After the skew correction, in order to remove the rotation noise, morphological operation is applied to the image. Next step is to estimate the dot size of halftone image. Here we assume that the shape of the dot is square although many other shapes are used in reality. The connected components analysis operation is applied to the image and each connected component size is recorded. Generally we can assume that there are many one-dot-sized components in a halftone image. So the most frequent component size might be the dot size. After the dot size is determined, we calculate the center of dot using edge information. By analyzing the distribution of the summation value of edge pixel along the x-axis and y-axis, we determine the boundary of dots. The center of dot is the half of dot size away from the boundary. Once the center of dot is found, all we have to do is to read the pixel value. After these preprocessing operations, we can obtain binary halftone image from the scanned image.

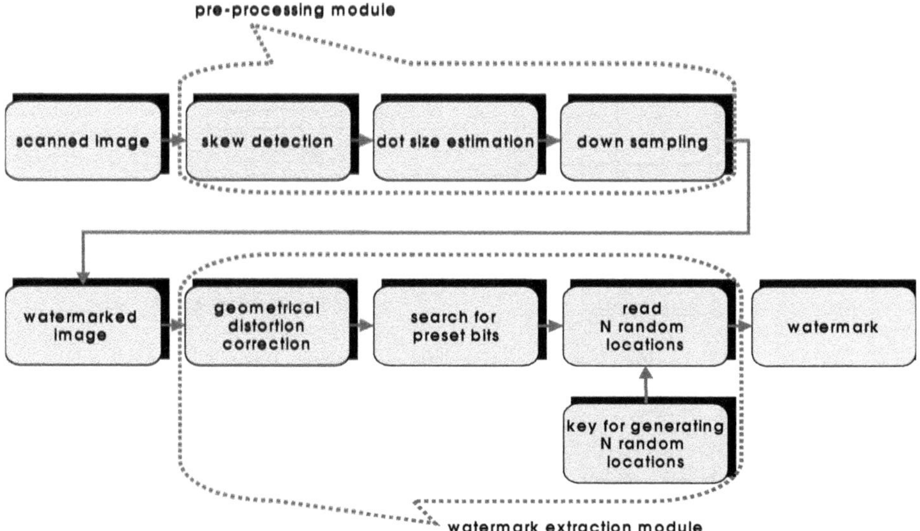

Fig. 6. The block diagram of watermark extraction system

In order to determine the watermark block size, autocorrelation function of binary halftone image is computed using the following equation

$$R_{g,g}(u,v) = \sum_m \sum_n g(m,n)g(m+u,n+v) \tag{2}$$

where $g(m,n)$ is the watermarked halftone image. If there are any periodic data in the watermarked image, there would be multiple peaks in autocorrelation function as shown Figure 7. To detect the peaks, the gradient of autocorrelation value is computed. These peaks are used to compute the size of the watermark block.

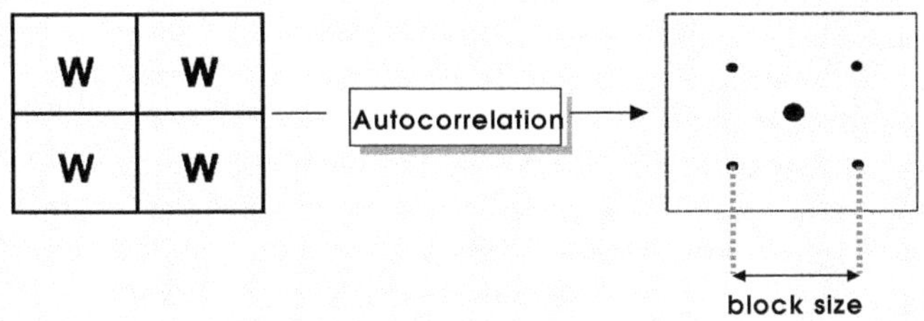

Fig. 7. The peaks of autocorrelation function can be used as reference points in computing transformation parameters.

After the watermark block size is determined, N pseudo-random locations are generated by a same key which was used in the embedding process. Knowing the information of these random locations, the corrected image is scanned sequentially to find the preset bits of the watermark. The concept of preset bits is used in order to be robust to translation and cropping. The first *P* bits of watermark are preset to known values. After finding the preset bits, the remaining watermark bits can be recovered simply by reading the pixel values at next random locations.

3 Experimental Results and Discussion

The proposed algorithm is tested with one test image in order verify its performance. The result was compared with that of Ming [7] [8]. Ming proposed DHED (Data Hiding Error Diffusion) method which inserted watermark by toggling the pixel value of halftone image. In DHED, the data hiding error is only compensated by the future pixel, that is, the next pixels in the scanning order, but in the proposed method, the error is spread out to its neighbor pixels by the HVS filtering more uniformly than DHED.

The test image is a 128x128 8-bit grayscale image cam eraman" shown in Figure 8(a). Figure 8(b) is the watermark image consisting of four non-overlapping blocks containing 96 watermark bits. The watermark bit "0" is shown as a black dot and "1" as a white dot. Figure 8(c) shows the initial halftone image generated by ordered dithering. It shows the salt and pepper type artifacts and the distribution of black and white pixels is not uniform. It is mainly due to the watermark bits which are forced at the pseudo-random locations. Figure 8(d) is the final halftone image generated by the proposed algorithm. As you can see, the black and white pixel distributions are more uniform than the initial halftone image and the number of salt and pepper type artifacts is significantly decreased. Moreover it is difficult to identify the watermark pixels. Figure 8(e) is the final halftone image without watermark data. Note that there is no

(a) (b)

(c) (d)

(e) (f)

Fig. 8. The results of "cameraman" image watermarking. (a) original image (b) watermark image (c) initial halftone image (d) final halftone image with watermark (e) final halftone image without watermark (f) final halftone image using DHED.

significant visual difference between Figure 8(d) and (e). Figure 8(f) is the final result of DHED algorithm. As you can see, the result of the proposed algorithm is better than that of DHED.

To test the robustness of the proposed algorithm to geometrical cropping and rotation, the final halftone was printed by HP LaserJet at 600 dpi and it was scanned by HP scanjet at 2400 dpi as shown in Figure 9(a). During scanning, it was deliberately rotated and cropped. In Figure 9(b), the skew was corrected using edge information and connected components were found in Figure 9(c). The dot centers were found using the projection value of edge as shown in Figure 9(d). Finally the binary halftone image was recovered by reading the value of each dot in Figure 9(e). In order to compute the watermark block size, the autocorrelation function of the final halftone image is calculated as shown in Figure 9(f). As you can see, the peaks can be identified and the watermark block size is equal to the distance between peak points in Figure 9(f). Then the final halftone image is scanned sequentially to find the preset bits of the watermark block. Once we find the preset bits, the remaining watermark bits can be recovered simply by reading the pixel values at next random locations.

4 Conclusion

In this paper, a new watermarking method for halftone images is proposed. The proposed method is based on iterative halftoning technique. It hides data at pseudo-random locations within a halftone image. The major problem of this method is to remove the artifacts and distortions due to the embedded watermark data effectively. The proposed method achieves the improved visual quality by using iterative error minimizing technique. By integrating data hiding into halftoning operation, relatively large amount of data can be hidden within a halftone image while the visual quality of final halftone image is maintained. Moreover the watermark data within the halftone images is not easily detectable by the eye.

To be robust to cropping and distortion, the watermark consists of several non-overlapping blocks. Each block contains the same watermark data. An image processing procedure has been developed to recognize the real printed binary image. After a series image processing operation, the skewed and cropped scanned image is corrected and the binary halftone image is recovered. Using autocorrelation function, we can determine the watermark block size and finally we can extract the watermark information form the watermark block. Experiments using real scanned images were conducted and experimental results show that the proposed algorithm generates halftone images with good visual quality and robust to the unintentional geometrical attacks. This new technique has great potential in printing security documents such as currency, coupon, on-line tickets and ID card as well as confidential documents.

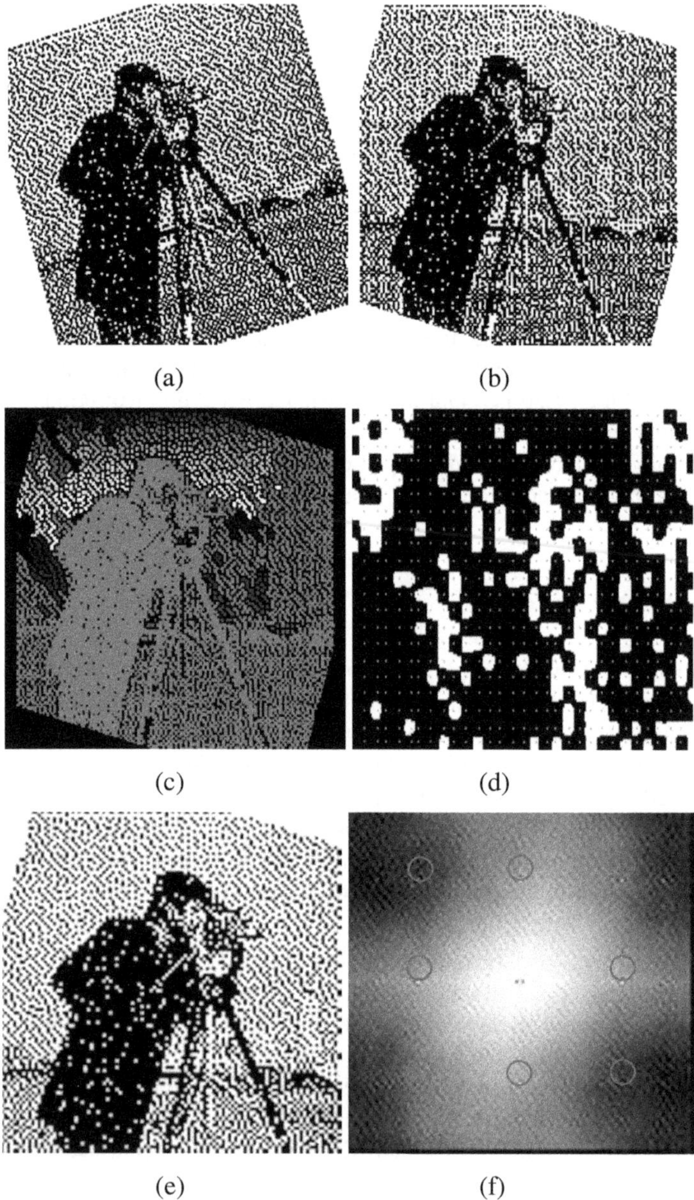

Fig. 9. Watermark extraction steps. (a) scanned halftone image (b) skew-corrected image (c) the result of connected component analysis (d) the detection of dot center (e) final binary halftone image (f) autocorrelation function of the final halftone image.

References

1. Ulichney, R. A.: Digital Halftoning. MIT Press, Cambridge, MA(1987)
2. Allebach, J. P.: DBS: Retrospective and Future Direction. Proceedings of SPIE Vol. 4300 (2001) 358–376
3. Hel-Or, H. Z.: Copyright Labeling of Printed Images. Proceedings of IEEE Int. Conf. on Image Processing (2000) 702–705
4. Wang, S.G. and Knox, K.T.: Embedding digital watermarks in halftone screens. Proceedings of SPIE Vol. 3971(2000) 218–227
5. Baharav, Z. and Shaked, D.: Watermarking of dither halftoned images. Proceedings of SPIE Vol.3657(1999) 307–316
6. Fu, M.S. and Au, O.C.: Data Hiding in Halftone Images by Stochastic Error Diffusion. Proceedings of IEEE Int. Conf. on Acoustics, Speech, and Signal Processing (2001) 1965–1968
7. Fu, M.S. and Au, O.C.: Hiding Data in Halftone Image using Modified Data Hiding Error Diffusion. Proceedings of SPIE Vol. 4067 (2000) 1671–1680
8. Fu, M.S. and Au, O.C.: Data Hiding for Halftone Images. Proceedings of SPIE Vol.3971, (2000) 228–236
9. Fu, M.S. and Au, O.C.: Halftone image data hiding with intensity selection and connection selection. Signal Proceeding: Image Communication 16(2001) 909–930
10. Kacker, D. and Allebach, J. P.: Joint Halftoning and Watermarking. Proceedings of IEEE Int. Conf. on Image Processing (2000) 69–72
11. Mese, M., Vaidyanathan, P. P.: Look-Up Table (LUT) Method for Inverse Halftoning. IEEE Trans. on Image Processing, Vol. 10 (2001) 1566–1578
12. Kutter, M.: Watermarking Resisting to Translation, Rotation, and Scaling. Proceedings of SPIE Vol. 3528 (1998) 423–431
13. Parker, J.R.: Algorithms for Image Processing and Computer Vision. John Wiley & Sons, Hoboken, NJ (1996)

A Feature-Watermarking Scheme for JPEG Image Authentication

Jinshen Wang[1], Yuewei Dai[1], Stefan Thiemert[2], and Zhiquan Wang[1]

[1]Department of Automation,
Nanjing University of Science & Technology, Nanjing, China 210094
[2]Fraunhofer IPSI, Department MERIT, Darmstadt, Germany
daiywei@mail.njust.edu.cn

Abstract. Feature-based watermark is a special kind of watermark, which reflects the features of the content, and these features are deliberately chosen in the way that they will keep invariant during "content preserving" modifications while being sensitive to "malicious" attacks. In this paper, a novel approach to content authentication for JPEG images is proposed. The image authentication method is based on partial energy relation between groups of 8×8 DCT blocks as features, while the strategies of watermark embedding and extraction is based on improved DEW algorithm. Our proposed scheme has the capability of differentiating "content preserving" modifications from "malicious" attacks and so can ascertain and locate the "malicious" attacks. Experimental results show the feasibility of the proposed scheme.

Keywords: authentication, features, watermarking, semi-fragile

1 Introduction

1.1 Watermarking Techniques for Image Authentication

Digital images are more and more widely used in nowadays society because of their ease of manipulation, processing, and storage. Meanwhile, the well-known proverb that "the photograph doesn't tell a lie" is no longer true since the development of powerful image manipulation software. The synthetic images are as natural as images appear in almost every TV program and film, which makes it hard to distinguish original images from manipulated ones. This technical development has decreased the credibility that photography used to achieve in the past. So the authentication of digital media including image and video is becoming a highlight, especially in medical, military and juristic occasions.

Image authentication verifies the originality of an image by detecting malicious manipulations. This goal is different from that of image watermarking which embeds into the image a signature surviving most manipulations.
The earlier technique for the authentication of a digital object is the digital signature, which is usually a hash of the corresponding object. This scheme is classified as

T. Kalker et al. (Eds.): IWDW 2003, LNCS 2939, pp. 212–222, 2004.
© Springer-Verlag Berlin Heidelberg 2004

complete authentication [3], which considers the whole piece of data and does not allow any manipulation. However, it is well known that digital images have some special requirements. For example, they are generally provided in compressed form of JPEG, and sometimes they need to be transformed from one form to the other, which causes the object to be changed. In these cases [3] the authentication schemes are required to be robust to these "content preserving" such as image type conversion, re-quantization, and re-encoding, etc. manipulations, while sensitive to "malicious" ones (content partly or totally removal/ replacement/ ruining within one image).

It should be noted that there is no absolute borderline between "content preserving" modifications and "malicious" manipulations [22]. As a matter of fact, whether a manipulation belongs to "content preserving" or "malicious" depends on applications as well as related requirements. For example, a filtering operation may be thought of as acceptable for a common picture but will be unacceptable for a medical picture. And even the same operation hops from one to the other when different parameters are used.

Authentication watermarks can be classified as fragile watermark [2], [3], [5], [10], [18], or semi-fragile watermark [3], [4], [5], [6], [12]. The former usually is designed to be very sensitive to every possible alteration in pixel values. In most cases fragile watermarking schemes embed a watermark by LSB modifications, which cannot survive "content preserving" manipulations. Semi-fragile watermarks are designed to differentiate between "content preserving" and malicious manipulations. It is important for a semi-fragile watermarking scheme to be "moderately robust" to some degrees. Feature-based watermarking is a "semi-fragile" watermarking.

1.2 The Main Contributions of This Paper

1) Scheme's outline

When an image is compressed with JPEG, its image pixels are transformed to DCT coefficients, quantized, and encoded. In this study, we have found by experiments that the energy relationship between two blocks (or group of blocks) remains invariable through repetitive JPEG compression. And we also found that the main parts of DCT block's energy are located in the lower frequencies, which determine the characteristic of the "content". We separate the 64 DCT coefficients of all blocks into a form of two regions. The lower region is used to form feature code while the higher is used to embed both content authentication watermarks and copyright protection watermarks. The former is based on the invariance of DCT energy relationship between different blocks when undergoing some processing manipulations, and this relationship is one-bit quantized for simplicity. The latter is inspired from DEW scheme [8] that used to embed robustly in image and video. Three keys controlling the group coupling, encrypting message, and block shuffling respectively guarantee the security of our scheme. Like the Ching-yung Lin' scheme [5], our scheme is also relatively fast since it needn't JPEG coding and decoding, all the disposing is implemented directly in compressed domain.

2) Arrangement of the paper
In section 2, we depict the proposed system in general, including feature extraction, watermark embedding/detection and content verification. In section 3, the feature extraction method will be described in detail, followed by the watermark embedding/detection scheme in section 4. In section 5, some discussions and analysis about the scheme are given out in its ability to detect and localize malicious manipulations and to tolerate acceptable changes. And conclusions will be given in section 6.

2 General System Designing

Now we describe the framework of our image authentication system. It can be divided into three parts as shown in Fig.1: feature extraction, watermark embedding/ detection and content verification.

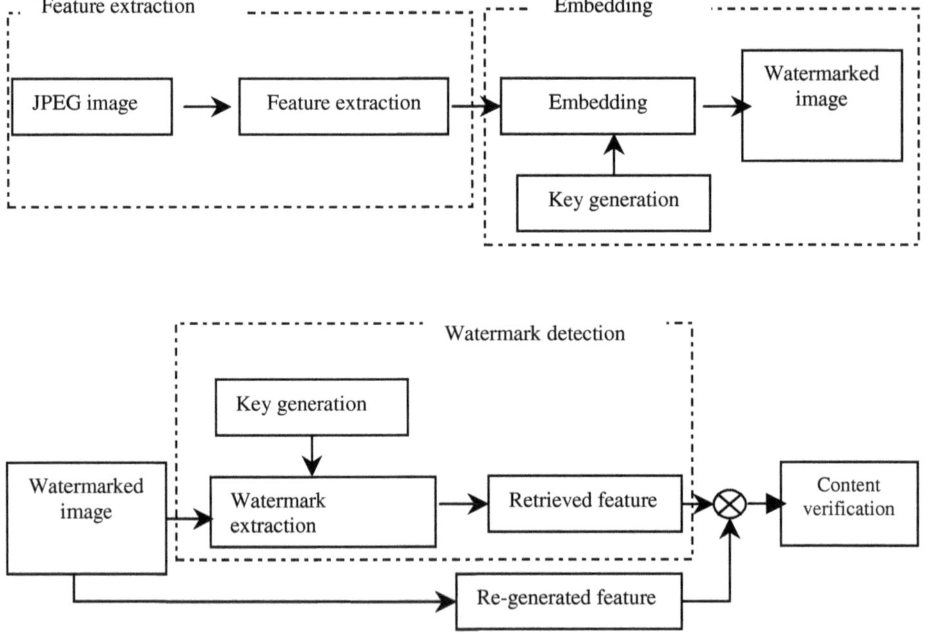

Fig. 1. The diagram of the image authentication system

3 Feature Extraction

In [3] and [5], the authentication signature of Ching-yung Lin et al. is based on the invariance of the relationship between DCT coefficients of the same position in separate blocks of an image. This relationship will be preserved when these coefficients are quantized in a JPEG compression process. Since using DCT coefficient pairs with two single coefficients generates the feature code, it will be fluctuated if their difference is small enough under some "content preserving" modifications. Although the author raised a margin value to avoid such situations, it caused another problem stated in the literature [6]. That is, if an attacker manipulates the image, making the absolute value of the difference below a margin value M, this attack will never be detected. So we believe that the relationships among the DCT coefficients in the neighborhood areas should be explored in the feature generation.

From the literature [1], we found that the partial energy relationship between two groups of DCT block will keep constant during recompression with different quality factors. Thus we do a one-bit quantization of this relationship to generate our Authentication Message (AM).

There are M 8×8 blocks in one image of JPEG format, $B=\{b_1, b_2, \ldots, b_M\}$. For each 8×8 block, $C_i=\{c_{i,0}, c_{i,2}, \ldots, c_{i,63}\}$ is the corresponding DCT coefficients. We separate $\{c_{i,j}\}_{j=0,\ldots,63}$ to two parts, $C_{i,f}=\{c_{i,1}, \ldots, c_{i,s}\}$; $C_{i,e}=\{c_{i,s+1}, \ldots, c_{i,63}\}$, where s can be adjusted according to the average energy of the whole image. We assign 2n blocks with some fixed arrangement in one group for feature extraction and watermark embedding. Thus one image also can be expressed as $G=\{g_1, g_2, \ldots, g_L\}$, and $M=2n\times L$.

The feature extraction procedure is as following:
Step 1: VLC decoding

Step 2: Block grouping:
Combine several adjacent blocks together as a group according to pre-defined number n, in which the blocks are arranged in rectangle style.

Step 3: Coupling two groups
A group pair is the basic unit for feature extraction and watermark embedding, and one group is separated into two parts with equal number of blocks. To enhance the security of the scheme, we couple two groups under the control of key 1. So the couple groups are selected randomly. Every group has its counterpart. Let N_1 be the total group pair number of an image. The coupled group pairs are re-indexed respectively as:

$$P =\{p_1, p_2, \cdots, p_{N_1}\}=\{(g_{1a}, g_{1b}), (g_{2a}, g_{2b}), \cdots, (g_{N_1 a}, g_{N_1 b})\} \qquad (1)$$

Step 4: Partial energy calculating

Partial energy of each group which consists of several DCT coefficients in each 8×8 block in one group is calculated by Equation (2),

$$E^s = \sum_{i=1}^{2n} \sum_{j=0}^{s} (\theta_{ij})^2 \quad (2)$$

Where $s = 0,1,2,...,63$, θ_{ij} is the DCT coefficient in 8×8 blocks.

Step 5: Selecting separating index s

We separate all 64 DCT coefficients of one image into two parts. The region, which has lower frequencies, is the feature-extraction region. The higher region is the watermark-embedding region. We use the following iteration procedure to search the separating index s_μ:

FOR s=1 to 63 DO

IF $\frac{\overline{E}^s}{\overline{E}^{63}} \geq \mu\%$ THEN GOTO end

END

Here μ is the reasonable energy value for both feature and embedding, which is suggested as 80~90. As can be seen the separation index s cannot have the value 0; otherwise the feature extraction region would be empty.

Step 6: One-bit quantization of partial energy relationship

Let image features be:

$$F = \{f_1, f_2, \cdots, f_{N_1}\},\ f_i \in (0,1) \ \text{i=1,2, ..., N}_1. \quad (3)$$

For each group pair, the feature is can be calculated by:

$$f_i = \begin{cases} 0 & \text{if } \overline{E}^s_{j,ia} - \overline{E}^s_{j,ib} \geq M_f \\ re-construct & -M_f < \overline{E}^s_{j,ia} - \overline{E}^s_{j,ib} < M_f \\ 1 & \overline{E}^s_{j,ia} - \overline{E}^s_{j,ib} \leq -M_f \end{cases} \quad (4)$$

Here M_f is minimum difference of energy for feature generator, when an energy difference is less than this value, the relations will be uncertain after recompression. We re-construct their relations by adjusting the DCT coefficient of the highest frequency in the lower region to force their energy difference to be larger than M_f.

4 Scheme Designing

4.1 Watermarking Embedding

Watermark formation and embedding procedure can be described as following:
Step1: Encrypting the message F to form watermark W.

$$W = F \oplus K_2 = (w_1, w_2, \cdots, w_{N_w}) \tag{5}$$

Here " $\oplus$ " is the encryption operation, K_2 is a pseudo-random sequence (public key or symmetric key), N_w is the total number of bits in the watermark.
Step 2: Pseudo-randomly shuffling the blocks within the range of one image to get better energy distribution.
The shuffling process is controlled by K_3. The blocks of this shuffled image are grouped again in the same way as in section 3 to form the label-bit-carrying region (lc-region), and each lc-region has two parts (A, B) with the same size (n blocks, the same as in feature extraction).
Step 3: Watermark embedding using DEW algorithm [8]:
FOR all watermark bits w_i in W, DO

- Separate an lc-region (a group with 2n blocks) into A, B two sub-regions
- Calculate cut-off index I_c

$$I_c = \max\{c_{min}, \max\{j \in (s_\mu, 63) \mid (\overline{E}_A^j - \overline{E}_A^{s_\mu}) \geq D\}, \max\{k \in (s_\mu, 63) \mid (\overline{E}_B^k - \overline{E}_B^{s_\mu})\}\} \tag{6}$$

- IF (w_i=0) THEN discard DCT coefficients of sub-region B from high to low until $(E_A - E_B) \geq D$, except for $c \leq Ic$.
- IF (w_i=1) THEN discard DCT coefficients of sub-region A from high to low until $(E_B - E_A) < D$.

Step 4: Shuffling all blocks back to their original locations.
Step 5: VLC coding and restore the JPEG data stream.

4.2 Watermark Detection

The watermark detection procedure is a blind one, which is designed as three parts,

- Extract the watermark
- Regenerate the feature and reconstruct the watermark
- Content Verification

1) Extracting watermark
   a) VLC decoding of the data stream
   b) Shuffle it randomly controlled by K_3
   c) Group it in the same way as in section 3.
   d) FOR all possible watermark bits w'_i in $W'(N_W$ bits), DO
   - Separate a lc-region (a group with 2n blocks) into A, B two sub-regions
   - Calculate cutoff index I'_c and energy difference threshold D'. Usually $D' \leq D$.

$$I_c = \max\{c_{min}, \max\{j \in (s_\mu, 63) \mid (\overline{E}_A^j - \overline{E}_A^{s_\mu}) \geq D\}, \max\{k \in (s_\mu, 63) \mid (\overline{E}_B^k - \overline{E}_B^{s_\mu})\}\} \tag{7}$$

- IF $(E'_A - E'_B) \geq D'$ THEN ($w'_i = 1$)
  ELSE IF $(E'_A - E'_B) \leq -D'$ THEN ($w'_i = 0$)
  ELSE ($w'_i =$ don't care)
  END

e) Decrypt the watermark using K_2 to get the image feature code F'

2) Regenerating feature and reconstructing watermark

We do the same thing as stated in section 3, and get image feature code:

$$F'' = \{f''_1, f''_2, \cdots, f''_{N_1}\},\ f''_i \in (0,1),\ i=1,2,\ldots,N_1. \tag{8}$$

$$f''_i = \begin{cases} 0 & \text{if } \overline{E}^s_{j,ia} - \overline{E}^s_{j,ib} \geq M'_f \\ don't\ care & -M_f < \overline{E}^s_{j,ia} - \overline{E}^s_{j,ib} < M'_f \\ 1 & \overline{E}^s_{j,ia} - \overline{E}^s_{j,ib} \leq -M'_f \end{cases} \tag{9}$$

Here we let $M'_f \leq M_f$. Since every selected group couple is fixed, and the embedded bit depends on the position of these blocks involved, so there is still a barrier of $2 \times M'_f$.

3) Content Verification

Compare the extracted feature code F'' with the re-generated feature code F' to find whether there are malicious manipulations to the object. And if it happens then try to ascertain the location of manipulation.

There are three possible scenarios. For the simplicity of discussion, we assume that the watermark is robust enough, which means the extracted watermark is exactly equal to the embedded one ($f' = f$).

a) " $f''=0$ and $f'=0$ " and " $f''=1$ and $f'=1$ "

When every bit of regenerated feature code is equal to extracted feature code, then the content can be taken as authentic.

b) " $f''=0$ and $f'=1$ " and " $f''=1$ and $f'=0$ "

When one or more mismatches appear, we may conclude that this image has been manipulated in some ways. Since the groups are numbered, we can locate the manipulations according to the group number. But one feature bit stands for the relation between two groups, how can we determine which group has been suffered attack? One possible answer is to observe those groups nearby around both groups. Usually a manipulation will affect more than one group because the group size is small.

c) " $f''=0$ and $f'=$ don't care " and " $f''=1$ and $f'=$ don't care "

This is an uncertain scenario when the original feature code bit is "0" or "1" but the regenerated code falls into "don't care region". Our goal is to make this region is as narrow as possible by deliberately choosing the combinations of feature generating/regenerating, watermarking embedding/extracting parameters.

5 Experiments and Analysis

To demonstrate the feasibility of our scheme, we designed a set of experiments. All the experiments will be applied on the luminance layer, and also can be applied to the other two layers.

In our experiments, the images used as cover images shown in Fig. 2, are JPEG formatted with an original quality factor 85, all of size 512×512 (group size 2n=16). The resulting stego-images are shown in Fig. 2, respectively. The PSNR (peak of signal to noise ratio) values of the stego-images are shown in Table 1 from which we can see that the stego-images still have good quality.

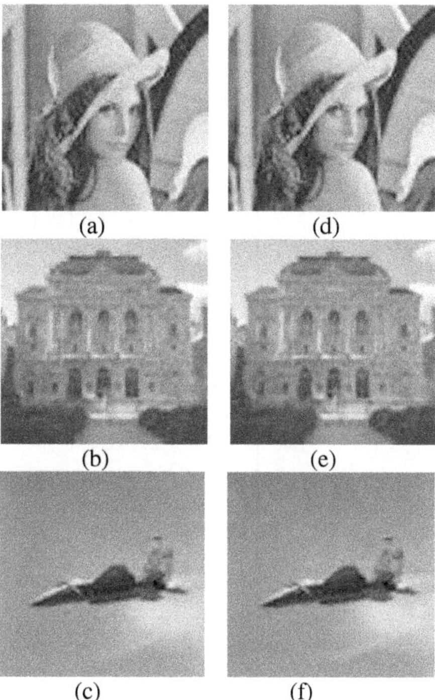

Fig. 2. (a) Cover image "Lena". (b) Cover image "Opera". (c) Cover image "F15" (d)-(f) The corresponding Stego-images

Table 1. The PSNR values of the stego-images

	Lena	Opera	F-15
PSNR	35.2	35.8	35.5

In evaluating the proposed image authenticator, we design three kinds of attacks: one part disappeared; one part is removed; and one part is replaced. We only took the "F-15" image as an example – the other two images are similar. Each image is first modified and then re-compressed. The results for the experiment items are given in table 2.

Table 2. Experimental results (group size 2n=16)

Manipulation	Manipulated image	Should be found	Actually be found
Part disappeared			
Part is removed			
Part is replaced			

From the results we may get the following conclusions:

- If the parameters are well selected, deliberately tampers can be found with a high probability by this scheme, i.e. the proposed scheme is semi-fragile to some extent. On the one hand, the scheme is sensitive to "content modifications"; on the other hand, it is robust to those "normal modifications" such as recompressions. So, this scheme is useful with a high probability of trust

- The ability of manipulation localization changes with the size of groups, which, when group size (2n blocks) decreases, the localization precision increases and the sensitivity increases. But the robustness to "normal modifications" will decrease at the same time because the averaging effect gets weaker.
- The embedding capacity also varies with the group size. The total embedding bits will decrease as the group size increase.
- It is necessary to make a trade-off among group size, energy difference and minimal cut-off index. From the experiments, we found out that the larger the enforced energy difference, the more robust the watermark would be. But too much energy difference will cause the perceptible decrease of visual quality because more DCT coefficients have to be discarded.

6 Conclusions

In this paper, we present a novel watermarking scheme to content authentication for JPEG images. The image authentication method is based on a semi-fragile feature, which has the ability to differentiate "content preserving" modifications from "malicious" attacks, so our proposed scheme can ascertain and locate the attacks. Experimental results have shown the feasibility of the proposed scheme. Our future effort will be focused on parameters optimization and finding some adaptive way to determine those parameters upon different applications.

References

1. Yuewei Dai, Stefan Thiemert, Martin Steinbach, Enric Hauer, Jana Dittmann. Feature-based watermarking scheme for MPEG-I/II video authentication. Conference on Security, Steganography, and Watermarking of Multimedia Contents VI, part of the IS&T/SPIE Symposium on Electronic Imaging 2004, 18–22 January 2004 in San Jose, CA USA (has been accepted)
2. Jessica Fridrich. Security of Fragile Authentication Watermarks with Localization, Proc. SPIE Photonic West, Vol. 4675, Electronic Imaging 2002, Security and Watermarking of Multimedia Contents IV, San Jose, California, January, 2002, pp. 691–700.
3. Ching-Yung Lin and Shih-Fu Chang, Semi-Fragile Watermarking for Authenticating JPEG Visual Content, SPIE Security and Watermarking of Multimedia Contents II, EI '00, San Jose, CA, Jan. 2000.
4. Mehmet U. Celik , Gaurav Sharma, A. Murat Tekalp and Eli Saber. Video authentication with self-recovery. Video Authentication with Self-Recovery, Proceedings of SPIE, Security and Watermarking of Multimedia Contents IV, January 2002.
5. Ching-Yung Lin and Shih-Fu Chang, Issues and Solutions for Authenticating MPEG Video, SPIE Security and Watermarking of Multimedia Contents, EI '99, San Jose, CA, Jan. 1999.
6. Kuato Maeno, Qibin Sun, Shih-Fu Chang, Masayuki Suto. New semi-fragile image authentication watermarking techniques using random bias and non-uniform quantization. Proceedings of SPIE, Security and Watermarking of Multimedia Contents IV, Vol.4675. Jan., 2002. pp. 659–670

7. Iwan Setyawan , Reginald L. Lagendijk. Low bit-rate video watermarking using temporally extended differential energy watermarking (DEW) algorithm. Proceedings of the SPIE. SPIE Security and Watermarking of Multimedia Contents III, San Jose, Jan. 21–26, 2001
8. A. Hanjalic, G.C. Langelaar, P.M.B. van Roosmalen, J. Biemond, R.L. Lagendijk. Image and video databases: restoration, watermarking and retrieval. First edition, Netherlands, ISBN: 0444505024.
9. Dittmann,, Jana, Stabenau, Mark, Steinmetz, Ralf: Robust MEG Video Watermarking Technologies, Proceedings of ACM Multimedia'98, The 6th ACM International Multimedia Conference, Bristol, England, pp. 71–80
10. J. Dittmann, A. Mukherjee, M. Steinebach, Media-independent Watermarking Classification and the need for combining digital video and audio watermarking for media authentication, Proceedings of the International Conference on Information Technology: Coding and Computing, 27–29 March, Las Vegas, Nevada, USA, pp. 62 - 67, IEEE Computer Society, ISBN 0 - 7695 - 0540–6, 2000
11. Jana Dittmann , Martin Steinbach. Joint watermarking of audio-visual data. 2001 IEEE Fourth Workshop on Multimedia Signal Processing, October 3 - 5, Cannes France, IEEE, Piscataway, NJ, USA, pp. 601–606, ISBN 0-7803-7025-2, 2001
12. Bijan G. Mobasseri, Aaron T. Evans. Content-dependent video authentication by self-watermarking in color space. Proceedings of the SPIE. SPIE Security and Watermarking of Multimedia Contents III, San Jose, Jan. 21–26, 2001
13. Lisa M. Marvel, George W. Hartwig , Jr. and Charles Boncelet, Jr. Compression-compatible fragile and semi-fragile tamper detection. Proceedings of the SPIE. SPIE Security and Watermarking of Multimedia Contents III, San Jose, Jan. 21–26, 2001
14. Eugene T. Lin , Christine I. Podilchuk , Edward J. Delp. Detection of image alterations using semi-fragile watermarks. Proceedings of the SPIE. International Conference on Security and Watermarking of Multimedia Contents II, Vol. 3971, January 23–28, 2000, San Jose, CA.
15. Chun-shien Liu, Hong-Yuan Mark Liao , and Chwen-Jye Sze. Combined watermarking for image authentication and protection. Proc. 1st IEEE Int. Conf. on Multimedia and Expo, New York City, NY, USA, Vol. III, pp. 1415–1418, Jul. 30 ~ Aug. 2, 2000
16. Dinu Coltue, Philippe Bolon, Jean-Marc Chassery. Fragile and robust watermarking by histogram specification. Proc. SPIE Photonic West, Vol. 4675, Electronic Imaging 2002, Security and Watermarking of Multimedia Contents IV, San Jose, California, January, 2002, pp. 701–710.
17. Chih-wei Tang and Hsueh-ming Hang. An image feature based robust digital watermarking scheme. Proceedings of SPIE, Security and Watermarking of Multimedia Contents, Vol.4675. Jan., 2002. pp. 584–595
18. Ping Wah Wong, Nasir Memon. Secret and public key authentication watermarking schemes that resist vector quantization attack. Proceedings of SPIE, Security and watermarking of multimedia contents II, 2000. pp. 417~427
19. M.M. Yeung and F. Mintzer, An invisible watermarking technique for image verification. Proceedings of ICIP, Oct., 1997.
20. Peng Yin, Hong Heather Yu. Classification of video tampering methods and countermeasures using digital watermarking. Invited paper for SPIE's International Symposium: ITCOM 2001, Denver, Colorado, USA, 2001.
21. Bruce Schneier. Applied cryptography—protocols, algorithms, and source code in C. John Wiley & Sons, Inc. 1996
22. Ingmar J. Cox, Matthew L. Miller, Jeffrey A. Bloom. Digital Watermarking. An Imprint of Academic Press. 2002.

An Intelligent Watermark Detection Decoder Based on Independent Component Analysis

Zhang Li[1], Sam Kwong[2], Marian Choy[2], Wei-wei Xiao [1], Ji Zhen[1], and Ji-hong Zhang[1]

[1] Faulty of Information Engineering, Shenzhen University, Shenzhen, China, 518060
[2]Department of Computer Science, City University of Hong Kong, China

Abstract. The detection errors undermine the credibility of a digital watermarking system. It is crucial to have a reliable detector such that false detection rate can be minimized before digital watermarking can be widely used in the real world. An intelligent watermark decoder using Independent Component Analysis (ICA) is proposed in this paper. The mathematical model of the detector is given in this paper. This intelligent decoder extracts a watermark correctly without using the original image. However, the accuracy of the watermarking extraction depends on the key and the statistical independence between the original image and the watermark. Experimental results have demonstrated that the proposed intelligent watermarking technique is robust against the attacks produced by Stirmark, such as cropping, filtering, image compression, rotation, scaling. It also has a good robustness against combination of several kinds of attacks. It is indicated that this new intelligent decoder has superior advantages over the existing ones in many aspects.

Keywords: intelligent detection, digital watermarking, independent component analysis

1 Introduction

Digital watermarking technique is an effective means to resolve copyright protection and information security problems by embedding additional information (watermark information) into the digital protected media [1,2]. Invisibility and robustness are the most important characteristics in watermarking. Since Cox [3] has proposed to apply the spread spectrum technique to the watermark embedding process, most of the watermarking algorithms adopt watermark detection based on a statistic correlation. Barni extended the correlation detection to public watermarking techniques so that the watermark detection no longer requires the original image [4]. The watermark detection is then to compute the correlation between the test image and the given watermark. However, it still needs the original image during the detection and thus known as semi-public watermarking. With this method, the detector can detect the existence of the watermark but could not estimate or extract it. In fact, the extraction of the secret message could be an even harder problem than detecting it. In general, the decoder must somehow base on a correlation coefficient called an optimum decision

T. Kalker et al. (Eds.): IWDW 2003, LNCS 2939, pp. 223–234, 2004.
© Springer-Verlag Berlin Heidelberg 2004

threshold such that the false alarm probability is equal to the leak detection probability. Usually it is not easy to obtain an optimum decision threshold of the corrupted watermark.

Recently, blind source separation by Independent Component Analysis (ICA) has received attention because of its potential applications in signal processing [5]. The goal of ICA is to recover independent sources given only sensor observations that are unknown linear mixtures of the unobserved independent source signals. The goal is to perform a linear transform, which makes the resulting variables as statistically independent from each other as possible. ICA is a fairly new and generic method in signal processing. It reveals a diversity of theoretical challenges and opens a variety of potential applications. Successful results in EEG, FMRI, speech recognition and face recognition systems indicate the power and optimistic hope in this new paradigm.

We propose a new intelligent watermark detector based on ICA, which will extract the watermark without using the original watermark and the original image during the detection. It is a completely blind method during watermark detection. Our method had gone through testing against all the attacks produced by the popular "Stirmark" attacks. Experimental results have shown that this intelligent watermark detector based on ICA is robust to all kinds of attacks produced by Stirmark, such as image compression, cropping, rotation, scaling, removal rows or/and columns. It can also extract multiple embedded watermarks during the detection. We compared the results in this paper to [6], which also adopts the ICA to the watermarking system in spatial domain. Our algorithm shows better results.

The organization of the paper is as follows.

Section 2 describes the realization of intelligent watermark detector based on ICA. In Section 3, we describe the performance of the intelligent detector proposed in this paper. Section 4 presents our experimental results. Finally, we draw our conclusion in Section 5.

2 Realization of Intelligent Watermarking Based on ICA

2.1 Intelligent Watermark Embedding Process

The watermark is embedded in Discrete Wavelet Transform domain (DWT), and 4 levels of DWT are conducted to the original image. The watermark can also be embedded in Discrete Cosine Transform (DCT), Discrete Fourier Transform (DFT) and spatial domain with different watermark embedding intensity. The watermark embedding intensity in different wavelet transform levels is usually determined by Just Noticeable Difference of the original image, which incorporates the characteristics of human visual system and can be computed in DWT domain as in [4]:

$$\log \alpha(\theta, f) = \log 0.495 + 0.466 (\log f - \log(0.401 g_\theta)) \tag{1}$$

Where, $\theta \in \{LL, HL, LH, HH\}$, $g_{LL} = 1.501$, $g_{HL} = g_{LH} = 1$, $g_{HH} = 0.534$. α is the initial embedding intensity of the watermark. The embedding steps of this intelligent watermarking system are described as follows:

Step 1: To creation and preprocess the watermark. The watermark is created randomly and expressed by W, that is, the watermark is independent to the original image. The watermark we used in this paper is an image having the same size as the original image. It is beneficial to preprocess the watermark before embedding to enhance the security of the watermark. In this paper the watermark is rearranged by Cat map, which can be expressed as follows.

$$\begin{pmatrix} x_{n+1} \\ y_{n+1} \end{pmatrix} = \begin{pmatrix} 1 & 1 \\ 1 & 2 \end{pmatrix} \begin{pmatrix} x_n \\ y_n \end{pmatrix} \pmod{1} \tag{2}$$

Cat map parameter can be used as private key during the watermark detection process.

Step 2: Watermark embedding process. Both original and watermark images are decomposed into 4 levels using DWT. The approximation components (LL1, LL2, LL3, LL4) in each level are not chosen as any change on the approximation details will seriously degrade the image quality. The other components of the watermark are added to the host image. Let the original vector of host image be *X*, the watermark image be *W*, the embedding strength be α (this can be computed from the human visual system in discrete wavelet domain from Equ.1), and the watermarked image be *Y*. The watermark embedding process can be expressed as:

$$Y(k,i,j) = X(k,i,j) + \alpha(k,i)W(k,i,j) \tag{3}$$

where
k= level of decomposition, *k*=1,2,3,4
i= decomposition component, *i*=1,2,3 indicates HL/LH/HH respectively
j= index of embedding coefficient in component *i*

Step 3: Perform the inverse DWT (IDWT) to retrieve the watermarked image.

2.2 Realization of Intelligent Watermark Detector Based on ICA

In this Section we will describe how the intelligent watermark detector works as shown in Fig.1.

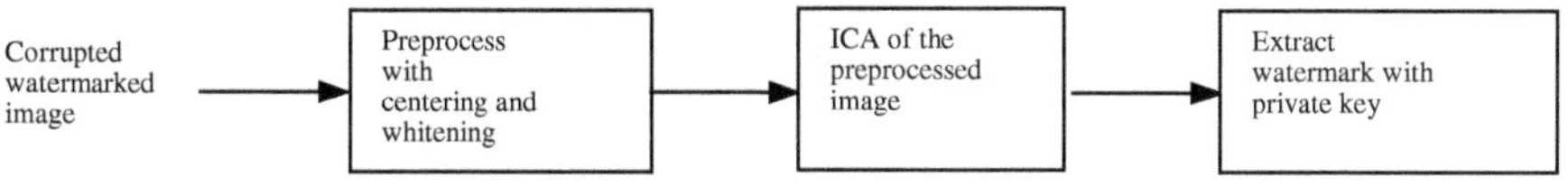

Fig. 1. The block diagram of the intelligent watermark detector

ICA process is the core of the intelligent detector accomplished by the FASTICA algorithm [5]. The reason that we are using the FASTICA algorithm is that it is proved to very robust and efficient. In addition, its Matlab™ implementation algorithm is available on the World Wide Web free of charge at http://www.cis.hut.fi/projects/ica/fastica/. Readers should refer to [5] for the detail about the algorithm. Assume that *n* observed linear mixtures $x_1, \cdots x_n$ of *n* independent components can be expressed as:

$$x_j = a_{j1}s_1 + a_{j2}s_2 + \cdots + a_{jn}s_n \text{ for all } j=1..n \tag{4}$$

Without loss of generality, both the mixture variables and the independent components can be assumed to have zero mean. We have:

$$X = AS \tag{5}$$

where *X* is the observed vector, *S* is original source vector and *A* being the mixed matrix, and both *S* and *A* are unknown. The statistical model expressed in Equ.5 is called independent component analysis, or the ICA model. *X* represents all the observed data, and both *A* and *S* must be estimated from it. If we know the separate matrix *L*, we can estimate the source signal easily. That is, we can estimate the source by:

$$S = LX \tag{6}$$

So, it is important to compute the correct separate matrix during the independent components analysis process. Before applying the ICA model, it is helpful to conduct preprocessing such as centering and whitening to simplify the ICA process. We can use a private key to extract the watermark after performing the ICA to the preprocessed watermarked image. The process of intelligent detector is described in detail as follows:

Step1: Preprocessing of the test image for centering and whitening[5]. The observed variable *x* is centered by subtracting the mean vector *m=E{x}* from the observed variable, this makes *x* a zero-mean variable. This preprocessing is designed to simplify the ICA algorithms. After estimating the mixing matrix *A* with centered data, we can complete the estimation by adding the mean vector of the original source signal back to the centered estimates of the source data. Another preprocessing is to whiten the observed variables. Whitening means to transform the variable *x* linearly so that the new variable $\tilde{x}$ is white, i.e., its components are uncorrelated, and their variances equal unity. In other words, variable $\tilde{x}$ is white means the covariance matrix of $\tilde{x}$ equals to the identity matrix: $E\{\tilde{x}\tilde{x}^T\} = I$, that is, $\tilde{x}$ is uncorrelated. Whitening can be computed by eigenvalue decomposition of the covariance matrix[5]:

$$E\{xx^T\} = EDE^T \tag{7}$$

Where, *E* is the orthogonal matrix of eigenvector of $E\{xx^T\}$. *D* is a diagonal matrix of its eigenvalues, that is $D = diag(d_1, \cdots, d_n)$. Note that $E\{xx^T\}$ can be estimated in a standard way from the availability of $x(1), \cdots, x(T)$.

Step2: Perform the FastICA[5] to the signal that has been centered and whitened, that is to find the separate matrix *L:*

Choose an initial (e.g., random) weight vector L;

i. Let $L^+ = E\{xG(L^T x)\} - E\{G'(L^T x)\}L$ and update $L = L^+ / \|L^+\|$, where, $E(\bullet)$ is the mean compute factor. $G(\bullet)$ is a non-linear function and the following choices of $G(\bullet)$ have proved to be very useful: $G_1(u)=\log \cosh u$, $G_2(u)=-\exp(-u^2/2)$[5].

ii. If the difference between the iterative results is less than the threshold, that is, $|L^+ - L| < \varepsilon$, we can say that the process is converged and the cycle will terminate; otherwise, go back to Step 2i until the result is converged. The threshold ε can be defined by user and we use $\varepsilon = 10^{-6}$ in our experiments. If the result is still not converged after 3000 cycles, then the process will be forced to terminate and we can conclude that there is no independent component for the corrupted watermarked image.

If there are multiple watermarks in the tested image, the extracted watermark must be subtracted before extracting the next one.

Step3: Extract the perfect watermark by using the key in the watermark embedding process.

3 Performance of the Intelligent Detector

Sometimes we not only interest in extracting the embedded watermark correctly but also to carry out the performance analysis of the intelligent detector. In this section, we describe how to analyze the performance of this watermarking system in detail.

3.1 Mathematical Model of Original Image

In order to analyze the performance of the proposed intelligent watermark detection, the mathematical model of the original image is proposed. Since the wavelet coefficients of image fit well with the characteristic of the human visual system, the intelligent detector based on wavelet domain is analyzed in this paper. On the other hand, the intelligent watermark detector based on DCT[9], DFT and spatial domain can be analyzed in a similar fashion with their respective mathematical model of the original image in the corresponding domain. In fact, our work is similar to the one done in the DCT domain by the authors in [9].For most images, wavelet coefficients of low passes can be modeled as a uniform distribution, and that of band passes are modeled as a generalized Laplacian density function expressed as follows.

$$f_{s,r}(x) = \frac{e^{-\left|\frac{x}{s}\right|^r}}{2s(\Gamma(1/r)/r)} \tag{8}$$

Where, $\Gamma(x) = \int_0^\infty t^{x-1} e^{-t} dt$ is a gamma function. Parameters s and r are computed from the original image and described in detail in [7]. They are needed if we want to conduct the performance analysis to the watermarking system. If we only want to extract the embedded watermark, these parameters are not required during the watermark detection process.

3.2 Definition and Distribution of the Likelihood Function

The performance analysis is an important grading indicator to mark the success of a watermark detector. In order to conduct performance analysis of the intelligent watermark detector proposed in this paper, we formulate the detection process as a binary hypothesis test. H_0: $Y(i,j)=X(i,j)$, $H_1: Y(i,j)=X(i,j)+W(i,j)$. H_0 indicates that the watermark W is not present in the test image Y and H_1 is to indicate that Y contains the watermark W. To do the performance analysis, we analyze the distribution of the likelihood function and measure the performance of the watermark detector in terms of its probabilities of a false alarm, p_F (i.e., false watermark detection) and a detection coefficient, p_D (i.e., success to detect the existing watermark) for a given original image. In order to compute the probabilities of false alarm and detection, we first analyze the likelihood function of the watermarking, $\Lambda(Y)$, which is defined as follows.

$$\Lambda(Y)=\frac{f(Y,W)}{f(Y)} \tag{9}$$

where W is the watermark and Y the test image. If $\Lambda(Y)>\eta$, then H_1 is true, otherwise H_0 is true. η is a predetermined decision threshold. The log likelihood function of sub-band wavelet coefficients is defined as follows.

$$l(Y)=\sum_{i,j}\left|\frac{Y(i,j)}{s}\right|^r+\ln\left(\prod_{k=1}^{N}\exp\left\{-\sum_{i,j}\left|\frac{Y(i,j)-W\alpha(i,j)c(i,j)}{s}\right|^r\right\}\right) \tag{10}$$

where α is the embedded intensity and c is the key of pseudorandom permutation. For a given original image, suppose c consists of a series of random independent equally probable values from the set $\{-1,1\}$, and assume $W=1$ for simplicity. We can rewrite the log likelihood function as:

$$l(Y)=\sum_{i,j}\left(\left|\frac{Y(i,j)}{s}\right|^r-\left|\frac{Y(i,j)-\alpha(i,j)c(i,j)}{s}\right|^r\right) \tag{11}$$

From the central limit theory: we know that if i,j is large enough then the distribution of $l(Y)$ tends to be a normal distribution. We can compute the mean and the variance of $l(Y)$ first. If H_0 is true, namely $Y(i,j)=X(i,j)$, then $l(Y)$ can be rewritten as:

$$l(Y) = \sum_{i,j} \left(\left| \frac{X(i,j)}{s} \right|^r - \left| \frac{X(i,j) - \alpha(i,j)c(i,j)}{s} \right|^r \right) \tag{12}$$

We can then calculate the mean and the variance as follows:

$$E(l(Y)/H_0) = \sum_{i,j} \left| \frac{X(i,j)}{s} \right|^r - \frac{1}{2} \sum_{i,j} \left(\left| \frac{X(i,j) - \alpha(i,j)}{s} \right|^r + \left| \frac{X(i,j) + \alpha(i,j)}{s} \right|^r \right) \tag{13}$$

$$Var(l(Y)/H_0) == \frac{1}{4} \left(\sum_{i,j} \left(\left| \frac{X(i,j) - \alpha(i,j)}{s} \right|^r + \left| \frac{X(i,j) + \alpha(i,j)}{s} \right|^r \right) \right)^2 \tag{14}$$

Similarly if H_1 is true, that is $Y(i, j) = X(i, j) + W(i, j)$, then:

$$l(Y) = \sum_{i,j} \left(\left| \frac{X(i,j) + \alpha(i,j)c(i,j)}{s} \right|^r - \left| \frac{X(i,j)}{s} \right|^r \right) \tag{15}$$

$$E(l(Y)/H_1) = \frac{1}{2} \left(\sum_{i,j} \left(\left| \frac{X(i,j) - \alpha(i,j)}{s} \right|^r + \left| \frac{X(i,j) + \alpha(i,j)}{s} \right|^r \right) \right) - \sum_{k} \left| \frac{X(i,j)}{s} \right|^r = -E(l(Y)/H_0) \tag{16}$$

$$Var(l(Y)/H_1) = Var(l(Y)/H_0) \tag{17}$$

So we know that in H_0, $l(Y)$ obeys normal distribution $N(E(l(Y)/H_0), Var(l(Y)/H_0))$, and in H_1, $l(Y)$ obeys the normal distribution $N(E(l(Y)/H_1), Var(l(Y)/H_1))$.

3.3 Computation of Detection Probability and False Alarm Probability

If H_1 is true, then the detection probability p_D is:

$$p_D = P\{l(Y) > \eta / H_1\} \tag{18}$$

From H_1, we know that $l(Y)$ obeys normal distribution and we can obtain p_D as follows:

$$p_D = \int_{\eta}^{\infty} \frac{1}{\sqrt{2\pi Var(l(Y)/H_1)}} \exp\left\{ -\frac{(l(Y) - E(l(Y)/H_1))^2}{2Var(l(Y)/H_1)} \right\} dl(Y) \tag{19}$$

Assume $t = \frac{l(Y) - E(l(Y)/H_1)}{\sqrt{Var(l(Y)/H_1)}}$, then p_D is as follows:

$$p_D = \int_{\frac{\eta - E(l(Y)/H_1)}{\sqrt{Var(l(Y)/H_1)}}}^{\infty} \frac{1}{\sqrt{2\pi}} e^{-\frac{t^2}{2}} dt \tag{20}$$

From H_0, we know that $l(Y)$ also obey the normal distribution $N(E(l(Y)/H_0), Var(l(Y)/H_0))$, so we can compute the false alarm probability p_F as follows:

$$\begin{aligned} p_F = P\{l(Y) > \eta / H_0\} &= \int_\eta^\infty \frac{1}{\sqrt{2\pi Var(l(Y)/H_0)}} \exp\left\{-\frac{(l(Y) - E(l(Y)/H_0))^2}{2Var(l(Y)/H_0)}\right\} dl(Y) \\ &= \int_\eta^\infty \frac{1}{\sqrt{2\pi Var(l(Y)/H_1)}} \exp\left\{-\frac{(l(Y) + E(l(Y)/H_1))^2}{2Var(l(Y)/H_1)}\right\} dl(Y) \end{aligned} \tag{21}$$

Assume $t = \frac{l(Y) + E(l(Y)/H_1)}{\sqrt{Var(l(Y)/H_1)}}$, we obtain:

$$p_F = \int_{\frac{\eta + E(l(Y)/H_1)}{\sqrt{Var(l(Y)/H_1)}}}^{\infty} \frac{1}{\sqrt{2\pi}} e^{-\frac{t^2}{2}} dt \tag{22}$$

We can see that for a given image and a fixed p_F, the larger $\frac{2E(l(Y)/H_1)}{\sqrt{Var(l(Y)/H_1)}}$ and p_D are, the better the watermarking performs. The intelligent watermark detector can be used in many special applications.

4 Experimental Results

In our experiments, all the attacks are produced by the watermark test software – Stirmark. The constraint is set to $p_F \leq 10^{-6}$ and we have done experiments on many images including Lena image having the size of 256×256. The watermark is produced randomly, that is the watermark is independent to the original image. Experimental results showed that this intelligent watermark detector can extract the watermark with good robustness without using the original image. We compare the results of our intelligent detector to reference [6], which adopts ICA in spatial domain. In order to analyze the similarity between the original watermark and the extracted watermark quantitatively, normalization correction [8] is applied. Fig.2 gives the original image and the watermark.

深圳大学
信息工程
学院

Fig. 2. Original Lena image watermark permuted watermark watermarked image

Experiments were performed to examine the robustness of the proposed intelligent watermark detection to the JPEG compression produced by Stirmark with different qualify factor Q and table 1 listed the results. Normalization Correlation (*NC*) is used to express the similarity between the original watermark w and the extracted watermark w^* quantitatively and use the Peak Signal to Noise Ratio (*PSNR*) to express the difference between the watermarked image $y_{i,j}$ and the compressed watermarked image $x_{i,j}$. It is observed that the higher *NC*, the more similarity between the extracted watermark and the original watermark. The definitions of the *NC* and *PSNR* are given below [8]:

$$PSNR = 10\log(x_{\max}^2 /(N^{-2}\sum_{i=1}^{N}\sum_{j=1}^{N}(x_{i,j} - y_{i,j})^2)) \tag{23}$$

$$NC = \frac{\sum_{i=0}^{256}\sum_{j=0}^{256} w(i,j)w^*(i,j)}{\sum_{i=0}^{256}\sum_{j=0}^{256}(w(i,j))^2} \tag{24}$$

Table 1. The experimental results to JPEG compression

Q	90	80	70	60	50	40	30	20	10
PSNR	72.8911	42.9237	41.4464	38.3789	36.9986	35.3863	34.1631	32.3656	29.4666
NC	0.9935	0.9929	0.9926	0.9911	0.9897	0.9803	0.9460	0.9303	0.8445
Extracted watermark									

We also carry out all kinds of attacks by Stirmark to test the robustness of intelligent watermark detector proposed in this paper. Table 2 listed some experimental results by the Stirmark attacks.

Fig.3 gives the normalization correction between the multiple (5 watermarks) extracted watermarks from the corrupted watermarked image and 1000 watermarks, which are produced randomly including the perfect five watermarks. The intelligent detector can extract the five perfect watermarks with high precision.

Table 2. The experimental results to Stirmark

Attack	Remove one row one column	Remove one row five columns	Remove seventeen rows five columns	Median filter	Convolution filter	Skew x 5.0%y5.0%	Scaling factor x1.0 y1.20	Rotation 2.00 degree with scaling 2.0 with crop
NC	0.9967	0.9957	0.9958	0.9989	0.9237	0.9977	0.9976	0.7825
Extraction watermark								

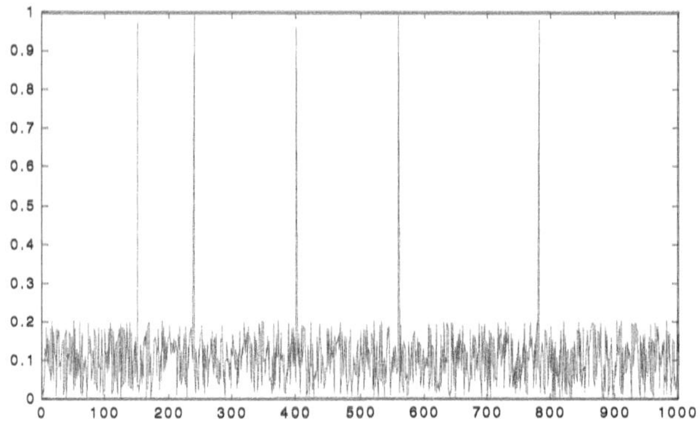

Fig. 3. Multi- watermark Extraction

We compared our results with that of reference [6]. The authors in [6] adopt the ICA in spatial domain. Fig 4 shows the comparisons on the attack of scaling and rotation. The experimental results have shown that the intelligent detector based on DWT domain in this paper has a much better robustness.

5 Conclusion

An intelligent watermark decoder based on ICA is proposed in this paper and it can be applied in any other domains such as DWT, DCT, DFT, or spatial domain. The intelligent decoder can extract the watermark correctly without using any information about the original image and embedded watermark. The attack and the accuracy of the watermarking extraction system depend on the key and statistical independence between the original image and the watermark. Experimental results have demonstrated that the proposed intelligent watermarking technique is robust with respect to attacks produced by Stirmark, such as cropping, filtering, image compression, rotation, and scaling. In addition, it has a good robustness against combination of several attacks. We compared the results of our method to reference [6] which adopts the ICA in spatial domain and the results have shown that this new intelligent decoder has superior advantages over the existing ones in many aspects.

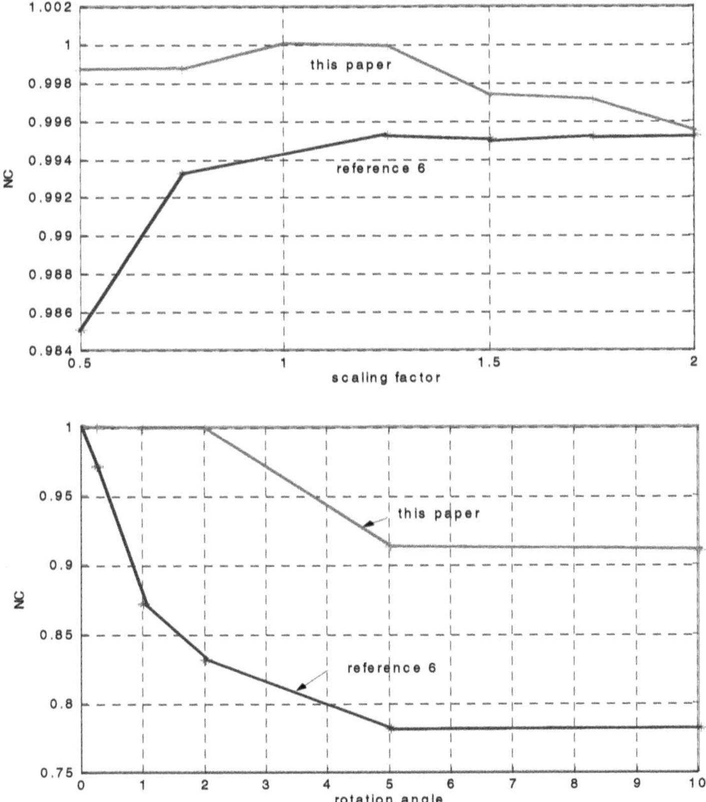

Fig. 4. NC comparison (scaling and rotation)

Acknowledgement. This work is partly supported by City University Strategic Grant 7001488.

References

1. Sviatolsav Voloshynovskiy, Shelby Pereira, Thierry Pun, Joachim J. Eggers and Jonathan K. Su.: Attacks on Digital Watermarks: Classification, Estimation-based attacks and benchmarks. IEEE Communications Magazine, August, (2001), pp.2~10
2. Pierre Moulin.: The role of information theory in watermarking and its application to image watermarking. Signal Processing. 81 (2001) 1121–1139
3. Cox I. J., Kilian J. Leighton T. et al.: Secure spread spectrum watermarking for multimedia. IEEE Tans. on Image Processing, (1997) 6(12):1673–1687

4. Barni M., Bartolini F., Cappelini V., et al.: A DCT domain system for robust image watermarking. Signal Processing, (1998) 66(3): 357–372
5. A. Hyvarinen, E. Oja.: Independent component analysis: a tutorial. Notes for International Joint Conference on Neural Networks (IJCNN'99), Washington D. C. http://www.cis.hut.fi/projects/iac/, (1999)
6. D. Yu, F. Sattar, K.K. Ma.: Watermark detection and extraction using independent compo nent analysis method. EURASIP Journal on Applied Signal Processing (2002) (1): 92–104
7. R. W. Buccigrossi and E. P. Aimoncelli.: Image compression via joint statistical characterization in the wavelet domain. IEEE Trans on Image Processing. (1999) 8(12): 1688~1701
8. C.T.Hsu, J.L.Wu.: Hidden digital watermarks in images. IEEE Transactions on Image Processing, (1999) 8(1): 58–68
9. Hernández Juan R., Amado Martín, and Fernando Pérez-González: DCT-Domain Watermarking Techniques for Still Images: Detector Performance Analysis and a New Structure. IEEE Transactions on Image Processing, vol. 9, no. 1, January 2000, pp.55–66

Coefficient Selection Methods for Scalable Spread Spectrum Watermarking

Angela Piper[1*], Reihaneh Safavi-Naini[1], and Alfred Mertins[2]

[1] School of Information Technology and Computer Science
University of Wollongong, NSW, Australia
[2] Faculty of Mathematics and Science
University of Oldenburg, Oldenburg, Germany

Abstract. With the increasing use of mobile and internet technology as a means of content distribution, we see a move towards scalable content distribution mechanisms, which allow the adaptation of content to the requirements of the target system. Adequate protection of scalable content requires the adoption of scalable watermarking algorithms. Many of the existing algorithms are based on the spread spectrum techniques, first presented in a watermarking context by Cox et al. [2]. The various algorithms often use quite different methods for coefficient selection, resulting in different watermark properties. We examine the effect of the coefficient selection method on watermark scalability by considering the quality and resolution scalability of seven simple selection methods when used as part of a spread spectrum watermarking algorithm.

1 Introduction

The internet is already seeing widespread use as a mechanism for content distribution. A growing number of devices are being connected via networks, all with differing capabilities and requirements in areas such as resolution, colour depth, storage capacity and processing ability. Furthermore, the users of these devices may also have differing needs or desires with regards to the display of such content. Finally, in order to provide delivery within acceptable time it is desirable that the transmitted content be as small as possible. As a result, in order to best distribute content over a network it is becoming increasingly necessary to tailor the content to the requirements of both the device and the user. That is, the content must be highly scalable.

Already there is a great deal of discussion about how to best protect the rights of the creator, owner or distributor of an image. Digital watermarking has the ability to provide such protection as well as offering a variety of other potential uses. However the process of tailoring the image to different device and user requirements means that the majority of devices will receive only parts of the image content, and different devices will receive different parts. This in

* Partial funding for this research was provided by the Smart Internet Technology Cooperative Research Centre, Australia.

T. Kalker et al. (Eds.): IWDW 2003, LNCS 2939, pp. 235–246, 2004.
© Springer-Verlag Berlin Heidelberg 2004

turn means that the majority of devices will receive only parts of the watermark and that different devices will receive different parts of the watermark. Thus, it is necessary to ensure that our watermarking algorithms are scalable, because each of these different devices must still be able to obtain sufficient data from its partial watermark to allow it to detect the embedded information at the required level.

Many of the existing watermarking algorithms are based on spread spectrum techniques. One of the components of any spread spectrum watermarking algorithm is its coefficient selection method. There are a seemingly endless variety of coefficient selection methods available, each with its own motivation, strengths and weaknesses. We consider seven simple coefficient selection methods and evaluate their scalability, both in terms of quality and resolution scalability.

2 Background

2.1 Spread Spectrum

Spread Spectrum modulates the signal with a pseudo-random noise sequence to produce the watermark X. Insertion requires both an embedding formula and a method for coefficient selection, and there are many options in each area.

Three embedding formulae are provided in [2]:

$$v_i' = v_i + \alpha x_i \tag{1}$$
$$v_i' = v_i(1 + \alpha x_i) \tag{2}$$
$$v_i' = v_i(e^{\alpha x_i}) \tag{3}$$

where α is a (potentially variable) scaling factor used to ensure visual undetectability and x_i is the ith element of X.

Although Cox et al offer only one coefficient selection method, the 1000 largest non-DC coefficients in the greyscale component, numerous other options have been implemented including non-LL subband wavelet coefficients which exceed a given significance threshold [3], blue component coefficients only [4] or coefficients in all three colour channels [7].

The detection of a spread spectrum watermark is achieved by examination of a correlation coefficient. In the case where the original image is available, the embedding process can be reversed and the correlation between the candidate and extracted marks can be calculated. A large correlation value corresponds to watermark presence and a small value indicates that the candidate watermark is absent from the image.

2.2 Scalability in Compression

A scalable image compression algorithm is one which allows an image to be compressed for a number of target bit rates such that an optimal image can be reconstructed, at any of those rates, using the relevant sections of the same compressed data.

There are two main types of scalability to consider in the case of still images: resolution scalability and quality scalability.

Resolution scalability (or *spatial scalability*) is achieved by encoding a low resolution version of the image separately from one or more layers of higher resolution data. This data can be combined with the appropriately scaled low resolution version to produce a higher resolution image. Typically each refinement-layer allows the display of an image at twice the horizontal and twice the vertical resolution previously obtainable.

Quality scalability is achieved by encoding a coarsely quantised version of the image separately from one or more layers of more finely quantised refinement data at the same resolution. The refinement-layers can be combined with the coarsely quantised version of the image to produce a higher quality image. Quality scalability is also termed *SNR scalability*, however the quality metric used to determine the layers need not be directly related to the signal-to-noise ratio (SNR).

The extent to which content is scalable depends on the number of refinement-layers. If few layers of refinement data are used then the resulting compressed bit stream will be optimal for only a few target bit rates. A larger number of refinement-layers will provide optimality for further bit rates, creating a stream with higher scalability at the cost of a slightly greater total length.

2.3 JPEG2000

JPEG2000 is a new wavelet-based image compression standard which has been developed to provide higher levels of consistency, performance and flexibility than the old DCT-based JPEG standard. An important feature of the standard as it applies to internet and mobile applications is that JPEG2000 offers greatly improved options for scalability.

As part of the compression process, a discrete wavelet transform is applied to decompose the image into four subbands: LL, LH, HL and HH. The LH, HL and HH subbands form the highest resolution layer. The LL subband can be further decomposed using the same procedure, and the resultant LH, HL and HH subbands form the second highest resolution layer. The decomposition process is continued until all desired resolution layers are obtained; the final LL subband forms the lowest resolution layer.

A context adaptive bit plane coder is independently applied to groups of coefficients from the same subband to produce a number of coding passes. These passes can then be arranged into quality layers so that those passes which provide the greatest amount of information about the image are in the lowest layer, those which provide slightly less information appear in the next layer and so on. Precisely how many passes are assigned to each layer will depend upon the compression rate set for that layer.

3 Scalability in Watermarking

3.1 Previous Work

The concept of scalable watermarking was first introduced by Wang and Kuo [10] as the watermarking component of an "integrated progressive image coding and watermarking system", allowing simultaneous image protection and image compression with progressive display. They provide no formal definition however, either here or in later work with Su[9].

Chen and Chen [1] explicitly emphasize that upon receipt of "more information of the watermarked image, the bit error rate (BER) of the retrieved watermark image decreases". They add that such an algorithm must "take into consideration the way the image is transmitted", tailoring the algorithm to the scalable transmission method rather than simply progressively transmitting a watermarked image.

The watermarking scheme of Steinder et al. [8] restricts the watermark to the base-layer only in the interests of early detection. While this will certainly provide early detection, all refinement layers remain unprotected by the watermark.

These papers focus on early detection as opposed to detection under a variety of possible rate constraints, which may be the reason that it is not until the discussion by Lin et al. [5] that explicit mention is made of the requirement implicit in [8] that the watermark be "detectable when only the base-layer is decoded".

3.2 Proposed Definition

The purpose of scalable watermarking is to suitably protect content regardless of which particular portions are delivered. Clearly then, such algorithms must protect the content in its base form, but the extra commercial value contained within the higher layers of the content warrants a greater amount of protection. Thus we define a scalable watermarking algorithm as follows:

A scalable watermarking algorithm is a combined watermark embedding and detection scheme intended for use with scalable content and possessing the following two properties:

1. The watermark is detectable in any portion of the scaled content which is of 'acceptable' quality.
2. Increased portions of the scaled content provide reduced error in watermark detection.

In this definition we do not include the point made by Chen and Chen that the watermark should be tailored to the scalable coding or transmission method because, while this may well be necessary to achieve the above properties, should it be possible to achieve the properties without such tailoring, the algorithm would still be well suited to the outlined purpose.

3.3 Applying the Definition

The proposed definition is useful in a conceptual sense; however in order to perform a meaningful evaluation of any watermarking schemes in light of this definition it is necessary to convert the qualitative terms into quantitative ones. As is the case with any such conversion, the particular selections made will be substantially application dependent. A consequence of this is that in any general study, such as this one, the choices made will always be somewhat arbitrary.

If the watermark is to be deemed detectable in any portion of the scaled content which is of acceptable quality, we require definitions for what constitutes *detection* and for what constitutes *acceptable* quality. The point at which a watermark is considered detectable will depend both on what rates of error are considered acceptable for the specific application and on the accuracy of the model of the detection statistic used to estimate the appropriate detection threshold for a given probability of false positive error. For this study we will follow Cox et al. in employing the similarity statistic as our measure of correlation, considering the candidate vector detectable if the similarity between it and the extracted vector exceeds the detection threshold corresponding to a false positive probability of 1×10^{-9}. Rather than employing the constant threshold used in [2] we apply the more accurate false positive model proposed by Miller and Bloom [6] which increases towards that proposed by Cox et al. as the size of the extracted watermark increases.

Precisely what constitutes acceptable quality is highly subjective. The author or distributor of the content will generally make some assessment as to the level of degradation that the content can be expected to sustain before it no longer holds either commercial value or artistic merit. Given that scalable encoding involves the selection of a base-layer or lowest quality version of the image, we can reasonably assume that this base-layer constitutes the least acceptable quality version. Thus the smallest portion of acceptable quality we might want to consider would be an image composed solely of the lowest quality or lowest resolution layer.

We also wish to ensure that increased portions of the scaled content provide *reduced detection error*. Although it is possible to obtain a far finer granularity, we can still obtain an accurate picture of a watermarking scheme's general behaviour by defining an *increased portion* of the content as a full added quality or resolution layer. The *error rate* is the proportion of the total detection attempts which are either false positive, where we detect a watermark which is not in fact present, or false negative, where we fail to detect a watermark which is present. It is not possible to obtain accurate estimates of the error rates for these systems using only a few trials. However, provided the shape of the distribution of the detection statistic does not change significantly, an *increase in average similarity value* will correspond to a *reduction in error rate*. So, rather than attempt to measure the error rate directly, we will consider the mean similarity value, for which it is far easier to obtain an accurate estimate.

Even with this defined, there still remains the problem as to what sort of increase in similarity is desirable. If we wish to ensure that all portions of the content are equally protected then we would require that equal amounts of the watermark vector be detectable from each single portion of the content. If this is the case, then the ideal detector response from an image constructed from the first k of n layers would be $\sqrt{\frac{kN}{n}}$ where N is the length of the watermark vector. However there is no particular reason for treating all resolution or quality layers uniformly. It is quite likely that particular resolution or quality layers contribute far more to the overall image than do others. Thus it might be preferable to employ some measure of the value of a given layer in determining what amount of the watermark should be used for the protection of that layer. In order to do this we would take a perceptual distortion measure D, such as the peak signal to noise ratio (PSNR), and determine the desired similarity based on the reduction in distortion provided by each layer. For example, if the PSNR for an image reconstructed from the first layer lies halfway between that of a mid-grey image[1] and that of an image reconstructed using the first and second layers, then we would want an equal amount of the watermark to be embedded in each of these layers. We would, of course, want the similarity value of an image composed of all n layers to equal the expected similarity value for the full length N watermark. Thus, if $D(k)$ is the distortion between the original image and the image reconstructed using the first k of n layers, the ideal detector response from the reconstructed image would be $\sqrt{\frac{(D(k)-D(0))N}{(D(n)-D(0))}}$, where the 0th layer consists of a mid-grey image.[2]

4 Coefficient Selection Methods

Now that we have outlined the desired behaviour of a scalable spread spectrum watermark we consider different methods for coefficient selection and investigate which, if any, match that desired behaviour. There are numerous possibilities for selecting the coefficients in which to embed and almost every watermark algorithm will use a different scheme. The following selection methods are an attempt to provide a variety of schemes, with some justification for each.

top: Embed in the 1000 largest magnitude coefficients, regardless of any other considerations. This scheme has the greatest freedom of coefficient selection and thus the most intrinsic robustness that can be provided when embedding proportionally to coefficient magnitude. However because there is no restriction on embedding in either the chrominance (C_b and C_r) components or the low resolution subbands, it risks visual detectability unless the embedding strength α is low.

[1] A mid-grey image is our best reconstruction based on no information.

[2] It should be noted that this calculation relies on the ability of the distortion measure to accurately reflect the relative visual quality of two images. If the distortion values obtained do not lie in the range where this is the case then the use of this calculation as an ideal value becomes suspect and an alternative should be found.

nolow: Embed in the 1000 largest magnitude coefficients, excluding the lowest resolution layer. The lowest frequency subband is often excluded from watermark embedding schemes due to the sensitivity of the human visual system to artifacts caused by the modification of these bands.

lum: Embed in the luminance component only. Many spread spectrum watermarking schemes are designed for greyscale images only. Embedding in the luminance (Y) component only avoids the risk of detectability through variations in colour, which can be quite apparent at strengths where variations in brightness are not detected. However this restricts the selection space to one third of the available coefficients.

lumnl: Embed in the luminance component only, excluding the lowest resolution layer. This is perhaps the scheme closest to that recommended for colour images in [2] and can be expected to share the advantages and disadvantages of both lum and nolow.

res: Embed in each resolution layer proportionally to the number of coefficients in that resolution. The number of coefficients added by the second resolution is three times that available at the first resolution and each subsequent addition provides four times that provided by the one before it. Furthermore, the sensitivity to modifications in each resolution is reduced as the resolution layer increases. Thus we can comfortably embed an increasing portion of the watermark in each additional resolution whilst maintaining quite a high embedding strength.

comp: Embed in each component proportionally to the number of coefficients in that component. This scheme allows embedding in colour components, which are commercially valuable and may warrant such additional protection, but it ensures that only one third of the watermark is embedded in any component in an attempt to avoid colour artifacts due to excessive embedding in a single component. However in images where colour coefficients are not large, this is likely to embed more of the watermark in the colour components than does the unconstrained embedding.

top2/5: Embed in those coefficients with magnitude greater than two fifths of the largest coefficient in their associated resolution layer. This selects coefficients which are fairly large for their resolution layer but has less emphasis on the lower resolution layers (which tend to have higher valued coefficients) than the unconstrained scheme. Strategies involving variable thresholds such as this generally do not specify a set watermark length, however for comparison purposes we maintain a length of 1000 and stop embedding once that length is reached.

5 Experimental Setup

To investigate the effects of the above mentioned coefficient selection methods on watermark scalability, the following experiment is performed:

We examine the three classic 512 × 512 RGB test images: lena, mandrill and peppers. Each image undergoes JPEG2000 compression using 6 resolution layers, precincts of size 128 × 128, and quality layers with rates 0.01, 0.02, 0.04, 0.06 and 0.9999. A transformation from RGB to YC_bC_r space is applied, as is usual, to decorrelate the colour channels and thus achieve better compression results. Given that the addition of a watermark will cause some degradation to the image there is no reason to employ a lossless filter. Thus the wavelet transformation uses the Daubechies 9,7 filter, as this is the lossy filter provided by the core of the JPEG2000 standard.

Directly preceding the quantisation stage of compression, a spread spectrum watermark of length 1000 is embedded into the wavelet domain coefficients. Following [2] we use Gaussian pseudo random noise with zero mean and unit variance, a single bit message, and

$$v_i' = v_i(1 + \alpha x_i)$$

as the embedding formula. In order to provide consistent grounds for comparison, the scalar embedding strength α is adjusted for each selection method and each image in order to ensure that the mean squared error of the resulting image is 6.5[3] given the full resolution and a rate of 0.9999.

Once an image has been watermarked and compressed we can produce from it a series of images which comprise the first k layers of the full image, where k ranges from 1 to 6 for a decomposition by resolution or from 1 to 5 for a decomposition by quality. These images represent what might be received by various devices with different resolutions or bandwidth. The watermark X' can be extracted from any of these images V' by taking it and the unwatermarked image V and applying the inversion of the embedding formula. The corresponding similarity value is then calculated using

$$sim(X, X') = \frac{X.X'}{\sqrt{X'.X'}}$$

To obtain a more accurate estimate of this value we perform the above procedure using 100 different Gaussian watermarks and record the average similarity value for each k-layer image. In each case, a threshold is calculated based upon the length of the extracted watermark, using the false positive model[4] described in [6], and whether or not the similarity value passes this threshold is recorded.

6 Experimental Results

6.1 Adjusted Embedding Strengths

We see low embedding strengths for top and comp, a somewhat higher embedding strength for lum, and much higher strengths for nolow, lumnl and res. The top and comp schemes are completely unconstrained with regards to resolution

[3] A mean squared error of 6.5 corresponds closely to a peak signal to noise ratio of 40, which should ensure visual undetectability.

[4] This model is adapted to work with similarity rather than normalised correlation

and select a large number of coefficients from the lowest resolution layer, thus requiring a low embedding strength to maintain a consistent level of distortion. While lum is also unconstrained with regards to resolution, the restriction to a single component ensures that no more than one third of the coefficients in the lowest resolution layer are available for selecting, thus it is impossible for the lum scheme to select as many lowest resolution coefficients as do top and comp, hence it is likely to produce lower distortion and allow a higher embedding strength. Interestingly, the top2/5 scheme shows embedding strengths very near to those of top and comp, showing that this scheme still selects a high number of the more visually detectable coefficients. The nolow, lumnl and res schemes, which are drastically restricted in their ability to select low resolution coefficients, all achieve a resultant increase in embedding strength.

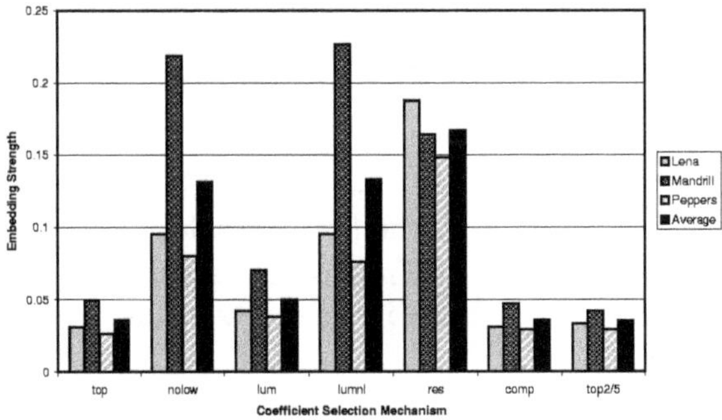

Fig. 1. Embedding Strengths

6.2 Detectability

We now examine whether or not the watermarks established using these selection methods are detectable in the scaled content. Given that we perform only a hundred trials on each image, we would not expect to see any missed detections for a scheme which achieves a reasonably low false negative error rate. Thus we consider the resolution and the quality layer at which each selection scheme first passes the detection threshold, on all trials and for all three images [Tab. 1].

Table 1. Layer at which detection threshold is exceeded for all images

	top	nolow	lum	lumnl	res	comp	top2/5
Resolution	1	5	5	5	4	1	1
Quality	2	1	2	1	1	3	2

Unfortunately, no scheme survives at both the lowest quality layer and the lowest resolution layer of all images. That is, none of the schemes examined here fully satisfy the first property of a scalable watermark: that the watermark be detectable in any portion of the content which is of acceptable quality. We cannot expect the nolow, lumnl and res schemes to be detectable in the lowest resolution layer, due to the resolution restrictions placed on these schemes, however undetectability until layer 4 is unacceptable. The detection results for decomposition by quality layer are reasonably good, although the low embedding strength schemes fail detection at the first layer. The two schemes which provide the best detectability overall are the top2/5 and top schemes, both of which are fully detectable at the lowest resolution layer and at the second quality layer.

6.3 Decreasing Error Rate – Resolution

For each selection method, we can compare the similarity value obtained from the image reconstructed upon receipt of resolution layer k with an ideal similarity value. As was discussed in Section 3.3, we calculate the ideal similarity value based on the reduction in distortion provided by each layer as $\sqrt{\frac{(D(k)-D(0))*1000}{(D(6)-D(0))}}$, where $D(k)$ is the distortion, in this case the PSNR, between the original image and the image reconstructed using the first k resolution layers.

It can be easily seen [Tab. 2] that none of the schemes provides a consistently close match to our ideal for all three images. The nolow, lumnl and res schemes

Table 2. Average squared deviation from the ideal - resolution

	top	nolow	lum	lumnl	res	comp	top2/5
Lena	9.37	67.29	7.06	67.30	184.12	31.70	3.40
Mandrill	23.47	123.37	45.87	129.59	77.88	3.18	36.73
Peppers	4.18	86.95	7.80	72.24	172.59	8.03	6.24
Average	12.34	92.53	20.24	89.71	144.86	14.30	15.46

are inherently disadvantaged due to the impossibility of obtaining close to the ideal value at the first resolution layer, and these schemes continue to remain well under the ideal until the final layers have been added. The top and comp schemes tend towards the opposite extreme, embedding too much of the watermark in the lowest layer and not enough in the final layers. This problem is less severe than that encountered by the highly constrained schemes and the match for top and comp is best on average. The moderately constrained schemes, top2/5 and lum, suffer in the average case from their poor performance on the mandrill image.

6.4 Decreasing Error Rate – Quality

The same examination can be performed using a quality decomposition. Again, similarity values obtained from the image reconstructed upon receipt of quality layer k are compared with an ideal similarity value based on the reduction in distortion provided by layer k.

As was the case with the resolution decomposition, there is no scheme which is closest to the ideal for all three images. Furthermore, while for the resolution decomposition the less constrained schemes were generally close to the ideal and the more constrained schemes were generally far from the ideal, there is no such consistency to be found in the quality decomposition.

Table 3. Average squared deviation from the ideal - Quality

	top	nolow	lum	lumnl	res	comp	top2/5
Lena	57.05	17.63	63.59	17.76	27.05	103.54	70.30
Mandrill	33.32	41.96	19.19	43.62	33.63	61.77	15.10
Peppers	106.28	21.56	101.82	29.74	10.65	141.16	96.91
Average	65.55	27.05	61.53	30.37	23.78	102.16	60.77

As was the case with detectability at low layers, the scalability of a given selection method with respect to error reduction favours, on average, the nolow, lumnl and res schemes under a quality decomposition. The schemes which do not have high embedding strengths, perform poorly in terms of quality scalability. However, even the highest strength schemes do not fit the ideal well and are outperformed by both lum and top2/5 on the mandrill image.

The most striking feature of the quality scalability results, however, is the exceedingly large deviation for the comp scheme. It seems that with only the most significant bits of the colour coefficients being assigned to low quality layers, the similarity values for comp are always far below the ideal, much more so than the other schemes which have much the same embedding strength but are free to select a higher number of coefficients from the luminance channel.

7 Conclusion

None of the selection methods examined in this experiment fully provide the properties of a scalable watermarking algorithm. The first property we require is that the watermark be detectable in any acceptable portion of the image. Unfortunately, while the high embedding strengths achievable using selection methods that provide minimal distortion (nolow, lumnl and res) allow watermark detectability in the lowest quality layer, we are not able to consistently detect a watermark embedded using such schemes in images of low or moderate resolution. Conversely, those selection methods which allow consistent detectability when an image is adapted for low resolution display (top, comp, and top2/5) require low embedding strengths and are not consistently detectable in our least acceptable quality image. The lum selection method, which allows embedding at a moderate strength, is consistently detectable at neither the base resolution nor the base quality layer. The top scheme, which selects the largest coefficients across all resolutions, and the top2/5 scheme, which selects the large coefficients within each resolution, have the best general results, both allowing detection at the lowest resolution layer and the second quality layer.

The same problems occur with reducing error rate as increased portions are received, and no selection scheme performs consistently well in this regard. The top, comp, top2/5 and, to a lesser extent, lum schemes provide quite a close match to our ideal rate of error reduction as resolution layers are added. However these schemes, particularly comp, deviate highly from our ideal during receipt of the quality scalable bit stream. The nolow, lumnl and res selection methods are closest to our ideal rate of error reduction as quality layers are added, but are far from the ideal in terms of resolution scalability.

Given the conflict between watermark scalability in terms of resolution and watermark scalability in terms of quality, it seems unlikely that a fully scalable watermarking algorithm can be achieved merely by altering the coefficient selection method. Instead, the better schemes, such as top and top2/5, should be used as a foundation from which to investigate whether added scalability might be achieved through alternate embedding formulae and variable strength embedding.

References

1. T. P.-C. Chen and T. Chen, "Progressive Image Watermarking"; Proc. IEEE Intl. Conf. on Multimedia and Expo., July 2000.
2. I. J. Cox, F. T. Leighton and T. Shamoon, "Secure spread spectrum watermarking for multimedia" IEEE Trans. Image Processing, 1997.
3. R. Dugad et al., "A New Wavelet-Based Scheme for Watermarking Images"; International Conference on Image Processing, vol 2, 1998.
4. Kutter et al., "Towards Second Generation Watermarking Schemes"; International Conference on Image Processing, 1999.
5. E. Lin, C. Podilchuk, T. Kalker, and E. Delp, "Streaming video and rate scalable compression: What are the challenges for watermarking?", Proceedings of the SPIE Security and Watermarking of Multimedia Contents III, January 2001
6. M.L. Miller and J.A. Bloom, "Computing the Probability of False Watermark Detection"; Proc. 3rd International Workshop on Information Hiding, 1999.
7. A. Piva et al., "Exploiting the cross-correlation of RGB-channels for robust watermarking of color images"; International Conference on Image Processing, vol 1, 1999.
8. M. Steinder, S. Iren and P. D. Amer, "Progressively Authenticated Transmission"; MILCOM, November 1999.
9. P.-C. Su, H.-J. M. Wang and C.-C. J. Kuo, "An Integrated Approach to Image Watermarking and JPEG2000 compression"; Journal of VLSI Signal Processing, vol. 27, 2001.
10. H.-J. M. Wang and C.-C. J. Kuo, "An Integrated Progressive Image Coding and Watermarking System"; Proc. Int. Conf. on Acoustics, Speech and Signal Processing, vol. 6, pages 3721–3724, March 1998.

Performance Analysis of Order Statistical Patchwork

Hyojeong Kuk and Yong Cheol Kim

Dept. of Electrical and Computer Eng, University of Seoul
teeming@sidae.uos.ac.kr yckim@uos.ac.kr

Abstract. In conventional patchwork, the difference of the mean values of two groups is compared for watermark detection. We propose order-statistical patchwork schemes, which achieves significant improvements over conventional patchwork. First, we show that, when the mean comparison in patchwork is replaced by the median comparison, we get PSNR improvement due to informed watermarking. Second, we propose a majority voting scheme of a sequential comparison of pixel pairs in a sorted order, which produces significantly lower BER. The performance improvements are mathematically analyzed and tested. In experimental results, PSNR is about 6dB $\sim$ 15dB higher in the first method and BER is about $1/5 \sim 1/2$ times lower in the second method than conventional patchwork.

1 Introduction

A straightforward method of image watermarking in the spatial domain is to add a pseudorandom pattern $W(m,n)$, to the pixel values of an image. Watermark pattern $W(m,n)$, multiplied by a factor of k, is added to the host image to generate the watermarked image $I_W(m,n)$ as follows:

$$I_W(m,n) = I(m,n) + kW(m,n) \tag{1}$$

In the detection process, we calculate the correlation between the watermarked image $I_W(m,n)$ and the pattern $W(m,n)$. The embedded watermark W is declared to exist in image I, if the ratio $(W \cdot W' / \sqrt{W' \cdot W'})$ is greater than a threshold[1].

Detection in this way provides only 1-bit type information, *i.e.* it makes a judgment whether the watermark W exists there, or not. When we want to insert several bits[2], we can separately embed each bit into one subimage. A simple way of embedding M bits, $\{s_1, s_2, \ldots, s_M\}$, is to split an image I into M subimages $\{b_1, b_2, \ldots, b_M\}$ and then embed each bit in a subimage. The actual embedding of a bit may be either in spatial-domain[3], or in frequency-domain[4].

T. Kalker et al. (Eds.): IWDW 2003, LNCS 2939, pp. 247–262, 2004.
© Springer-Verlag Berlin Heidelberg 2004

1.1 Informed Watermarking

Watermarking is closely analogous to digital communication. From the detector's viewpoint, the data to send is the watermark and the host signal is the channel noise, which distorts the watermark information. However, there is a meaningful difference between the two. In communication, the exact value of the channel noise is not available either to the sender or to the receiver. On the contrary, in watermarking, the exact value of noise (host signal) is completely known in the embedding process.

In watermarking, we combat two noise sources[5] as shown in Fig.1. One is the host signal itself(S_1) and the other is the intentional attack(S_2). S_1 is completely known in the embedding process. Image fidelity and detection capability can be significantly improved if this side information (knowledge of S_1) is properly used. For example, in the case of block-by-block bit embedding, if a block exhibits strong (+1) characteristics even before embedding a (+1) bit, we do not need to modify the image block at all.

Since dirty-paper channel model[6] proved that the noise S_1, caused by the host signal, does not degrade the communication performance, several works of watermarking with side information have been published, such as dithered indexed modulation[7].

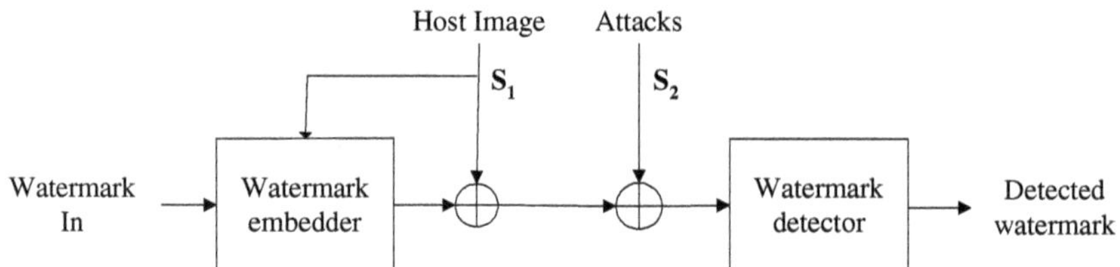

Fig. 1. Dirty-paper channel model

1.2 Patchwork: Detection by Mean Comparison

In the original patchwork method as introduced in [8], the existence of watermark is detected in a correlation-based way. We can extend patchwork method to embed a digital signature as follows:

The signature is a sequence of M bits, $S = \{s_1, s_2, \cdots, s_M\}$. An image is divided into M blocks, $\{b_1, b_2, \cdots, b_M\}$, each of which will embed one bit. Each block is pseudo-randomly divided into two equal-sized groups of N pixels, group A and group B, depending on the value of pseudo-random pattern $w_{m,n}$

$$A = \{a_{m,n} | w_{m,n} = 1\}$$

$$B = \{b_{m,n} | w_{m,n} = 0\}$$

The luminance of pixels of two groups is modified as shown in eq. (2). Let A* and B* represent the watermarked versions of A and B, then

$$\left.\begin{aligned} a^*_{m,n} &= a_{m,n} + d \cdot k \\ b^*_{m,n} &= b_{m,n} - d \cdot k \end{aligned}\right\} \quad \text{where} \quad d = \begin{cases} +1 & \text{if} \quad s = 1 \\ -1 & \text{if} \quad s = 0 \end{cases} \tag{2}$$

1.3 Contribution of Paper

In this paper, we present a performance analysis of order statistics-based patchwork method. Significant improvements are obtained both in the image quality and in the detection capability. The performance is measured both in BER (robustness) and PSNR (perceptibility). BER includes both false-positives and false-negatives in the detection of a single bit.

First, we show that, if we use the median in patchwork instead of the mean, PSNR can be significantly improved. The value of the median is the same in the following two cases: a) when we modify all the pixels and b) when we modify only those pixels whose values are close to the median. Hence, the detection performance in both cases is the same. This way, we have a large improvement in PSNR by virtue of the side information, *i.e.* the knowledge of pixel distribution. The cost for this improvement is none, except for the sorting.

Second, we have a significant improvement in BER when the bit detection is by a majority voting of comparison of sorted pairs. The N pixels in each group, A^* and B^*, are sorted and then they are consecutively compared in pairs in a sorted order. The improvement factor is in the order of $O(N^{1/4})$.

The reason why we selected patchwork method in spatial-domain is for an easy comparison of performance to show an improvement due to informed watermarking. The framework of order statistical watermarking is not limited to patchwork only, but can be extended to general watermarking methods, including frequency-domain methods and geometrical attack-robust methods.

The organization of this paper is as follows: In the next section, we briefly describe the conventional patchwork method and the two proposed methods. Detailed analysis is presented in section 3. Experimental results on standard test images are described in section 4.

2 Embedding and Detection in the Proposed Methods

First, a conventional patchwork method is described. Then, we describe two proposed methods, *method I* by median-comparison and *method II* by voting of sorted comparison.

2.1 Patchwork Method

In patchwork, the mean luminance of each group is compared. If D is larger than 0, we decide that the embedded bit is 1, otherwise, 0.

$$D = \frac{1}{N}\left[\sum_{i=1}^{N} a_i^* - \sum_{j=1}^{N} b_j^*\right]\begin{cases} > 0 & \text{decide as} \quad 1 \\ < 0 & \text{decide as} \quad 0 \end{cases} \tag{3}$$

2.2 Method I

The bit decision is based on the comparison of the median α^* of group A^* and the median β^* of group B^*.

$$D = \alpha^* - \beta^* \begin{cases} > 0 & \text{decide as} \quad 1 \\ < 0 & \text{decide as} \quad 0 \end{cases} \tag{4}$$

By using the median, the PSNR is significantly improved since we need to modify only a small fraction of the pixels. Still, we get the same detection performance as when we modify all the pixels.

Fig. 2 shows that the median of both cases is the same. Let the original median be α and β. Now, a value of k is added to and subtracted from group A and group B as in Fig.2 (b). The medians are now $\alpha^* = (\alpha + k)$ and $\beta^* = (\beta - k)$, respectively. In Fig.2 (c), when only those pixels are modified which are in $[med - k \cdot\cdot med + k]$, the values of the medians are the same as in Fig.2 (b).

Hence, we have a large improvement in PSNR. In a simple approximation of uniformly distributed luminance in $[0 \cdot \cdot 255]$, the percentage of modified pixels $(3 + 1 - (-3))/255 = 3\%$ for $k = 3$. Then, the improvement in PSNR is about 15.6 dB.

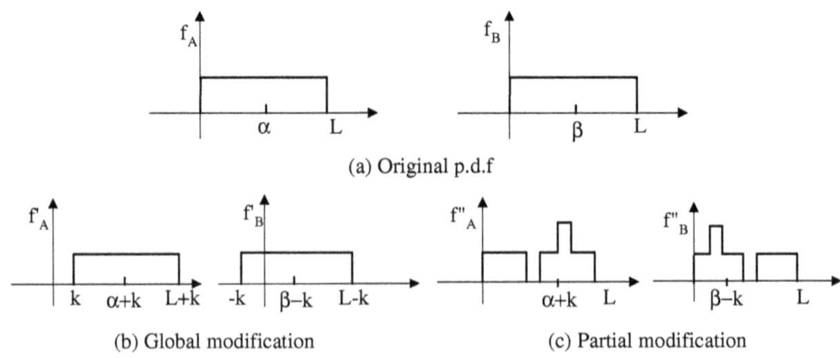

Fig. 2. The position of median in method I

2.3 Method II

Fig.3 shows the process of embedding and extracting of a bit. In the extraction process, the pixels of both groups are sorted by the luminance value. Let X_i and Y_i be the i-th largest pixel value of A^* and B^*, respectively. Then, we consecutively compare X_i and Y_i and sum the comparison results. If the sum is larger than 0, then we decide the data bit is 1, otherwise 0.

$$Z = \sum_{i=1}^{N} sgn(X_i - Y_i) \begin{cases} > 0 & \text{decide as} \quad 1 \\ < 0 & \text{decide as} \quad 0 \end{cases} \tag{5}$$

Method I can be considered as a special case of this method, where the decision is dependent only on the comparison of two medians.

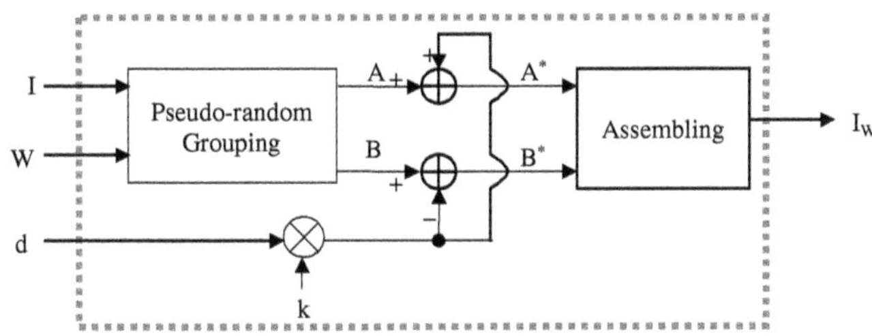

(a) Embedding process

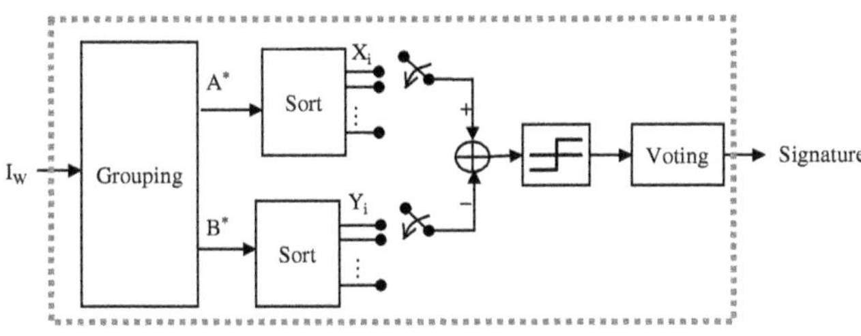

(b) Extraction process

Fig. 3. Embedding and Extraction process for method II

3 Performance Analysis of the Proposed Methods

In the analysis, we make a simple assumption that the distribution of luminance values is uniform in $[0 \cdot \cdot L]$. In all of the three methods, the decision of the watermark bit is based on the distance, D, which is obtained by comparing two groups, A^* and B^*. We use a test statistic q as the performance measure[3]:

$$q = \frac{\text{Mean}[D]}{\text{standard dev}[D]}$$

In the following analysis, the embedded bit is assumed to be '1', without loss of generality. Hence, A^* is the *brighter* group and B^* is the *darker* group.

3.1 Patchwork Method

We compare the mean values of group A and group B.

$$D_m = \sum_{i=1}^{N} a_i^* - \sum_{j=1}^{N} b_j^* = \sum_{i=1}^{N} (a_i + k) - \sum_{j=1}^{N} (b_i - k)$$

Then, $E[D_m] = N\{E[a+k]\} - N\{E[b-k]\} = 2kN$

$$var[D_m] = \sum_{i=1}^{N} var[a_i + k] + \sum_{j=1}^{N} var[b_j - k] = N\left(\frac{L^2}{12}\right) + N\left(\frac{L^2}{12}\right) = \frac{NL^2}{6}$$

The test statistic q is as follows:

$$q = \frac{E[D_m]}{|var[D_m]|^{1/2}} = \frac{2kN}{\sqrt{N/6} \cdot L} = 2\sqrt{6}\sqrt{N}\frac{k}{L} \tag{6}$$

3.2 Method I

When the sequence $\{X_1, X_2, \cdots, X_N\}$, which is uniformly distributed over $[0 \cdot\cdot L]$, is sorted in descending order into a sequence $\{Y_1, Y_2, \cdots, Y_N\}$, the mean and variance for Y_i is shown in eq.(7). Detailed steps are in the Appendix.

$$E[Y_i] = \frac{N-i+1}{N+1} L \quad \text{and} \quad var[Y_i] = \frac{i(N-i+1)}{(N+1)^2(N+2)} L^2 \tag{7}$$

The index i of the median is $\left\lfloor \frac{n+1}{2} \right\rfloor$, hence $E[Y_{Med}] \approx \frac{L}{2}$ and $var[Y_{Med}] \approx \frac{L^2}{4N}$.

Let D_d be the difference of the two medians, then:

$$D_d = (\alpha + k) - (\beta - k)$$

$$E[D_d] = E[\alpha + k] - E[\beta - k] = \left(\frac{L}{2} + k\right) - \left(\frac{L}{2} - k\right) = 2k$$

$$var[D_d] = var[\alpha + k] + var[\beta - k] = \frac{L^2}{4N} + \frac{L^2}{4N} = \frac{L^2}{2N}$$

The test statistic q is as follows:

$$q = \frac{E[D_d]}{|var[D_d]|^{\frac{1}{2}}} = \frac{2k}{\sqrt{L^2/2N}} = 2\sqrt{2}\sqrt{N}\frac{k}{L} \tag{8}$$

3.3 Method II

We add k to pixels in A, normalize by L and sort them in descending order into a sequence $X = \{X_1, X_2, \cdots, X_N\}$. The pixel values of group B decrease by k, then are normalized by L and sorted in descending order into a sequence $Y = \{Y_1, Y_2, \cdots, Y_N\}$. Since the luminance has a uniform distribution in [0..1], the mean and the variance of (normalized) X_i and Y_i are given by eq. (A-2) and eq. (A-3).

$$\begin{aligned} E[X_i] &= \frac{N-i+1}{N+1} + \Delta \\ E[Y_i] &= \frac{N-i+1}{N+1} - \Delta\,, \quad \text{where } \Delta = \frac{k}{L} \end{aligned} \tag{9}$$

$$var[X_i] = var[Y_i] = \frac{i(N-i+1)}{(N+1)^2(N+2)} \leq \frac{N^2/4}{N^3} = \frac{1}{4N} \tag{10}$$

Let C_i be a binary random variable, which indicates the comparison of X_i and Y_i.

$$C_i = sgn(X_i - Y_i) = \begin{cases} +1 & \text{if} \quad X_i > Y_i \\ -1 & \text{if} \quad X_i < Y_i \end{cases}$$

The final decision for the data bit is obtained as follows:

$$Z = \sum_{i=1}^{N} C_i \begin{cases} > 0 & \text{decide as} \quad 1 \\ < 0 & \text{decide as} \quad 0 \end{cases} \tag{11}$$

Assuming $C_1, C_2, \ldots, C_N$ are independent, the mean and variance of Z are as follows:

$$E[Z] = \sum_{i=1}^{N} E[C_i] = \sum_{i=1}^{N} [P_+ \cdot (+1) + P_- \cdot (-1)] = N(1 - 2P_-) \tag{12}$$

$$var[Z] = \sum_{i=1}^{N} var[C_i] = \sum_{i=1}^{N} \{E[C_i^2] - E[C_i]^2\} = 4N \cdot P_-(1 - P_-) \tag{13}$$

where $P_+ = \text{Prob}[C_i > 0]$ and $P_- = \text{Prob}[C_i < 0]$.

The test statistic q is as follows:

$$q = \frac{E[Z]}{\sqrt{var[Z]}} = \frac{\sqrt{N}(1-2P_-)}{2\sqrt{P_-(1-P_-)}} \tag{14}$$

Since P_- is the probability of making a wrong decision based on comparing pixels of the brighter group A^* and the darker group B^*, the value of P_- is small.

Hence, $\frac{1-2P_-}{\sqrt{P_-(1-P_-)}} \approx \frac{1}{\sqrt{P_-}}$

And we get,

$$q \approx \frac{\sqrt{N}}{2} \cdot \frac{1}{\sqrt{P_-}} \tag{15}$$

Now, we derive the key probability P_-. The probability that $C_i \leq 0$ is given as follows[9]:

$$\begin{aligned} P_- &= \text{Prob}[C_i < 0] = \text{Prob}[Y_i > X_i + 2\Delta] \\ &= \int_0^{1-2\Delta} \int_{x+2\Delta}^{1} f_i(x) \cdot f_i(y) dx dy \\ &\text{where,} \quad f_i(x) = \frac{n!}{(n-i)!(i-1)!} x^{n-i}(1-x)^{i-1} \end{aligned} \tag{16}$$

Instead of numerically computing eq. (16), we make a simple Gaussian approximation. Let $D_i = X_i - Y_i$, then from eq.(9) and eq.(10),

$$E[D_i] = E[X_i] - E[Y_i] = 2\Delta$$

Assuming X_i and Y_i are independent,

$$var[D_i] = var[X_i] + var[Y_i] = 2\frac{i(N-i+1)}{(N+1)^2(N+2)} \approx \frac{2i(N-i)}{N^3} \leq \frac{1}{2N}$$

Assuming D_i is Gaussian,

$$P_- \leq Q\left(\frac{E[D_i]}{\sqrt{var[D_i]}}\right) = Q\left(2\sqrt{2}\sqrt{N}\Delta\right) < \frac{1}{4\sqrt{\pi}\sqrt{N}\Delta} \exp(-4N\Delta^2) \tag{17}$$

Substituting eq. (17) into eq. (15),

$$q \approx \frac{\sqrt{N}}{2} \cdot \frac{1}{\sqrt{P_-}} = \pi^{1/4} N^{3/4} \frac{k}{L} \cdot \exp\left(2N\frac{k^2}{L^2}\right) \tag{18}$$

3.4 Summary and Discussion

Table 1 is a list of how the block size N affects the performance. BER is lower in method II (voting) since the detection which is dependent on all N pairs is less likely to produce an error than a comparison of just one pair of means or medians. A mean value, too, is dependent on all the pixels in a group. However, the mean is heavily affected by outliers. On the other hand, in method II, the effect of a few outliers is ignorable since the weighting factor of every comparison is the same.

The actual PSNR improvement by method I(median) is smaller than the analysis in section 2, because we need to modify pixels in a wider range than the minimum range of $[med - k \cdot \cdot med + k]$, in order to be provided against possible attacks as will be described section 4.

Table 1. Effect of size N on the detection performance

Methods	Test statistic	Remarks	PSNR
Patchwork	$2\sqrt{6}\sqrt{N}\frac{k}{L}$	$O\left(N^{1/2}\right)$	normal
Method I	$2\sqrt{2}\sqrt{N}\frac{k}{L}$	$O\left(N^{1/2}\right)$	higher
Method II	$\pi^{1/4}N^{3/4}\frac{k}{L} \cdot \exp\left(2N\frac{k^2}{L^2}\right)$	$O\left(N^{3/4}\right)$	normal

4 Experimental Results

We tested the proposed methods for 16 standard test images with 256-gray levels. The test images are shown in Fig.4. BER and PSNR are measured both without attack and under attacks. Table 2 is a list of the parameters of the attacks in the test.

First, in order to determine the value of N, BER without attack is measured as a function of N and the result for ($N = 32$ 131072) is in Fig.5. In the following experiments, we use $N = 512$. When N is larger than 2048, BER converges to almost zero.

Fig. 6 shows a comparison of BER without attack for method I, method II and conventional patchwork. BER in method I is in the range of $1\% \sim 10\%$, except for one test image(image 16). Though BER in method I is higher than patchwork case, PSNR is considerably improved as will be described shortly. As expected, BER in method II is in the range from 0% (no error) to 4%, except for one test image(image 16), which is about 1/5 of the patchwork method. For some of the test images, BER in method II is 0% while conventional patchwork produces BER of about 1% $\sim$ 5% for them.

Secondly, we compared the robustness of the three methods against various attacks, including noise addition, filtering and compression. Fig.7 shows BER for three of the 16 images. All three methods exhibit strong robustness against additive noise. Under all cases of attack, BER in method II is 1/5 $\sim$ 1/2 times lower than the BER in the conventional patchwork.

Thirdly, improvement of PSNR by informed watermarking in method I is tested. Without attack, BER is the same whether all the pixels are modified or only 20% of them are modified since both cases produce the same median values. Under attack, however, the robustness depends on the modification ratio, as shown in Fig.8. In order to make the best use of informed watermarking, we use an adaptive modification ratio. We continue to raise the modification ratio for attack-sensitive blocks from 20% until they exhibit the same robustness as 100% modification. As a result, only half of all the image blocks are modified with a modification ratio of 20% $\sim$ 100%. PSNR under attacks is shown in Fig.9, for 20% ratio, for 100% ratio and for the adaptive ratio. Improvement by using an adaptive modification ratio is in the range of 6 dB $\sim$ 10 dB.

5 Conclusion

We proposed two order-statistical patchwork schemes, which achieves significant improvements over conventional patchwork. In method I, the bit decision is based on the comparison of the median values of two groups of pixels. Median comparison results in PSNR improvement, due to informed watermarking. In method II, the pixels are sorted and then pixel pairs from two groups are sequentially compared and the bit decision is by a majority voting. Significantly lower BER is obtained in method II.

The improvements are mathematically analyzed under an assumption of uniform luminance distribution of image pixels. In experiments with standard test images, PSNR improvement is about 6dB $\sim$ 10dB (in method I) and BER improvement is about 1/5 $\sim$ 1/2 times lower (in method II) than in the conventional patchwork method.

(a) Lena (b) Baboon (c) Peppers (d) Barbara
(e) Texmos (f) Airfield (g) Airplane (h) Pentagon
(i) Airport (j) Binder (k) Bird (l) Bubble
(m) Couple (n) Debbie (o) Girl (p) Key

Fig. 4. Test images

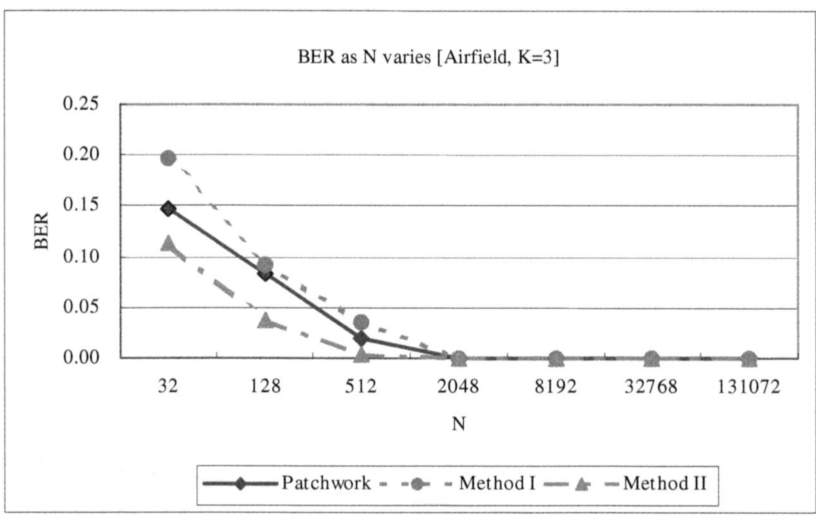

(a) Airfield Image

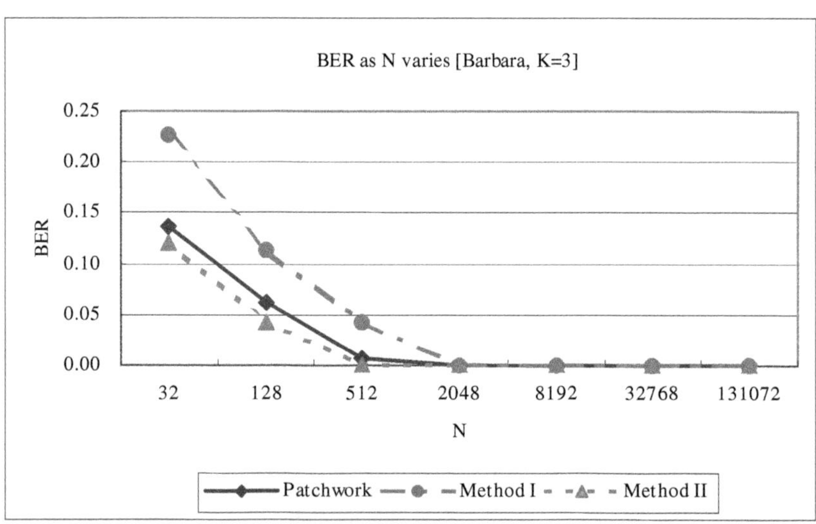

(b) Barbara Image

Fig. 5. BER as N varies (k=3)

Table 2. List of Tested Attacks

Attack	Description	Parameter
None	No	-
Noise Addition (Gaussian noise)	N1	$\sigma^2 = 0.0001\sigma_I^2$
	N2	$\sigma^2 = 0.0005\sigma_I^2$
	N3	$\sigma^2 = 0.001\sigma_I^2$
Median filtering	M1	Window size=2*2
	M2	Window size=3*3
Low Pass filtering (Gaussian LPF)	L0.5	$\sigma = 0.5$
	L1	$\sigma = 1$
	L2	$\sigma = 2$
JPEG	J70	Q=70
	J50	Q=50
	J30	Q=30
Histogram Equalizer	Heq	-

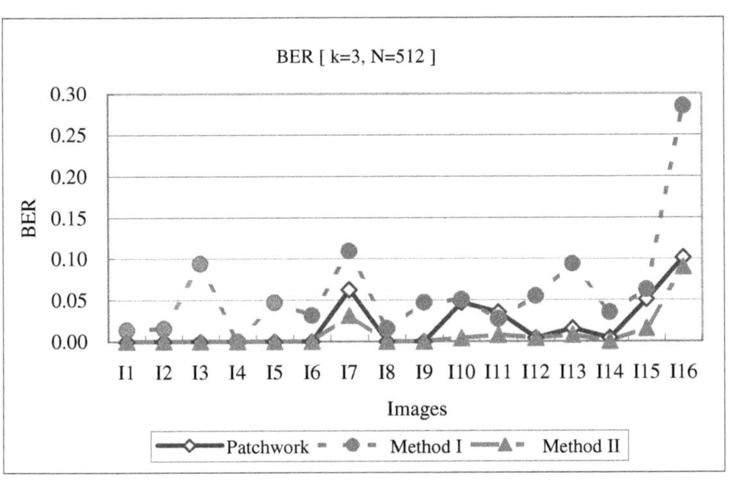

Fig. 6. BER for various images

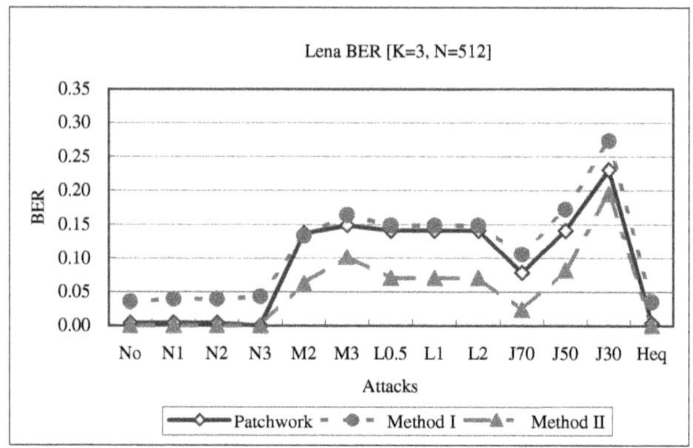

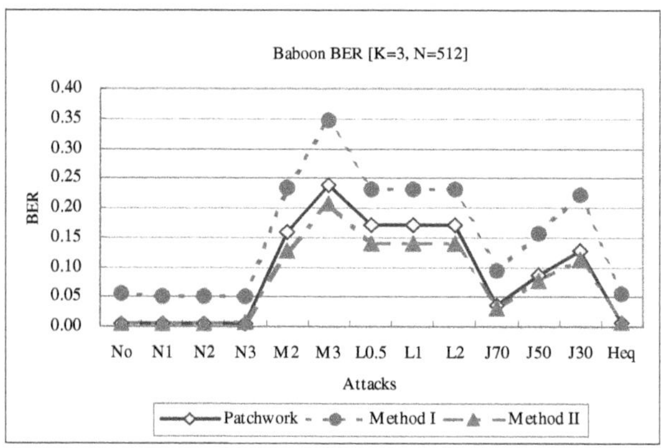

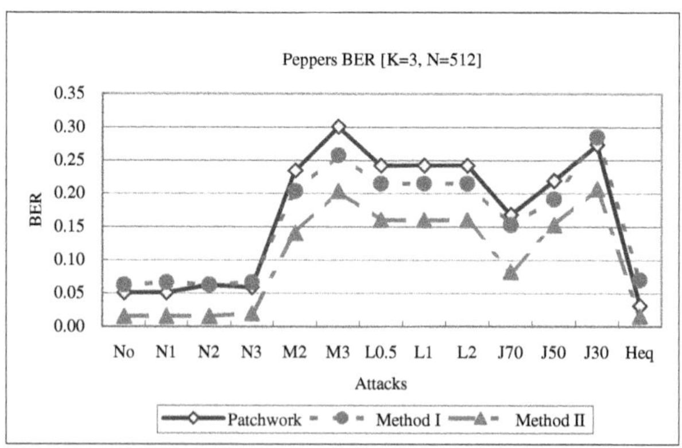

Fig. 7. BER under various attacks

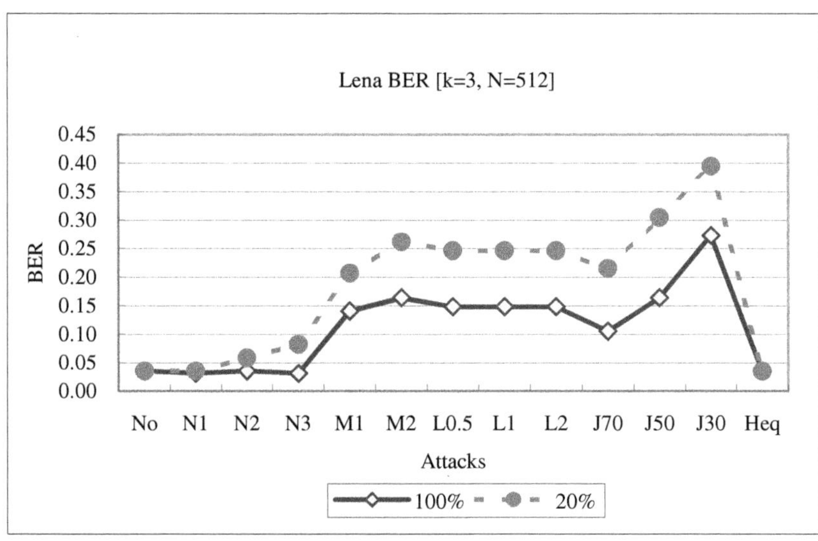

Fig. 8. BER as modification ratio varies in method I (for Lena)

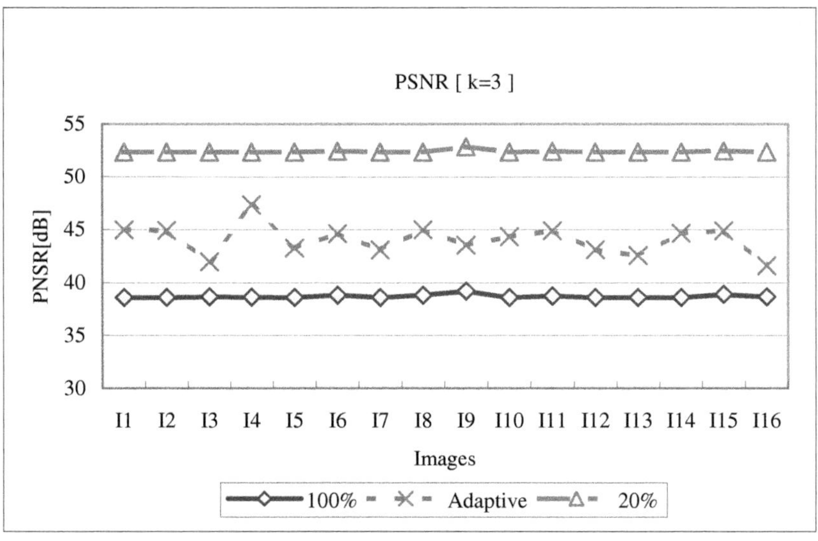

Fig. 9. PSNR improvement in method I

References

1. I.Cox *et al.*, "Secures spread spectrum watermarking for Multimedia", IEEE Transactions on Image processing, Vol.6, No.12, December 1997
2. J.Smith and B.Comiskey, "Modulation and information hiding in images", Information Hiding, University of Cambridge, U.K., May 1996
3. N.Nikolaidis and I.Pitas, "Robust image watermarking in the spatial domain", EURASIP 66(3), pp 385–403, May 1998
4. Y.Kim and B.Choi, "Two-step detection algorithm in a HVS-based blind watermarking of still images", IWDW2002, pp.278–292, 2002
5. I.Cox, M.Miller and J.Bloom, "Digital Watermarking", Morgan Kaufmann, 2002
6. M.Costa. "Writing on Dirty Paper", IEEE Transactions on Information Theory, 29: pp.439–441, 1983
7. B.Chen and G.W.Wornell, "Digital watermarking and information embedding using dither modulation", IEEE 2nd Workshop on Multimedia Signal Processing, pp.273–278, 1998
8. W.Bender *et al.*, "Techniques for data hiding", IBM Systems Journal, Vol.35, NOS 3&4,1996
9. A. Papoulis, "Probability, Random Variables and Stochastic Processes", 2nd Ed. McGraw-Hill, 1984

Appendix: Mean and Variance of Order Statistic

Let X_i, $i = 1, \cdots, n$ be independent random variables which are uniformly distributed over [0..1]. Sorting X_is in descending order, we get Y_i, $i = 1, \cdots, n$ such that $Y_1 \geq Y_2 \geq \cdots \geq Y_n$. The p.d.f. of Y_i is given by [9],

$$f_i(y) = \frac{n!}{(i-1)!(n-i)!} F_X^{i-1}(y)[1 - F_X(y)]^{n-i} f_X(y)$$

where $F_X(x)$ is the c.d.f. of the random variable X.

Since $F_X(x) = x$, $0 \leq x \leq 1$, we get

$$f_i(y) = \frac{n!}{(i-1)!(n-i)!} y^{i-1}[1-y]^{n-i}, \quad 0 \leq y \leq 1 \tag{A-1}$$

Then, the mean and variance of Y_i are obtained as follows.

$$E[Y_i] = \int_0^1 y f_i(y) dy = \frac{n-i+1}{n+1} \tag{A-2}$$

$$var[Y_i] = \int_0^1 y^2 f_i(y) dy - \{E[Y_i]\}^2 = \frac{i(n-i+1)}{(n+1)^2(n+2)} \tag{A-3}$$

In the derivation of eq. (A-2) and Eq. (A-3), we used the derived result for beta function $B(x, y)$:

$$B(x, y) = \int_0^1 t^{x-1}(1-t)^{y-1} dt = \frac{\Gamma(x)\Gamma(y)}{\Gamma(x+y)} = \frac{(x-1)!(y-1)!}{(x+y-1)!}$$

Rotation-Tolerant Watermark Detection Using Circular Harmonic Function Correlation Filter

Hyungshin Kim[1] and B.V.K. Vijaya Kumar[2]

[1] Department of Computer Engineering,
Chungnam National University,
220 Gung-dong, Yuseong-gu Daejeon, 305-764, South Korea
ispace2000@yahoo.co.kr

[2] Department of Electrical and Computer Engineering,
Carnegie Mellon University,
Pittsburgh, PA 15213 USA
kumar@ece.cmu.edu

Abstract. Almost all of the previous watermarking methods utilize some form of correlation or matched filter during watermark detection. The conventional correlation detector provides optimal performance when the watermarked image goes through additive white noise. In this paper, we propose to use a circular harmonic function (CHF) correlation filter instead of the conventional matched filter at the detector. In this way, we can achieve rotation tolerant correlation peak at the detector. During the filter design, conflicting filter design parameters can be optimally traded off while achieving desired correlation peak in response to rotation of the image. The proposed detector can be used with any watermarking method where rotation of the watermark should be detected. As the filter design can be done off-line, the proposed method can be used in real-time watermark detectors.

1 Introduction

Since the beginning of the research on digital watermark, much work has been reported [1][2]. Watermarking schemes robust to geometric distortions have received great attention recently. It is because a simple geometric distortion can de-synchronize watermark detector without losing image fidelity, which results in detection failure [3]. Many watermarking methods resilient to geometric distortions were reported. One approach is to embed a known template into images along with the watermark [4][5]. During detection, the inserted template pattern is used to invert the distortion that the watermarked images went through and the watermark is extracted after compensating for the distortion. The process of embedding the template reduces information capacity and image fidelity. Invariant watermarks can be designed using the Fourier-Mellin transform [6][7] or geometric moment functions [8]. They utilize invariant functions or parameters that are invariant to geometric transformation. Watermarks using image features are reported [9] [10]. The invariant watermarks and feature-based methods have

T. Kalker et al. (Eds.): IWDW 2003, LNCS 2939, pp. 263–276, 2004.
© Springer-Verlag Berlin Heidelberg 2004

difficulties in insertion and detection as their watermarks are not white noise-like. In this paper. we propose a method to achieve rotation tolerance by using a new correlation detector. Rotation tolerance means that our method provides rotation invariance only within a limited range of rotation angle.

There have been many optimal detectors for each different watermark embedding method. The correlation detector is the optimum structure for additive watermarks [11]. For multiplicative watermarks, other optimal detectors are reported [12][13]. We propose a new watermark detector using the Optimal Trade-off Circular Harmonic Function (OTCHF) filters [14]. The circular harmonic function (CHF) is useful in representing the rotational property of an image as any image expressed in polar coordinates is periodic in angle with period 2π and thus can be expressed in terms of a Fourier series expansion in angle. We can design a correlation detector which achieves rotation tolerant correlation peak with the CHFs. During filter design, we can optimally trade off among various quadratic correlation filter performance criteria. The correlation filter is optimal in that no other correlation filter can simultaneously improve in all performance criteria while providing the specified rotation response. In this way, our correlation detector exhibits tolerance to noise and rotation. The designed correlation detector can be used with any watermarking method that requires rotation invariance of the watermark. As the OTCHF filters can be designed off-line, we can still maintain the real-time computation speed at the detector.

The rest of this paper is organized as follows. The relevant CHF basics are explained in Section 2. Section 3 describes the OTCHF filter design method. We show how we can apply the OTCHF filter design method into a watermark detector in Section 4. In Section 5, we apply the OTCHF detector to a watermark method and show the implementation results. Concluding remarks are made in Section 6.

2 Circular Harmonic Functions (CHF) [14]

Let $\hat{f}(x,y)$ denote the reference image with its 2-D Fourier transform (FT) by $\hat{F}(u,v)$. Here, the hat is used to indicate a function of Cartesian coordinates. We can transform $\hat{F}(u,v)$ into polar frequency to obtain $F(\rho,\phi)$. Since $F(\rho,\phi)$ is periodic in ϕ with period of 2π, we can use a Fourier series expansion in ϕ as follows:

$$F(\rho,\phi) = \sum_k F_k(\rho) e^{jk\phi}$$

$$F_k(\rho) = \frac{1}{2\pi}\int_0^{2\pi} F(\rho,\phi) e^{-jk\phi} d\phi \qquad (1)$$

where $F_k(\rho)$ is the k-th circular harmonic function (CHF) of $\hat{F}(u,v)$. Note that we use CHF's of the Fourier transform of the image rather than CHF's of the image itself. Let $\hat{H}(u,v)$ denote the correlation filter in Cartesian frequencies. Its polar coordinate transformed version also lends itself to a CHF decomposition as follows:

$$H(\rho,\phi) = \sum_k H_k(\rho)e^{jk\phi}$$

$$H_k(\rho) = \frac{1}{2\pi}\int_0^{2\pi} H(\rho,\phi)e^{-jkl}d\phi \tag{2}$$

Let c denote the correlation value at the origin when the input is $\hat{f}(x,y)$ and the correlation filter $\hat{H}(u,v)$. Using Eq. 1 and Eq. 2, we obtain the following expression for the correlation peak in terms of the filter and the input CHF's:

$$\begin{aligned} c &= \int\int \hat{F}(u,v)\hat{H}^*(u,v)dudv \\ &= \int_0^{2\pi} d\phi \int_0^{\infty} \rho d\rho F(\rho,\phi)H^*(\rho,\phi) \\ &= \int_0^{\infty} \rho d\rho \int_0^{2\pi} d\phi \left[\sum_k F_k(\rho)e^{jk\phi} \right. \\ &\quad \left. \times \sum_l H_l^*(\rho)e^{-jl\phi}\right] \end{aligned} \tag{3}$$

As the integral $\int_0^{2\pi} e^{j(k-l)\phi}d\phi$ is zero for $k \neq l$, only a single summation is needed leading to the following simpler expression for the correlation output:

$$c = \sum_{k=-\infty}^{\infty} C_k \quad C_k = 2\pi\int_0^{\infty} F_k(\rho)H_k^*(\rho)\rho d\rho \tag{4}$$

The correlation output c is the sum of C_k, which we call as CHF weights and can be obtained from the knowledge of the k-th CHFs of $\hat{F}(u,v)$ and the filter function $\hat{H}(u,v)$. Eq. 4 shows how we can control C_k values by choosing the filter CHF's $H_k^*(\rho)$.

When we rotate the input image $\hat{f}(x,y)$ by angle θ in the clockwise direction, $\hat{F}(u,v)$ is rotated by angle θ leading to $F(\rho,\phi+\theta)$. From Eq. 1, the CHF's of the FT of this rotated image are then given by $F_k(\rho)e^{jk\theta}$. Since the filter is unchanged, its circular harmonics do not change and the correlation output as a function of input rotation is given as follows:

$$c(\theta) = \sum_{k=-\infty}^{\infty} C_k e^{jk\theta} \tag{5}$$

Eq. 5 has the similar form as the frequency response of a finite impulse response (FIR) filter. This enables us to use FIR filter design methods for the determination of CHF filter weight C_k. Hence we can use any FIR filter design method to assign CHF weights.

3 Optimal Tradeoff Circular Harmonic Function (OTCHF) Filter Design

Once the CHF weights C_k are determined, the next task is to find the filter CHF's $H_k(\rho)$ so that the correlation filter $H(\rho,\phi)$ can be determined. As $H_k(\rho)$ is not completely determined by Eq. 4, we can optimize other relevant correlation output criteria [15]. We will express below three correlation filter performance criteria. We have shown here only the final forms of each parameters and full developments can be found in [14].

1. *Output Noise Variance (ONV)*: This is the variance at the output due to additive noise in the input image. It measures the sensitivity of the filter to additive input noise. If we assume that the input noise power spectrum $\hat{P}_n(u,v)$ is isotropic, then the ONV can be expressed as follows using CHF's:

$$\begin{aligned} ONV &= \int\int |\hat{H}(u,v)|^2 \hat{P}_n(u,v)dudv \\ &= 2\pi \sum_k \left[\int_0^\infty |H_k(\rho)|^2 P_n(\rho)\rho d\rho\right] \end{aligned} \tag{6}$$

2. *Average Correlation Energy (ACE)*: For each possible input rotation, it is desired that the resulting correlation output exhibit a sharp correlation peak at the center with relatively little energy elsewhere in the correlation output. ACE represents the average of the correlation energies as the input is rotated through full 360° and must be made as small as possible to reduce the sidelobes in the correlation plane. The ACE can be expressed with CHF's as follows:

$$\begin{aligned} ACE &= \frac{1}{2\pi}\int_0^{2\pi} d\theta \left\{\int_0^{2\pi} d\phi \int_0^\infty \rho d\rho \right. \\ &\quad \left. \times |F(\rho,\phi+\theta)|^2 |H(\rho,\phi)|^2\right\} \\ &= 2\pi \sum_k \left[\int_0^\infty |H_k(\rho)|^2 P_{avg}(\rho)\rho d\rho\right] \end{aligned} \tag{7}$$

where $P_{avg}(\rho)$ is the power spectrum of input image and it can be shown as:

$$P_{avg}(\rho) = \sum_{l=-\infty}^{\infty} |F_l(\rho)|^2 \tag{8}$$

3. *Average Similarity Measure (ASM)*: ASM measures the average squared distance from individual correlation outputs $\hat{c}(x,y,\theta)$ to the average $\bar{c}(x,y) = (1/2\pi)\int_0^{2\pi} \hat{c}(x,y,\theta)d\theta$ of all these correlation outputs. ASM is really a dissimilarity measure. It is desired that a correlation filter make all its correlation outputs as similar as possible so that we make ASM as small as possible.

$$ASM = \frac{1}{2\pi}\int_0^{2\pi} d\theta \left[\int\int |\hat{c}(x,y,\theta) - \bar{c}(x,y)|^2 dxdy\right]$$
$$= 2\pi \sum_{k=-\infty}^{\infty}\left[\int_0^{\infty} |H_k(\rho)|^2 P_{ASM}(\rho)\rho d\rho\right] \tag{9}$$

where

$$P_{ASM}(\rho) = \sum_{l\neq 0} |F_l(\rho)|^2 \tag{10}$$

In [16], it is shown that we can design one filter that can optimally trade off among those three criteria by minimizing a weighted sum, $\alpha \cdot ONV + \beta \cdot ACE + \gamma \cdot ASM$. Thus, the OTCHF filter $H(\rho,\phi)$ is obtained by solving the following minimization problem.

$$\text{minimize} \quad \int_0^{\infty} |H_k(\rho)|^2 P_{FOM}(\rho)\rho d\rho$$
$$\text{subject to} \quad \int_0^{\infty} F_k(\rho) H_k^*(\rho)\rho d\rho = C_k \tag{11}$$

where

$$P_{FOM}(\rho) = \alpha P_n(\rho) + \beta P_{avg}(\rho) + \gamma P_{ASM}(\rho) \tag{12}$$

This minimization leads to the following filter CHFs $H_k(\rho)$.

$$H_k(\rho) = \lambda^* \frac{F_k(\rho)}{P_{FOM}(\rho)} \quad \text{where } \lambda_k = \frac{C_k}{\int_0^{\infty} \frac{|F_k(\rho)|^2}{P_{FOM}(\rho)}\rho d\rho} \tag{13}$$

After we have $H_k(\rho)$, we can get $H(\rho,\phi)$ using Eq. 1, and then we get $H(u,v)$ by inverse polar mapping.

Fig. 1 shows the designed OTCHF correlation filter's impulse response h. The corresponding watermark and the correlation output is shown in Fig. 2. Note that the designed filter's impulse response has very little similarity to the watermark.

4 Proposed OTCHF Watermark Detector

In the previous section, we have shown how an optimal tradeoff rotation-tolerant correlation filter can be designed. In this section, we show how we apply the OTCHF filter to watermark detection within a simple additive watermarking method.

Let's consider a rectangular image X of size $N = N_1 N_2$ pixels. We consider a white watermark W of size N embedded into the spacial domain of the image by simple addition. Then the watermarked image Y becomes,

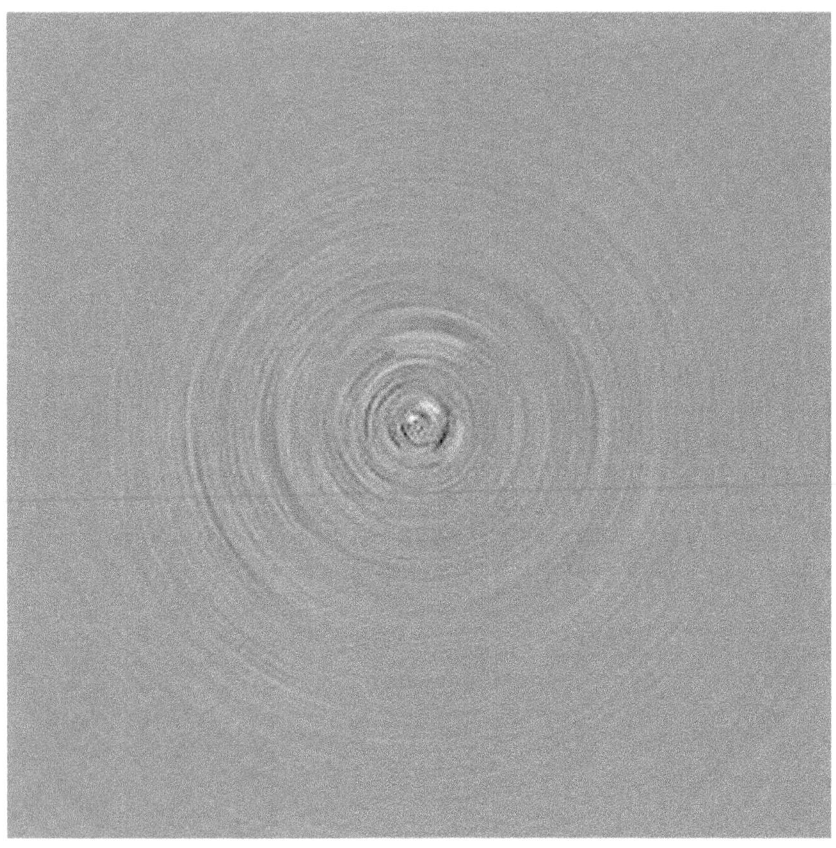

Fig. 1. Computed OTCHF filter point spread function h in image domain

$$Y = X + W \tag{14}$$

As practiced by [17], we modulate the watermark using a simple perceptual masking matrix Λ,

$$\Lambda = |L * X| \tag{15}$$

where $*$ denotes a convolution and

$$L = \begin{bmatrix} -1 & -1 & -1 \\ -1 & 8 & -1 \\ -1 & -1 & -1 \end{bmatrix}$$

With a scaling factor s, we get the final watermarked image Y as follows,

$$Y = X + s\Lambda W \tag{16}$$

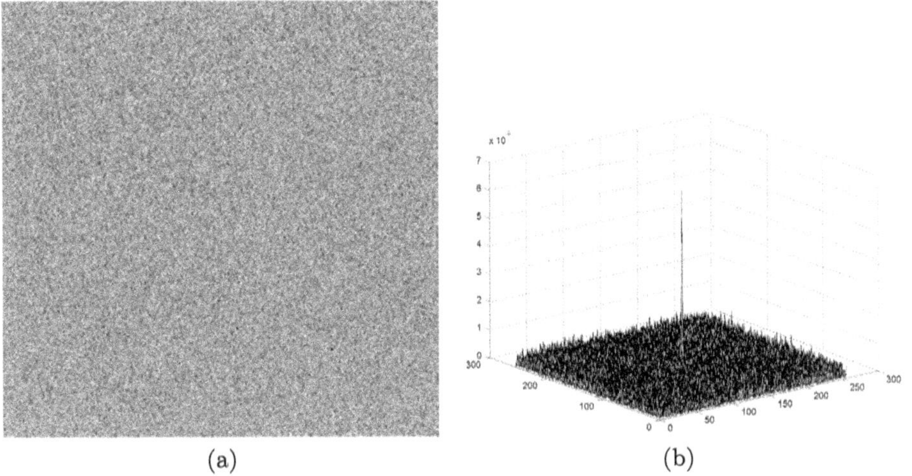

(a) (b)

Fig. 2. Embedding example : (a) A Gaussian watermark W (b) Computed correlation output between h and W

After embedding a watermark, we generate the OTCHF filter h and it can be expressed by the filter design function f_o as follows:

$$h = f_o(W, c(\theta)) \tag{17}$$

with a given rotation tolerance specification $c(\theta)$,

$$c(\theta) = \begin{cases} 1, & \text{for } |\theta| \leq \theta_t \\ 0, & \text{for } |\theta| > \theta_t \end{cases} \tag{18}$$

where θ_t is the tolerance angle. We don't use $\theta_t = 360°$ which might provide complete rotation invariance.

It is because if we set $\theta_t = 360°$, we get only one non-zero C_k from the filter design and the resulting filter will have extremely poor discrimination capability. Fig. 3 shows the overall embedding module.

At detector, we measure the correlation d between the test image Y and the OTCHF filter h as follows,

$$\begin{aligned} d &= < Y, h > \\ &= < X, h > + s\Lambda \cdot < W, h > \\ &= d_{org} + d_{wmk} \end{aligned} \tag{19}$$

where,

$$< Y, h > = \frac{1}{N} \sum_{n=1}^{N} Y(n)h(n)$$

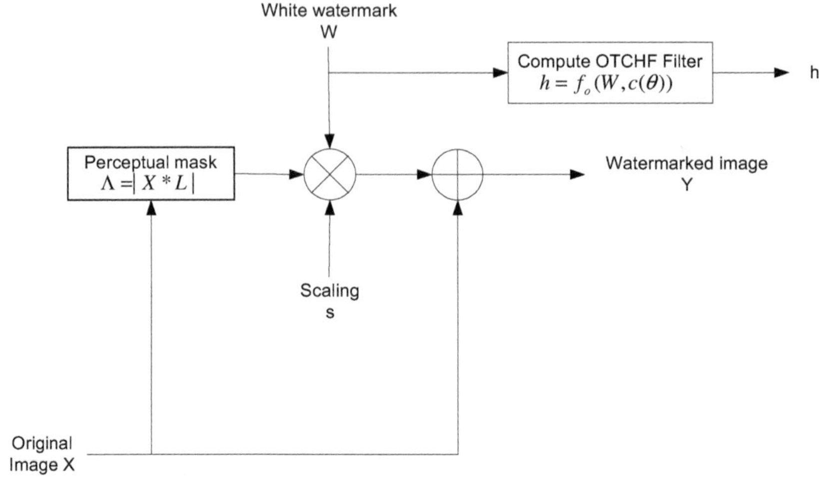

Fig. 3. An Additive embedding structure

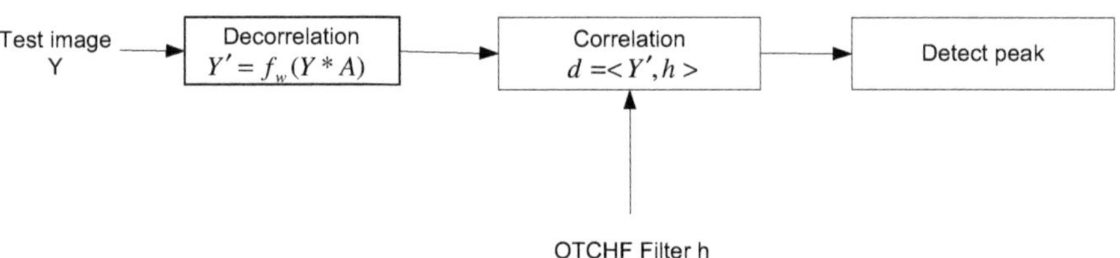

Fig. 4. OTCHF Correlation detector

When we correlate W with Y as in other conventional detector, the expected value of the correlation contribution by the original unmarked image d_{org} is equal to zero. However, as we now have generated a new signal h which may not be as white as the watermark W, we are not sure if d_{org} will still have small contribution to d. To reduce the magnitude of d_{org}, as suggested by [17], we may apply a whitening filter to de-correlate host image from the watermark.

As we will be using this whitening procedure f_w at detector, we also whiten the watermark before the OTCHF filter design. This can be shown as,

$$\begin{aligned} h &= f_o\{f_w(W), c(\theta)\} \\ &= f_o\{W * A, c(\theta)\} \end{aligned} \tag{20}$$

where A is a decorrelation filter. Various decorrelation filters can be practiced to find the best performance.

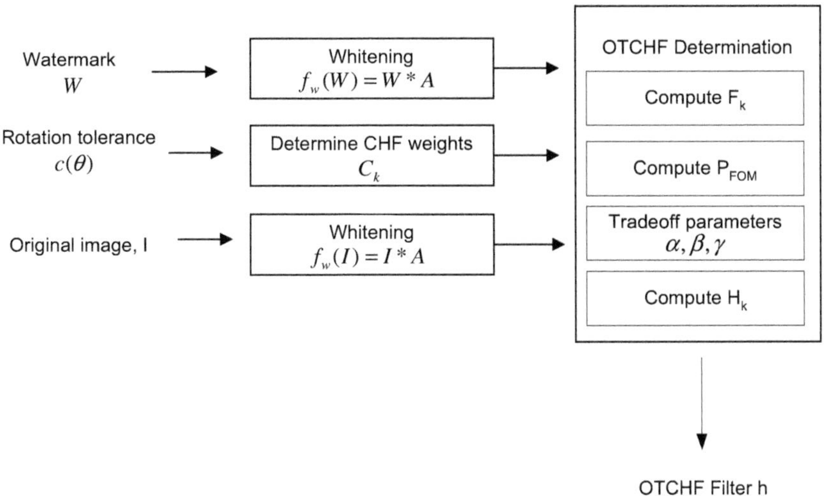

Fig. 5. OTCHF Correlation filter determination

Now the correlation value d at detector becomes,

$$\begin{aligned} d &= < f_w(Y), h > \\ &= < f_w(X + s\Lambda W), f_o(f_w(W), c(\theta)) > \\ &= < f_w(X), f_o(f_w(W), c(\theta)) > +s\Lambda \cdot < f_w(W), f_o(f_w(W), c(\theta)) > \\ &= d'_{org} + d'_{wmk} \end{aligned} \tag{21}$$

The contribution of the original unmarked image d'_{org} is expected to show relatively smaller value than d'_{wmk}. The contribution of the watermark d'_{wmk} remains almost unchanged. Fig. 4 shows the detector structure.

The effort to reduce the interference from the original image can be also implemented within the OTCHF design parameters. At ONV, the additive noise at the detector is considered as $P_n(\rho)$. Other than channel noise, we know exact characteristics of the noise, which in this case is the power spectrum density of the original image. Hence, we use $P_n(\rho)$ as follows,

$$\begin{aligned} P_n(\rho) &= \sum_{\phi} P_n(\rho, \phi) \\ &= \sum_{\phi} F(\rho, \phi) F^*(\rho, \phi) \end{aligned} \tag{22}$$

where $F(\rho, \phi)$ is the Fourier transform of the original image in polar coordinate.

The OTCHF filter design procedure is shown in Fig. 5. We take the 2-D FFT of the whitened watermark and carry out a polar transform. After the polar transform, we carry out 1-D FT's along the angular axis to obtain the CHF components. Once these CHF components are obtained, they can be used with any choice of α, β and γ parameters. From the given rotation tolerance specification $c(\theta)$, CHF weight C_k is determined using FIR filter design method. The original image I is whitened and its power spectrum is computed as a noise input for OTCHF filter. The CHF form of the OTCHF filter H_k is achieved by evaluating Eq. 13 with C_k, P_{FOM} and the CHF's of the watermark, F_k. The filter $H(\rho, \phi)$ is computed using Eq. 1.

5 Experimental Results

To demonstrate the performance of the OTCHF correlation detector, we implemented the watermark embedding and detection as in Fig. 3 and Fig. 4.

Experiments are performed with 100 images from the Corel image library [18]. We have cropped images into the size of 240 × 240 and luminance components are extracted from the RGB color images. The watermark is generated from a

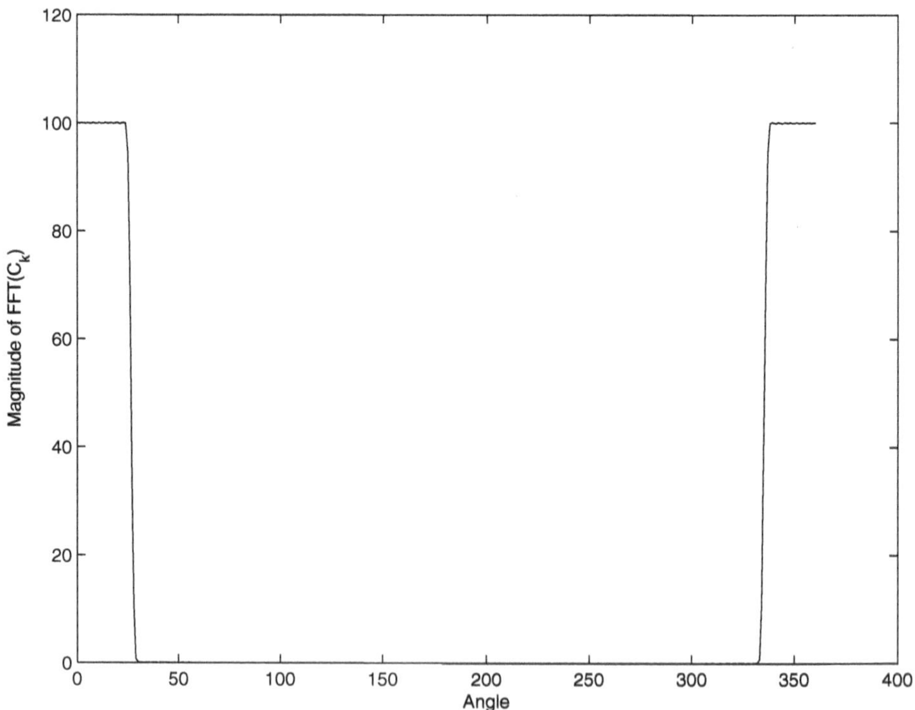

Fig. 6. Rotation response provided by the designed CHF weights

Gaussian distribution using a random number generator. This watermark is perceptually masked using L. Watermark insertion strength is controlled by scaling factor s so that $PSNR > 36dB$ is maintained along the test. The watermark is added directly into the intensity image. The OTCHF filter is determined as in Fig. 5. For our test, we used the rotation tolerance as follows:

$$c(\theta) = \begin{cases} 1, & \text{for } |\theta| \leq 25^{\circ} \\ 0, & \text{for } |\theta| > 25^{\circ} \end{cases} \tag{23}$$

We used the REMEZ function in $MATLAB^{©}$ to determine the CHF weights C_k. Magnitudes of the resulting FIR filter coefficients are shown in Fig. 6. We use the decorrelation filter A which was suggested in [17]. After computing $F_k(\rho)$ of the whitened watermark W, we determine $H_k(\rho)$ as in Eq. 13. For this test, we used values $\alpha = 0.0001$, $\beta = 0.999$, $\gamma = 0.0001$. The reason of choosing these values is to focus on sharpness of the correlation peak rather than noise robustness.

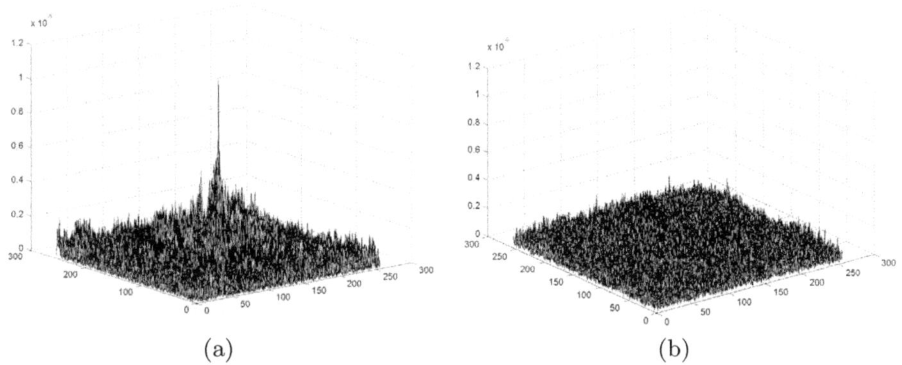

(a) (b)

Fig. 7. Correlation output : (a) after 10° rotation (b) after 60° rotation

Fig. 7 shows the correlation output from the detector using the watermarked image and the OTCHF filter h after applying whitening filter. Since 10° is within the specified tolerance range, we observe high peak at the center while the correlation peak is small after 60° rotation which is out of the specified range. However, due to the correlation of the original image, there are some relatively high peaks. To reduce the correlation noise, we need to refine our whitening filter at the detector for future application.

Watermarked images are rotated in 360 degrees with one-degree increments and we measured the resulting correlation performances in terms of peak-to-sidelobe ratio (PSR) which is defined as the ratio of correlation peak to the standard deviation in a small area away from the correlation peak. Fig. 8 shows average PSR values averaged over 100 test images. Theese PSR's appear to follow the prescribed rotation tolerance $c(\theta)$.

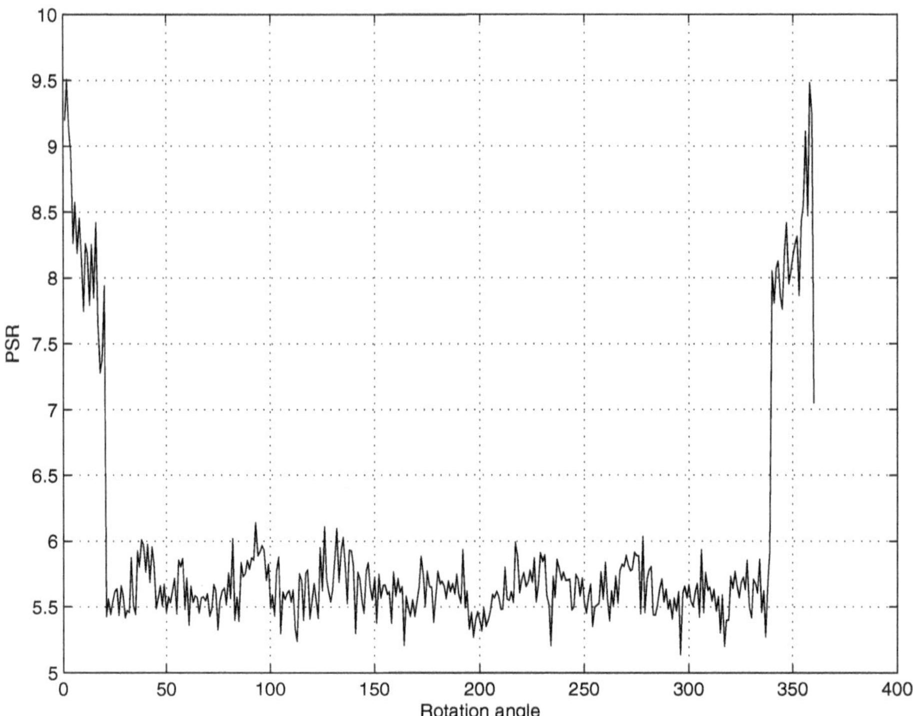

Fig. 8. Averaged PSR values of correlation outputs from 100 images

Another experiments were performed with large number of images to investigate the robustness of the designed detector. A watermark is embedded into 2000 images. We did not use the whitening filter for this experiment. The trade off parameters are used as, $\alpha = 1 \times e^5, \beta = 1 \times e^{-5}, \gamma = 0$. We have used those values to reduce the interference of the original image at detector. The OTCHF filter h is designed with $\theta_t = 10°$. Each original and watermarked images are rotated $0.25°, 1°, 2°, 5°, 10°$, respectively. We compute correlation between h and each image and PSR value is computed. Empirical detector response can be shown by drawing histogram of PSR values. Fig. 9 shows the PSR histogram of unrotated images and rotated images. PSR's from the correlation between filters and unmarked images are distributed within a narrow region of $3.5 \sim 11$. The PSR's from the correlation between filters and watermarked images are distributed in relatively wider region of $5 \sim 25$. As we are using very simple additive watermarking, we get some overlapped region even before any rotation of the watermarked image. Considering the fact that additive white watermark loose almost complete correlation by rotation, these plots show that the designed filter can provide rotation tolerance to the detector.

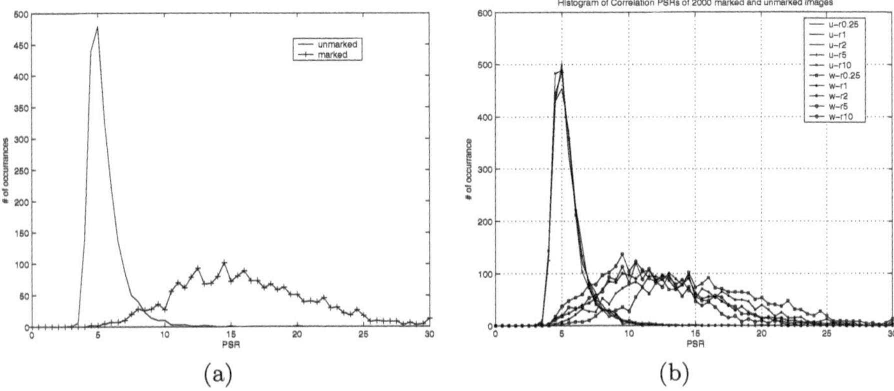

(a) (b)

Fig. 9. Empirical detector performance : (a) before rotation (b) after rotations

6 Conclusions

In this paper, we introduced a new correlation filter known as OTCHF filter for rotation tolerant watermark detection. The rotation tolerance is achieved by the filter design procedure that utilizes the property of CHF and optimal trade off of ONV, ACE and ASM parameters. We have demonstrated the robustness of OTCHF correlation detector by applying to a very simple additive watermarking method. As the OTCHF filter design process is performed off-line, the watermark detection can be done without causing extra delay. Hence, it is suitable for any real-time watermark detector. Though the characteristics of the designed filter is not white, the interference with the original image can be reduced by exploring preprocessing and OTCHF control parameters. However, further research toward better decorrelation will be carried out in near future. The parameters used for trade-off should be further reviewed for better correlation performance.

Acknowledgements. This work was supported by the Post-Doctoral Fellowship Program of Korea Science and Engineering Foundation (KOSEF) and by the center for communications and computer security (C3S) at Carnegie Mellon University.

References

1. I. J. Cox and M. L. Miller, "Eletronic watermarking:The first 50 years," *Proc. IEEE Int. Workshop on Multimedia Signal Processing* pp. 225–230, 2001.
2. F. Hartung and M. Kutter, "Multimedia watermarking technique," *Proc. IEEE*, Vol 87, pp. 1079–1107, July, 1999.
3. F. A. P. Petitcolas, R. J. Anderson, and M. G. Kuhn, "Attacks on copyright marking systems," *in Proc. 2nd Int. Workshop on Information Hiding*, pp. 218–238 , 1998.

4. S. Pereira and T. Pun, "Robust template matching for affine resistant image watermarksI," *IEEE Trans. Image Processing*, Vol 9, pp. 1123–1129, July, 2000.
5. G. Csurka, F. Deguillaume, J. J. K. O'Ruanaidh, and T. Pun, "A Bayesian approach to affine transformation resistant image and video watermarking, " *Proc. 3rd Int. Workshop on Information Hiding* pp. 315–330, 1999.
6. J. J. K. O'Ruanaidh and T. Pun, "Rotation, scale, and translation invariant spread spectrum digital image watermarking", *Signal Processing*, Vol 66, pp. 303–317, 1998.
7. C. Y. Lin, M. Wu, J. A. Bloom, I. J. Cox, M. L. Miller and Y. M. Lui, "Rotation, scale, and translation resilient watermarking for images," *IEEE Trans. Image Processing*, Vol 10. May, pp. 767–782, 2001.
8. M. Alghoniemy and A. H. Tewfik, "Image watermarking by moment invarinat," *IEEE Int. Conf. Image Processing*, pp. 73–76, 2000.
9. M. Kutter, S. K. Bhattacharjee, and T. Ebrahimi, "Towards second generation watermarking schemes," *Proc. IEEE Int. Conf. Image Processing*, pp. 320–323, 1999.
10. Hyung-Shin Kim, Yunju Baek, Heung-Kyu Lee and Young-Ho Suh, "Robust image watermark using Radon transform and bispectrum invariants," Lecture Notes in Computer Science, 2578, Springer-Verlag, pp.145–159 2003
11. J. R. Hernandez and F. Perez-Gonzalez, "Statistical analysis of watermarking schemes for copyright protection of images," *Proc. IEEE*, Vol 87, July pp. 1142–1166 1999.
12. Q. Cheng and T. S. Huang, "Robust optimum detection of transform domain multiplicative watermarks" *IEEE Trans. Signal Processing.* Vol.51, No.4, Apr., pp.906–924, 2003.
13. M. Barni, F. Bartolini, A. D. Rosa, and A. Piva, "Optimum decoding and detection of multiplicative watermarks" *IEEE Trans. Signal Processing.* Vol.51, No.4, Apr., pp.1118–1123, 2003.
14. B.V.K.Vijaya Kumar, A. Mahalanobis, and A. Takessian, "Optiaml tradeoff circular harmonic function correlation filter methods providing controlled in-plane rotation response," *IEEE Trans. Image Processing.* Vol.9, No.6, Jun., pp.1025–1034, 2000.
15. B.V.K.Vijaya Kumar, D. Carlson, and A. Mahalanobis, "Optimal tradeoff synthetic discriminant function (OTSDF) filters for arbitrary devices," *Opt. Lett.*, vol.19, pp.1556–1558, 1994
16. P. Refregier, "Filter design for optical pattern recognition: Multicriteria optimization approach," *Opt. Lett.* Vol. 15, pp. 854–856, 1990
17. M. Maes, T. Kalker, J. P. M. G. Linnartz, J. Talstra, G. F. G. Depovere, and J. Haitsma, "Digital watermarking for DVD video copy protection" *IEEE Signal Processing Magazine.* Sep., pp.47–57, 2000.
18. Corel Corporation, Corel Stock Photo Library 3.

On Perceptual Quality of Watermarked Images – An Experimental Approach

Bassem Abdel-Aziz[1] and Jean-Yves Chouinard[2]

[1] University of Ottawa, Canada
bm_attar@canada.com
[2] Université Laval, Canada
chouinar@gel.ulaval.ca

Abstract. One challenge in designing content authentication watermarks is how to achieve a good balance between robustness against incidental distortions, fragility to tampering attacks, and maintaining an acceptable visual quality. In this paper, we present a performance analysis of a wavelet-based semi-fragile watermarking algorithm in terms of its impact on the perceptual quality of watermarked images. We use three different quality metrics to measure the degradation of the test images' visual quality. Based on our experimental results, we propose limits on the algorithm parameters in order to achieve an acceptable balance between good robustness and minimal perceptual quality impact. We also present a sliding-window technique that helps in choosing appropriate wavelet decomposition levels for embedding the watermark bits.

1 Introduction

As opposed to analog media, replication of digital media usually produces perfect copies of the original digital content. Digital watermarks are used as a method for embedding a known piece of digital data within another piece of digital data. Content authentication watermarks are a category of digital watermarks that are semi-fragile in nature. A well-designed semi-fragile watermark should be able, to some extent, to distinguish between malicious attacks and incidental distortions undergone by a watermarked image.

In section 2, we present the three image quality metric used in our simulations. The telltale watermarking algorithm used, based on Kundur et al. algorithm [1] is presented in section 3. In section 4, we present our simulations set-up and experimental results, followed by a conclusion.

2 Visual Quality Metrics

As an invisible watermark should not affect the visual quality of an image, a measure by which one can judge how the quality of an image is degraded after embedding a watermark is essential. Among several metrics [2], we choose three different metrics for measuring the visual impact of Kundur-based telltale watermark:

T. Kalker et al. (Eds.): IWDW 2003, LNCS 2939, pp. 277–288, 2004.
© Springer-Verlag Berlin Heidelberg 2004

A. Peak Signal-to-Noise Ratio

The Peak Signal-to-Noise Ratio (PSNR) metric is widely used to measure the difference between two images based on pixel differences [3]. In the watermarking case, we consider the difference between the watermarked and the original images. For a $N \times M$ pixels image with pixels' luminance values ranging from zero (black) to L_{max} (white), PSNR is defined as:

$$PSNR = 10\log_{10}\left(\frac{L_{\max}}{RMSE}\right)^2, \tag{1}$$

where RMSE is the root mean square error defined as:

$$RMSE = \sqrt{\frac{\sum_{i=1}^{N}\sum_{j=1}^{M}\left[l_o(i,j) - l_w(i,j)\right]^2}{N \times M}}, \tag{2}$$

where l_o and l_w are the respective luminance values of the original and watermarked images. Raw error measures work best when the error is due to additive noise. Unfortunately, they do not necessarily correspond to all aspects of the human visual perception of the errors [4].

To provide accurate measurements, image quality metrics should take into account the characteristics of the Human Visual System (HVS). If we apply the same amount of distortion to a textured area of an image, it will be much less noticeable by a human observer than if it is applied to a smooth "clear" area. The value of PSNR will be the same in both cases. This calls for a quality measure that applies a model of the human visual system.

B. Weighted Peak Signal-to-Noise Ratio

The weighted PSNR (wPSNR) is a different quality metric that was suggested in [5]. The wPSNR metric uses an additional parameter called the Noise Visibility Function (NVF) which is a texture masking function. NVF arbitrarily uses a Gaussian model to estimate how much texture exists in any area of an image. The value of NVF ranges from close to zero, for extremely heavily textured areas, and up to one, for clear smooth areas of an image. The wPSNR equation is a modified version of the regular PSNR equation that uses the value of NVF as a penalization factor:

$$wPSNR = 10\ \log_{10}\left(\frac{L_{\max}}{RMSE \times VNF}\right)^2 \tag{3}$$

For flat, smooth areas, NVF is equal to one, which represents the maximum penalization case: the wPSNR has the same value as the PSNR. For any value of NVF less than one, the wPSNR will be slightly higher than the PSNR to reflect the fact that the human eye will have less sensitivity to modifications in textured areas than in smooth areas.

C. Watson Perceptual Metric

To get a better understanding of perceptual models, we refer to an important parameter: the Just Noticeable Difference (JND) which is defined in psychophysics as the level of distortion that can be noticed in 50% of experimental observatory trials [6]. A distortion below a JND threshold of one is considered imperceptible by an average human observer.

In his work [7], Watson defines JNDs as linear multiples of a noise pattern that produces a JND distortion measure of one. Human perception to visuals and audio is not uniform. Human ear responds differently depending on loudness and frequency of input audio. Terhardt's model of the Human Auditory System (HAS) [8] indicates that the human ear is most sensitive to frequencies between 2-4 kHz. It also shows that sensitivity substantially declines at very low and very high frequencies.

The HVS has the same type of variable sensitivity based on properties of its input. These properties could include spatial frequency, luminance contrast, and color (spectral frequency) [6, 9]. Several different factors affect the human eye sensitivity. Watson model relies on two components in order to create a response similar to that of a human eye:

- **Context masking:** It is defined as a measure of a human observer's response to one visual stimulus when a second masking stimulus is also present.
- **Pooling:** The second important issue is how a perceptual model can merge individual sensitivity models into one global model that can simulate a human perceptual system. The model must also be able to combine the sensitivity and context masking information for different frequencies.

A standard feature of current visual models is the so-called β-norm or Minkowski summation. It is a method to combine the perceptibilities of separate errors to give a single estimate for the overall visual distortion of an image. Let $d[i]$ be an estimate of the probability that a human observer will notice the difference between an original image c_o and a watermarked one c_w in an individual perceptual parameter. Minkowski summation $D(c_o, c_w)$ representing the perceptual distance between c_o and c_w is defined as:

$$D(c_o, c_w) = \left(\sum_i |d[i]|^\beta \right)^{\frac{1}{\beta}}, \tag{4}$$

where the exponent β represents the degree of pooling. When $\beta \rightarrow \infty$, the pooling rule works in such a way that only the largest error matters while all other errors are ignored. When $\beta = 1$, the pooling becomes a linear summation of absolute error values. $\beta = 2$ allows individual perceptual errors to be combined in a standard deviation type measure [7]. We refer to the per-block perceptual error estimate as the Local Perceptual Error (LPE) in our simulations.

Although Minkowski summation is widely accepted and used in several perceptual models, some researchers suggest that it is not a good enough measure and suggest modeling image degradation as structural distortions instead of errors [10].

3 Wavelet-Based Telltale Watermarking

Telltale watermarks exploit the fact that the watermark undergoes the same transformations that the host content does. By analyzing a telltale watermark, we get information on "how" the host was attacked rather than on "whether" it was attacked or not. A good use for telltale watermarks is when we can not easily draw the line between legitimate and illegitimate distortions. An example of telltale fragile watermark embedded in the DCT domain is proposed in [11]. This scheme can detect different types of tampering in the watermarked image and can also locate where the tampering has occurred.

Transforming an image into the Discrete Wavelet Domain (DWT) will give us information about the scale which can be used to perform frequency domain analysis.

It is already known that Fourier analysis can be used for that purpose. The advantage of wavelet analysis over Fourier analysis is that in the wavelet domain we don't lose spatial information about the image. More information about the DWT and the roots of wavelet analysis can be found in [12] and [13].

Wavelet decomposition of an image will generate a group of coefficient subsets. Each subset corresponds to a scale or a frequency sub-band. By inspecting how the coefficients of each sub-band are changed from their values in the un-attacked image, we get a good measure on how severely each frequency sub-band was attacked.

For instance, by inspecting the coefficients of the high-frequency sub-bands we can determine whether or not the image had undergone a low-pass filtering attack. Taking advantage of the spatial information in the DWT domain, we can also detect cases where all frequencies in a narrow spatial region have been equally distorted. This implies to a high degree of certainty that this region was edited [6]: one can consider cases where attackers maliciously change the license plate number in a digital photo of a car that was involved in a fatal crash.

Telltale watermarks can generally tell us about various other things. We can build an exhaustive list of all known practical and hypothetical attacks; then, we can design a telltale watermark that is able to distinguish between a subset of these attacks depending on the application at hand. A special case of telltale watermarks is a localization watermark that can tell us which times (for audio content) and regions (for video and images) were distorted.

We choose the telltale algorithm by Kundur et al. [1, 14] as an example of wavelet-based watermarking algorithms for our simulations. An L-level discrete wavelet transform of the original image is taken using Haar bases (a special case of the Daubechies family of wavelets, identified as “db-1”) [13]. Watermark bits are inserted to selected coefficients by quantizing them to even or odd multiples of a step size. A key is used to make sure that the odd/even mapping is random. Watermark extraction uses the same quantization technique.

4 Performance Evaluation of the Telltale Watermarking Scheme

In this paper, we evaluate the performance of telltale watermarking through several simulations that involve embedding watermarks into ten test images, Fig. 1, using different embedding parameters. We follow that by measuring the effect of the watermark signal on the host image's visual quality. We use three different quality metrics, PSNR, wPSNR, and the Watson metric. In that simulation, we also attempt to evaluate the limitations and advantages of each of these metrics. We also suggest a modified version of the embeddor that takes advantage of our perceptual metrics simulations to improve the watermark robustness to incidental distortions while keeping visual artifacts within acceptable levels.

Fig. 1. Set of test images

A. Test Setup

Our simulations use the "C++" language to analyze the test images as well as Matlab™ language to embed, extract, and analyze telltale watermarks. We also use the Checkmark benchmark tool [16].

We use ten grayscale 512×512 pixel images with 256 grayscale levels per pixel. We choose to only use grayscale images without loss of generality as the algorithm can be used with color images. The algorithm modifies the pixel intensities, which is directly applicable to grayscale images without prior preparation. In the case of color images, we would have to convert the image from the RGB color model, where the luminance has no separate channel, into a suitable model such as YIQ, where Y represents luminance of the image pixels [3]. We can then apply the algorithm to the Y component.

As Fig. 1 shows, we select the images such that they have different features. For instance, while the "Bear" image has heavy textures and a dark area near the lower center, we can see that the "Watch" image has sharp edges and many smooth areas.

B. Simulation Set 1 – Effect of the Number of DWT Levels

In this test set, we embed a watermark in each of the ten test images. We repeat the process using the same starting wavelet decomposition level (level one) while incrementing the ending decomposition level (from one to eight). Using more decomposition levels to embed the watermark bits means that the total watermark energy will be higher. It also means that we can get more information about attacks. We use a watermark energy scaling factor $\Delta=1$ for all tests in this simulation set.

Table 1 shows the effect of embedding watermark bits into more decomposition levels on the PSNR of the original image compared to the watermarked one. The quality of the image degrades as we use more embedding levels. We also note that the rate of quality degradation is decreasing. This is mainly due to the fact that higher decomposition levels (corresponding to lower frequency ranges) have less coefficients which means that less watermark bits can be embedded into them.

One should note that we only use the details levels (horizontal, vertical, and diagonal) to embed the watermark bits. Approximation coefficients are not used as the image quality is very sensitive to the slightest change in them. They correspond to the DC components of the DCT of an image.

Table 1. PSNR (dB) values for watermarked images using different decomposition levels

	L1-L1	L1-L2	L1-L3	L1-L4	L1-L5	L1-L6	L1-L7	L1-L8
Baboon	51.10	48.17	46.39	45.16	44.26	43.47	42.77	42.08
Bear	51.23	48.28	46.51	45.30	44.26	43.53	42.95	42.46
Entrance	51.13	48.17	46.47	45.18	44.24	43.47	42.72	42.19
F16	51.06	48.14	46.39	45.18	44.23	43.36	42.60	42.19
Boat	51.05	48.17	46.45	45.21	44.15	43.44	43.01	42.13
Opera	51.09	48.16	46.39	45.12	44.03	43.43	42.68	41.70
Pills	51.10	48.15	46.40	45.15	44.12	43.44	42.53	42.36
Rose	51.07	48.15	46.37	45.17	44.15	43.27	43.06	42.46
Watch	51.13	48.15	46.41	45.14	44.16	43.60	42.67	41.88
Water	51.06	48.16	46.38	45.18	44.22	43.52	42.88	42.44

Table 2 depicts the effect of embedding watermark bits into more decomposition levels on the wPSNR of the original image compared to the watermarked one.

We note that wPSNR for the "Bear" image is slightly lower than that for the other images, even though that image has texture in many areas. The reason for that is the large smooth dark area representing the bear's chest. Because this area is black and smooth, any changes to that area will be highly penalized by the NVF, thus causing the quality metric to drop. For the "Water" image, we note that the wPSNR value is significantly higher than the PSNR one. This reflects the heavy details and textures of that image and its capacity to absorb more modifications without showing visual artifacts. We also note that even when all decomposition levels are used, the overall quality of the images doesn't heavily degrade. This indicates that we can use any set of levels to embed the watermark bits.

We finally use the Watson metric to generate a perceptually lossless quantization matrix of the DCT transform of each of our test images. The entries of this matrix represent the amount of quantization that each coefficient can withstand without affecting the visual quality of the image. This matrix, referred to as the "visibility threshold matrix", uses three different visual aspects in order to model the human visual system: the contrast sensitivity, the contrast masking, and the luminance masking. We choose to build that matrix for blocks of 16×16 pixels each as a human face scaled below a 16×16 block is of such a low resolution that recognition becomes impossible [15]. We then compare blocks of the watermarked image with the corresponding blocks of the original image using the visibility threshold matrix as a reference in order to judge which blocks have been modified to the extent that the modifications can be visible to humans. We also calculate the average of all block errors and use it as an estimate of the Total Perceptual Error (TPE) of the watermarked image. As the simulation results will show, the TPE is not accurate and it is much better to use the per-block error matrix, LPE, values instead. We refer to the following parameters of the Watson metric as they are essential for interpreting the results:

Table 2. wPSNR (dB) values for watermarked images using different decomposition levels

	L1-L1	L1-L2	L1-L3	L1-L4	L1-L5	L1-L6	L1-L7	L1-L8
Baboon	55.94	53.01	51.24	50.06	49.05	48.35	47.58	46.98
Bear	52.75	49.79	48.01	46.79	45.75	45.00	44.42	43.91
Entrance	53.51	50.52	48.83	47.55	46.59	45.79	45.03	44.48
F16	52.26	49.35	47.59	46.36	45.41	44.56	43.76	43.46
Boat	53.22	50.36	48.64	47.40	46.32	45.61	45.12	44.29
Opera	53.40	50.46	48.69	47.45	46.34	45.76	45.00	43.89
Pills	52.33	49.41	47.65	46.39	45.35	44.65	43.72	43.53
Rose	51.80	48.88	47.09	45.89	44.85	43.99	43.79	43.15
Watch	52.56	49.56	47.81	46.53	45.55	45.01	44.20	43.29
Water	53.24	50.34	48.57	47.37	46.41	45.73	45.10	44.63

- Local Perceptual Error (LPE):

LPE is a two-dimensional array of values in units of Just Noticeable Differences (JNDs). Since in our simulation we use block sizes of 16×16, the size of the LPE array will be 32×32 entries. We can scale the values of that array to make it suitable for viewing as a bitmap by using a suitable scaling integer value *S*. The resulting bitmap will have 32×32 blocks where darker blocks represent low visual error and lighter blocks represent high visual errors. From that bitmap representation, which we can call the Block Visual Error (BVE) bitmap, we can determine which blocks took more visual damage due to the watermark embedding.

- Total Perceptual Error (TPE):

The value of TPE gives a rough estimate of the overall visual distortion of the image due to the embedding of the watermark. It is calculated as the mean value of the entries of the LPE array. It should be noted that the value of TPE can be misleading as heavy distortion of few blocks can render the image visually unusable, while the TPE will still report a total error value that is not perceptible. This is because blocks of the image that didn't suffer any distortion will dilute the total error through averaging. In other cases, images with smooth areas could report an overall high TPE while in fact only smooth areas have visible artifacts. To give a practical example that supports our argument, we show the "Bear" image watermarked with a relatively high quantization

step value ($\Delta = 5$). The TPE for the watermarked image is 2.852 JNDs, which give a strong indication about the visual damage in the image.
As shown in Fig. 2, the watermarked image has only heavy visual artifacts in the dark smooth areas of the image, while the textured areas of the image, despite having been modified, are showing much less distortions. Using the BVE bitmap, calculated from the LPE matrix, we get a more sensible and accurate estimate about the amount of visual error in every 16×16 pixels block of the image.
The total perceptual error values for simulation 1 are shown in Table 3. All values are shown to be less than one JND, indicating that the watermarked images have no global distortions and are generally usable.

Fig. 2. Watermarked "Bear" image and its Block Visual Error bitmap representation

Table 3. TPE in units of JNDs of simulation set 1

	L1-L1	L1-L2	L1-L3	L1-L4	L1-L5	L1-L6	L1-L7	L1-L8
Baboon	0.11	0.19	0.22	0.23	0.24	0.25	0.26	0.26
Bear	0.30	0.50	0.57	0.60	0.60	0.64	0.62	0.64
Entrance	0.12	0.21	0.23	0.25	0.26	0.27	0.28	0.28
F16	0.10	0.17	0.20	0.21	0.22	0.23	0.23	0.24
Boat	0.12	0.20	0.23	0.24	0.25	0.26	0.27	0.27
Opera	0.12	0.21	0.24	0.26	0.27	0.28	0.29	0.29
Pills	0.11	0.19	0.21	0.23	0.24	0.25	0.26	0.26
Rose	0.11	0.20	0.22	0.24	0.25	0.26	0.26	0.26
Watch	0.13	0.22	0.25	0.27	0.28	0.28	0.29	0.30
Water	0.13	0.22	0.25	0.27	0.28	0.29	0.29	0.30

Fig. 3 depicts the BVE bitmap for watermarked "Entrance" image using all decomposition levels. It is obvious from the BVE bitmap that highly textured and high-contrast areas show less visual errors than darker smoother areas. We also observe that visual errors in the brighter area near the center of the image are the lowest compared to other image areas. This observation matches Watson's use of luminance masking, where his perceptual model accounts for the fact that brighter regions of an image can be changed by a larger amount before being noticed [7].

We also observe that textured areas of the image tend to have less perceptual errors. This confirms Mannos' observations [9] about the human eye's Contrast Sensitivity Function (CSF), which implies that human eyes are most sensitive to luminance differences at mid-range frequencies. The eye's sensitivity decreases significantly at lower and higher frequencies.

From results of simulation set 1, we observe that: (1) wPSNR gives a better estimate of distortion than PSNR, (2) the best visual metric among the three metrics we used seems to be the Watson metric. The reason is its ability to give localized visual error estimates. The BVE bitmap representation of Watson's LPE gives the most realistic and detailed estimates on visual distortion of the host image due to watermark embedding, and (3) using all decomposition levels doesn't badly affect the visual quality compared to using just one or two levels. This means that we can embed the watermark bits at any decomposition level as long as this improves the algorithm's performance.

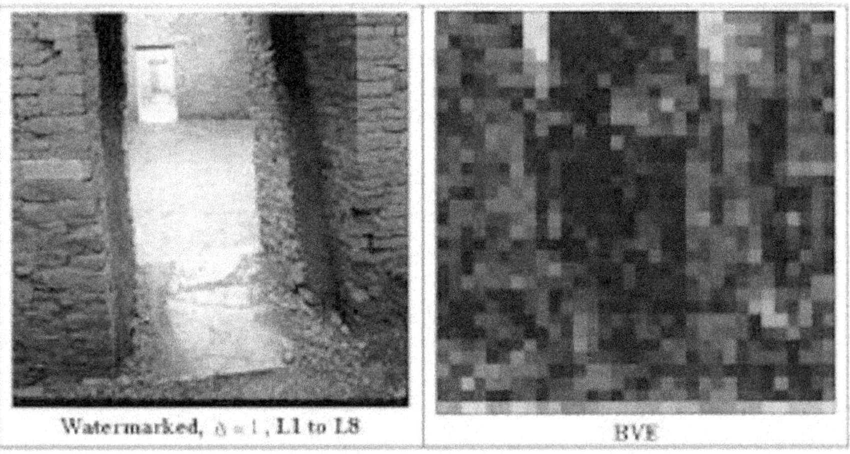

Fig. 3. Watermarked "Entrance" image and its Block Visual Error bitmap representation

C. Simulation Set 2 – Effect of the Quantization Step Size

In this simulation set, we watermark the test images using different values of the quantization step Δ and decomposition levels one to five. We study the visual effect of embedding telltale watermarks by comparing PSNR, wPSNR, and the Watson metric results.

Table 4 shows the effect of embedding watermark bits using different values of the quantization step Δ on the PSNR (dB) of the original image compared to the watermarked one.

The slight difference in PSNR values in that table and those in the fifth column (L1-L5) of Table 1 is due to the fact that every time we embed the watermark, a new random key is used to select the exact locations of the coefficients to quantize in order to embed the watermark bits.

Table 4. PSNR (dB) values for watermarked images using different quantization step sizes

	Δ=1	2	5	10	20
Baboon	44.14	38.16	30.14	24.30	18.16
Bear	44.25	38.23	30.46	24.43	18.64
Entrance	44.13	38.18	30.22	24.35	18.53
F16	44.17	38.17	30.16	24.17	18.37
Boat	44.11	38.14	30.17	24.27	18.34
Opera	44.28	38.11	30.20	24.14	18.23
Pills	44.04	38.16	30.20	24.21	18.21
Rose	44.18	38.16	30.20	24.17	18.22
Watch	44.24	38.02	30.24	24.37	18.48
Water	44.30	38.12	30.08	24.08	18.11

Table 5 depicts the results of the same simulation applied in order to measure effect of watermark embedding on wPSNR (dB). TPE results for this simulation indicate that except for "Bear" image, all test images can be watermarked using Δ value of one or two without damaging the visual quality of the images.

Table 5. wPSNR (dB)

	Δ=1	2	5	10	20
Baboon	48.94	43.05	34.98	29.19	23.01
Bear	45.74	39.73	31.97	25.98	20.19
Entrance	46.49	40.50	32.59	26.75	21.00
F16	45.36	39.33	31.32	25.33	19.66
Boat	46.29	40.32	32.35	26.49	20.57
Opera	46.57	40.43	32.48	26.46	20.54
Pills	45.26	39.38	31.43	25.45	19.45
Rose	44.90	38.88	30.92	24.89	18.95
Watch	45.67	39.42	31.63	25.78	19.94
Water	46.49	40.32	32.27	26.24	20.33

The TPE error values for the "Bear" image are generally higher than other test images due to the fact that the watermarking algorithm embeds watermark bits into the totally dark (almost black) areas of that image. This leads to highly visual distortions in these areas. Since the TPE is the mean value taken over all of the image blocks, the highly distorted dark areas account for the higher TPE for "Bear" image.

D. Simulation Set 3 – Effect of DWT Decomposition Levels Window

We embed the watermark using $\Delta = 1$. We set the number of decomposition levels we use to embed the watermark bits. In that specific simulation, we used a fixed window size, $L_{end} - L_{start} + 1$, of *4*. Therefore, the first iteration of our simulation set will embed a watermark with $\Delta = 1$ into levels from one and up to level four into all test images. The second iteration will embed a watermark with $\Delta = 1$ into decomposition levels from level two and up to level five into all test images. This goes on until we approach the last iteration, where we embed a watermark with $\Delta = 1$ into levels from five and up to level eight into all test images. In other words, we use a "sliding window" of a fixed size that moves across the image's spatial frequency spectrum starting from higher frequencies and stopping at lowest ones to investigate the relative significance of embedding the watermark bits within a specific frequency range of the image. It is known [9] that modifications in lower frequency channels of an image generally introduce more visible artifacts. On the other hand, lower frequency components of an image represent most of the image's energy. If distortions are able to render a low-frequency-embedded watermark undetectable, this usually means that the visual quality of the image was also severely damaged.

Table 6. TPE in units of JNDs for different DWT decomposition levels windows

	L1-L4	L2-L5	L3-L6	L4-L7	L5-L8
Baboon	0.23	0.18	0.08	0.04	0.04
Bear	0.59	0.45	0.23	0.14	0.19
Entrance	0.25	0.19	0.08	0.05	0.05
F16	0.21	0.16	0.06	0.04	0.04
Boat	0.25	0.18	0.07	0.04	0.04
Opera	0.26	0.19	0.08	0.05	0.04
Pills	0.23	0.17	0.07	0.04	0.05
Rose	0.24	0.18	0.07	0.04	0.04
Watch	0.27	0.20	0.08	0.05	0.05
Water	0.27	0.20	0.09	0.05	0.05

Embedding a watermark into the higher frequency spectrum is equivalent to adding Gaussian noise to the image, assuming the watermark data has the same statistical properties as Gaussian noise. Since Gaussian noise can usually be alleviated using a smoothing filter, this means that our watermark will also be weak against filtering.
Table 6 depicts the resulting TPE, in units of JNDs, of simulation set 3. All errors are fairly below the one JND threshold. Table 6 also indicates the fact that the overall perceptual error for watermarked images drops as we embed more watermark bits towards the lower frequency range. This confirms our assumption that using lower frequency ranges (embedding watermark bits into higher decomposition levels) is more likely to introduce visual artifacts, but at the same time it also means we are adding less watermark energy. The overall effect of these two contradicting factors manifests itself as an overall drop of the perceptual error as we slide the window towards the higher level, lower frequency, and lesser coefficients decomposition levels.

Conclusion

The perceptual performance of a wavelet-based semi-fragile watermark was evaluated. The use of perceptual quality metrics helps in tuning the algorithm parameters by setting acceptable perceptual limits. This implies that adaptive watermarks should perform better in general. There are however some drawbacks of using the wavelet domain for watermarking. These watermarks are not tolerant to timing errors. Synchronization is critical during watermark extraction. The perceptual impact of watermark embedding was studied, and suitable ranges for algorithm parameters were suggested. Our simulation results also indicated that to properly calibrate the watermark parameters, appropriate perceptual metrics are essential. The telltale watermark was shown to be usable in real-work applications given that the right algorithm parameters are used.

References

1. D. Kundur and D. Hatzinakos. Digital Watermarking for Telltale Tamper Proofing and Authentication. Proceedings of the IEEE, 87(7), pp. 1167–1180, 1999
2. M. Kutter and F. A. P. Petitcolas, "A fair benchmark for image watermarking systems," in Proc. SPIE Security & Watermarking Multimedia Contents, Vol. 3657, pp. 226–239, San Jose, CA, USA, Jan. 1999
3. R. C. Gonzalez and R. E. Woods. Digital Image Processing, 2e. Prentice Hall, 2002
4. I. Avcıbaş, B. Sankur, K. Sayood. Statistical Evaluation of Image Quality Measures. Journal of Electronic Imaging, Vol. 11, pp. 206–223, April, 2002
5. S. Voloshynovskiy, A.Herrigel, N.Baumgärtner, and T.Pun. A stochastic approach to content adaptive digital image watermarking. International Workshop on Information Hiding, Dresden, Germany, 29 September-1 October 1999, Lecture Notes in Computer Science, Ed. Andreas Pfitzmann.
6. I. J. Cox, M. L. Miller, J. A. Bloom. Digital Watermarking. Morgan Kaufmann, 2002
7. A. B. Watson. DCT quantization matrices visually optimized for individual images. Human Vision, Visual Processing, and Digital Display IV, Proc. SPIE 1913–14, (1993)
8. E. Terhardt. Calculating Virtual Pitch. Hearing Research. 1:155–182. 1979
9. J. L. Mannos and J. J. Sakrison. The Effects of a Visual Fidelity Criterion on the Encoding of Images. IEEE Transactions on Information Theory. IT-4:525–536. 1974
10. Z. Wang, A. C. Bovik and L. Lu. Why is Image Quality Assessment So Difficult? IEEE International Conference on Acoustics, Speech, & Signal Processing. May 2002
11. M. Wu and B. Liu. Watermarking for image authentication. IEEE International Conference on Image Processing, October 1998
12. G. Strang and T. Nguyen. Wavelets and Filter Banks, Revised Edition. Wellesley-Cambridge Press, 1997
13. Y. T. Chang. Wavelet Basics. Kluwer Academic Publishers, 1995
14. D. Kundur and D. Hatzinakos. Towards a telltale watermarking technique for tamper proofing. Proc. IEEE Int. Conf. On Image Processing, vol. 2, pp. 409–413, 1998
15. J. Fridrich. Methods for Detecting Changes in Digital Images. IEEE Workshop on Intelligent Signal Processing and Communication Systems. Melbourne, Australia. November 1998
16. Shelby Pereira, Sviatoslav Voloshynovskiy, Maribel Madueño, Stéphane Marchand-Maillet and Thierry Pun, Second generation benchmarking and application oriented evaluation, In Information Hiding Workshop, Pittsburgh, PA, USA, April 2001

Audio Watermarking Based on Music Content Analysis: Robust against Time Scale Modification

Wei Li and Xiangyang Xue

Department of Computer Science and Engineering
University of Fudan, 220 Handan Road
Shanghai 200433, P. R. China
weili_fd@yahoo.com, xyxue@fudan.edu.cn

Abstract. Synchronization attacks like random cropping and time scale modification are crucial to audio watermarking technique. To combat these attacks, a novel content-dependent temporally localized robust audio watermarking method is proposed in this paper. The basic idea is to embed and detect watermark in selected high energy local regions that represent music transition like drum sounds or note onsets. Such regions correspond to music edge and will not be changed much for the purpose of maintaining high auditory quality. In this way, the embedded watermark is expected to escape the damages caused by audio signal processing, random cropping and time scale modification etc, as shown by the experimental results.

Keywords: music content analysis, localized watermarking, synchronization attacks

1 Introduction

Synchronization is a serious problem to any watermarking scheme, especially to audio watermarking scenario. Audio processing such as random cropping and time scale modification cause displacement between embedding and detection in the time domain and is hence difficult for watermark to survive.

Generally speaking, synchronization problem can be alleviated by the following methods: exhaustive search [1], synchronization pattern [2], invariant watermark [3], and implicit synchronization [4].

Time scale modification is a serious attack to audio watermarking, very few algorithms can effectively resist this kind of synchronization attack. According to the SDMI (Secured Digital Music Initiative) Phase-II robustness test requirement [5], a practical audio watermarking scheme should be able to withstand time scale modification up to ±4%. In the literature, several existing algorithms aimed at solving this problem. Mansour et al. [6] proposed to embed watermark data by changing the relative length of the middle segment between two successive maximum and minimum of the smoothed waveform, the performance highly depends on the selection of the threshold, and it is a delicate work to find an appropriate threshold. In [7], Mansour et al. proposed another algorithm for embedding data into audio signals by changing the interval lengths between salient points in the signal, the extrema of the wavelet coefficients of the envelope are adopted as salient points. The proposed

T. Kalker et al. (Eds.): IWDW 2003, LNCS 2939, pp. 289–300, 2004.
© Springer-Verlag Berlin Heidelberg 2004

algorithm is robust to MP3 compression, low pass filtering, and can be made robust to time scaling modification by using adaptive quantization steps. The errors are primarily due to thresholding problems. For modification scales lower than 0.92 or higher than 1.08, the bandwidth of the envelope filter as well as the coarsest decomposition scale should be changed accordingly. Tachibana et al. [1] introduced an audio watermarking method that is robust against random stretching up to ±4%. The embedding algorithm calculates and manipulates the magnitudes of segmented areas in the time-frequency plane of the content using short-term DFTs. The detection algorithm correlates the magnitudes with a pseudo-random array that corresponds to two-dimensional areas in the time-frequency plane. Tachibana et al. [8] further improved the performance up to ±8% by using multiple pseudo-random arrays, each of which is stretched assuming a certain amount of distortion. Since most of the detection process for the multiple arrays is shared, the additional computational cost is limited.

The above mentioned methods share one common problem, that is, they all highly depend on adjusting some parameters like thresholds or some assumed factors, this is really a delicate and hard work. In this paper, we present a novel music content dependent temporally localized robust audio watermarking method, focusing on combating audio signal processing and the synchronization problems caused by random cropping and time scale modification. The key point lies in determining the embedding and detection regions by applying content analysis of the music. These regions, selected as music transitions such as percussion instruments like drum and note onset, are closely related to the sensation of rhythm, and they have to be left unchanged or altered very little under time scale modification, in order to keep high auditory quality. Moreover, watermark embedded in such local areas shows natural resistance to random cropping, because cropping happened at these regions will degrade the audio quality significantly. Therefore, by embedding the watermark in these relatively safe regions, we can expect the watermark to elude all kinds of attacks, especially those challenging time domain synchronization attacks.

2 Motivation and Embedding Regions Selection

Since the main purpose of this paper is to combat time scale modification, it is necessary to know something about the existing time scale modification algorithms, and see why watermark embedded in selected regions representing music transition can be hoped to elude this challenging attack.

2.1 TSM Attack and Countermeasure

Recently developed TSM algorithms are usually performed on the harmonic components and residual components separately [10]. The harmonic portion is time-scaled by demodulating each harmonic component to DC, interpolating and decimating the DC signal, and remodulating each component back to its original frequency. The residual portion, which can be further separated into transient (edges) and noise components in the wavelet domain, is time-scaled by preserving edges and relative distances between the edges while time-scaling the stationary noise components between the edges. The edges are related to attacks of musical notes, transitions, or non-harmonic instruments such as castanets, drums and other percussive instruments. Such information may be related to temporal aspects of a music signal such as tempo and timbre. Special care must be taken when manipulating the time-scale of the residual component. First, it is important to preserve the shape or slope of the attacks (edges). If the slope is not preserved, the instruments tend to sound dull because the high frequency information is lost. Second, it is important to preserve the relative distances between the edges while maintaining synchronization with the harmonic component, because this contains the information relative to tempo [9].

Based on the above knowledge, we know that TSM algorithms stretch audio signals only in regions where there is minimum transient information and strive to preserve music edges. If we embed watermark in regions representing music transitions such as percussion instruments like drum and note onset, which are highly correlated with the feeling or mood of a musical work, it is possible to elude time scale modification without delicately adjusting parameters like thresholds or predefined scale factors.

2.2 Selection of Embedding Regions

The selection of embedding regions is crucial to digital watermarking. If the embedding regions can not be identified correctly, the watermark detection procedure is bound to be failed, because it will detect the watermark in areas where there do not exist watermark at all. The best regions should be able to stand common audio processing and time domain synchronization attacks, keeping unchanged as much as possible. Also, the detection algorithm should tolerate small amount of changes of the embedding regions in the time domain.

In modern music, musical instruments like electric guitar, electronic organ, bass and drum etc are usually played together, the time domain waveform is a mixer of all kinds of instrument sounds and the singer's vocal voice. Often, the sound of one instrument is masked by another, it is not so easy to distinguish the sound of a particular instrument in the time domain. From the general knowledge of music, we know that different musical instruments take up different frequency band and play different roles in understanding the whole music. The frequency band name, rough frequency partition, and possible musical instruments included are listed in Table 1.

Table 1. Frequency band name, partition, and corresponding musical instruments

Frequency band name	Frequency partition	Musical instruments possibly included
Bass area	$\leq$ 200 Hz	kick drum and bass guitar
Mid range	200 Hz – 2 kHz	guitar, vocal voice
	2 kHz – 6 kHz	snare drum, tambourine, side drum, piano, organ, trumpet, vocal voice, guitar
	6 kHz – 10 kHz	stringed instruments
High range	$\geq$ 10 kHz	cymbals and hi-hats

In order to verify the content of Table 1, we use five-level Discrete Wavelet Transform (DWT) to calculate an octave decomposition in frequency of a piece of piano music with the 'db4' wavelet basis, then the power spectrum is calculated at each subband, as shown in Figure 1. It can be seen that the main energy at the d3 subband distributes from 3 kHz to 5 kHz approximately, which is just in the main frequency range of drum according to Table 1. Our listening test also demonstrates that the d3 subband is mainly composed of sound of drum, while sound of other instruments like electric guitar, bass, or electronic organ are significantly depressed.

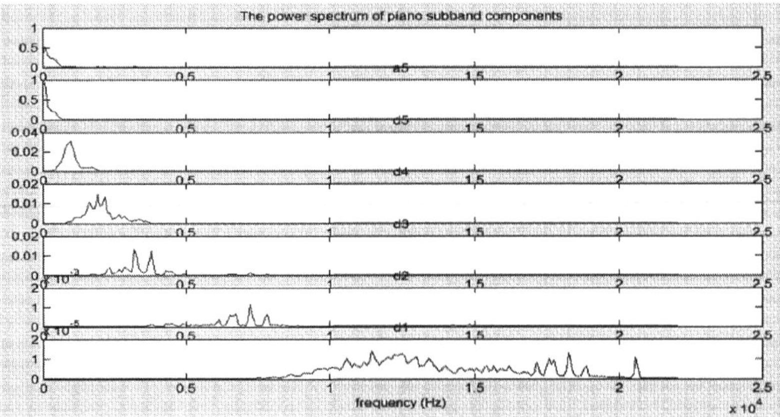

Fig. 1. The power spectrum of piano at each subband after five-level wavelet decomposition

Through extensive listening tests on different kinds of modern music like pop, rock, light music etc, we come to the conclusion that in most cases, after five-level wavelet decomposition of the original music, drum sounds mainly concentrate on the d3 subband, taking the form of apparent local maximal peak as shown in Figure 2 in black color, while other instrument and vocal voices are usually negligible.

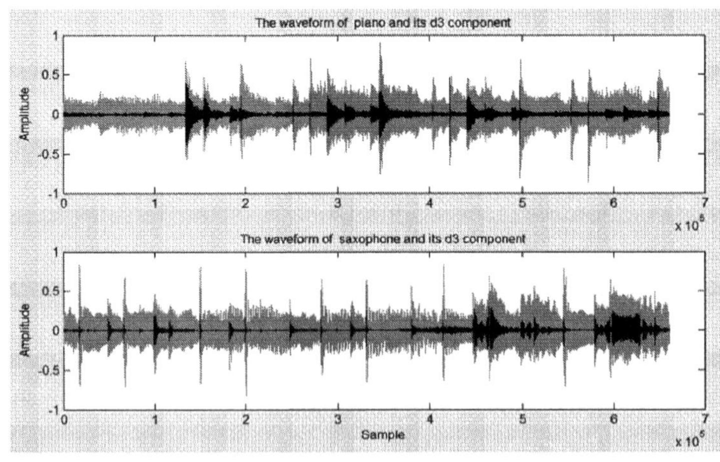

Fig. 2. The original waveform (green) and the waveform at the d3 subband (black) of piano and saxophone.

The above observations initiate the idea of selecting the small regions in the original waveform (green in Figure 2) with the same coordinate scope as those local maximal peaks at the d3 subband as the regions of watermark embedding. These regions represent the sounds of drum in most cases, and occasionally correspond to note onset or attack. Whether such regions are suitable to embed and detect watermark depends on their ability to stand audio signal processing and time domain synchronization attacks. Figure 3 shows an example of the d3 subband of piano and saxophone after +10% time scale modification, compared with Figure 2, it can be seen that although the absolute position of these peaks shifts a little due to time expanding, the local region around each peak does not change much. This means that the watermark detection can be performed at almost the same regions as that of embedding, even after serious synchronization attacks.

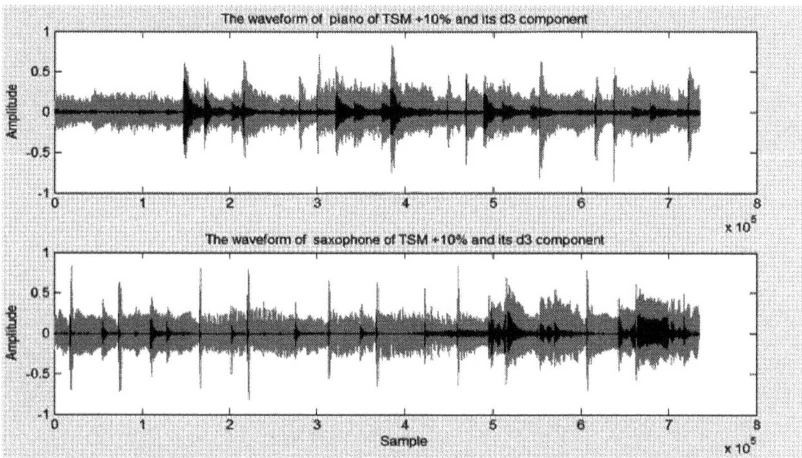

Fig. 3. The original waveform (green) and the waveform at d3 subband (black) of piano and saxophone after +10% time scale modification.

To sum up, the concrete steps of selecting watermark embedding regions are described as follows:

(a). Five-level wavelet decomposition is performed on the input audio.

(b). The d3 subband is smoothed by denoising, making the peaks more apparent.

(c). A peak-picking algorithm as shown in Figure 4 is adopted to select all local maximal peaks $\{ROICenter_i\}$ at the d3 subband.

(d). Corresponding watermark embedding regions $\{R_i\}$ at the original waveform are calculated according to (1):

$$R=\{R_i \mid R_i = ROICenter_i - ROILength/4 : ROICenter_i + ROILength*3/4-1\} \quad (1)$$

where *ROILength* is the length of each small embedding region, it is 4096 samples in our experiment.

The time signature of pop music is typically 4/4, and the average Inter-Beat Interval (IBI) is about 500 ms, which is 22050 samples under the sampling rate of 44100 Hz. After detecting the first peak, the pointer should jump forward by an interval between 1/3 to 1/2 IBI, i.e., moves to the next local drum region, under the assumption that beats generally have more energy than offbeats and that the tempo is roughly constant. It is our observation that the duration of a drum sound is about 0.1s-0.05s, which approximately corresponds to 4400-2200 samples, under the sampling rate of 44.1 kHz. So, it is appropriate to select the length of each embedding region as 4096 samples long.

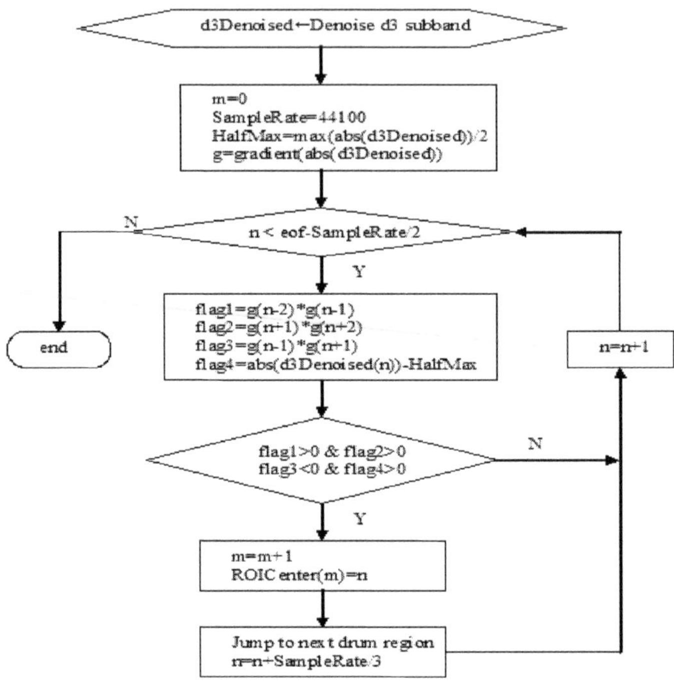

Fig. 4. Flow chart of the d3 subband peak-picking algorithm, used for embedding regions selection.

3 Embedding Strategy

(a). First, five-level wavelet decomposition of the original music is performed, then a peak-picking method at the d3 subband as mentioned above is conducted. Let *iPeakNum* be the number of all detected peaks, then the number of embedding regions *ROINum* is calculated as follows, to ensure its being odd when applying the majority rule in detection.

$$\text{ROINum} = \text{iPeakNum} + (\text{iPeakNum} \,\%\, 2 - 1) \qquad (2)$$

(b). The corresponding regions at the original audio waveform are calculated according to (1)

(c). After determining all the watermark embedding regions, Fast Fourier Transformation is performed to each region, AC FFT coefficients from 1kHz to 6kHz are selected as the dataset for watermark embedding.

(d). The watermark adopted in our experiment is a 64-bit pseudorandom number sequence *W*, denoted by (3), it is mapped into an antipodal sequence *W'* before embedding using BPSK modulation (1 → -1, 0 → +1) according to (4), for the convenience of applying majority rule in detection. Experimental results show that a 64-bit watermark can maintain high audio perception quality, while a 128-bit or bigger watermark will introduce annoying distortion, that is, exceeding the watermark capacity of some 4096-sample embedding regions.

$$W = \{w(i) \mid w(i) \in \{1,0\},\ 1 \le i \le 64\} \tag{3}$$

$$W' = \{w'(i) \mid w'(i) = 1 - 2 * w(i),\ w'(i) \in \{+1,-1\},\ 1 \le i \le 64\} \tag{4}$$

(e). Each watermark bit, *w'(k)*, is repeatedly embedded into all the selected ROI regions by exchanging the corresponding AC FFT coefficient pair according to (5)

$$\begin{aligned} & for\ \ l=1:ROINum \\ & \quad for\ \ k=1:64 \\ & \quad\ flag = ROIFFTR(off+2*k-1) < ROIFFTR(off+2*k) \\ & \quad\ \begin{cases} if\ \ w'(k)=1\ \ and\ \ flag=1 \\ \quad exchange\ \ the\ \ absolute\ \ value \\ if\ \ w'(k)=-1\ \ and\ \ flag=0 \\ \quad exchange\ \ the\ \ absolute\ \ value \end{cases} \\ & \quad end \\ & end \end{aligned} \tag{5}$$

where *ROIFFTR(off+2*k-1)* and *ROIFFTR(off+2*k)* are the AC FFT coefficients at the low-middle frequency band ranging from 1kHz to 6kHz, *off* is a user defined offset. Because most of these coefficients are in the same order of magnitude, exchanging them while preserving the biggest low frequency (<1kHz) coefficients will not introduce annoying auditory quality distortion.

(f). Inverse Fast Fourier Transformation (IFFT) is applied to the modified AC FFT coefficients in each ROI region to transform them back to the waveform in the time domain.

4 Detection Strategy

The detection algorithm is straightforward and blind, without resorting to the original audio signal or the original watermark.

(a). First, the same method with embedding is used to determine all watermark detection regions. Let *iPeakNum1* be the number of calculated local high energy peaks, then the number of detection regions *ROINum1* can be calculated as (6), to ensure its being odd when applying the majority rule in detection. Note that the number of detection regions (*ROINum1*) may be different from that of embedding regions (*ROINum*), since it is usually changed more or less after undergoing all kinds of distortions such as audio signal processing or time domain synchronization attacks.

$$\mathrm{ROINum1} = \mathrm{iPeakNum1} + (\mathrm{iPeakNum1} \,\%\, 2 - 1) \tag{6}$$

(b). Next, Fast Fourier Transform is performed to each detection region, obtaining a series of AC FFT coefficients for watermark detection.

(c). The embedded watermark bits in each region are extracted based on the following rule (7), then the BPSK modulated antipodal watermark bits are determined based on the majority rule according to (8), since it is equal to global redundancy to embed the same watermark into all embedding regions.

$$
\begin{aligned}
&for \quad m = 1 : ROINum1 \\
&\quad for \quad n = 1 : 64 \\
&\qquad flag = FFTR(2*n-1+off) > FFTR(2*n+off) \\
&\qquad \begin{cases} if & flag = 1 \quad then \quad w'(m,n) = 1 \\ if & flag = 0 \quad then \quad w'(m,n) = -1 \end{cases} \\
&\quad end \\
&end
\end{aligned} \tag{7}
$$

$$
w'(n) = sign\left(\sum_{m=1}^{m=ROINum1} w'(m,n) \right) \quad 1 \le n \le 64 \;, \; 1 \le m \le ROINum1 \tag{8}
$$

where m is the *m-th* embedding region, n means the *n-th* watermark bit embedded in the *m-th* region, and *ROINum1* is the number of all detection regions.

(d). Finally, BPSK demodulation is used to obtain the original watermark bits:

$$
w(i) = (1 - w'(i)) \;/ 2 \qquad 1 \le i \le 64 \tag{9}
$$

5 Experimental Results

The algorithm was applied to a set of audio signals including pop, saxophone, rock, piano, and electronic organ (15s, mono, 16 bits/sample, 44.1 kHz). The waveform of the original and the watermarked rock music is shown in Figure 5, with the signal noise rate (SNR) of 32.4 dB, which is rather high to show that little apparent distortions have been introduced.

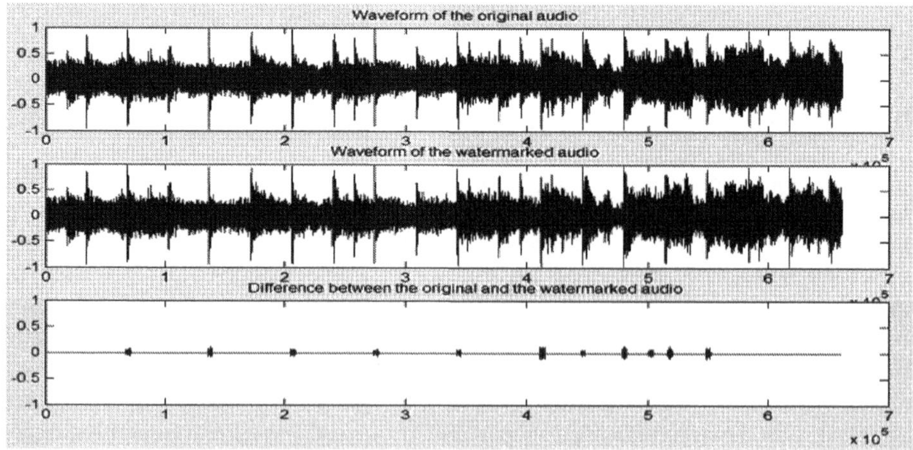

Fig. 5. (a) The original rock waveform, (b) The watermarked rock waveform, (c) The difference between (a) and (b).

5.1 Robustness Test

To evaluate the performance of the proposed watermarking algorithm, we tested its robustness according to the SDMI (Secured Digital Music Initiative) Phase-II robustness test procedure [5]. The audio editing and attacking tools adopted in experiment are Cool Edit Pro v2.0, GlodWave v4.26 and Stirmark for Audio v0.2. The experimental conditions and robustness test results under common audio signal processing, random cropping, time scale modification and Stirmark for Audio are listed in Table 2-4.

From Table 2 it can been seen that this algorithm is very robust to high strength audio signal processing, for example, it can resist MP3 compression up to 32kbps (22:1), low pass filtering with the cutoff frequency of 4kHz, noise addition that can be heard clearly by everybody, resample, echo, denoise etc. Table 2 shows strong robustness to random cropping, as long as one or more embedding regions are not cropped, the detection will succeed. In our experiment, even 10000 samples are cropped at each of 8 randomly selected positions, it does not make any affection to the watermark detection.

Table 2. RCDR(Ratio of Correctly Detected Regions), sim, BER of rock under audio signal processing and random cropping

Attack Type	RCDR	Sim	BER
UnAtacked	11/11	1	0%
MP3 (32kbps)	8/17	0.9701	3.13%
MP3 (48kbps)	8/17	0.9852	1.56%
MP3 (64kbps)	7/19	0.9718	3.13%
MP3 (96kbps)	8/17	0.9852	1.56%
MP3 (128kbps)	9/17	1	0%
Low pass (4khz)	5/17	1	0%
Low pass (8khz)	9/13	1	0%
Equalization (Bass Boost)	9/15	1	0%
Resample (44100->16000->44100)	6/9	1	0%
Resample (44100->22050->44100)	8/11	1	0%
Echo (100ms, 40%)	10/13	1	0%
Noise (audible)	10/11	1	0%
Denoise (Hiss Removal)	5/13	0.9235	7.81%
Jittering (1/500)	1/13	0.8861	12.50%
Jittering (1/1000)	5/11	0.9553	4.69%
Crop1 (10000*8)	10/11	1	0%

Pitch-invariant time scale modification is a challenging problem in audio watermarking technique, it can be viewed as a special form of random cropping, removing or adding some parts of audio signal while preserving the pitch. In our test dataset, the algorithm shows strong robustness to this attack up to at least ±10%, far beyond the ±4% standard requested in the SDMI phase-II proposal. Based on the introduction in section 2.1, this is mainly due to the relative invariance of the high energy regions under such attacks. The test results of rock under time scale modification from -20% to +20% are tabulated in Table 3 (– means that watermark detections in all embedding regions are failed).

Table 3. RCDR, sim, BER of rock under time scale modification

Attack Type	RCDR	Sim	BER	Attack Type	RCDR	Sim	BER
TSM-1%	8/11	1	0%	TSM+1%	8/11	1	0%
TSM-2%	7/13	1	0%	TSM+2%	5/11	1	0%
TSM-3%	7/7	1	0%	TSM+3%	6/9	1	0%
TSM-4%	6/11	1	0%	TSM+4%	7/13	1	0%
TSM-5%	8/11	1	0%	TSM+5%	8/11	1	0%
TSM-6%	7/13	1	0%	TSM+6%	8/15	1	0%
TSM-7%	2/11	0.9701	3.13%	TSM+7%	8/15	1	0%
TSM-8%	4/11	1	0%	TSM+8%	7/13	1	0%
TSM-9%	6/11	1	0%	TSM+9%	6/11	1	0%
TSM-10%	5/13	1	0%	TSM+10%	3/11	1	0%
TSM-11%	9/15	1	0%	TSM+11%	5/9	1	0%
TSM-12%	3/9	1	0%	TSM+12%	5/11	0.9718	3.13%
TSM-13%	2/5	1	0%	TSM+13%	4/9	0.9852	1.56%
TSM-14%	2/9	0.9080	9.38%	TSM+14%	4/11	1	0%
TSM-15%	0/11	0.9276	7.81%	TSM+15%	4/11	1	0%
TSM-16%	4/11	0.9701	3.13%	TSM+16%	8/13	1	0%
TSM-17%	1/5	0.8072	18.75%	TSM+17%	0/11	–	–
TSM-18%	0/9	–	–	TSM+18%	4/11	0.9852	1.56%
TSM-19%	4/11	1	0%	TSM+19%	5/13	0.9852	1.56%
TSM-20%	3/11	1	0%	TSM+20%	0/11	–	–

Stirmark for Audio is a standard robustness evaluation tool for audio watermarking technique. All operations are performed by default parameter except that the MP3 compression bit rate is changed to 32kbps. From Table 4, we can see that most results are satisfactory. In the cases of failure, the auditory quality is also distorted severely.

6 Conclusion

In this paper, by embedding the watermark in the perceptually important localized regions of interest through music content analysis, we obtained high robustness against common audio signal processing and synchronization attacks such as random cropping and time scale modification. The selection of the embedding regions is the most important step in this algorithm, to what extent these regions can be invariant against attacks like time scale modification directly determines how robust this algorithm is. It should be noted that this method has its inherent limitation. Although it is suitable for most modern music with obvious rhythm, it does not work well on jazz and some classical music without apparent rhythm, in this circumstance, there are not obvious peaks on the d3 subband. To seek more steady embedding regions is our further work.

Table 4. RCDR, sim, BER of rock under Stirmark for Audio

Attack Type	RCDR	Sim	BER
write_addbrumm_100	11/11	1	0%
write_addbrumm_1100	11/11	1	0%
write_addbrumm_2100	8/9	1	0%
write_addbrumm_3100	8/9	1	0%
write_addbrumm_4100	8/11	1	0%
write_addbrumm_5100	3/7	1	0%
write_addbrumm_6100	5/11	0.9718	3.13%
write_addbrumm_7100	3/11	0.9566	4.69%
write_addbrumm_8100	1/7	0.8956	10.94%
write_addbrumm_9100	1/9	0.8792	12.50%
write_addbrumm_10100	1/15	0.8792	12.50%
write_addnoise_100	11/11	1	0%
write_addnoise_300	11/11	1	0%
write_addnoise_500	11/11	1	0%
write_addnoise_700	11/11	1	0%
write_addnoise_900	11/11	1	0%
write_addsinus.wav	10/11	1	0%
write_amplify	11/11	1	0%
write_compressor32KBPS	7/15	0.9852	1.56%
write_copysample	0/3	–	–
write_cutsamples	0/13	–	–
write_dynnoise	5/9	1	0%
write_echo	6/17	0.9553	4.69%
write_exchange_30	11/11	1	0%
write_exchange_50	11/11	1	0%
write_exchange_70	11/11	1	0%
write_fft_hlpass	9/11	1	0%
write_fft_invert	11/11	1	0%
write_fft_real_inverse	9/11	1	0%
write_fft_stat1	2/11	0.9393	6.25%
write_fft_test	2/11	0.9393	6.25%
write_flippsample	1/11	0.9393	6.25%
write_invert	11/11	1	0%
write_lsbzero	11/11	1	0%
write_normalize	11/11	1	0%
write_nothing	11/11	1	0%
write_original	11/11	1	0%
write_rc_highpass	10/11	1	0%
write_rc_lowpass	11/13	1	0%
write_smooth2	9/11	1	0%
write_smooth	10/13	1	0%
write_stat1	10/13	1	0%
write_stat2	11/11	1	0%
write_zerocross	11/11	1	0%
write_zerolength	7/9	0.9553	4.69%
write_zeroremove	7/13	1	0%

Acknowledgement. This work was supported in part by Natural Science Foundation of China under contracts 60003017 , 60373020 and 69935010, China 863 Plans under contracts 2001AA114120 and 2002AA103065, and Shanghai Municipal R&D Foundation under contracts 03DZ15019 and 03DZ14015, Fudan Graduates Innovation Fund.

References

[1] R. Tachibana, S. Shimizu, T. Nakamura, and S. Kobayashi, "An audio watermarking method robust against time and frequency fluctuation," in SPIE Conf. on Security and Watermarking of Multimedia Contents III, San Jose, USA, January 2001, vol. 4314, pp. 104–115.
[2] http://amath.kaist.ac.kr/research/01-11.pdf.
[3] W. Li, X.Y. Xue, "Audio Watermarking Based on Statistical Feature in Wavelet Domain", in Poster Track of the Twelfth International World Wide Web Conference (WWW2003). Budapest, Hungary, May 2003.
[4] C. P. Wu, P. C. Su, and C-C. J. Kuo, "Robust and efficient digital audio watermarking using audio content analysis," in SPIE Int. Conf. on Security and Watermarking of Multimedia Contents II, San Jose, USA, January 2000, vol. 3971, pp. 382–392.
[5] http://www.sdmi.org/download/FRWG00022401-Ph2_CFPv1.0.pdf, SDMI Phase II Screening Technology Version 1.0, Feb 2000.
[6] M. Mansour, A. Tewfik, "Time-Scale Invariant Audio Data Embedding". Proc. IEEE International Conference on Multimedia and Expo, ICME, 2001.
[7] M. Mansour and A. Tewfik, "Audio Watermarking by Time-Scale Modification", Proc. IEEE International Conference on Acoustics, Speech and Signal Processing, ICASSP, Salt Lake City, May 2001.
[8] R. Tachibana, "Improving audio watermarking robustness using stretched patterns against geometric distortion," Proc. of the 3rd IEEE Pacific-Rim Conference on Multimedia (PCM2002), pp. 647–654.
[9] K. N. Hamdy, A. H. Tewfik, T. Chen, and S. Takagi, "Time-Scale Modification of Audio Signals with Combined Harmonic and Wavelet Representations," ICASSP-97, Munich, Germany.
[10] C. Duxbury, M. E. Davies and M. B. Sandler, "Separation of Transient Information in Musical Audio Using Multiresolution Analysis Techniques", the 4th International Workshop on Digital Audio Effects, Limerick, December 2001.

Wei Li is a Ph.D. candidate of Fudan University, China and the corresponding author, whose research interest includes audio watermarking, retrieval/classification.
Xiangyang Xue is a professor of Fudan University, China, whose research interest includes image/video retrieval, multimedia application etc.

Multi-bit Video Watermarking Based on 3D DFT Using Perceptual Models

Young-Yoon Lee, Han-Seung Jung, and Sang-Uk Lee

School of Electrical Eng. and Computer Science, Seoul Nat'l Univ., Korea
{yylee,jhs,sanguk}@ipl.snu.ac.kr

Abstract. In this paper, we propose a multi-bit watermarking technique for video sequences. An N-bit message is embedded in one unit of video fragment, in which a scene is employed as a watermarking unit. The proposed algorithm is fundamentally based on the three-dimensional discrete Fourier transform (DFT). In order to generate a watermark and optimum weighting factors, the perceptual properties for all the three-dimensional DFT coefficients should be computed. This strategy may require not only high computing complexity but also be undesirable. So, we design a perceptual model of an image in the DFT domain, and apply it to the video watermarking. The proposed perceptual model is expected to give high fidelity, and also its simplified version for video watermarking, estimating visual masks from a reference mask, is effective compared to fully calculated visual masks. Through the computer simulations, it will be shown that the proposed watermarking algorithm with the perceptual model yields effective performance for fidelity. Moreover, it will be also shown that the proposed scheme provides robustness against various attacks, such as compression, geometric attacks, and collusion attacks.

1 Introduction

The increasing utilization of digital media and its traits lead to illegal use of copyrighted material, *i.e.*, unrestricted duplication and dissemination via the Internet. Despite of all these undesirable trend, digital media itself is widely used and substituted for the analog ones, and these unlimited usage of the digitally recorded material may incur copyright issues. In order to cope with these possible copyright issues, a great number of techniques, including digital watermarking, have been studied and proposed in the last few decades.

Digital watermarking methods modify the original work and convey the copyright information safely. Thus, watermarking techniques should embed messages imperceptibly into the cover work, which is called transparency or fidelity, and also detect the message in spite of inevitable signal processing or malicious attacks, which is called robustness. With these two requirements being satisfied fundamentally, the payload of the watermark should be also considered. In many cases, in order to protect intellectual property rights, copyright information, including the year of copyright, the permission granted on the work, and the rating for it, may require about 60 bits or 70 bits in the cover work [17]. Moreover, it is

T. Kalker et al. (Eds.): IWDW 2003, LNCS 2939, pp. 301–315, 2004.
© Springer-Verlag Berlin Heidelberg 2004

important that one watermark message should be embedded in one unit of host data fragment. For video sequences, one unit of watermark information may be embedded in each frame or spread over seconds of frames. But, spreading the watermark over seconds of frames may not be desirable because some parts of the watermarked video could be taken by a pirate, where the watermark might be unavailable any longer. Thus, watermark information should be embedded within a few seconds, and moreover, detected even with a second of video. Generally, it is recommended that the watermark bit rate be ideally more than 70 bits per second.

There has been some works on a video watermarking. In [9], a three-dimensional DFT watermarking uses template in the log-log-log map of the 3D DFT magnitude and is robust against frame-rate changes, aspect-ratio modification and rescaling of frames. To aim of enhancing watermark capacity, we exploit the characteristics of the human visual system in DFT domain and design a novel perceptual model.

This paper addresses a multi-bit watermarking for video sequences. An N-bit message is embedded in one unit of video fragment, where we use a scene as watermarking unit of video. Segmentation into video scenes allows the watermarking procedure to consider the temporal redundancy. That is, frames from the same scene are so analogous that a consistent watermark can be easily detected with a part of the scene in the proposed algorithm. It is often the case that the watermark should be extracted from the frames without knowledge of the location of the video or from the pirated video, which may be a part of a scene (possibly one or two seconds of the video). Thus, a scene-based video watermarking technique must be reasonable. From a viewpoint of watermark security, due to a great number of analogous frames, watermarks in video signal may be vulnerable to pirate attacks, *i.e.* frame averaging, frame dropping, interframe collusions, statistical analysis, etc. However, these attacks are not effective, since the watermarks are not only hidden by pseudo-noise sequence but also preserved by the scene-based approaches. The proposed algorithm is fundamentally based on three-dimensional DFT. First, one-dimensional DFT is applied along the temporal axis of a video scene, which leads to a temporal representation of the video scene. Generally, we need mid-band frequency frames that a watermark is embedded into, and these frames are transformed using two-dimensional DFT, yielding three dimensional DFT as a result. In order to generate a watermark and the corresponding weighting parameters, the perceptual properties for all the three-dimensional DFT coefficients should be derived, but this strategy may require high computing complexity and be undesirable. Thus, we design a perceptual model of an image in the DFT domain, and extend the proposed model to the video watermarking. This strategy is expected to improve fidelity, and the simplified version for video, estimation of visual masks from a reference mask, is effective compared to fully calculated visual masks. Next, an N-bit message is embedded to the DFT magnitude based on pseudo-random sequences to make the message noise-like signals, which is statistically undetectable against interframe-collusions or other statistical analysis. Each bit is spread and also weighted by a given visual mask, which makes it possible to detect the watermark even with a part of the watermarked scene. The detector determines '1' or '0' for each bit using correlation-based algorithm.

This paper is organized as follows. In Section 2, a perceptual model in the DFT domain is presented, which is derived from the two-dimensional DFT of an image. The proposed perceptual model is employed in the three-dimensional DFT of video watermarking system. In Section 3, multi-bit watermark embedding and detection algorithm will be explained in detail. Watermark embedding can be achieved using spread spectrum, in which pairs of the DFT magnitude are modified to represent watermark bit information. In the process of detecting watermark signals, a correlation coefficient is employed as a similarity measure. Section 4 presents the performance of the proposed algorithm. It is shown that the proposed algorithm is robust against various attacks, such as compression, cropping, scaling, rotation, and frame-based attacks. In Section 5, we present the conclusion of this paper.

2 Visual Masking

Recently, many watermarking techniques take advantage of the research results on developing useful visual models for image or video compression. The JND (just noticeable difference) thresholds, one of the remarkable visual models, determine optimum quantization step sizes or bit allocations for compression applications. But, it is often the case that all the masking information obtainable from a visual model cannot be fully exploited in image compression due to the limited bit rate (or side information). However, since this limitation does not exist for the watermarking application, it is known that we can fully make use of a visual model for the local threshold values [5,7,10]. Therefore, a lot of researches, applying the human visual system (HVS) to the watermarking algorithm, are carried out with developing the watermarking systems. In many cases, the HVS is modeled in the DCT or wavelet domain, as mentioned above [2,18,10,7]. However, no useful visual models have been developed yet in the DFT domain. The reason is partly that there is no successful try of image compression in the DFT domain. In this section, we will investigate the DFT and use its properties in our video watermarking algorithm.

First of all, considering the spatial effects of DFT basis, the two-dimensional DFT of an $N \times N$ image $\{u(m,n)\}$, and its inverse transform are defined as

$$v(k,l) = \sum_{m=0}^{N-1}\sum_{n=0}^{N-1} u(m,n) W_N^{km} W_N^{ln}, 0 \le k,l \le N-1, \tag{1}$$

$$u(m,n) = \frac{1}{N^2}\sum_{k=0}^{N-1}\sum_{l=0}^{N-1} v(k,l) W_N^{-km} W_N^{-ln}, 0 \le m,n \le N-1. \tag{2}$$

And, the spatial effects of DFT basis are shown in Fig. 1. In case that the DFT element $v(\pm 8, \pm 16)$ of 256×256 Lena image is added by $10N^2$, then the wave appears as in Fig. 1(b). If the component of the wave number $\pm\kappa$ in DFT domain is excited, *i.e.*, $v(\pm\kappa') = Ae^{\pm j\theta_v}$, we can rewrite the inverse Fourier transform

(a) (b)

Fig. 1. (a) Lena image and (b) Lena image with the modification of the DFT coefficients.

of (2) as the wave equation, given by

$$u(\mathbf{x}) = \frac{2A}{N^2} \cdot \phi\left(2\pi\kappa \cdot \mathbf{x} - \theta_v\right) = \frac{2A}{N^2} \cdot \phi\left(2\pi\rho_\kappa\rho_\mathbf{x}\cos(\theta_\kappa - \theta_\mathbf{x}) - \theta_v\right), \tag{3}$$

where $\phi(x) = \cos x$, $\kappa = \kappa'/N = (k/N, l/N) = \rho_\kappa e^{j\theta_\kappa}$, and $\mathbf{x} = (m,n) = \rho_\mathbf{x} e^{j\theta_\mathbf{x}}$. Here, the basis images can be derived from (3), which is shown in Fig. 2. The wave patterns in the basis images can be characterized by the wave length and its directions. From (3), the amplitude of the wave pattern is $\frac{2A}{N^2}$ and the wavelength λ is the reciprocity of wave number κ, *i.e.*, $\lambda = |\frac{1}{\kappa}| = \frac{1}{\rho_\kappa}$ and its direction θ is $-\theta_\kappa$. From the literatures of the HVS, maximal invisible disturbance can be determined by three factors: the wave length and its directions, and the statistical property of images.

For a given image, the modification of the DFT components yields certain patterns of a periodic function in the spatial domain, called spatial frequency patterns, as mentioned above. A critical threshold of the modification powers, which we may not perceive, varies according to the spatial frequency of the pattern [18], its direction [19, 20, 21], and the context of the image. As a result, a visual mask α for measuring visual fidelity can be derived as

$$\alpha = \alpha_r \cdot \alpha_\theta \cdot \alpha_u, \tag{4}$$

where α_r is given by a function of spatial frequency, α_θ presents the effect of its direction, and α_u is a luminance component of the image, respectively. The contrast sensitivity function (CSF) $A_r(f_r)$ for spatial frequency (in cycles/degree) f_r [18] is given by

$$A_r(f_r) \approx \left[c + (f_r/f_0)^{k_1}\right] \exp\left[-(f_r/f_0)^{k_2}\right], \tag{5}$$

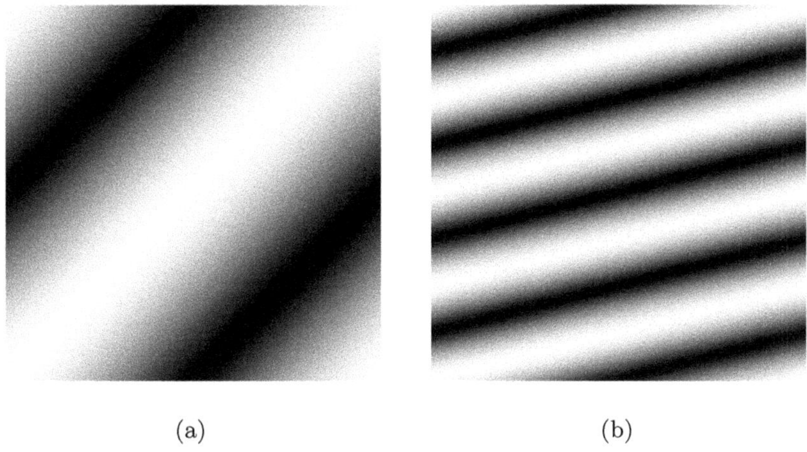

(a) (b)

Fig. 2. The DFT basis images in cases of (a) κ'=(1,1), and (b) κ'=(1,4).

where $c = 0.0192$, $f_0 = 8.77$, $k_1 = 1$, and $k_2 = 1.1$. And the corresponding plots are shown in Fig. 3. As shown in the figure, this function gives a peak value at $f_r = 8.0$ cycles/degree.

Let the DFT-manipulated images be viewed at a distance where $n_s = 65$ pels subtended 1° of viewing angle, and the wavelength of the pattern be λ, then the spatial frequency f_r can be written as

$$f_r = \frac{n_s}{\lambda} = n_s \rho_\kappa. \tag{6}$$

As a result, the sensitivity of human perception for spatial frequency is represented by a function α_r, which is an inverse function of the CSF, given by

$$\alpha_r(\rho_\kappa) = \frac{1}{A_r\left(n_s \rho_\kappa\right)}. \tag{7}$$

The HVS is most sensitive to vertical/horizontal lines and edges in an images, and least sensitive to the lines and edges with 45-degree orientation, being less than the vertical/horizontal ones by approximately 3dB [19]. This sensitivity can be represented as

$$\alpha_\theta(\theta) = \frac{1}{2} + \frac{8}{\pi^2}\left(\theta - \frac{\pi}{4}\right)^2. \tag{8}$$

Also, the eye is less sensitive to brighter signals. Brightness sensitivity is known to be nonlinear and concave [18]. In our algorithm, we use the cube root relationship, given by

$$\alpha_u(u) = \sqrt[3]{u}. \tag{9}$$

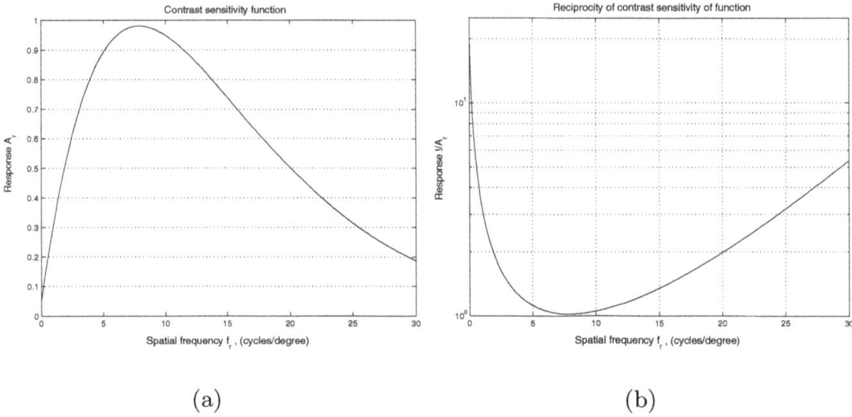

Fig. 3. (a) Contrast sensitivity function (CSF), and (b) the reciprocity of the CSF.

Since the video is the concatenation of the similar images, the statistical property of one frame is similar to that of the others. So, we can use this statistical property of one reference visual mask to estimate the others of the subsequence temporal frequency frames, which are obtained by one-dimensional DFT along the temporal axis, and we employ this approach in order to reduce computing complexity finding visual masks of all frequency frames in three-dimensional DFT domain. Fig. 4 shows the estimation of perceptual properties of subsequent temporal frequency frames from a given (computed) visual mask using statistical properties. That is, the prediction gain is derived using regression method. As shown in Fig. 4, we can observe that the estimation error decreases by six times, which means that the visual mask, extracted from a reference frame in the DFT domain, can be applied effectively as those of subsequent frequency frames in a video scene.

3 Watermarking Algorithm

In the proposed algorithm, a scene should be extracted before watermark embedding. We employ the scene-change detection algorithm. Video sequence is divided into scenes, using the distance function in [11,12], in which the measuring functions employing the luminance projection vectors, instead of full frames, are used for efficiency. This approach is known to be robust to video compression thanks to the utilization of DC images. Using a scene as a unit of watermarking fragment gives robustness against video-oriented attacks, such as frame averaging, frame dropping, interframe collusion, statistical analysis, etc.

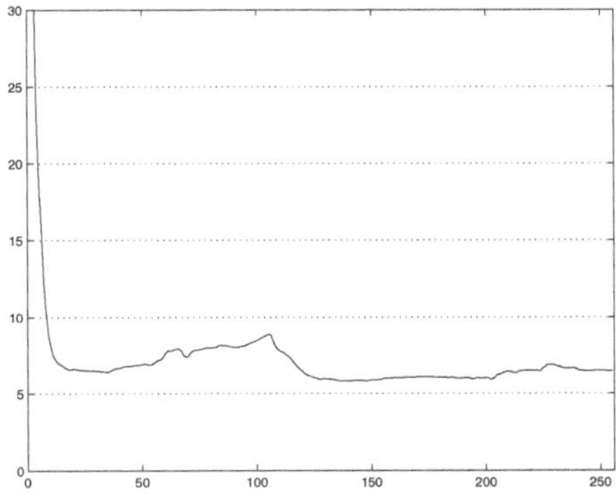

Fig. 4. Prediction gain : signal power per residual power

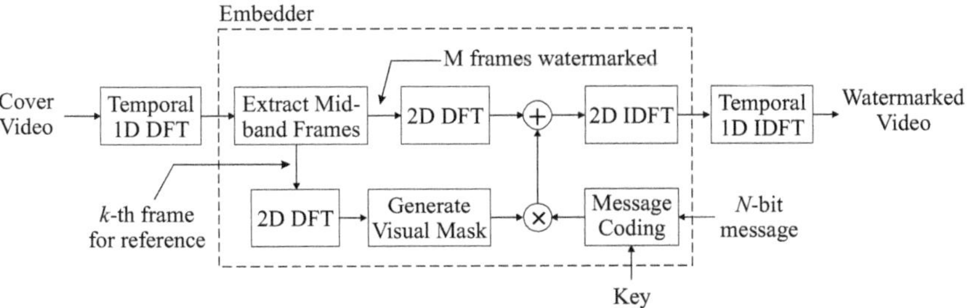

Fig. 5. Video watermarking system.

3.1 Watermark Embedding

The proposed watermarking technique is designed for copyright protection, in which the watermark message, encoded with N-bits, asserts the intellectual property rights of a given digitally recorded video. The N-bit message is encoded using pseudo-random sequences in order to obtain a spread spectrum signal. This strategy is a well known approach to ensure security against various attacks [3,4]. That is to say, spreading the watermark throughout the spectrum of an cover data guarantees its security or robustness against noise-like distortions as well as statistically analysis attacks. The location of the watermark is not obvious. Also, degrees of frequency modification may be controlled in such a way that ensures severe degradation of the original data by attacks on the watermark or ensures the robustness of the watermark. Besides the robustness against attacks, spreading achieves imperceptibility through placing a watermark in the frequency domain, where the energy in the spread watermark is small enough to be imperceptible.

The watermark embedding process is outlined in Fig. 5. A segmented scene is firstly transformed using one-dimensional DFT along the temporal axis, which yields a temporal representation of the video scene. It is often the cases that mid-band frequency components are preferred because of its robustness and fidelity. Consequently, three-dimensional DFT can be achieved by applying two-dimensional DFT to mid-band frequency frames, not all the video frames, which is thanks to the separable properties of the DFT. As shown in Fig. 5, one frame is selected to induce a perceptual mask, which is used as a reference perceptual mask for the other frequency frames. Generally, this reference frame may be the first (lowest frequency) frame in mid-band frequency frames, and each perceptual mask of the mid-band frequency frames is thought to be a subset of that of the reference frame. The N-bit watermark message is encoded using a pseudo-noise sequence key, which is weighted using the extracted perceptual mask, and added to the cover data. And then, the watermarked video sequence is obtained from inverse DFT. The proposed watermark embedding algorithm is summarized as follows:

1. Perform one-dimensional DFT along the temporal axis. Assuming a scene is composed of M frames, the 1D DFT produces temporal frequency frames of length M' by zero-padding. We use l mid-band frequency frames of $f_1, f_2, \cdots, f_l$ for watermark embedding.
2. From the frame f_1, which is the lowest frequency frame, a visual mask is computed. This visual mask is used as an initial value to generate visual mask with time component.
3. A watermark message is generated and encoded with a pseudo-random sequence for a given key. Let the N-bit message be $\mathbf{m} = [m_1 \; m_2 \; \cdots \; m_N]^T$, with $m_i \in \{1, -1\}$ in binary form. For kth message bit m_k, a pseudo-random sequence $\mathbf{p} = [p_1 \; p_2 \; \cdots \; p_L]^T$, of which the order is r with the length $L = 2^r - 1$, spreads the message bit. Firstly, the magnitudes of DFT coefficients to be watermarked, $\mathbf{c}_A = [c_A^1 \, c_A^2 \; \cdots \; c_A^L]^T$ and $\mathbf{c}_B = [c_B^1 \, c_B^2 \; \cdots \; c_B^L]^T$, are selected according to a given secret key $\mathbf{K}$. As shown in Fig. 6(a), pairs of $A(x, y)$ and $B(-x, -y)$ are modified at the same time to indicate $\{-1, 1\}$. That is, in case of kth watermark message bit $m_k = 1$, if $p_i = 1$, then we modify c_A^i and c_B^i to satisfy $c_A^i - c_B^i > \tau_w$, and if $p_i = -1$, then c_A^i and c_B^i are modified to satisfy $c_A^i - c_B^i < -\tau_w$. On the other hand, if $m_k = -1$, the reverse properties should be satisfied. As a result, The watermarked DFT coefficient vectors $\mathbf{c}_{wA}$ and $\mathbf{c}_{wB}$ are given by

$$\begin{aligned} \mathbf{c}_{wA} &= \mathbf{c}_A + \mathbf{w}_A m_k \mathbf{p} \\ \mathbf{c}_{wB} &= \mathbf{c}_B - \mathbf{w}_B m_k \mathbf{p}, \end{aligned} \tag{10}$$

where

$$\begin{aligned} \mathbf{w}_A &= \operatorname{diag}\left(\alpha_A^1, \alpha_A^2, \cdots, \alpha_A^L\right) \\ \mathbf{w}_B &= \operatorname{diag}\left(\alpha_B^1, \alpha_B^2, \cdots, \alpha_B^L\right). \end{aligned} \tag{11}$$

Here, $\mathbf{w}_A$ and $\mathbf{w}_B$ are watermarking strength, given by generated perceptual mask from step 2. Note that the symmetric points, as shown in Fig. 6(b), should be manipulated by the exact same values as well in order to produce real-valued frames after DFT modification and inverse DFT.

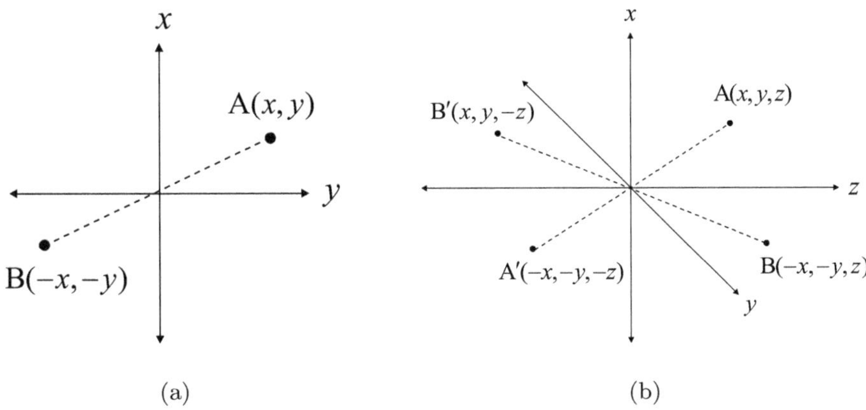

Fig. 6. One bit embedding.

3.2 Watermark Detection

In order to decode the watermarking message, we first extract watermarking feature vectors $\mathbf{c}_{wA}$ and $\mathbf{c}_{wB}$ for each message bit. Extracting the kth message bit m_k can be achieved by multiplying the correct pseudo-noise sequence $\mathbf{p}$ to the difference vector between $\mathbf{c}_{wA}$ and $\mathbf{c}_{wB}$, or $(\mathbf{c}_{wA} - \mathbf{c}_{wB})$, given by

$$\begin{aligned} d(\mathbf{c}_{wA}, \mathbf{c}_{wB}, \mathbf{p}) &= \frac{1}{L}\mathbf{p}^T(\mathbf{c}_{wA} - \mathbf{c}_{wB}) \\ &= \frac{m_k}{L}\sum_{i=1}^{L}(\alpha_A^i + \alpha_B^i) + \frac{1}{L}\mathbf{p}^T(\mathbf{c}_A - \mathbf{c}_B) \end{aligned} \tag{12}$$

Thus, each decoded message bit $\widehat{m_k}$ can follows m_k, which can be retrieved as follows.

$$\widehat{m_k} = \begin{cases} 1, & \text{if } d(\mathbf{c}_{wA}, \mathbf{c}_{wB}, \mathbf{p}) > T_d \\ -1, & \text{if } d(\mathbf{c}_{wA}, \mathbf{c}_{wB}, \mathbf{p}) < -T_d \end{cases} \tag{13}$$

To determine T_d we adopt the Neyman-Pearson criterion: we minimize the probability of missing the watermark subject to a given false detection rate. Given an image $\widetilde{I}$ and PN sequence $\mathbf{p}$, three cases are possible.

1. H_0 : image is not watermarked.
2. H_1 : image is watermarked with a PN sequence $\mathbf{p}'$ other than $\mathbf{p}$.
3. H_2 : image is watermarked with a PN sequence $\mathbf{p}$.

From the literatures of statistical decision theory, decision analysis should be preceded by some assumptions for given random variables used to the test statistics d. Let each feature vector $\mathbf{c}_A$ and $\mathbf{c}_B$ have the same mean and variance, and assuming that they are independent, then the test statistics d has a normal distribution from the central limit theorem. Consequently, the expectation of d for each hypotheses can be given by

$$\begin{aligned} H_0 &: \mu_{d0} = 0, \\ H_1 &: \mu_{d1} = m_k \frac{E[\mathbf{p'}^T \mathbf{p}]}{L} \left(E[\alpha_A] + E[\alpha_B]\right) = 0, \\ H_2 &: \mu_{d2} = m_k \left(E[\alpha_A] + E[\alpha_B]\right) \end{aligned} \tag{14}$$

To estimate the probability of false detection, $P_f = Prob(|d| > T_d | H_0 \bigcup H_1)$, we need to compute the variance of the random variable d in H_0 and H_1. The variances of H_0 and H_1 are, respectively, given by

$$\sigma_{d0}^2 = 2E[\mathbf{c}^2], \tag{15}$$

$$\sigma_{d1}^2 = 2E[\mathbf{c}^2] + \left(E[\alpha_A^2] + E[\alpha_B^2]\right). \tag{16}$$

Here, since the variance of H_1 is much larger than that of H_0, we expect that the false positive probability increases according to the increase in the variances. As a result, the false positive probability can be written by

$$P_f \leq \mathrm{erfc}\left(\frac{T_d}{\sqrt{2}\sigma_{d1}}\right). \tag{17}$$

In many cases, in order to decode the watermark information, a correlation-based detection approach can be widely used. That is, a correlation coefficient, derived from a given watermark pattern and a signal with/without the watermark, is used to determine the message bit. In the simulation, we employ a correlation coefficient to detect the message information, which is a normalized version of (12). Let a vector $\mathbf{v} = \mathbf{c'}_{wA} - \mathbf{c'}_{wB}$, then the correlation-based distance metric $d'(\mathbf{v}, \mathbf{p})$ can be given by

$$d'(\mathbf{v}, \mathbf{p}) = \frac{E[\mathbf{v}^T \mathbf{p}]}{\sqrt{E[\mathbf{v}^T \mathbf{v}] E[\mathbf{p}^T \mathbf{p}]}}. \tag{18}$$

If the metric $d'(\mathbf{v}, \mathbf{p})$ is larger than a threshold τ_d, the message bit is declared to be '1', and if the metric is smaller than a threshold $-\tau_d$, we can claim that the message bit is '-1'.

4 Simulation Results

For tests, we use two H.263 videos: Salesman and Carphone, which are in the standard QCIF format (176×144) with the frame rate of 25 frames/sec. Each sequence is composed of 125 frames (5 seconds of video) artificially. Fig. 7 shows correlation-based detection results for various watermark message bits, and reveal maximum message bits for a given fidelity and detection ratio. For an example, in order to achieve detection correlation 0.9 and fidelity of about 40dB, 48 bits for Salesman and 32 bits for Carphone might be recommended. This is always dependent on the characteristics of videos and the length of pseudo-noise

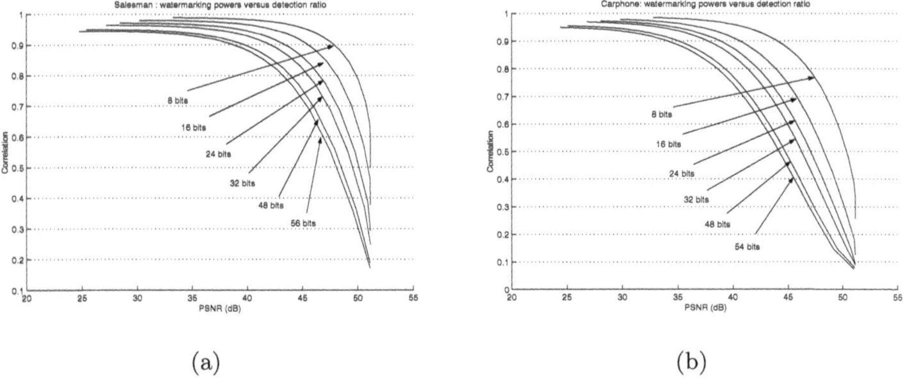

(a) (b)

Fig. 7. Watermarking power versus correlation-based detection ratio for (a) Salesman sequence, and (b) Carphone sequence.

sequences. In this simulation, the pseudo-noise sequence has the length of 127 (the order is 7), and we choose 48 bits for Salesman and 32 bits for Carphone.

The robustness against incidental or intentional distortions can be measured by the correlation values. In the computer simulation, various attacks, including video compression as well as intentional geometric distortions, are applied to test the robustness. For these attacks, the overall performance may be evaluated by the relative difference between the correlation values when a message bit is '1' or '0'. An experimental threshold is chosen to be $\tau_d = 0.55$, which yields the false positive probability 10^{-10} or less. In Fig. 8, we show the correlation results and bit errors after various attacks. Each detection test of a message bit is performed with 400 randomly generated watermark keys. Note that numbers in parentheses are the number of erroneous bits due to the corresponding attacks. Also, false negative values (the maximum correlation values by randomly generated incorrect keys) are observed in the error bar.

Due to the restricted transmission bandwidth or storage space, video data might suffer from a lossy compression. More specifically, video coding standards, such as MPEG-1/2/4 and H.26x, exploit the temporal and spatial correlations in the video sequence to achieve high compression ratio. We test the ability of the watermark to survive video coding for various compression rates. Each sequence is considered as a scene, where an identical watermark message is embedded, and each watermarked scene is encoded with the H.263 and JPEG, called motion-JPEG. First, we employ the H.263 to encode QCIF videos at the variable bit rate (VBR). That is, the H.263 encoding results with the fixed quantizer parameters (QP=5$\sim$13) are shown in Tables 1. For Salesman sequence, the H.263 coder encodes the video to yield average bit rates of 21.91 kbps $\sim$ 91.50kbps, and also the JPEG coder is applied to achieve the compression ratio (CR) of 15.44 $\sim$ 3.15. The correlation results and bit errors after JPEG and H.263 compression are shown to Fig. 8(a) and (b). Bit errors occur for severe compression, say, 1-bit

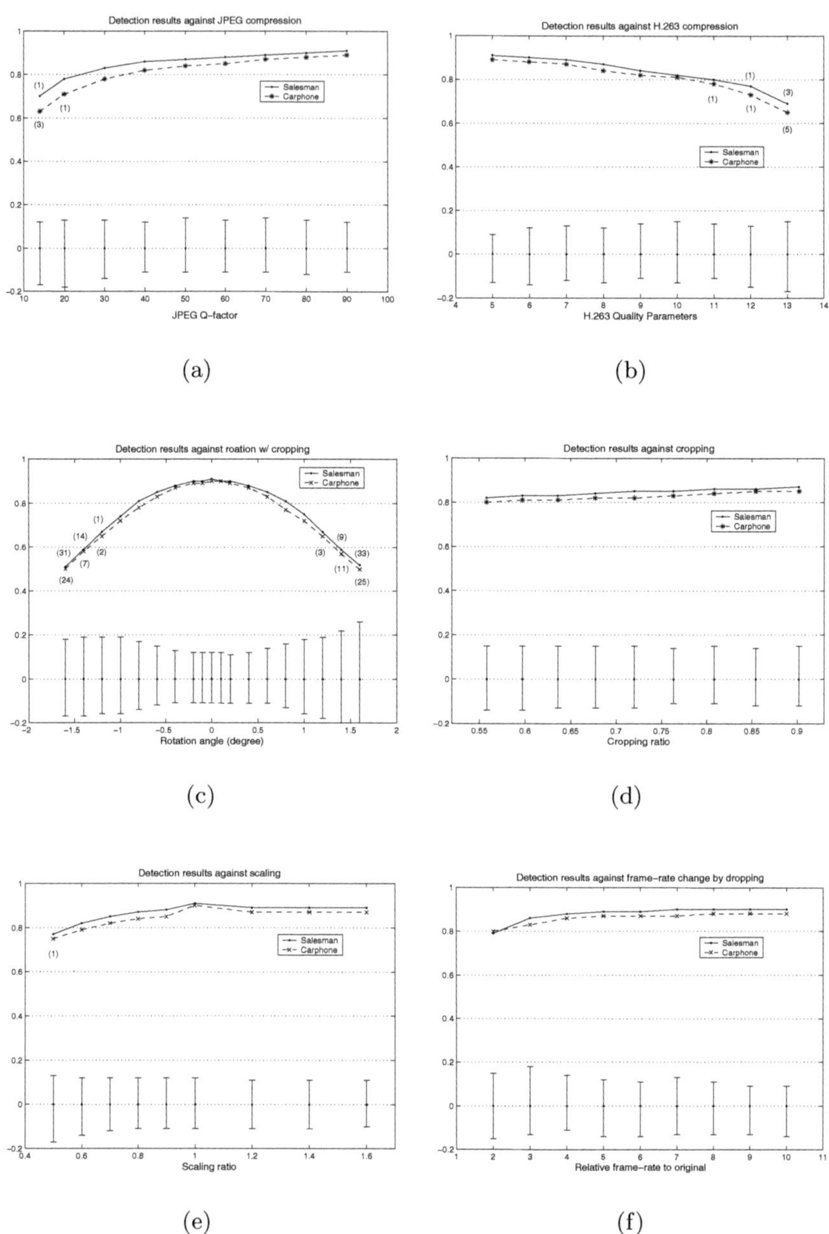

Fig. 8. Correlation values after (a) JPEG compression, (b) H.263 compression, (c) rotation with cropping, (d) cropping, (e) scaling, (f) frame-rate change for Salesman sequence and Carphone sequence.

Table 1. Image fidelity versus compression ratio.

JPEG compression					H.263 compression				
	Salesman		Carphone			Salesman		Carphone	
Q	PSNR (dB)	Comp. Ratio	PSNR (dB)	Comp. Ratio	QP	PSNR (dB)	bitrate (kbps)	PSNR (dB)	bitrate (kbps)
14	28.29	15.44:1	29.54	16.16:1	13	31.00	21.81	31.96	41.53
20	29.40	12.44:1	30.75	13.49:1	12	31.17	23.93	32.32	45.29
30	30.56	9.84:1	31.82	11.15:1	11	31.57	27.88	32.87	52.97
40	31.33	8.39:1	32.48	9.68:1	10	31.68	31.33	33.23	59.20
50	32.01	7.36:1	33.05	8.55:1	9	32.05	37.90	33.90	71.71
60	32.67	6.52:1	33.63	7.67:1	8	32.52	44.05	34.41	82.56
70	33.54	5.56:1	34.32	6.65:1	7	33.47	55.72	35.33	104.93
80	34.69	4.51:1	35.15	5.51:1	6	34.30	67.50	36.07	125.98
90	36.57	3.15:1	36.32	3.92:1	5	35.65	91.50	37.47	171.63

error for the JPEG with Q=14, 3-bit error for the H.263 with QP=13, and 1-bit error for the H.263 with QP=12 for Salesman sequence. In the other cases, no bit error can be observed.

In order to illustrate the robustness of the proposed scheme, RST attacks may be effective enough to distort the watermarked video not to detect the watermark due to losing its sync-position. The compression is an essential procedure to transmit or store any digital media, but RST distortions may be categorized into illegal or malicious attacks to remove the embedded watermark. In most cases, RST distortions are accompanied by cropping. For the proposed algorithm, both the cropping and scaling can be viewed as the distortion of the extracted signal due to additive noise. As such, it is expected that these attacks may degrade the detection value. In case of translation, the upper-left of each frame may be cropped, which is another version of cropping. We can expect that distortions by translation are the same as those by cropping, and this is easily shown to be true through computer simulations.

First, in the simulation, each frame is modified with rotations from $-1.6°$ to $1.6°$, with maximum cropping of about 6.5%. Since any template signals that recover the parameters of RST distortions are not embedded, a slight degree of rotation may possibly prevent detecting the watermark by removing synchronization, not watermark itself. Moreover, the DFT itself might be RST invariant, but it is often the case that the rotation with or without cropping yields noise-like distortions on the image. Fig. 8(c) shows the detection performance according to degrees of rotation. For the rotation angles from $-1°$ to $1°$, it is shown that the proposed algorithm can detect all bits successfully without errors. This makes it possible to extract the watermark message without a template. That is, through some trials of rotating the watermarked video by 1 or less degree of rotation, we can extract the watermark from manipulated video by rotation. However, rotation of more than one degree leads to errors in most of message bits, *e.g.* 31-bit errors by $-1.6°$ rotation, and 14-bit errors by $-1.4°$ rotation for Salesman sequence, where we embed 48 bits for a watermark message. Similar detection results are observed for Carphone sequence.

The correlation detections on cropping attacks are performed, and the plots are shown in Fig. 8(d). In case of cropping, the upper-left and lower-right of each frame is equally cropped, and the cropping ratio in Fig. 8(d) means non-cropping ratio. Fig. 8(e) shows the correlation values after scaling for various video sequences. Also, all bits of the embedded watermark message are easily determined. Despite loss of about 50 % by the cropping or scaling, the correlation results are maintained without much variance.

Some of the distortions of particular interest in video watermarking are those associated with temporal processing, e.g., frame-rate change, temporal cropping, frame dropping, and frame interpolation. To test frame dropping and interpolation, we dropped the odd index frames from the test sequences, which means that the frame-rate decreases to the half, in which the synchronization problems can be overcome using template embedding approaches. For simulations, the first half or the last half frames removed from the sequences. For the case of frame averaging, the missing frames are replaced with the average of the two neighboring frames. In these cases, the proposed algorithm detects the watermark perfectly. The detection results after frame-rate change, which can be achieved by dropping subsequent frames corresponding to the frame rate, are shown in Fig. 8(f), in which no bit error is observed. It can be easily expected that frame dropping and averaging does not affect detection ratio, considering the properties of the DFT. Our simulation results in this case are all similar to Fig. 8(f), while yielding no bit error. We can see that the proposed algorithm is robust against the temporal processing.

5 Conclusion

This paper addressed a multi-bit video watermarking technique. An N-bit message is embedded in one unit of video fragment, where we use a scene as watermarking unit of video. The proposed algorithm is fundamentally based on the three-dimensional DFT. In order to generate a watermark, the visual masking properties for all the three-dimensional DFT coefficients should be computed, but this strategy may require high computing complexity and be undesirable. So, we designed a visual mask of an image in the DFT domain, and this perceptual model is extended to video watermarking. This visual model can give high fidelity in video watermarking and the simplified version for video, using the estimation of visual masks from that of a reference frame, is effective compared to fully calculated visual model based watermarking. Through the computer simulations, it was shown that the watermarking algorithm with the proposed perceptual model yields effective performance about both fidelity and robustness. The simulation results demonstrated that the proposed scheme provides robustness to compression, cropping, scaling, rotation, and frame-based attacks.

References

1. S. Katzenbeisser, and F.A.P Petitcolas, *Information hiding: techniques for steganogrphy and digital watermarking*, Artech House, 2000.
2. I.J. Cox, M.L. Miller, and J.A. Bloom, *Digital watermarking*, Morgan Kaufmann, 2001.
3. I.J. Cox, M.L. Miller, A.L. Mckellips, "Watermarking as communication with side information", *Proceedings of the IEEE*, vol. 87, no. 7, pp. 1127–1141, July 1999.
4. I.J. Cox, J. Kilian, T. Leighton, and T. Shamoon, "Secure spread spectrum watermarking for multimedia", *IEEE Trans. on Image Processing*, vol. 6 , no. 12, pp. 1673–1687, Dec. 1997.
5. C.I. Podilchuk, and W. Zeng, "Image-adaptive watermarking using visual models", *IEEE Journal on Selected Areas in Comm.*, vol. 16, no. 4, pp. 525–532, May 1998.
6. K. Su, D. Kundur, and D. Hatzinakos, "A novel approach to collusion-resistant video watermarking," *Security and watermarking of multimedia contents, Proc. of SPIE*, vol. 4675, Jan. 2002.
7. M.D. Swanson, B. Zhu, and A.H. Tewfik, "Multiresolution scene-based video watermarking using perceptual models," *IEEE Journal on Selected Areas in Comm.*, vol. 16, no. 4, pp. 540–550, May 1998.
8. W. Zhu, Z. Xiong, and Y.-Q. Zhang, "Multiresolution watermarking for images and video," *IEEE Trans. on Circuits and Systems for Video Technologies*, vol. 9, no. 4, June 1999.
9. F. Deguillaume, G. Csurka, J. O'Ruanaidh, and T. Pun, "Robust 3D DFT video watermarking," *Security and watermarking of multimedia contents, Proc. of SPIE*, vol. 3657, pp. 113–124, Jan. 1999.
10. R.B. Wolfgang, C.I. Podilchuk, and E.J. Delp, "Perceptual watermarks for digital images and video," *Proceedings of the IEEE*, vol. 87, no. 7, pp. 1108–1126, July 1999.
11. M.M. Yeung and B. Liu, "Efficient matching and clustering of video shots," in *Proc. IEEE ICIP'95*, vol. 1, pp. 338–341, Oct. 1995.
12. H.S. Chang, S. Sul, and S.U. Lee, "Efficient video indexing scheme for content-based retrieval," *IEEE Trans. on Circuits and Systems for Video Technologies*, vol. 9, no. 8, pp. 1269–1279, Dec. 1999.
13. F. Goffin, J.F. Delaigle, C. De Vleeschouwer, B. Macq, J.-J. Quisquater, "A low cost perceptive digital picture watermarking method", *Storage and Retrieval for Image and Video Databases (SPIE)*, pp. 264–277, 1997.
14. G. Depovere, T. Kalker, J.P. Linnartz, "Improved watermark detection reliability using filtering before correlation," in *Proc. IEEE ICIP'98*, 1998.
15. A.K. Jain, *Fundamentals of digital image processing*, Prentice Hall, 1989.
16. P. Weyner, *Disappearing cryptography; Information hiding: steganography & watermarking*, 2nd Ed., Morgan Kaufmann, 2002.
17. G.C. Langelaar, I. Setyawan, and R.L. Lagendijk, "Watermarking digital image and video data," *IEEE Signal Processing Magazine*, pp. 20–46, Sept. 2000.
18. J. L. Mannos and J. J. Sakrison, "The effects of a visual fidelity criterion of the encoding of images", *IEEE Transaction on Information Theory*, vol. IT-20, no. 4, pp. 525–536, July 1974.
19. F. W. Campbell and J. J. Kulikowski, "Orientation selectivity of the human visual system", *Journal of Physiology*, 187:437–445, 1966.
20. F. W. Campbell, J. J. Kulikowski, and J. Levinson, "The effect of orientation on the visual resolution of gratings", *Journal of Physiology*, 187:427–436, 1966.
21. M. M. Taylor, "Visual discrimination and orientation", *Journal of the Optical Society of America*, 53:763–765, 1963.

EM Estimation of Scale Factor for Quantization-Based Audio Watermarking

Kiryung Lee[1], Dong Sik Kim[2], Taejeong Kim[3], and Kyung Ae Moon[1]

[1] Electronics and Telecommunications Research Institute, Daejeon 305-350, Korea
{kiryung,kamoon}@etri.re.kr

[2] Hankuk University of Foreign Studies, Yongin, Kyonggi-do 449-791, Korea
dskim@hufs.ac.kr

[3] Seoul National University, Seoul 151-742, Korea
tkim@snu.ac.kr

Abstract. The blind watermarking scheme extracts the embedded message without access to the host signal. Recently, efficient blind watermarking schemes, which exploit the knowledge of the host signal at the encoder, are proposed [1,2,3]. Scalar quantizers are employed for practical implementation. Even though the scalar quantizer can provide simple encoding and decoding schemes, if the watermarked signal is scaled, then the quantizer step size at the decoder should be scaled accordingly for a reliable decoding. In this paper, we propose a preprocessed decoding scheme, which uses an estimated scale factor. The received signal density is approximated by a Gaussian mixture model, and the scale factor is then estimated by employing the expectation maximization algorithm [6]. In the proposed scheme, the scale factor is estimated from the received signal itself without any additional pilot signal. Numerical results show that the proposed scheme provides a reliable decoding from the scaled signal.

1 Introduction

The blind watermarking scheme extracts the embedded message without access to the host signal, which is the original signal without the watermark. Early blind watermarking schemes employ the spread spectrum technique in the communication. The spread spectrum watermarking schemes regard the host-signal interference as an additive random noise, and reduce the interference by using a long pseudo random sequence. Recently, more enhanced blind watermarking schemes, which exploit the knowledge of the host signal at the encoder, are proposed [1,2,3].

Chen and Wornell [1] proposed the *quantization index modulation*, which achieves very efficient trade-offs among the rate and distortion of watermarking. Eggers, *et al.* [2] proposed a blind watermarking scheme called the *scalar Costa scheme* (SCS). A structured codebook, which is constructed by the uniform scalar quantizers, is used for encoding and decoding of the watermark. Moulin, *et al.* [3] proposed a blind watermarking scheme that maximizes the watermarking

T. Kalker et al. (Eds.): IWDW 2003, LNCS 2939, pp. 316–327, 2004.
© Springer-Verlag Berlin Heidelberg 2004

capacity by exploiting the knowledge of the host signal at the encoder. They also used uniform scalar quantizers for practical implementation. These schemes can reduce or possibly cancel the host-signal interference. Note that, in order to implement a practical blind watermarking scheme, the uniform scalar quantizers are used as shown in [1,2,3].

The watermarking schemes, which employ the uniform scalar quantizers, are practical in that they are simple to implement. However, they cannot extract the embedded message well when the amplitude of the watermarked signal is modified. Since the applied modification is generally not known to the decoder, the decoder uses the quantizer step size at the encoder, which is not matched to the received signal at the decoder. As a result, the decoding performance can be degraded. Hence, for a reliable decoding, the quantizer step size at the decoder should be adjusted accordingly. Moreover, the amplitude modification of multimedia signals occurs frequently in real applications. Thus, it is necessary to find a good estimate of the modification in order to successfully decode the watermark. A normalization of the audio signals with respect to the root mean square value of the amplitude is an example of the amplitude modification.

In order to extract the embedded message from the amplitude modified signal, Eggers, *et al.* [4] proposed a pilot-based estimation scheme. They embedded a pilot signal along with SCS watermarking, and then estimate the scale factor based on a Fourier analysis of the received pilot's histograms. For accurate estimation of the scale factor, the number of the pilot signal's samples should be large enough. However, since the size of the host signal is finite, the space for embedding the payload decreases as the size of the pilot signal increases.

In this paper, we propose a preprocessed decoding scheme with estimation of the scale factor using the *expectation maximization* (EM) algorithm. The proposed scheme is similar to the scheme in [4], where the decoding is performed using an estimated scale factor. However, the proposed scheme does not embed any pilot signal, which encroaches on the watermarking capacity. Instead of the pilot signal, we use the received signal itself for the estimation of the scale factor. We approximate the received signal density as a Gaussian mixture model, and the scale factor is estimated by employing the EM algorithm.

2 Watermarking with Scalar Quantizers

In this section, we review the blind watermarking schemes with scalar quantizers, which are proposed by Eggers, *et al.*, [2], and Moulin, *et al.* [3]. The watermarked signal is obtained by embedding the watermark signal into the original host signal. Attacks are then applied to the watermarked signal, yielding the attacked signal. Here, we consider an additive white Gaussian noise (AWGN) as the attack. The distortion between the host signal and the watermarked signal should be within a predetermined constant D_1, and the distortion between the host signal and the attacked signal should be within another constant D_2. Under this constraint, efficient blind watermarking schemes with scalar quantizers are proposed in [2] and [3]. Further, Kesal, *et al.*, [5] added several error correcting codes to the blind watermarking scheme of [3] for a more reliable decoding.

The watermark encoding process is implemented with a dithered scalar quantizer $\mathcal{Q}_{\Delta,d}(x)$, which is defined as

$$\mathcal{Q}_{\Delta,d}(x) := \Delta\left(\left\lfloor \frac{x}{\Delta} - \frac{d}{2} + \frac{1}{2}\right\rfloor + \frac{d}{2}\right), \tag{1}$$

for a constant x, where $\lfloor c \rfloor$, $c \in \mathbb{R}$, is the largest integer less than or equal to c. Here, the positive constant Δ is the step size, and $d \in \{0, 1\}$ is a binary dither. Let the sequence (x_n) denote the host signal, where x_n are i.i.d. random variables with a zero-mean Gaussian density having a variance σ_x^2. Let a binary sequence of $d_n \in \{0, 1\}$ denote the watermark signal, and the sequence (s_n) denote the watermarked signal. Here, we suppose that d_n are i.i.d. and independent of x_n. The watermarked signal is then obtained by the following encoding process:

$$s_n = (1-\alpha)x_n + \alpha\mathcal{Q}_{\Delta_e,d_n}(x_n) \tag{2}$$

where α $(0 < \alpha < 1)$ and Δ_e $(\Delta_e > 0)$ are encoding parameters determined from D_1 and D_2. (2) can be rewritten as

$$s_n = x_n + \alpha\left[\mathcal{Q}_{\Delta_e,d_n}(x_n) - x_n\right]. \tag{3}$$

As shown in (3), the watermarked signal s_n is obtained by adding the α-scaled quantization error of $[\mathcal{Q}_{\Delta_e,d_n}(x_n) - x_n]$ to the host signal. Note that the constant D_1 is given by $\alpha^2\Delta_e^2/12$. In the scheme of Moulin, *et al.* [3], α can be determined by $\alpha = D_1/D_2$, when $D_1, D_2 \ll \sigma_x^2$. Thus, Δ_e is equal to $\sqrt{12D_2^2/D_1}$. (Eggers, *et al.*, [2] obtained α and Δ_e in a different approach based on a numerical optimization technique.)

Let the sequence (v_n) denote an AWGN, which are i.i.d. random variables with the Gaussian density. Here, v_n has the zero-mean and the variance of σ_v^2, which is given by

$$\sigma_v^2 := D_2 - D_1. \tag{4}$$

The attack is conducted by adding v_n to the watermarked signal s_n. In other words, the attacked signal is equal to $s_n + v_n$. If we scale the attacked signal by a scaling factor g, then the received signal, which is denoted by the sequence (r_n), is given by

$$r_n = g(s_n + v_n). \tag{5}$$

Here, g is a positive constant.

The decoding process from the received signal r_n is as follows. We quantize r_n with the quantizer $\mathcal{Q}_{\Delta_d,0}(r_n)$, which has the quantization step size Δ_d and the dither $d = 0$. If g is known to the decoder, then the decoding is performed with $g\Delta_e$ as the step size Δ_d. However, since the scale factor g is generally unknown to the decoder, an estimated $\hat{g}$ is used for deriving Δ_d, i.e., the decoding process uses $\hat{g}\Delta_e$ as the step size Δ_d. (Note that an approach on estimation of g will be shown in the following section.) Suppose that $\tilde{r}_n$ denotes the quantization error of r_n. The quantization error is then given by

$$\tilde{r}_n := r_n - \mathcal{Q}_{\Delta_d,0}(r_n). \tag{6}$$

Here, two decoding schemes, the hard-decision decoding and the soft-decision decoding, are available. The hard-decision decoding provides much less computational complexity with efficient decoding algorithms, such as the syndrome decoding for the block codes, even though the soft-decision decoding always provides a better performance. In the hard-decision decoding, the absolute value of each $\tilde{r}_n$ should be compared to $\Delta_d/4$ in order to obtain the estimated watermark signal, $\hat{d}_n$, as follows:

$$\hat{d}_n = \begin{cases} 0, & |\tilde{r}_n| < \Delta_d/4 \\ 1, & |\tilde{r}_n| \geq \Delta_d/4. \end{cases} \tag{7}$$

The embedded message is now extracted from the estimated binary watermark signal $\hat{d}_n$. In the soft-decision decoding, the estimated watermark signal $\hat{d}_n$ is obtained by

$$\hat{d}_n = \frac{4|\tilde{r}_n|}{\Delta_d} - 1. \tag{8}$$

The embedded message is then extracted by searching the code that shows the maximum correlation with $\hat{d}_n$. As shown in both decoding schemes (7) and (8), the step size Δ_d plays an important role in obtaining the estimated watermark signal $\hat{d}_n$.

3 Proposed Scheme

3.1 Modeling for Received Signal Density

The encoding process of (2) can be rewritten by

$$s_n = \mathcal{Q}_{\Delta_e,d_n}(x_n) + (1-\alpha)\left[x_n - \mathcal{Q}_{\Delta_e,d_n}(x_n)\right]. \tag{9}$$

By substituting (9) into (5), we can obtain another representation for the received signal as

$$r_n = g\mathcal{Q}_{\Delta_e,d_n}(x_n) + u_n + gv_n, \tag{10}$$

where u_n is the quantization noise defined as

$$u_n := g(1-\alpha)\left[x_n - \mathcal{Q}_{\Delta_e,d_n}(x_n)\right]. \tag{11}$$

Here, we suppose that the quantization noise u_n is uniformly distributed under the smoothness assumption on the input density. Thus, u_n can be assumed uniformly distributed on $[-\Delta_u/2, \Delta_u/2)$, where $\Delta_u := g(1-\alpha)\Delta_e$. Note that u_n has the zero-mean and the variance of σ_u^2, which is given by

$$\sigma_u^2 = \frac{\Delta_u^2}{12} = \frac{g^2(D_2 - D_1)^2}{D_1}. \tag{12}$$

Since the decoding process is performed based on the quantized value $g\mathcal{Q}_{\Delta_e,d_n}(x_n)$, (10) can be interpreted as a signal constellation from $g\mathcal{Q}_{\Delta_e,d_n}(x_n)$ that is corrupted by the two additive noises u_n and gv_n. Note that the quantized values and the quantization noise are uncorrelated. Hence, $g\mathcal{Q}_{\Delta_e,d_n}(x_n)$ and u_n are uncorrelated. Consequently, u_n and gv_n can be regarded as two uncorrelated noises of uniform and Gaussian distributions, respectively. Let z_n denote the sum of the two uncorrelated noise signals u_n and gv_n, i.e., $z_n = u_n + gv_n$. In order to simplify the algorithm, we approximate the density of z_n to a Gaussian density, where the mean is zero and the variance σ_z^2 is given by

$$\begin{aligned}\sigma_z^2 &= \sigma_u^2 + g^2\sigma_v^2 \\ &= g^2\left[\frac{(D_2 - D_1)^2}{D_1} + (D_2 - D_1)\right].\end{aligned} \tag{13}$$

Under the Gaussian-density assumption on z_n, the density of r_n, which is denoted by $p(r)$, can be approximated as a Gaussian mixture:

$$p(r) \approx \sum_{m\in\mathbb{Z}} \eta_m p_m(r; \mu_m, \sigma_m^2), \tag{14}$$

where η_m is the probability that the sample is generated by the mth mixture component, and $p_m(r; \mu_m, \sigma_m)$ is the mth mixture component density, defined as

$$p_m(r; \mu_m, \sigma_m^2) := \frac{1}{\sqrt{2\pi}\sigma_m} \exp\left(-\frac{(r-\mu_m)^2}{2\sigma_m^2}\right). \tag{15}$$

Note that z_n and $g\mathcal{Q}_{\Delta_e,d_n}(x_n)$ are uncorrelated. Therefore, the variance of mth mixture component density σ_m^2 can be assumed to have constant value of σ_z^2 regardless of m, i.e., $\sigma_m^2 = \sigma_z^2, \forall m \in \mathbb{Z}$. Further, we may ignore the mixture components having very small η_m. If we consider only M mixture components with significant η_m, then (14) can be approximated as

$$p(r) \approx \sum_{m=1}^{M} \eta_m p_m(r; \mu_m, \sigma_z^2), \tag{16}$$

and (15) becomes

$$p_m(r; \mu_m, \sigma_z^2) = \frac{1}{\sqrt{2\pi}\sigma_z} \exp\left(-\frac{(r-\mu_m)^2}{2\sigma_z^2}\right). \tag{17}$$

In the following section, we will estimate $\hat{g}$ of the scale factor g from a linear regression fit based on the estimates of μ_m and σ_z^2, by employing the EM algorithm.

3.2 EM Estimation of Scale Factor

The EM algorithm in [6] is used for estimating the mean of each mixture component density, μ_m, where the expectation and maximization steps are merged into an updating equation. The scale factor is estimated from the estimates of μ_m using a linear regression fit and then σ_z is updated using the estimated scale factor $\hat{g}$. Let us consider an observation of $r_1, r_2, \cdots, r_N$ for the estimation, where N is a positive integer. The proposed estimation scheme is the iterations of the following steps. We first consider the updating steps for η_m and μ_m as

$$\eta_m^{(i)} = \frac{1}{N}\sum_{n=1}^{N} p(m|r_n, \Theta^{(i-1)}), \text{ for } m = 1, 2, \cdots, M, \tag{18}$$

$$\mu_m^{(i)} = \frac{\sum_{n=1}^{N} r_n p(m|r_n, \Theta^{(i-1)})}{\sum_{n=1}^{N} p(m|r_n, \Theta^{(i-1)})}, \text{ for } m = 1, 2, \cdots, M, \tag{19}$$

where the vector $\Theta^{(i-1)}$ includes $\eta_m^{(i-1)}$ and $\mu_m^{(i-1)}$, for $m = 1, 2, \cdots, M$, and $\sigma_z^{(i-1)}$. Here, $p(m|r_n, \Theta^{(i-1)})$ denotes the posterior probability with $\Theta^{(i-1)}$. Based on a linear regression fit, the ith estimate $g^{(i)}$ is then obtained by minimizing the mean squared error, which is given by

$$\sum_{m=1}^{M} \eta_m^{(i)} \left[\mu_m^{(i)} - g^{(i)}\mu_m^{(i-1)}\right]^2. \tag{20}$$

Thus, $g^{(i)}$ is given by

$$g^{(i)} = \frac{\sum_{m=1}^{M} \eta_m^{(i)} \mu_m^{(i)} \mu_m^{(i-1)}}{\sum_{m=1}^{M} \eta_m^{(i)} \left[\mu_m^{(i-1)}\right]^2}. \tag{21}$$

$\sigma_z^{(i)}$ is now updated by substituting (21) into (13). Here, the updating equation is given by

$$\sigma_z^{(i)} = g^{(i)}\sqrt{\frac{(D_2 - D_1)^2}{D_1} + (D_2 - D_1)}. \tag{22}$$

In the proposed scheme, the initial values of the parameters are set as follows.

$$\sigma_z^{(0)} = \sqrt{\frac{(D_2 - D_1)^2}{D_1} + (D_2 - D_1)}, \tag{23}$$

$$\mu_m^{(0)} = \frac{\Delta_e}{2}\left(m - \left\lfloor \frac{M-1}{2} \right\rfloor\right), \text{ for } m = 1, 2, \cdots, M, \tag{24}$$

and

$$\eta_m^{(0)} = \frac{1}{M}, \text{ for } m = 1, 2, \cdots, M. \tag{25}$$

The updating steps, (18), (19), (21), and (22), are iterated by L times, where L is the number of iterations. The estimated scale factor is then given by

$$\hat{g} = g^{(L)}. \tag{26}$$

With the estimated $\hat{g}$, the decoding process is straightforward with the scaled step size $\Delta_d = \hat{g}\Delta_e$ as shown in (6).

4 Audio Watermarking Application

In this section, we applied the proposed estimation scheme to the audio watermarking. The embedder and the extractor of the proposed scheme are presented in Fig. 1.

At the embedder, the audio signal is decomposed into 32 subbands by the polyphase filter bank of MPEG1 [7]. Considering the robustness against the lossy compression and the inaudibility, the watermark signal is embedded onto the subbands which correspond to the middle frequency. (The subbands between the 4th and the 19th are chosen as the cover data.) Further, in order to prevent the attacker's attempt to estimate the quantizer step size, the embedding is performed on the scrambled signal, which can be obtained by applying the random permutation and the Hadamard transform to each subband. According to the frequency of each subband, the degree of the robustness against the lossy compression and the amplitude modification varies. Hence, the same watermark signal is repeatedly embedded on the 16 subbands. In order to make the embedded watermark signal inaudible, the embedding depth is determined from the psychoacoustic model I in MPEG1 [7].

At the extractor, the applied scaled factor is estimated, and then the watermark decoding is performed independently for each subband. The result of each subband is obtained by the soft-decision decoding and the average of the normalized correlation values is compared to the predetermined threshold.

5 Numerical Results

In this section, the numerical results on the proposed scheme are shown. First, the relevance of the Gaussian mixture model approximation on the received signal density is shown and then the performance of the proposed decoding scheme is compared to the conventional decoding schemes.

The relevance of the Gaussian mixture model approximation on the received signal density is numerically observed. Fig. 2 shows the approximation of the received signal density with the Gaussian mixture model. As shown in Fig. 2,

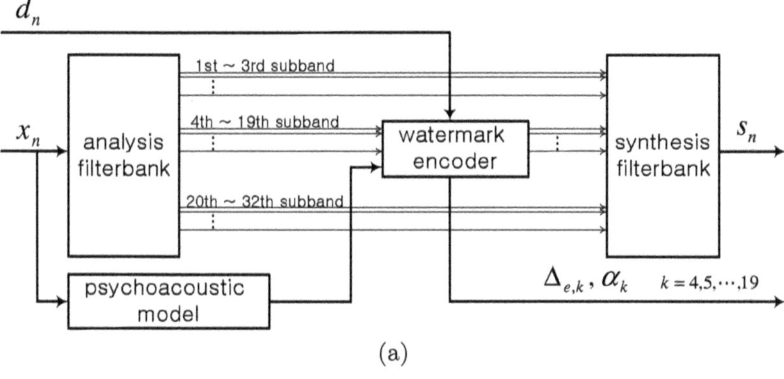

(a)

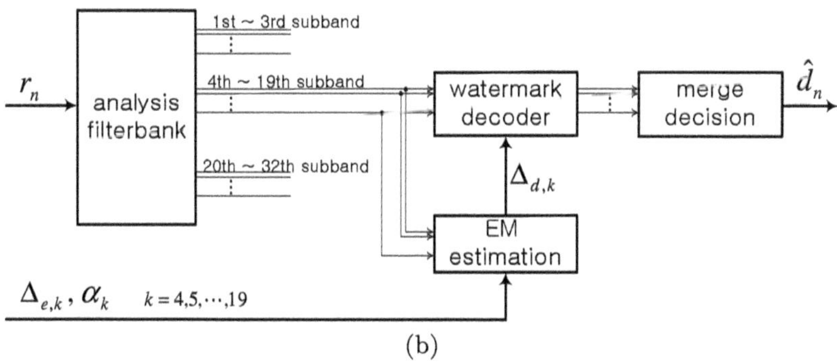

(b)

Fig. 1. Proposed audio watermarking scheme. (a) Embedder. (b) Extractor.

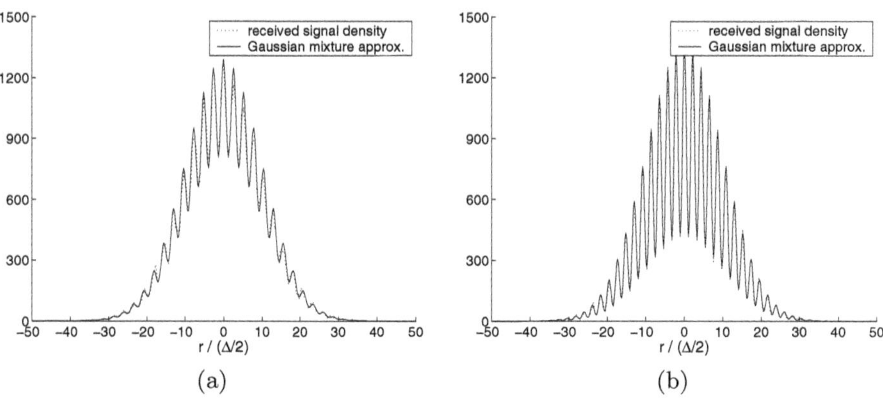

(a) (b)

Fig. 2. Received signal density and Gaussian mixture model approximation. (a) $D_2/D_1 = 1.5$. (b) $D_2/D_1 = 1.25$.

we may notice that the Gaussian mixture model (solid line) approximates well with the real densities (dotted line).

Fig. 3 shows the mean squared error (MSE) of the estimate with respect to the ratio D_2/D_1. Here, the MSE of the estimated scale factor is defined by $\mathrm{MSE}_g := E\{(\hat{g} - g)^2\}$. As shown in Fig. 3, the MSE increases as D_2/D_1 increases. Thus, when the AWGN becomes relatively strong, e.g., $D_2/D_1 \geq 1.5$, the estimation might provide inaccurate results.

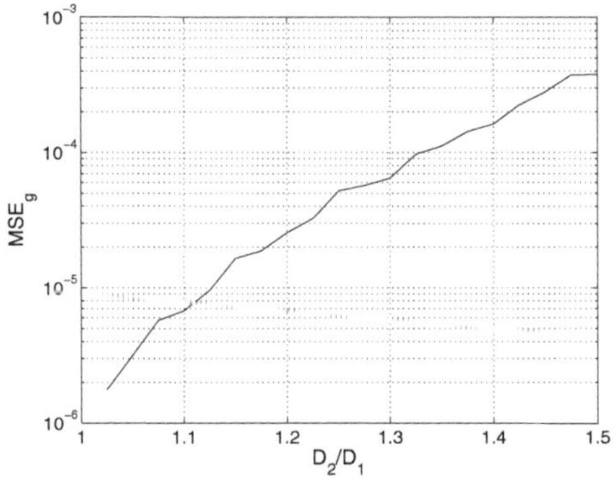

Fig. 3. MSE_g with respect to D_2/D_1 ($g = 1.05$, $N = 10^3$).

Fig. 4 shows the performance of the proposed scheme in terms of the bit error rate (BER). The *conventional scheme* with the step size Δ_e and the *ideal scheme* with the exactly scaled step size $\Delta_d = g\Delta_e$ are compared to the *proposed scheme* with the estimated scaling factor $\hat{g}$. Though iterative error-correcting codes can enhance the performance of the watermarking scheme [5], since we focus on cancelling the effect of scaling the watermarked signal, only the BER of the estimated watermark signal is considered. Here, the ratio σ_x^2 to D_1 is set as 20 dB, which is reasonable for most watermarking applications, and the estimation is performed using $N = 10^3$ received signal samples for various g. When scaling is applied, the conventional scheme makes some error even when the AWGN is very weak, e.g., $D_2/D_1 \approx 1.0$. Further, as shown in Fig. 4, the scaling by a scale factor of 1.20 nearly disables the decoding in the conventional scheme. On the contrary, the proposed scheme can approximately achieves the performance of the ideal scheme. As the ratio D_2/D_1 increases, the estimation becomes inaccurate and the gap between the proposed scheme and the ideal scheme increases. However, when the AWGN is weak, e.g., $D_2/D_1 \leq 1.5$, the proposed scheme can provide an affordable performance.

Fig. 5 shows a comparison of the proposed schemes for the different number of samples N. As shown in Fig. 5, when $N = 10^4$, the estimation becomes more accurate, and results in less BERs than the $N = 10^3$ case. However, the number of samples used for the estimation can be restricted depending on applications. Even though the scheme with 10^4 samples provides a better performance, the complexity could be impractical. The number of the samples N should be determined depending on the applications.

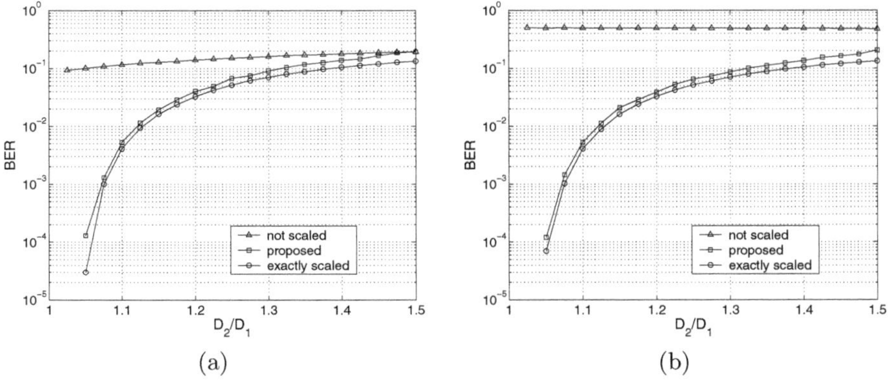

Fig. 4. BER with respect to D_2/D_1 ($N = 10^3$). (a) $g = 1.05$. (b) $g = 1.20$.

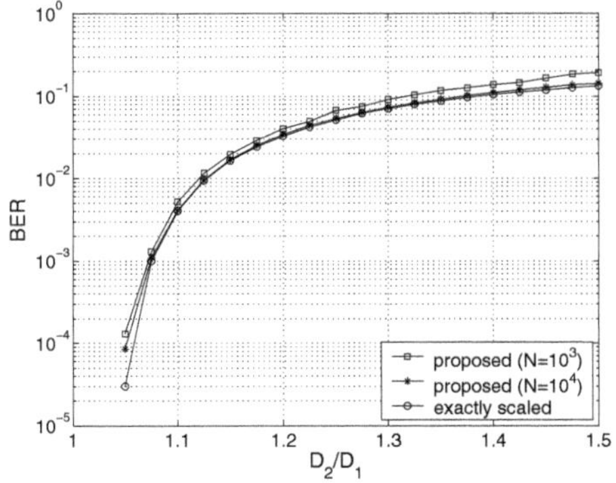

Fig. 5. BER for different N. ($g = 1.05$).

Fig. 6 shows the performance of the proposed audio watermarking scheme. For the conventional decoder, which does not employ the estimation scheme, the BER increases as the applied scale factor increases. On the contrary, the BER of the proposed scheme is nearly constant regardless of the applied scale factor. The BER of the proposed scheme is also nearly constant even when the lossy compression is applied.

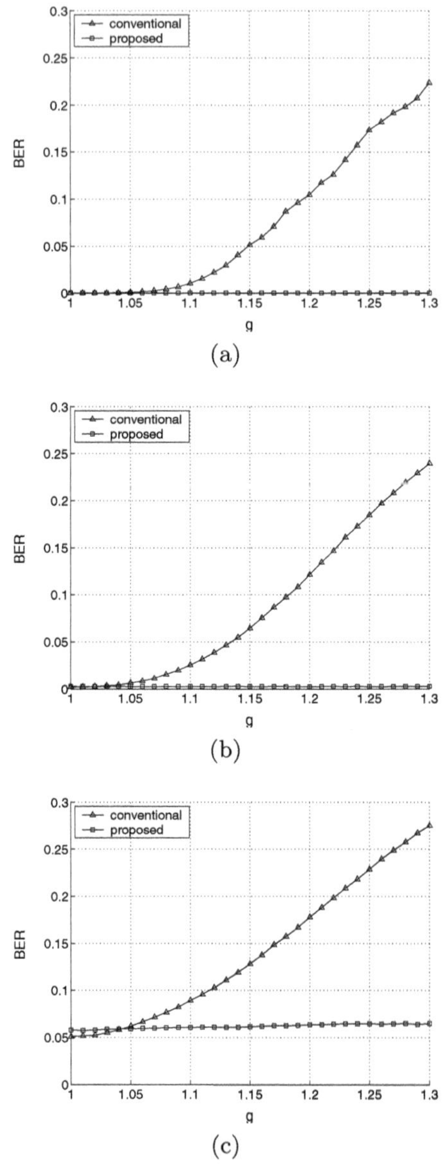

Fig. 6. BER for compressed audio signals. (a) No compression. (b) MP3 (192 kbps). (c) MP3 (128 kbps).

6 Conclusion

A preprocessed decoding scheme is proposed in order to extract the embedded message properly when the watermarked signal is scaled. Scaling the watermarked signal can disable the decoding of the watermark signal. Thus, estimation of the scale factor is required for a proper decoding. Further, since the normalization of the amplitude is usual with the digital audio signals, the scaling attack is important in the audio watermarking application. In the proposed scheme, the scale factor is estimated by employing the EM algorithm. Since the estimation uses the received signal itself, embedding pilot signal is not necessary. It is shown that the proposed scheme can estimate the scale factor accurately under a weak AWGN condition, and yield lower BERs than the conventional case. The numerical results show that the proposed audio watermarking scheme is robust against both the scaling attack and the lossy compression.

References

1. B. Chen and G. W. Wornell. Preprocessed and postprocessed quantization index modulation methods for digital watermarking. In *Proc. SPIE: Security and Watermarking of Multimedia Contents II*, vol. 3971, pages 48–59, San Jose, USA, January 2000.
2. J. J. Eggers, J. K. Su, and B. Girod. A blind watermarking scheme based on structured codebooks. In *Proc. IEE Colloquium*, pages 4/1–4/6, London, UK, April 2000.
3. P. Moulin, M. K. Mihçak, and G. I. Lin. An information-theoretic model for image watermarking and data hiding. In *Proc. IEEE Int. Conf. on Image Proc.*, volume 3, pages 10–13, Vancouver, B. C., September 2000.
4. J. J. Eggers, R. Bäuml, and B. Girod. Estimation of amplitude modifications before SCS watermark detection. In *Proc. SPIE : Multimedia Systems and Applications IV*, volume 4675, pages 387–398, San Jose, USA, January 2002.
5. M. Kesal, M. K. Mihçak, R. Kötter, and P. Moulin. Iterative decoding of digital watermarks. In *Proc. 2nd Symp. on Turbo Codes and Related Topics*, Brest, France, September 2000.
6. J. A. Bilmes. A gentle tutorial on the EM algorithm and its application to parameter estimation for gaussian mixture and hidden markov models. Technical Report ICSI-TR-97-021, University of Berkeley, 1998.
7. ISO/IEC 11172-3. Coding of moving pictures and associated audio for digital storage media at up to about 1.5 Mbit/s, Part 3: Audio 1993.

Semi-fragile Watermarking for Tamper Proofing and Authentication of Still Images

Sang-Jin Han[1], In Su Chang, and Rae-Hong Park

Department of Electronic Engineering, Sogang University, C.P.O. Box 1142
Seoul 100-611, Korea
Atilas2@hanmail.net, cisms@sogang.ac.kr,
rhpark@ccs.sogang.ac.kr

Abstract. In this paper, a novel semi-fragile digital watermarking method for tamper proofing and authentication in the discrete wavelet transform (DWT) domain is proposed. It is a blind algorithm for detection of malicious alterations made on still images. A binary authentication watermark is embedded in the DWT domain of an image, especially in the lower frequency (*LL*) band using block sum quantization (BSQ), which leads to the proposed algorithm tolerant to lossy compression with slight perceptual visual degradation. The proposed algorithm provides information on spatial localization and frequency regions that have been modified. Also, it is possible to detect various alterations made on the host image and to distinguish malicious changes such as replacement/insertion/deletion/forgery from non-malicious changes like lossy compression. Experimental results with various test images show that it is effective for detecting malicious changes, satisfying transparency and robustness to joint photographic experts group (JPEG) and JPEG 2000 compression.

1 Introduction

Development of the digital image and graphics editing software leads to easy manipulations of multimedia contents such as text, audio, graphics, image, and video. Multimedia contents manipulations have inherent problems, for example intentional alterations of contents and forgery of certificates or documents. Thus, nowadays verification of the integrity of the multimedia contents has gained importance in such applications [1]. In this paper, we focus on tamper proofing and authentication of digital still images using digital watermarking.

Digital watermarking is a process of imperceptibly altering multimedia contents by embedding authentication data [2]. It has been developed for copyright protection, fingerprinting, copy control, and content authentication. Generally digital watermarking techniques are classified into perceptible and imperceptible ones [3]. Perceptible watermarks cause noticeable changes in the original image when they are embedded, whereas imperceptible watermarks do not create any perceptible artifacts in the host image. Imperceptible watermarks are divided into robust, fragile, and semi-fragile watermarks. Robust watermarks are embedded in the host image so that removal is

[1] He is currently affiliated with LG Electronics Inc.

T. Kalker et al. (Eds.): IWDW 2003, LNCS 2939, pp. 328–339, 2004.
© Springer-Verlag Berlin Heidelberg 2004

difficult, designed to resist various attacks such as lossy compression, filtering, and geometric distortion. In contrast, fragile watermarks are added to the host image so as to be easily altered or destroyed when the host image is modified through various transformations. Semi-fragile watermarks are appropriately robust: robust to legitimate attacks, but fragile to illegitimate attacks [2]. In this paper, we propose a novel semi-fragile watermarking technique that detects the unauthorized alterations and malicious manipulations.

Until now, a large number of robust watermarking techniques have been proposed, whereas fragile and semi-fragile watermarking techniques have been received less attention. But, image tamper proofing and authentication using fragile or semi-fragile watermarking techniques are very useful and required to verify that no tampering has occurred during transmission [4,5] that can be applied to courtroom evidence [3], journalistic photography [6], commerce [7], and trustworthy camera [8].

Generally, tamper proofing systems require following features to effectively detect malicious modifications in images [9].

- *Tampering detection*: A tamper-proofing scheme should determine with high probability whether an image has been altered or not. This is most fundamental and required to reliably test image authenticity.
- *Detection of modifications*: Authentication watermark data can locate any modifications made on the image.
- *Integration*: An authentication system should embed authentication data into a host image rather than storing them separately as additional information.
- *Perceptual imperceptibility*: An embedded watermark should be perceptually invisible.
- *Blindness*: Because the original image may not exist, a host image is not required.
- *Tolerance to lossy compression*: The embedded watermark should be robust to lossy compression such as JPEG or JPEG 2000.

Therefore tamper proofing systems are not only sensitive to forgery and alterations, but must be tolerant to lossy compression that is unavoidable in various environments.

The rest of the paper is structured as follows. In Section 2 presents the proposed embedding and verification methods using block sum quantization (BSQ) in the band of the DWT domain. In Section 3, simulation results are shown and lastly, in Section 4 conclusions are given.

2 Proposed Algorithm

We propose a novel semi-fragile watermarking technique in the DWT domain for tamper proofing and authentication of still images. Compared to other transform domains, the DWT domain has many advantages. First the wavelet functions have a better space-frequency localization characteristic, thus they provide the capability to localize information both in space and frequency, which makes the wavelet based methods more robust against geometric attacks such as cropping and scaling. Also they are hierarchical and suitable for the human visual system (HVS) and used in JPEG 2000 [10].

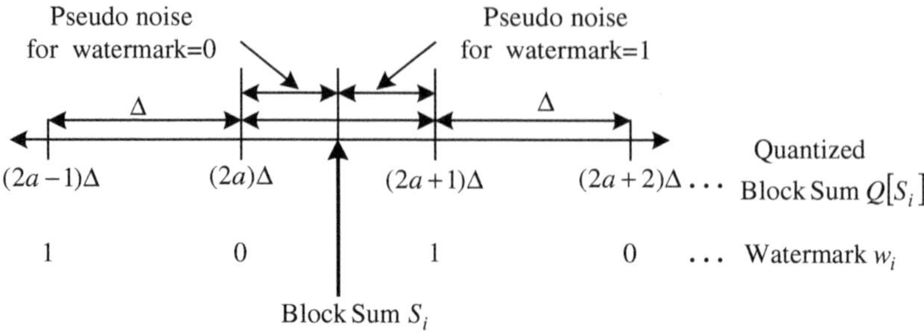

Fig. 1. Experimental results and discussions

2.1 Watermark Embedding in the Lower Frequency Band

A host image can be wavelet decomposed into a number of coefficient subbands in which LH_l, HL_l, HH_l, and LL_L, $1 \le l \le L$, represent the l-th level vertical, horizontal, diagonal, and lower frequency bands, respectively, where L denotes the total number of levels for decomposition. 2-level pyramid structured DWT decomposition $(L = 2)$ [11] is adopted in the proposed method.

Conventional DWT domain methods [3,12] embed watermarks into middle or high frequency bands such as LH_l, HL_l, HH_l bands, $1 \le l \le L = 5$, rather than into lower frequency LL_L bands. They show better perceptual invisibility, since human eyes are less sensitive to middle or higher frequency details. However, since the energy of most images is concentrated on the lower frequency region, the higher frequency components are discarded after quantization in JPEG or JPEG 2000. Thus their methods are not effective in practical network applications, in which data compression such as JPEG or JPEG 2000 is unavoidable. Therefore watermark embedding in the lower frequency region is desirable to survive against JPEG 2000 and JPEG. In this respect, Huang *et al.* embedded a watermark only into the DC components in the DCT domain [13]. However, in general the visual artifact becomes noticeable if the watermark is embedded in lower frequency bands [2]. The proposed method is to improve the previous works that have the trade-off between lossy compression and visual transparency [14]. By embedding watermarks using BSQ in the *LL* band of the DWT, the proposed algorithm minimizes the perceptual artifact. It satisfies the localization property and tolerance to lossy compression such as JPEG 2000 and JPEG. Also it can detect the malicious modifications.

2.2 BSQ in the *LL* Band

The proposed BSQ algorithm for watermark insertion is shown in Fig. 1, in which Δ denotes the quantization level of the block sum and S_i indicates the sum of the *i*th

If $S_i > 0$

$r_i = S_i \bmod \Delta$

$q_i = \text{abs}((S_i - r_i)/\Delta)$

Processing block sum quantization algorithm

else

$r_i = S_i \bmod \Delta + \Delta$

$q_i = \text{abs}((S_i - r_i)/\Delta)$

Processing block sum quantization algorithm

where *block sum quantization algorithm* is

if $q_i \bmod 2 == w_i$

$$B'_{i,k} = B_{i,k} - \text{int}\left(\frac{r_i}{K^2}\right) - 1 \quad \text{if } 0 \le k < r_i \bmod K^2$$

$$B'_{i,k} = B_{i,k} - \text{int}\left(\frac{r_i}{K^2}\right) \quad \text{if } r_i \bmod K^2 \le k < K^2$$

else

$$B'_{i,k} = B_{i,k} - \text{int}\left(\frac{r_i}{K^2}\right) \quad \text{if } 0 \le k < r_i \bmod K^2$$

$$B'_{i,k} = B_{i,k} - \text{int}\left(\frac{r_i}{K^2}\right) + 1 \quad \text{if } r_i \bmod K^2 \le k < K^2$$

Fig. 2. Embedding rules for BSQ

$K \times K$ block data. After block sum S_i is calculated, BSQ is performed using the procedure shown in Fig. 2, where $B_{i,k}$ signifies the *k*th coefficient value in the *i*th block and $B'_{i,k}$ is the watermark embedded coefficient value, with $k \in \{0,1,\dots,K^2-1\}$. In this procedure 1-bit authentication data is embedded in each $K \times K$ block, and the proposed watermark embedding technique is performed in the LL_L band, $1 \le L \le 2$, that contains the important information of an image. Note that the maximum length of watermarks is 4096 bits for a 512×512 image.

The overall procedure of the proposed semi-fragile watermarking technique for image tamper proofing and authentication is shown in Fig. 3. The embedding steps as shown in Fig. 3(a) are described as follows.

Step 1: DWT and initialization

- After the *L*-level DWT decomposition of the host image $f(m,n)$, the LL_L band is divided into $K \times K$ blocks, e.g., $L = 2$ and $K = 2$.
- The author binary watermark w_i, $w_i \in \{0,1\}$, $1 \le i \le N_w$, is generated as many as the number of blocks, where N_w signifies the total watermark length.
- The user-defined quantization level Δ is set to 16.

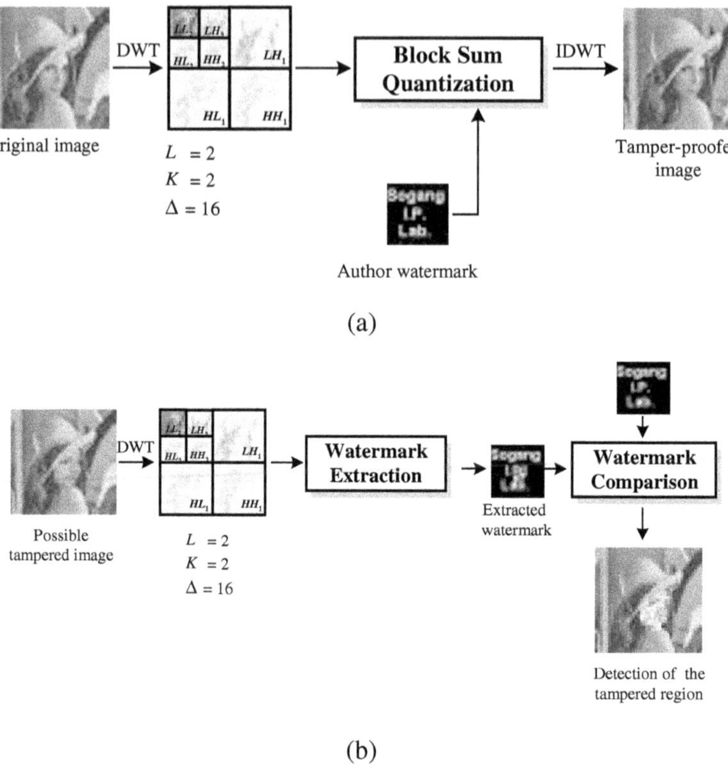

Fig. 3. Block diagram of the proposed tamper proofing procedure. (a) Embedding procedure. (b) Verification procedure

Step 2: Block sum calculation

· Calculate the block sum S_i of the LL_L band wavelet coefficients in each block.

Step 3: Block sum quantization

· By adding the pseudo random noise, the block sum S_i is quantized to $(2a+w_i)\Delta$, where a be an integer.

Step 4: IDWT

· Perform the *L*-level inverse DWT (IDWT) on the watermarked coefficients.

The overall amount of the pseudo random noise N_i to be added to the *i*th block $f_{LL_L,i}(m,n)$ in the LL_L band is represented by the difference between the quantized block sum $Q[S_i]$ and the original block sum S_i

$$N_i = \left|\sum_{m=0}^{K-1}\sum_{n=0}^{K-1} n_i(m,n)\right| = \left|Q[S_i]-S_i\right| = \left|(2a+w_i)\Delta - \sum_{m=0}^{K-1}\sum_{n=0}^{K-1} f_{LL_L,i}(m,n)\right|, \tag{1}$$

where $n_i(m,n)$ is the pseudo random noise to be added to pixel (m,n) in the *i*th block, and $Q[\cdot]$ represents the quantization function.

2.3 Watermark Verification

The watermark verification procedure shown in Fig. 3(b) is described as follows:

Step 1: DWT

· Perform the L-level DWT decomposition on the modified image $\hat{f}(m,n)$ and divide the LL_L band into $K \times K$ blocks, e.g., $L = 2$ and $K = 2$.

Step 2: Watermark extraction

· Extract watermarks by the following procedure rule:

$$\hat{w}_i = \left\lfloor \frac{|\hat{S}_i|}{\Delta} \right\rfloor \bmod 2 = \begin{cases} 0, & \text{if } Q[|\hat{S}_i|] = (2a) \cdot \Delta \\ 1, & \text{if } Q[|\hat{S}_i|] = (2a+1) \cdot \Delta, \end{cases} \tag{2}$$

where $\hat{w}_i$ is an extracted watermark, and $\hat{S}_i$ is the $K \times K$ block sum of the LL_L band wavelet cocfficients, of the possible tampered image, given by

$$\hat{S}_i = \sum_{m=0}^{K-1} \sum_{n=0}^{K-1} \hat{f}_{LL_L,i}(m,n). \tag{3}$$

Step 3: Tamper proofing and authentication

In this procedure, the hidden data are extracted fast. To detect whether tampering has occurred or not, the tamper assessment function (TAF) [3,12] is used, which is defined by

$$TAF(w,\hat{w}) = \frac{1}{N_w} \sum_{i=0}^{N_w-1} w_i \oplus \hat{w}_i, \tag{4}$$

where w is the true embedded watermark, $\hat{w}$ is the extracted watermark, and N_w is the total length of the watermark. The $TAF(w,\hat{w})$ value ranges between 0 and 1. If it is 0 (1), then the modified image is considered to be unchanged (tampered).

3 Experimental Results and Discussions

We evaluate the performance of the proposed tamper proofing and authentication technique in terms of the imperceptibility and tolerance to JPEG and various tampering such as replacement, insertion, deletion, and forgery of specific image regions. First we test the transparency in terms of the peak signal-to-noise ratio (PSNR).

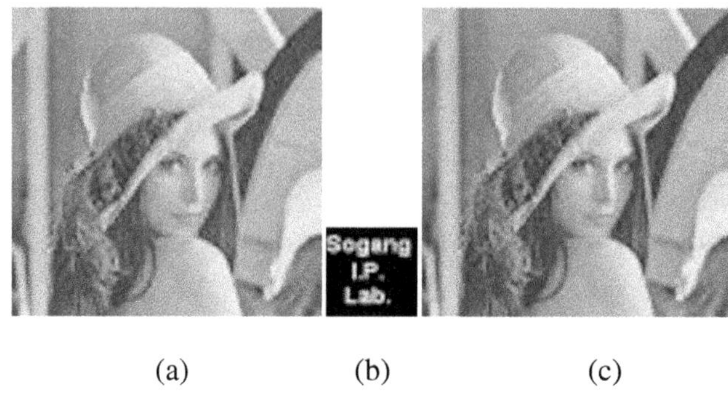

(a) (b) (c)

Fig. 4. Imperceptibility tests. (a) original Lena image. (b) binary authentication image. (c) Tamper-proofed image

Fig. 4 shows the results of the imperceptibility test for the Lena image. Fig. 4(a) is the 512×512 original Lena image quantized to 8 bits used as a host image $(M = N = 512)$. Fig. 4(b) is a 64×64 binary authentication watermark image $(N_w = 4096)$, and Fig. 4(c) is a tamper-proofed image when 2-level wavelet decomposition $(L = 2)$ and $\Delta=16$ are employed. In this case, the PSNR is 40.61dB and we cannot perceptually distinguish the original Lena image from the tamper-proofed watermark embedded image. Fig. 4 shows that the tamper-proofed image satisfies the imperceptibility in terms of the quantitative measure and subjective observation.

The proposed BSQ algorithm can be performed in each of four bands in the DWT domain. In each band, in order to compromise the invisibility, tolerance against JPEG 2000 and JPEG compression, and effective malicious tamper detection, we vary parameters such as the number of decomposition levels, block size, and quantization level.

Table 1 shows the PSNR of the 512×512 Lena and Baboon images for different Δ values. For 1-level decomposition cases $(L=1)$, the block size is set to 4×4 $(K=4)$, whereas 2×2 for 2-level cases. Total of 4096 bits $(N_w = 4096)$ are embedded in each case, with one bit of watermark embedded in each block. Table 1 shows that the smaller (larger) the quantization level, the higher (lower) the PSNR. As expected, watermark embedding in the LH_l, HL_l, HH_l bands, $1 \le l \le L = 2$, gives the PSNR higher than that in the LL_L band. Considering the visual degradation, $\Delta = 32$ and 64 are not suitable when $L = 2$.

Fig. 5 shows the results for JPEG 2000 and JPEG compression with two sets of parameter values: $(L=1, \Delta=64)$ and $(L=2, \Delta=16)$. Figs. 5(a) and 5(b) show the Lena image cases against JPEG 2000. When $\Delta=64$ and $L=1$, performing BSQ in the LL_1 band is most tolerant as shown in Fig. 5(a), and this trend is the same as the cases with $L=2$ and $\Delta=16$, as shown in Fig. 5(b). In the Baboon image cases against JPEG the results shown in Figs. 5(c) and 5(d) are similar to those of the Lena image cases against JPEG 2000. Fig. 5 shows that the LL_L band is most tolerant to JPEG 2000 and JPEG compression, where $L = 1$ or 2. In our experiments, 1- or 2-

Table 1. PSNR performance of the proposed algorithm for different parameter values (unit: dB)

Image	Decomposition level	Subband	Δ			
			8	16	32	64
Lena	L=1	LL_1	53.88	50.97	46.23	40.60
		LH_1	54.45	52.30	49.00	44.25
		HL_1	54.57	52.76	49.53	44.54
		HH_1	55.10	53.55	50.01	44.76
	L=2	LL_2	45.84	40.61	35.09	28.74
		LH_2	47.38	43.11	38.04	32.64
		HL_2	48.06	43.95	38.70	32.86
		HH_2	48.51	44.16	38.80	32.91
Baboon	L=1	LL_1	53.98	50.87	46.22	40.75
		LH_1	53.96	51.26	47.62	43.59
		HL_1	53.77	51.04	46.98	42.99
		HH_1	54.17	51.67	48.33	44.25
	L=2	LL_2	45.96	40.70	34.77	28.87
		LH_2	45.93	41.31	36.43	32.50
		HL_2	45.88	41.21	36.21	31.53
		HH_2	46.27	42.01	37.67	32.77

level wavelet decomposition is used since our watermark length N_w is 4906. For 3-level wavelet decomposition with 512×512 images, the block size is $1 \times 1 (K = 1)$, which is meaningless.

Fig. 6 shows the results for JPEG 2000 and JPEG compression simulations of the proposed algorithm that embeds watermarks only in the LL_L band, where $L = 1$ or 2. Fig. 6(a) shows the JPEG 2000 result whereas Fig. 6(b) indicates the JPEG result. In the case of the Lena image containing both high and low frequency components, when $\Delta = 16$ and $L = 2$, the result is most tolerant to JPEG 2000 compression up to 20:1 compression as shown in Fig. 6(a). Also in the case of the Baboon image containing mostly high frequency components, when $\Delta = 16$ and $L = 2$, the result is most robust to up to 8:1 JPEG compression ratio with small error as shown in Fig. 6(b). From Fig. 6, it is noted that as Δ and L become large, our semi-fragile watermarking method becomes tolerant to JPEG 2000 and JPEG.

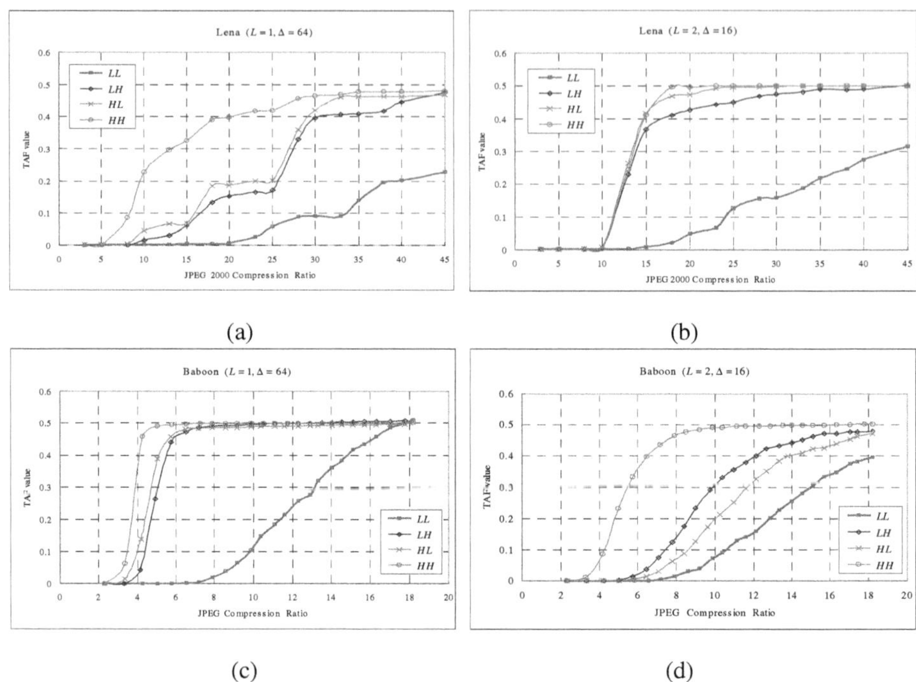

Fig. 5. JPEG 2000 and JPEG compression tests. (a) Lena ($L=1$, Δ =64) against JPEG 2000. (b) Lena ($L=2$, Δ =16) against JPEG 2000. (c) Baboon ($L=1$, Δ =64) against JPEG. (d) Baboon ($L=2$, Δ =16) against JPEG

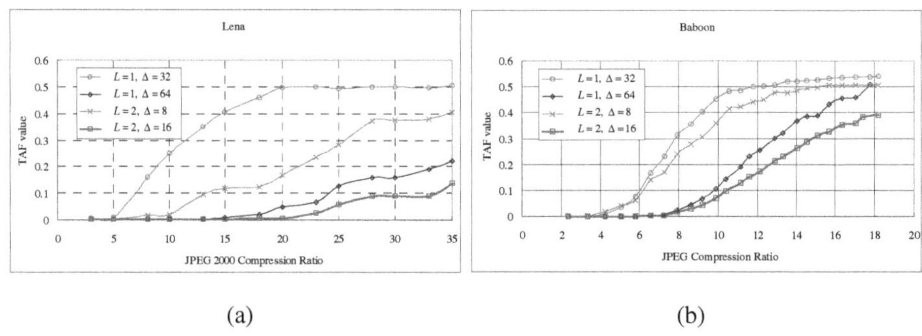

Fig. 6. TAF as a function of the JPEG 2000 and JPEG compression ratio. (a) Lena image against JPEG 2000. (b) Baboon image against JPEG

Table 2 shows the PSNR result of invisibility tests in the LL_L band for various 512×512 Barbara, Couple, Bridge, F16, Pepper, and Sailboat test images. We use the same parameter values shown in Table 1: $L, K,$ and Δ. Considering the trade-off

Table 2. PSNR performance test for the lower frequency bands (unit: dB)

band \ image \ Δ		8	16	32	64
LL_1	Barbara	53.93	50.94	46.19	40.67
	Couple	53.97	50.93	46.16	40.66
	Bridge	53.97	50.92	46.17	40.55
	F16	53.61	50.53	46.08	40.66
	Pepper	53.91	50.89	46.21	40.74
	Sailboat	53.83	50.87	46.19	40.78
LL_2	Barbara	45.91	40.54	34.92	28.93
	Couple	46.08	40.65	37.77	28.80
	Bridge	46.03	40.67	34.74	28.87
	F16	45.51	40.36	34.92	28.37
	Pepper	45.92	40.65	34.87	28.95
	Sailboat	45.89	40.78	34.59	28.61

between the quality of the watermarked image and the tolerance to JPEG 2000 and JPEG compression from Fig. 6 and Table 2, the optimal parameters that satisfy both perceptual transparency and tolerance to JPEG 2000 and JPEG are as follows: the block size is $2\times2\,(K=2)$, block sum quantizatoin step size Δ is 16 with 2-level wavelet decomposition $(L=2)$. We use the same parameters to meet the requirement, however, the user can vary the parameters according to their appropriate applications: for example, small Δ can be used to satisfy good perceptual invisibility and large Δ for tolerance to JPEG 2000 and JPEG.

Fig. 7 shows the detection results of various modifications such as replacement, insertion, deletion, and forgery. Figs. 7(a1)-7(a5) show experiments for object replacement, Figs. 7(b1)-7(b5) for region insertion, Figs. 7(c1)-7(c5) for object deletion, and Figs. 7(d1)-7(d5) for the malicious forgery, which are very likely to occur in practical situations. Figs. 7(a1), 7(b1), 7(c1), and 7(d1) are 512×512 original Lena, Couple, Sailboat, transcript images, respectively. Figs. 7(a2), 7(b2), 7(c2), and 7(d2) are tamper-proofed images with the PSNR equal to 40.61, 40.65, 40.78, and 40.68 dB, respectively. Fig. 7(a3) is a modified image in which a face region is replaced by the original Lena's face, Fig. 7(b3) is an altered image in which a picture frame is inserted, Fig. 7(c3) is a modified image in which a sailboat is deleted, and Fig. 7(d3) is an altered transcript image in which a grade is changed from A_- to A_+ and the CGPA is modified from 3.76 to 3.94. Figs. 7a(4), 7(b4), 7(c4), and 7(d4) are extracted watermark images from which we notice the modified region visually. Figs. 7(a5), 7(b5), 7(c5), 7(d5) show the tampered regions (marked by white pixels)

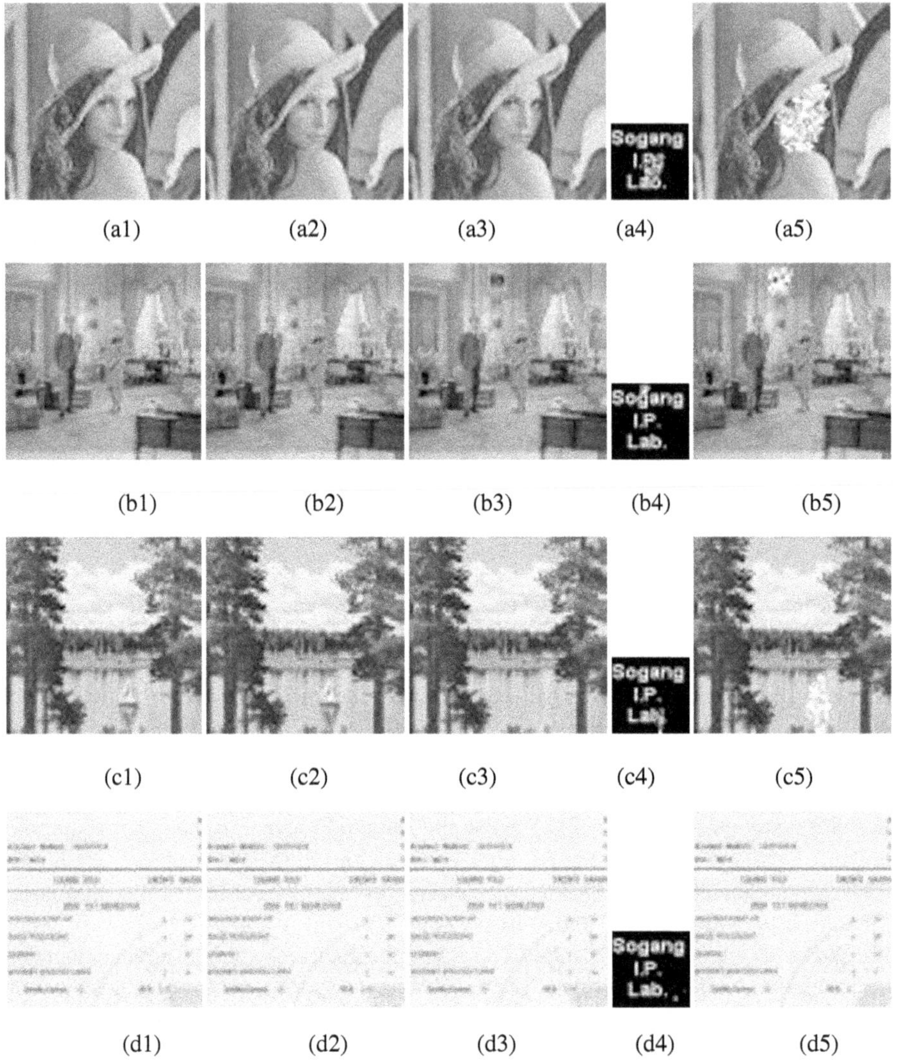

Fig. 7. Tamper detection tests. (a1) Original Lena image. (b1) Original Couple image. (c1) Original Sailboat image. (d1) Original Transcript image. (a2, b2, c2, d2) Tamper-proofed images of (a1, b1, c1, d1). (a3) Tampered image in which a face region is replaced by the original Lena's face. (b3) Changed image in which a picture frame is inserted. (c3) Modified image by deleting a sailboat. (d3) Altered image in which a grade is changed from A_{-} to A_{+} and CGPA is altered from 3.76 to 3.94. (a4, b4, c4, d4) Extracted watermark from (a3, b3, c3, d3). (a5, b5, c5, d5) Detected tampered region

detected from Figs. 7(a3), 7(b3), 7(c3), and 7(d3), respectively. In Fig. 7, the proposed algorithm detects exactly the tampered regions (marked by white pixels) such as a replaced object, inserted area, deleted region, and malicious forgery. Fig. 7 shows that the proposed method can be used widely for various applications.

4 Conclusion

In this paper a novel semi-fragile watermarking algorithm for tamper proofing and authentication of still images has been presented. The proposed watermarking algorithm embeds an authentication binary image by modifying the coefficients in the lower band of an image. Using BSQ in the LL_2 band of the DWT domain, our proposed method satisfies the imperceptibility and robustness to JPEG 2000 and JPEG compression, and correctly detects various image modifications. Experiments with various test images show that the proposed tamper proofing and authentication method shows desirable characteristics. Future work will concentrate on applications of the proposed algorithm to various multimedia contents.

Acknowledgement. This work was supported by the Brain Korea 21 Project.

References

1. Wolfgang, R.B., Podilchuk, C.I., Delp, E.J.: Perceptual watermarks for digital images and video. Proc. IEEE Vol. 87 (1999) 1108-1126
2. Cox, I.J., Miller, M.L., Bloom, J.A.: Digital Watermarking, Morgan Kaufmann, San Francisco (2001)
3. Kundur, D., Hatzinakos, D.: Digital watermarking for telltale tamper proofing and authentication, Proc. IEEE Vol. 87 (1999) 1167–1180
4. Li, C.-T., Lou, D.-C., Chen, T.-H.: Image authentication and integrity verification via content-based watermarks and a public key cryptosystem, Int. Proceedings of the IEEE ICIP Vol. 3 (2000) 694–697
5. Inoue, H., Miyazaki, A., Katsura, T.: Wavelet-based watermarking for tamper proofing of still images, Int. Proceedings of the IEEE ICIP Vol. 2 (2000) 88–91
6. Lin, E.T., Delp, E.J.: A review of fragile image watermarks, Int. Proceedings of the Multimedia and Security Workshop at ACM Multimedia (1999) 36–39
7. Wong, P.W.: A public key watermark for image verification and authentication, Int. Proceedings of the IEEE ICIP Vol. 1 (1998) 455–459
8. Friedman, G.: The trustworthy digital camera. Restoring credibility to the photographic image, IEEE Trans. Consumer Electronics Vol. 39 (1993) 905–910
9. Wu, M., Liu, B.: Watermarking for image authentication, Int. Proceedings of the IEEE ICIP Vol. 2 (1998) 437–441
10. Caramma, M., Lancini, R., Mapelli, F., Tubaro, S.: A blind and readable watermarking technique for color images, Int. Proceedings of the IEEE ICIP Vol. 1 (2000) 442–445
11. Mallat, S.: A Wavelet Tour of Signal Processing, Academic Press, San Diego (1999)
12. Kundur, D., Hatzinakos, D., Towards a telltale watermarking technique for tamper proofing, Int. Proceedings of the IEEE ICIP Vol. 2 (1998) 409–413
13. Huang, J., Shi, Y.Q., Shi, Y.: Embedding image watermarks in DC components, IEEE Trans. Circuits and Systems for Video Technology Vol. 10 (2000) 974–979
14. Chang, I.S., Park, R.-H.: Image retrieval based on data hiding, Int. Proceedings of the SPIE 4314 (2001) 321–328

Secure Video Watermarking via Embedding Strength Modulation

Gwenaël Doërr and Jean-Luc Dugelay

Eurécom Institute
Department of Multimedia Communications
2229, route des Crêtes BP 193
06904 Sophia-Antipolis Cédex, FRANCE
{doerr,dugelay}@eurecom.fr
http://www.eurecom.fr/~image

Abstract. Straightforward adaptations of results for still images watermarking have led to non-secure video watermarking algorithms. The very specific nature of digital video has indeed to be considered so that robustness and security issues are handled efficiently. As a result, a novel video watermarking scheme is presented in this paper: security is achieved by using a smooth time-dependent strength and payload is encoded in the phase difference between several signals transmitted along non-interfering communication channels. Moreover, temporal synchronization can be done in a blind manner on the detector side. The proposed scheme is finally proven to be secure against traditional intra-video collusion attacks and robust against MPEG compression.

1 Introduction

Digital watermarking has been introduced in the 90's as a complementary technology to protect digital multimedia data along its lifetime. Protecting digital data is necessary since it can be copied rapidly, perfectly, at a large scale and without any limitation on the number of copies. Consequently, encryption is usually enforced to render the data useless for people not having the correct decryption key. Nevertheless, encrypted digital data has to be decrypted sooner or later to be finally presented to a human observer/listener. In others terms, encryption protects digital data along its transport but this protection falls during content presentation. As a result, digital watermarking comes as a second line of defense to fill this *analog gap*. It basically embeds a secret invisible and robust watermark, which should be closely tied to the data so that it survives Digital/Analog conversion. This hidden signal encodes a message related to the targeted application: rights associated with the data for copyright protection, client signature for traitor tracing, data signature for authentication. There exists a complex trade-off between several conflicting parameters (*visibility*, *payload*, *robustness*, *security*) and a compromise has to be found which is often tied to the targeted application. The fresh watermarker is redirected towards existing books [1,2] for further insight regarding those issues.

T. Kalker et al. (Eds.): IWDW 2003, LNCS 2939, pp. 340–354, 2004.
© Springer-Verlag Berlin Heidelberg 2004

If digital watermarking has been mostly devoted to still images at the beginning, watermarking other types of multimedia data is now being investigated and digital video is one of those *new objects* of interest. Many applications can indeed benefit from digital watermarking in the context of video [3]. Cinema studios own very high valued video films. However, disseminating them is highly hazardous since released videos are then likely to be freely exchanged on popular peer-to-peer networks, leading thus to a drastic loss of royalties for the majors. Large amounts of money are at stakes and security mechanisms have to be introduced to safeguard the rights of the copyright owners. Digital watermarking has consequently been evocated to enforce copy and playback control [4] in the Digital Versatile Disk (DVD). The upcoming introduction of the digital cinema format also raises some concerns, in particular regarding camcorder capture of the screen [5,6]. As a result, it has been proposed to embed a watermark during show time to identify the cinema and the presentation date and time to be able to trace back the source of the leak in the distribution network. In the same fashion, digital watermarking can be inserted in Pay-Per-View (PPV) and Video-On-Demand (VOD) frameworks [7]. Thus, when an illegal copy is found, the customer who has broken his/her license agreement can be identified and sanctioned. Digital watermarking can also be exploited for broadcast monitoring [8] i.e. to check that video items are effectively broadcasted during their associated booked air time.

To date, video watermarking is mainly considered as an extension of still image watermarking. Some algorithms address the specificities of a compression standard [9,10] or embed a watermark in a three dimensional domain [11,12]. Nevertheless, watermarking digital video content is still regarded most of the time as watermarking a sequence of images. Unfortunately, this straightforward adaptation has led to weak algorithms in terms of security [13,14] i.e. resistance of the watermark against hostile intelligence. Depending on the specifications of the targeted application, such a weakness can be critical. A novel watermarking scheme is consequently presented in this article to address this issue. In Section 2 an original embedding strategy is proposed. It basically consists in encoding the payload in the phase difference between several signals transmitted along non-interfering communication channels. A self-synchronized detection procedure is then described in Section 3. The performances of the system are then evaluated in terms of security (intra-video collusion) and robustness (MPEG compression). Finally, conclusions are drawn and tracks for future work given in Section 5.

2 Watermark Embedding

Hartung and Girod [15] have described one of the pioneer video watermarking systems based on the Spread Spectrum theory [16]. In few words, a pseudo-random watermark encoding the payload is scaled by an embedding strength and added to the video signal. This approach is still used in recent video watermarking schemes. Either a different watermark is embedded in each video frame [17], or the same watermark is embedded in each video frame [8]. Unfortunately, both strategies have been shown to be weak against intra-video collusion attacks [13,14]. As a result, a novel approach based on embedding strength modulation instead of watermark modulation is proposed in Subsection 2.1 so that the inserted watermark is immune against traditional collusion attacks. An application based on sinusoidal modulation is then presented in Subsection 2.2 and a discussion is conducted to show how multibit payload can be obtained.

2.1 Time-Dependent Embedding Strength

To date, video watermarking has mostly inherited from the results obtained for still images and many algorithms rely on the insertion of a spread-spectrum watermark in the luminance channel in a frame by frame fashion. Such approaches can be basically summarized with the following equation:

$$\check{F}_k = F_k + \alpha W_k \quad W_k \sim \mathcal{N}(0,1) \tag{1}$$

where F_k is the kth video frame, $\check{F}_k$ its watermark version and α the embedding strength. The pseudo-random watermark W_k has a normal distribution with zero mean and unit variance and has been pseudo-randomly generated with a secret key K used as a seed. Perceptual shaping can be subsequently introduced to improve the invisibility of the watermark by making for example the embedding strength α dependent of the local content of the frame [18]. On the receiver side, a simple correlation-based detector permits to assert the presence or absence of the watermark.

Depending on the evolution of the embedded watermark W_k in time, two well-known systems can be obtained, each one having its strengths and weaknesses in terms of security. When a different watermark is inserted in each video frame [15,17], averaging successive video frames spreads the watermark signal amongst neighbor frames, which makes the detector fail to detect the underlying hidden signal. On the other hand, if the same watermark is embedded in each video frame, it can be finely estimated and a simple remodulation removes the watermark signal [19]. Both approaches can be regarded as specific cases of a more general framework, where the embedder switches between P orthogonal watermarks [14]. The detector should then be slightly modified to obtain robust performances against traditional intra-video collusion attacks. Nevertheless, such a scheme is potentially weak against an attack, which combines watermark estimation remodulation and vector quantization.

The security issue is consequently not entirely solved and further investigations have to be conducted to securely embed a watermark in a video. Previous approaches basically rely on a modulation of the watermark W_k to achieve security. However, to the best knowledge of the authors, no study has been conducted which considers the temporal modulation of the embedding strength to achieve security as described by the following equation.

$$\check{F}_k = F_k + \alpha_k W \quad W \sim \mathcal{N}(0,1) \tag{2}$$

On the receiver side, each video frame is correlated with the fixed watermark W and the detector checks if the received temporal signal matches the expected α_k.

For security issues, the modulation law should respect some constraints. On one hand, α_k should be zero mean to be immune against the watermark estimation / remodulation attack. On the other hand, α_k should vary smoothly in time to be immune against temporal frame averaging. This approach is further discussed by considering a sinusoidal modulation law in the remaining of the article.

2.2 Achieving Payload with Multiple Sinusoids

For invisibility reasons, the watermarking process should introduce the same distortion in all the video frames, which will not be the case if a single sinusoid is embedded as given by Equation 2. A basic idea consists then in using several watermarks W_i to carry the same sinusoidal signal modulo a phase difference ϕ_i as written below:

$$\check{F}_k = F_k + \alpha \sum_{i=0}^{P-1} \sin\left(\frac{2\pi k}{T\tau} + \phi_i + \phi_r\right) W_i \tag{3}$$

where τ is the frame rate e.g. 25 frames/sec, T the sinusoid period in seconds, ϕ_r a random phase shared by all the W_i's and ϕ_i a phase specific to each W_i. The P watermarks are also orthonormalized with the Gram-Schmidt algorithm [20] to prevent cross-talk on the detector side i.e. $W_i \odot W_j = \delta_i^j$ if $\odot$ denotes the linear correlation and δ the Kronecker delta. The W_i's can be regarded as spatial carrier signals carrying the same temporal signal modulo a phase difference. In other terms, the same signal is transmitted along several non-interfering communication channels with a phase difference between them. The Mean Square Error (MSE) between a video frame of dimension $W \times H$ and its watermarked version is given by:

$$\begin{aligned} MSE_k &= \frac{1}{WH} \sum_{x=1}^{W} \sum_{y=1}^{H} \left[\check{F}_k(x,y) - F_k(x,y)\right]^2 \\ &= \frac{\alpha^2}{WH} \sum_{x=1}^{W} \sum_{y=1}^{H} \left[\sum_{i=0}^{P-1} \sin(2\pi k\rho + \phi_i + \phi_r)\, W_i(x,y)\right]^2 \\ &= \alpha^2 \sum_{i=0}^{P-1} \sin^2(2\pi k\rho + \phi_i + \phi_r) \\ &= \frac{\alpha^2}{2}\left[P - A(k) \sum_{i=0}^{P-1} \cos(2\phi_i) + B(k) \sum_{i=0}^{P-1} \sin(2\phi_i)\right] \end{aligned} \tag{4}$$

where $1/\rho = T\tau$ is the sinusoid period in number of frames, $A(k) = \cos(4\pi k\rho + 2\phi_r)$ and $B(k) = \sin(4\pi k\rho + 2\phi_r)$. In order to make the distortion independent of the temporal index k, it is necessary to chose the ϕ_i's so that both sums in Equation 4 are equal to zero and the Pth roots of unity in $\mathbb{C}$ are good candidates. As a result, the several ϕ_i's can be defined as follows:

$$\forall i \in [1, P-1] \qquad 2\phi_i = \frac{i2\pi}{P} \pmod{2\pi}$$

$$\forall i \in [1, P-1] \quad \phi_i = \frac{i\pi}{P} \quad \text{or} \quad \phi_i = \left(\frac{i}{P}+1\right)\pi \pmod{2\pi} \tag{5}$$

The problem is underconstrained i.e. for each watermark W_i, there are two alternatives to choose the associated phase ϕ_i. This ambiguity will be exploited in the remaining of the article to encode the payload. Depending on the binary value of the ith bit b_i of the payload, a phase can be associated to the ith watermark according to the following equation:

$$\phi_i = \left(\frac{i}{P}+b_i\right)\pi \qquad b_i \in \{0,1\} \tag{6}$$

On the detector side, it will be necessary to estimate the ϕ_i's in a blind manner to obtain back the payload. In other terms, a temporal reference is required and the first sinusoid will be dedicated to that purpose. As a result, b_0 is set to 0 and it is then necessary to use $P+1$ watermarks to transmit a P bits payload. An example of the resulting mixture of sinusoids is shown in Figure 1.

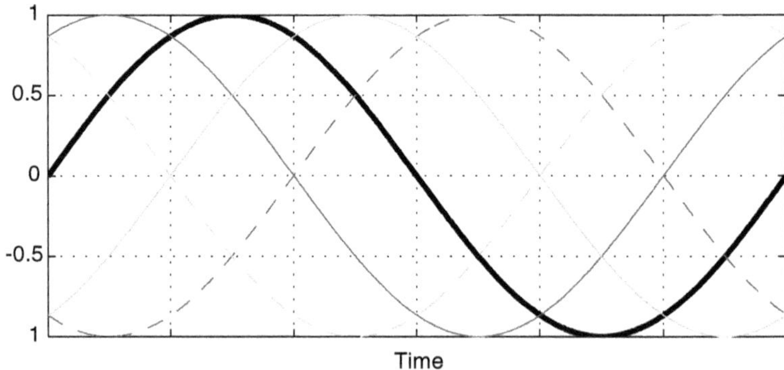

Fig. 1. Example of a mixture of sinusoids for a two bits payload. The bold line will be used for synchronization during detection. Dark (resp. light) gray lines suggest the two possible positions (plain and dash line) of the sinusoid associated with the first (resp. second) bit. Plain lines indicate the positions to encode the payload 01.

Once the ϕ_i's have been set as defined in Equation 6, the watermark embedding process introduces the same distortion in each video frame. The MSE is indeed equal to $\alpha^2 P/2$ according to Equation 4. This relation expresses the traditional trade-off in digital watermarking between payload, distortion and embedding strength, which is often related with robustness. For example, if the MSE is fixed to 9 and the payload to 16 bits, then the embedding strength is determined by the previous relation and should be around 1.

3 Watermark Retrieval

Once a content owner has embedded a secret digital watermark in a video, this later one can be transmitted over a digital network and delivered to customers.

If the content owner finds one day an illegal copy, he/she can check the presence of an underlying watermark and extract the payload to determine the rights associated with this video. This quite novel embedding strategy calls for a new detection procedure. The framework of the detector can be divided in three major modules. In a first step, the several temporally sinusoidal signals transmitted along non-interfering communication channels are extracted (Subsection 3.1). Next, the period of the reference sinusoid is estimated (Subsection 3.2). Finally, the phase differences between the different sinusoids and the reference one are estimated to evaluate the bit carried by each sinusoid (Subsection 3.3).

3.1 Parallel Signal Extraction

As previously pointed out, the embedding process can be regarded as the transmission of the same temporally sinusoidal signal, modulo some phase differences ϕ_i's, along several non-interfering communications channels, whose carrier signals can be assimilated to the watermarks W_i's. The first task of the detector is consequently to separate those several hidden temporal signals. This can be easily done by performing parallel linear correlations between the incoming video frames $\check{F}_k$ and the set of watermarks W_i as follows:

$$\begin{aligned}\beta_i(k) &= \check{F}_k \odot W_i \\ &= F_k \odot W_i + \alpha \sum_{j=0}^{P-1} \sin(2\pi k\rho + \phi_j + \phi_r)\, W_j \odot W_i \\ &= F_k \odot W_i + \alpha \sin(2\pi k\rho + \phi_i + \phi_r) \\ &\approx \alpha \sin(2\pi k\rho + \phi_i + \phi_r)\end{aligned} \tag{7}$$

where $\beta_i(.)$ is the extracted temporal signal associated with the ith watermark W_i. It should be noted that the orthonormalization of the set of watermarks has played a key role to simplify the previous equation. Moreover, it has been assumed that all the video frames have no correlation with each one of the watermarks ($F_k \odot W_i \approx 0$). Since this hypothesis is not necessarily true in practice, a preprocessing step [21] can be introduced before the embedding process which removes any interfering correlation from the original video frames. The obtained temporal signals β_i's are then normalized to have zero mean and a variance equal to 0.5 i.e. the average energy of a sinusoidal signal of amplitude 1 over a period. This normalization allows to compensate some alterations of the transmitted signals and the resulting normalized signals $\bar{\beta}_i(.)$'s should be almost equal to $\sin(2\pi k\rho + \phi_i + \phi_r)$. Thus, this first module outputs P normalized sinusoidal signals $\bar{\beta}_i(.)$ which only differ by some phase differences ϕ_i's. The next two modules will consequently be devoted to the estimation of those phase differences in order to extract the hidden payload.

3.2 Self-Synchronization

The estimation of the several phase differences ϕ_i's will rely on the unbiased cross-correlations between the reference signal $\bar{\beta}_0$ and the other ones. Since those correlations output phase differences in number of frames, it is necessary to estimate the period $1/\rho$ of the sinusoidal signals to get back the phase differences in radians. Even if the period T used during embedding is known on the detector side, it cannot be used directly since the video may have experienced temporal attacks e.g. small increase / decrease of the video speed. The period of the reference signal $\bar{\beta}_0$ should consequently be estimated and the autocorrelation $\bar{\beta}_0 \otimes \bar{\beta}_0$ of this signal is computed, with $\otimes$ the unbiased cross-correlation operator defined as follows:

$$f \otimes g\,(\delta) = \frac{1}{N - |\delta|} \sum_{n=\max(0,-\delta)}^{\min(N,N-\delta)} f(n)\, g(n+\delta) \qquad \delta \in \mathbb{Z} \tag{8}$$

where δ is a varying lag used in the cross-correlation and N the shared length of the signals f and g. Since the reference signal $\bar{\beta}_0$ is expected to be almost sinusoidal, basic trigonometric addition formulas insure that $\bar{\beta}_0 \otimes \bar{\beta}_0\,(\delta) \approx \cos(2\pi\delta\rho)/2$ i.e. the autocorrelation is sinusoidal and has the same period as the reference signal. The estimated period $1/\tilde{\rho}$ is then twice the average distance between two extrema. This estimation is performed on the autocorrelation instead of the extracted reference signal $\bar{\beta}_0$ because it is often far less noisy which facilitates extrema detection.

Such a procedure will always output an estimation of the period $1/\rho$ even if $\bar{\beta}_0$ is not sinusoidal or even periodic e.g. when a video is not watermarked. A matching criterion has consequently to be defined to determine if the extracted reference signal is effectively a sinusoid with a period $1/\tilde{\rho}$ or not. For example, one can compute the cross-correlation between $\bar{\beta}_0$ and a generated sinusoid of period $1/\tilde{\rho}$ with a lag δ varying between 0 and $\lceil 1/\tilde{\rho} \rceil$. The resulting signal is expected to be a period of a cosinusoid oscillating between -0.5 and 0.5. As a result, the maximum value M of this cross-correlation can be compared to a threshold ζ_{match} to assert whether the estimated sinusoidal signal matches the extracted reference one or not. If M is lower than ζ_{match}, the detector assumes that the estimated period $1/\tilde{\rho}$ does not match the periodicity of the extracted reference signal $\bar{\beta}_0$ and reports that no watermark has been detected. Otherwise, the detection procedure continues with the estimated period $1/\tilde{\rho}$. At this point, it should be noted that the detector can estimate the temporal distortions that the video has been subjected to, if it has access to the period $1/\rho$ used during the embedding process.

3.3 Payload Extraction

Once the period of the underlying sinusoidal signals has been estimated, the detector can then performed its final task, which is to estimate the phase differences ϕ_i between the different extracted $\bar{\beta}_i$'s and the reference $\bar{\beta}_o$ to estimate the payload bits b_i. The process will again rely on the unbiased cross-correlation operator. Since the extracted temporal signals are expected to be almost sinusoidal, trigonometric addition formulas insure that $\bar{\beta}_i \otimes \bar{\beta}_0(\delta) \approx \cos(2\pi\delta\rho - \phi_i)/2$.

As a result, the phase difference between the temporal signal carried by W_i and the one carried by W_0 can be estimated according to the following equation:

$$\tilde{\phi_i} = 2\pi\tilde{\rho} \ \arg \max_{\delta \in [0, \lceil 1/\tilde{\rho} \rceil]} \left(\bar{\beta}_i \otimes \bar{\beta}_0(\delta) \right) \tag{9}$$

This estimated $\tilde{\phi_i}$ is then compared with the only two possible phase differences for this specific communication channel given by Equation 6. The detector finally concludes that the bit, associated with the phase difference which is the nearest from the estimated one, has been embedded. This can be mathematically written as follows:

$$\tilde{b_i} = \arg \max_{b \in \{0,1\}} \left(\left| \tilde{\phi_i} - \left(\frac{i}{P} + b \right) \pi \right| \right) \tag{10}$$

As soon as the detector has asserted that the period $1/\rho$ has been correctly estimated, a sequence of bits is extracted in a blind manner, whatever the phase differences ϕ_i are. Whether the estimated $\tilde{\phi_i}$'s are near the phase differences given by Equation 6 or not, this will have no influence at all on the detector and the output result. Reliability measures $\mathcal{R}_i$ should consequently be introduced to indicate how confident the detector is for each estimated bit $\tilde{b_i}$. For example, the absolute difference Δ_i between the estimated phase difference $\tilde{\phi_i}$ and the expected one $\left(\frac{i}{P} + \tilde{b_i}\right)\pi$ can be considered. When this difference Δ_i is around 0, the estimated phase difference is really close to the expected one and the associated reliability should be very high. On the other hand, when Δ_i is around $\pi/2$, the estimated phase difference is almost in the middle of the expected one and the bit $\tilde{b_i}$ should be regarded as unreliable. Several functions can be used to obtain such reliability measures e.g. a triangular function ($\mathcal{R}_i = 1 - 2\Delta_i/\pi$) or a Hanning function ($\mathcal{R}_i = 0.5 + 0.5\cos 2\Delta_i$). Those reliability measures are then averaged to obtain a global reliability score $\mathcal{R}$, which is then then compared to a threshold $\zeta_{reliable}$ to determine if a message has been effectively embedded or not.

4 Performances

Watermarked videos experience various non hostile video processings when they are transmitted on a network: noise addition, frame filtering, chrominance re-sampling (4:4:4, 4:2:2, 4:2:0), lossy compression, transcoding, changes of spatio-temporal resolution (NTSC, PAL, SECAM), etc. Such processings can even be performed by content providers. Moreover, high-valued watermarked videos are also likely to be submitted to strong hostile attacks. Basically, several water-marked contents can be colluded to produce unprotected content [13,14]. Collusion traditionally occurs when a clique of malicious customers gathers together to produce unwatermarked content. That is *inter-videos* collusion i.e. several watermarked video are required to produce unprotected content. Additionally, successive frames of a watermarked video can be regarded as several watermarked images. Thus, a single malicious user can collude several watermarked frames to produce an unprotected video. That is *intra-video* collusion i.e. a watermarked video alone permits to stir out the watermark signal from the video stream. This section will consequently be devoted to the evaluation of the performances of the presented video watermarking algorithm. In particular, Subsections 4.1 and 4.2 will focus on the security of the embedded watermark against two basic intra-video collusion attacks to demonstrate the superiority of the presented algorithm in comparison with previous ones [8,15,17]. Subsequently, the algorithm is also checked to be robust against moderate lossy compression with the popular MPEG standard in Subsection 4.3.

4.1 Temporal Frame Averaging

Digital watermarks are generally localized mostly in high frequencies since the Human Visual System (HVS) is less sensible to noise addition. As a result, one of the earliest proposed attacks to remove hidden watermarks is to apply a low-pass filter to the protected data [22]. Spatial filtering has been investigated extensively and most watermarking algorithms for still images are robust against it today. In the context of video, since neighbor video frames are highly similar, temporal low-pass filtering can be used to obtain an estimate of the original video frames i.e. without the underlying watermark. This can be written:

$$\dot{F}_k = \mathcal{L}_w(E_k), \quad E_k = \{F_{k+d}, -w \leq d \leq w\} \tag{11}$$

where w is half the size of the temporal window, $\mathcal{L}_w$ is the used temporal low-pass filter and $\dot{F}_k$ is the resulting k^{th} attacked video frame. In practice, a simple temporal averaging filter is often used even if non-linear operations can be performed [23]. Previous works [13,14] have shown that such an attack succeeds in trapping video watermarking systems which always embed a different watermark in each video frame [15,17]. This result has to be contrasted with the content of the video scene. Indeed, averaging several successive frames may result in a video of poor quality if fast moving objects are present in the scene or if there is a camera global motion. As a result, this attack is particularly relevant in static shots even if it can be adapted to cope with dynamic ones thanks to frame registration [24].

Now, if a video watermarked with the previously presented scheme is attacked, the following video frames are obtained:

$$\begin{aligned}
\dot{F}_k &= \frac{1}{2w+1} \sum_{d=-w}^{w} \check{F}_{k+d} \\
&= \frac{1}{2w+1} \sum_{d=-w}^{w} F_{k+d} + \frac{\alpha}{2w+1} \sum_{i=0}^{P-1} W_i \sum_{d=-w}^{w} \sin\left(2\pi(k+d)\rho + \phi_i + \phi_r\right) \\
&= \underline{F_k} + \alpha\gamma \sum_{i=0}^{P-1} \sin\left(2\pi k\rho + \phi_i + \phi_r\right) W_i
\end{aligned} \tag{12}$$

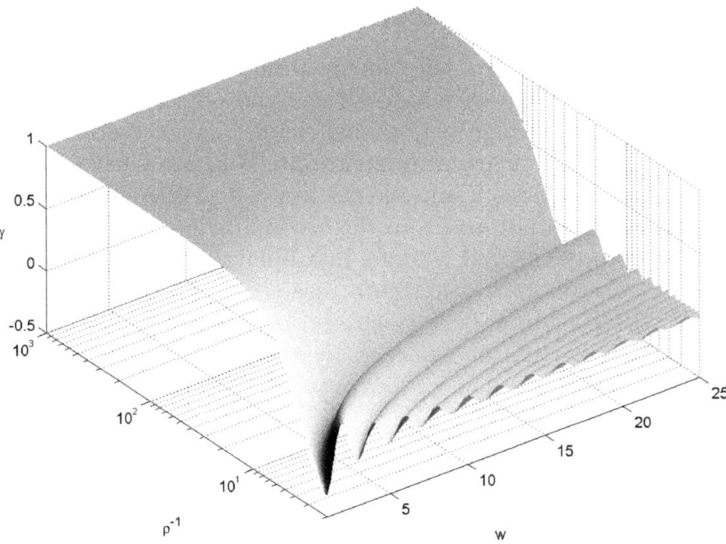

Fig. 2. Variations of the signed attenuation factor γ due to temporal frame averaging with the period of the sinusoid $1/\rho$ and w which is half the size of the temporal window.

where $\underline{F_k}$ is the kth original video frame after temporal frame averaging and $\gamma = \mathrm{sinc}\big((2w+1)\pi\rho\big)/\mathrm{sinc}(\pi\rho)$. Regarding Equation 3, one can notice that temporal frame averaging has basically scaled the watermark signal by a factor γ. Since the absolute value of this scaling factor is always lower than 1, it can be regarded as a signed attenuation factor whose variations are depicted in Figure 2. For a given sinusoid period $1/\rho$, this attenuation factor decreases before oscillating around zero as the temporal window size increases. On the other hand, for a given temporal window size, γ decreases before oscillating around zero as the period $1/\rho$ of the sinusoid decreases. Such a behavior could have been predicted, since the values of the sinusoid are almost equal inside the temporal window when the period of the sinusoid is large. The period $1/\rho$ can consequently be chosen in such a way that the attenuation factor γ is always higher than a given value γ_{lim} as long as the temporal window size is below a given value w_{max}. For example, a content provider can estimate that the watermark is not required to survive if more than 11 successive frames are averaged ($w_{max} = 5$) since the resulting video has very poor visual quality. As a result, if the period $1/\rho$ is chosen to be greater than 30, then the attenuation factor γ is guaranteed to be always greater than 0.8. In other terms, the parameters w_{max} and γ_{lim} give a lower bound for the period of the sinusoid. Thus, temporal frame averaging only results in a relatively small attenuation of the hidden temporal signal and experiments have shown that the detector can counterbalance it thanks to the normalization.

4.2 Watermark Estimation Remodulation

When all the video frames carry the same watermark, the attacker can estimate the embedded watermark in each video frame and obtain a refined estimation of the watermark by combining (e.g. taking the average) those different estimations [13]. The ideal watermark estimator consists in computing the difference between a watermarked video frame and the associated original one. However, in practice, an attacker has not access to the original video frames and the watermark estimation process should be done in a blind manner. Previous work [19] has been done to estimate a watermark inserted in an image. As previously mentioned, a digital watermark is generally localized in high frequencies and a reasonable estimation can be obtained by computing the difference between a watermarked video frame and its low-pass filtered version[1]. As a result, the estimated watermark is given by:

$$\tilde{W}_T = \frac{1}{T}\sum_{n=1}^{T}\left[\check{F}_{\psi(n)} - \mathcal{L}(\check{F}_{\psi(n)})\right] \tag{13}$$

where T is the number of combined watermark estimations and $\mathcal{L}(.)$ a spatial low-pass filter. The mapping function $\psi(.)$ indicates that the frames providing an estimation of the watermark are not necessarily adjacent. Once the embedded watermark has been estimated, it is subtracted from each watermarked video frame $\check{F}_t$ with a remodulation strength β. In practice, an attacker sets this remodulation strength so that the visual distortion introduced by the attack is equal to the one introduced by the watermark embedding process. As a result, the following attacked video frames are obtained:

$$\dot{F}_k = \check{F}_k - \sqrt{\frac{MSE_{embed}}{\tilde{W}_T \odot \tilde{W}_T}}\,\tilde{W}_T \tag{14}$$

Previous work [13,14] has shown that this attack is particularly efficient against video watermarking schemes which always embed the same watermark [8]. Furthermore, the more the video frames are different, the more each individual watermark estimate refines the final one. In other terms, this attack is more efficient in dynamic scenes.

In the context of the watermarking scheme presented in Section 2, such an attack is doomed to fail since there is more than a single watermark to be estimated. Assuming that the attacker has access to the perfect watermark estimator $\check{F}_k - F_k$, the resulting estimated watermark will be a linear combination of the several W_i's as written below:

$$\tilde{W}_T = \sum_{i=1}^{P-1}\left(\frac{\alpha}{T}\sum_{n=1}^{T}\sin\left(2\pi\psi(n)\rho + \phi_i + \phi_r\right)\right)W_i = \sum_{i=1}^{P-1}\lambda_i(T)W_i \tag{15}$$

[1] In practice, some samples are badly estimated e.g. around the edges and in textured regions. An additional thresholding operation can consequently be performed to remove those non-pertinent samples.

If the frames providing the individual estimates are chosen randomly, then the coefficients $\lambda_i(T)$ are drawn from a truncated Gaussian distribution with zero mean and a variance equal to $\alpha^2/2T$. In other terms, the more video frames are considered, the more the λ_i's are close to zero. Since the attacker has not access to the perfect watermark estimator, each watermark estimation is noisy and accumulating several watermark estimations decreases the power of the watermark signal. Thus, combining several individual watermark estimates hampers the final estimation of the embedded watermark, which is in complete contradiction with the paradigm behind the original attack and experiments have shown that the embedded watermark is completely immune to the watermark estimation remodulation attack. Nevertheless parameters need to be chosen cautiously to prevent new security breaches. First the period $1/\rho$ of the sinusoid should remain secret or pseudo-secret. Otherwise the attacker would be able to separate the video frames in distinct sets of frames carrying the same watermark. Then he/she would only have to perform a simple watermark estimation remodulation attack on each set to remove the watermark. Moreover, the period $1/\rho$ should not be an integer. Otherwise, the attacker may be able to perform an attack based on watermark estimations clustering [14]. In the best case, $1/\rho$ should be chosen irrational ($\mathbb{R} - \mathbb{Q}$) so that a given mixture of sinusoidal coefficients is never used twice.

4.3 MPEG Compression

One hour of a video coded at 25 frames per second, with a frame size of 704×576 and pixels coded with 3 bytes, requires around 100 Gbytes for storage. In practical video storage and distribution systems, video sequences are consequently stored and transmitted in a compressed format. As a result, the behavior of the presented watermarking scheme against lossy compression, and in particular against MPEG-2 compression, has been investigated. Video sequences of 375 frames of size 704×576 at 25 frames per second have been watermarked with the embedding algorithm presented in Section 2 before being compressed with a freely available MPEG-2 encoder at 6 Mbits/s with a GOP of 12 (IBBPBBPBBPBBI) with default parameters. Figure 3 depicts one of the extracted sinusoids before and after the lossy compression in a given video sequence. First of all, it should be noted that the hidden sinusoid has been globally attenuated, which is a well-known behavior of spread-spectrum watermarks facing low-pass filtering or DCT coefficients quantization. However, this attenuation is stronger in dynamic scenes (frames 0-80 and 331-374) than in static shots (frames 80-330). This can be explained by the fact that more bits are allocated to motion vectors in dynamic scenes, thus reducing the number of bits allocated to details i.e. the hidden watermark located in high frequencies. Furthermore, it should be noted that the attenuation factor seems to be dependent of the MPEG frame type (I, P or B). In fact, the zoomed area reveals that the watermark signal is more attenuated in B frames than in P or I ones, which could have been expected since B frames are predicted from P frames, which are themselves predicted from I frames. In few words, MPEG compression basically more or less attenuates the hidden signal depending of the content of the scene with a factor which is dependent of the MPEG frame type. As a result, the *shape* of the hidden signal is slightly altered. Nevertheless, the detector estimates the several phase differences from the cross-correlated signal which is far much smoother and experiments have shown that the detector still succeeds in extracting the payload with a good confidence score (95%). Of course, the more periods of the sinusoid are considered for detection, the smoother are the cross-correlated signals and the more accurate is the detection.

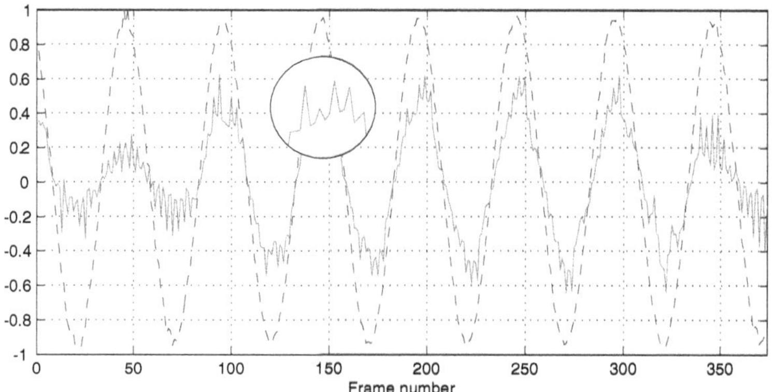

Fig. 3. Visualization of a given embedded sinusoid before (dashed line) and after (plain line) MPEG compression with the video sequence *pingpong*.

5 Conclusions and Perspectives

Digital video watermarking has mostly relied for the moment on direct adaptations of results for still image i.e. a video clip is regarded as a sequence of still images, which are watermarked with either an *embed always the same watermark* strategy, or an *embed always a different watermark* one. Unfortunately, such extensions have opened security breaches, in particular against collusion attacks. An innovative embedding strategy based on embedding strength modulation has consequently been presented in this paper to achieve security: the detector only considers a finite set of pseudo-random watermarks while the attacker views the video frames as carrying each one a different watermark. Furthermore, a moderate payload has been hidden in the video by introducing some phase differences between several non-interfering communication channels carrying the same temporal signal. Finally, this approach has been proven to be secure against traditional intra-video collusion attacks. It has also been shown to be robust against moderate MPEG compression and future work will evaluate the robustness of the algorithm against other non-hostile attacks.

Security against collusion has been notably enhanced with the proposed approach in comparison with previous systems. However, it can still be broken by an attacker with a higher level of expertise. First, the attacker can try to estimate the scene background, e.g. via video mosaicing [24], and then to generate a video similar to the original one from this estimated scene. Alternatively, it can be noticed that, for a given secret key, the inserted watermarks always lie in the same low dimensional subspace $\mathcal{W}$ generated by the W_i's. As a result, an attacker can estimate $\mathcal{W}$, e.g. by computing the PCA of the several individual watermark estimates obtained from each frame, and remove the part of the frame projected on this subspace. As a result, *informed coding* should be investigated to make the watermarks spread all over the watermarking space and not only a low dimensional subspace of it.

References

1. Katzenbeisser, S., Petitcolas, F.: Information Hiding: Techniques for Steganography and Digital Watermarking. Artech House (1999)
2. Cox, I., Miller, M., Bloom, J.: Digital Watermarking. Morgan Kaufmann Publishers (2001)
3. Doërr, G., Dugelay, J.-L.: A guide tour of video watermarking. Signal Processing: Image Communication **18**(4) (2003) 263–282
4. Bloom, J., Cox, I., Kalker, T., Linnartz, J.-P., Miller, M., Traw, C.: Copy protection for DVD video. Proceedings of the IEEE **87**(7) (1999) 1267–1276
5. Haitsma, J., Kalker, T.: A watermarking scheme for digital cinema. In: Proceedings of the IEEE International Conference on Image Processing. Volume 2. (2001) 487–489
6. Bloom, J.: Security and rights management in digital cinema. In: Proceedings of the IEEE International Conference on Acoustics, Speech, and Signal Processing. Volume IV. (2003) 712–715
7. Griwodz, C., Merkel, O., Dittmann, J., Steinmetz, R.: Protecting VoD the easier way. In: Proceedings of the ACM Multimedia Conference. (1998) 21–28
8. Kalker, T., Depovere, G., Haitsma, J., Maes, M.: A video watermarking system for broadcast monitoring. In: Proceedings of SPIE 3657, Security and Watermarking of Multimedia Contents. (1999) 103–112
9. Jordan, F., Kutter, M., Ebrahimi, T.: Proposal of a watermarking technique for hiding/retrieving data in compressed and decompressed video. In: JTC1/SC29/WG11 MPEG97/M2281, ISO/IEC (1997)
10. Langelaar, G., Lagendijk, R., Biemond, J.: Real-time labelling of MPEG-2 compressed video. Journal of Visual Communication and Image Representation **9**(4) (1998) 256–270
11. Deguillaume, F., Csurka, G., Ó Ruanaidh, J., Pun, T.: Robust 3D DFT video watermarking. In: Proceedings of SPIE 3657, Security and Watermarking of Multimedia Contents. (1999) 113–124
12. Swanson, M., Zhu, B., Tewfik, A.: Multiresolution scene-based video watermarking using perceptual models. IEEE Journal on Selected Areas in Communications **16**(4) (1998) 540–550
13. Su, K., Kundur, D., Hatzinakos, D.: A novel approach to collusion resistant video watermarking. In: Proceedings of SPIE 4675, Security and Watermarking of Multimedia Contents IV. (2002) 491–502

14. Doërr, G., Dugelay, J.-L.: Switching between orthogonal watermarks for enhanced security against collusion in video. Technical Report RR-03-080, Eurécom Institute (2003)
15. Hartung, F., Girod, B.: Watermarking of uncompressed and compressed video. Signal Processing **66**(3) (1998) 283–301
16. Pickholtz, R., Schilling, D., Millstein, L.: Theory of spread spectrum communications - a tutorial. IEEE Transactions on Communications **30**(5) (1982) 855–884
17. Mobasseri, B.: Exploring CDMA for watermarking of digital video. In: Proceedings of SPIE 3657, Security and Watermarking of Multimedia Contents. (1999) 96–102
18. Voloshynovskiy, S., Herrigel, A., Baumgärtner, N., Pun, T.: A stochastic approach to content adaptive digital image watermarking. In: Proceedings of the Third International Workshop on Information Hiding (LNCS 1768). (1999) 211–236
19. Voloshynovskiy, C., Pereira, S., Herrigel, A., Baumgärtner, N., Pun, T.: Generalized watermarking attack based on watermark estimation and perceptual remodulation. In: Proceedings of SPIE 3971, Security and Watermarking of Multimedia Contents II. (2000) 358–370
20. Cohen, H.: A Course in Computational Algebraic Number Theory. Springer-Verlag (1993)
21. Cox, I., Miller, M.: Preprocessing media to facilitate later insertion of a watermark. In: Proceedings of the International Conference on Digital Signal Processing. Volume 1. (2002) 67–70
22. Kutter, M., Petitcolas, F.: A fair benchmark for image watermarking systems. In: Proceedings of SPIE 3657, Security and Watermarking of Multimedia Contents. (1999) 226–239
23. Zhao, H., Wu, M., Wang, Z., Liu, K.: Non-linear collusion attacks on independent fingerprints for multimedia. In: Proceedings of the IEEE International Conference on Acoustics, Speech, and Signal Processing. Volume V. (2003) 664–667
24. Doërr, G., Dugelay, J.-L.: New intra-video collusion attack using mosaicing. In: Proceedings of the IEEE International Conference on Multimedia and Expo. Volume II. (2003) 505–508
25. Kutter, M.: Watermarking resisting to translation, rotation and scaling. In: Proceedings of SPIE 3528, Multimedia Systems and Applications. (1998) 423–431
26. Herrigel, A., Voloshynovskiy, S., Rytsar, Y.: The watermark template attack. In: Proceedings of SPIE 4314, Security and Watermarking of Multimedia Contents III. (2001) 394–405

On the Insecurity of Non-invertible Watermarking Schemes for Dispute Resolving

André Adelsbach[1], Stefan Katzenbeisser[2]*, and Ahmad-Reza Sadeghi[3]

[1] Saarland University, Department of Computer Science, D-66123 Saarbrücken, Germany, adelsbach@cs.uni-sb.de
[2] Technische Universität München, Institute for Informatics, D-85748 Garching bei München, Germany, skatzenbeisser@acm.org
[3] Ruhr-Universität Bochum, Chair for Communication Security, D-44780 Bochum, Germany, asadeghi@crypto.ruhr-uni-bochum.de

Abstract. Robust watermarking is an important and powerful technology with several applications in the field of copyright protection. Watermarking schemes were proposed as primitives for dispute resolving schemes and direct proofs of authorship. However, it was shown that watermark-based dispute-resolving schemes are vulnerable to inversion attacks where an adversary exploits the invertibility property of the underlying watermarking scheme to lead the dispute-resolving mechanism to a deadlock. One of the proposed countermeasures is to make watermarking schemes "non-invertible" by incorporating cryptographic primitives, such as one-way functions, into the watermark embedding process. However, this solution ignores the fact that the security strongly depends on the false-positives probability of the underlying watermarking scheme, i.e., the probability to find a detectable watermark which has never been embedded into the considered content.
In this paper, we analyze the impact of the false-positives rate on the security of dispute-resolving applications that use "non-invertible" watermarking schemes. We introduce a general framework for non-invertibility and show that previous constructions based on cryptographic one-way functions, such as [6,11], are insecure, if the false-positive rate is non-negligible.

1 Introduction

The rapid growth of the Internet as a distribution medium for digital goods increased the risk of copyright infringements. From an economic point of view, this risk makes the commercialisation of digital works difficult, if not impossible. Therefore, the need for technical copyright protection solutions has increased steadily over the last years.

Robust digital watermarking is a promising technology in the context of copyright protection and was proposed as a central building block in dispute-resolving schemes, proofs of authorship, copy protection systems or fingerprinting.

* This work was performed while the author was visiting the Otto-von-Guericke Universität Magdeburg, Germany.

T. Kalker et al. (Eds.): IWDW 2003, LNCS 2939, pp. 355–369, 2004.
© Springer-Verlag Berlin Heidelberg 2004

When using digital watermarking schemes in such applications, it is important to consider the statistical properties of the watermark detector and assess their impact on the overall security of the application. In contrast to cryptographic primitives, whose strengths and limitations are well-known, there is currently no adequate theory of security for watermark detectors.

Dispute-resolving protocols form important applications of watermarking schemes and aim at resolving authorship-disputes, where two or more parties, called *authorship disputants*, claim to be the rightful author of a *disputed work* W_{dis}. There are numerous proposals for dispute-resolving schemes by means of watermarking. Early proposals, such as [7,9,10], focused on developing robust watermarking schemes and treated authorship disputes in a rather informal and simplistic way. The common belief was that embedding the author's identity as a watermark into all his works prior to publication and proving the presence of this watermark later in some disputed work would be sufficient for the author to prove rightful authorship.

Later, Craver et al. [6] investigated the process of watermark-based dispute resolving in more detail and demonstrated that previous proposals are insecure by showing that many watermarking schemes are *invertible*. Given a work W, an inversion attack attempts to compute a fake original work, a fake watermark and a fake watermarking key such that this watermark is detectable in W and also in the rightful author's original work. An attacker can exploit inversion attacks to fake proof tokens, which hinder disputes from being resolved.

As a solution to this problem, Craver et al. [6] proposed cryptographic constructions for making watermarking schemes *non-invertible* and argued that such non-invertible schemes would be sufficient for dispute resolving. The basic idea of these proposals is to compute the watermark or the watermarking-key in a one-way manner from the original work. The authors argued that these systems are more secure, as an attacker would have to invert the one-way function in order to compute a suitable fake original, fake watermark and fake watermarking-key.

Since the work of Craver et al. there are two main approaches in the context of dispute resolving. The first one follows the idea of Craver et al. and focuses on dispute resolving solely by means of non-invertible watermarking schemes [16,11,14]. Here, the main goal is to construct non-invertible watermarking schemes from standard (invertible) watermarking schemes by applying cryptographic primitives, such as digital signatures and one-way functions, to the watermark- or key-generation. The second approach involves the use of trusted third parties, such as registration or timestamping authorities, which works even with invertible watermarking schemes [15,8,2].

In this paper we analyze the first approach, namely the construction of non-invertible watermarking schemes and their use in dispute resolving. In particular, we discuss the impact of the watermarking scheme's false-positives rate on the security of the non-invertibility construction and that of the overall dispute-resolving process.

Ramkumar and Akansu [13] introduced an attack against the construction of Craver et al. [6], which works because of the non negligibility of the false-positives probability. Our contribution is an extension of their work in [13]. We introduce a general framework for non-invertibility constructions, which fits most of the previous constructions. We show that such non-invertibility constructions, which uses cryptographic one-way functions to compute a watermark and watermarking key from the original work, an identity string and an optional cryptographic key, are insecure unless the false-positives rate of the watermarking scheme is very small (negligible in the security parameter). This is a substantial result, as, firstly, most of the previous proposals for dispute resolving followed this general non-invertibility construction principle and, secondly, known robust watermarking schemes tend to have comparatively large false-positives probabilities.[1]

Loosely speaking, the insecurity in presence of a large false-positives probability is due to the fact that an attacker does not have to invert the cryptographic one-way function. Instead, he can mount an iterative attack, which consists of deriving some "fake" original by adding a small random error-vector to the disputed work, computing the corresponding fake watermark and fake watermarking-key and checking whether the computed data forms a false-positive of the disputed work. If the false-positives rate of the watermarking scheme is non-negligible, this iterative attack is polynomial (efficient). Further contributions of this paper are rigorous computational definitions of positives probabilities and invertible watermarking schemes. This type of definition is standard in cryptographic security proofs and may be a suitable basis for rigorous security proofs of watermarking schemes as well.

In Section 2 we give the necessary formal definitions of watermarking schemes, dispute-resolving schemes, (false-)positives probabilities and invertibility attacks. In Section 3 we summarize some previously proposed non-invertibility constructions and introduce a general framework, in which most previous proposals fit. Furthermore, we show that this general construction, and consequently the corresponding concrete instantiations, are insecure if the (false-)positives rate of the underlying watermarking scheme is non-negligible. Finally, we address future research topics in Section 4.

2 Basic Definitions and Conventions

We denote the set of all works, watermarks and watermarking-keys with $\mathcal{W}$, $\mathcal{WM}$ and $\mathcal{K}$ respectively. We assume the existence of a similarity function $sim()$: $\mathcal{W} \times \mathcal{W} \rightarrow \{\top, \bot\}$, that, given two works W_1 and W_2, outputs $\top$ iff W_1 is perceptibly similar to W_2.

For an algorithm $\mathtt{M}$, $[\mathtt{M}()]$ denotes the set of all output values of algorithm $\mathtt{M}()$, which occur with non-zero probability and $\leftarrow [\mathtt{M}()]$ denotes sampling an output according to the probability distribution resulting from $\mathtt{M}()$. Furthermore, $s \in_R \mathcal{S}$ for a set $\mathcal{S}$ denotes the uniform and random selection of an element s of $\mathcal{S}$ and $|\mathcal{S}|$ denotes the cardinality of $\mathcal{S}$. Finally, $\mathbf{Prob}[\mathsf{pred}(v_1, \ldots, v_n) :: \mathsf{assign}(v_1, \ldots, v_n)]$ denotes the probability that the predicate pred holds when the probability is

[1] For instance in watermarking schemes with correlation-based detector the robustness and the negligibility of the false-positives rate are conflicting requirements.

taken over a probability space defined by the formula assign on the n free variables v_i of the predicate pred. For example, $\mathbf{Prob}[v \equiv 0 \pmod 2 :: v \leftarrow_R \mathbb{Z}_n]$ denotes the probability that a random element of $\mathbb{Z}_n$ is even.[2]

We call a function $f(k)$ *negligible* if the inverse of any polynomial is asymptotically an upper bound, i.e., $\forall d > 0\ \exists k_0\ \forall k > k_0 : f(k) < 1/k^d$. We denote this by $f(k) <_\infty 1/\mathtt{poly}(k)$. A function $f(k)$ is called *non-negligible* if it can be asymptotically lower bounded by the inverse of some polynomial, i.e., $\exists d>0\ \exists k_0\ \forall k>k_0 : f(k) \geq 1/k^d$. We denote this by $f(k) \geq_\infty 1/\mathtt{poly}(k)$.[3]

2.1 Watermarking Schemes

A (detecting) watermarking scheme consists of four polynomial-time algorithms:

- *Generation algorithms*: On input of the security parameters $par^{\mathtt{wm}}_{sec}$, the probabilistic key generation algorithm $\mathtt{GenKey}(par^{\mathtt{wm}}_{sec})$ generates the keys $(K^{\mathtt{emb}}, K^{\mathtt{det}})$ required for watermark embedding and detection. The watermark generating algorithm $\mathtt{GenWM}(par^{\mathtt{wm}}_{sec})$ generates the watermark WM.
- *Embedder*: On input of the cover-work W, the watermark WM to be embedded and the embedding key $K^{\mathtt{emb}}$, the embedding algorithm $\mathtt{Embed}(W, WM, K^{\mathtt{emb}})$ outputs the watermarked work (*stego-work*) W'.
- *Detector*: On input of a (possibly modified) stego-work W'', the watermark WM, the original cover-work W, also called *reference-work*, and the detection key $K^{\mathtt{det}}$, the detection algorithm $\mathtt{Detect}(W'', WM, W, K^{\mathtt{det}})$ outputs a boolean value $ind \in \{\top, \bot\}$. Here, $\top$ indicates the presence and $\bot$ the absence of the watermark.

An ideal detecting watermarking scheme is a tuple $(\mathtt{GenKey}(), \mathtt{GenWM}(), \mathtt{Embed}(), \mathtt{Detect}())$ such that $\forall W \in \mathcal{W}, \forall WM \in [\mathtt{GenWM}()], \forall (K^{\mathtt{emb}}, K^{\mathtt{det}}) \in [\mathtt{GenKey}()]$:

$$W' = \mathtt{Embed}(W, WM, K^{\mathtt{emb}}) \implies \mathtt{Detect}(W', WM, W, K^{\mathtt{det}}) = \top \wedge sim(W', W) = \top.$$

We call this scheme *ideal*, because it assumes that watermark embedding and detection is successful for all (watermarked) works, watermarks and keys and ignores error-probabilities. However, in the rest of the paper we work with *robust* watermarking schemes, which have a negligible false-negative probability, implicitly bounded by the robustness requirement (see below). We postpone the discussion of (false-)positives probabilities to Section 2.3.

We call a watermarking scheme *symmetric* iff $K^{\mathtt{det}} = K^{\mathtt{emb}}$ and in this case, we usually denote this key as $K^{\mathtt{wm}}$. *Blind* watermarking schemes do not require the cover-work W as an input to $\mathtt{Detect}()$. In the remainder of this paper, we

[2] This notion is standard to define error- and success-probabilities of attackers in cryptography. We will apply this formalism in the context of watermarking schemes and dispute resolving.

[3] Note that "not negligible" is *not* the same as "non-negligible", as there are functions which are neither negligible nor non-negligible.

restrict ourselves to non-blind symmetric watermarking schemes. However, we want to stress that our definitions and attacks can be easily adapted to blind and asymmetric watermarking schemes.

Robust Watermarking Schemes. A *robust* watermarking scheme can detect watermarks even if the underlying digital work has been (maliciously) modified, as long as the work is perceptibly similar to the cover-work. More formally, a watermarking scheme is called *computationally robust*, iff

$$\forall W \in \mathcal{W}, \forall WM \in \mathcal{WM}, \forall \text{ probabilistic polynomial-time attacker } \mathtt{A}$$

$$\begin{aligned}
&\textbf{Prob}[\mathtt{Detect}(W'', WM, W, K^{\mathtt{wm}}) = \bot \wedge sim(W'', W') = \top :: \\
&\quad K^{\mathtt{wm}} \leftarrow [\mathtt{GenKey}(par^{\mathtt{wm}}_{sec})]; \\
&\quad W' = \mathtt{Embed}(W, WM, K^{\mathtt{wm}}); \\
&\quad W'' \leftarrow [\mathtt{A}(W', par^{\mathtt{wm}}_{sec})]; \\
&\ ] \\
&<_{\infty} 1/\mathtt{poly}(par^{\mathtt{wm}}_{sec})
\end{aligned}$$

This definition resembles computational security requirements of cryptographic primitives, such as encryption schemes. Note, however, that currently no watermarking scheme fulfills this ideal computational robustness definition. Nevertheless, it is a suitable abstraction (similar to the marking assumption in fingerprinting [4]) which can be used to design applications, such as dispute-resolving protocols. Furthermore, we want to stress that the robustness definition, especially the input available to the attacker $\mathtt{A}$, depends on context of the targeted application.

2.2 Dispute Resolving

In this section we give a short summary of authorship disputes and the general approach for resolving authorship disputes with non-invertible watermarking schemes. For a more formal and detailed discussion of dispute resolving schemes and strategies for proving authorship in disputes we refer to [2].

An authorship-dispute between two disputants C_1 and C_2 about a disputed work W_{dis} is a scenario where C_1 and C_2 claim to be the exclusive rightful authors of W_{dis}. Informally, the goal of a dispute-resolving scheme is to allow a third party, the *dispute resolver* D, to resolve authorship-disputes in a "fair" way, by comparing the authorship proof tokens presented by the disputants.

A *dispute-resolving scheme* consists of three protocols: the first protocol **Initialize**() initializes the whole system. This may, among other things, comprise generating cryptographic keys and the authentic distribution of necessary public keys. The second protocol is the preparation protocol **Prepare**() in which the rightful author, say C_1, prepares a newly created original work W_1, prior to its publication, for possibly arising disputes. As an output of this protocol, the rightful author C_1 receives a tuple $(W_1', proof_{C_1,W_1})$. Here, W_1' is a possibly modified (e.g. watermarked) version of W_1 and $proof_{C_1,W_1}$ is a proof token, which C_1 can use to prove his rightful authorship in subsequent disputes for works W_{dis}, derived from W'_1. The third protocol is the actual dispute-resolving protocol Resolve(), where the two disputants C_1, C_2 input their proof tokens. This protocol allows the dispute resolver D to resolve the authorship-dispute for the disputed work W_{dis}.

The basic security requirement of dispute-resolving schemes is the *completeness of* Resolve(), requiring that all disputes are resolved in favor of the rightful author *if*[4] he participates in the Resolve() protocol and inputs the proof token obtained in Prepare().

Classic watermark-based dispute resolving schemes require the rightful author C_1 to prepare his original work W_1 by embedding a watermark WM_{C_1,W_1} into W_1, using watermarking key $K^{\mathtt{wm}}_{C_1,W_1}$. The resulting marked version is denoted as W'_1. Here, $proof_{C_1,W_1} := (W_1, WM_{C_1,W_1}, K^{\mathtt{wm}}_{C_1,W_1})$. C_1 has to keep this proof token as well as his original work W_1 secret and must only publish W'_1 (or works derived thereof).

In order to resolve a dispute, both disputants and the dispute resolver run the Resolve()-protocol together. The disputants start this protocol by sending their proof tokens, corresponding to the disputed work, $proof_{C_1,W_1} = (W_1, WM_{C_1,W_1}, K^{\mathtt{wm}}_{C_1,W_1})$ and $proof_{C_2,W_2} = (W_2, WM_{C_2,W_2}, K^{\mathtt{wm}}_{C_2,W_2})$, to D. Then, D verifies the presence of WM_{C_1,W_1} and WM_{C_2,W_2} in W_{dis}, using the detection algorithm Detect(). If only one watermark, say WM_{C_1,W_1}, is present in W_{dis}, the dispute is resolved in favor of C_1. Otherwise, if both watermarks are detectable in W_{dis}, D checks which of the alleged originals W_1, W_2 is the *true* original. This is done by checking the presence of WM_{C_1,W_1} in W_2 and the presence of WM_{C_2,W_2} in W_1 respectively. The dispute is resolved in favor of the disputant who presented an "original" that does not contain the other disputants watermark.

2.3 Positives Probability

Since the watermark detection process generally relies on statistical tests, false alarms are possible, i.e., situations where the watermark detector incorrectly reports a watermark to be present. Here, "incorrectly" intuitively means that the watermark has actually not been embedded. The probability for such a false alarm was commonly named false-positives probability.

Although the notion of "false-positives" is standard in the watermarking literature, we prefer to use the notion of "positives" instead. This is, because the detecting party cannot distinguish "true" positives from "false" positives on its own, since pure watermarking schemes generally lack a checkable legality criterion.[5] Furthermore, the detector (or the party who detects watermarks) in adversarial environments, such as the dispute resolver, commonly did not embed the watermark himself and, as a consequence thereof, does not know whether the watermark has been truly embedded.

[4] This restriction has been commonly neglected in literature (see [1,2]).

[5] This is why non-invertibility constructions augment pure watermarking schemes by additional legality criteria (see Section 3.1).

We define the *positives set* of a watermarking scheme as the set of all input tuples $(W', WM, W, K^{\text{wm}})$ yielding a positive detection result (*positive tuple*)

$$\mathcal{PS} := \{(W', WM, W, K^{\text{wm}}) \mid \texttt{Detect}(W', WM, W, K^{\text{wm}}) = \top\}$$

and we define the *positives rate* as the fraction of positive tuples to all such tuples:

$$pr = \frac{|\mathcal{PS}|}{|\mathcal{W} \times \mathcal{WM} \times \mathcal{W} \times \mathcal{K}|}$$

Note that this rate is completely determined by the watermarking scheme and does not depend on the application context, in which the watermarking scheme is being used. In contrast, the *positives probability* is not completely determined by the watermarking scheme, but additionally depends on the probability distribution of works, watermarks and watermarking keys (see [5]), which itself depends on the context given by the application in which the watermarking scheme is being used. In particular, the application's security requirements (or equivalently the attacker's goals) and the underlying trust model play a central role in defining an adequate positives probability.

Depending on the above aspects, we can distinguish different types of positives probability. The following positives probabilities are suitable for non-adversarial environments or for adversarial environments, where an attacker has no incentive to cause a "false" positive:

1. **Random-Work Positives Probability**: For a reference work W, watermark WM and watermarking key K^{wm}, we define the corresponding *random-work* positives probability as:

   $$\begin{aligned} &pp(W, WM, K^{\text{wm}}) := \\ &\quad \textbf{Prob}[\texttt{Detect}(W', WM, W, K^{\text{wm}}) = \top :: W' \leftarrow [\texttt{GenWork}(par^{\text{wm}}_{sec})];]. \end{aligned}$$

   Here, GenWork() must be chosen in a way that the resulting probability distribution resembles that of the application. The blind version of this positives probability $\textbf{Prob}[\texttt{Detect}(W', WM, K^{\text{wm}}) = \top :: W' \leftarrow [\texttt{GenWork}(par^{\text{wm}}_{sec})];]$ is suitable for copy-control applications in video delivery (e.g., DVD), where GenWork() has to resemble Hollywood movies as accurate as possible.[6]
2. **Random-Watermark Positives Probability**: For works W, W' and a watermarking key K^{wm}, we define the corresponding *random-watermark* positives probability as:

   $$\begin{aligned} &pp(W, W', K^{\text{wm}}) := \\ &\quad \textbf{Prob}[\texttt{Detect}(W', WM, W, K^{\text{wm}}) = \top :: WM \leftarrow [\texttt{GenWM}(par^{\text{wm}}_{sec})];]. \end{aligned}$$

   This definition of the positives probability is suitable for transactional watermarks, such as fingerprints. However, we want to stress that this definition

[6] Note that in copy-protection applications, attackers do not have an incentive to find works in which the "don't copy" watermark is detectable.

is problematic in application scenarios where an attacker does not generate watermarks correctly by using GenWM(). For example, in fingerprinting, a dishonest seller may want to falsely blame innocent buyers by choosing watermarks using arbitrary strategies.[7]

3. **Random-Input Positives Probability**: We define the random-input positives probability formally as: $\textbf{Prob}[\texttt{Detect}(W', WM, W, K^{\texttt{wm}}) = \top :: W' \leftarrow [\texttt{GenWork}(par^{\texttt{wm}}_{sec})]; WM \leftarrow [\texttt{GenWM}(par^{\texttt{wm}}_{sec})]; W \leftarrow [\texttt{GenWork}(par^{\texttt{wm}}_{sec})]; K^{\texttt{wm}} \leftarrow [\texttt{GenKey}(par^{\texttt{wm}}_{sec})];]$ and note that it is identical to the positives rate pr as defined above, if all generation algorithms produce a uniform distribution.

In security applications with possibly cheating parties (attackers), these probabilities are generally not realistic, because they assume certain parts of the inputs to the detection algorithm to have special probability distributions, e.g., Gaussian normal or uniform. In most security applications, at least parts of the inputs to Detect() can be chosen freely by the attacker without adhering to a pre-defined distribution. Therefore, we additionally define a new type of positives probability, which is realistic in the dispute-resolving scenario:

Positives Probability for Dispute Resolving. In dispute-resolving, as described in Section 2.2, an attacker, given a prepared work W', can choose the watermark, reference work and watermarking key arbitrarily. This attack strategy is formulated by an arbitrary polynomial-time machine A. Given the security parameter and a given prepared work W', A computes the watermark $WM_{\texttt{A}}$, the reference-work $W_{\texttt{A}}$ and the watermarking key $K^{\texttt{wm}}_{\texttt{A}}$ according to the probability distribution induced by the random choices of A. We define the *positives probability for dispute resolving* $pp_{dis}(\texttt{A})$ as:[8]

$$\begin{aligned}&\textbf{Prob}[\texttt{Detect}(W', WM_{\texttt{A}}, W_{\texttt{A}}, K^{\texttt{wm}}_{\texttt{A}}) = \top ::\\ &\quad W \leftarrow [\texttt{GenWork}(par^{\texttt{wm}}_{sec})];\ W' \leftarrow [\texttt{Prepare}(W)];\\ &\quad (WM_{\texttt{A}}, W_{\texttt{A}}, K^{\texttt{wm}}_{\texttt{A}}) \leftarrow [\texttt{A}(W', par^{\texttt{wm}}_{sec})];\\ &\ ]\end{aligned}$$

2.4 Impact of Invertibility

It was shown by Craver et al. [6] that dispute resolving, as described in Section 2.2, fails in case the watermarking scheme is *invertible*. Intuitively, a watermarking scheme is invertible iff an attacker $\texttt{A}_{inv}$, on input of a prepared work W_1' can find works W_{dis}, W_f (fake original) similar to W_1', a fake watermark WM_f and a fake watermarking key $K^{\texttt{wm}}_f$ such that the watermark WM_f is detectable in both W_{dis} and W_1 with non-negligible probability, where W_1 is

[7] A more realistic definition would not assume a specific distribution of watermarks, but allow an attacker algorithm to choose watermarks arbitrarily, as in the positives probability for dispute resolving.

[8] Note that in contrast to the above positives probabilities, this positives probability depends on the concrete attacker (formalized by algorithm A) and the attacker can use an arbitrary strategy to compute the positive tuple.

the true original work. Formally, we call a watermarking scheme invertible, iff

$\exists$ probabilistic polynomial-time algorithm $\mathtt{A}_{inv}$ such that

$$\begin{aligned}
&\mathbf{Prob}[\mathtt{Detect}(W_{dis}, WM_f, W_f, K_f^{\mathtt{wm}}) = \top \wedge \mathtt{Detect}(W_1, WM_f, W_f, K_f^{\mathtt{wm}}) = \top \wedge \\
&sim(W_{dis}, W_1') = \top \wedge sim(W_1', W_f) = \top :: \\
&\quad W_1 \leftarrow [\mathtt{GenWork}(par_{sec}^{\mathtt{wm}})];\ \ W_1' \leftarrow [\mathtt{Prepare}(W_1)]; \\
&\quad (W_{dis}, W_f, WM_f, K_f^{\mathtt{wm}}) \leftarrow [\mathtt{A}_{inv}(W_1', par_{sec}^{\mathtt{wm}})]; \\
&\quad] \\
&\geq_\infty 1/\mathtt{poly}(k)
\end{aligned}$$

Note, that this non-invertibility definition fits dispute-resolving applications, because it assumes W_1' to be a work, which has been prepared by a dispute-resolving scheme. More general non-invertibility definitions are possible, but are omitted due to lack of space.

Assume that the rightful author C_1 published a prepared work W_1' for which he knows the original work W_1, a watermark WM_{C_1,W_1} and a watermarking key $K_{C_1,W_1}^{\mathtt{wm}}$ (i.e. a $proof_{C_1,W_1}$) such that $\mathtt{Detect}(W_1', WM_{C_1,W_1}, W_1, K_{C_1,W_1}^{\mathtt{wm}}) = \top$. If the dispute resolving scheme uses an invertible watermarking scheme, an attacker C_2 can use the inversion algorithm $\mathtt{A}_{inv}$ to come up with a work W_{dis} (similar to W_1') and a corresponding proof token, i.e., a fake original W_f, a fake watermark WM_f and a watermarking key $K_f^{\mathtt{wm}}$, such that his newly computed watermark will be both detectable in W_{dis} and in C_1's original W_1.

In a dispute over the work W_{dis} no order of insertion can be established, as C_1's original W_1 contains C_2's fake watermark, although it is the true original and has not been derived from C_2's fake original W_f. Consequently, the classical watermark-based dispute resolving process fails and is insecure if invertible watermarking schemes are being used.

From an abstract point of view, inverting a watermarking scheme can be interpreted as *finding a special positive of the watermarking scheme*. Consequently, the following simplifying implication holds: *The higher the positives rate of the watermarking scheme, the "easier" the inversion of the watermarking scheme.*

3 Non-invertibility

Since the need for *non-invertible* watermarking schemes as basis for dispute-resolving protocols has been noted early, several authors tried to prevent inversion attacks by incorporating cryptographic primitives (like one-way functions) in the watermark- or key-generation process.

Qiao and Nahrstedt [12] presented a watermarking scheme that they claimed to be non-invertible. Their scheme is based on the idea to construct the watermark *WM* from the DES encryption of the original work. The DES key is chosen by the rightful author during the watermark embedding mechanism. The constructed watermark is then embedded in the work by using a traditional watermarking scheme. A successful inversion attack requires the computation of a

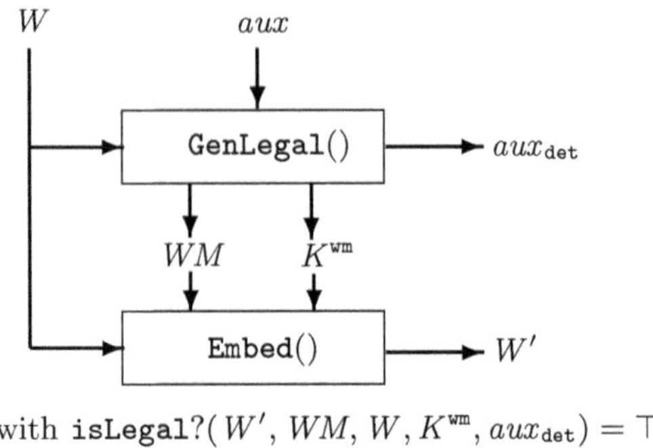

with $\texttt{isLegal?}(W', \mathit{WM}, W, K^{\texttt{wm}}, aux_{\texttt{det}}) = \top$

Fig. 1. The embedding mechanism of the general non-invertibility construction.

detectable mark WM that is the DES encryption of the fake original and was, therefore, believed to be impossible.

A different system, proposed by Craver et al. [6], uses a one-way hash-function H and a cryptographically secure pseudorandom number generator PRNG. In their system, WM is constructed as the output of PRNG, seeded with a one-way hash of the original work $\mathit{WM} = \mathit{PRNG}(H(W))$. The authors claimed that this system is secure, as an attacker would have to find a detectable mark that conforms to the above restriction.

3.1 The General Non-invertibility Construction

In this section we introduce a general framework for non-invertibility constructions, which aims at reducing the positives rate of the watermarking scheme by introducing a *complementary legality criterion.* For this, the watermarking scheme is extended by two algorithms $\texttt{GenLegal}()$ and $\texttt{isLegal?}()$ for generating and testing legal detection tuples. A detection tuple is considered *legal,* if the legality test, specified by $\texttt{isLegal?} : \mathcal{W} \times \mathcal{WM} \times \mathcal{W} \times \mathcal{K} \times \{0,1\}^{par^{\texttt{ni}}_{sec}} \rightarrow \{\top, \bot\}$ outputs $\top$. Here, $par^{\texttt{ni}}_{sec}$ represents the security parameter of the non-invertibility construction.

During the extended watermark embedding procedure, a legal watermark is computed by an algorithm $\texttt{GenLegal}()$, which takes a work W and some auxiliary information aux (which may contain an identity string or a cryptographic key), and outputs a legal watermark WM, a watermarking key $K^{\texttt{wm}}$ and an auxiliary bit-string $aux_{\texttt{det}}$ that satisfy $\texttt{isLegal?}(W', \mathit{WM}, W, K^{\texttt{wm}}, aux_{\texttt{det}}) = \top$. This procedure is depicted in Figure 1. Note that in some concrete constructions the output of $\texttt{GenLegal}()$ may not depend on all inputs, specifically aux may be empty. $\texttt{GenLegal}()$ typically involves cryptographic primitives so that it cannot be easily inverted by an attacker.

The legality criterion is verified during an *extended watermark detection process.* Typically, this extended detection process outputs $\top$ iff both $\texttt{Detect}(W', \mathit{WM}, W, K^{\texttt{wm}}) = \top$ and $\texttt{isLegal?}(W', \mathit{WM}, W, K^{\texttt{wm}}, aux_{\texttt{det}}) = \top$, where $aux_{\texttt{det}}$

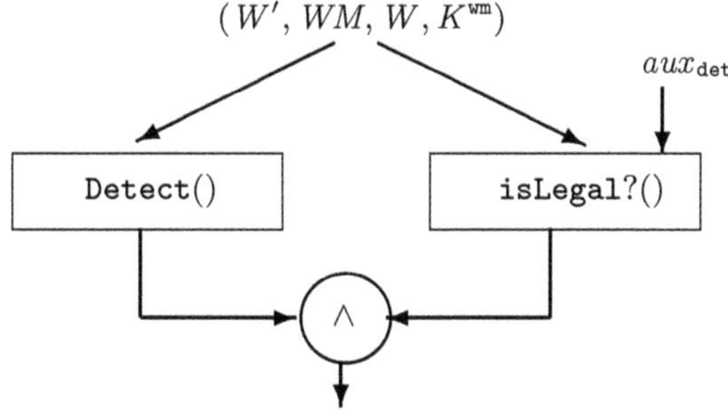

Fig. 2. The detection mechanism of the general non-invertibility construction.

denotes the auxiliary input that was generated in the extended embedding step. That is, the "legality" of the inputs to `Detect()` must be verified in the extended detection phase. The extended detection procedure is shown in Figure 2. Note that the previous proposals for "non-invertible" watermarks quoted above are special cases of this general construction.

An attacker who wants to perform an inversion attack now faces to produce a detectable mark that also passes the legality criterion. It was commonly believed that this construction makes it more difficult to perform an inversion attack against the extended watermarking scheme, because any possible inversion amounts to inverting the algorithm `GenLegal()`, which can be made infeasible by applying a cryptographic one-way function. In the following, we will show that this reasoning is wrong if the positives rate of the underlying watermarking scheme is non-negligible. We define

$$\mathcal{LS} := \{(W', WM, W, K^{\mathtt{wm}}, aux_{\mathtt{det}}) \mid \mathtt{isLegal?}(W', WM, W, K^{\mathtt{wm}}, aux_{\mathtt{det}}) = \top\}$$

and refer to it as the *legals set*. The *legal positives set* of the extended detection is the intersection of the extended detector's positives set $\mathcal{PS}_{\mathtt{ext}} := \mathcal{PS} \times \{0,1\}^{par^{\mathtt{ni}}_{sec}}$ and the legals set $\mathcal{LS}$, as illustrated in Figure 3. Introducing the additional legality criterion obviously reduces the *positive rate* $\frac{|\mathcal{PS}|}{|\mathcal{W}\times\mathcal{WM}\times\mathcal{W}\times\mathcal{K}|}$ of the original watermarking scheme to the *legal positives rate* $\frac{|\mathcal{PS}_{\mathtt{ext}} \cap \mathcal{LS}|}{|\mathcal{W}\times\mathcal{WM}\times\mathcal{W}\times\mathcal{K}\times\{0,1\}^{par^{\mathtt{ni}}_{sec}}|}$ of the extended detection process, because input tuples have to pass *both* the detection and the legality test.

If the legality criterion is selected suitably, e.g., such that the watermarking key or the watermark itself has to be an one-way image of the original work and some auxiliary input (e.g., a cryptographic key or the identity of the rightful author), the legals set, and consequently the legal positives set as well, is small. However, a small legal positives set (or positives rate) does not necessarily imply that legal positives are "hard" to find.

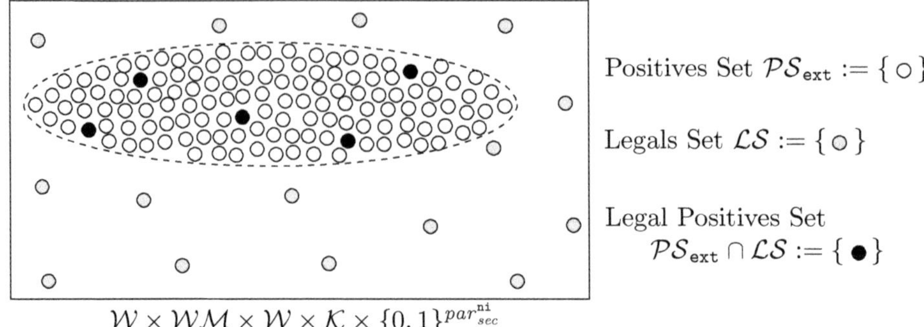

Fig. 3. Simplified illustration: The legal positives set of the extended detection process.

3.2 Insecurity of the General Construction

As stated above, the goal of an attacker is now to find a *legal positive*. In the remainder of this section, we consider the success probabilities of two specific attack strategies, one of which breaks the security of non-invertibility constructions following the framework of Section 3.1 if the watermarking scheme's positive rate is non-negligible.

1. **Generate positives and check for legality.** An attacker following this strategy iteratively generates random positives and checks them for legality. Due to the invertibility of the underlying basic watermarking scheme, the generation of positives is possible in polynomial time. However, since only a small fraction of the positives also fulfills the legality criterion, the randomly selected positive fails to be legal with overwhelming probability. Therefore, this concrete attacker strategy fails in finding legal positives. This made several researchers believe that inverting the extended watermarking scheme (i.e., finding legal positives) is infeasible. Formally, the success probability of this attacker strategy is given by the *legal positives rate*, defined as $\frac{|\mathcal{PS}_{\mathtt{ext}} \cap \mathcal{LS}|}{|\mathcal{PS}_{\mathtt{ext}}|}$. However, the fact that one specific attacker strategy is infeasible is no security proof, since there may be other strategies, such as the following, which are successful.
2. **Generate legals and check for positivity (detectability).** A more efficient attacker strategy is to iteratively generate legal tuples and check them for positivity/detectability.
   Since generating legals and deciding positivity (using `Detect`) is efficient, the overall attack is also efficient, if the expected number of iterations required is polynomial in the security parameter. The latter holds if the probability that a generated legal tuple is also positive is non-negligible. If `GenLegal`() produces uniformly distributed legals, as is the case when applying cryptographic primitives such as hash-functions, signature schemes or encryption schemes, the success probability of each round is given by the *positive legals rate*, defined as $\frac{|\mathcal{PS}_{\mathtt{ext}} \cap \mathcal{LS}|}{|\mathcal{LS}|}$. This rate is non-negligible, because a

non-negligible fraction of $\mathcal{LS}$ lies also in $\mathcal{PS}_{\mathtt{ext}}$.[9] Consequently, this attack strategy is successful in finding a legal positive in expected polynomial time.

Truly non-invertible watermarking schemes need to prevent this attack. To achieve this for dispute resolving applications, the positives probability for dispute resolving $pp_{dis}(\mathtt{A})$, as defined in Section 2.3, must be negligible for all probabilistic polynomial-time attackers $\mathtt{A}$. Note, however, that this is only a necessary requirement, that does not guarantee the non-invertibility of the scheme alone. In fact, it seems to be questionable whether one can prevent such attacks at all by means of cryptography and without involving a trusted third party.

Now, it is straightforward to translate this successful attack strategy against the general framework to attacks against concrete non-invertibility constructions.

To attack the scheme by Qiao and Nahrstedt [12], the attacker chooses a *new* DES key K, implying that the DES encryption does not provide any additional security.[10] He then takes the work W' in dispute, tweaks some of its bits, while preserving perceptual similarity, and obtains W''. He then encrypts W'' with his DES key K to obtain a watermark WM_f and tests whether this watermark is detectable in the attacked work W'. If this is the case, the attack succeeds and he outputs W'' as his fake original and WM_f as his fake watermark. Otherwise, he discards W'' and iterates the procedure. Because of the properties of DES, the attacker produces a large number of different (statistically independent) watermarks WM_f as test candidates.

Analogously, Ramkumar and Akansu [13] presented an attack against the proposal of Craver et al. [6]. Here, the attacker can take the work W' in question, modify some of its bits to obtain the work W_f which he uses to produce the corresponding legal watermark $WM_f = PRNG(H(W_f))$. This process is iterated, until the constructed fake watermark WM_f is detectable in W' relative to the fake reference-work W_f.

Note that both attacks do not break the cryptographic mechanisms used in the embedding process. Instead, they circumvent the cryptographic primitives by producing a large number of "candidates" for fake original works, which they use to come up with a large number of corresponding "fake" legal watermarks. If the positives rate is large enough, the attacker obtains — in both attacks — a legal detectable mark in polynomial time.

4 Conclusion and Further Research

In this paper we analyzed the impact of the (false-)positives probability on the security of proposed non-invertibility constructions. For this, we introduced an

[9] This is due to the uniform distribution of $\mathcal{LS}$ and the non-negligibility of the watermarking scheme's positive rate.

[10] Already the fact that the construction does not prevent an attacker from choosing the key contradicts the security definition of encryption schemes and pseudo-random functions. Consequently, this construction cannot draw its security from the security of DES.

abstract general non-invertibility framework that subsumes many previous proposals for non-invertible watermarking schemes. We then showed that the general framework is insecure despite the use of cryptographic primitives, such as one-way functions, if the positives rate of the underlying watermarking scheme is non-negligible. This result is a generalization of the attack of Ramkumar and Akansu [13] and is of great importance, since it shows that non-invertible watermarking schemes are more difficult to construct than previously believed and thus many proposals for dispute-resolving, which relied on certain non-invertible watermarking schemes, are insecure.

Having identified the insecurity of previous dispute-resolving proposals, some natural further research topics arise. One question is how one can construct truly non-invertible watermarking schemes or dispute-resolving protocols that draw their security *not* from non-invertible watermarks. One way to construct truly non-invertible watermarking schemes may be the use of non-cryptographic legality criteria, e.g., as proposed by Ramkumar and Akansu [13], or to strictly limit the degrees of freedom in choosing watermarks [16]. Unfortunately, it is generally difficult to formally assess the security of such approaches and again it is quite likely, that similar attacks work for such schemes as well. Another way is to make the computation of a legal watermark hard by involving a trusted third party [3].

Protocols for dispute-resolving that do not draw their security from non-invertible watermarking schemes can be constructed by using trusted timestamping-services or registration services for determining the true original (see e.g., [15,2]). An overview over possible approaches can be found in [2].

Acknowledgments. We would like to thank Ton Kalker for inspiring discussions on types of false-positives probabilities.

References

1. André Adelsbach, Birgit Pfitzmann, and Ahmad-Reza Sadeghi. Proving ownership of digital content. In Andreas Pfitzmann, editor, *Information Hiding—3rd International Workshop, IH'99*, volume 1768 of *Lecture Notes in Computer Science*, pages 126–141, Dresden, Germany, October 2000. Springer-Verlag, Berlin Germany.
2. André Adelsbach and Ahmad-Reza Sadeghi. Advanced techniques for dispute resolving and authorship proofs on digital works. In *Proceedings of the SPIE vol. 5020, Security and Watermarking of Multimedia Contents V*, pages 677–688, 2003.
3. André Adelsbach Adelsbach, Stefan Katzenbeisser, and Helmut Veith. Watermarking schemes provably secure against copy and ambiguity attacks. In *Proc. of ACM CCS-10 Workshop on Digital Rights Management*, October 2003.
4. Dan Boneh and James Shaw. Collusion-secure fingerprinting for digital data. In Don Coppersmith, editor, *Advances in Cryptology – CRYPTO '95*, volume 963 of *Lecture Notes in Computer Science*, pages 452–465. International Association for Cryptologic Research, Springer-Verlag, Berlin Germany, 1995.
5. Ingemar Cox, Matthew L. Miller, and Jefferey A. Bloom. *Digital Watermarking*. Morgan Kaufmann Publisher, 2002.

6. Scott Craver, Nasir Memon, Boon-Lock Yeo, and Minerva M. Yeung. Resolving rightful ownerships with invisible watermarking techniques: Limitations, attacks, and implications. *IEEE Journal on Selected Areas in Communications*, 16(4):573–586, May 1998.
7. Eckhard Koch and Jian Zhao. Towards robust and hidden image copyright labeling. In *Proceedings of IEEE Workshop on Nonlinear Signal and Image Processing*, pages 452–455, 1995.
8. Martin Kutter and Frank Leprevost. Symbiose von Kryptographie und digitalen Wasserzeichen: Effizienter Schutz des Urheberrechtes digitaler Medien. In *Tagungsband des 6. Deutschen IT-Sicherheitskongress, Bundesamt für Sicherheit in der Informationstechnik*, pages 1–4, May 1999.
9. Nikos Nikolaidis and Ioannis Pitas. Copyright protection of images using robust digital signatures. In *IEEE International Conference on Acoustics, Speech and Signal Processing (ICASSP-96)*, volume 4, pages 2168–2171, May 1996.
10. Ioannis Pitas and George Voyatzis. Applications of toral automorphisms in image watermarking. IEEE Signal Processing Society, 1996.
11. Lintian Qiao and Klara Nahrstedt. Watermarking methods for MPEG encoded video: Towards resolving rightful ownership. In *International Conference on Multimedia Computing and Systems (ICMCS)*, pages 276–285, Austin, Texas, USA, 1998. IEEE, IEEE, Washington Brussels Tokyo.
12. Lintian Qiao and Klara Nahrstedt. Watermarking schemes and protocols for protecting rightful ownerships and customer's rights. *Journal of Visual Communication and Image Representation*, 9(3):194–210, 1998.
13. Mahalingam Ramkumar and Ali Akansu. Image watermarks and counterfeit attacks : Some problems and solutions. In *Symposium on Content Security and Data Hiding in Digital Media*, pages 102–112, Newark, NJ, USA, May 1999. New Jersey Institute of Technology.
14. Mitchell D. Swanson, Mei Kobayashi, and Ahmed H. Tewfik. Multimedia data-embedding and watermarking technologies. *Proceedings of the IEEE*, 86(6), June 1998.
15. Raymond Wolfgang and Edward Delp. Overview of image security techniques with applications in multimedia systems. In *Proceedings of the SPIE International Conference on Voice, Video, and Data Communications*, pages 297–308, 1997.
16. Wenjun Zeng and Bede Liu. On resolving rightful ownerships of digital images by invisible watermarks. In *4th International Conference on Image Processing (ICIP)*, pages 552–555, Santa Barbara, CA, USA, October 1997. IEEE.

RST-Resistant Image Watermarking Using Invariant Centroid and Reordered Fourier-Mellin Transform

Bum-Soo Kim[1], Jae-Gark Choi[2], and Kil-Houm Park[1]

[1] Department of Electronic Engineering, Kyungpook National University, 1370, Sankyug-Dong, Buk-Gu, Daegu, 702-701, Korea,
bskim0@hanafos.com, khpark@ee.knu.ac.kr

[2] Department of Computer Engineering, Dongeui University, Gaya-Dong, Busanjin-Gu, Busan, 614-714, Korea
cjg@dongeui.ac.kr

Abstract. This paper proposes a new image watermarking scheme which is robust to RST attacks by improving Fourier-Mellin transform based Watermarking (FMW). The proposed scheme reorders and modifies function blocks of FMW for improvement of realization and performance. Unlike FMW, our method uses Log-Polar Map (LPM) in the spatial domain for scaling invariance, while translation invariance is provided by the use of an invariant centroid as the origin of LPM. Invariant centroid is a gravity center of a central area on gray scale image that is invariant although an image is attacked by RST. For this, its calculation method is proposed. Also since LPM includes the property which transforms rotation of Cartesian coordinates system into a cyclic shift, 2-D DFT is performed on the LPM image and the magnitude spectrum extracted to provide a domain that is rotation invariant. The resulting domain, which is invariant to RST, is then used as the watermark-embedding domain. Experimental results demonstrate that the proposed scheme is robust to RST attacks.

1 Introduction

The past decade has seen an explosion in the use and distribution of digital multimedia data. PCs with Internet connections have made the distribution of digital data and applications much easier and faster. However, this has also had a serious effect on copyright encroachment, thereby creating a new demand for copyright protection of digital data [1-5]. To provide copyright protection for digital data, two complementary techniques have been developed: encryption and watermarking. Encryption can be used to protect digital data during the transmission process from the sender to the receiver. However, after the receiver has received and decrypted the data, it becomes identical to the original data and is no longer protected. Watermarking can compliment encryption by embedding a secret imperceptible signal, a watermark, into the original data in such a way that it always remains present.

T. Kalker et al. (Eds.): IWDW 2003, LNCS 2939, pp. 370–381, 2004.
© Springer-Verlag Berlin Heidelberg 2004

Generally digital image watermarking has certain requirements, the most important being robustness and invisibility. Robustness means that the embedded watermarks cannot be removed by intentional or unintentional digital data changing, called attacks. Although robustness can be obtained based on significant modifications to the host data, such modifications are noticeable and thus do not satisfy the requirement of invisibility. As such, a tradeoff is needed between the different requirements so that an optimal watermarking can be developed for each type of application.

The conventional digital image watermarking methods include robustness to waveform attacks such as JPEG compression, filtering, and noise addition, yet they are not robust to geometrical attacks such as rotation, scaling, and translation (RST). To solve this problem Fourier-Mellin transform-based Watermarking (FMW) is proposed [6,7].

FMW is theoretically robust to RST attacks as it uses 2-D DFT and LPM as follows. First, it calculate the magnitude of 2-D DFT to obtain a translation-invariant domain. Then, for every point of 2-D DFT magnitude a corresponding point in LPM is determined. The polar coordinate system converts a rotation of Cartesian coordinate system into a cyclic shift and also includes a scaling invariance. By taking the 2-D DFT magnitude of this LPM, a RST-invariant domain is obtained to which a spread spectrum watermark is added. However, FMW performs LPM on DFT domain, which requires interpolation of 2-D DFT magnitudes with a large dynamic range between neighboring coefficients [8]. As result, the efficiency of interpolation becomes very poor. Therefore it is difficult to implement FMW in practice. Also FMW requires 2-D DFT twice, which involves a high computation cost. FMW embeds a watermark in the magnitude of the second 2-D DFT. The watermark-embedded frequency band may not be the middle frequency band of the original image i.e., it means that FMW doesn't meet the trade-off between robustness and invisibility. To solve the difficulty of practical implementation, Lins et al. proposed an improved FMW scheme [10]. This scheme can solve the implementation difficulty of FMW. However it cannot solve other problems such as the frequency localization problem.

Accordingly, this paper improves FMW scheme to overcome above problems. The proposed scheme reorders and modifies function blocks of FMW as followings. First it obtains LPM of an original image. LPM in the spatial domain can overcome the interpolation problem because it has a similar scale between neighboring pixels. LPM can guarantee scaling and translation invariance if the origin of LPM can be obtained invariantly. Therefore the calculation method of invariant centroid as the origin of LPM is proposed in this paper. The invariant centroid can be always detected under any RST attack, even if the image is cropped. Second, the LPM image is transformed by 2-D DFT and the magnitude is used as the watermark-embedding domain, because LPM transforms a rotation attack into a cyclic shift and the magnitude of 2-D DFT is invariant to cyclic shift. As a result, the proposed scheme exhibits robustness to RST attacks. Also the calculation cost is reduced as only one 2-D DFT is performed. Furthermore, to prevent the watermarked image from degrading due to the coordinate system conversion, only LPM image of watermark signal is inverse mapped to Cartesian coordinates and add to the original image.

The remainder of the paper is structured as follows. The properties of 2-D DFT and LPM, as used in the proposed method, are described in section 2. Section 3 introduces the proposed watermarking scheme and experimental results are presented in section 4. Section 5 contains the final conclusions.

2 Properties of 2-D DFT and LPM

The properties of 2-D DFT and LPM, as described below, are used to make a domain that is invariant to RST.

2.1 Properties of 2-D DFT

An important property of DFT is translation invariance of its magnitude. Shifts in the spatial domain only cause a linear shift in the phase component. Therefore, this property can be used for translation invariance of watermarking. If a two-dimensional signal $f(x, y)$ in the spatial domain is shifted, yet only the phase of its 2-D DFT is shifted, while the magnitude remains invariant as follows:

$$f(x,y) \leftrightarrow F(u,v),\ \ f(x+a,y+b) \leftrightarrow F(u,v)exp[-j(au+bv)] \tag{1}$$

where a and b are the amount of shifts on the x and y axis respectively, and $F(u, v)$ is 2-D DFT of $f(x, y)$.

The rotation of $f(x, y)$ is represented by the rotation of $F(u, v)$, that is

$$f(x\cos\theta - y\sin\theta, x\sin\theta + y\cos\theta) \leftrightarrow F(u\cos\theta - v\sin\theta, u\sin\theta + v\cos\theta) \tag{2}$$

and the scale change in the spatial domain increases the resolution of the spectrum and reduces the magnitude inverse proportionally as follows:

$$f(ax, by) \leftrightarrow \frac{1}{ab}F(u/a, v/b) \tag{3}$$

2.2 Properties of LPM

The properties of LPM include scaling invariance and the conversion of a rotation on Cartesian coordinates into a cyclic shift on log-polar coordinates. The scale of an image on log-polar coordinates is not changed, if the sampling rates, N_r and N_θ, of LPM on the radial and angular direction, are constant. Eq. (4) represents the use of LPM to transform the point (x, y) on Cartesian coordinates into (r, θ) on log-polar coordinates as follows:

$$x - x_0 = exp(r\Delta_r)\cos(\theta\Delta_\theta),\ \ y - y_0 = exp(r\Delta_r)\sin(\theta\Delta_\theta) \tag{4}$$

where (x_0, y_0) are the Cartesian coordinates used as the origin of the log-polar coordinates, $\Delta_r = ln(max.distancefromorigin)/N_r - 1$ and $\Delta_\theta = 2\pi/N_\theta$ are

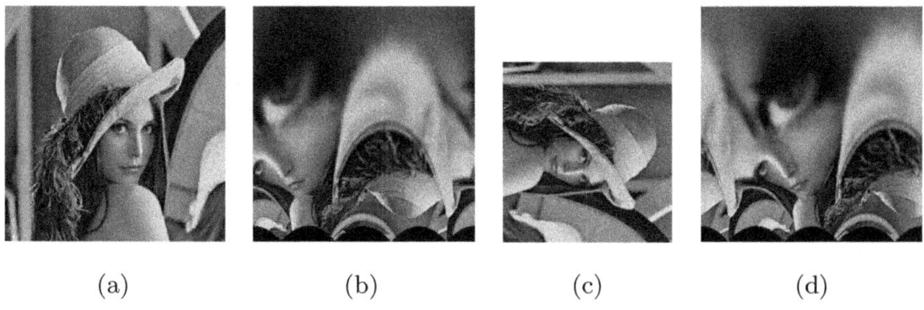

(a) (b) (c) (d)

Fig. 1. Properties of LPM: (a) original Image; (b) LPM of (a); (c) 90 degrees rotation and 75(d) LPM of (c)

the sampling step size for the r and θ axis respectively, and $r = \{0, 1, \ldots, N_r - 1\}$, $\theta = \{0, 1, \ldots, N_{\theta-1}\}$. The Fig. 1 shows a visual representation of the properties of LPM. The original image is shown in Fig. 1 (a), while the rotation and scaling-attacked image is shown in Fig. 1 (c). LPM results of Fig. 1 (a) and (c) are represented by Fig. 1 (b) and (d), respectively, which exhibit LPM properties of scaling invariance and the conversion of rotation on Cartesian coordinates into a cyclic shift.

3 Embedding and Detection of Watermark

The proposed watermarking scheme uses the properties of 2-D DFT and LPM in a similar way to FMW scheme as regards making a domain that is robust to RST attacks. However, the proposed scheme only uses 2-D DFT once so as to reduce the calculation complexity and embed the watermark into the intended frequency bands, and LPM is used in the spatial domain to prevent interpolation problems in the frequency domain. For LPM, the origin should be selected very carefully as different results can occur depending on the location of the origin. As such, this method proposes a calculation method of an invariant centroid, which remains unchanged under various attacks. After the above processes, LPM of an image becomes invariant to translation and scaling, yet rotation is still presented as a cyclic shift. Therefore, to make a domain that is also invariant to rotation, 2-D DFT magnitude is extracted and used as the watermark-embedding domain. In watermark detection, copyright is determined based on the presence or absence of the watermark without the original image.

3.1 Invariant Centroid

The proposed scheme uses LPM provide scaling invariance. Although scaling invariance can be easily satisfied by LPM, deciding on the origin of LPM is very important as if the origin changes, LPM of the image will also change. In FMW, the origin is always DC of 2-D DFT magnitude, however, in the proposed

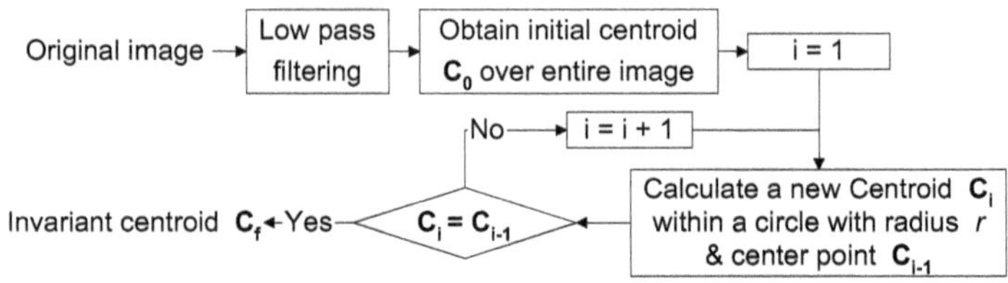

Fig. 2. Scheme for deriving invariant centroid

scheme, the origin is decided in the spatial domain. If the center of an image is used as the origin, this can cause different results if the image is cropped for some reason. Therefore, an invariant point that remains unchanged after geometrical or waveform attacks is needed. In conventional feature point finding techniques, it is difficult to find an invariant point that is not changed by geometrical transformations, image processing, and compression. Therefore, in the proposed scheme, an invariant centroid derived by an iterative method is used as the origin as it can also provide translation invariance. The method of deriving the invariant centroid is depicted in Fig. 2. The centroid $\mathbf{C} = (C_x, C_y)$ of an image $I(x, y)$ is calculated as follows:

$$C_x = \sum_x \sum_y f(x,y)x, \; C_y = \sum_x \sum_y f(x,y)y \tag{5}$$

where $f(x,y) = I(x,y)/\sum x \sum y I(x,y)$ and $(x,y) \in \Re^2$ is the region of the image $I(x,y)$.

Eq. (5) shows that the centroid of an image can differ if the image is cropped by geometrical attacks or the pixel values are changed due to waveform attacks. Therefore, the initial centroid of the image $\mathbf{C_0}$ is calculated using Eq. (5) after performing low pass filtering so as to reduce the effects of waveform attacks, as most waveform attacks, e.g. JPEG compression and noise addition etc., do not affect the low frequency bands. Thereafter, Eq. (5) is used to calculate the centroid $\mathbf{C_1}$ based on a circular region with radius r and center point $\mathbf{C_0}$. The region used to calculate the centroid position must be circular so that it will not change although rotation occurs. $\mathbf{C_1}$ is also used as the center point for another circle with radius r, so as to calculate $\mathbf{C_2}$. A comparison is then made between $\mathbf{C_2}$ and $\mathbf{C_1}$ and the above process is repeated until the centroids converge on the same point, thereby becoming an invariant centroid $\mathbf{C_f}$. Geometrical or waveform attacks will have no effect on the location of this point due to the use of low pass filtering and the fact that the point was not extracted from the entire image but rather from a restricted area inside the image.

3.2 Watermark Embedding

The proposed watermark-embedding scheme is shown in Fig. 3. The image $I(x,y)$ is transformed into LPM $LM(r,\theta)$ using the invariant centroid $\mathbf{C_f}$ as

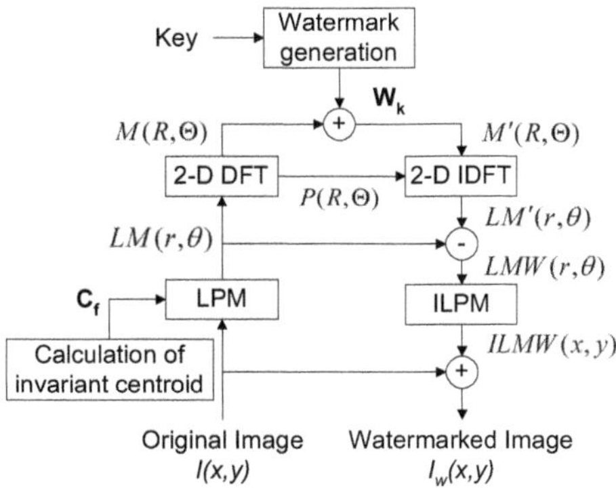

Fig. 3. Proposed watermark embedding scheme

the origin. As a result, $LM(r, \theta)$ is invariant to translation and scale changes in the image on Cartesian coordinates. However, a rotation of the image is still transformed into a cyclic shift. Therefore, to create a domain that has an invariant property to cyclic shifts, 2-D DFT is performed since the magnitude of 2-D DFT, $M(R, \Theta)$, is cyclic shift invariant due to the properties of 2-D DFT, as mentioned in the previous section. Consequently, since $M(R, \Theta)$ becomes a domain that is invariant to geometrical attacks, the watermark generated from the copyright owner's key k is embedded in this domain.

The embedded watermark $\mathbf{W_k}$ is generated from the copyright owners key as follows:

$$\mathbf{W_k} = \{w1, w2, \ldots, w_N\}, \; w_i \in \{-1, 1\} \tag{6}$$

where it is a binary pseudo-random sequence of length N. The generated watermark $\mathbf{W_k}$ is embedded in N points of $M(R, \Theta)$ selected based on the k and which satisfy the frequency bands $f_1 < \sqrt{R_i^2 + \Theta_i^2} < f_2$ using the formula

$$M'(R_i, \Theta_i) = M(R_i, \Theta_i)(1 + \alpha w_i) \tag{7}$$

where α is the embedding strength and $1 \leq i \leq N$. The watermark is also embedded in $M(-R_i, -\Theta_i)$ because the magnitude of 2-D DFT is symmetric to DC.

Furthermore, The watermark is not embedded in the frequency domain directly but rather LPM image of the watermark signal $LMW(r, \theta)$ is inverse mapped to Cartesian coordinates and added to $I(x, y)$. The reason for using indirect embedding is that LPM and inverse LPM can cause a loss of image quality. In fact, the change of coordinate system requires some form of interpolation. The intention of the proposed inverse processing is that only the additional watermark signal is damaged by the coordinates conversion.

3.3 Watermark Detection

In the proposed watermark detection scheme, copyright is determined based on the presence or absence of the watermark without the original image. The

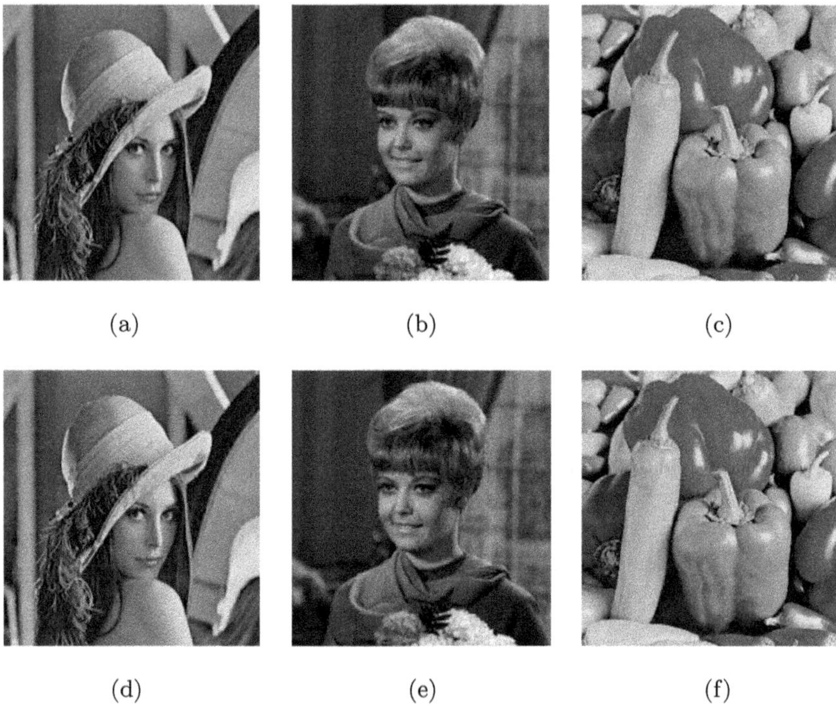

Fig. 4. Original and watermarked images: (a), (b), & (c) original images; (d), (e), & (f) watermarked images of (a), (b), & (c), respectively

test image is transformed into log-polar coordinates based on LPM using an invariant centroid as its origin, then we obtain 2-D DFT magnitude of LPM image, $M'(R,\Theta)$. Next, the number of N points, $M'(R_1,\Theta_1),\ldots,M(R_N,\Theta_N)$, are selected using the key and the similarity with the watermark $\mathbf{W_k}$ is calculated using the formula

$$S = \frac{\sum_{i=1}^{N} w_i M'(R_i,\Theta_i)}{\sqrt{\sum_{i=1}^{N} \left(M'(R_i,\Theta_i)\right)^2}} \tag{8}$$

and whether the watermark is present or not is determined based on the similarity S compared with a threshold T.

4 Experimental Results

To evaluate the performance of the proposed watermarking scheme experiments were conducted using the Lena, Girl, and Pepper (256 × 256) images and the results compared with Alghoniemy and Tewfik's method [9] and Lin's et al.'s method [10]. Alghoniemy and Tewfik's method is normalizes an original image into a standard form using its moments, then a watermark is embedded in the

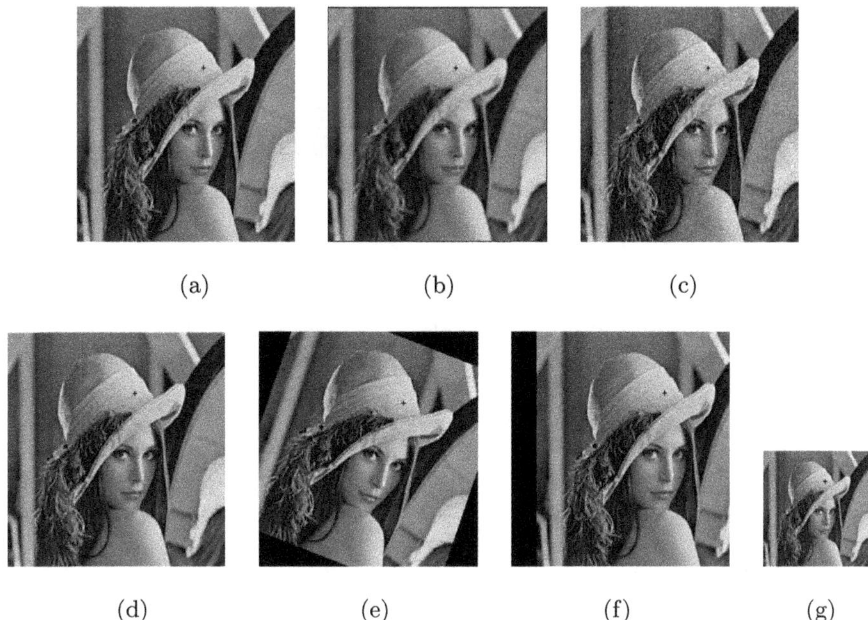

Fig. 5. Invariant centroids which are marked as cross: (a) original image; (b) 3 × 3 average filtered; (c) 5% gaussian noise added; (d) JPEG compressed image with compression ratio of 70; (e) 20 degree clockwise rotation of image plus cropping; (f) 30 pixels translated along x axis; (g) scaled image based on scaling factor of 0.5.

normalized image. It exhibits robustness to geometrical attacks since the normalized image is not changed by RST as long as the image is not cropped. On the other hand, Lin's et al.'s method is one of FMW and use exhaustive search instead of using LPM in 2-D DFT magnitude.

When finding the invariant centroid, the radius of the circle r was 64, and sampling rates, N_r and N_θ, for transforming to LPM were both 512. Also the watermark embedding bands f_1 and f_2 were 50 and 70, respectively. The embedding strength α was 0.2 for Lena and Pepper images, and 0.3 for Girl image. The length N of the watermark was 3000 and the decision threshold T, used to determine the presence of the watermark, was 3.

Fig. 4 shows the images and their watermarked images used in the experiments. Fig. 4 (a), (b) and (c) are the original images and (d), (e), (f) are the watermarked images with PSNRs of 41.40dB, 41.78dB, and 40.08dB, respectively. Fig. 4 demonstrates that the invisibility requirement was satisfied by the proposed scheme.

The most important part of the proposed scheme, which identifies an invariant centroid as the origin of LPM, was found to be efficient and robust to various attacks, see Fig. 5. Fig. 5 (a) shows the invariant centroid of the original image, while Fig. 5 (b) to (g) represent the robustness of the invariant centroid to var-

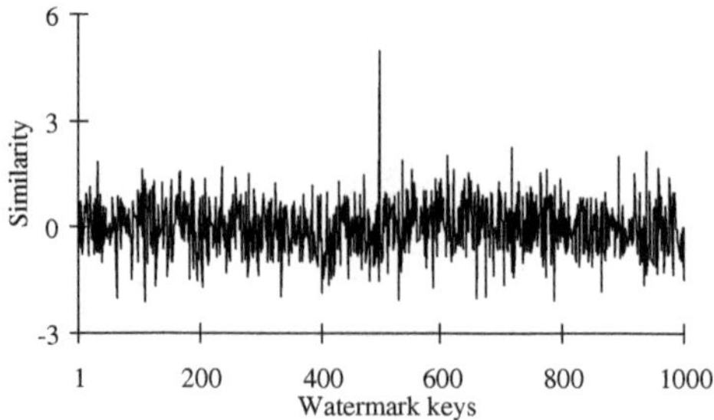

Fig. 6. Similarity in Lena image with watermarks of 1000 different keys

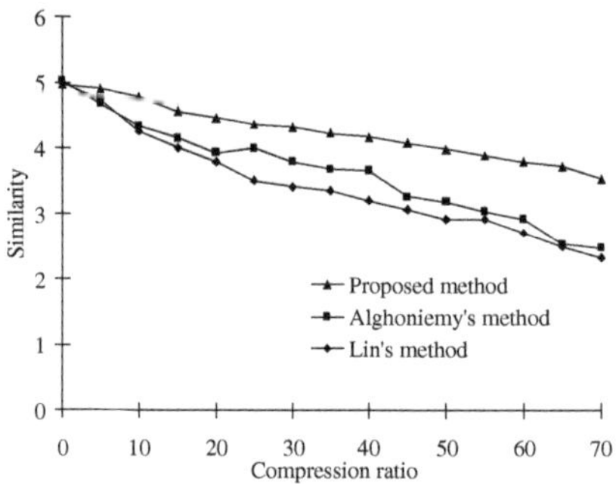

Fig. 7. Similarity in Lena image after JPEG compression

ious attacks, including 3 × 3 average filtering (Fig. 5 (b)), addition of 5JPEG compression based on compression ratio of 70 (Fig. 5 (d)), clockwise rotation of 20 degrees with cropping (Fig. 5 (e)), translation of 30 pixels along x-axis (Fig. 5 (f)), and scale changing based on scaling factor of 0.5 (Fig. 5 (g)), respectively. In Fig. 5 (a)-(g), invariant centroid is marked as cross and we can see that although various geometrical and waveform attacks are given, each centroid in Fig. 5 (a)-(g) are positioned on the similar point which is on the band of hat. The 500th watermark was embedded in the Lena image among 1000 watermarks generated using different keys and the computed similarities between the watermarks and the watermarked Lena image are shown in Fig. 6. The result shows that the similarity with the 500th watermark was the highest, which also satisfied the threshold. Therefore, the person with the 500th key can insist on their copyright ownership of the image.

To demonstrate the robustness of the proposed scheme, experiments were performed based on waveform and geometrical attacks. Fig. 7 and 8 show that the proposed scheme is robust to waveform attacks. In Fig. 7, the watermark could still be well detected even after the image was compressed using a compression

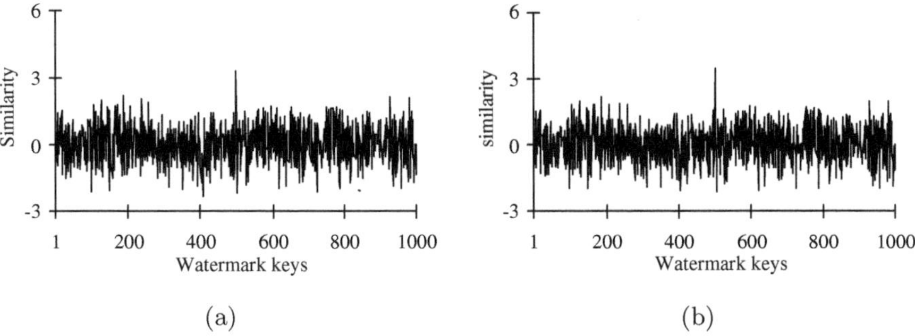

Fig. 8. Similarity in Pepper image with watermarks of 1000 different keys: (a) after 3×3 average filtering; (b) after 3×3 median filtering

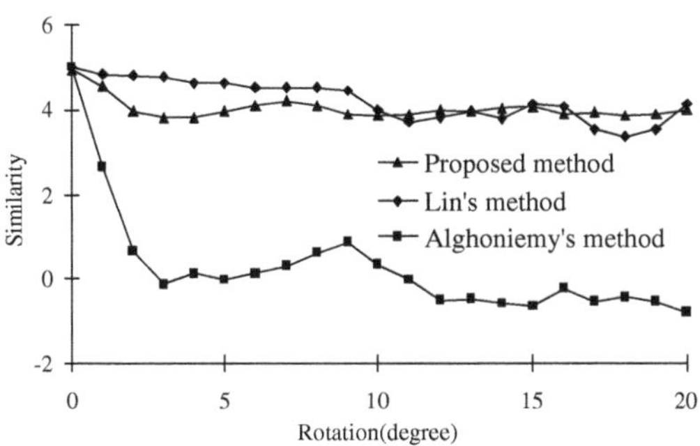

Fig. 9. Similarity in Lena image after rotation attacks

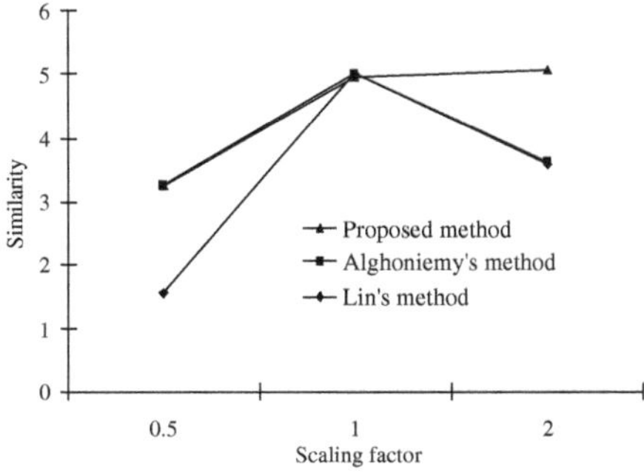

Fig. 10. Similarity in Lena image after scaling attacks

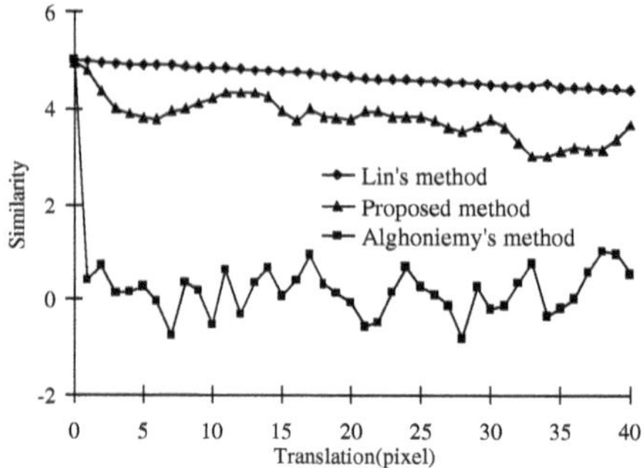

Fig. 11. Similarity in Lena image after translation attacks

ratio of 70, although the similarity values were satisfied given threshold. However Lin's et al.'s method has lower similarity values than threshold after compression ratio 45 because Lin's et al.'s method embeds the watermark into all frequency bands. Also the proposed scheme was found to be robust to low pass filtering as shown in Fig. 8. Fig. 8 (a) and (b) present the similarities in the pepper image including a watermark after average and median filtering using a size of 3×3. Although the similarity was lower after filtering, since they were higher than the threshold, the copyright could still be proved.

Figs. 9, 10, and 11 show that the proposed watermarking scheme was robust to geometrical attacks. The similarities after a rotational attack are shown in Fig. 9. Fig 9 (a) depicts the results of rotational attacks without cropping. All methods used in experiments did not lose any watermark information after rotation of the image. In contrast, Fig. 9 (b) represents the results of rotational attacks with cropping. Although Alghoniemys method was known to be robust to rotational attacks, however, this was not the case when the image was cropped because the image moments were not preserved. The similarities computed using different scaling factors are shown in Fig. 10. The similarities with the proposed method were theoretically uniform in spite of a scale change, although the similarity was lower when the scale was reduced, as a certain loss of information is unavoidable in a discrete signal. However, when the scaling factor was 0.5, the similarities still satisfied the threshold. In this case, Alghoniemys method performed well as there was no cropping, however Lin's et al.'s method cannot have sufficient similarity value since this method cannot have the properties of frequency localization and the scale downed image has the effect of LPF. Fig. 11 represents the similarities after translation attacks on 40 pixels along the x-axis, and shows that the proposed scheme was robust to translation. A translation of a digital image consequently involves cropping. Therefore, the watermark could be detected as long as the region used to acquire the invariant centroid was not cropped. Accordingly, the experimental results confirmed that the proposed watermarking scheme was robust to geometrical and waveform attacks based on the use of an invariant centroid and the properties of LPM and 2-D DFT.

5 Conclusion

This paper proposed a watermarking scheme, which is robust to geometrical attacks including cropping by improving FMW, and that is based on transforming an image to a domain that is invariant to rotation, scale, and translation. This domain is made by LPM using invariant centroid and 2-D DFT. LPM of an image provides invariance to scaling, plus translation invariance is included through the use of an invariant centroid as the origin of LPM. Since LPM transforms an image rotation into cyclic shift, 2-D DFT is performed on LPM image and the magnitude extracted to make a domain that is also invariant to cyclic shifts. Consequently, a domain is created that is invariant to rotation, scaling, and translation. A watermark generated from a copyright owners key is then embedded in this domain of visually significant bands. The resulting watermark is thus robust to both geometrical and waveform attacks. To prevent any image degradation due to the coordinate system conversion, we use indirection embedding method that only LPM image of watermark signal is inverse mapped to Cartesian coordinates and add to the original image.

References

1. Swanson, M.D., Kobayashi, M., Tewfik, A,H.: Multimedia data-embedding and watermarking technologies, Proceedings of IEEE, **86** (1998) 1064–1087
2. Bender, W.R., Gruhl, D., Morimoto, N., Lu, A.: Techniques for data hiding, IBM Systems Journal, **35** (1996) 313–336
3. Pitas, I.: A method for watermark casting on digital images, IEEE Transactions on Circuits and Systems for Video Technology, **8** (1998) 775–780.
4. van Schyndel, R. G., Tirkel, A. Z., and Osborne, C. F.: A digital watermark, Proceedings of ICIP, **2** (1994) 86–89.
5. Pereira, S. and Pun, T.: Robust template matching for affine resistant image watermarks, IEEE Transactions on Image Processing, **9** (2000) 1123–1129.
6. O'Ruanaidh, J. J. K. and Pun, T.: Rotation, scale and translation invariant digital image wa-termarking, Proceedings of ICIP, **1** (1997) 536–539.
7. O'Ruanaidh, J. J. K. and Pun, T.: Rotation, scale and translation invariant spread spectrum digital image watermarking, Signal Processing, **66** (1998) 303–317.
8. Langelaar, G. C., Setyawan, I., and Legendijk, R. L.: Watermarking digital image and video data, IEEE Signal Processing Magazine, **17** (2000) 20–46.
9. Alghoniemy, M. and Tewfik, A. H.: Geometric distortion correction through image normalization, Proceedings of ICME, **3** (2000) 1291–1294.
10. Lin, C.-Y., Wu, M., Bloom, J. A., Cox, I. J., Miller, M. L., and Lui, Y. M.: Rotation, scale, and translation resilient watermarking for images, IEEE Transaction on Image Processing, **10** (2001) 762–782

Robust Audio Watermarking Using Both DWT and Masking Effect

Won Young Hwang[1], Hwan Il Kang[1], Seung Soo Han[1], Kab Il Kim[1], and Hwan Soo Kang[2]

[1] Myongji University, Division of Electrical Information Control Engineering
San 38-2, Namdong, Yongin Kyunggido 449-728, South Korea
1978polo@hanmail.net, {hwan, shan, kkl}@mju.ac.kr

[2] Dongyang Technical College, Department of Electronic Commerce
62-160 Gochuk-Dong, Kuro-Ku Seoul, South Korea
hskang@dongyang.ac.kr

Abstract. In this paper, we propose a new digital audio watermarking technique with the wavelet transform. The watermark is embedded by eliminating unnecessary information of audio signal based on human auditory system (HAS). This algorithm is an audio watermarking method, which does not require any original audio information in watermark extraction process. In this paper, the masking effect is used for audio watermarking, that is, post-temporal masking effect. We construct the window with the synchronization signal and we extract the best frame in the window by using the zero-crossing rate (ZCR) and the energy of the audio signal. The watermark may be extracted by using the correlation of the watermark signal and the portion of the frame. Experimental results show good robustness against MPEG1-layer3 compression and other common signal processing manipulations. All the attacks are made after the D/A/D conversion.

1 Introduction

With the rapid spread of computer networks and the further progress of digital contents (audio, image, video, document [1] etc.), security and legal issues of copyright protection have become important. Digital watermark method is one promising technique for effectively protecting the copyright of digital contents. The important properties of the embedded watermark are the quality of the contents having embedded watermark data, the robustness of the watermark against modification of the contents, resistance to intentional removal of or tampering with the watermark, and the reliability of extracted watermark data. In case of audio watermark, the standard work is in process by SDMI (secure digital music initiative). Compared to the video signal, the audio signal can be represented as the small number of samples per time. It represents that there is no enough room for the watermark information, compared to the video signal. Another problem in the audio watermarking is that the HAS (Human Auditory System) is more sensitive than the HVS (Human Visual System). Many researchers have developed the audio

T. Kalker et al. (Eds.): IWDW 2003, LNCS 2939, pp. 382–389, 2004.
© Springer-Verlag Berlin Heidelberg 2004

watermarking methods. In echo hiding, the echo signal is embedded into the original audio signal [2]. Some algorithms use the patchwork method [3], and the spread spectrum is one of the most general audio watermarking method [4]. The spread spectrum technique is designed to encode a stream of information by spreading the encoded data across as much of the frequency spectrum as possible. This allows the signal survival excellent, even if there are interferences on some frequencies. But it has a fatal weakness in the asynchronous attack. A solution to overcome such a problem is one of the most difficult matters in audio watermarking method. In the algorithm proposed in this paper, the degradation of sound quality can be minimized using some characteristics of HAS and the wavelet transform can be obtained by utilizing zero-crossing rate (ZCR) and the energy of audio signal. Technologies of the audio watermarking have using the masking effect of the human auditory system [5] [6]. The masking effect of the HAS is secure of high quality in technologies of audio watermarking. The robustness of this algorithm was tested by applying several attacks such as cropping, quantization, time stretch, MPEG layer3, WMA [7], VQF [8] compression. All the attacks are made after the D/A/D conversion.

2 Proposed Audio Watermarking Algorithm

The algorithm proposed in this paper uses the HAS and the psychoacoustics model [9]. This algorithm embeds the watermark into the audio signal by DWT, ZCR-energy analysis, and the post-temporal masking effect. The watermark embedding region was selected by using the time domain post-masking effect. When extracting the embedded watermark, the first process is the synchronization, which means finding the watermarked region by searching the post-masking region.

2.1 Background

2.1.1 Psychoacoustic Model

The proposed method is to seek and remove the unnecessary information by using the HAS characteristic and the masking effect. The unnecessary information represents an element which can not be extracted by the human hearing, but the real sound exists. To find this information, the absolute threshold of hearing [10], the critical band analysis [11], and the simultaneous-temporal masking effects [12] are utilized. The frequency characteristic of the human auditory system is an essential factor of MPEG audio encoder.

Masking effect

The masking effect is related to the limitation of the certain sound according to the noise and distortion. The audio masking is the effect by which the faint but audible sound becomes inaudible in the presence of another louder audible sound. The masking effect is consisted of the temporal masking in the time domain and simultaneous masking in the frequency domain. The simultaneous masking is divided into two, the tone-masking-noise and the noise-masking-tone. The tone-masking-noise is a phenomenon that the noise became masking in center of critical band. The temporal masking refers to both pre- and post- temporal masking. The pre-masking effect make weaker signals inaudible before the stronger masker make turned on and the post-masking effect make weaker signals inaudible after the stronger masker make turned off. In this paper, the watermark is embedded using the post-temporal masking

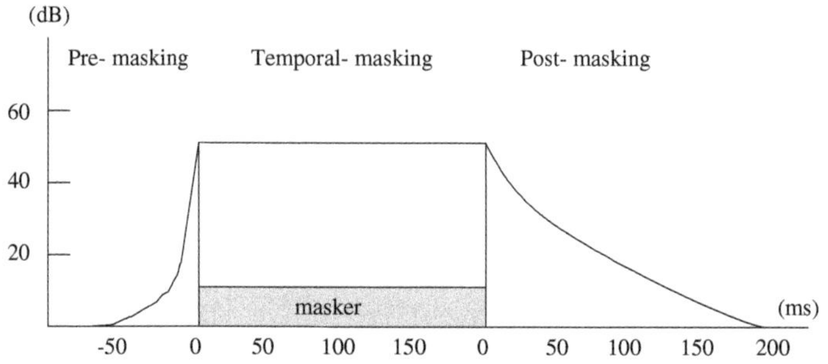

Fig. 1. Post-temporal masking.

2.1.2 Zero-Crossing Rate (ZCR) and Energy Analysis

By applying the appropriate size of the window to the audio signal in the time domain, the audio signal is divided into several frames and the ZCR and energy of each frame are obtained. These two factors are used for the start-end point detection of the watermark. In this paper, these two factors are used to search regions to embed the watermark. The frames with the high-energy with the low-ZCR are selected as the post-temporal masking regions. This region is selected as a good point to embed the watermark.

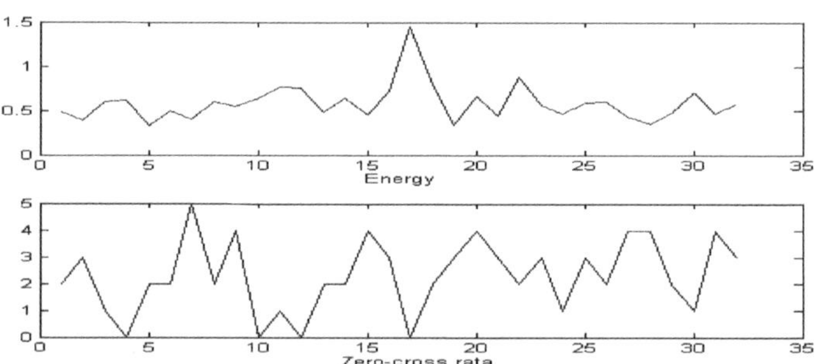

Fig. 2. Energy and ZCR analysis.

2.1.3 Discrete Wavelet Transform (DWT)

The wavelet Transform (WT) is a technique for analyzing signals. It was developed as an alternative to the short time Fourier Transform (STFT) to overcome problems related to its frequency and time resolution properties. More specifically, unlike the STFT that provides the uniform time resolution for all frequencies the DWT provides high time resolution and low frequency resolution for high frequencies and high frequency resolution and low time resolution for low frequencies. In that respect, it is similar to the human ear which exhibits similar time-frequency resolution characteristics. The Discrete Wavelet Transform (DWT) is a discrete case of the WT that provides the compact representation of a signal in time and frequency that can be computed efficiently.

The DWT is defined by the following equation:

$$W(j,k) = \sum_j \sum_k x(k) 2^{-j/2} \varphi(2^{-j} n - k) \tag{1}$$

In the above equation, $\varphi(t)$ is a time function with finite energy and fast decay called the mother wavelet. The DWT analysis can be performed using a fast and pyramidal algorithm related to multirate filterbanks [13].

As a multirate filterbank, the DWT can be viewed as a constant Q filterbank with octave spacing between the centers of the filters. Each subband contains half the samples of the neighboring higher frequency subband. In the pyramidal algorithm the signal is analyzed at different frequency bands with different resolution by decomposing the signal into a coarse approximation and detail information. The coarse approximation is then further decomposed using the same wavelet decomposition step. This is achieved by successive highpass and lowpass filtering of the time domain signal and is defined by the following equations:

$$\begin{aligned} y_{high}[k] &= \sum_n x[n] g[2k-n] \\ y_{low}[k] &= \sum_n x[n] h[2k-n] \end{aligned} \tag{2}$$

In the above equation, $y_{high}[k]$, $y_{low}[k]$ are the outputs of the highpass (g) and lowpass (h) filters, respectively after subsampling by 2. Because of the downsampling the number of resulting wavelet coefficients is exactly the same as the number of input points. [14] [15] In this paper, the watermark is embedded using DWT.

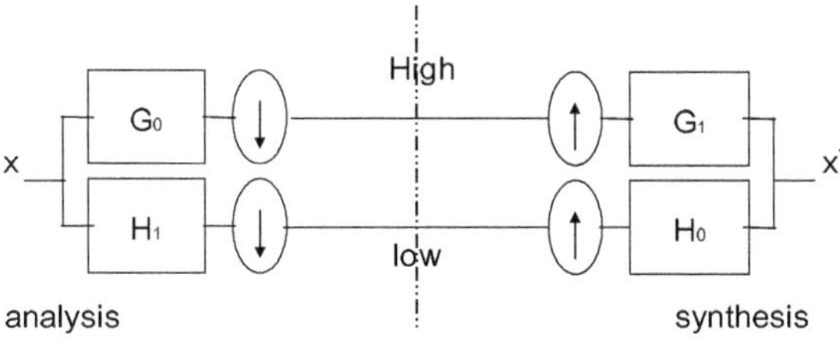

Fig. 3. One-level analysis and synthesis system.

2.2 Sync Embedding and Extractions

STEP1. The synchronization signal is created from the random noise of length 1024 bits.

STEP2. We embed the synchronization signal in the time domain by using the ZCR and the energy. Then the signal is transform to the signal by DWT and we insert the watermark.

STEP3. The new signal (Cn) is made through inverse DWT.

STEP4. We extract the synchronization signal from the region that has the highest similarity among regions. The similarity calculation is calculated by shifting the window in the right direction one by one in the new signal. (Fig. 4)

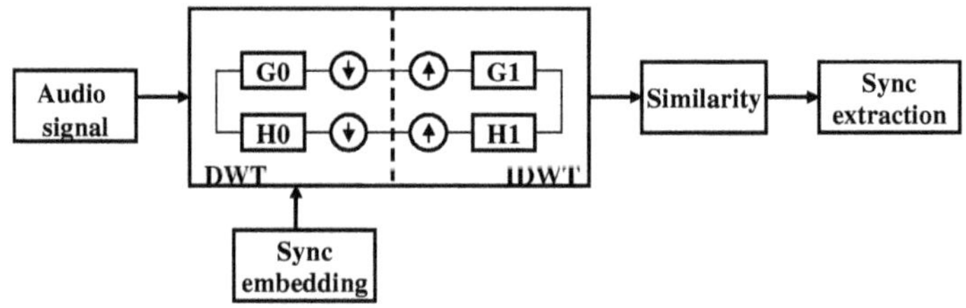

Fig. 4. Sync embedding and extractions procedure.

2.3 Watermark Embedding and Extractions

STEP1. The window is divided into the length 1024 bits from the synchronization extraction point. (32 by 32)(Fig. 5)

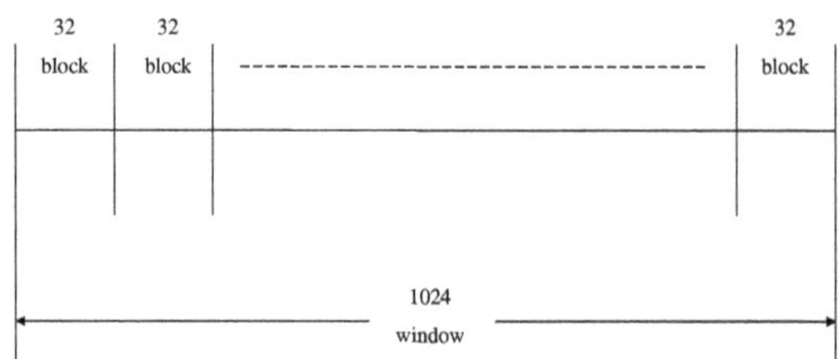

Fig. 5. Window select to watermark embed.

STEP2. We obtain the energy and ZCR from each frame.

STEP3. We embed the part of watermark in the frame of the high-energy with the low-ZCR. (Co)

STEP4. We embed process of the additive watermark in the wavelet domain by multiplying watermark signal (Ws) with embedding strength.

STEP5. The new signal (Con) is made through inverse DWT.

STEP6. The extract process of watermark is performed from similarity of Con and watermark signal. (Fig. 6)

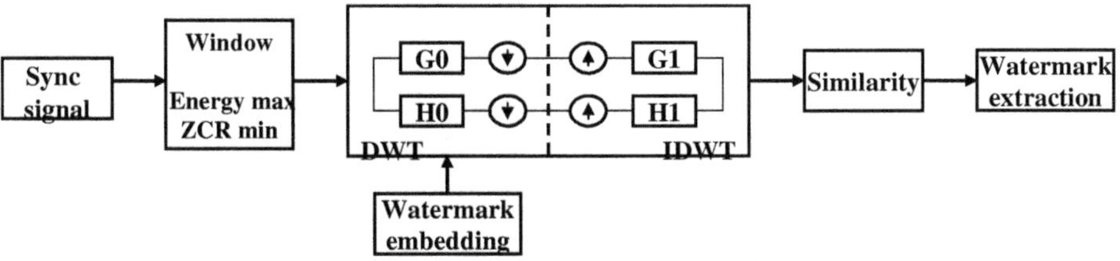

Fig. 6. Watermark embedding and extractions procedure.

3 Experimental Results

The experiments were performed according to the requirements of SDMI [16]. The audio signals under test were 16 bits mono signal sampled at 44.1 kHz.
All the experiments are performed using the analog signal passed through the speaker but not using the digital signal. The audio samples include Ballade (Audio1), Rock (Audio2), Metal (Audio3), and Classic (Audio4) music. To test the robustness of the propose watermarking algorithm against various types of attacks. All the attacks are made after the D/A/D conversion.
Table 1 shows the results of the no manipulation, clipping, quantization, MPEG1 layer, WMA, VQF compression, time stretch and echo addition attacks. Watermark extraction rata is more than 90%. But with the VQF compression process, the watermark extraction rata is 70%.

Table 1. Watermark extraction results for the attacks.

	Audio1	Audio2	Audio3	Audio4	Extraction rate
No manipulation	10	10	10	10	100%
Clipping	9	10	9	8	90%
Quantization	9	10	10	9	95%
MPEG1 layer 3	9	10	9	8	90%
Time stretch (+10%)	8	10	10	8	90%
Time stretch (-10%)	8	9	9	10	90%
WMA	9	10	10	9	95%
VQF	5	9	8	6	70%
Echo addition (3%)	9	10	9	10	95%

Table 2 shows the results of the performance comparison between the proposed watermarking algorithm and the spread spectrum method, which is proposed by Cox. Et. Al. Spread spectrum method spreads data in frequency domain using by the discrete cosine transform (DCT). An obvious weakness appears in spread spectrum method with the asynchronous attacks (quantization, MPEG1 layer, WMA and VQF). Comparatively, the proposed algorithm show robust results in asynchronous attacks.

Table 2. Proposed algorithm vs. spread spectrum method.

	proposed algorithm extraction rata	Spread spectrum method rata
No manipulation	100%	100%
Clipping	90%	90%
Quantization	95%	15%
MPEG1 layer 3	90%	15%
Time stretch (+10%)	90%	90%
Time stretch (-10%)	90%	90%
WMA	95%	20%
VQF	70%	10%
Echo addition (3%)	95%	90%

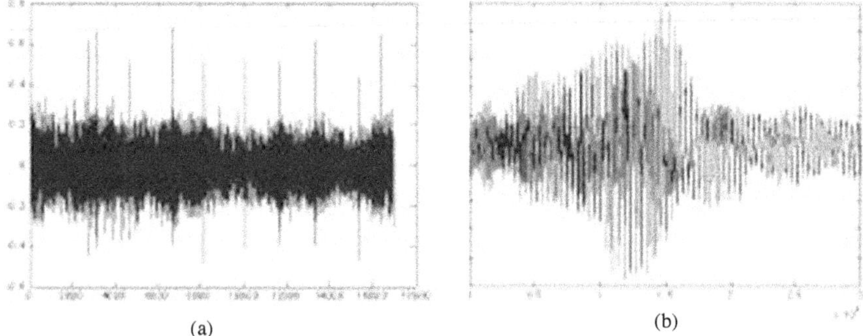

(a) (b)

Fig. 7. Proposed algorithm vs. spread spectrum method: (a) watermark extraction of DWT after mp3 compression; (b) watermark extraction of DCT after mp3 compression

4 Conclusions

In this paper, we proposed a new HAS and DWT based algorithm for the audio watermarking. This algorithm utilizes the ZCR and the energy analysis, and the post-temporal masking effect for embedding the watermark. The watermark may be detected by using the correlation of the watermark signal and the portion of the frame. By applying several attacks proposed by SDMI, the robustness of the proposed algorithm is tested, and the experiments shows good performance in the synchronization and the other audio signal manipulation with minimal audio quality degradation. Also, the proposed algorithm is shown to make good performance in D/A/D conversion.

Acknowledgements. This work was supported in part by the Myongji University in the framework of the project during the sabbatical year of the second author.

References

[1] Hwan Il Kang, Jong Uk Choi, Kab Il Kim, "A vector watermarking using the generalized square mask", Information Technology: Coding and Computing, 2001. Proceedings. International Conference on, Apr 2001 pp.234–236

[2] Say Wei Foo, Theng Hee Yeo, and Dong Yan Huang "An adaptive audio watermarking system," Electrical and Electronic Technology, 2001. TENCON. Proceedings of IEEE Region 10 International Conference, vol.2, (2001) 509–513

[3] H. Kii J. Onishi, and S. Ozawa, "The digital watermarking method by using both patchwork and DCT", Multimedia Computing and System, 1999 IEEE International Conference on, vol.1 (1999) 895–899

[4] I. Cox, J. Kilian, T. Leighton, and T. Shamoon, "Secure Spread Spectrum Watermarking for Multimedia", IEEE Transaction on Image Processing, vol. 6, pp.1673–1687, Dec. 1997.

[5] Yong-Hun Kim, Seung-Soo Han, Hwan-Il Kang, Kab-Il Kim 'A Digital Watermarking Using Two Masking Effects' Third IEEE Pacific Rim Conference on Multimedia, - PCM2002. Hsinchu, Taiwan, Dec. 2002. pp.655–662

[6] Mitchell D. Swanson, Bin Zhu, Ahmed H. Tewfik, Laurence Boney 'Robust audio watermarking using perceptual masking' Signal Processing 66 (1998) 337–355

[7] http://www.microsoft.com

[8] http://www.vqf.com

[9] ISO/IEC IS I1I172, Information technology - coding of moving pictures and associated audio for digital storage up to about 1.5Mbits/s

[10] Fletcher, 'Auditory Patterns' Re. Mod. Phys., pp. 47–65. Jan. 1940

[11] Zwicker, E, & Fastl. 'Psychoacoustics Facts and Models.' Springer-Verlag . 1990

[12] Schroeder,M. 'Optimizing digital speech coders by exploiting masking properties of the human ear.' J Axoust. Sco. Am. Dec.1979. pp.1647–1652

[13] S.G Mallat "A Theory for Multiresolution Signal Decomposition: The Wavelet Representation" IEEE. Transactions on Pattern Analysis and Machine Intelligence, Vol.11, 1989, 674–693

[14] I.Daubechies "Orthonormal Bases of Compactly Supported Wavelets" Communications on Pure and Applied Math. Vol.41 1988, 909–996

[15] Tzanetakis, G., Essl, G., Cook, P.R., "Audio Analysis using the Discrete Wavelet Transform," In Proc. WSES Int. Conf. Acoustics and Music: Theory and Applications (AMTA 2001) Skiathos, Greece, 2001.

[16] http://www.sdmi.org/

Normalization Domain Watermarking Method Based on Pattern Extraction

Si-Woong Lee[1], Jae-Gark Choi[2], Hyun-Soo Kang[3], Jin-Woo Hong[4], and Hyoung Joong Kim[5]

[1] Div. of Info. Comm. and Computer Eng., Hanbat National University, San 16-1, Dukmyung-Dong, Yusong-Gu, Taejeon, 305-719, Korea
swlee69@hanbat.ac.kr

[2] Dept. of Computer Eng., Dongeui University, Gaya-Dong, Busanjin-Gu, Busan, 614-714, Korea
cjg@dongeui.ac.kr

[3] Graduate School of AIM, Chung-Ang University, 221, Heuksuk-dong, Dongjak-ku, Seoul, 156-070, Korea
hskang@cau.ac.kr

[4] Radio & Broadcasting Tech. Lab., ETRI, 161 Gajeong-Dong, Yuseong-Gu, Daejeon, 305-350, Korea
jwhong@etri.re.kr

[5] Dept. of Control and Instrumentation Eng., Kangwon Natioanl University, Chunchon, 200-701, Korea
khj@kangwon.ac.kr

Abstract. This paper presents a new watermarking scheme using the pattern-based image normalization. The proposed method extracts an image-adaptive binary pattern (BP) composed of inner regions, and the geometric moments are computed using the BP rather than the source image itself. This approach avoids any misalignment between the normalized images on both sides of embedding and detection, which is inevitable when the source image itself is used.

1 Introduction

Recently, extensive efforts have been devoted to the development of robust digital watermarking for the copyright protection of digital assets. Nonetheless, several critical issues still need improving to match the quality of service available in commercial fields. One of these problems in the image watermarking area is robustness to geometrical attacks. Conventional watermarking schemes are most vulnerable to geometrical attacks, such as rotation and scaling, as they can completely change the alignment of the watermark with respect to the pixels[1].

Accordingly, the current paper proposes a new watermarking scheme using moment-based image normalization[2] to provide robustness to geometrical distortions. Normalization involves synchronizing two images before and after geometric transformation based on computing a standard form for them that is invariant under geometrical attack if and only if the attack causes a variation in

T. Kalker et al. (Eds.): IWDW 2003, LNCS 2939, pp. 390–395, 2004.
© Springer-Verlag Berlin Heidelberg 2004

the pixel positions rather than the pixel values. However, normalization that uses moments computed from gray scale images[2] has two failure modes: 1) Signal disturbances in a boundary area resulting from disappeared and newly inserted pixels and, 2) signal distortion introduced by added watermarks or other kinds of value-metric attacks. Therefore, to accommodate these problems, a pattern-based image normalization scheme is proposed that uses an image-adaptive binary pattern rather than a gray scale image to compute the moments.

2 Image Normalization Based on Pattern Extraction

In moment-based normalization, the normalization criterion is imposed on the moments of an image. The moment of order (p, q) of a gray scale image is defined as

$$m_{p,q} = \int\int_{\Gamma} x^p y^q g(x, y) dx dy \tag{1}$$

where Γ is the support of the image[2]. However, in the proposed method, the moment is computed as

$$m_{p,q} = \int\int_{\Gamma} x^p y^q b_g(x, y) dx dy \tag{2}$$

where $b_g(x, y)$ is the binary pattern of $g(x, y)$. Two conditions are imposed on generating $b_g(x, y)$ to solve the above-mentioned problems:

1) $b_g(x, y)$ should only be composed of the interior pixels, i.e., not connected to the image boundary and
2) the additive noise, including a watermark signal, should have negligible influence on the shape of $b_g(x, y)$.

The proposed watermarking scheme is shown in Fig. 1. Prior to the BP extraction step, the input signal is low-pass filtered. The purpose of the filtering operation is to remove noise power in high frequencies to accommodate the second condition imposed on the BP generation above. Since the BP for normalization purposes does not need to have a meaningful shape, the filter can have a very narrow pass-band as long as it can produce an efficient correlation between BP shapes on both sides. From the filtered image, $b_g(x, y)$ is generated. In the current paper, two possible methods of generating $b_g(x, y)$ are presented: threshold method and segmentation method.

Threshold method: The binary image is obtained using the threshold process in the equation below:

$$b_g(x, y) = \begin{cases} 1, if\ T - \Delta \leq g(x, y) \leq T + \Delta \\ 0, \text{otherwiae} \end{cases} \tag{3}$$

where T and Δ are constants determined from observing the pixel luminance in a circle area whose the center is the image center. The connected white pixels

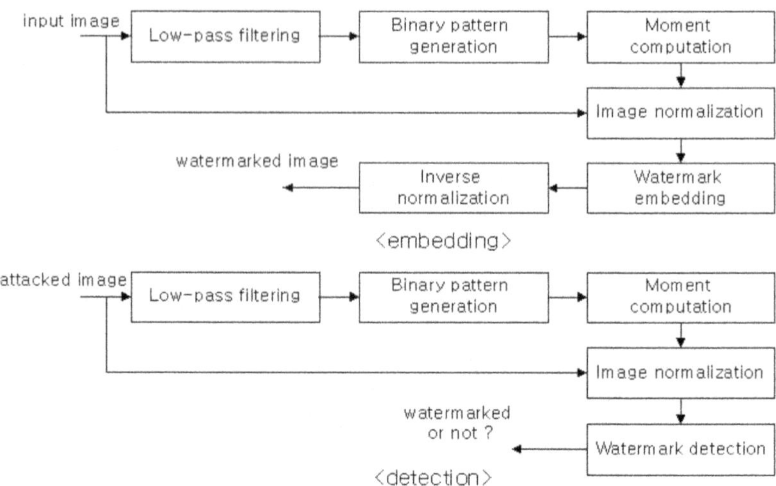

Fig. 1. Proposed watermarking scheme

are grouped into regions, then the region with the closest center to the image center and not connected to the image boundary is chosen as the BP of $g(x, y)$.

Segmentation method: This method is more sophisticated as the image is segmented into homogeneous luminance regions larger than the size boundary using morphological tools. The connection of those regions that are not connected to the image boundary then constitutes the BP of $g(x, y)$.

Once the BP of an image is obtained, moments through the second order are computed using Eq. (2). Thereafter, normalization is performed and $g(x, y)$ is geometrically transformed into a standard form $g_n(x, y)$. There are already a variety of image normalization algorithms. Among them, the current study used the method described in [3] that is applied to a binary image using the concepts of a centroid, principal axis, and independent scale.

3 Watermark Embedding and Verification

The proposed watermarking scheme operates in the frequency domain based on a similar approach to Barnis method[1]. From the zig-zag ordered DCT coefficients of the normalized image, $T = \{t_{L+1}, t_{L+2}, \ldots, t_{L+N}\}$ from the $(L+1)th$ to the $(L+N)th$ are taken. The marking is performed on the selected coefficients by changing the magnitude component according to the following rule using a scaling parameter α :

$$t'_{L+i} = t_{L+i} + \alpha \, |t_{L+i}| \, x_i, \; i = \{1, 2, \cdots, N\} \tag{4}$$

where x_i is the $i - th$ random number of a watermark of length N .. In the last stage of embedding, inverse normalization restores the original orientation

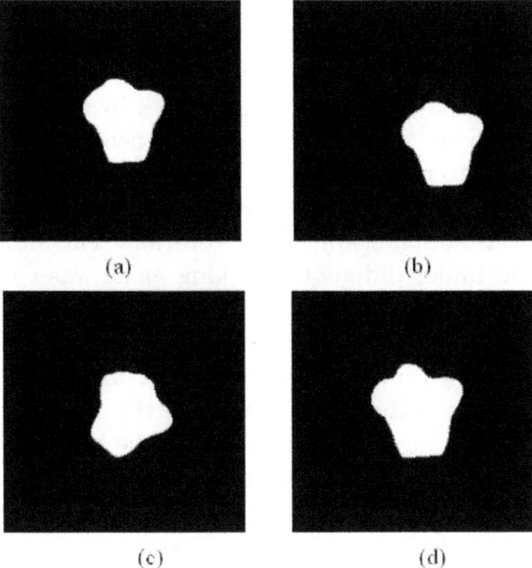

Fig. 2. Extracted BP: (a) original image; (b) translation attack; (c) rotation attack; (d) scale attack

and scale. Since this process involves the appearance of new pixels, they are substituted with the original signal.

The presence of a watermark can be reliably verified in the normalized domain. Given a test image, the LPF and BP generation are applied successively. From the moments of the BP, the normalized image is obtained in the same manner as the embedding. Then the similarity (s) between the coefficients and the pseudo-random sequence (X) is calculated as follows,

$$s = \frac{1}{N} \sum_{i=1}^{N} t^{*}_{L+i} x_i \tag{5}$$

To decide the presence of a given mark, it should be determined whether $s > T$, where T is the threshold.

4 Experimental Results

In the simulation, a 256x256 Miss America image was used to demonstrate the effectiveness of the proposed method. For the BP generation, the threshold method was used and the normalized image was marked with $L = 1000$, $N = 3000$, and $\alpha = 0.2$ to obtain the watermarked image.

Fig. 2 shows the binary patterns of the original and attacked images with various geometrical distortions. It can be seen that the patterns were still highly correlated in their shapes, thereby enabling an exact synchronization of the normalized images. A watermark should still be detectable after common signal distortions, such as JPEG compression, filtering, etc, are applied to the data. Since the proposed scheme embeds the watermark by modifying the DCT coefficients, it is unaffected by the common signal processing. Specifically the proposed method was able to resist JPEG compression down to a compression ratio of about 32:1. In addition, a watermark should also be able to withstand geometric distortions, such as shifts, scaling, and rotation. The similarity variation of the proposed method under different attacking angle was compared with those of methods in [1] and [2] in Fig.3. At a two-degree angle, the Barnis method was unable to exhibit a sufficient similarity to verify the existence of the watermark. By adapting the normalization scheme in [2] that uses the gray-level image in computing the moments to the Barnis method, the watermark was verified to the 8-degree angle. For a large attacking angle, the method also failed to verify the watermark with the reason that the moments suffer the boundary effects severely. However, no watermark information was lost with the proposed method regardless of the degree of the rotation attack, since the watermark information is verified in the accurately synchronized domain.

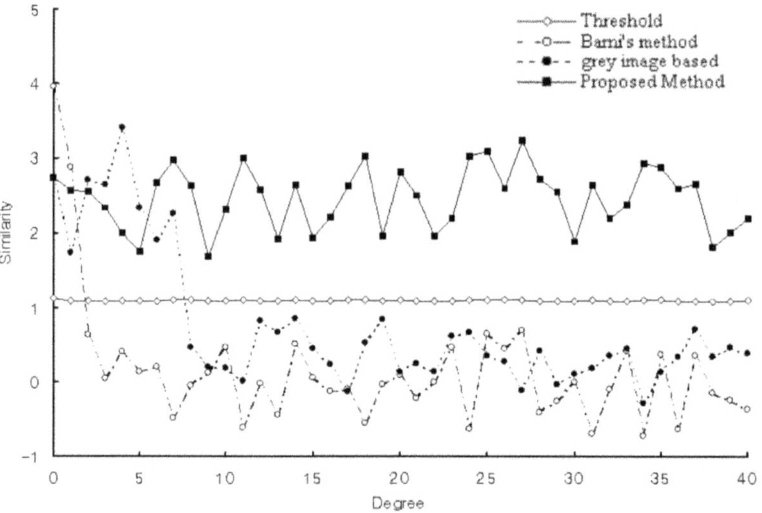

Fig. 3. Similarity relative to rotation angle

5 Conclusion

The current paper proposed a new watermarking scheme that operates in the normalization domain. As such, the proposed pattern-based image normalization enables the watermark embedding and detection domains to be synchronized, regardless of shifts, scaling, and rotation. Experimental results confirmed that the proposed scheme could reliably verify the existence of a watermark from an image that has been degraded due to geometrical attacks.

Acknowledgement. This work was supported in part by the IT Research Center (ITRC), Ministry of Information and Communication, Korea.

References

1. M. Barni, F. Bartolini, V. Cappellini, A. Piva,: A DCT-domain system for robust image watermarking, Signal processing (1998) 357–372.
2. M. Alghoniemy and A .H. Tewfik,: Geometric distortion correction through image normalization, vol.2, in Proc. of ICIP (2000) 1291 1294.
3. Y. S. Abu-mostafa and D. Psaltis,: Image normalization by complex moments, vol.PAMI-7, no.1, IEEE Trans. PAMI (1985) 46–55.

Robust Watermarking with Adaptive Receiving

Xiangui Kang[1, 2], Jiwu Huang[1], Yun Q. Shi[3], and Jianxiang Zhu[1]

[1]Dept. of Electronics, Sun Yat-Sen University, Guangzhou 510275. P. R. China
{isskxg, isshjw}@zsu.edu.cn
[2]National Laboratory of Pattern Recognition, Beijing 10080, P. R. China

[3]Dept. of ECE, New Jersey Institute of Technology, NJ 07102, U. S. A.
shi@njit.edu

Abstract. This paper presents a watermarking scheme with enhanced robustness owing to adaptive receiving and turbo code in addition to other measures. We embed a training sequence with informative watermark in the original image. A new adaptive receiver is developed, which is adjusted adaptively according to the responsive distribution of the training sequence. Together with carefully designed data embedding techniques, concatenated coding of direct sequence spread spectrum (DSSS) and Turbo code, 2-D interleaving, our newly developed resynchronization technique and incorporated with the registration technique based on motion estimation technique developed by Loo and Kinsbury, our proposed algorithm can successfully resist almost all the StirMark testing functions including both common signal processing, such as JPEG compression and median filtering, and geometric distortions. The watermarking is robust against the combination of geometric distortion and JPEG_10, the combination of large global distortion and arbitrary local small distortion. To our best knowledge, we use adaptive receiving to combat the fading of host media feature (watermark carrier) for the first time.

1 Introduction

Digital watermarking has emerged as a potentially effective tool for multimedia copyright protection, authentication and tamper proofing [1, 2]. Robustness is one of the key issues in watermarking for many applications. Robustness against both common signal processing and geometric distortion at the same time remains challenging, and robustness to the combination of large distortion (such as rotation by a large angle, scaling by a large factor, and/or cropping by a large quantity) and random small local distortion (such as randomization-and-bending in StirMark 3.1) remains an open problem. In our previous work, we developed non-blind [3] and blind technique [4] to make watermark robust to geometric distortion. But the watermark in [3, 4] is not robust against some of the testing functions in StirMark 3.1, such as median filtering and randomization-and-bending. It is noted that the test functions of watermark robustness against common signal processing in StirMark 3.1 include median filtering and the related test results have not been reported in detail in

T. Kalker et al. (Eds.): IWDW 2003, LNCS 2939, pp. 396–407, 2004.
© Springer-Verlag Berlin Heidelberg 2004

the literature. According to our work, robustness to median filtering is a tough problem to handle in watermarking [3, 4] because median filtering damages the watermark severely and the PSNR of median filtered image versus the non-filtered image is rather low. For example, the PSNRs of 2×2, 3×3 and 4×4 median filtered image versus non-filtered image are as low as 25.9dB, 28.9dB and 20.9dB respectively for Baboon image. As an extension of our work in [3, 4], we develop watermarking with adaptive receiving to improve the robustness of watermark against median filtering in this paper. Note that the adaptive receiving was first introduced in [5] to handle the fading of the watermark extracted from a corrupted marked image. In this paper, however, we use adaptive receiving to combat the fading of host media feature (watermark carrier), thus enhancing the watermark robustness against median filtering for the first time. We also incorporate the resynchronization based on minimum distance [3] and the motion estimation technique developed by Loo and Kinsbury [6] to solve the combination of large distortion such as rotation, scaling, translation and/or cropping (RST) and arbitrary local small distortion such as randomization-and-bending. The proposed watermarking technique can resist almost all attacks in StirMark 3.1 including median filtering and randomization-and-bending.

The remaining of this paper is organized as follows. In Section II, we introduce the watermark embedding. Section III describes the resynchronization of the watermark. Section IV is about watermark extraction based on adaptive receiving. The experimental results are presented in Section V. Conclusion is drawn in the last section.

2 Watermark Embedding

To survive all kinds of attacks, we encode the message $\boldsymbol{m}$ $\{m_i;\ i=1, \ldots, L,\ m_i \in \{0,1\}\}$ with concatenated coding of DSSS coding and turbo code. To cope with bursts of errors possibly occurred with watermarked image, 2D interleaving [7] is exploited. We embed informative watermark (the encoded message) into LL_4 subband in DWT domain to make it robust while keeping the watermark invisible [2, 3]. To achieve adaptive receiving, we embed a training sequence randomly together with the informative watermark.

The watermark embedding is implemented as follows.

The 60-bit message $\boldsymbol{m}$ is first encoded using turbo code with rate 1/2 to obtain the message $\boldsymbol{m_c}$ $\{m_{ci};\ i=1, \ldots, L_c,\ m_{ci} \in \{0,1\}\}$of length L_c =124 [8]. Then each bit m_{ci} of $\boldsymbol{m_c}$ is DSSS encoded using an N_1-bit bi-polar PN-sequence $\boldsymbol{p}=\{p_j;\ j=1, \ldots, N_1,\ N_1=7$ in our work}, where "1" is encoded spreadly as $\{+1 \times p_j;\ j=1, \ldots, N_1\}$, "0" as $\{-1 \times p_j;\ j=1, \ldots, N_1\}$, thus obtaining a binary string $\boldsymbol{W}$.

$$m_{ci} \xrightarrow{DSSS\ coding} W_i\{w_{ij};\ w_{ij} \in \{-1,+1\}, 1 \le j < N_1\}, 1 \le i < L_c \tag{1}$$

The training sequence $\boldsymbol{T}$ $\{T_n;\ n=1, \ldots, 152\}$, $T_n \in \{-1,1\}$ should be distributed all over the image randomly based on a key. In our work, $\boldsymbol{T}$ is composed of 152 bits "1". The watermark embedding process is shown in Fig.1.

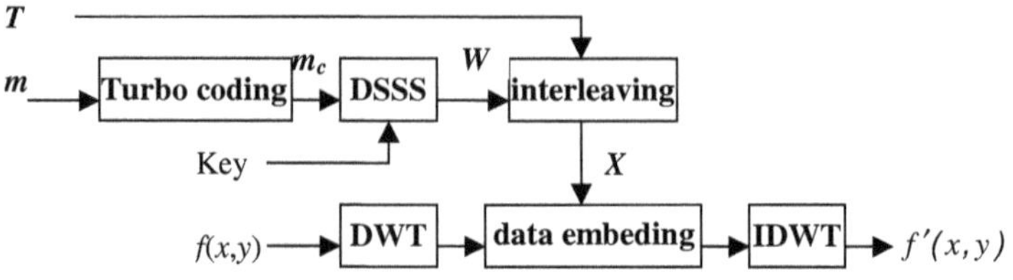

Fig. 1. The watermark embedding process

In implementation, we put 152-bit sequence ***T*** into a 32x32 2-D array randomly based on a key, the binary string ***W*** is filled into the remaining portion of the above-mentioned array. By applying 2-D interleaving technique [7] to this array, we obtain another 2-D array. Scanning this 2-D array, say, row by row, we convert it into a 1-D array $\boldsymbol{X}=\{x_i\}$ ($1<i<1024$). We perform a 4-level DWT on an original 512x512 image $f(x, y)$ by using the Daubechies 9/7 bi-orthogonal wavelet filters. The DWT coefficients in the LL_4 subband are scanned in the same fashion as mentioned above to form a 1-D array ***C***. We adopt quantization-based embedding [9], expressed in Equation (2), to embed the binary data ***X*** into ***C*** to obtain $\boldsymbol{C'}$. Here $C(i)$, $C'(i)$ denotes the ith element in ***C***, and $\boldsymbol{C'}$, respectively. The quantizer $q(.)$ is a uniform, scalar quantization function of step size S, and $q(x)= kS+0.5S$, $k=\left\lfloor \frac{x}{S} \right\rfloor$ ($k\in Z$), where $\lfloor . \rfloor$ means *floor* operation. Equation (2) indicates that the proposed embedding method tries to output a $C'(i)$ value which is closest to $C(i)$ and whose corresponding embedding bit value equals to x_i (Fig. 2). The parameter S can be chosen so as to make a good compromise between the contending requirements of imperceptibility and robustness. Note that the difference between $C(i)$ and $C'(i)$ is between $-0.5S$ and $+0.5S$. Performing inverse DWT on the modified image, we obtain a watermarked image $f'(x, y)$.

$$\begin{cases} C'(i) = q(C(i) - \frac{1}{4}S) + \frac{1}{4}S, \text{ if } x_i = 1 \\ C'(i) = q(C(i) + \frac{1}{4}S) - \frac{1}{4}S, \text{ if } x_i = -1 \end{cases} \tag{2}$$

(a) $C'(i)$ $(k\text{-}1)S+0.5S$ kS $kS+0.5S$ $(k+1)S$ $(k+1)S+0.5S$

|-----x-----|-----x-----|-----x----|-----x-----|

(b) embedded bit x_i = "1"   "-1"   "1"   "-1"

Fig. 2. Graphical illustration of data embedding. (a) "x" indicates a possible $C'(i)$ value after one bit is embedded. (b) the corresponding embedded bit.

3 Resynchronization

In order for the watermark to be robust against large distortion such as rotation by a large angle, scaling by a large factor, and/or cropping by a large quantity, we perform an anti-RST operation [3] to remove the RST distortion applied to the watermarked image by searching for the minimum distance (best matching) between the attacked watermarked image and the reference image $f(x, y)$. If the searched minimum distance is less than a threshold, in our work, we choose it to be 5 (empirically determined), then the RST distortion recovered image, must be further registered based on motion estimation [6] to remove other small distortion such as shearing, small general linear transform, and randomization-and-bending testing functions in StirMark 3.1. Otherwise, the RST distortion removed image is used for watermark extraction directly.

4 Watermark Extraction

The watermark extraction is the inverse process of the watermark embedding. First, perform the 4-level DWT on the resynchronized test image. The coefficients of the LL_4 subband are scanned according to the same way as used in data embedding and turned into a 1-D array, denoted by $\boldsymbol{C}^*=\{C^*(i)\}$. In most cases the results of attacks are assumed to be additive noise (with zero mean), so we can extract the hidden binary data $\boldsymbol{X}^*$ according to Equation (3) [9, 3] with the best decision level 0.5S. Here *mod* denotes signed remainder after division. Equation (3) indicates that if r ($r = C^*(i) \bmod S$) is in the interval (0, 0.5S), then the decision is made in favor of "–1", that is, (0, 0.5S) represents the hidden data bit "–1". The interval representing "1" is (0.5S, S). Next we perform 2-D de-interleaving, which is the inverse process of 2-D interleaving [7], to $\boldsymbol{X}^*$ to obtain the binary sequences $\boldsymbol{W}^*$. We segment $\boldsymbol{W}^*$ by N_1 bits per sequence, correlate the obtained sequence with the original *PN*-sequence $\boldsymbol{p}$. If the correlation value is larger than 0, the recovered bit is "1", otherwise, "–1", we then obtain the binary bit sequence $\boldsymbol{m}^*_c$. $\boldsymbol{m}^*_c$ is further turbo decoded [8], the message $\boldsymbol{m}$ can thus be recovered.

$$x_i^* = \begin{cases} +1, & r = C^*(i) \bmod S > \dfrac{S}{2} \\ -1, & otherwise \end{cases} \tag{3}$$

Unfortunately, the above extraction method does not take into account the practically important case of channel fading (image feature fading). Thus extracted watermark is not robust enough or its imperceptibility is not very high. For example, to be robust to 3x3 median filtering, we must adopt a high watermark strength with S equal to or greater than, say, 260 for Baboon image, the PSNR of the obtained watermarked image versus original image is less than 33.9dB and the generated watermark's invisibility is not very well. The hidden data bit x_i is transmitted via a

DWT coefficient $C'(i)$ in the LL_4 subband. When the channel is fading, e.g., as the image is median filtered, the equivalent channel model can be presented as:

$$C^*(i) = F \cdot C'(i) + \beta \tag{4}$$

where F denotes the generalized fading and β denotes the generalized additive noise in the equivalent channel. Fig. 3 to Fig. 5 show the distribution of r (refer to Equation 3) associated with the training sequence ***T***, which is composed of 76 binary "1" and 76 binary "–1" bits here. In these figures, the r values corresponding to binary "1" and "–1" of ***T*** are sorted respectively according to their values from small to large. That is, the x-coordinate denotes the sorting order number, the y-coordinate denotes the value of r in the unit of embedding strength related parameter S. Because the training sequence is embedded randomly together with informative watermark, the distribution of r with respect to the training sequence is similar to the distribution of r with respect to the informative watermark. Fig. 3 shows the distribution of ***T*** in the unattacked marked image, the value of r corresponding to "1" of ***T*** is 0.75S, the value of r corresponding to "–1" of ***T*** is 0.25S. Fig. 4 shows the distribution of the training sequence in a 3x3 median filtered image, we can see that because of the fading of the

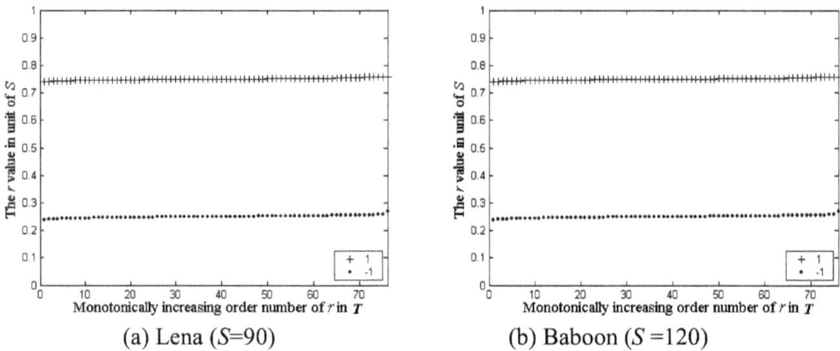

(a) Lena (S=90) (b) Baboon (S=120)

Fig. 3. The distribution of training sequence in the unattacked marked image.

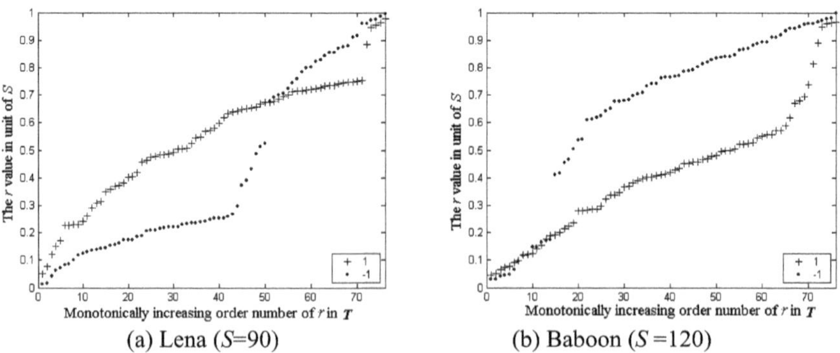

(a) Lena (S=90) (b) Baboon (S=120)

Fig. 4. The distribution of training sequence in 3x3 median filtered image.

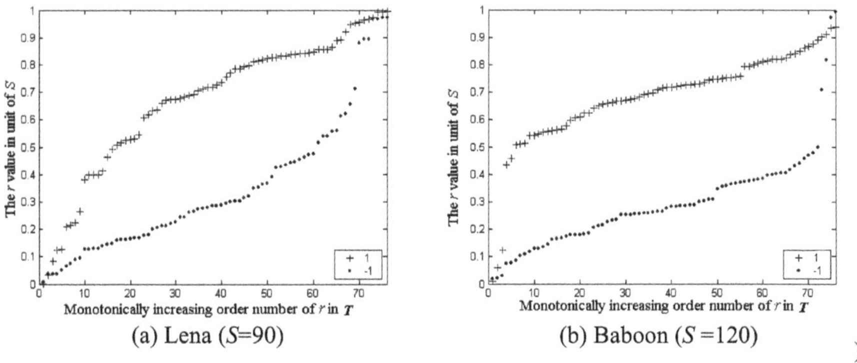

(a) Lena (S=90) (b) Baboon (S =120)

Fig. 5. The distribution of training sequence in JPEG_10 compressed image.

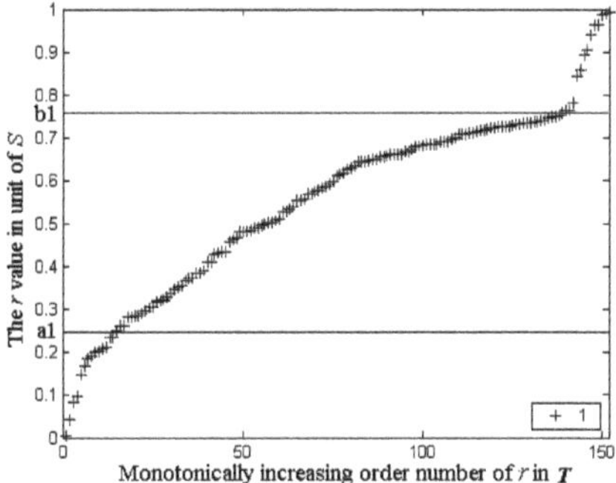

Fig. 6. Determining the interval (a_1, b_1) representing "1" (a_1=0.25S, b_1=0.75S).

DWT coefficients in the LL_4 subband of the filtered image, the interval (0.5S, S) does not contain most of r corresponding to "1" of $\boldsymbol{T}$, and the interval (0, 0.5S) does not contain most of r corresponding to "–1" of $\boldsymbol{T}$. So the above extraction method, that is, the interval (0, 0.5S) representing "–1" and (0.5S, S) representing "1", may not be the best for hidden data bit extraction when the test image is median filtered. We hence propose the following method to determine the interval representing binary "1" or "–1" adaptively.

From Fig. 3 to Fig. 5, it is observed that the curves corresponding to binary "1" and "–1" exhibit similar behavior except that due to the *mod S* operation the average values of two curves differ by 0.5S. Therefore in the embedding, the training sequence $\boldsymbol{T}$ is composed of 152 bits "1". In this way the distribution of r values is expected more accurate since double data are available. In the extraction, we calculate the r with respect to the 152 bits of training sequence first, then we determine the two intervals representing "1" and "–1", respectively according the distribution of the r described below.

We search for an interval that contains the most r values associated with the training sequence bits among all the intervals with a fixed width 0.5S. The interval can be in the form of (a_1, b_1), where $0<a_1<b_1<S$, a_1-b_1=0.5S, as shown in Fig. 6 or in

the form of $(c_1, S) \cup (0, d_1)$, where $0<d_1<c_1<S$, $d_1+S-c_1=0.5S$. Interval corresponding to "1" is then determined. The remaining interval within $(0, S)$ is the interval representing "–1".

In implementation, we divide the whole interval $(0, S)$ into 20 subdivisions: $(0, 0.05S)$, $(0.05S, 0.1S)$, …, $(0.95S, S)$ with the width of each division being $0.05S$. Then we can find an interval (Fig. 6) with width of $0.5S$ (equal to 10 divisions) that contains the most r of the training sequence bits among all the intervals with the width of $0.5S$. If we find several intervals with width of $0.5S$ which contain the most r of the training sequence bits simultaneously, for example, there are three intervals: $(0.30S, 0.80S)$, $(0.35S, 0.85S)$, and $(0.40S, 0.90S)$, each contains the most r values associated with the training sequence bits, then the middle interval $((0.30S +0.40S)/2, (0.30S +0.40S)/2+0.5S)=(0.35S, 0.85S)$ is chosen as the interval representing "1". The remaining interval of $(0, S)$ subtracting $(0.35S, 0.85S)$, that is, $(0.85S, S) \cup (0, 0.35S)$, is the interval associated with "–1".

Next we extract the hidden data. If r is in the interval representing "1", the recovered hidden data bit value is 1; if r falls in the interval representing "–1", the recovered bit value is –1. Next we perform 2-D de-interleaving, which is the inverse process of 2-D interleaving [7], to $\boldsymbol{X}^*$ to obtain the binary sequences $\boldsymbol{W}^*$. We segment $\boldsymbol{W}^*$ by N_1 bits per sequence, correlate the obtained sequence with the original *PN*-sequence $\boldsymbol{p}$. The obtained correlation value is regarded as the soft decision value and is inputted to the log-MAP decoder for turbo code [8]. The message can thus be recovered.

5 Experimental Result

We have tested the proposed watermarking algorithm on various 512x512x8 images. A 60-bit message is embedded into each of the images. The parameter S for each image that we used in our work and the PNSR of the marked image versus the original image are shown in Table 1. The watermarks are perceptually invisible (Fig. 7 and Fig. 8). The PSNRs of marked images are larger than 40 dB. Table 2 shows the test results with our proposed algorithm using StirMark 3.1. In Table 2, "1" represents the embedded 60-bit message can be recovered with no error while "0" means the embedded message cannot be recovered correctly.

Table 1. The S which we choose and the PNSR of the marked image versus original image

	Lena	*Baboon*	*Plane*	*Boat*	*Drop*	*Pepper*	*Lake*	*Bridge*
S	90	120	90	90	90	90	110	90
PSNR(dB)	42.0	40.0	42.2	42.2	42.0	42.1	40.6	42.3

Table 2. Experimental results with StirMark 3.1

StirMark functions	*Lena*	*Baboon*	*Plane*	*Boat*	*Drop*	*Pepper*	*Lake*	*Bridge*
JPEG_10~100	1	1	1	1	1	1	1	1
scaling	1	1	1	1	1	1	1	1
jitter	1	1	1	1	1	1	1	1
cropping_25	1	1	1	1	1	1	1	1
aspect ratio	1	1	1	1	1	1	1	1
rotation (auto-crop, scale)	1	1	1	1	1	1	1	1
general linear transform	1	1	1	1	1	1	1	1
shearing	1	1	1	1	1	1	1	1
Gauss filtering	1	1	1	1	1	1	1	1
sharpening	1	1	1	1	1	1	1	1
FMLR	1	1	1	1	1	1	1	1
randomization-and-bending	1	1	1	1	1	1	1	1
2x2median_filter	1	1	1	1	1	1	1	1
3x3median_filter	1	1	1	1	1	1	1	1
4x4median_filter	0	0	1	0	1	0	0	0

(a)

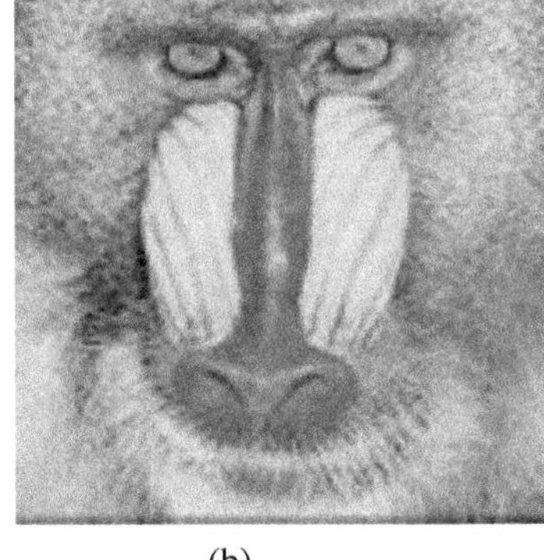

(b)

Fig. 7. Watermarked (a) Lena image (S=90, 42dB) and (b) Baboon image (S=120, 40 dB)

Fig. 8. Watermarked images

Fig. 9. (a) A distorted version of Figure 7a due to RST + randomization-and-bending. (b) Th recovered image (padded with the original image). The message (60bits) can be recovered.

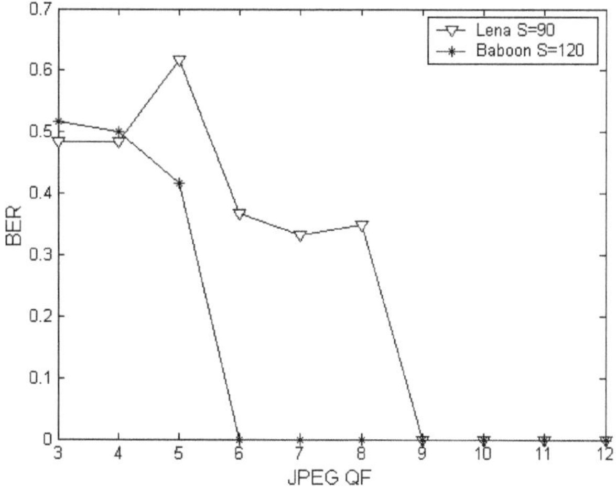

Fig. 10. The results obtained for Lena and Baboon image for JPEG compression.

It is observed that the watermark is robust against almost all of geometrical distortion related test function, specifically, rotation (auto-crop, auto-scale), scaling, jitter attack (random removal of rows and/or columns), general linear transform, shearing, cropping, aspect ratio and randomization-and-bending. It is noted that it can simultaneously resist large RST distortion and random, small, local geometric distortion such as randomization-and-bending (Fig. 9). In addition, it is noted that our proposed technique can resist common signal processing such as JPEG compression, Gauss filtering, FMLR, sharpening and 3x3 median filtering very well. In particular, it can recover watermark signal with no error after JPEG compression with quality factor less than 10, specifically, 9 for Lena and 6 for Baboon (Fig. 10). Furthermore, the watermark can resist the combination of RST distortion and JPEG with quality factor 10 (JPEG_10) (Fig. 11). We can recover the message when the PSNR of the Gaussian noise corrupted image is merely 20.2dB for Lena and 17.3 dB for Baboon.

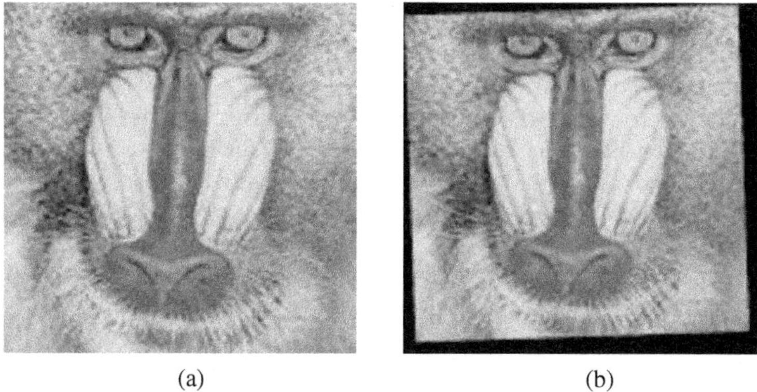

(a) (b)

Fig. 11. (a) A distorted version of Figure 7b due to JPEG_10+RST. (b) The recovered image (padded with 0). The message (60bits) can be recovered.

6 Conclusions and Discussions

The main contributions reported and some discussions made in this paper are as follows.

(1) We proposed a watermarking algorithm with enhanced robustness due to adaptive receiving and turbo code in addition to the newly developed registration, 2-D interleaving techniques, the concatenated coding of turbo code and DSSS, and the new embedding strategy in the LL subband in DWT domain.

(2) By adaptive receiving using a training sequence, we model the data extraction as channel of additive noise non-zero mean or zero-mean due to fading. This seems particularly promising in enhancing robustness of watermarking against median filtering and other distortion having fading nature. Note that we have to increase the embedding strength related parameter S largely (larger than or equal to 260 in our work) to in order to overcome 2x2 and 3x3 median filtering if without using the proposed adaptive receiving. This demonstrates the effectiveness of adaptive receiving. To our best knowledge, the difficulty of watermark robustness against median filtering and the success in overcoming this difficulty have not been reported in the literature, and we use adaptive receiving to combat the fading of host media feature for the first time.

(3) Robustness of the proposed watermark algorithm against 4x4 median filtering, however, is more challenging. It is noted that the PSNR of a 4x4 median filtered image versus the non-filtered marked image is as low as 20.9 dB for Baboon, and 23.7dB for Lena. Note that the filtered images are rather blurred and hence their commercial value has been lowered. According to our experiments, if we adopt S=190 for Baboon (the PSNR of the marked image is 35.6 dB) and S=120 for Lena (the PSNR of the marked image is 40 dB), the watermarking is robust to 4x4 median filtering while the watermark is still almost invisible but with a little low frequency pattern in the marked image. We can obtain the similar result for Boat, Pepper, Lake, Bridge images. So it is observed that robustness against 4x4 median filtering can be enhanced by increasing the strength of the watermark using adaptively embedding [10, 11, 12, 13]. The issue of 4x4 median filtering is currently being under further investigation.

(4) It is robust to common signal processing such as signal enhancement (including Gaussian filtering, 3x3 median filtering, FMLR) and JPEG compression with quality factor less than 10.

(5) Incorporated with our newly developed registration technique [3] and the existing registration based on motion estimation [6], the proposed watermarking can cope with both large distortion and small local distortion such as randomization-and-bending. The proposed watermarking is also robust against the geometric distortion combined with JPEG_10.

In the resynchronization, we use an original image or an undistorted watermarked image as a reference, so the proposed watermarking is non-blind.

Acknowledgments. This work is supported by NSFC (69975011, 60172067, 60133020), "863" Program (2002AA144060), NSF of Guangdong (013164); Funding of China National Education Ministry; New Jersey commission of Science and Technology via NJWINS.

References

1. Hartung, F., Kutter, M.: Multimedia watermarking techniques. Proceeding of the IEEE, 87(7) (July 1999) 1079–1107
2. Cox, J., Killian, J., Leighton, F. T., Shamoon, T.: Secure spread spectrum watermarking for multimedia. IEEE Transactions on Image Processing, 6(12) (1997) 1673–1687
3. Kang, X., Huang, J. and Shi, Y., Q.: An image watermarking algorithm robust to geometric distortion, In Lecture Notes in Computer Science: Proc. of Int. Workshop on Digital Watermarking 2002 (IWDW2002), vol. 2613, Seoul, Korea, (2002) 212–223
4. Kang, X., Huang, J. and Shi, Y., Q, Lin, Y.: A DWT-DFT composite watermarking scheme robust to both affine transform and JPEG compression. IEEE Transactions on Circuits and Systems for Video Technology, 13(8), (2003) 776–786
5. Voloshynovskiy, S., Deguillaume, F., Pereira, S. and Pun, T.: Optimal adaptive diversity watermarking with channel state estimation. Proceeding of SPIE: Security and watermarking of Multimedia content III, vol.4314, San Jose, CA, USA, (22-25, Jan. 2001) 673–685
6. Loo, P. and Kingbury, N.: Motion estimation based registration of geometrically distorted images for watermark recovery. In: Proc. SPIE Security and Watermarking of Multimedia Contents IIII, Vol. 4314, CA, USA (Jan., 2001)
7. Shi, Y., Q. and Zhang, X., M: A new two-dimensional interleaving technique using successive packing. IEEE Transactions on Circuits and Systems, Part I: Fundamental Theory and Application, 49(6)(June 2002) 779–789
8. Berrou, C. and Glavieux, A.: Near optimum error correcting coding and decoding: turbo-codes. IEEE transactions on communications. 44(10)(Oct. 1996) 1261–1271
9. Chen, B. and Wornell, G., W: Quantization index modulation: A class of provably good methods for digital watermarking and information embedding. IEEE Transactions On Information Theory, 47(4) (May 2001) 1423–1443
10. Huang, J. and Shi, Y., Q.: An adaptive image watermarking scheme based on visual masking. Electronics letters, 34(8) (1998) 748–750
11. Huang, J. and Shi, Y., Q. and Shi, Y.: Embedding image watermarks in DC components. IEEE Transactions on Circuits and Systems for Video Technology, 10(6)(2000) 974~979
12. Podilchuk, C., I. and Zeng, W.: Image-adaptive watermarking using visual models. IEEE Journal on Selected Areas in Communications, 16(4)(1998) 525–539
13. Voloshynovskiy, S., Deguillaume, F. and Pun, T.: Content adaptive watermarking based on a stochastic multiresolution image modeling. In Tenth European Signal Processing Conference (EUSIPCO 2000), Tampere, Finland, (September 5–8, 2000)

A Robust Logo Multiresolution Watermarking Based on Independent Component Analysis Extraction

Thai D. Hien[1], Zensho Nakao[1], and Yen-Wei Chen[1, 2]

[1]Department of Electrical & Electronics Engineering, University of the Ryukyus, Okinawa 903-0213, Japan.
[2] Institute for Computational Science and Engineering, Ocean University of China, China.
{tdhien, nakao, chen }@augusta.eee.u-ryukyu.ac.jp

Abstract. This paper proposes a novel blind logo multi-resolution watermarking technique based on independent component analysis (ICA) for extraction. To exploit the human visual system (HVS) and the robustness, a perceptual model is applied with a stochastic approach based on noise visibility function (NVF) for adaptive watermarking algorithm. A logo watermark is embedded by modifying middle-frequency sub-bands of wavelet transform. The new detection technique based on ICA is introduced during the extraction phase to ensure a blind watermark. The proposed algorithm is checked for the robustness to several compression algorithms such as Jpeg, jpeg 2000, SPIHT, EZW, and principal components analysis (PCA) based compression and also robust against various image and digital processing operators.

1 Introduction

Digital watermarking aims to hide the secret messages in digital objects for the copyright protection. In recent years it has been recognized that embedding information in a transform domain such as DCT, FFT and DWT leads to more robust watermark. The advantage of the DWT relative to DFT or DCT is that it allows for localized watermarking of the image. Many image watermarking algorithms based on wavelet transform are proposed. [2, 3, 4, 7]. Some other method exploited the relationship to image coding: in [5] Xie *et al* present a watermark scheme which integrated into set partitioning in hierarchical trees (SPIHT) coder with purposes of authentication. Inoue *et al* [6] embed the watermark to DWT coefficients, based on embedded image coding using zero-tree (EZW).

In order to insert an invisible watermark, the current trend has been to model the human visual system (HVS) and specify as a perceptual masking function which yields the allowable distortion of any pixels. This complex function compiles contrast, luminance, color, texture and edges. We must embed carefully the watermark in sufficient amounts in order to maximize the strength of the watermark and to guarantee the imperceptibility. There are several different perceptual models and visual quality measures adapted to the HVS. Barni *et al* [1] proposed a weighting factor in the embedding function, and the weighting factor depends on the resolution

T. Kalker et al. (Eds.): IWDW 2003, LNCS 2939, pp. 408–422, 2004.
© Springer-Verlag Berlin Heidelberg 2004

level, the orientation of the sub-bands, and the texture area of the image. A concept shared between image compression and a watermarking system is "just noticeable difference" (JND) threshold which was proposed in [10] by Podichuk, and the JND threshold is an upper bound on the quantization step size and the watermark intensity, and determines the amount of distortion that can be added to each coefficient without being visible. It is possible to compute a JND map, containing a weighting factor for each transform domain coefficient to be modified. Delaigle *et al* [8] proposed a perceptual masking model that guarantees the invisibility of the watermark in combination of an edge and textures discrimination to determine the embedding level of maximal length sequence (MLS). The method in [1], [8], and [10] are very significant and reasonable to take HVS into account because of its inherent features. If one can modify an image based on one rule taken from the HVS, then it will be easier to generate an imperceptible watermark with maximum modification, and the length strength of the watermark can be adaptive to the host image. In this proposed method, each watermark value is multiplied by a strength parameter and is used in combination with the mask function (NVF) which is computed based on a stochastic model for adaptive embedding and the HVS [9].

With the coming Jpeg 2000 standard and in order to fit the Jpeg2000 coding, watermarking system has to be robust to Jpeg 2000 compression, furthermore we need to note that wavelet transform is closer to the HVS than the DCT because it splits the signal into multi-resolution bands of particular scale and orientation that can be processed independently. This proposed scheme will be based on wavelet transform in order to adapt to that objective. A watermark is a signature $\{+1,-1\}$ text image, is permuted to become a pseudo-random sequence, and added to the DWT coefficients at the two I_l^{LH}, I_l^{HL} sub-bands of the host image, where l is final decomposition level.

It is known that most of the existing watermark techniques are based on some assumptions for watermark detection and extraction, and some require the previous knowledge of the watermark, the watermark location, the strength, the threshold, and the original image. The proposed watermarking scheme does not rely on the information such as the original image, the watermark, the strength... for recovering the watermark, which was embedded in the DWT domain. For the watermark detection, a novel and simple method based on ICA is proposed, where with only the de-mix key, one can extract the watermark. The method could perform extraction watermark perfectly.

Experimental results show the validity of the technique both from the point of view of watermark invisibility and from the point of view of robustness against most common attacks: the proposed system is robust against image compression such as Jpeg and Jpeg2000 [19], SPIHT [18], EZW [17] and PCA based compression, is demonstrated to be resistant to median filtering, low-pass filtering, adding noise, denoising, cropping and resizing.

In the next two sections, we introduce the basic concepts of the proposed watermark embedding and extraction. Experimental results are given in section 4. Finally section 5 includes discussion and conclusion.

2 The Embedding Algorithm

The embedding of the watermark requires three main steps: the scrambling of the watermark image, calculation of visual mask, and finally insertion of the watermark.

2.1 Scrambling of the Watermark

We use a binary text logo image $\{+1,-1\}$ as a watermark. With such a watermark, more robustness can be obtained against attacks because the signatures can always preserve a certain degree of structural information, which are meaningful and recognizable, and the extracted watermark also can be easier to verify with human eyes rather than by the correlation method. To decrease the effectiveness of the image cropping attacks, and to prevent the watermark from tampering or unauthorized access by attackers, a scrambling watermark method with a user-selected "seed" is performed. For scrambling of the watermark, pixels of the watermark are permuted pseudo-randomly to form a new watermark image. The pseudo-random permutation can be done by using a linear feedback shift register "seed". By setting the state of the shift register, a pseudo-random sequence can be generated which is then recoverable by resetting the shift register to its original state. Once the binary watermark is scrambled, it can be inserted into the host image. Let W and W_p be the original and permuted watermark, that is $W_p = \{w_p(i,j) = w(i',j') | 0 < i,i' < M \text{ and } 0 < j,j' < N\}$, where the pixel at (i',j') is mapped to pixel at (i,j) in a pseudo-random order, M and N are size of the watermark. The permutation function and its inverse can be presented by the following equation:

$$W_p = Permute(W, seed).$$

$$W = Inverse\_permutation(W_p, seed). \quad (1)$$

Fig.1 shows the text binary image of size 64x64 which is used for a watermark and its corresponding permutation. The permutation of watermark can be used for embedding, and inverse permutation is required in the detection phase to recover the text image.

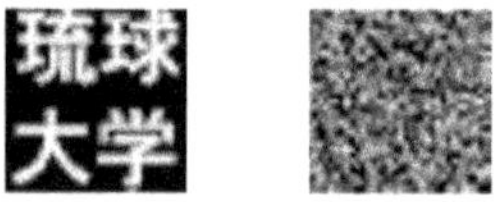

琉球
大学

(a) (b)

Fig. 1. (a) A watermark, (b) A permutation of the watermark

2.2 Embedding Watermark

Firstly the image to be watermarked is decomposed into a number of levels by wavelet transform (l = 1, 2, 3…). A watermark is inserted in the mid frequency sub-bands by modifying the wavelet coefficients belonging to the two detail bands at final level. (I_l^{LH} , I_l^{HL}). Fig 2 depicts three levels decomposition of "Lena" image, $l = 3$,

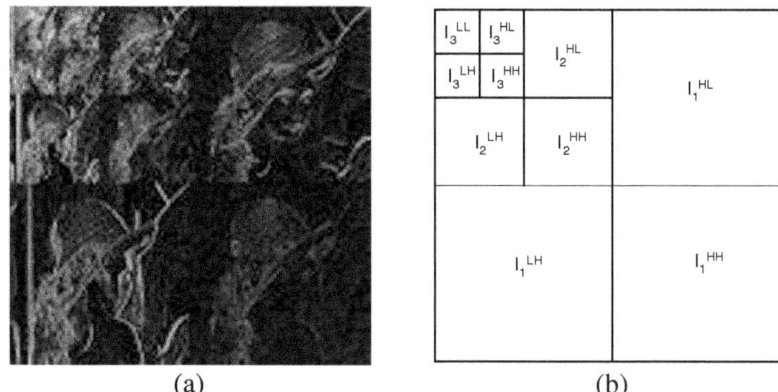

(a) (b)

Fig. 2. DWT of "Lena" in three resolution level.

where I_l^{LH} I_l^{HL} sub-bands are used for embedding watermark. This choice has been made based on an optimal compromise among robustness, invisibility and the attack. With this choice the watermark could be made more robust and effective against image degrading. The watermark is permutated as a pseudorandom binary $\{+1,-1\}$ sequence, is inserted by modifying the wavelet coefficients belonging to I_l^{LH} , and I_l^{HL} sub-bands at final level l.

The stochastic models of cover image is applied to content adaptive watermark by computation of an NVF [9]. We consider either locally i.i.d. (independent identically distributed) non-stationary Gaussian or globally Generalized Gaussian (GG) models. Based on information of the host image, one can compute the NVF function. Fig 3 shows the (a) permuted watermark, (b) NVF function of "Lena", (c) masks at texture, edge areas and (d) masks at flat areas.

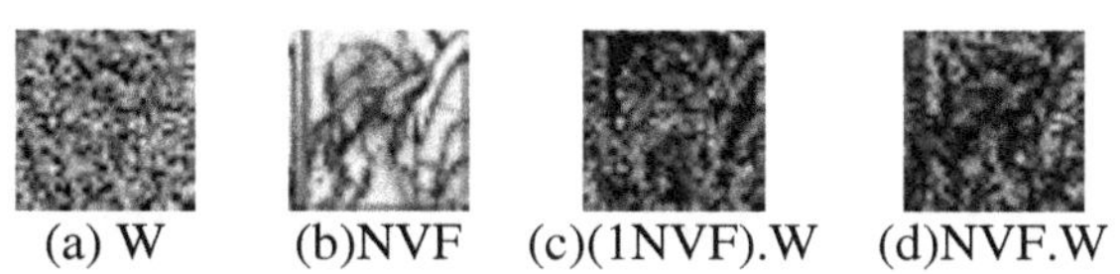
(a) W (b)NVF (c)(1NVF).W (d)NVF.W

Fig. 3. (a) Watermark, (b) NVF masking function of "Lena", (c) Watermark at edge and texture region, (d) Watermark at flat regions

The watermark is embedded by the following more detailed formula:

$$I_l^{'LH}(i,j) = I_l^{LH}(i,j) + A^{LH}.\alpha(1-NVF(i,j))W(i,j) + B^{LH}.\beta.NVF(i,j)W(i,j)$$
$$I_l^{'HL}(i,j) = I_l^{HL}(i,j) + A^{HL}.\alpha(1-NVF(i,j))W(i,j) + B^{HL}.\beta.NVF(i,j)W(i,j) \quad (1)$$

where $I_l^{'LH}$, $I_l^{'HL}$ are watermarked transform coefficients, A^{LH} B^{LH}, A^{HL} B^{HL} denote the watermark strengths of texture and edge regions and flat regions at I_l^{LH} I_l^{HL} sub-bands; α, β are smoothing factors at the texture regions and flat regions, β is fixed to 0.1, where α is adapted to control the smoothness. The above rule embeds the watermark in highly textured areas and the areas containing the edges stronger than in the flat regions and it can be controlled by both of strength parameters and smoothing factors for adaptive watermark.

Table 1. Strength parameters of "Lena", "Peppers" and "Baboon"

Image	A^{LH}	B^{LH}	A^{HL}	B^{HL}
Lena	42.46	4.24	24.12	2.41
Peppers	40.09	4.10	33.16	3.31
Baboon	46.32	4.63	45.61	4.56

Table 2. PSNR, MSE corresponding to smooth parameter α of images "Lena", "Peppers" and "Baboon "

α	Lena		Peppers		Baboon	
	PSNR	MSE	PSNR	MSE	PSNR	MSE
0.05	60.95	0.05	60.40	0.06	58.47	0.09
0.1	55.19	0.20	54.64	0.22	52.71	0.35
0.15	51.76	0.43	51.21	0.49	49.27	0.77
0.20	49.30	0.76	48.75	0.87	46.81	1.35
0.25	47.38	1.19	46.83	1.35	44.90	2.10
0.30	45.81	1.70	45.26	1.93	43.33	3.02
0.35	44.49	2.31	43.94	2.63	42.00	4.10
0.4	43.34	3.02	42.79	3.42	40.85	5.35
0.45	42.32	3.81	41.77	4.33	39.83	6.76

In this proposal the strengths of watermark A^{LH} and A^{HL} are calculated by the mean of the absolute value at I_l^{LH} and I_l^{HL} sub-bands where $A^{LH} = \mu|I_l^{LH}|$, $A^{HL} = \mu|I_l^{HL}|$ and $B^{LH} = A^{LH}/10$, $B^{HL} = A^{HL}/10$. The watermark image I' is obtained by the inverse DWT. Table 1 shows strength parameters of "Lena", "Peppers" and "Babbon" and table 2 shows the PSNR and MSE of "Lena", "Peppers", and "Babbon" with respect to smooth parameter and strengths. In this proposes α is set to 0.2 to ensure the invisible. Fig (7b) shows the watermarked image "Lena" with PSRN = 49.30dB.

In order to apply ICA for blind watermark detection, the embedding process need to create a de-mix key for the detection phase. The following equation is used to create the de-mix key:

$$I_l^{*LH}(i,j) = I_l^{LH}(i,j) + A^{LH}\alpha_k.K(i,j)$$
$$I_l^{*HL}(i,j) = I_l^{HL}(i,j) + A^{HL}.\alpha_k.K(i,j) \quad (2)$$
$$demix\_key(i,j) = I_l^{*HL}(i,j) + I_l^{*HL}(i,j) + K(i,j)$$

where I_l^{*LH}, I_l^{*HL} are the wavelet transform coefficients where the key K are embedded, and $\alpha_k = 0.5$ is used as strength of the mixture. Using only the de-mix key and the key, the owner can claim the ownership on any watermarked versions and the other copies. The original image is kept in secret and the de-mix key is used for user detection. Fig 4 shows the embedding scheme, and the de-mix key is created during the embedding phase.

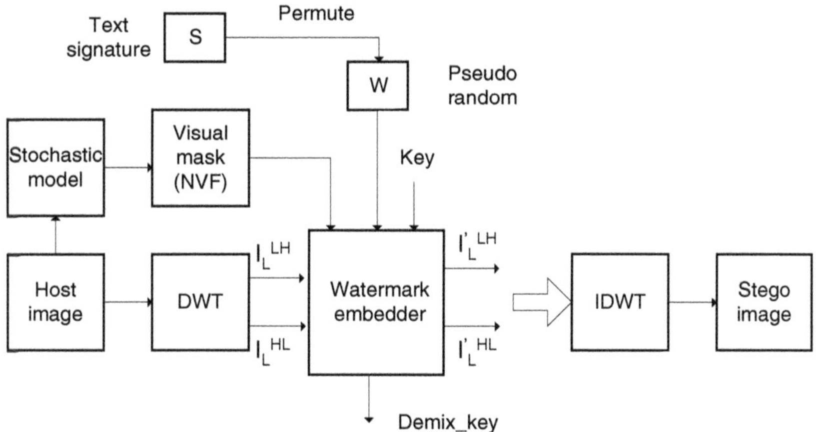

Fig. 4. The proposed watermark embedding scheme

3 ICA Based Watermark Extraction

3.1 Independent Component Analysis

Independent Component Analysis (ICA) is a method for extracting independent sources, given only mixtures of the unknown sources. This method has a wide range of applications in signal- and image processing issues. We will present the assumptions in ICA and explain how algorithms can be used for watermarking issues. The algorithms are applied to watermark extraction from the watermarked version. The results suggest that ICA can extract exactly watermark that were hidden in image. The simplest model of ICA, we observe m signal $X = [x_1, x_2, \dots x_m]$ and n sources $S = [s_1, s_2, \dots s_n]$, $(n \le m)$ in the mixture system. The relation between sources and the observation are linear combination of n sources, which can be written as:

$$X = A.S \quad (3)$$

where A is unknown matrix of full rank called the mixing matrix:

$$A = \begin{bmatrix} a_{11}a_{12} & \cdots & a_{1n} \\ a_{21}a_{21} & \cdots & a_{2n} \\ \vdots \ \vdots & \ddots & \vdots \\ a_{m1}a_{m2} & \cdots & a_{mn} \end{bmatrix}$$

The goal of ICA is to estimate the original components s_i from the mixture x_j by finding the matrix W called un-mixing matrix, which estimate from m observation X. The independent components are obtained as:

$$S = W.X \tag{4}$$

It is to be noted that the watermark, and the original can be regarded as unknown sources and the watermarked is a mixture, and by creating a different mixtures, one can perform ICA to extract the watermark. Fig. 5 denotes the ICA model, which can reconstruct the sources (independent components) by estimating a basic matrix W from its mixtures.

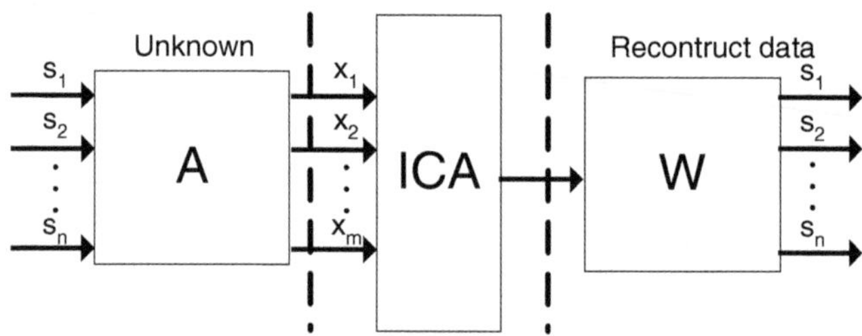

Fig. 5. ICA modelling

Several algorithms for ICA have been introduced recently. Bell & Sejnowski recommend "Infomax" algorithm [13]. The Independent component analysis (ICA) algorithm of Bell and Sejnowski is an information-theoretic unsupervised learning algorithm which can be applied to the problem of separating multi-channel signal data. An efficient batch algorithm called "JADE" has been originally developed by Cardoso [14] based on the (joint) diagonalization of cumulant matrices. A robust ICA algorithm proposed by Cichocki [15], takes into account the temporal information of the sources, works in a batch fashion, is quite simple and fast, and separates signals which have low or even zero kurtosis. This paper applies fast ICA algorithm for the watermark extraction: fixed point or Fast ICA algorithm has been originally developed by Aapo Hyvärinen and Erkki Oja [11] [12] which is based on the following two states: first is PCA whitening process of the input and the next employs the fast ICA algorithm by using the fourth-order statistics of the signal [12]. Fast ICA is chosen because it has a number of desirable properties compared to the existing methods for ICA, which includes fast convergence, easy to implement and suitable for watermarking applications.

3.2 Watermark Extraction

The usefulness of this new proposed method is that it does not require the knowledge of the watermark, and other parameters such as strengths, smooth factors, etc. By using only the de-mix key, one can identify their ownership of any copy version of the watermarked image. To extract the watermark, it is necessary to create mixtures from watermarked copy version. The following step is used to extract the watermark:

Step 1: The stego (watermarked) image is decomposed through DWT in l levels (l = 1, 2, 3), in order to obtain the wavelet coefficients $I_l^{\#LH}$ and $I_l^{\#LH}$ sub-bands.

Step 2: From $I_l^{\#LH}$ and $I_l^{\#LH}$ sub bands create mixture signals to input ICA.

$$\begin{aligned} X_1 &= I_l^{\#LH} + demix\_key \\ X_2 &= I_l^{\#HL} + demix\_key \\ X_3 &= I_l^{\#LH} + I_l^{\#HL} \\ X_4 &= demix\_key + K \end{aligned} \tag{5}$$

In equation (5), X_1, X_2, X_3, X_4 are observation mixtures s of the wavelet transform coefficients of the original (I_i^{LH}, I_i^{HL}), the watermark, and the key. They can be rewritten as:

$$\begin{aligned} X_1 &= a_{11} I_l^{LH} + a_{12} I_l^{HL} + a_{13} w + a_{14} k \\ X_2 &= a_{21} I_l^{LH} + a_{22} I_l^{HL} + a_{23} w + a_{24} k \\ X_3 &= a_{31} I_l^{LH} + a_{32} I_l^{HL} + a_{33} w + a_{34} k \\ X_3 &= a_{41} I_l^{LH} + a_{42} I_l^{HL} + a_{43} w + a_{44} k \end{aligned} \tag{6}$$

where $a_{i,j} (i = 1,2,3,4; j = 1,2,3,4)$ are the unknown mixture parameters. As described earlier, it is possible to perform ICA for those mixtures to extract the watermark.

Step 3: The above four mixtures are input to fastICA [12] algorithm and the watermark W is extracted from those mixtures. The copyright can be claimed from the watermarked image or the copy version of the watermarked image.

Fig.6 shows the ICA blind watermarked extraction method based on the de-mix key. Fig. (7d) shows the extracted watermark from the watermarked image "Lena", it is noted that watermark could be perfectly extracted by our method (NC =1.00).

After extraction of the watermark, users can compare the extracted one with the reference watermark subjectively. A similarity measurement of the extracted, $W'(i, j)$, and the reference watermarks, $W(i, j)$, can be defined by the normalized correlation (NC):

$$NC = \frac{\sum_{i=1}^{M_w} \sum_{j=1}^{N_w} \left[W(i,j) W'(i,j) \right]}{\sum_{i=1}^{M_w} \sum_{j=1}^{N_w} \left[W(i,j) \right]^2} \tag{7}$$

The value of NC lies in $[0,1]$, and if we acquire higher NC values, the embedded watermark is more similar to the extracted one.

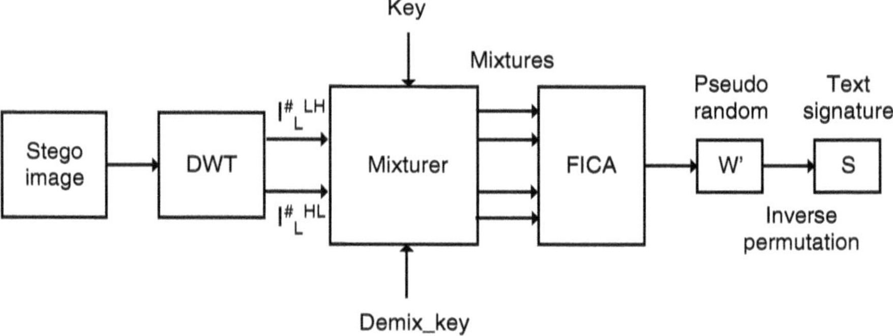

Fig. 6. The proposed extraction scheme

4 Experimental Results

There are several important requirements for an effective watermarking scheme: transparency, robustness and capacity. The proposed watermarking method was tested on some standard images, those were watermarked and processed to try removing the watermark. Haar filters have been used for computing DWT with 3 levels where the highest sub-bands I_3^{LH} , I_3^{HL} are used for embedding watermark. The Japanese logo text signature meaning "*University of the Ryukyus*" of sizes 64x64 is used as watermark.

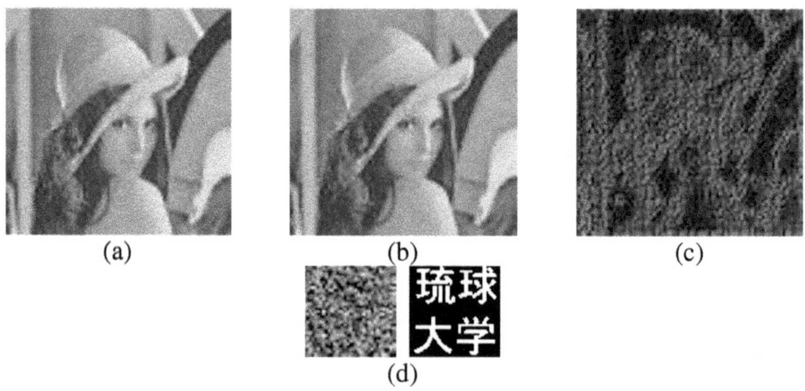

Fig. 7. (a) The original "Lena" image, (b) Watermarked "Lena" with PSNR = 49.30 (c) Difference between the original "Lena" and the watermarked "Lena" (d) Extracted watermark by ICA before permutation and after permutation (NC = 1.00).

First the invisibility is evaluated: in Fig. 7(a) the original image "Lena" with size 512x512 is presented, while in Fig. 7(b) the watermarked copy is shown. The two images are evidently undistinguishable, the watermarked image has PNSN = 49.30 dB. The effectiveness of the spatial masking function on the watermarked image are shown in Fig 7(c) which is the difference between the original image and the watermarked one, magnified by a factor 8, and it is evident that the watermark in textured and edges areas are stronger than in flat regions. Fig 7 (d) is extracted 64x64 random sequence and its inverse permuted version. Table 3 shows PSNR and NC values for 3 standard images "Lena", "Peppers", and "Baboon" which were watermarked by our proposed method, The extractor could extract exactly the watermark with NC = 1.00.

Table 3. PSNA and NC value of watermarked "Lena", "Peppers", and "Baboon"

Image	PSNR	NC
Lena	49.30	1.00
Peppers	48.75	1.00
Baboon	46.81	1.00

The experimental results are presented in the following, to demonstrate the robustness of the proposed system with respect to various common image/signal processing techniques and geometric distortions.

A watermarked image was filtered with low-pass and median filters. Figure (8a) and (8b) show the watermarked image "Lena" under filters with window size 5x5, and Figures (8c), (8d) show corresponding ICA watermark extracted.

Fig. 8. (a) (b) Watermarked image "Lena" low-pass and median filtered 5x5, and coresponding PSNR results, (c) (d) The corresponding ICA watermark extracted and NC results.

During the image manipulation, different parts of a "Lena" image are cropped where the missing portion is filled in with zeros and croped parts are replaced with the "Peppers" image. It is noted that by our technique the watermark is distributed over the entire image and it is suitable for the robustness to cropping attack.

Fig. 9 shows the cropping attacked "Lena" in experiments and the PSNR of cropped results: (9a) crop 25% lower-right surroundings, (9b) crop 25% lower-left quarter, (9c) crop 25% up-left surroundings, (9d) crop 45% of the surrounds and replace with "Peppers" image, (9e) crop 25% lower-right surroundings and replaced with "Peppers" image , (9f) crop 25% lower-left quarter and replaced with "Peppers" image, (9g) crop 25% up-left surroundings replaced with "Peppers" image, (9h) center crop 10% and replaced with "Peppers" image. Fig. 10 shows the corresponding extractor output of Fig.9 and NC values of the extracted results.

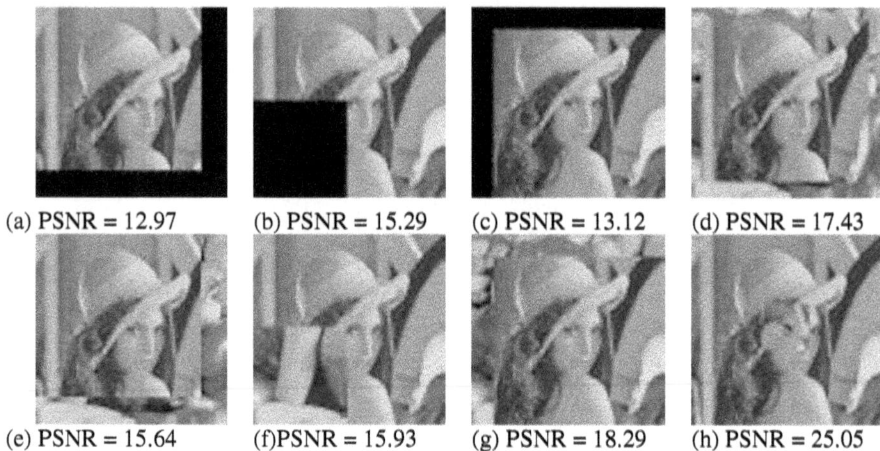

Fig. 9. The cropping attacked versions "Lena" in experiment and the PSNR of crop results.

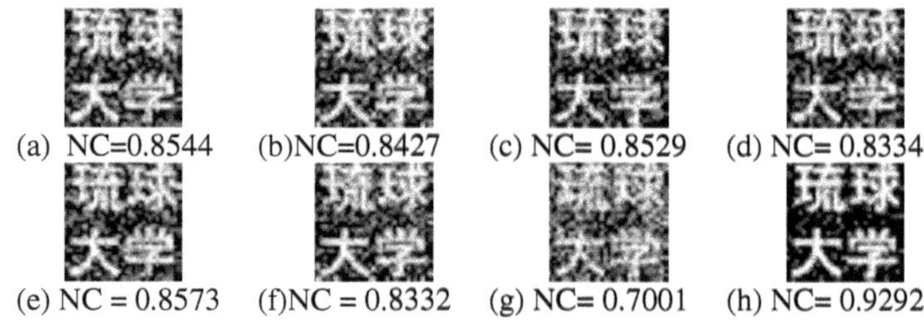

Fig. 10. The corresponding extractor output of Fig 4 and NC of the extracted results.

Fig.11 shows the extracted results from Jpeg compression, JPEG-2000 compression [19], Wavelet-SPIHT (set-partitioning in hierarchical trees) compression [18], Embedded Zero-tree Wavelet compression (EZW) [17] and PCA based compression. The PCA based compression is applied on each 8x8 sub-block of the image. The images are reconstructed by retaining only coefficients corresponding to the energy components of the sub-block.

Table 4 summarizes the PSNR and NC results from Jpeg compression with quality factors down from 85 to 15. Table 5 summarizes the PSNR and NC results from Jpeg 2000, SPIHT, EZW coding and compression with bit rates down from 2.0 to 0.4. Table 6 summarizes the PSNR and NC results from PCA compression with number of retained coefficients at each 8x8 blocks pixels down from 49 to 9 corresponding of fig. 11.

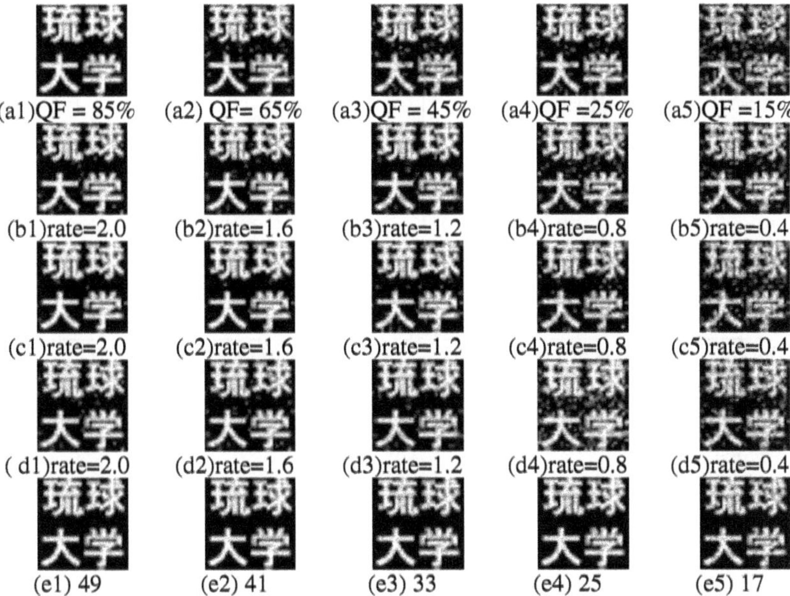

Fig. 11. The extracted watermark from jpeg, jpeg 2000, SPITH, EZW, and PCA based compression versions of the watermarked "Lena" with different compression ratio: (a1), (a2), (a3), (a4) extracted watermarks from Jpeg compression with QF down from 85% to 15%. (b1), (b2), (b3), (b 4) extracted watermarks from Jpeg 2000 compression with bit rates down from 2.0 to 0.4 bpp. (c1), (c2), (c3), (c4) extracted watermarks from SPIHT compression with bit rates down from 2.0 to 0.4 bpp. (d1), (d2), (d3), (d4) extracted watermarks from EZW compression with bit rates down from 2.0 to 0.4 bpp. (e1), (e2), (e3), (e4) extracted watermarks from PCA based compression with different number of coefficients retained.

Table 4. PSNR, NC values of JPEG compression Standard (lossy DCT), (The higher NC values indicate the more robustness)

Attacks Jpeg	PSNR(dB)	NC
Quality factor (%)		
85	40.1262	0.9946
65	37.5320	0.9395
45	36.1419	0.9033
25	34.2576	0.8890
15	32.4162	0.7628

Table 5 shows PSNR and NC values after random noise addition, viewer filter denoise, and resize of the watermarked version "Lena" to difference sizes.

Table 5. PSNR, NC values of Jpeg 2000, SPITH, and EZW attacks with different bit rate (lossy DWT), (The higher NC values indicate the more robustness)

Attacks	JPEG 2000		SPIHT		EZW	
Rate (bits/pixel.)	PSNR(dB)	NC	PSNR(dB)	NC	PSNR(dB)	NC
2.0	43.2850	0.9717	44.6622	0.9917	43.9432	0.9818
1.6	42.2459	0.9624	43.2156	0.9844	42.6815	0.9432
1.2	40.8149	0.9507	41.6627	0.9536	41.0173	0.9231
0.8	39.1757	0.9053	39.7531	0.9097	38.7320	0.9012
0.4	36.0245	0.8647	36.5377	0.8335	35.7217	0.8161

Table 6. PSNR, NC values of PCA compression attack, (The higher NC values indicate the more robustness)

Attacks PCA based compression	PSNR(dB)	NC
Number of coefficients retained in 8x8 sub-block		
49	47.3614	0.9968
41	44.7083	0.9907
33	42.2195	0.9854
25	39.6317	0.9780
17	36.8136	0.9314
9	32.9693	0.9137

Table 7. NC values vs. the attackings method. (The higher NC values indicate the more robustness)

Attacks	PSNR(dB)	NC
Adding random noise Power = 200	28.1321	0.8163
Random noise + denoising by wiener filter	34.0117	0.8089
Resize to 448x448	37.6637	0.9702
Resize to 640x640	39.5429	0.9585
Resize to 256x256	32.3801	0.8628

5 Conclusion and Discussion

5.1 Comparison and Discussion

Hsu and Wu [20] presented a technique for embedding the logo digital watermark into the images, the embedding and extraction method of the DCT based approach, and middle frequencies part were selected for modification using residual mask. Their method has been shown to be effective for large images and for Jpeg based compression at high bit rate. Lu and Huang [21] proposed a logo watermark system called "Cocktail watermark" which was tested under various type of attacks and showed results for the robustness. Both [20] [21] require the original image during the extraction. Huang et al [22] presented a watermark method which is based on vector quantization to embed three difference logo watermarks, and their method could perfectly extract watermarks under no attacks, and showed the robustness under intentional attacks. In [23] Dan Yu introduced a dewatermarking method by ICA when watermark is embedded and detected in spatial domain. It may not be robust to jpeg and jpeg2000 image compression and nor effective much for image quality because of spatial domain watermarking technique. Here we presented a new blind watermark scheme with higher invisibility based on wavelet decomposiotion. Under attacks our system extracted exactly the watermark by ICA based detection, We checked the robust against various compression algorithms attacks such as JPEG, JPEG2000, SPIHT, EZW, and PCA based compression. The experiment shows that our system is robust under almost all compression domains. The system was also checked under other types of attacks and showed the robustness. Our system can be added to the existing watermark algorithms with regard building a real world applications.

5.2 Conclusion

In this paper, we proposed a novel watermark technique. The watermarked images were obtained by modifying the mid band frequency of wavelet transform. The HVS model is taken into account in order to perform the optimal embedding with regard to the robustness. Our algorithm is based on wavelet domain that is suitable for the upcoming Jpeg 2000 compression algorithm. We used ICA for blind extraction. By using ICA, even without information on the embedding such as original image, strength, watermark as well as threshold, the watermark can be perfectly extracted. Our method may be more secured by incorporating an encryption algorithm to de-mix key. The experimental results show the proposed technique can survive under almost all compression domains such as DCT, DWT and PCA based compression. The robustness was also checked under various types of attacks including cropping of an image, low-pass and median filtering, adding noise, image resize. Further work will concentrate on enhancement of the proposed algorithm to protect the original source more effectively againts other kind of attacks such as rotation, copy attacks which are more challenging as our future work.

References

1. M. Barni, F. Bartolini, and A. Piva, "Improved Wavelet-Based Watermarking Through Pixel-Wise Masking," IEEE Trans., Image Process., vol.10, no. 5, pp. 783–791, 2001.
2. R. Dugad, K. Ratakonda, and N. Ahuja. " A new wavelet-based scheme for watermarking images," Proc. of the IEEE, ICIP '98, Chicago, IL, USA, 1998.

3. X.G Xia, C. G. Boncelet, and Gonzalo R.Arce, "Wavelet transform based watermark for digital images," Optics Express, pp. 497–450, 1998.
4. J. R. Kim, Y.Shik Moon, "A robust wavelet-based digital watermark using level-adaptive thresholding," Proc., of IEEE , ICIP 99, pp 202, Kobe, Japan,1999.
5. L. Xie, Gonzalo R.Arce, "Joint wavelet compression and authentication watermarking," In Proceedings of the IEEE, ICIP 98, Chicago, IL, USA, 1998.
6. H. Inoue, A. Miyazaki, A. Yamamoto, and T. Katsura, "A Digital Watermark based on the wavelet Transform and its Robustness on Image Compression," In Proc., of IEEE, ICIP98, pp.391–395, 1998.
7. D.Kundur, D. Hatzinakos, "Digital watermarking using multiresolution wavelet decomposition," Proc., of IEEE, ICASSP98, vol.5, pp.2969–2972, Seattle, WA, USA, 1998.
8. JF Delaigle, C De Vleeschouwer and B Macq, "Watermarking based on a human visual model," Signal process., Special Issue on Watermarking, vol.66, no.3, pp.319–336, 1998.
9. S. Voloshynovskiy, A. Herrigel, N. B., and T. Pun, "A stochastic approach to content adaptive digital image watermarking," Lecture Notes in Computer Science, vol.1768, pp. 212–236, September 2000.
10. Christine I. Podilchuk, Wenjun Zeng, "Image-Adaptive Watermarking Using Visual Models," IEEE Journal Selected Areas of Communications (JSAC), vol.16, No.4,pp. 525–539, 1998.
11. E. Bingham and A. Hyvärinen, "A fast fixed-point algorithm for independent component analysis of complex-valued signals," Int. Journal of Neural Systems, vol.10, no.1, pp.1–8, 2000.
12. A. Hyvärinen and E. Oja, "Independent Component Analysis: Algorithms and Applications," Neural Networks, vol. 13, Issue 4, pp. 411–430, 2000.
13. Bell A.J. and Sejnowski T.J, "An information maximization approach to blind separation and blind deconvolution," Neural Computation, vol.7, no.6, pp.1129–1159, 1995.
14. J.-F. Cardoso, "High-order contrasts for independent component analysis," Neural computation, Vol.11, no 1, pp.157–192, 1999.
15. Cichocki, Andrzej, Barros, and A Kardec, "Robust Batch Algorithm for Sequential Blind Extraction of Noisy Biomedical Signals," Fifth Int., Sym., on Signal Process., and App., (ISSPA99), Vol.1, pp.363–366, 1999.
16. S. Cruces, L. Castedo, A. Cichocki, "Robust blind source separation algorithms using cumulants," Neurocomputing, vol.49, pp.87–118, 2002.
17. M Shapiro, "Embedded image coding using zerotree of wavelet coefficients," IEEE Trans., Signal Proc., vol.41, no.12, 1993.
18. Amir Said and William A. Pearlman "A New Fast and Efficient Image Codec Based on Set Partitioning in Hierarchical Trees," IEEE Trans., Circuits and Systems for Video Tech., vol. 6, pp.243–250, 1996.
19. C. Christopoulos, A. Skodras, and T. Ebrahimi, "The JPEG2000 still image coding system: An Overview," IEEE Trans., Consumer Electronics, Vol. 46, No. 4, pp. 1103–1127, 2000.
20. C.T Hsu and Ja-Ling Wu, "Hidden Digital Watermarks in Images," IEEE Trans. On Image Process., vol.8, No.1, pp.58–68, 1999.
21. C-Shien Lu, S-Kun Huang, C-Jye Sze, and H-Y.Mark Liao "Cocktail Watermarking for Digital Image Protection," IEEE Trans., Multimedia, Vol. 2, No. 4, pp.209–224, 2000.
22. H.C. Huang, F.H.Wang, and J.S Pan, "A VQ-Based Robust Multi-Watermarking Algorithm," IEICE trans., fundamentals vol E85-A,N0.7,JULY 2002.
23. D. Yu, Farook Sattar and K. Ma, "Watemarking Detection and Extraction using Independent Component Analysis Methods," EURASIP Journal on Applied Signal Processing 2002:1, pp.92–104.

Highly Reliable Stochastic Perceptual Watermarking Model Based on Multiwavelet Transform

Ki-Ryong Kwon[1], Ji-Hwan Park[2], Eung-Joo Lee[3], and Ahmed H. Tewfik[4]

[1]Department of Electronic and Computer Engineering, Pusan University of Foreign Studies, 55-1 Uam-dong, Nam-gu, Pusan 608-738, Republic of Korea,
krkwon@taejo.pufs.ac.kr

[2] Division of Electronic and Telecom. Engineering, Pukyung National University, 55-9 Daeyun-dong, Nam-gu, Pusan, 608-810, KOREA
jpark@pknu.ac.kr

[3]Dept. of Information/Comm. Eng., Tongmyong University of Information Technology, Pusan 608-711, Korea
ejlee@tit.ac.kr

[4]Dept. of Electrical and Computer Engineering, University of Minnesota, 4-174 EE/CSci Building 200 Union Street S.E. Minneapolis, MN55455,
tewfik@ece.umn.edu

Abstract. This paper presents highly reliable adaptive image watermark embedding using a stochastic perceptual model based on multiwavelet transform. To embedding watermark, the original image is decomposed into 4 levels using a discrete multiwavelet transform, then a watermark is embedded into the only JND (just noticeable differences) of the image each subband. The perceptual model is applied with a stochastic multiresolution model for watermark embedding. This is based on the computation of a NVF (noise visibility function) that have local image properties. The perceptual model that has adaptive image watermarking algorithm embed at the texture and edge region for more strongly embedded watermark by the JND. This method uses not only stationary GG (Generalized Gaussian) model characteristic but also nonstationary JND model because watermark has noise properties. The experiment results of simulation of the proposed watermark embedding method using stochastic perceptual model based on multiwavelet transform techniques was found to be excellent invisibility and robustness more than Podilchuk's algorithm.

Keywords: JND(just noticeable difference), NVF(noise visibility function), Digital watermarking, Multiresolution, Multiwavelet , Perceptual model

1 Introduction

There has been a lot of Internet in the digital watermarking research over the last few years, mostly due to the fact that digital watermarking might be used as a tool to protect the copyright of multimedia data. A digital watermark is an imperceptible signal embedded directly into the media content, and it can be detected from the host media for some applications. The insertion and detection of digital watermarks can help to identify the source or ownership of the media, the legitimacy of its usage, the

T. Kalker et al. (Eds.): IWDW 2003, LNCS 2939, pp. 423–434, 2004.
© Springer-Verlag Berlin Heidelberg 2004

type of the content or other accessory information in various applications. Specific operations related to the status of the watermark can then be applied to cope with different situations.

One of the important requirements of watermark embedding systems is to compromise between the invisibility and robustness of the embedding algorithm [1]. First of all, the watermark must be embedded in invisible way to avoid degrading the perceptual quality of the host image. Users should not distinguish the existence of the watermark by viewing of the watermarked image. Secondly, the watermark must be robust against watermark attacks in which applied to the image content for the purposes of editing, storage or even circumventing watermark detection. These attacks include but are not limited to lossy compression, filtering, noise-adding, geometrical modification. The HVS (human visual system) is less sensitive to changes in the neighborhood of the edges than in the smooth regions of the image [2]. This is called the spatial masking effect, and can be exploited in data embedding by increasing the strength of the watermark around the edges and high textured areas of the image, and reducing the strength in smooth regions with low luminance. Swanson *et al.*[3] was proposed to method using blocks in DCT (discrete cosine transform) domain using property of human perceptual system. It used in the context of image compression using perceptually based quantizers. Kutter[4] have developed content adaptive schemes on the basis of luminance sensitivity function of the human visual system. The masking function is based on the estimation of the image luminance for embedding is not efficient against wavelet compression or denoising attacks. Podilchuk and Zeng[5] were developed to a content adaptive scheme, where the watermark is adjusted for each DCT block and wavelet domain. This approach is very limited the practical applications since it can be shown that the usage of the cover image will results in watermark schemes which can be easily broken. Delaigle *et al.* [6] proposed a perceptual modulation function to overcome the problem of visibility of the watermark around edges. This method developed a content adaptive criterion that may easily be applied to any watermarking technique in coordinate, Fourier, DCT or wavelet domains. Voloshynovskiy *et al.*[7] were proposed to adequate stochastic modeling for content adaptive digital image watermarking. Knowing stochastic models of the watermark and the cover image, one can formulate the problem of watermark estimation/detection according to the classical Bayessian and multiresolution paradigm and estimate the capacity issue of the image watermark.

The conventional watermarking approach, based on global information about the image characteristic, embed the watermarking signal as random noise in the whole cover image with the same watermark strength regardless of the local property of image. Therefore, this embedding method is leaded in practice to visible artifacts in the flat regions that are characterized by small variability [8]. In order to decrease these artifacts, the given watermark strength has to be decreased. This reduces the robustness of the watermark against several attacks, since the image region that generate the most visible artifacts determine the final maximum strength of the watermark signal to be embedded.

This paper presents highly reliable adaptive watermark embedding using a stochastic multiresolution model based on multiwavelet transform. Multiwavelet using this paper is DGHM multiwavelet with approximation order 2 for the reduction of artifacts in the reconstructed image. To embedding watermark, the original image is decomposed into 4 levels using a discrete multiwavelet transform, then a watermark is embedded into the JND(just noticeable differences) of the image each subband. The perceptual model is applied with a stochastic approach for watermark embedding. This is based on the computation of a NVF that have local image properties. The perceptual model with adaptive watermark embedding algorithm embed at the texture and edge region for more strongly embedded watermark by the JND. This methods use stationary GG model and nonstationary Gaussian characteristics because watermark has noise properties. The experiment results of simulation of the proposed watermark embedding method using stochastic perceptual model based on multiwavelet transform techniques was found to be excellent invisibility and robustness

2 Stochastic Perceptual Model

2.1 Multiwavelet Transform

Multiwavelet are a new addition to realize as vector-valued filter banks leading to wavelet theory. Multiwavelet is an advantage, since it offers simultaneous compactly support, orthogonality, symmetry, and vanishing moments [9-11]. Its system can simultaneously provide perfect reconstruction (orthogonality), good performance at the boundaries (linear-phase symmetry), and high order of approximation (vanishing moments). But a single wavelet cannot possess all these properties at the same time.

One of the great challenges to successful watermark embedding of orthogonal multiwavelet is to construct the space spanned by the multiscaling function with a higher approximation order usually leads to better energy compaction than single wavelets. And it contributes the reduction of checkboard artifacts in the reconstructed image. For a tree-structured vector filter bank in multiwavelet transforms, the lowpass and highpass properties for the two vector filters are not as clear as those for the two filters in single wavelet transforms.

The scaling vector $\mathbf{\Phi}(t)=[\phi_1(t),\cdots,\phi_N(t)]^T$, will denote a compactly supported orthogonal scaling vector of length N with a matrix dilation equation.

$$\mathbf{\Phi}(t)=\sqrt{2}\sum_{k\in Z}\mathbf{H}[k]\mathbf{\Phi}(2t-k). \tag{1}$$

Where, the multiwavelet coefficients $\mathbf{H}[k]$ are N by N real matrices.

An orthonormal basis of W_0 of where $W_0=V_{-1}\oplus V_0$ is generated by N wavelets vector $\mathbf{\Psi}(t)=[\varphi_1(t),\cdots,\varphi_N(t)]^T$, satisfying the matrix wavelet equation

$$\mathbf{\Psi}(t)=\sqrt{2}\sum_{k\in Z}\mathbf{G}[k]\mathbf{\Psi}(2t-k). \tag{2}$$

The $\mathbf{G}[k]$ are also N by N real matrices. The scaling vectors with $\boldsymbol{H}$ and $\boldsymbol{G}$ from matrix finite impulse response (FIR) filters have orthogonality, stability, smoothness, and good approximation property.

2.2 JND Paradigm

The JND thresholds determined by a model of human visual system and local image characteristics. JND threshold is dependent, as long as, the watermark values remain below JND threshold to achieve watermark transparency. Watermark embedding to perceptually significant coefficients is following.

$$X^{*}_{u,v,l,f} = \begin{cases} X_{u,v,l,f} + t^{F}_{l,f}\, w_{u,v,l,f}, & if\ X_{u,v,l,f} > t^{F}_{l,f} \\ X_{u,v,l,f} & otherwise \end{cases} \tag{3}$$

Where a weight $t^{F}_{l,f}$ is determined for each frequency band based on typical viewing condition. l denotes the resolution level where l=1,2,3,4 and f denotes the frequency orientation where f=1,2,3. The resulting weights in this paper use the Watson model [12]. $X_{u,v,l,f}$ refers to the wavelet coefficient at position (u,v) in resolution level l and frequency orientation f. The selected PSCs (perceptually significant coefficients) for Lena and Barbara images are represented in Fig. 1.

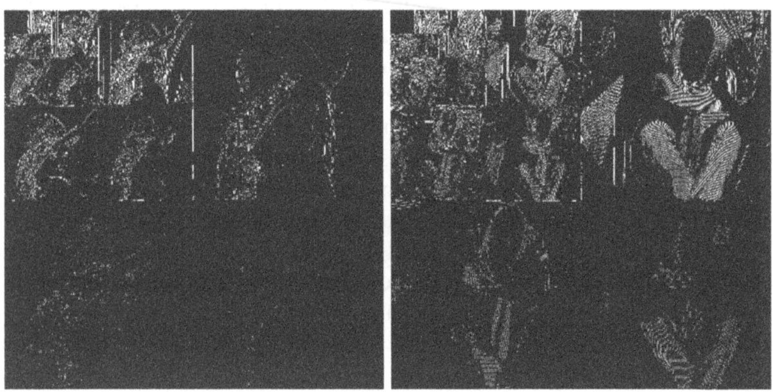

Fig. 1. Watermark embedded region by JND selection.

2.3 Stochastic Perceptual Model

The proposed watermark model is shown by block diagram of Fig. 2.

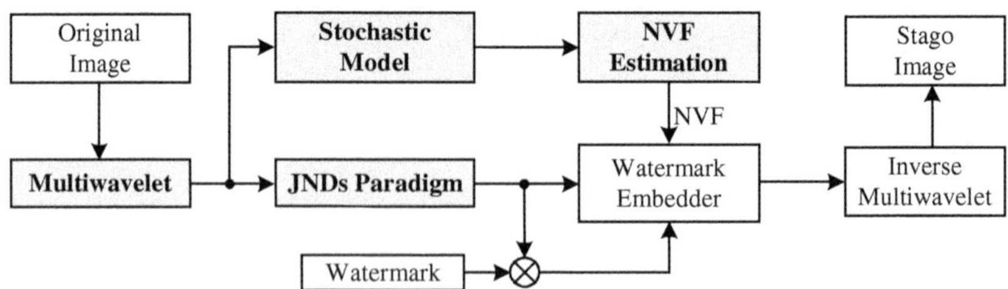

Fig. 2. The proposed adaptive watermark embedding model.

NVF function with stationary GG model. For optimal NVF decision, stationary GG model use shape parameter and variance of each subband in order to decrease visible artifact according to local properties of image. In the case of stationary GG model, NVF can be written in the (4):

$$NVF(i,j)=\frac{w(i,j)}{w(i,j)\ +\sigma_x^2(i,j)} \tag{4}$$

$$w(i,j)=\gamma[\eta(\gamma)]^{\gamma}\frac{1}{\|a(i,j)\|^{2-\gamma}} \tag{5}$$

$$a(i,j)=\frac{x(i,j)-\bar{x}(i,j)}{\sigma_x},\quad \eta(\gamma)=\sqrt{\frac{\Gamma(\frac{3}{\gamma})}{\Gamma(\frac{1}{\gamma})}} \tag{6}$$

Where $\sigma_x^2(i,j)$ denotes the variance of image. $\bar{x}(i,j)$ is mean of image and γ is shape parameter. In this paper, the estimated shape parameter use the γ=0.67. $\Gamma(t)$ is Gamma function. The watermark embedding use shape parameter and variance of each subband regions of multiwavelet domain, it is derived content adaptive criteria according to edge and texture.

NVF with non-stationary Gaussian model. In the case of non-stationary Gaussian model, NVF can be written in the (7):

$$NVF(i,j)=\frac{1}{1\ +\sigma_x^2(i,j)} \tag{7}$$

Where $\sigma_x^2(i,j)$ denotes the local variance of the image in a window centered on the pixel with coordinates $(i,j), 1\le i,j\le M$. The watermark is an *i.i.d.*(independent identically distributed) Gaussian process with unit variance, i.e. $N(0, 1)$. The NVF is the output of the perceptual model to a noise $N(0, 1)$. In order to estimate the local image variance the maximum likelihood (ML) estimate can be used. Assuming that image is a locally *i.i.d.* Gaussian distributed random variable, the ML estimate is given by:

$$\sigma_x^2(i,j)=\frac{1}{(2L+1)^2}\sum_{m=-L}^{L}\sum_{n=-L}^{L}(x(i+m,j+n)-x(i,j))^2 \tag{8}$$

with

$$x(i,j)=\frac{1}{(2L+1)^2}\sum_{m=-L}^{L}\sum_{n=-L}^{L}x(i+m,j+n) \tag{9}$$

Where $(2L+1)\times(2L+1)$ is a window of size.

2.4 Adaptive Watermark Embedding

The final equation with adaptive watermark embedding is following:

$$X^{*}_{u,v,l,f} = X_{u,v,l,f} + \{(1 - NVF)\cdot S_{ET} + NVF \cdot S_{F}\} w_{u,v,l,f} \tag{10}$$

Where $X^{*}{}_{u,v,l,f}$, $X_{u,v,l,f}$, and $w_{u,v,l,f}$ denote the watermarked image, original image, and watermark. S_{ET} denotes the watermark strength of texture and edge regions. S_F denotes the watermark strength of flat region. In this paper, S_{ET} is used for perceptually quantization and bit allocation for image compression [12] from Fig. 3(a). S_F is according to the perceptual criteria employed in the perceptual subband image coder by R. J. Safranek, *et al*,[13] by Fig. 3(b). The above rule embeds the watermark in highly textured areas and areas containing edges stronger than in the flat regions.

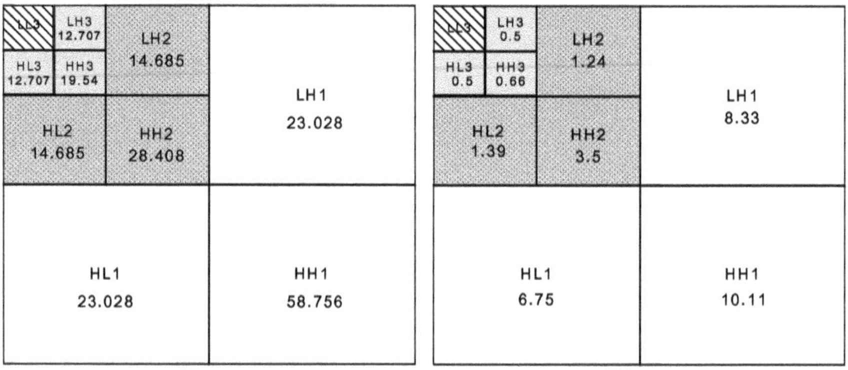

Fig. 3. Watermark strength of (a) edge or texture regions, (b) flat regions.

2.5 Watermark Detection

The watermark detection is the following.

$$w^{*}{}_{s,u,v,l,f} = X_{u,v,l,f} - \hat{X}^{*}{}_{u,v,l,f} \tag{11}$$

$$w^{*}{}_{u,v,l,f} = \frac{w^{*}{}_{s,u,v,l,f}}{t^{C}{}_{u,v,l,f}} \tag{12}$$

$$\rho_{\omega\omega^{*}}(l,f) = \frac{w^{*}_{l.f}\cdot w_{l,f}}{\sqrt{E_{w_{l,f}} E_{w_{l,f}}}}, \quad \text{for } l\text{=1,2,3,4 and } f\text{=1,2,3} \tag{13}$$

Where $w^{*}_{s,u,v,l,f}$ is different value between original multiwavelet coefficients and watermarked and attacked multiwavelet coefficients.

3 Experimental Results

To illustrate the main features of the proposed adaptive watermarking method using the stochastic perceptual model in the multiwavelet domain, we simulated our algorithm on several images of 512×512 size. The DGHM multiwavelet is decomposed the original image into 4 levels. The length of used watermark is variable to dependent image characteristics.

The length of watermark sequence using the proposed and Podilchuk algorithms is shown the Table 1. As the shown Table 1, we note the watermark length varies significantly depending on the particular image characteristics. The watermark lengths of stationary GG model and non-stationary Gaussian model are the same. Also, the watermark length of proposed method is more embedding than the Podilchuk's method. This is more robustness than the Podilchuk's. The PSNR of the visual quality of the stego images according to watermark strength variation for Lena and Peppers images are shown the Table 2. This means that quality of image is decided by embedding strength of watermark. At the Table 2, when heightened embedding strength more than 30, we could know that quality of image fall off rapidly. Also, watermark is embedded in state that characteristics of low frequency bands and high frequency bands are ignored as fixed embedding strength. This method can derive higher PSNR as decision embedding strength of watermark as adaptively in each subband.

Table 1. Length of watermark sequence using the proposed and Podilchuk algorithms.

		Lena	Barbara	Baboon	Peppers	Airplane
Proposed	Stationary	8,311	18,706	38,062	9,660	11,565
	Non-stationary					
Podilchuk		7,973	17,749	37,655	7,458	10,318

Table 2. The PSNR comparison according to watermarked strength.

Image	Lena (512×512)		Peppers (512×512)	
Watermark Strength	**Stationary** PSNR[dB]	**Non-stationary** PSNR[dB]	**Stationary** PSNR[dB]	**Non-stationary** PSNR[dB]
10	43.97	43.93	43.32	43.26
20	37.95	37.91	37.30	37.25
30	34.43	34.39	33.78	33.73
40	31.93	31.89	31.28	31.23
50	30.00	29.96	29.34	29.29
60	28.41	28.37	27.76	27.71
70	27.08	27.03	26.42	26.37
80	25.92	25.87	25.26	25.21
90	24.92	24.85	24.23	24.18
100	23.98	23.94	23.32	23.27

To establishment the robustness of the watermarked image under JPEG attack, we compressed it by JPEG with a Q factor varying 10% to 90%. We know that the result shows the resilience of the watermarking scheme against the JPEG compression. As the PSNR comparison of JPEG in Fig. 4, the Podilchuk's method showed higher PSNR in the 90% compression rate, but in different compression rates, the proposed method displayed higher PSNR. So we can say that proposed model is excellent PSNR than the Podilchuk's method, In the meantime, correlation response of proposed model shows that more superior than the Podilchuk's method in all compression rates.

To evaluation the robustness of the watermarked image under cropping attack, we randomly cropped a region with size of a 10% to 90% from the watermarked image and then compressed it by JPEG with a quality factor varying 80%. So, we could know that the result shows resilience of the watermarking scheme against the combination of cropping and JPEG compression as shown in Fig. 5. For the cropping attack, the proposed and Podilchuk methods are similar to PSNR and correlation response for the cropping ratio. As shown by he results in Table 3, the proposed algorithm remained robust against all these attacks when compared to the Podilchuk's algorithm.

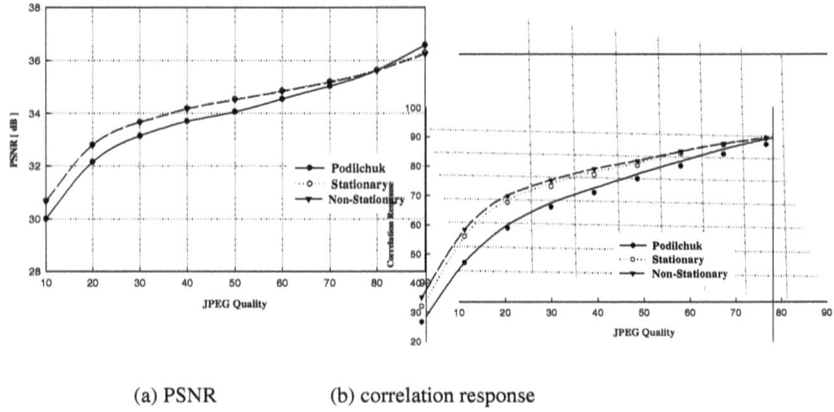

(a) PSNR (b) correlation response

Fig. 4. The robustness test of JPEG attacks.

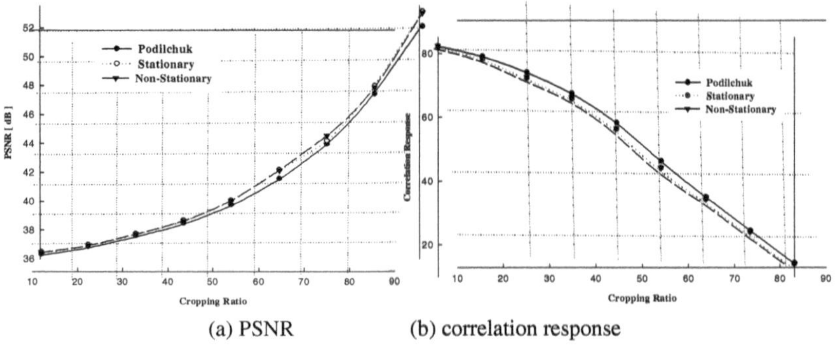

(a) PSNR (b) correlation response

Fig. 5. The robustness test of cropping attack after JPEG compression Q=80%.

The correlation response for watermarked image, no attack, non-stationary and stationary GG models are shown in Fig. 6. We used the 200th watermark seed among 1000 watermark seed for experiments. As can know in Fig. 6, proposed method could detect correlation response of high numerical value to various image processing. This means that the proposed method is robustness in various attacks.

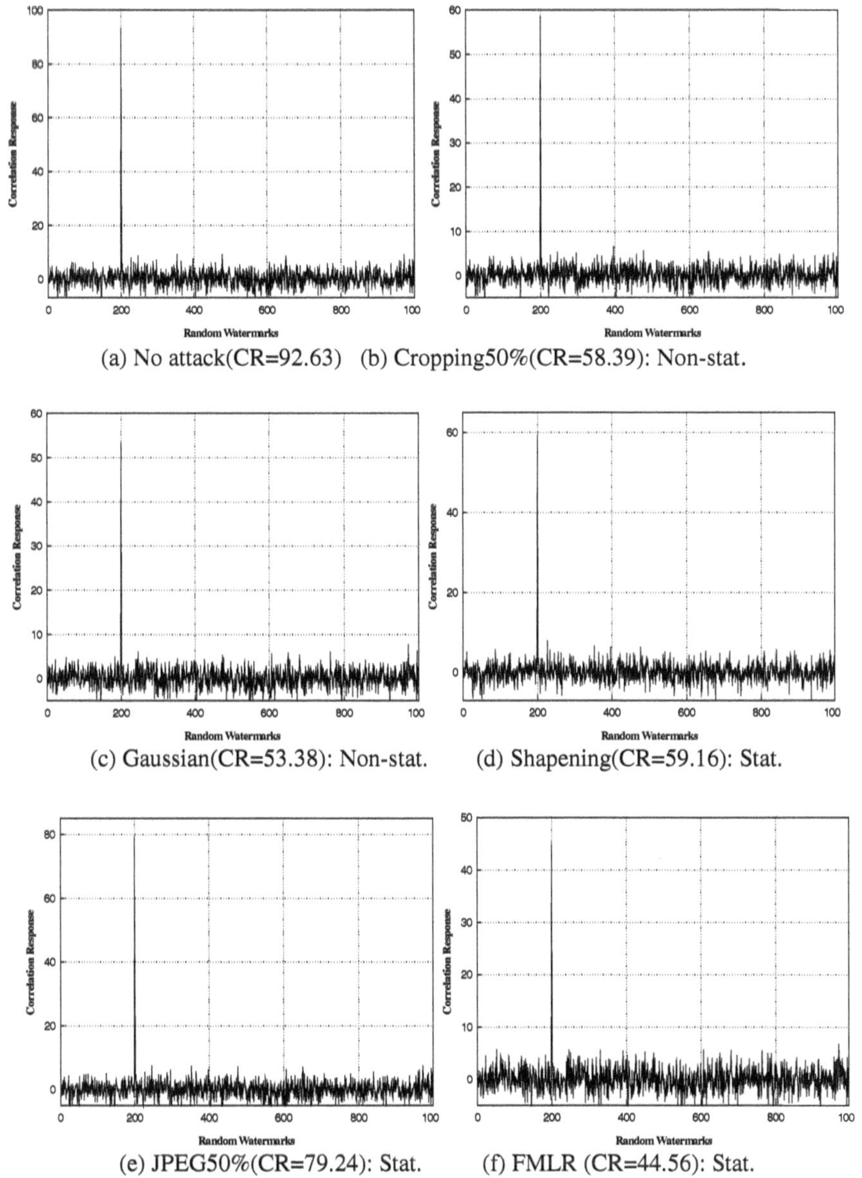

(a) No attack(CR=92.63) (b) Cropping50%(CR=58.39): Non-stat.

(c) Gaussian(CR=53.38): Non-stat. (d) Shapening(CR=59.16): Stat.

(e) JPEG50%(CR=79.24): Stat. (f) FMLR (CR=44.56): Stat.

Fig. 6. The correlation response for attacks.

We displayed the result in Table 3 after we compare to non-stationary and stationary GG models and the Podilchuk methods about several attacks. We could know certainly that proposed method is superior more than the Podilchuk's method. And it showed that non-stationary model overmatches in equal PSNR.

The extracted watermark for the Peppers and Barbara images using the proposed model are shown in Fig. 7. The extracted watermark of proposed model is embedding the edge and textured regions as shown to Fig. 7(c)-(f).

Table 3. The correlation response according to attacks.

	PSNR[dB]			Correlation Response		
	Podilchuk	Non-stat.	Stationary	Podilchuk	Non-stat.	Stationary
No Attack	38.67	37.91	37.95	90.87	92.63	92.62
median	30.25	30.67	30.66	51.05	59.97	59.59
sharpening	21.39	21.68	21.69	51.24	61.45	59.16
gaussian	32.97	33.82	33.83	45.60	53.38	51.76
FMLR	31.93	32.65	32.66	36.02	45.76	44.56
crop50	42.12	41.94	41.99	61.57	58.39	58.36
jpeg50	34.16	34.52	34.54	73.14	81.21	79.24

4 Conclusions

In this paper, we have presented a new approach for highly reliable adaptive watermark embedding using stochastic perceptual model based on multiwavelet domain. To embedding watermark, the original image was decomposed into 4 levels using the DGHM multiwavelet transform, then a watermark is embedded into the JND of the image each subband. The perceptual model is applied with a stochastic approach of stationary GG model and non-stationary Gaussian model for watermark embedding. This is based on the computation of a NVF that have local image properties. The stochastic perceptual model with adaptive watermark embedding algorithm embed at the texture and edge region for more strongly embedded watermark by the JND. This method uses stationary GG model and nun-stationary Gaussian model because watermark has noise properties. The experiment results of the proposed watermark embedding based on multiwavelet transform techniques was found to be excellent invisibility and robustness.

Acknowledgements. This work was supported by grant No. (R01-2002-000-00589-0) from the Basic Research Program of the Korea Science & Engineering Foundation.

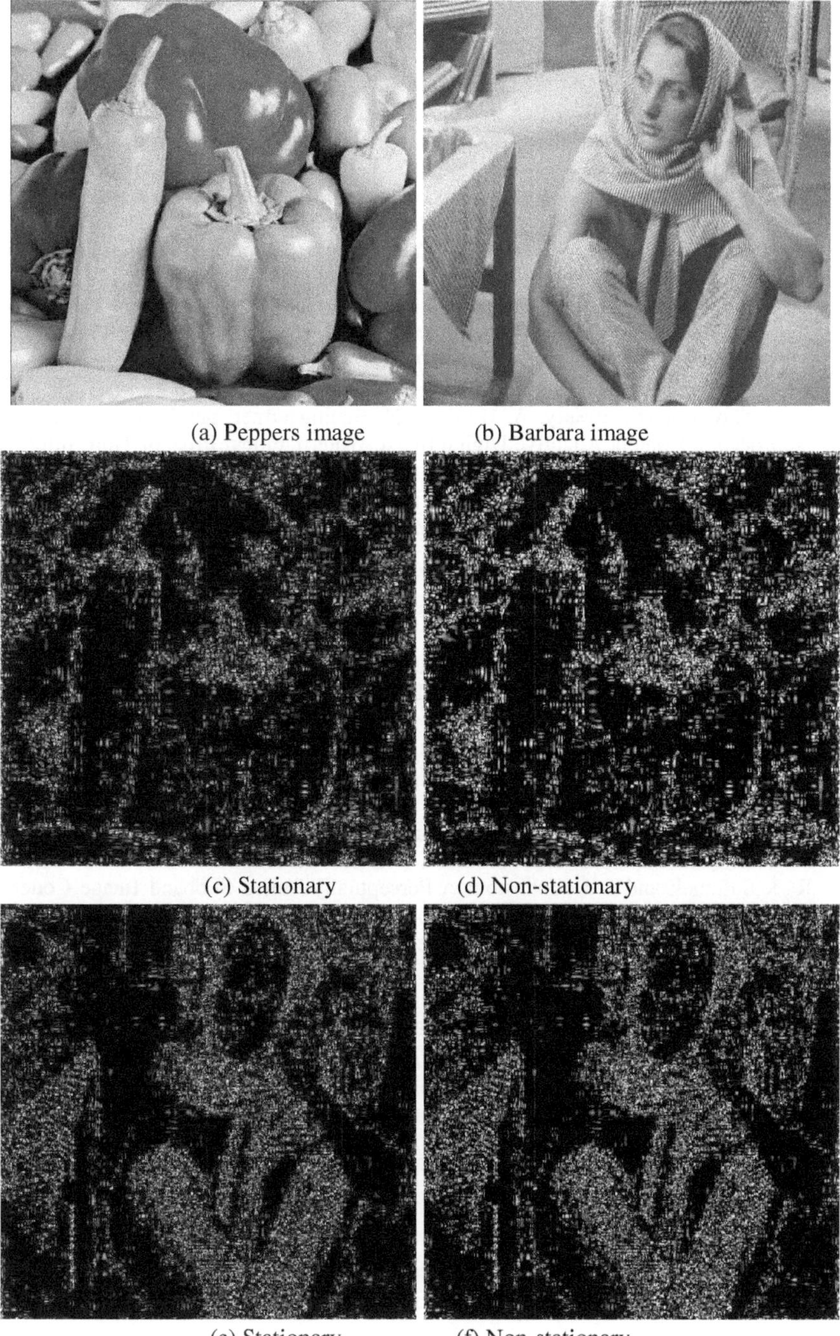

(a) Peppers image (b) Barbara image

(c) Stationary (d) Non-stationary

(e) Stationary (f) Non-stationary

Fig. 7. Extracted watermark images.

References

1. I.Cox, J.Kilian, T.Leighton, and T.Shamoon.: Secure Spread Spectrum Watermarking for Multimedia. NEC Research Institute Tech Rep. 95–10, (1995)
2. J.Huang and Y.Shi: Adaptive Image Watermarking Scheme Based on Visual Masking. Electronic Letters, Vol. 34, No. 8, (1998) 748–750
3. M. Swanson, B. Zhu, and A. Twefik.: Transparent Robust Image Watermarking. IEEE International Conference on Image Processing ICIP96, Vol. 3 (1996) 211–214
4. M. Kutter: Watermarking Resisting to Translation, Rotation and Scaling. Proc. of SPIE, Boston, USA (1998)
5. C.Podilchuk and W.Zeng.: Image Adaptive Watermarking Using Visual Models. IEEE Journal on Selected Areas in Communication, Vol. 16, No. 4 (1998) 525–539
6. J.F.Delaigle, C.De Vleeschouwer, and B.Macq: Watermarking Algorithm Based on a Human Visual Model. Signal Processing, Vol.66, (1998) 319–335
7. Sviatoslav Voloshynovskiy, A. Herrigel, N. Baumgaertner, and T. Pun.: A Stochastic Approach to Content Adaptive Digital Image Watermarking. Proc. of Third Information Hiding Workshop (1999)
8. Ki-Ryong Kwon and Ahmed H. Tewfik: Adaptive Watermarking Using Successive Subband Quantization and Perceptual Model Based on Multiwavelet Transform. Proc. of SPIE, 4675–32, (2002)
9. V. Strela, P. N. Heller, G. Strang, P. Topiwala, and C. Heil: The Application of Multiwavelet Filterbank to Image Processing. IEEE Trans. On Image Processing, Vol. 8, No. 4, (1999) 548–563
10. X. G. Xia, J. S. Geronimo, D. P. Hardin, and B. W. Suter: Design of Prefilters for Discrete Multiwavelet Transforms. IEEE Trans. on Image Processing, Vol. 44, No. 1, (1996) 25–35
11. Douglas P. Hardin and David W. Roach: Multiwavelet Prefilters I: Orthogonal Prefilters Preserving Approxima-tion order p ≤2. IEEE Trans. On Circuits and Systems II, Vol. 45, (1998) 1106–1112
12. A. B. Watson, G. Y. Yang, J. A. Solomon, and J. Villasenor: Visual Thresholds for Wavelet Quantization Error, Proc. SPIE, Vol. 2657, (1996) 381–392
13. R. J. Safranek and J. D. Johnston: A Perceptually Tuned Subband Image Coder with Image Dependent Quantization and Post-quantization Data Compression. IEEE Intl. Conf. Acoustics, Speech and Signal Processing-ICASSP 89, (1989) 1945–1948

Metadata Hiding for Content Adaptation

Yong Ju Jung, Ho Kyung Kang, and Yong Man Ro

Multimedia Information and Communication Group, Information and Communications University (ICU), P.O.Box 77. Yusong, Daejeon, 305-600, Korea
{yjjung,kyoung,yro}@icu.ac.kr

Abstract. In this paper, we propose an application of data hiding, especially for content adaptation, where one can reduce computational time and get better transcoding results or quality. Hiding some useful information for content adaptation can help content transcoder to do effective transcoding so that one can achieve lower complexity as well as better quality in content adaptation. Experimental results show that the proposed method, based on data hiding, gives effectiveness to content adaptation with reasonable subjective quality.

1 Introduction

Data hiding mainly concerns embedding some proprietary data into digital media for the purpose of identification, annotation, and message transmission. Applications can often be found in various fields. Those are (1) the digital watermarking, which provides the protection of intellectual property rights, (2) secret communications, (3) error concealment, (4) controlling digital signals, etc. Especially, controlling digital signals is to embed customizing information that allows personalized delivery of video and image or enhances the video watching experience by giving viewers the capability to control and personalize what they view. Every data hiding technique is constrained by a minimum amount of perceivable degradation of the host signal, which can be an image, audio, or video. It may be possible because the human auditory and visual systems are imperfect detectors. Hidden data must be able to be retrieved from attacked host signals.

Another topic, Universal Multimedia Access (UMA), deals with delivery of image, video, audio, and multimedia content under different network conditions, user characteristics, and capabilities of terminal devices [1]. The objective of universal access systems is to create different presentations of the same information, from a single content-base, so as to provide the best possible presentation to the user [2]. This can be done by content adaptation.

Actually, content adaptation, which is conventionally called transcoding, has been studied extensively in recent years. To transcode a content effectively, there have been studies of transcoding mechanisms, such as transcoding hints in MPEG-7 Multimedia Description Scheme (MDS), which allows content authors or providers to guide the processes of manipulating and adapting multimedia material [1]. However, little work has been done to combine metadata hiding and content adaptation, which could result in more effective techniques.

T. Kalker et al. (Eds.): IWDW 2003, LNCS 2939, pp. 435–446, 2004.
© Springer-Verlag Berlin Heidelberg 2004

Although metadata could help content transcoding, it sometimes requires an additional storage and management in case of a separate file of metadata. However, by using metadata hiding into the content, one can have the following advantages over storing the metadata in a separate file or multiplexing them into a system format, *i.e.*, putting them in the header [10]. First, the management cost of storage and bandwidth for metadata could be additionally saved. Second, header data may be easily lost under a cropping-like attack, and it is very difficult to maintain the header data when the video format is changed. So, hiding metadata rather than openly carrying them into the header has an advantage in some applications. Third, once some valuable side information is embedded into the original data, one can extract and use it in the only case that it is needed.

In this paper, our focus is on metadata hiding for content adaptation which can reduce computational time and get better quality for adapting contents. Hiding some useful information for content adaptation can help resource tailor to do effective transcoding so that it can result in lower complexity and better quality.

The paper is organized as follows: In Sect. 2, we shall propose a new metadata hiding system for content adaptation. We introduce and discuss our adaptation approaches using the proposed system, which are syntactical and semantic information hiding to help content adaptation. In Sect. 3, we show experimental results and the effectiveness of the proposed system. Finally, we draw conclusions in Sect. 4.

2 Proposed Metadata Hiding System

In this section, we discuss and propose a new metadata hiding system for content adaptation. In our previous work [3], we introduced an application of metadata hiding, which was a multimedia indexing/retrieval system containing MPEG-7 metadata. The MPEG-7 descriptors and description schemes are inserted into the original data using a data hiding technique. In this multimedia system, the extraction of MPEG-7 metadata for every query can be replaced by simple extraction of the hidden data. Once database is built in a way that the metadata is hidden into the original content, it is useful for fast and efficient retrieval of multimedia database, *i.e.*, for an image as a query, extraction time is saved, and storage of meta data could be saved as well.

In this manner, our approach starts from answering the following question: which information to be embedded can be useful for specific application?

Under this consideration, we propose that some useful side information can be embedded into the original data in order to help content adaptation become effective in time and quality. In the following subsections, after briefly mentioning the methodology of our proposed system, we discuss which information can be embedded for content adaptation.

2.1 Methodology

Before delving into our proposed metadata hiding system, we will mention briefly MPEG-7 transcoding hints in order to compare with our proposed system. MPEG-7 transcoding hints support effective transcoding of content. These metadata allow content authors or providers to guide the processes of manipulating and adapting multimedia material [1]. Figure 1 shows the generic application scenario of transcoding hints.

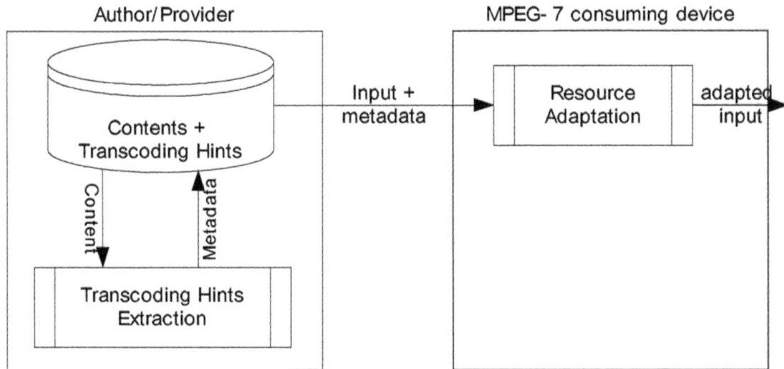

Fig. 1. Generic illustration of transcoding hints application scenario [6].

Alternatively, as shown in Fig. 2, our proposed content adaptation system uses some hidden side information which can help transcoding. Once a database is built in such a way that the metadata is hidden into the original content, it is useful for fast and efficient transcoding of multimedia contents, *i.e.*, extraction time to get some useful transcoding information is saved like the transcoding hints scenario. Also, unlike the transcoding hints scenario, the management cost of storage and bandwidth for metadata could be additionally saved as well. Even though metadata hiding itself can affect content quality, it can be tolerant or reasonable depending on the specific application.

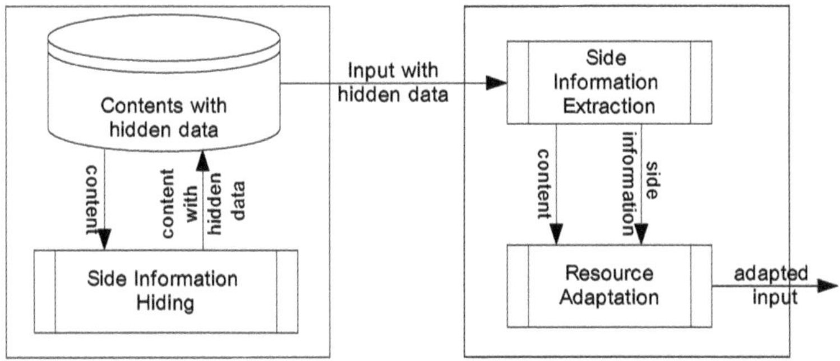

Fig. 2. Generic illustration of data hiding system for content adaptation.

In general, the metadata or side information has a small amount of data compared with the original content. Therefore, the small amount of metadata can be embedded into the original content, especially video, using conventional data hiding techniques.

Under the proposed methodology, we perform and discuss two kinds of side information hiding for content adaptation. One is syntactical information hiding for content adaptation, and the other is semantic information hiding.

2.2 Syntactical Information Hiding for Content Adaptation

In [4], a fast approach with data hiding was proposed to derive a new MPEG stream with the half spatial resolution from an original MPEG stream. After downsizing the original four-block residues to one-block, the authors use subblock motion information to improve the image quality. As the syntax of MPEG does not allow subblock motion information to be included, it is sent as side information using data hiding so as to be compliant with the video encoding standard.

We see it can be one of the examples of content adaptation with data hiding. Now, our concern is which other side information can be used for content adaptation. To find this side information, we need to revisit content adaptations one by one.

In general, content adaptations can be listed as follows (see MPEG-7 VariationSetDS in [5]): Summarization, Abstraction, Extraction, ModalityTranslation, SpatialReduction, TemporalReduction, SamplingReduction, RateReduction, QualityReduction, ColorReduction, Substitution, AltanativeView, etc.

Among the above adaptations, we can see what needs the side information, which can help the adaptation. That side information is similar to MPEG-7 transcoding hints.

Transcoding hints consist of the motion hint, the difficulty hint, the importance hint, the shape hint, the coding hint, and the spatial resolution hint [5].

Also, in [9], the authors suggested three classes to help MPEG video transcoding, which can transcode an MPEG video bitstream into various MPEG video bitstreams with different characteristics. Those are Temporal Similarity, Spatial Complexity and Region Perceptibility, which are very similar to MPEG-7 media transcoding hints. Even though the proposed characteristics in [9] are redundant with transcoding hints, these can be also used effectively for content adaptation. Most information, mentioned above, can be directly obtained without fully decoding MPEG bitstreams. However, if it is not possible or is very time-consuming to get useful information, hiding side information can have advantages.

2.2.1 Metadata Hiding for Adaptations Regarding Spatial Reduction, Temporal Reduction, and Quality Reduction

One side information can be the region perceptibility in [9], the importance hint in MPEG-7 transcoding hints. The importance hint specifies the relative semantic importance of video segments within a video sequence, or of regions or objects within an image, and can be used by a rate control mechanism to improve subjective quality [6]. This hint allows the transcoder to allocate more bits to important parts of the content.

Although importance regions and values can be obtained by contents-based methods depending on specific application or by manual methods according to user preference, the contents-based method does not result in better performance than the manual one does. So, an application in which users give the importance information, specified by user preference values, is more effective sometimes. This information can be hidden into host content to obtain better transcoding result, which has higher subjective quality. That means users, including authors or publishers, provide importance hints so that they can control the adaptation of content [6].

Figure 3 shows the architecture of this adaptation system with the importance information hiding.

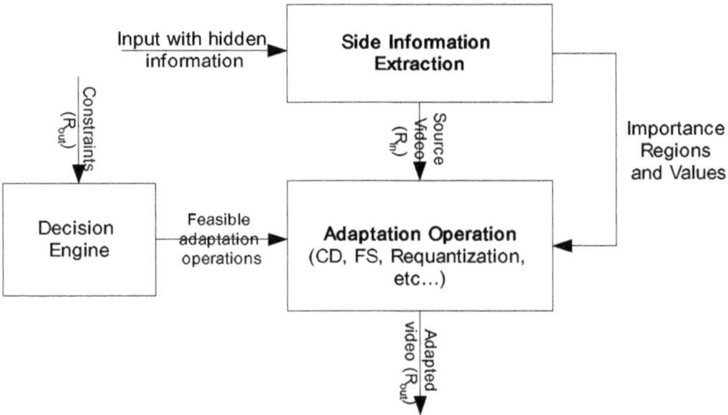

Fig. 3. The architecture of the proposed content adaptation system using the hidden side information, *i.e.*, the importance information.

The procedure of this system is as follows:
(1) Obtain importance regions and values by automatic or manual method.
(2) Hide the obtained importance information: The metadata to be hidden are the positions of bounding boxes, within which important spatial segments are located, or the positions of important temporal segments and their importance values [7].
(3) Send or retrieve the stream with hidden information to the adaptation server. This situation depends on a specific application.
(4) Extract the hidden importance information.
(5) Process content adaptation.

For spatial reduction, there is a transcoding algorithm using this importance information in [8], which can be adopted into this system.

```
if (inside temporal region marked with importance)
then
    skip very few frames according to importance value or keep all frames;
else
    skip many frames (much more than the inside region)
```

Fig. 4. Procedure of a frame skipping method with importance information.

For quality reduction, some adaptation operator, e.g., coefficient dropping (CD) or requantization, can work. We can drop fewer coefficients or requantize more coarsely for the important segment according to importance values. Otherwise, we can drop more coefficients or requantize finely. In Fig. 3, R_{in} means the input rate of a source stream, and R_{out} means the output rate of the adapted stream.

Also, for temporal reduction, we can use frame skipping (FS) methods. Figure 4 shows the psuedo code of a frame skipping method with the extracted importance information.

2.2.2 Metadata Hiding for Adaptations Regarding Summarization, Abstraction, and Extraction

This idea starts from which scene description of a video sequence can be side information so that those adaptations can be easily done with computational reduction in adaptation time. Our approach is hiding scene descriptions, which may contain the number of shots, the shot index number, key frame and shot boundary information.

In recent years, key frame extraction and shot boundary detection have been fundamental tools for research on video summarization. These basic descriptions could be generated manually, semi-automatically, or automatically. Manual generation is too costly; however, it is the most accurate method. Both manual and automatic methods have trade offs between cost and accuracy. The automatic summarization approach, which is normally used, is as follows: The AV data is analyzed to extract basic features, such as shots or key frames, using low-level features such as motion and color, and to assess their relative importance. Then, the most important components are selected, possibly condensed further, and organized to generate a summary [6].

In our paper, our concern is not for automatic extraction method of shot boundary and key frame in adaptation time. Instead of that, we just focus on data hiding as side information, assuming that we already have key frame and shot boundary information for video summarization or abstraction, which is one kind of content adaptation. Actually, due to inborn characteristics of shot, shot boundary information can be easily obtained in the creation time of a video. For example, shot boundary can be identical with camera operation of creator or editing operation in editing time. Obviously, if scene changes can be extracted easily in the whole adaptation procedure, the adaptation time to get summary is reduced.

The whole procedure is as follows: At first, basic features, like key frame and shot boundary information, are embedded into the original video signal itself. Then, the video stream with hidden information is delivered to the adaptation server. In the content adaptation procedure, after extracting this information, it is used to determine video segments, and further, to extract a video summary.

Like this approach, hiding key frame and shot boundary information to directly host video signal will help resource tailor to do online transcoding. It fits well for the application having a real-time requirement.

2.3 Semantic Information Hiding for Content Adaptation

One of metadata hiding applications is to embed customizing information that allows personalized delivery of video and image or to allow viewers to control and personalize what they view [10]. That means data hiding allows users to tailor a video to their needs. The hidden data can be made accessible to different levels of users, depending on the wishes of the author.

In addition to the syntactical information, semantic information can also be embedded so that it can help semantic content adaptation. For example, marking or describing violence or sexual scenes in video, semantic adaptation can be performed by eliminating, changing to other scenes, or embedding subtitles according to the user's level, such as the user's age [11]. We believe that this kind of semantic information hiding can be applied under our above system, like syntactic information hiding in the previous subsection.

3 Experiments

A series of experiments was conducted to evaluate the overall efficiency of the proposed side information hiding for content adaptation.

Generally, digital watermarking typically requires very few bits, 1% or less of the host data size. But in this paper, we consider applications that require significantly larger amounts of data embedding because of metadata hiding. So, we need to construct an appropriate embedding algorithm to meet our approach.

Several interesting data hiding techniques have been developed in various approaches so far [10], [12], [13]. Most of those techniques are performed in MPEG DCT domain. In this paper, since our concern is not the development of effective data hiding techniques, we will choose and adopt one of the conventional methods for our experiments.

Embedding data into the DCT coefficients of I or P-frame results in error propagation within a GOP. So it is reasonable to embed the side information into the DCT residues of B-frame. Since modifications of high frequency DCT coefficients yield less observable artifacts, it is also reasonable to embed in the high frequency coefficients of B-frame [4].

In general, the adaptation system can be placed at the server, proxy, and client side according to the situation. An exemplary application system of server-adaptation server-client 3-tier architecture is utilized in our experiments. The operation flow is as follows: The content generator creates information for transcoding, such as the above syntactic and semantic information. Data hiding is also executed. Precisely, an author extracts side information for transcoding manually, semi-automatically, or automatically. That side information is embedded into the host data. Then, that hidden information is extracted and used in the real transcoder, as a content provider. Finally, a user in the client device consumes the adapted content, which has the best possible quality.

3.1 Experimental Settings

In our experiments, we have used a golf video sequence included in an MPEG-7 video contents set. Its frame size is 352 x 240, and its total length is 5000 frames (3min 19sec) with a 12-frame GOP structure, IBBBPBBBPBBBI in display order. We have conducted two kinds of experiments for metadata hiding, which are syntactical information hiding for content adaptation as mentioned in Sect 2.2. In Table 1 to Table 3, side information for experiments is shown.

First, Table 1 shows importance information for still regions. This information is just for the selected temporal region for the purpose of simulation. Currently, it consists of frame number, still region, and importance value.

Table 1. Side information to be embedded into an original video, which are frame number, importance still region, and values.

Frame number	Still region			Importance value
	Width	Height	Center(x,y)	
1400	100	80	155,75	0.8
1800	100	200	176,105	0.8
2216	45	100	172,126	0.8
2216	50	22	268,44	1.0
2713	50	90	179,136	1.0
3200	120	200	184,110	0.9
3400	120	200	184,110	0.9
3700	80	80	78,78	0.9

Table 2 shows importance information for temporal regions. This side information is embedded into the original video, and it consists of shot index, temporal region, and its importance value.

Table 2. Side information to be embedded into an original video, which is shot index, start frame, end frame, and importance value.

Shot index	Start frame	End frame	Importance value	Shot index	Start frame	End frame	Importance value
0	1	263	0.1	6	2714	2874	1.0
1	294	882	1.0	7	2875	3687	0.9
2	912	1299	0.9	8	3688	4037	0.7
3	1324	2267	0.8	9	4038	4312	0.2
4	2268	2561	0.6	10	4313	4378	0.8
5	2562	2713	0.2	11	4404	5000	0.8

Table 3 shows shot boundary information consisting of start frame, end frame, and shot type. This information to be embedded into an original video sequence is used for another kind of content adaptation experiment, which is summarization, abstraction, and extraction. Actually, embedded data is represented by each symbol.

3.2 Experimental Results

For the experiment of metadata hiding for adaptations regarding spatial, temporal and quality reduction, we embed importance information of still regions and temporal regions, such as side information in Table 1 and 2. The exact embedded information is the following set:

(1) (frame number, width, height, center position, importance value)

(2) (shot index, start frame, end frame, importance value),

where (1) is for still region, and (2) is for temporal region.

This information is embedded by the method mentioned above into the high frequency band coefficients of DCT residues in B-frames. Figure 5 shows the data hiding procedure adopted in our experiment. DH marker is a unique data to mark or

Table 3. Side information to be embedded into an original video, which is shot boundary information consisting of start frame, end frame, and shot type.

Shot boundary index	Start frame	End frame	Shot type	DH-frame	Start frame symbol	End frame symbol	Shot type symbol
0	264	293	Dissolve	264	0	-29	1
1	883	912	Dissolve	888	5	-24	1
2	1299	1324	Wipe	1308	9	-16	2
3	2267	2268	Cut	2268	1	0	0
4	2561	2562	Cut	2568	7	6	0
5	2713	2714	Cut	2724	11	10	0
6	2874	2875	Cut	2880	6	5	0
7	3687	3688	Cut	3696	9	8	0
8	4037	4038	Cut	4044	7	6	0
9	4312	4313	Cut	4320	8	7	0
10	4378	4404	Wipe	4380	2	-24	2

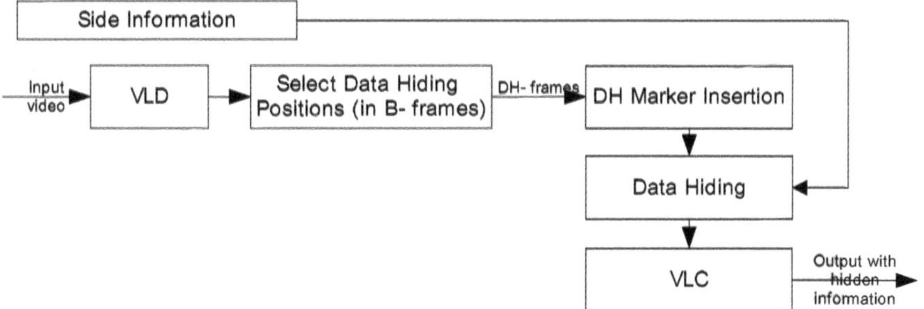

Fig. 5. Data hiding procedure.

indicate the existence of hidden data in current frame or GOP. DH-frame is the selected frame to embed data, which is indicated by DH marker.

Table 4 shows that the extracted side information is the same as the original. So, this extracted information is used for the effective content adaptation.

By performing spatial reduction using this extracted importance information for still region, better result can be achieved. Figure 6 shows the spatially reduced result of the 2216th frame with (2216, 45,100, 172, 126, 0.8) and (2216, 50, 22, 268, 44, 1.0) importance information pairs, which are rectangular box in the (a) figure. As seen from (b) and (c) results in Fig. 6, the adaptation result performed with importance information has the amplified region in which the user is more interested. The frame size of the reduced-resolution sequences is 176 x 120, which is half of the original. These results illustrate the effectiveness of the data hiding method for content adaptation.

And by performing temporal reduction using this extracted importance information for temporal region, we can achieve better results. In this case, frame dropping is performed in the above manner. Also, in order to get quality-reduced results, coefficient dropping is performed. As in the spatial reduction, the extracted importance information is used to get improved subjective quality.

Table 4. Part of the extracted side information.

Frame number	Still region			Importance value
	Width	Height	Center(x,y)	
1400	100	80	155,75	0.8
1800	100	200	176,105	0.8
2216	45	100	172,126	0.8
2216	50	22	268,44	1.0
2713	50	90	179,136	1.0
..	..	..	..	..

(a) size: 352 x 240

(b) size: 176 x 120

(c) size: 176 x 120

Fig. 6. (a) Original frame and transcoding results (b) without using information hiding (c) using importance information hiding.

For the experiment of metadata hiding for adaptations regarding summarization, abstraction, and extraction, we embed shot boundary information for each shot, such as side information shown in Table 3. The real embedded information is the following set: (start frame symbol (SFS), end frame symbol (EFS), shot type symbol (STS)), where $SFS = SF(i) - DHF(i)$, $EFS = EF(i) - DHF(i)$, and $SF(i)$ means the number of the start frame, $EF(i)$ the number of the end frame, and $DHF(i)$ the number of the data hiding frame of the ith shot boundary. These symbol sets are embedded by the data hiding procedure shown in Fig. 5.

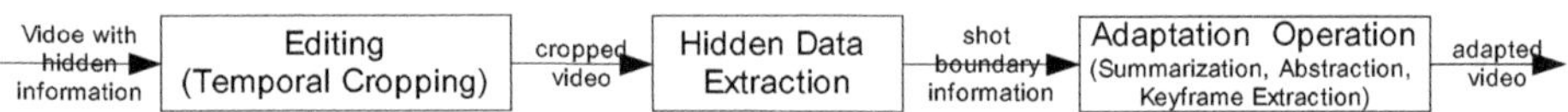

Fig. 7. Data extraction procedure under editing operation which is temporal cropping attack.

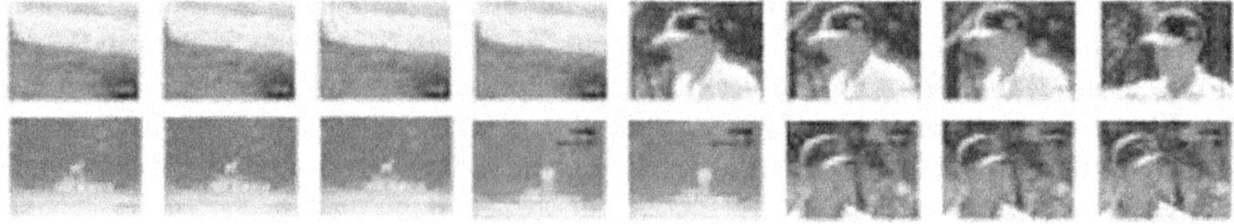

Fig. 8. 4 shots between 2561st and 3635th frame of the original video.

To show the effectiveness of our proposed method, the hidden data undergoes an editing operation, specifically the temporal cropping attack. After that, the hidden data is extracted, and adaptation operations are executed. The experimental procedure

Table 5. Extracted shot boundary information.

Shot boundary index	Start frame symbol	End frame symbol	Shot type symbol	DH-frame	Start frame	End frame	Shot type
3	1	0	0	2268	2267	2268	CUT
4	7	6	0	2568	2561	2562	CUT
5	11	10	0	2724	2713	2714	CUT
6	6	5	0	2880	2874	2875	CUT

is shown in Fig.7. Figure 8 shows that there are 4 shots between the 2561st and 3635th frame of the original video. These shots are used for this experiment.

Table 5 shows the extracted shot boundary information, which is the (SFS, EFS, STS) set from each DH-frame and the obtained exact shot boundary information which is the number of start frame, end frame, and shot type calculated from each symbol set. When one shot among the above 4 shots is deleted by an editing operation, the result is shown in Fig. 9. The shot boundary information extracted from the remaining 3 shots is shown in Table 6. As seen from Table 6, DH-frame values are changed by the editing operation. However, the obtained information, which is the number of the start frame, the end frame, and the shot type calculated from each symbol pair, matches exactly with the shots shown in Fig. 9. So, our proposed method is very useful under cropping-like attack and the hidden data can survive when the video format is changed.

From the above experiments, we believe that other content adaptations with useful side information can also perform well by the use of the data hiding technique. Intuitively, we feel that, in order to obtain better quality, decoder can be customized. To overcome error propagation, when there is considerable motion and/or a large GOP, the GOP structure can be modified to reduce the number of frames between two successive I-frames, as in [4]. In our experiment, we have not adopted and performed this kind of customization, but we believe it can be very useful for improving quality. Therefore, our approach can become more reasonable.

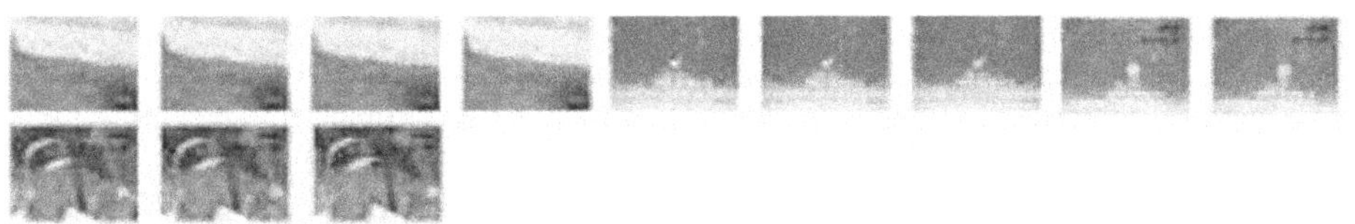

Fig. 9. Remaining 3 shots after editing operation of the original 4 video shots.

Table 6. Extracted shot boundary information after editing operation.

Shot boundary index	Start frame symbol	End frame symbol	Shot type symbol	DH-frame	Start frame	End frame	Shot type
3	1	0	0	2268	2267	2268	CUT
5	11	10	0	2572	2561	2562	CUT
6	6	5	0	2728	2772	2723	CUT

4 Conclusion

In this paper, we have proposed a metadata hiding system for content adaptation, which can reduce computational time and get better transcoding quality. We have also introduced our adaptation approaches using the proposed system, which are syntactical and semantic information hiding to help content adaptation. Hiding some useful information for content adaptation can help content transcoder to do effective transcoding so that it can result in lower complexity and better quality. Experimental results show that the proposed method based on data hiding gives effectiveness to content adaptation with reasonable content quality.

Once a database is built in such a way that the metadata is hidden into the original content, adaptation time, as well as the storage of metadata, could be saved. In our paper, we have seen that data hiding can provide effective content adaptation without extra bandwidth or storage requirements.

References

1. MPEG-7 Applications Document v.8.1, ISO/IEC JTC1/SC29/WG11/M4839, MPEG99, Vancouver, BC, July 1999
2. MPEG-7 application: Universal Access Through Content Repurposing and Media Conversion, ISO/IEC JTC1/SC29/WG11/M4433, MPEG99, Seoul, Korea, March 1999
3. Ho Kyung Kang, Yong Ju Jung, Hee Kyung Lee and Yong Man Ro: Multimedia database system with embedding MPEG-7 meta data. SPIE Electronic Imaging (2001)
4. Peng Yin, Min Wu, and Bede Liu: Video Transcoding by Reducing Spatial Resolution. Proc. ICIP, Vol. 1. (2000) 972–975
5. Information Technology - Multimedia Content Description Interface - Part 5: Multimedia Description Schemes, ISO/IEC JTC1/SC29/WG11/N4242, Sydney, Australia, July 2001
6. van Beek, P., Smith, J. R., Ebrahimi, T., Suzuki, T., and Askelof, J.: Metadata-Driven Multimedia Access. IEEE Signal Processing Megazine, Vol. 20. No. 2. (2003) 40–52
7. Report on the CE on the Transcoding Hint DS, ISO/IEC JTC1/SC29/WG11/M6002, Geneva, CH, May 2000.
8. Improving the Media Transcoding Hint DS by adding an attribute for spatial resolution reduction, ISO/IEC JTC1/SC29/WG11/M6267, Beijing, CN, July 2000.
9. Huang, K., Tung, Y., Wu, J., Hsiao, P., and Chen, H.: A Frame-based MPEG Characteristics Extraction Tool and Its Application in Video Transcoding. IEEE Trans. on Con. Electronics, Vol. 48. No. 3. (2002) 522–532
10. Swanson, M.D., Bin Zhu, and Tewfik, A.H.: Data Hiding for Video-in-Video. Proc. ICIP'97, Vol. 2. (1997) 676–679
11. Nam, J., Alghoniemy, M., and Tewfik, A.H.: Audio-Visual Content-Based Violent Scene Characterization. Proc. ICIP'98, Vol. 1. (1998) 353–357
12. Chae, J.J., and Manjunath, B.S.: Data Hiding in Video. Proc. ICIP'99, Vol. 1. (1998) 311–315
13. Min Wu, Heather Yu, and Alex Gelman: Multi-level Data Hiding for Digital Image and Video. SPIE Photonics East'99 (1999)

Echo Watermarking in Sub-band Domain

Jae-Won Cho[1], Ha-Joong Park[1], Young Huh[2], Hyun-Yeol Chung[1], and Ho-Youl Jung[1*]

[1]Dept. of Info. and Comm. Eng., University of Yeungnam, KOREA
ram56@image.yu.ac.kr
[2]Korea Electrotechnology Research Institute, KOREA

Abstract. Echo hiding is a method for embedding information, called watermark, into an audio signal. In general, echo hiding is processed in the time domain by convolving audio signal with echo kernel, without any consideration of the frequency characteristics. In this paper, we propose an echo hiding technique, which inserts echo into sub-band signal so as to take account into the frequency characteristics. The proposed echo hiding enables to embed high-energy echo, while minimizing the host audio quality distortion. In addition, the proposed allows increasing watermark capacity, since it is possible to embed simultaneously some watermark bits into different sub-band signals. The simulation results show that the proposed is more effective than the conventional echo hiding, in terms of watermark capacity and robustness against various attacks.

1 Introduction

Recently, the outstanding progress of digital multimedia data has increased the ease with which it is reproduced and retransmitted [1]. This kind of trend increases the requirement of copyright protection. Traditional data protection techniques such as encryption are not adequate for copyright enforcement, because the protection cannot be ensured after the data is decrypted [2]. Unlike encryption, digital watermarking does not restrict access to the host data, but ensures the hidden data remain inviolate and recoverable [3]. Watermarking is a copyright protection technique to embed information, so-called watermark, into host data. Several audio watermarking techniques have been developed; phase coding [4], spread spectrum modulation [2],[4], low bit coding [4], echo hiding [4],[5], etc.

Echo hiding embeds watermark data into a host audio signal by interposing an echo. It is motivated by the fact that HAS (Human Auditory System) cannot distinguish an echo from the original audio signal when delay and amplitude of echo are appropriately controlled. Since echo hiding firstly introduced by D. Gruhl and W. Bender [5], there have been several trials to improve the performance in terms of transparency and robustness against intentional or non-intentional attacks

"This work was supported by Yeungnam Uiversity Research Grant (105602)."

* Corresponding author. Tel.:+82-53-810-3545, *E-mail* : hoyoul@yu.ac.kr (H.Y. Jung)

T. Kalker et al. (Eds.): IWDW 2003, LNCS 2939, pp. 447–455, 2004.
© Springer-Verlag Berlin Heidelberg 2004

[4],[5],[6],[7],[8]. Theses trials have mainly focused on finding efficient echo filters (kernels). In usual echo hiding techniques, watermarked signal is obtained by convolving audio signal with echo filter, where one of two echo filters is selected, frame-by-frame, according to the watermark bit to be embedded. Since the watermark encoding process is done in time domain, the identical echo filter pair is applied to whole frequency components of audio signal. Note that frequency characteristics of HAS and host signal should be considered in the process of echo hiding.

In this paper, we propose an echo hiding technique, which interposes echo into sub-band signal, so as to take account into the frequency characteristics. For such purposes, the host signal is decomposed into several sub-band signals by using WT (Wavelet Transform), and a pair of echo filter with different amplitude is applied to each sub-band signal. It means that the amplitude of echo can be adjusted in each sub-band according to energy distributions of host signal and frequency characteristics of HAS. Thus, the proposed echo hiding enables to embed high-energy echo, while minimizing the host audio quality distortion. In addition, the proposed allows increasing the watermark capacity, since some watermark bits can be simultaneously embedded.

This paper is organized as follows. Section 2 describes in brief the usual echo hiding technique. In section 3, we propose an echo hiding, which interposes echo into sub-band signal. Section 4 shows the simulation results of the proposed and usual echo hiding. In this simulation, blind detection method is employed. Finally, we conclude this paper in section 5.

2 Previous Echo Hiding

In general, echo hiding can be represented by the convolution of audio signal and echo filter, where a pair of echo filter is used in order to embed binary data. Fig. 1 shows the echo hiding process. Host audio signal $x[n]$ is divided into smaller frames $x_m[n]$, for $m = 1, 2, \cdots, M$, where M is the number of frame. Each frame then is encoded with the desired watermark bit by considering each as an independent signal. Individual frame $x_m[n]$ passes through the echo filter, $e_i[n]$, for $i \in \{0,1\}$, that is selected according to watermark bit $\omega_m \in \{0,1\}$.

$$\hat{x}_m[n] = x_m[n] * e_i[n] \tag{1}$$

where $\hat{x}_m[n]$ denotes the m-th frame of watermarked signal, and $*$ indicates convolution. Various kinds of filters have been developed for echo hiding. These include positive single echo filter, positive multiple echo filter, a negative single echo filter, negative multiple echo filter, and PN(Pseudo Noise) sequence echo filter [5],[6],[7],[8]. In general, the delay of echo is chosen within the range of 0.9ms to 3.4ms [12]. In this paper, only positive single echo filter is applied for the purpose of evaluating the proposed. The transfer function of the positive single echo filter is given by

$$E_i(z) = 1 + \alpha \cdot z^{d_i}, \qquad for \;\; i \in \{0,1\}, \tag{2}$$

where α and d_i indicate the amplitude and delay of echo, respectively. The final watermarked signal, $\hat{x}[n]$, is the recombination of all independently echoed frames. To prevent abrupt changes around boundary of echoed frames, smoothing processing is applied. It should be noted that usual echo hiding process is done in the time domain and it does not consider the frequency characteristics.

Watermark extraction is to detect the position of echo in each frame of watermarked audio signal. In this case, auto-cepstrum (or autocorrelation) is available, because a peak is occurred at the location of echo [6]. Auto-cepstrum is obtained by

$$F^{-1}\left(\ln\left(F\left(\hat{x}_m[n]\right)\right)^2\right), \tag{3}$$

where F and F^{-1} denote FT(Fourier Transform) and its inverse. The watermark data is obtained by detecting the peak of auto-cepstrum, frame by frame.

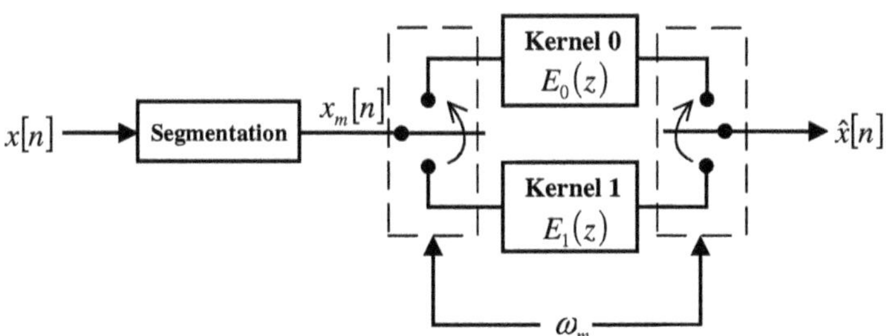

Fig. 1. Diagram of usual echo hiding in time domain

3 Echo Hiding into Sub-band Signal

Main idea of this paper is to embed echo into sub-band signal. Host signal is decomposed into several sub-band signals by using WT (Wavelet Transform), and echo is embedded into sub-band signals.

For the simplicity, let's consider only two-channel echo embedding system as show in Fig. 2. Host signal $x[n]$ is decomposed into low frequency and high frequency band signals by analysis filter bank, $H_L(z)$ and $H_H(z)$. The band signals are divided into smaller frames, respectively, and a pair of echo filter, $E_0'(z)$ and $E_1'(z)$, is applied to each frame of band signal. The echoed sub-band signals are transformed into echoed audio signal passing through reconstruction filter bank, $G_L(z)$ and $G_H(z)$. If the same watermark bit stream is applied to both band signals, the system is the same as usual echo hiding as mentioned in Fig. 1. It is proved in appendix that echo hiding in time domain can be represented by convolution of sub-band signals and echo filters with appropriate delay. This proof demonstrates that the proposed echo hiding is an alternative to usual one. In addition, the amplitude of echo embedded in individual band can be appropriately adjusted according to the frequency characteristics. Thus, the proposed echo hiding technique enables to embed high-energy echo, while minimizing the host audio quality distortion. By applying iteratively the two channel sub-band encoding, echo can be embedded into multiple sub-band signals.

Fig. 3 shows the proposed watermark extraction process. Echoed audio signal is decomposed into sub-band signals by using the same analysis filter bank as used in encoding. Watermark is extracted from each sub-band signal by using auto-cepstrum. Since watermark bit stream is independently extracted from each band signal, different bit streams can be embedded into individual band signal in echo hiding process. It means that the proposed allows increasing the watermark capacity. If different watermark sequences are embedded into sub-band signals by using the same pair of echo filter, interference between echoed sub-band signals can be occurred. This causes to reduce the watermark detection rate. To cope with it, different pair of echo filter can be applied to respective band signal.

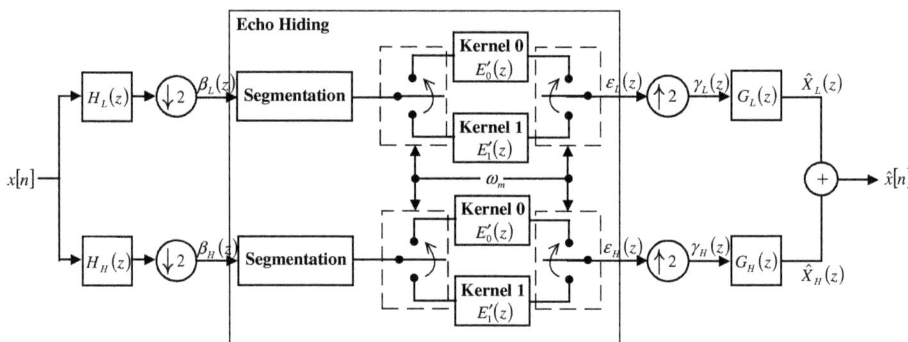

Fig. 2. Echo hiding process into two channel sub-band signals.

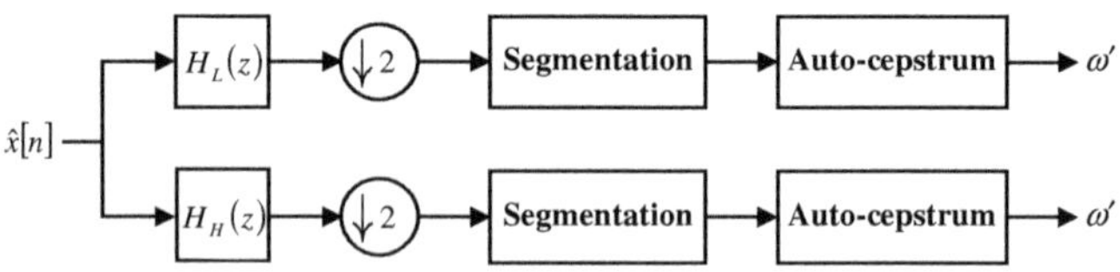

Fig. 3. Watermark extraction process from two channel sub-band signals

4 Simulation Results

The simulations are carried out on mono classic music with 16-bits/sample and sampling rate of 44.1KHz. The quality of audio signal is measured by *SNR* (Signal to Noise Ratio)

$$SNR = 10\log_{10}\left(\sum_{n=0}^{L} x[n]^2 \Big/ \sum_{n=0}^{L} (x[n] - \hat{x}[n]))^2\right) \tag{4}$$

where L is the length of audio signal. Employing blind watermarking technique, watermark detection is measured by *DR* (Detection Ratio)

$$DR = \frac{\textbf{\# of watermark bits correctly extracted}}{\textbf{\# of watermark bits placed}} \tag{5}$$

For sub-band decomposition, 5/3-tap bi-orthogonal perfect reconstruction filter bank [9] is applied recursively to low frequency band signal. Here, host audio signal is decomposed into five sub-bands (four multi-resolution levels). The filter bank can be implemented by fast operation algorithm, called lifting [10]. The frequency ranges of each sub-band are listed in table 1. One frame consists of 46.44 msec (2048 samples) in time domain, in order to embed about 22 bits/sec [11]. The delay of echo is experimentally selected over 0.9~3.4 msec in time domain. To obtain the same echo effects in sub-band domain, the length of frame and the delay of echo should be reduced by power of two proportional to multi-resolution level. As mentioned in section 2, only single positive echo filter is used.

Table 1. Frequency range of sub-band(KHz)

1st-band	2nd-band	3rd-band	4th-band	5th-band
0.0~1.3	~2.7	~5.5	~11.0	~22.0

Table 2. Comparative evaluation of the proposed (in sub-band domain) and the conventional (in time domain), in terms of SNR and DR, when using the fixed amplitude of echo (0.3).

Attacks		Time Domain		Sub-band Domain									
				1st-band		2nd-band		3rd-band		4th-band		5th-band	
		SNR	DR	SNR	DR	SNR	DR	SNR	DR	SNR	DR	SNR	DR
No Attack		10.46	0.87	10.73	0.80	26.64	0.81	33.21	0.87	41.77	0.93	52.97	0.98
Add Noise		10.42	0.81	10.69	0.80	25.80	0.79	30.28	0.84	32.79	0.79	33.33	0.67
Amplify		5.11	0.87	5.14	0.80	6.00	0.81	6.02	0.86	6.02	0.92	6.02	0.97
Band Pass Filter		8.00	0.86	8.17	0.81	9.82	0.78	9.93	0.78	9.95	0.70	9.95	0.55
Echo		3.48	0.66	3.56	0.72	4.68	0.72	4.72	0.77	4.73	0.84	4.73	0.91
MP3	64Kbps	10.45	0.85	10.71	0.80	26.06	0.79	31.32	0.83	33.79	0.87	36.13	0.71
	128Kbps	10.46	0.86	10.73	0.80	26.65	0.80	33.19	0.86	41.38	0.91	49.42	0.90
Average		8.34	0.83	8.53	0.79	17.95	0.79	21.24	**0.83**	24.35	**0.85**	27.51	0.78

To evaluate robustness, we consider various attacks such as adding noise, amplifying (by a half), band-pass filtering (0.1~6KHz), echo embedding (amplitude of 0.5, delay of 100msec), and MP3 compression (64Kbps, 128Kbps).

Table 2 shows the performance of the proposed echo hiding (in sub-band domain), in terms of SNR and DR, assuming that watermark is embedded, at a time, into only one sub-band signal. That is, pre-determined sub-band signal is encoded to echoed sub-band signal, but others be kept intact. To give a reference for comparisons, we also simulated the usual echo hiding (in time domain) which can be considered as embedding echo into whole frequency signal. For pair comparison, the same pair of echo filter with fixed amplitude of 0.3 is applied to both usual and the proposed. The simulations show that the proposed echo hiding is superior, in term of audio quality measured by SNR, to the usual method, since the distortion caused by echo hiding is limited within one sub-band signal. In addition, DR of the proposed is very similar to that of time domain based method. The results demonstrate that echo embedding in whole frequency is waste of resource. Note that the third and forth sub-bands are the best place to hide echo, in terms of both transparency and robustness.

Next simulation was carried out to find appropriate amplitude of echo in each sub-band. The amplitude of echo is chosen heuristically with also analyzing SNR. The amplitude in each band is listed in table 3 and simulation results are given in table 4. This demonstrates that the proposed achieves higher robustness at the expense of slight quality degradation. In addition, it is possible to embed simultaneously different watermark bit into every individual sub-band signals. It means that the watermark capacity can be increased up to five times.

Table 3. Appropriately selected amplitude of echo in each sub-band

1st-band	2nd-band	3rd-band	4th-band	5th-band
0.33	0.45	0.45	0.70	0.70

Table 4. Evaluation of the proposed, when using appropriately selected amplitude of echo in each sub-band as shown in table 3

Attacks		Sub-band Domain									
		1st-band		2nd-band		3rd-band		4th-band		5th-band	
		SNR	DR	SNR	DR	SNR	DR	SNR	DR	SNR	DR
No Attack		9.90	0.82	23.12	0.88	29.69	0.93	34.41	0.98	45.65	1.00
Add Noise		9.87	0.82	22.72	0.87	28.14	0.90	30.85	0.93	33.13	0.80
Amplify		5.03	0.82	5.99	0.88	6.02	0.93	6.02	0.98	6.02	1.00
Band Pass Filter		7.81	0.83	9.70	0.79	9.91	0.84	9.94	0.84	9.95	0.62
Echo		3.34	0.74	4.63	0.87	4.71	0.86	4.72	0.93	4.73	0.95
MP3	64Kbps	9.89	0.82	22.86	0.87	28.79	0.90	31.04	0.96	35.67	0.87
	128Kbps	9.90	0.82	23.13	0.88	29.70	0.92	34.37	0.98	44.81	0.99
Average		7.96	0.81	16.02	**0.86**	19.57	**0.90**	21.62	**0.94**	25.71	**0.89**

Table 5. Evaluation of the proposed, when embedding two watermark bits, frame-by-frame, into the third and fourth sub-bands, respectively

Attack		SNR	DR
No Attacks		28.42	0.96
Add Noise		27.22	0.92
Amplitude		6.01	0.96
Band Pass Filter		9.93	0.82
Echo		4.71	0.87
MP3	64Kbps	27.22	0.92
	128Kbps	28.44	0.96
Average		18.85	0.92

For evaluation of watermark capacity, we carried out the final simulation that embeds two watermark bits, frame-by-frame, into the third and fourth sub-bands, respectively. Here, two different pairs of echo filter (with different delay) are applied, to cope with interference between echoed sub-band signals. The same amplitude of echo is selected as given in table 2. As shown in table 5, the results indicate that the proposed allows increasing the watermark capacity with maintaining high detection rate.

5 Conclusions

In this paper, we proposed a new echo hiding technique, which inserts echo into sub-band signal. Through the simulations, we proved that the proposed echo hiding enables to embed high-energy echo, minimizing the host audio quality distortion. In addition, the proposed allows increasing the watermark capacity, since several watermark bits can be simultaneously embedded. As results, the proposed is a good alternative to the conventional echo hiding in time domain.

References

1. Paraskevi Bassia, Ioannis Pitas, Nikos Nikolaidis : Robust Audio Watermarking in the Time Domain. IEEE Transactions on Multimedia, Vol.3, No.2, (2001) 232–241
2. Darko Kirovski, Henrique Malvar : Robust Spread-Spectrum Audio Watermarking. Proceedings of IEEE ICASSP 01, Vol.3, (2001) 1345–1348
3. Say Wei FOO, Theng Hee YEO, Dong Yan HUANG : An Adaptive Audio Watermarking System. Proceedings of IEEE Region 10, Vol.2, (2001) 509–513
4. W.Bender, D.Gruhl, N.Morimoto, A.Lu : Techniques for data hiding. IBM Systems Journal, Vol.35, Nos 3&4, (1996) 313–336
5. D.Gruhl, W.Bender : Echo Hiding. Proceedings of Information Hiding Workshop, (1996) 295–315
6. Hyen O Oh, Jong Won Seok, Jin Woo Hong, Dae Hee Youn : New Echo Embedding Technique for Robust and Imperceptible Audio Watermarking. Proceedings of IEEE ICASSP 01, Vol.3, (2001) 1341–1344

7. Byeong-Seob KO, Ryouichi NISHIMURA, Yoiti SUZUKI : Time-spread Echo Method for Digital Audio Watermarking using PN sequences. Proceedings of IEEE ICASSP 02, (2002) 13–17
8. C.Xu : Applications of Digital Watermarking Technology in Audio Signals. J.Audio Eng. Soc., Vol.47, No.10, (1999)
9. Gilbert Strang, Truong Nguyen : Wavelets and Filter Banks. Wellesley Cambridge Press, (1997)
10. Sweldens W. : The lifting Scheme : A Custom-Design Construction of Biothogonal Wavelets. Applied and Computational Harmonic Analysis, Vol.3, No.2, (1996) 186–200
11. Xin Li, Hong Heather Yu : Transparent and Robust Audio Data Hiding in Sub-band Domain. Proceedings of IEEE Coding and Computing, (2000) 74–79
12. Hyen-O Oh, Hyun-Wook Kim, Dae-Hee Youn, Jong-Won Seok, Jin-Woo Hong : New Echo Embedding Technique for Robust Audio Watermarking. The Journal of the Acoustical Society of Korea, Vol. 20, No.2, (2001) 66-76

Appendix

Excluding echo hiding phase, the proposed sub-band domain based echo hiding system shown in Fig. 2 is the same as two-channel sub-band coding system. Perfect reconstruction requires the following conditions

$$\begin{aligned} H_L(z)G_L(z) + H_H(z)G_H(z) &= 2 \\ H_L(-z)G_L(z) + H_H(-z)G_H(z) &= 0 \end{aligned} \tag{A-1}$$

Echoed sub-band signals can be represented as

$$\begin{aligned} \varepsilon_L(z) &= \frac{1}{2}\cdot E_i'(z)\cdot\left(X(z^{\frac{1}{2}})H_L(z^{\frac{1}{2}}) + X(-z^{\frac{1}{2}})H_L(-z^{\frac{1}{2}})\right) \\ \varepsilon_H(z) &= \frac{1}{2}\cdot E_i'(z)\cdot\left(X(z^{\frac{1}{2}})H_H(z^{\frac{1}{2}}) + X(-z^{\frac{1}{2}})H_H(-z^{\frac{1}{2}})\right) \end{aligned} \tag{A-2}$$

Thus, the echoed audio signal $\hat{X}(z)$ can be driven as

$$\begin{aligned} \hat{X}(z) &= \varepsilon_L(z^2)G_L(z) + \varepsilon_H(z^2)G_H(z) \\ &= E_i'(z^2)\cdot\{(X(z)H_L(z) + X(-z)H_L(-z))\cdot G_L(z) \\ &\quad + (X(z)H_H(z) + X(-z)H_H(-z))\cdot G_H(z)\} \\ &= E_i'(z^2)\cdot\{(H_L(z)G_L(z) + H_H(z)G_H(z))\cdot X(z) \\ &\quad + H_L(-z)G_L(z) + H_H(-z)G_H(z)\cdot X(-z)\} \end{aligned} \tag{A-3}$$

Assuming that analysis and reconstruction filter banks satisfy the above perfect reconstruction condition, $\hat{X}(z)$ is written as

$$\hat{X}(z) = E_i'(z^2)X(z). \tag{A-4}$$

If echo filter in time domain $E_i(z)$ (shown in Fig. 1) is equal to $E_i'(z^2)$, i.e., $E_i(z) = E_i'(z^2)$, the time domain based echo hiding can be represented by convolution of sub-band signals and echo filters with a half delay.

Modification of Polar Echo Kernel for Performance Improvement of Audio Watermarking

Siho Kim, Hongseok Kwon, and Keunsung Bae

School of Electronic & Electrical Engineering, Kyungpook National University,
1370 Sankyuk-dong, Puk-gu, Taegu, 702-701, Korea
{si5, hskwon}@mir.knu.ac.kr
ksbae@ee.knu.ac.kr
http://mir.knu.ac.kr/

Abstract. In this paper, we present a new echo kernel, which is a modification of polar echo kernel, to improve the detection performance and robustness against attacks. Polar echo kernel may have the advantage of large detection margin from the polarity of inserted echo signal, but its poor frequency response in low frequency band degrades sound quality. To solve this problem, we applied bipolar echo pulses to the polar echo kernel. Using the proposed echo kernel, the distributions of autocepstrum peaks for data '0' and '1' are located more distant and improvement of detection performance is achieved. It also makes the low frequency band flat so that the timbre difference in the polar echo kernel can be removed to reproduce the imperceptible sound quality. Informal listening tests as well as robustness test against attacks were performed to evaluate the proposed echo kernel. Experimental results demonstrated the superiority of the proposed echo kernel to both conventional unipolar and polar echo kernels.

1 Introduction

Recently the availability of digital audio content has been grown quickly and low cost digital equipments and Internet allow people to easily create, modify, and copy it. However, these technologies also make it easy to illegally copy and redistribute it without regard to copyright ownership. So, a need has arisen for protecting copyright ownership of digital content. Digital audio watermarking is the technique that a watermark signal is added to the original audio content as imperceptible as possible. It is now drawing much attention as a new method of providing copyright protection to digital audio content. Over the last few years, considerable audio watermarking algorithms have been proposed such as spread spectrum coding [1], phase coding [2], echo hiding [2,3,4], and so on. Among them, spread spectrum and echo hiding schemes are paid more attention than phase coding scheme, because they do not need the original audio for detecting watermarks. Especially, echo hiding is considered to be better in terms of imperceptibility since it just adds delayed and attenuated version of the original signal

T. Kalker et al. (Eds.): IWDW 2003, LNCS 2939, pp. 456–466, 2004.
© Springer-Verlag Berlin Heidelberg 2004

itself. Of course, time-delay and strength of echo should be decided carefully for trade-offs between imperceptibility and robustness. To increase the ability of detection and robustness against attack, it requires a larger echo, which results in distortion and timbre change of the audio signal. Therefore it is important to design the echo kernel that can have imperceptibility to original digital content as well as improved detection performance and robustness against attacks. In this paper, we present a new echo kernel that shows improved detection rate and robustness compared to the conventional echo kernels. The newly designed echo kernel has the form of modified polar echo kernel with two pulses having different signs. Experimental results are given with our findings and discussion. This paper is organized as follows. In section 2, we briefly explain audio watermarking schemes with echo kernels. In the next section the proposed echo kernel and its characteristics are presented. In section 4, the experimental results are shown and discussed, and finally we make a conclusion in the last section.

2 Audio Watermarking with Echo Kernels [2,3]

Audio watermarking schemes based on echo kernels embed data into a host audio signal in the form of delayed and attenuated version of the original signal, that is, an echo. There are three parameters to be considered in the echo kernel: initial amplitude, decay rate, and offset delay. The quality and robustness of watermarked signal depend on the amplitude and offset delay of the echo. The initial amplitude and decay rate are desired to be smaller than the audible threshold of the human ear. In general, the human ear cannot distinguish echo from the original for most sounds if offset delay is around 1 msec. There are two ways to represent data, i.e., binary symbols with single pulse as an echo: one is using different delay times (or offset delay) for each binary symbol, the other is using the sign (or polarity) of the pulse. Figure 1 and 2 show typical echo kernels with single pulse as an echo. In Figure 1 the coder uses two delay times, one to represent a binary '0'(offset 0, δ_0) and the other to represent a binary '1'(offset 1, δ_1). On the other hand, in Figure 2, the coder uses positive polarity to represent a binary '0' and negative polarity to represent a binary '1'.

Information is embedded into a signal by echoing the original signal with one of two kernels. Let the kernel represent the system function for encoding a binary data. Then processing a signal through either '0' kernel or '1' kernel will result in an encoded signal. In order to encode more than one bit, the original signal is divided into smaller portions. Each individual segment can then be echoed with the desired bit by considering each as an independent signal. The final encoded signal is the recombination of all independently encoded signal portions. To prevent abrupt changes between portions encoded with different bits, the encoded signals of each portion are added using mixed signal. Extraction of the embedded information involves the detection of delay position or polarity of the echoes. In order to do this, the cepstrum of watermarked signal is generally calculated. Then larger peak at offset delay is determined by taking the autocorrelation of the cepstrum, which is denoted as autocepstrum and can be obtained from the Equation (1).

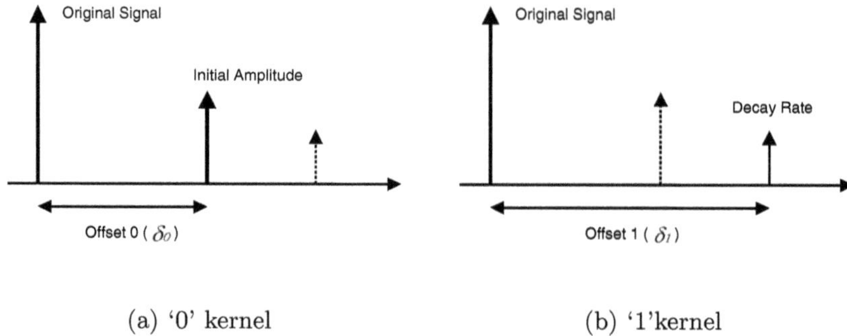

Fig. 1. Impulse responses of unipolar echo kernel

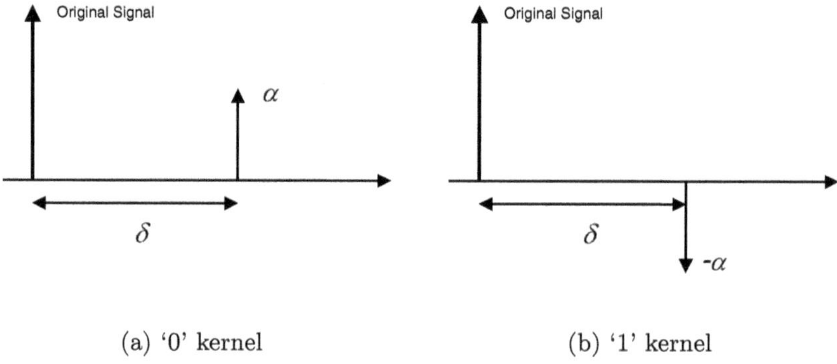

Fig. 2. Impulse responses of polar echo kernel

$$s_{AC}(n) = F^{-1}\left(ln_{cmplx}\left(F\left(s_{wm}(n)\right)\right)^2\right) \tag{1}$$

where F means Fourier Transform and F^{-1} its inverse transform. s_{wm} is watermarked audio signal and s_{AC} is its autocepstrum. In each frame, the embedded binary data is decoded by comparing the autocepstrum peak at offset positions.

Figure 3 shows the distributions of autocepstrum peak at offset 0 and offset 1 for the watermarked signal using the unipolar echo kernel. In case of using '0' kernel, the large peak value exists at δ_0 and small values distribute around zero at δ_1 as shown in Figure 3(a). On the contrary, in case of '1' kernel, the distribution of peaks shows the property similar to '0' kernel except the exchanged offset delay like Figure 3(b). The peak value increases in direct proportion to the amplitude of echo signal inserted and the shape of distribution has a property similar to Gaussian distribution due to the influence of audio signal noises. When we draw

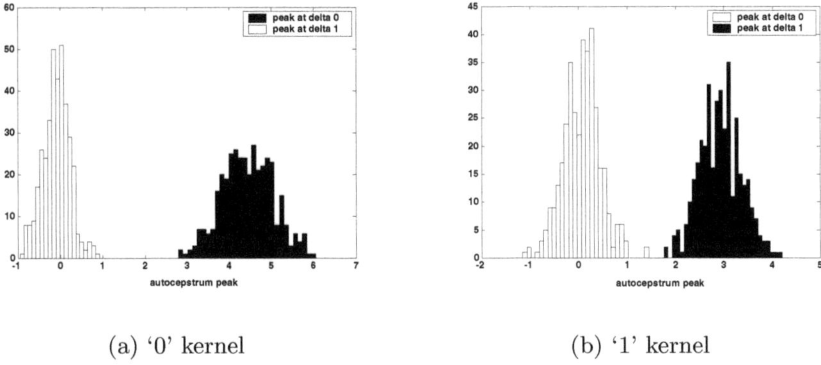

(a) '0' kernel (b) '1' kernel

Fig. 3. Distributions of autocepstrum peak with unipolar echo kernel

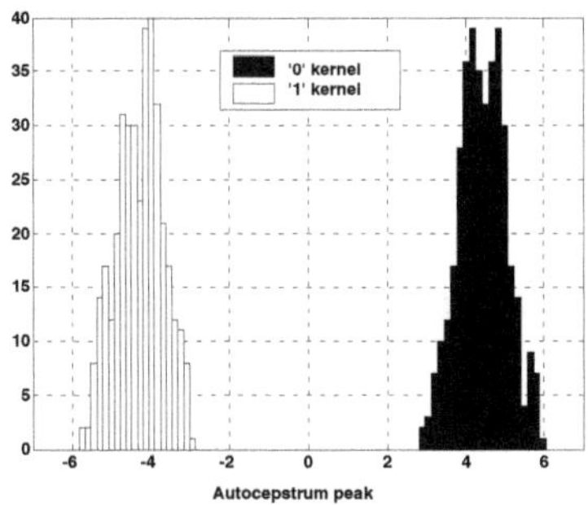

Fig. 4. Distributions of autocepstrum peak with polar echo kernel

a comparison with relative distance for peaks distribution in δ_0 and δ_1, we can verify that the relative distance is closer in case of '1' kernel's than '0' kernel's as shown in Figure 3(a) and (b). It is because that in case '1' kernel, the echo amplitude is designed to be smaller than '0' kernel considering the auditory property of human ear. Hence the probability of detecting incorrectly '1' as '0' is higher than the opposite case.

Using the polar echo kernel with the same delay, we can increase the relative distance for the distribution of autocepstrum peak two times and reduce the detection error occurred asymmetrically in the unipolar echo kernel as shown in Figure 4. It can be expected that polar echo kernel has more margins than unipolar echo kernel in the detection of hidden data since the former can have large difference in autocepstrum, as shown in Figure 4. But polar echo kernel has a critical disadvantage in the sense that it results in the timbre alteration of the audio signal caused by the negative echo pulse. The negative echo pulse

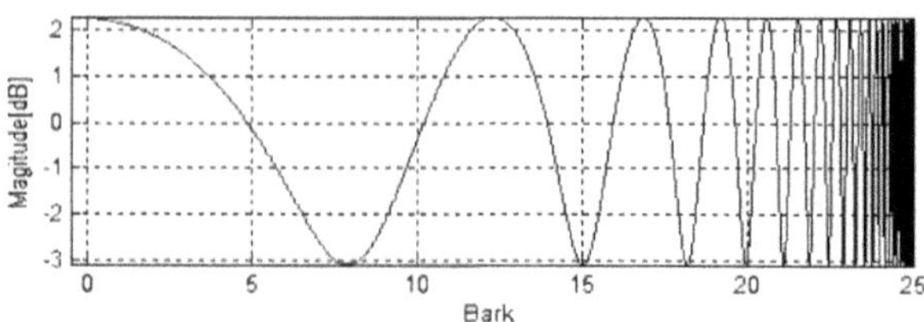

(a) Positive echo kernel

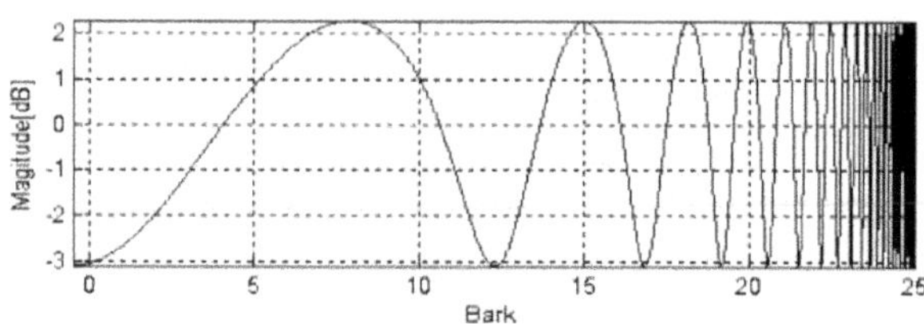

(b) Negative echo kernel

Fig. 5. Frequency responses of positive and negative echo kernel

functions as a high pass filter and poor frequency response at lower band distorts the original signal, and makes the sound slightly sharp. Figure 5 shows the frequency responses of the polar echo kernel in Bark scale [5], positive echo kernel and negative echo kernel, respectively, where offset delay, δ, is set to 50 samples (1.1 msec at 44.1 kHz sampling rate).

In Figure 5, the frequency responses of positive and negative echo kernel are contrary to each other. Especially the frequency band below 500 Hz(corresponding to about 5 Bark) is boosted in case of positive echo kernel but weakened in case of negative echo kernel. Low frequency band below 500 Hz is narrow band in comparison with whole frequency band of 22,050 Hz, but it is relatively important band considering the property of human auditory system. Hence watermarked sound shows more abundant timbre than original sound in case of positive echo but sharper and keener in case of negative echo. In general, people have a preference for abundant timbre so that the sound using positive echo is preferred to negative echo. And it is also concerned that the different timbre in adjacent frame may cause the deterioration of sound quality. Therefore it is necessary to make up for the weakness of low frequency band caused by negative echo and reduce the timbre difference between positive and negative echo kernel.

3 Proposed Echo Kernel with Bipolar Echo

Since the major cause of timbre alteration in polar echo kernel is the opposite property at low frequency band, we can solve this problem by applying one more pulse having opposite polarity to the preceding one. It is similar idea to [4], which is kind of a modification of unipolar echo kernel, what they call a bipolar echo kernel. It makes the low frequency band flat so that it increases the imperceptibility. We apply this bipolar echo to the polar echo kernel as shown in Figure 6. The frequency responses are shown in Figure 7 where offset delay, δ, and Δ are set to 50 samples and 1 sample, respectively. Consequently it makes the low frequency band of each kernel flat so that the defect of negative echo might be complemented and the timbre difference can be reduced considerably.

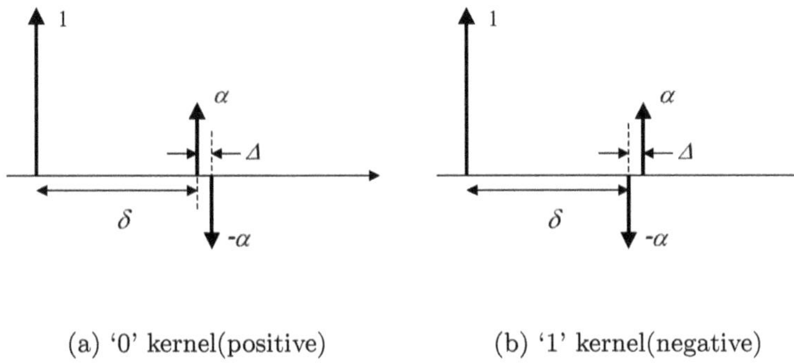

(a) '0' kernel(positive) (b) '1' kernel(negative)

Fig. 6. Proposed echo kernel with bipolar echo

The watermark detection procedure with the proposed echo kernel is similar to that of conventional methods, that is, the detection and comparison of the autocepstrum peaks at the offset position. However, in the proposed echo kernel, the sign of autocepstrum plays an important role in detection, so it is calculated by Equation (2).

$$s_{AC}(n) = Re\left(F^{-1}\left(\left|ln_{cmplx}(S_{wm})\right|^2\right)\right) \tag{2}$$

where S_{wm} denotes the discrete Fourier transform of the watermarked audio signal. Figure 8 shows the results of autocepstrum with the proposed echo kernel for offset delay, δ, of 50 samples and Δ of 1 sample. As shown in Figure 8, in case of '0' echo kernel the negative peak follows the positive one consecutively, and in case of '1' echo kernel it has reverse pattern. It seems to be more robust if the difference between the peaks of autocepstrum at δ and $(\delta + \Delta)$ are used for detection. Therefore we define the detection parameter *peak_diff* as given in

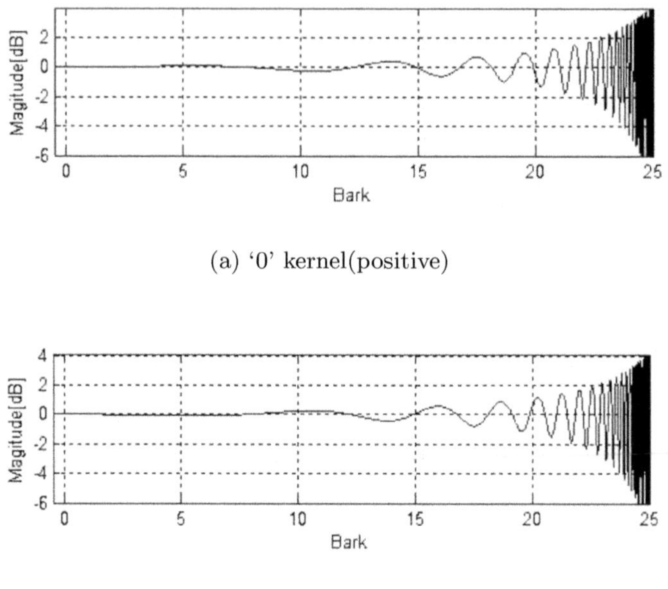

(a) '0' kernel(positive)

(b) '1' kernel(negative)

Fig. 7. Frequency responses of the positive and negative echo kernel with bipolar echo

Equation (3). For example, when the sign of *peak_diff* is positive, the '0' echo kernel is detected and conversely negative, '1' echo kernel.

$$peak\_diff = s_{AC}(\delta) - s_{AC}(\delta + \Delta) \quad (3)$$

4 Experimental Result

In order to evaluate the performance of the proposed echo kernel, robustness test and informal listening test were performed. The echo kernels used in this experiment are denoted as follows:

- Unipolar Echo Kernel (UEK): Offset of the echo is used.
- Polar Echo Kernel (PEK): Polarity of the echo is used.
- Modified Polar Echo Kernel (MEK): Polarity of the bipolar echo is used.

The parameters used in each echo kernel are shown in Table 1. The audio signals used in the experiments are sampled at 44.1 kHz with 16 bits resolution. Information was embedded into the audio signal at a rate of 28.7109 (in case that frame length is 1024 samples and overlap is 512 samples) bits per second.

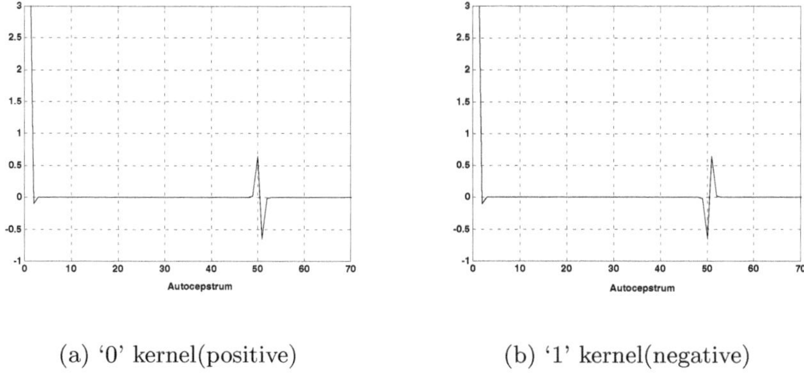

(a) '0' kernel(positive)

(b) '1' kernel(negative)

Fig. 8. Autocepstrum of the positive and negative echo kernel with bipolar echo

Table 1. Parameters for each echo kernel [samples]

Echo Kernel	'0' echo kernel Delay(Amplitude)	'1' echo kernel Delay(Amplitude)
UEK	50(α)	70(0.7α)
PEK	50(α)	50(-α)
MEK	50(α), 51(-α)	50(-α), 51(α)

4.1 Robustness Test

First we evaluated the detection error rate (BER: Bit Error Rate) according to the echo amplitude, α, with no attack and Figure 9 shows the result. It is shown that as α increases the error rate decreases, as expected. But for increasing imperceptibility, small value of α is desirable. We can see, therefore, that the proposed echo kernel gives the best result among them. In other words, the proposed echo kernel can obtain the improved sound quality for the limited BER.

We have investigated the robustness of the proposed echo kernel for several attacks as follows:

- MPEG compression: MPEG-1 Audio Layer 3 (MP3) with 56 kbps/ch
- Band-pass filtering: FIR filter with bandwidth 100 Hz $\sim$ 8 kHz
- Equalizer: General 'rock' which boosts low and high frequencies
- Linear time scale modification: Linear speed change with the amount of $\pm 2\%$

Figure 10 shows the detection results for each type of attacks. It can be seen that, on the whole, the proposed echo kernel shows more robustness to attacks in comparison with other types of echo kernels. But it shows the abrupt degradation of BER in time scale modification attack as conventional method.

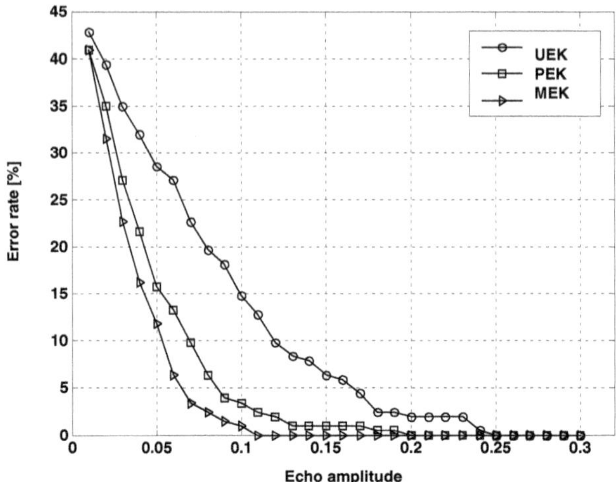

Fig. 9. BER according to echo amplitude, α

4.2 Quality Test

In order to estimate the audio quality after watermark embedding, we performed informal subjective tests of sound quality using the procedure presented in ITU-R BS-1116 [6]. The listening test procedure is like this: The listener could listen freely between 'Reference', 'A', and 'B', where 'A' and 'B' are the processed version and the hidden reference, randomly allocated. The listener was asked to judge the 'Basic Audio Quality (graded as five-point from 0 to 5)' of the 'A' and 'B' versions in each trial and any difference from the reference was considered as impairment. Finally we use the DiffGrade as evaluation measurement which is the value subtracting the score of hidden version from that of processed version. The test was performed for the several amplitudes of echo and four kinds of music (rock, ballad, dance, and classic).

Table 2. Results of subjective quality test (DiffGrade)

	0.1			0.3			0.5		
	UEK	PEK	MEK	UEK	PEK	MEK	UEK	PEK	MEK
Rock	0.091	-0.09	-0.18	0.182	-0.36	-0.09	-0.82	-2.55	-0.55
Ballad	-0.09	-0.27	0	-0.64	-1.27	-0.27	-2	-2.64	-1.09
Dance	-0.09	0.09	0	-0.55	-0.55	0	-1	-2.18	-0.64
Classic	-0.09	-0.36	-0.09	-0.64	-1.64	-0.45	-1.82	-2.91	-1
Average	-0.05	-0.16	-0.07	-0.41	-0.95	-0.2	-1.41	-2.57	-0.82

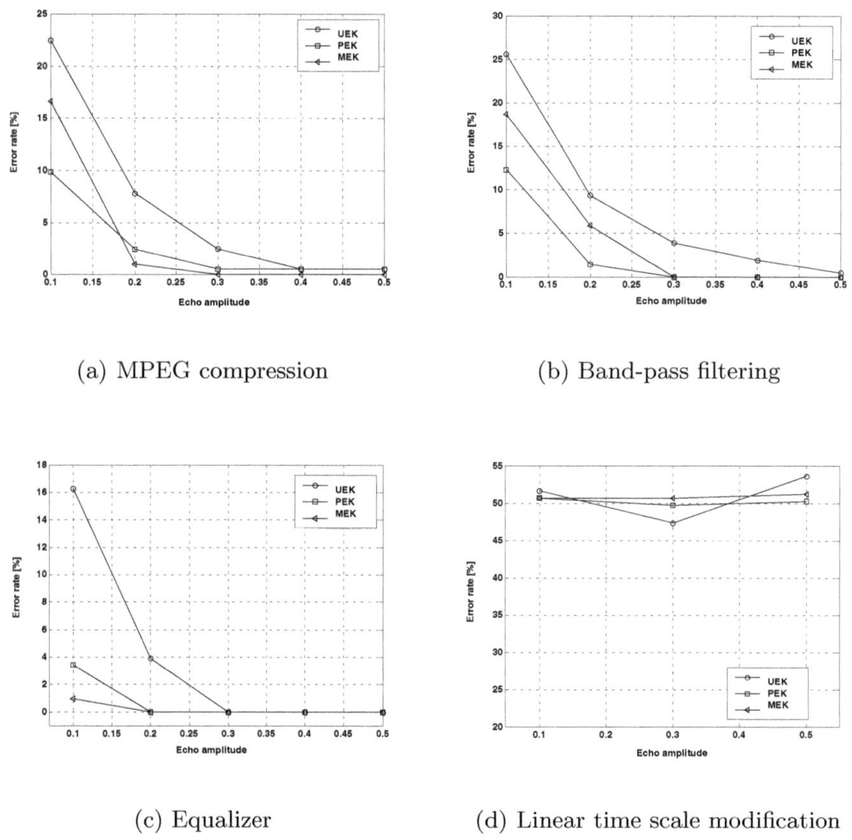

(a) MPEG compression (b) Band-pass filtering

(c) Equalizer (d) Linear time scale modification

Fig. 10. BER according to echo amplitude, α, under several attacks

The results of subjective quality test are shown in Table 2. From the test results, the watermarked signal is inaudible perceptually with echo amplitude 0.1 for all the kernels. Although the score changes depending on the type of music for echo amplitude of 0.3, the proposed echo kernel shows nearly imperceptible to the original sound, while the conventional unipolar kernel and polar kernel are distinguished from original sound a little. Finally in case of echo amplitude of 0.5, it is easy to distinguish difference in all methods and especially unipolar and polar echo kernels are accompanied with some degradation of sound quality. The impairment of sound quality results from the different timbre of kernels in adjacent frame. Considering the results of robustness and quality tests, we can say that the proposed echo kernel is the best one among them.

5 Conclusions

We could confirm that the polar echo kernel improves the performance of detection to be more robust, but its poor frequency response in low frequency band degrades sound quality. To solve this problem, we applied bipolar echo pulses to the polar echo kernel. It makes the low frequency band flat so that the timbre difference in the polar echo kernel can be removed to reproduce the imperceptible sound quality. We performed informal subjective tests of sound quality and robustness test against attacks. Experimental results demonstrated the superiority of the proposed echo kernel to both conventional unipolar and polar echo kernels. Nevertheless the weakness for time-scale attack is still remained in proposed method like conventional method.

References

1. Boney, L., Tewfik, A. H., Hamdy, K. N.: Digital Watermarks for Audio Signals. Third IEEE International Conference on Multimedia Computing and Systems (1996) 473–480
2. Bender, W., Gruhl, D., Morimoto, N., Lu, A.: Techniques for data hiding. IBM Systems Journal, Vol.35, Nos 3&4 (1996) 313–336
3. Gruhl, D., Lu, A.: Echo Hiding. Information Hiding Workshop, Cambridge University, U.K. (1996) 295-315
4. Oh, H. O., Youn, D. H., Hong, J. W., Seok, J. W.: Imperceptible Echo for Robust Audio Watermarking. AES 113th Convention, Los Angeles, CA, USA, Oct. (2002)
5. Rabiner, L., Juang, B. H.: Fundamentals of speech recognition. Prentice-Hall, Englewood Cliffs, New Jersey (1993)
6. ITU-R Recommendation BS.1116, Methods for the Subjective Assessment of Small Impairments in Audio Systems Including Multi-channel Sound Systems. ITU, Geneva, Switzerland (1994)

Increasing Robustness of an Improved Spread Spectrum Audio Watermarking Method Using Attack Characterization

Nedeljko Cvejic and Tapio Seppänen

MediaTeam Oulu Group, P.O. Box 4500, Information Processing Laboratory, FIN-90014 University of Oulu, Finland
{cvejic, tapio}@ee.oulu.fi

Abstract. We propose a novel robust audio watermarking algorithm in time domain that uses perceptually tuned ISS method and attack characterization at the embedding side. Attack characterization is used for prediction of distortions in the watermark channel in order to improve watermark detection reliability. The proposed algorithm has decreased bit error rate in comparison with the watermarking system that uses SS and has simple tools to tune the algorithm to the maximum available watermark capacity for a fixed detection bit error rate.

1 Introduction

Digital watermarking is a process that embeds an imperceptible and statistically undetectable signature to multimedia content (e.g. images, video and audio sequences). Embedded watermark contains certain information (signature, logo, ID number, etc.) related uniquely to the owner, distributor or the multimedia file itself. In the past few years, several algorithms for embedding and extraction of watermarks in audio sequences have been presented. In a number of the developed algorithms, watermark embedding and extraction are carried out using spread-spectrum (SS) technique. SS sequence can be added to the host audio samples in time domain [1], to FFT coefficients [2], in wavelet domain [3] or to cepstral coefficients [4]. Watermark is spread over a large number of coefficients and distortion is kept below the just noticeable difference level (JND) by using occurrence of masking effects of the human auditory system (HAS). Change in each coefficient can be small enough to be imperceptible, because correlator detector output still has a high signal to noise ratio (SNR), as it de-spreads the energy present in a large number of coefficients.

In [5] authors describe the importance of decreasing the influence of the host signal on the watermark extraction process, analyzing a spread spectrum system with the fixed cross correlation value. Analysis of the watermark detection performance clearly shows improved detection robustness, compared with the case of uninformed watermark embedding, where the host signal itself is considered as a source of interference in the watermark channel. However, in [5] there is no detailed description of the practical issues concerning the watermark embedding process, e.g. control of the perceptual quality of the signal when a

T. Kalker et al. (Eds.): IWDW 2003, LNCS 2939, pp. 467–473, 2004.
© Springer-Verlag Berlin Heidelberg 2004

fixed cross-correlation is forced. Using given framework from, in [6] authors have derived three different watermarking approaches, corresponding to the cases of "maximized robustness", "maximized correlation coefficient" and "constant robustness". Still, the problem of minimizing bit error rate, at a fixed average distortion level during watermark embedding process, is not addressed. Recently, an improved spread spectrum (ISS) method has been proposed [7] that removes the host signal as a source of interference, gaining significantly on robustness of watermark detection. The improvement obtained using ISS over standard SS method is in the range of gains if the quantization index modulation (QIM) is compared to standard SS methods. ISS method does not suffer from the same sensitivity to amplitude scaling as QIM method, as ISS is insensitive to amplitude scaling as SS method. However, ISS method cannot keep the distortion caused by watermark embedding at a constant level as in SS method. Although it delivers the same average distortion as in SS method, forced cross-correlation minimization may cause large local distortion of the host signal, which is an unacceptable property for most of audio watermarking applications. In addition, all the results presented in [7] are theoretically derived, without subjective test and measuring bit error rate in the presence of attacks other than Additive White Gaussian noise.

In this paper, we propose a novel robust audio watermarking algorithm in time domain that uses perceptually tuned ISS method and attack characterization at the embedding side. Distortion caused by ISS method is spread to a predefined number of samples using threshold obtained from perceptual model derived from temporal masking phenomenon of the human auditory system (HAS). Attack characterization is used for prediction of distortions in the watermark channel in order to improve watermark detection reliability. The proposed algorithm has a simple trade off tools to keep a predefined bit error rate with variable watermark capacity or obtain constant watermark capacity if a variable BER is allowed.

2 Method

The overall scheme of the watermark embedding algorithm is given in Figure 1. Samples of the host audio sequence are forwarded simultaneously to the masking analysis module and attack characterization module. Masking threshold in time domain is derived for every input block of host audio (length 205 samples=4.65ms). With reference to temporal masking curves and the length of analyzed audio frames, it was concluded that the spread watermark sequence should be at least 24 dB below the power level of the audio maximum in the frame. The length of frame and power level of watermark are chosen in line with the requirements of HAS regarding inaudibility and to give the watermark highest possible amplitude before it is added to the host signal.

Attack characterization section has the purpose of analysis of the signal for the watermark removal attacks with different signal processing methods. Beside detection desynchronization attack, the most malicious attacks for the contemporary audio watermarking algorithms are mp3 compression and LP filtering. In order to find the level of introduced noise by these distortions, these spectrum modifications are simulated at the embedding side. Therefore, each

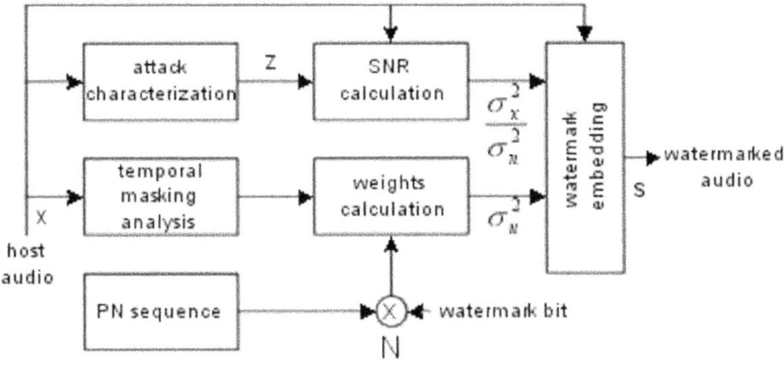

Fig. 1. Watermark embedding scheme

data hiding block undergoes mp3 compression and LP filtering. A distortion measure SNR is defined as

$$SNR = 10 \cdot \log \frac{\sum_n x^2(n)}{\sum_n [x(n) - z(n)]^2} \tag{1}$$

is calculated for blocks of host audio with predefined length N and forwarded to the watermark embedding block. x(n) stands for the original host audio samples and z(n) are samples of audio after the given modification.
We assume that one bit of hidden information is embedded in a vector **s** of N samples in time domain, resulting in watermark bit rate of 1/N bits/sample. Watermark bits are perceptually tuned using weight coefficients form HAS time domain masking analysis and embedded into host audio sequence using ISS modulation. The power of watermark sequence in a block with length N, after spreading and perceptual tuning, is σ_u^2. We used the linear version of ISS method, as it is the simplest to analyze, but still provides a significant part of the gains in relation to traditional SS method. In this case the host audio is watermarked according to:

$$\mathbf{s} = \mathbf{x} + (\alpha b - \lambda x)\mathbf{u} \tag{2}$$

where **x** stands for the original host signal vector, **s** stands for watermarked audio vector and **u** holds for the PN sequence after the perceptual adaptation process. Weighted PN sequence is added or subtracted from the signal **x** according to variable b, where b can be either +1 or -1, according to the watermark bit embedded into host audio. Parameters α and λ control the distortion level and removal of the host signal influence on the detection statistic, respectively. Standard SS method is achieved by setting $\alpha = 1$ and $\lambda = 0$. Inner product and norm are defined as [7]:

$$\langle \mathbf{x}, \mathbf{u} \rangle = \frac{1}{N} \sum_{i=0}^{N-1} x_i u_i \tag{3}$$

and $\|\mathbf{x}\| = \langle \mathbf{x}, \mathbf{x} \rangle$, where N is the dimension of vectors $\mathbf{x}$, $\mathbf{u}$, $\mathbf{s}$, $\mathbf{n}$ and $\mathbf{y}$ in Figure 1. Variable x is defined as $x = \langle \mathbf{x}, \mathbf{u} \rangle / \|\mathbf{u}\|$.

For watermark detection, we assume that the modification of the watermarked audio can be modeled as addition of noise. This assumption is not always valid, especially in the case of mp3 compression that tends to modify frequency spectrum in a fading-like manner. On the other hand, analysis of the system's performance is far simpler if the distortion is modelled as Additive White Gaussian Noise (AWGN), due to its convenient statistical properties. Therefore, theoretical analysis will give only upper bounds for detection performance, as the model underestimates the level of the introduced distortion. Thus, the channel is modelled as

$$\mathbf{y} = \mathbf{s} + \mathbf{n} \tag{4}$$

where $\mathbf{n}$ stands for the attack noise vector and $\mathbf{y}$ denotes the vector that is received at the watermark extraction side. Detection is performed by computing the normalized sufficient statistic r:

$$r = \frac{\langle \mathbf{y}, \mathbf{u} \rangle}{\langle \mathbf{u}, \mathbf{u} \rangle} = \frac{\langle b\mathbf{u} + \mathbf{x} + \mathbf{n}, \mathbf{u} \rangle}{\sigma_u^2} = \alpha b + (1 - \lambda)x + n \tag{5}$$

It is clear that as λ tends to 1, the less influence x has on r. The detector is the same as that in standard SS, its estimate of the embedded bit is $b^{'} = sign(r)$. The expected average distortion introduced by embedding of one watermark bit is:

$$E[D] = E[\|\mathbf{s} - \mathbf{x}] = \left(\alpha^2 + \frac{\lambda^2 \sigma_x^2}{N\sigma_u^2}\right) \sigma_u^2 \tag{6}$$

To make the average distortion of the new system to be equal to the distortion in the standard SS, we force $E[D] = \sigma_u^2$ and derive expression for α:

$$\alpha = \sqrt{1 - \lambda^2 \frac{\sigma_x^2}{N\sigma_u^2}} \tag{7}$$

The error probability p can be computed [7] as:

$$p = \frac{1}{2} \cdot erfc\left(\frac{1}{\sqrt{2}} \sqrt{\frac{\frac{N\sigma_u^2}{\sigma_x^2} - \lambda^2}{\frac{\sigma_n^2}{\sigma_x^2} + (1 - \lambda)^2}}\right) \tag{8}$$

This is a function of λ, signal to noise ratio $(\sigma_x/\sigma_n)^2$ and the relative power of the perceptually tuned SS sequence $N(\sigma_u/\sigma_x)^2$. By proper selection of the parameter λ, bit error rate of the system using ISS can be made several orders of magnitude smaller than system using traditional SS modulation. Error probability can be minimized for the optimum value of λ, computed from the error probability p by setting $dp/d\lambda = 0$ and is given by:

$$\lambda_{opt} = \frac{1}{2}\left[\left(1 + \frac{\sigma_x^2}{\sigma_x^n} + \frac{N\sigma_u^2}{\sigma_x^2}\right) - \sqrt{\left(1 + \frac{\sigma_x^2}{\sigma_n^2} + \frac{N\sigma_u^2}{\sigma_x^2}\right)^2 - 4\frac{N\sigma_u^2}{\sigma_x^2}}\right] \tag{9}$$

Watermark embedding scheme uses the derived equation for λ_{opt} for adjustment of the desired properties and overall performance of the watermarking system. Attack characterization module can include several sections that would simulate expected attacks that appear in the transmission channel. Test results included in this paper are obtained using attack characterization module that consisted of mp3 and low pass filtering characterization sections, as they caused the largest bit error rate on the original SS watermarking system [8], as well as on other contemporary audio watermarking methods [1,2,3]. Masking analysis module computes the highest allowed value for σ_u^2 under the constraints of time domain masking of the HAS. The estimate of the signal-to noise ratio in the watermark channel from the attack characterization block $(\sigma_x/\sigma_n)^2 = 10^{\frac{SNR}{10}}$ is forwarded to the embedding module.
Using attack characterization, even by a simple parameter as SNR, we were able to implement watermarking system that is able to make a trade-off between good statistical properties of ISS modulation and requirement for robust watermark detection. As we tend to improve an algorithm using blind watermark detection (without access to the original host audio sequence), it is a convenient way to estimate channel noise $\mathbf{n}$ without knowledge of the statistical model of the noise. For desired watermark capacity, determined by variable N, λ_{opt} is calculated and variable a derived from the equation 7. Therefore, using attack characterization block we can derive upper bounds for system's performance under a particular watermark removal attack and determine the upper bound for capacity of the watermark channel for a given bit error rate. On the other hand, it is possible to design a system with predefined upper bound for bit error rate and derive λ_{opt} and variable watermark capacity determined by block length N.

3 Experimental Results

Developed audio watermarking algorithm has been tested using a large set of songs from different music styles (pop, rock, techno, jazz). All music pieces have been watermarked using the described algorithm, with overall SNR ranging from -25.5 dB to -27.3dB. Subjective quality evaluation of the watermarking method has been done by blind listening tests involving ten persons that listened to the original and the watermarked audio sequences and were asked to report dissimilarities between the two signals, using a 5-point impairment scale. (5: imperceptible, 4: perceptible but not annoying, 3:slightly annoying, 2:annoying 1: very annoying.) The average mean opinion score was 4.6, standard deviation 0.42. The watermarked audio sequences have then been attacked using mp3 compression (bit rate 32 kbps mono, maximum bandwidth 7634 Hz) and low pass filtering (cut-off frequency 6 kHz, 60 dB stop band attenuation). The results of the tests have been plotted for the mp3 compression attack in Figure 2, and in Figure 3 for the low pass filter attack. Beside measured bit error rate Figures 2 and 3 contain theoretically calculated bit error rate if the informed ISS watermark scheme is used.
Both mp3 and low pass filtering attacks have dramatically increased detection bit error rate, as these attacks cannot be modelled as AWGN, due to unpredictability

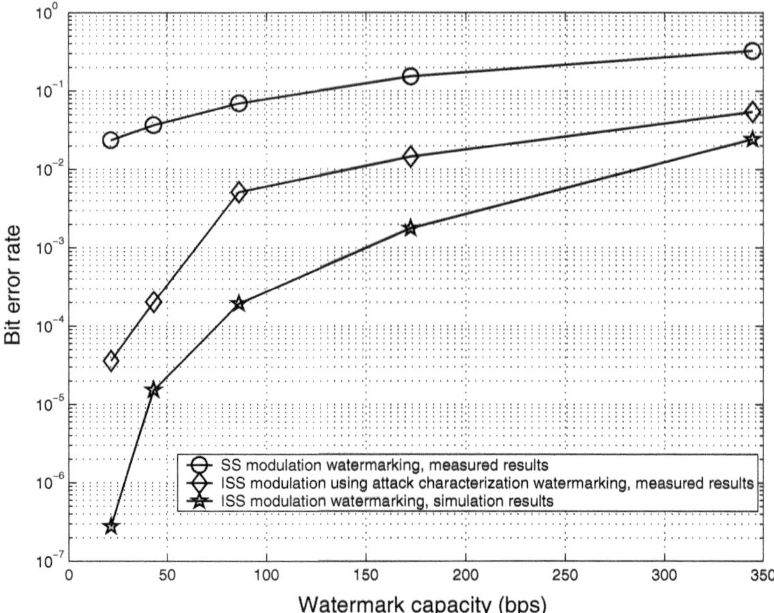

Fig. 2. Detection reliability in the presence of mp3 compression (32 kbps mono)

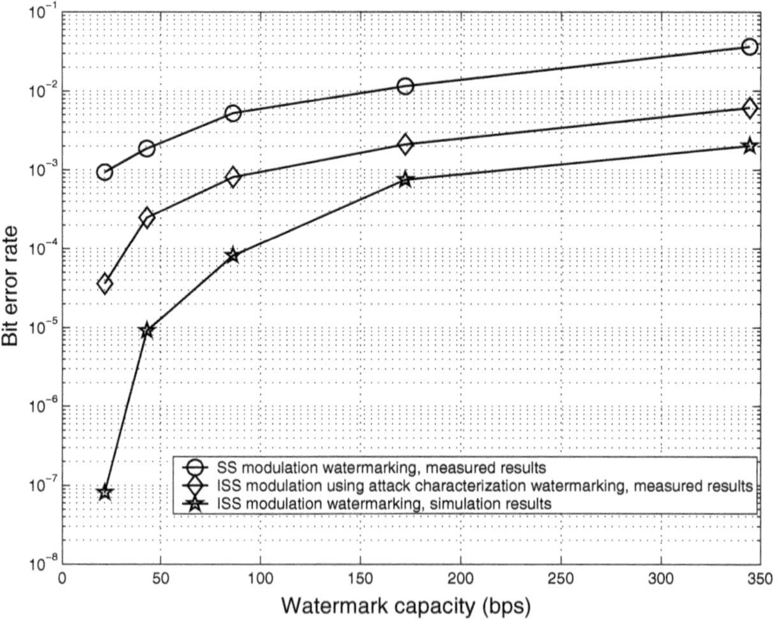

Fig. 3. Detection reliability in the presence of low pass filtering (cut-off freq. 6 kHz)

of SNR variations, including complete fade of the particular frequency subbands, during the watermark data transmission. It is clear that detection performance of the system using attack characterization and ISS modulation is significantly higher compared to the method using standard SS modulation. At lower watermark capacities gains are equal to a few orders of magnitudes in detection bit error rate. However, bit error rate of the described system was, as expected, still larger than in the case of the ISS modulation system with informed detection. Test results have confirmed algorithm's property to take advantage of the statistical properties of ISS modulation while maintaining blind detection during the watermark extraction process.

References

1. Bassia P., Pitas I.: Robust audio watermarking in the time domain. IEEE Transactions on Multimedia, Vol. 3. No. 2. (2001) 232–241
2. Swanson M. D., Zhu B.,Tewfik A. H.: Robust audio watermarking using perceptual masking. Signal Processing, Vol. 66. No. 3. (1998) 337–355
3. Mansour M. F., Tewfik A. H.: Audio watermarking by time-scale modification. Proc. IEEE International Conference on Acoustics, Speech, and Signal Processing (2001) 1353–1356
4. Lee S. K., Ho Y. S.: Digital audio watermarking in the cepstrum domain. IEEE Transactions on Consumer Electronics, Vol. 46. No. 3. (2000) 744–750
5. Cox I. J., Miller M. L., McKellips A. L.: Watermarking as communications with side information. Proceedings of the IEEE, Vol. 87. No. 7. (1999) 1127–1141
6. Miller M. L., Cox I. J., Bloom J.: Informed embedding: Exploiting image and detector information during watermark insertion, Proc. IEEE International Image Processing Conference, (2000) 1–4
7. Malvar H. S., Florencio D.: Improved spread spectrum: A new modulation technique for robust watermarking, IEEE Transactions on Signal Processing, Vol. 52. No. 4. (2003) 898–905.
8. Cvejic N., Keskinarkaus A., Seppänen T.: Audio watermarking using m-sequences and temporal masking, Proc. IEEE Workshop on Applications of Signal Processing to Audio and Acoustics, (2001) 227–230

Enhancement Methods of Image Quality in Screen Mark Attack

Ki Hyun Kim[1,2] and Yong Man Ro[2]

[1] Network Security Dep., Electronics and Telecommunications Research Institute
161, Gajeong-dong, Yuseong-gu, Daejeon, Korea
kihyun@etri.re.kr

[2] Image and Video System Lab., Information and Communications University,
58-4, Hwaam-dong, Yuseong-gu, Daejeon, Korea
yro@icu.ac.kr

Abstract. In this paper, we propose an Enhancement Screen Mark System (ESMS) that improves image quality better than the current Screen Mark System (SMS). Screen mark attack is similar in copy attack method and creates a good quality image that contains a watermark of the attacker. A copy attack does not destroy a watermark that is embedded in target image, and does not impair its detection. Attacker inserts his watermark into the target image by a method that copies his watermark to the target image. Attacker does not need to know any information about the watermark system of target image; it creates new challenges, especially when watermarks are used for copyright protection and identification. The proposed system uses the Gaussian Blur Filter (GBF) to remove a watermark in the target image and create a screen mark. It selects the most efficient screen mark and includes Image Quality Enhancement Module (IQEM). As a result, we get an improved result of about 0.8db to 2.3db on test images.

1 Introduction

Paper watermarks appeared in the art of handmade papermaking nearly 700 years ago in Fabriano, Italy. After the invention, watermarks quickly spread in Italy and then over Europe, although they were initially used to indicate the paper brand or paper mill. They later served as indication for paper format, quality, and strength, and were also used as the basis for dating and authenticating paper. Now, this concept is applied to digital media, such as audio, video, and image [1][2]. Recently, developers of digital contents or Intelligent Property (IP) want more and more efficient solutions for protection from illegal counterfeiting, tracking, and monitoring their multimedia contents. The digital watermark is a solution.

The digital watermark has been progressed to develop a more and more robust method. Some researchers have also been investigating ways to attack digital watermarks. Usually, researchers who study about watermark attack, research new watermark insertion technology that overcomes new attack methods. The General

T. Kalker et al. (Eds.): IWDW 2003, LNCS 2939, pp. 474–482, 2004.
© Springer-Verlag Berlin Heidelberg 2004

purpose of an attack is to destroy the embedded watermark in a digital watermark. In this case, the attacked image has a very serious distortion phenomenon.

In this paper, we propose an enhancement of the watermark attack system that minimises the distortion phenomenon. The system uses a screen mark attack algorithm. The algorithm is improved by adding new module to improve the quality of attacked image. In section 2, we describe a screen mark attack. In section 3, we describe enhancement methods that use a variable filter for an oracle attack, select screen mark of difference image concerned with quality of attacked images, and add IQEM. We conclude the paper in section 4.

2 Screen Mark Attack on Watermarking System

Screen mark attack uses overmarking attack as its basic idea. The overmarking attack is a watermark attack method for inserting another watermark into the image, which already contains a watermark. Nobody can distinguish who is the owner of the image, actually. A common public watermark system, such as Picturemarc 1.6 of Digimarc Co. or Suresign 3.1 of Signum Technologies Co., cannot insert a new watermark in an image that includes an original watermark because after the public watermark systems check whether there is some watermark in image or not, inserts its watermark in the image in case of there is no watermark. So, we cannot use the overmarking attack method to insert a new watermark in an image that already includes a watermark.

However, in the case of using the Screen mark attack, the attack is possible that attacker inserts his watermark to image that already includes watermark using public watermark system. [3]. The attack method is included as a protocol attack method according to watermark attack classification.

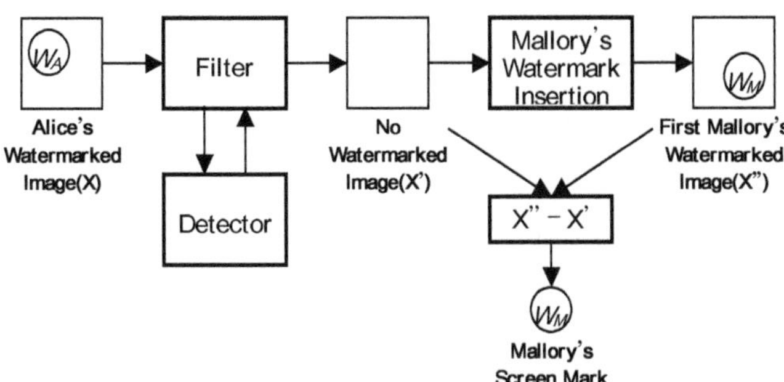

Fig. 1. First step for Screen mark attack

Screen mark attack consists of two steps. In the first step, an attacker makes a screen mark. Next, the attacker inserts the screen mark, which was created in the first step, in target image. We can see that Mallory attacks Alice's watermarked image as shown in Figure 1. Mallory uses a Filter and a detector to remove Alice's watermark, e.g., an *oracle attack* [4][5][7].

2.1 Oracle Attack

The lexical meaning of "Oracle" is intent, which asks solutions and seeks answers from God by "a divine message". An Oracle attack erases a watermark in target image using a filter and a detector. Most watermark attack methods have a watermark detector. This detector can consist of the hardware part of electronic equipment such as a DVD being included in a program such as image processor software. The attacker attacks the watermark that is included in the image without information about inserting a watermark. It is same with Figure 2.

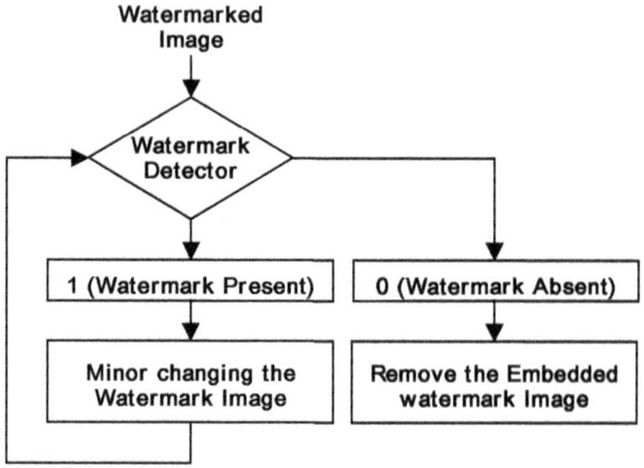

Fig. 2. Oracle attack schemes

Linnartz detailedly construed this method. The target image is inputted into the detector, and then the detector start to check the image that includes the watermark. If the result of "1 (there is watermark)" appears in the detector, the attacker impalpably changes pixel values in target image. Then the result image is inputted into the detector again. It is continued and repeated until "0 (there is no watermark)" is the result. As a result, the detector does not detect the watermark of the target image. There is a changer that increases the value of pixels by 0.5. "Blurring" is a method to change watermarked images impalpably or change the Gray value of images gradually. The calculation complexity of an oracle attack is very high because the attack is achieved to change the elemental area. In the Figure 1, Mallory uses a filtering attack such as Blurring, impalpably to attack target image (X), which includes Alice's watermark (W_A). It is an Oracle Attack. Mallory gets image X' that Alice's watermark is erased. Mallory inserts his watermark using a public watermark system in a no watermarked image X'. Mallory can obtain its watermark signal, a subtraction image, from two image: image X'', which has Mallory's watermark (W_M), and image X'. The watermark signal is called screen mark.

In Figure 3, we can see a change in baboon image and a screen mark. Oracle attack was applied in Alice's watermark image a) and received in image b). Also, at this point, we can see a decrease of picture quality through the change of PSNR. The decrease of PSNR in image c) is happened because Mallory inserts his watermark in image b). Screen mark is obtained through subtracting pixel value of image b) from c), and the resulting has a range from -5 to 5. The pixel value of image d) is a value that is multiples by 10 after adding 10 in the pixel value of screen mark so that we can see the screen mark pattern easily.

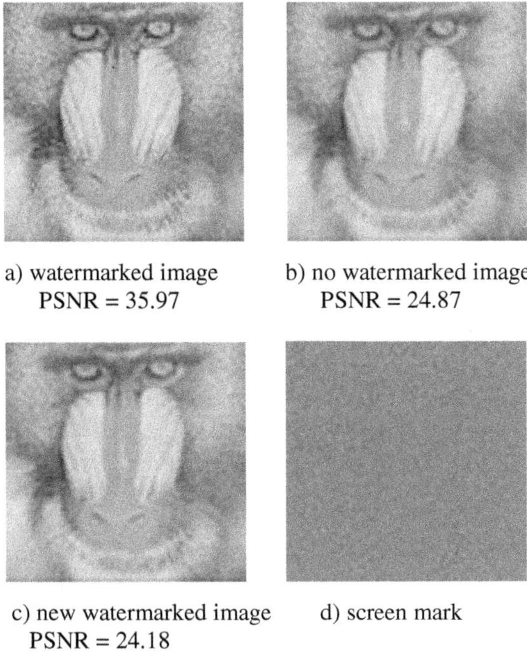

a) watermarked image PSNR = 35.97

b) no watermarked image PSNR = 24.87

c) new watermarked image PSNR = 24.18

d) screen mark

Fig. 3. Image change by flowing of screen mark first step

In the second step of the screen mark attack system, the Mallory's screen mark (W_M) is amplified by the weighting value α and the result is added to image. Then Mallory creates a screen mark attack image (X*) in Figure 4[1][5].

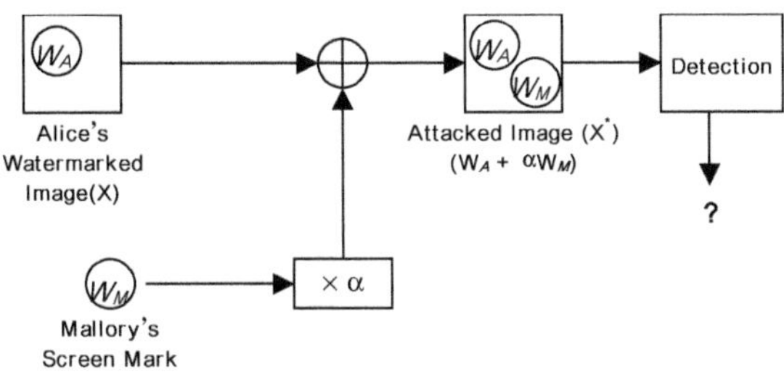

Fig. 4. Second step for screen mark attack

Alice's watermark W_A and Mallory's watermark (W_M) exist at the same time in image (X*). The watermark detector can't distinguish the normal author. The screen mark attack, a kind of copy attack method, can attack without knowledge of the algorithm or the technique of watermark system that wishes to attack. Mallory does not need information about topology of Alice's watermark. We reference some papers about a *copy attack* [1][2][6].

2.2 Copy Attack

A copy attack is an attack belonging to the group of protocol attacks. The goal of a copy attack is not to remove the watermark or impair its detection, but to estimate a watermark from a watermarked image and copy it to some other image called target data [2]. The estimated watermark is adapted to the local features of the target data. The copy attack is an applicable method when a valid watermark in the target data can be produced with neither knowledge of the watermarking technology nor knowledge of the watermarking key.

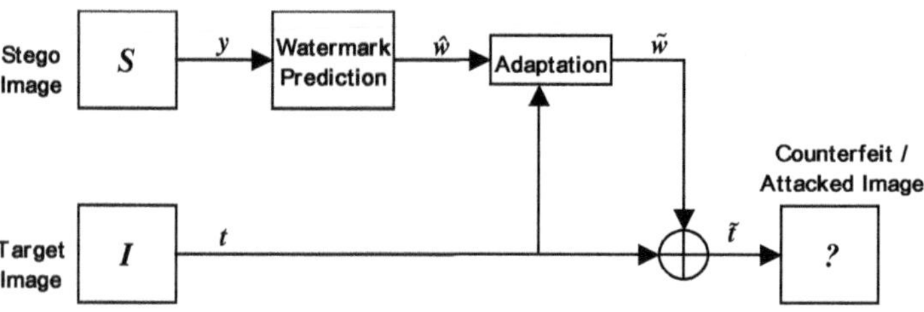

Fig. 5. The block of Copy attack

Figure 5 shows the functional blocks of the copy attack. One input to the system is called the stego image, which contains the watermark of the attacker, and another input is called the target image, into which the watermark form the stego image is to be copied. Copy attack consists of three technical steps. In the first step, the watermark in the stego image is predicted, resulting in $\hat{w}$. The prediction is processed in the next step. The goal of this processing is to adapt the watermark to the target image in order to maximize its energy under the constraint of keeping it imperceptible after insertion in the target image. In the last step, the predicted and processed image is added to the target image.

3 Enhancement in Screen Mark Attack

In this section, we propose three methods to improve the quality of an image that is the result of a screen mark attack. In the first and second step of a screen mark attack method, we wish to propose each method to improve the performance of an attack. Performance elevation of a screen mark attack means that PSNR of an attacked image is improved more than the existent method. In this paper, we use Adobe Photoshop 6.0 to insert and detect watermarks. Gray image such as a baboon, bear, lena, and watch are used. The size of an image is 256 x 256.

3.1 Enhancement Method at First Step

For the first step, we must find a new filter that can erase Alice's watermark and improve image quality more than the existent method in Oracle attack. We experimented with various filters, such as smooth filter, blur filter, motion blur filter, high pass filter, and Gaussian blur filter. Table 1 reports the results of using several filters. The smooth filter generally uses 3x3 filter.

Table 1. PSNR measures for Oracle attack

	Smooth Filter	Blur filter	Gaussian Blur filter	Result 1	Result 2
baboon	17.95	24.87	25.48	29.51	30.02
bear	20.81	26.15	26.24	31.32	31.51
lena	23.98	28.28	28.86	33.65	34.70
watch	22.22	26.88	27.17	32.58	33.51

In the case of Blur filter, the filter attacks a target image. This attack is continuously repeated until a watermark inserted in the target image is not detected (Adobe Photoshop 6.0). Table 1 reports the PSNR. The value of the results is calculated by the original image that has no watermark and estimated image. The results indicate that Gaussian blur filter is better than the blur filter. We realize that the Gaussian blur filter is a solution that gets image of better picture quality than the Blue filter solution presented in Table 1. A column of Result 1 presents the results of the screen mark system using the blue filter. By the same method, a column of Result 2 presents the results that are gotten in the case of the Gaussian blur filter. We can see improvement effects to about 0.1db to 1.0db by the Gaussian method. As a result, the first step of a Screen mark attack is useful when using a Gaussian blur filter.

3.2 Enhancement Method at Second Step

In this section, we suggest two methods for improvement of image quality at second steps of a screen mark attack. In the first method, a different value of the target image and stego image is used. That is, we use a screen mark that is gotten by another target image in the second-stage attack. We can see the results in Table 2.

Table 2. PSNR measures for variable Screen mark

	Baboon SM	Bear SM	Lena SM	Watch SM
Baboon	**30.021**	30.203	30.047	30.125
Bear	32.086	**31.501**	32.444	31.921
Lena	35.410	35.264	**34.705**	34.890
Watch	34.092	34.352	34.135	**33.510**

In the case of using a screen mark of another image, we get improved image rather than when we use a screen mark of its image. If an attacker wishes to get an image of good image quality, he must prepare screen marks of other images. However, we need to research about the cause.

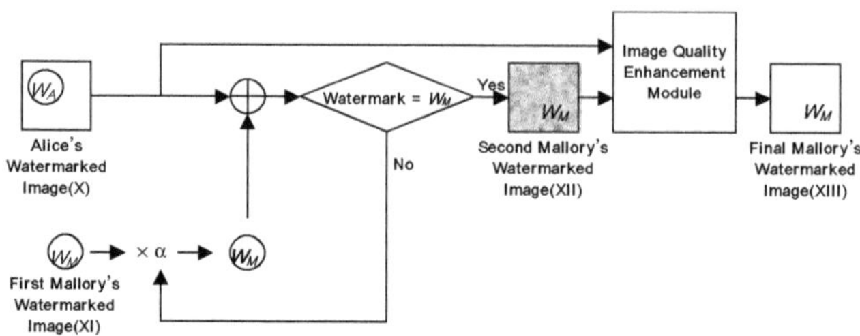

Fig. 6. Proposing Screen Mark second step

The second method of the second step uses a target image that differs from stego image in copy attack. Through Image Quality Enhancement Module (IQEM), image quality of image XII is improved similarly with the image quality of Alice's watermarked image (X). Attacker attacks X to use XI. The detector cannot detect target image's watermark according to the weighting value α. If the weighting value increases continually, the detector detects XI. Next, we improve the image quality to use the IQEM that is embodied in the approximation algorithm. The algorithm is displayed in Figure 7 [8].

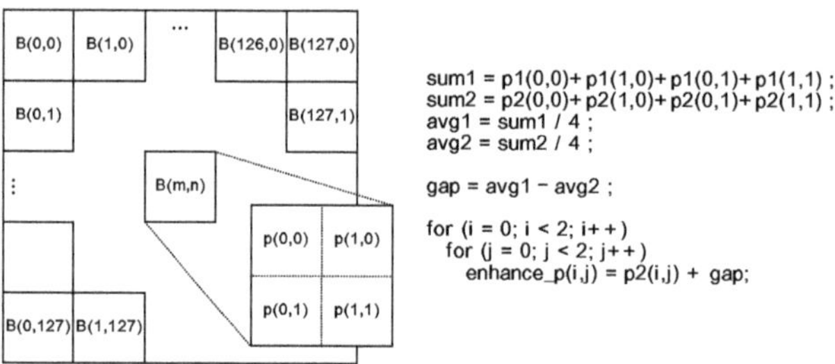

Fig. 7. Approximate method algorithm

A size of the image that is used in this paper is 256 x 256, and a block size is 2 x 2. A block size can use 4 x 4 or 8 x 8, etc. In the case of the baboon, we get the best result in 2 x 2. Sum1 is the sum of 4-pixel value in block B (m, n) of image X, and Sum2 is the sum of 4-pixel value in block B (m, n) of image XII. These sum values are divided into 4, and we obtain a mean value of each block. The difference value of two average values is called "gap". Such calculated gap value is reflected in each pixel value in block B (m, n) of image XII. In Figure 8, we show performance result of IQEM in case of the baboon image. First, we check the performance of IQEM through PSNR value of images. We understand the performance of IQEM through similarity of histograms. In the Fig8, IQEM changes from the shapes in two circles of the histogram in image (b into the shapes in two circles of histogram in image (c.

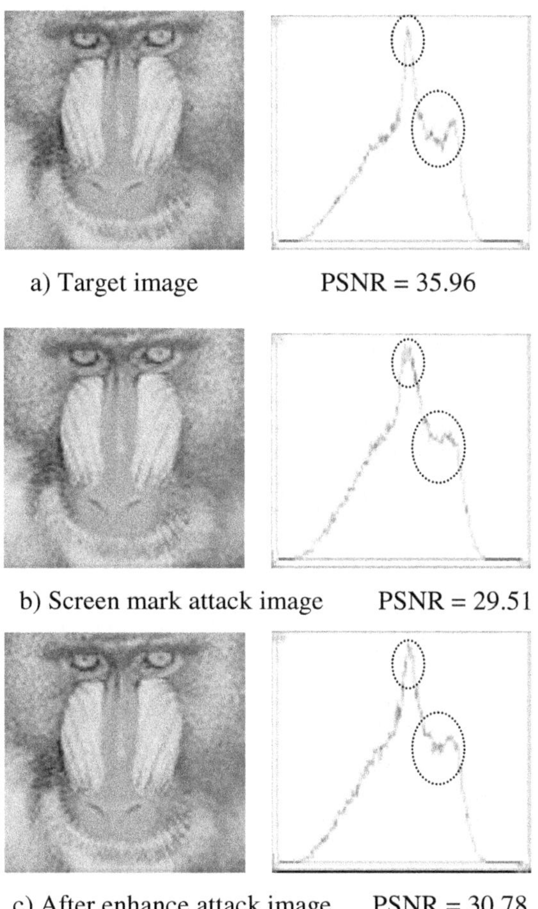

a) Target image PSNR = 35.96

b) Screen mark attack image PSNR = 29.51

c) After enhance attack image PSNR = 30.78

Fig. 8. Result of approximate method process

When the Enhancement screen mark attack method consisted of a Gaussian blur filter, a bear's screen mark, and IQEM is used to attack a baboon image, image quality improves to 1.27db in baboon image. We get improved results of about 0.8db to 2.3db in other images as well as the baboon image.

4 Conclusion

Attack technologies in digital watermarks have been developed by watermark insertion technologies, translations and counterfeit methods of watermark. Common attacks to watermarks usually aim to destroy the embedded watermark or to impair its detection. However, copy attack does not destroy a watermark or impair its detection; it creates new challenges, especially when watermarks are used for copyright protection and identification. The Screen mark attack seems like a copy attack.

In this paper, we proposed methods that make better image quality in screen mark attack and we make the system. The methods are to use the Gaussian Blur filter to remove watermark in target images, to use screen marks of other images, and to add IQEM. As a result, we get improved results of about 0.8db to 2.3db through test images. Present, we are studying about a new attack solutions that create an attacked image that has an image quality similar to quality of a target image.

References

1. Stefan Katzenbeisser, Fabien A.P. Petitcolas, *Information Hiding Techniques for Steganography and Digital Watermarking* (Artech house, INC. 2000)
2. Martin Kutter, Sviatoslav Voloshynovskiy, Alexander herrigel, The Watermark Copy Attack : *Security and Watermarking of Multimedia Content II,Vol.3971 of SPIE Proceedings*, San Jose, California USA, 23–28 January 2000.
3. H.J. Park, C.H. Lee, H.K. Lee, Screen Mark Attack : A New Image Watermarking Attack, *The Korean Society of Broadcast Engineers,* 01-6-1-07, 2001, 58–65
4. Michalewicz, Z.: Genetic Algorithms + Data Structures = Evolution Programs. 3rd edn. Springer-Verlag, Berlin Heidelberg New York (1996)
5. Linnartz, M. van Dijk, Analysis of the Sensitivity Attack Against Electronic Watermarks in Images, *Proceedings of the Second International Workshop of Information Hiding*, vol. 1525 of Lecture Notes in Computer Science, Springer, pp. 258–272, 1998
6. S. Voloshynovskiy, S. Pereira, V. Iquise, & T. Pun, Attack Modelling : Towards a Second Generation Watermarking Benchmark, *Preprint submitted to Elsevier Science*, 20 June 2001.
7. Min Wu, Bede Liu, Attacks On Digital Watermarks, IEEE, 1999, 1508–1512.
8. Sung Kon Oh, Jeong Hyun Yoon, & Yong Man Ro, Image Enhancement with Attenuated Blocking Artifact in transform Domain, *IEICE Trans. Inf. & Syst. Vol. E85-D, No. 1*, January 2002, 291–297.

A Method to Improve the Stego-Image Quality for Palette-Based Image Steganography

Mei-Yi Wu[1], Yu-Kun Ho[1], and Jia-Hong Lee[2]

[1] Department of Electrical Engineering, National Cheng Kung University, Tainan, Taiwan, R.O.C.
barbara@mail.cju.edu.tw

[2] Department of Information Management, Kun Shan University of Technology, Tainan, Taiwan, R.O.C.
jhlee@mail.ksut.edu.tw

Abstract. This article presents a method of palette-based image steganography that minimizes the RMS error between an original image and its stego-image. The proposed method is based on a palette modification scheme, which can iteratively embed one message bit into each pixel in a palette-based image. In each iteration, both the cost of removing a entry color in a palette and the benefit of generating a new one to replace it are calculated. If the maximal benefit exceeds the minimal cost, an entry color is replaced. Experimental results show that the proposed method can remarkably reduce the distortion of the carrier images (stego-images) to other palette-based methods.

1 Introduction

The hiding of data is frequently called "*steganography*". Data are embedded into digital media to identify, annotate, protect copyright, and deliver secret data. These embedded data travel along with the host media. The hiding of data is a highly multidisciplinary field that combines image and signal processing with cryptography, communication theory, coding theory, signal compression, and the theory of visual perception.

Depending on the form of type of information hidden in digital images, data hiding schemes can be roughly divided into two major categories [1]: non-robust, undetectable data hiding, and robust image watermarking. In the first application, a digital image contains a secret message. For example, when the least significant bit of each pixel is replaced by an encrypted bit-stream, the changes to a typical image will be imperceptible and the encrypted message will be masked by some innocent looking image. The main applications of such a scheme are to transmit secret data [2][3]. In the second application, a short message (a watermark) is embedded in the image in a robust manner. Many robust techniques including statistical methods [4], signal transformation [5], the spread spectrum method [6], Discrete Cosine Transform (DCT)[7], Discrete Fourier Transformation (DFT)[8], a wavelets-based technique [9],

T. Kalker et al. (Eds.): IWDW 2003, LNCS 2939, pp. 483–496, 2004.
© Springer-Verlag Berlin Heidelberg 2004

Fourier-Mellin transformation [10], fractal-based methods [11], and a content based method [12] can be efficiently applied to watermark digital images. The stego-images generated by these methods can survive common image processing operations, such as lossy compression, filtering, the adding of noise, geometrical transformation, and others. For a comprehensive description of watermarking methods, please refer to [13].

The Internet provides a huge channel for the mass communication of digital multimedia including text and images. One of the most fascinating method of hiding data embeds information in digital images[14]. Digital image steganography is one such method whose primary purpose is to embed and deliver secret messages in digital images without raising any suspicion. The secret messages may be compressed and encrypted before the embedding is begun. Many image steganographic techniques have been presented. A number of steganographic methods are based on replacing the least-significant-bits (LSBs) of the cover images [1][3]. Some methods that are based on human visual perception capability have been proposed to achieve higher embedding capacity[15][16]. Other methods modify small details in images to reduce the visibility of the watermark, such as for example , the text marking method[4], texture block coding[4], and the fractal based method[11].

The choice of image format plays an important role on the design of secure steganographic systems. Uncompressed image formats, including BMP, provide a very larg space in which to embed messages, but their obvious redundant data makes them very suspicious to steganalysts. Therefore, the commonly used JPEG and GIF images on Internet web sites have become more popular for steganographic applications[14].

Steganographers tend not to like to use palette-based images, because the limitation on the colors available in a finite palette causes difficulties in hiding data. Two approaches to embedding messages in palette-based images have been described; they include embedding messages into the palette and embedding messages into image data. The main advantage of the first approach is that is easy to implement. Freeware Gifshuffle [17] shuffles the color entries and uses different combinations of color entries to hide messages. The stego-image remains visibly intact, only the orders of the colors in the palette are changed. However, it's capacity is limited by the size of palette, and a long message cannot be thus embedded. The second approach has high capacity but is generally difficult to use without distorting of the stego-images.

A convention scheme for hiding data in palette-based images is called the EZ Stego method [18], in which the colors in the palette are first sorted by luminance, which is a linear combination of three colors R, G, B in the palette , such as is given by $R + G + B$. In the reordered palette, most neighboring palette entries are close to each other in the color space. The method embeds the messages in a binary form into the LSB of indices (pixels) pointing to the palette colors. However, this method works not well in creating high quality stego-images. The main reason is that colors with similar luminance values may be relatively far from each other (e.g. colors [9, 28, 202] and [202,9,28] have the same luminance but represent two extremely different colors).

To avoid this problem, Fridrich [19] presents a new method to hide message bits into the parity bit of close colors. The parity bit of the color *R*, *G*, *B* is calculated as $(R + G + B)$ *mod 2*. For each pixel of an image, a message bit is embedded by searching the closest colors in the palette till a palette entry with the desired parity bit. Since the parity bits of palette entries corresponding to real images are more or less randomly distributed, this will guarantee that the original colors are not modified too much within the stego-image. However, there exists false contouring and noises in the output stego-images by using Fridrich's method, especially to embed data for hand-drawing images (such as cartoon pictures). Since only few colors are used in this kind of images, the color difference between an entry and others will become larger in the embedding process. Fredrich and Du[20] also proposed modified approach, including a non-adaptive method and an adaptive method, to improve the security of palette steganography.

Some steganalytic methods for detecting the presence of hidden messages in images, such as visual attacks and statistical attacks, have also been explored in [21]. Fridrich, Goljan and Du[22] recently proposed a steganalysis method which can detecting even small changes to bitmap images that originated as JPEGs. Johnson and Jajodia[23] pointed out some steganographic methods for palette images that preprocess the palette before embedding are very vulnerable. For example, S-Tools[17] or Stash[17] create clusters of close palette colors that can be swapped for each other to embed message bits. The characteristics of some other steganography software are also identified[24]. Provos and Honeyman[25] presented a detection framework to retrieve two million JPEG images from eBay auctions and automatically detect whether they might contain secret messages.

In this paper, an iterative method is derived to minimize the RMS error between the original image and the stego-image. The method will iteratively modify both the palette content and image data in the original palette-base image. Then, Fridrich's method is applied to embed messages into the modified image and achieve a less distorted stego-image. The motivation of the method is to replace the "*less important*" colors in the image with the neighboring color to spare palette entries for some " *more important*" colors. Thus, we can greatly reduce the root-mean-square (RMS) error during the embedding process of Fridrich's method. Finally, we compare the original images with their corresponding stego-images produced by EZ Stego, Fridrich's method and the proposed method by using the RMS distance. Experimental results show that the proposed method produces significantly better results.

The rest of the paper is organized as follows. In the next section, we briefly review the EZ Stego and Fridrich's methods to data hiding. Section 3 details our new approach to minimize the RMS error between the original image and the stego-image. Section 4 presents the experimental results and a modification is employed to improve the security of the proposed method. A general case study is also given. The final section summarizes our work.

2 Related Work about Data Hiding for Palette-Based Images

2.1 EZ Stego Method

EZ stego method is similar to the generally used LSB method for 24 bit color images (or 8 bit grayscale images). After sorting the palette colors by luminance, this method embeds the message in a binary form into the LSB of indices pointing to the palette colors. The detail steps are listed as follows:

Step1: Reorder the palette color according to the luminance of each palette entry.
Step2: Find the index of the pixel's RGB color in the reordered palette.
Step3: Get one bit from the embedding binary message and replace the LSB of the index.
Step4: Find the new RGB color that the index now points to the reordered palette.
Step5: Find the index of the new RGB color in the original palette.
Step6: Replace the pixel with the index of the new RGB color.

The receiver can simply recover the message by collecting the LSBs of all indices in the image file.

2.2 Fridrich's Steganographic Method

Fridrich proposes a steganographic method to hide message bit into the parity bit of close colors. First, the distance of two colors in a palette is given as follows:

Definition 1: Let i, j be two color entries in palette P with $C_i=(r_i, g_i, b_i)$ and $C_j=(r_j, g_j, b_j)$ respectively, the color distance between C_i and C_j (in Euclidean norm) is denoted as

$$d(i,j)=\sqrt{(r_i-r_j)^2+(g_i-g_j)^2+(b_i-b_j)^2} \quad (1)$$

Let f be a palette-based image of size n by n, there is totally $n\times n$ message bits can be embedded by using Fridrich's method. For each pixel with color palette index i in f, one data bit d("0" or "1") of embedded bit stream will be "coded" by keeping the following principle. If $(r_i + g_i + b_i + d) \bmod 2 = 1$, a searching for other entries is performed to find the closest color entry with different parity such that $(r_i + g_i + b_i + d) \bmod 2 = 0$. Otherwise, nothing requires to do.

Message recovery is simply achieved by checking the color parity of the corresponding palette indices. For each pixel in a received image (stego-image) with palette index i, if $(r_i + g_i + b_i) \bmod 2 = 0$, an embedded message bit "0" will be decoded. Otherwise, message bit "1" is decoded. This method never replace a pixel color by a completely different color, which could occasionally happen in EZ Stego because ordering of the palette by luminance may derive discontinuities in neighboring colors.

3 The Proposed Method

Our approach can be regarded as a preprocessing work of some palette baseFridrich's method. We minimize the RMS error by iteratively updating a palette color before starting the Fridrich's embedding process. It can be also regarded as a replacement operation to remove a specified entry of the palette and then to create a new color to occupy the removed entry.

Within the iteration, the calculation of removing an entry and the benefit of creating a new one color is done. If the obtained benefit is larger than the loss of removal cost, we remove the selected entry to be an "*empty*" one by taking a replacement for the corresponding image data in the image. Then, a new color is created to occupy the *empty* position by which we can greatly reduce the RMS error in the embedding process. When the iteration algorithm is finished, Fridrich's method is employed for data embedding and recovery.

Assume that the embedded message is encrypted by a traditional encryption algorithm (such as 56-bit key DES) and output random pattern consisting of "0" and "1" with approximately the same size respectively. The following definitions are given before we introduce the details of the method:

Definition 2: Let f be a palette-based image with palette size L (with entries 0 to L-1), the occurrence frequency for each entry in f is denoted as $N(i)$, where i=0 to L-1.

Definition 3: In a palette P, C_x is the closest color for C_y, if entry x satisfies the following equation:

$$d(x, y)=\text{Min}\{\, d(n, y): n=0,1,\ldots,L-1 \text{ and } n\neq y \,\} \text{ where } L \text{ is the size of } P. \quad (2)$$

We say that x is the first referenced entry for entry y in P and is denoted as

$$x= R^{first}(y)$$

Definition 4: In a palette P, C_x is the closest color for C_y with *different parity* (parity bit of the color C_x (r_x, g_x, b_x) is $r_x+g_x+b_x$ mod 2), if entry x satisfies the following equation:

$$d(x, y)=\text{Min}\{\, d(n, y): n=0,1,\ldots,L-1 \text{ and } (r_y+r_n+g_y+g_n+b_y+b_n) \bmod 2=1\} \quad (3)$$

We say that x is the first referenced entry for entry y in P and is denoted as

$$x = R_{DP}^{first}(y)$$

Definition 5: In a palette P, if C_x is the first closest color for C_y with *different parity*, then the second closest color C_z for color C_y is defined as follows:

$$d(z, y)=\text{Min}\{\, d(n, y): n=0,1,\ldots,L-1.\ n\neq x \text{ and } (r_y+r_n+g_y+g_n+b_y+b_n) \bmod 2=1\} \quad (4)$$

We say that z is the second referenced entry for entry y in P, and is denoted as

$$z = R_{DP}^{second}(y)$$

3.1 Cost of Removing an Entry

According to the above definitions, we can estimate the removal cost with three items (Fridrich's error cost, removal of one color entry from the palette, and the reference error by removing the palette entry) for each entry i in a palette. Assume that the embedded message is encrypted and consisting of the same size of "0" and "1", there is about half of the number of pixel with color entry i will be replaced with another color entry in the embedding process. The first item denoted as $COST_{\text{Fridrich}}(i)$ is the embedding error of Fridrich's method.

$$COST_{Fridrich}(i)=\frac{1}{2}N(i)\times d(i,R_{DP}^{first}(i)) \tag{5}$$

where $N(i)$ is the total number of entry i distributed in the original image f.

The second item denoted as $COST_{\text{self}}(i)$, is the cost derived from the replacement error for updating the color entry i to the closest color with entry k and the embedding error of the updated entry k.

$$COST_{self}(i)=N(i)\times d(i,R^{first}(i))+\frac{1}{2}N(i)\times d(k,R_{DP}^{first}(k)) \tag{6}$$

where $k=R^{first}(i)$

The third item denoted as $COST_{\text{ref}}(i)$ is the reference error derived by other entries in the palette which select entry i as their closest color during the embedding process.

$$COST_{ref}(i)=\frac{1}{2}\sum_{\substack{k=0\cdots L-1\\ R_{DP}^{first}(k)=i}}\left\{N(k)\times\left[d(k,R_{DP}^{second}(k))-d(k,R_{DP}^{first}(k))\right]\right\} \tag{7}$$

Finally, the total error cost is given by

$$\Delta COST(i)=COST_{self}(i)+COST_{ref}(i)-COST_{\text{Fridrich}}(i) \tag{8}$$

3.2 Benefit of Creating a New Entry

For an entry i of the palette with index color $C_i(r_i,g_i,b_i)$, a new entry j is created to make a *referenced pair* which will reduce the embedding error into distance 1 by using the following equation.

$$\begin{aligned} r_j &= r_i \\ g_j &= g_i \\ b_j &= \begin{cases} 1 & \text{if} \quad b_i=0 \\ b_i-1 & \text{otherwise} \end{cases} \end{aligned} \tag{9}$$

Therefore, the benefit of creating a new entry for entry i is given as follows:

$$Benefit(i)=\frac{1}{2}N(i)\times\left[d(i,R_{DP}^{first}(i))-1\right] \tag{10}$$

where $d(i,R_{DP}^{first}(i))$ is the embedding error of Fridrich's method.

To implement the proposed method, the following algorithm is given:

Algorithm: An Iterative Method for Palette-Based Image Steganography

Input: a palette-based image f, the occurrence frequency $N(i)$ of each color entry in f
a entry set $S=\phi$
Output: a palette-based image g
Step1: While $Benefit_{max}$ -$COST_{min} > 0$
an entry replacement is performed (from step 2 to step 5)
Step2: For each palette entry i, if $i \notin S$ then
calculate$\Delta COST(i)$ and $Benefit(i)$
Find the minimum cost (denoted as $COST_{min}=\Delta COST(p)$)
Find the maximum benefit (denoted as $Benefit_{max} = Benefit(q)$);
Step3: Replace the palette color $C_p(r_p, g_p, b_p)$ and then copy this modified palette to image g, where
/* palette color with index p will be updated by index q */
$r_p = r_q$
$g_p = g_q$

$$b_p = \begin{cases} 1 & \text{if} \quad b_q = 0 \\ b_q - 1 & otherwise \end{cases}$$

Step4: Sequentially scan the image data of $f(i, j)$ and output a new image $g(i, j)$ according to the following condition:
/* $f(i, j)$, $g(i, j)$ denote the corresponding palette indices on pixel location (i, j), respectively */
Case $f(i, j) = p$: $g(i, j) = R^{first}(p)$
Case $f(i, j)= q$: if cnt < $N(q)$ / 2 then
$g(i, j) = p$;
cnt=cnt+1 ;
end if
Otherwise:
$g(i, j) = f(i, j)$
Step5: Add p, q to set S and update the occurrence frequencies of each color entry in the modified image for next iteration.
$N(R^{first}(p))= N(R^{first}(p)) + N(p)$
$N(p)= N(q)/2$
$N(q)= N(q)- N(q)$

Step6: Stop

4 Experimental Results and Discussions

4.1 Experimental Results

To evaluate the performance of different steganographic methods, two images (Fruit and Swimmer) with 256 and 128 color palette entries respectively are employed. Both these images of size 256×256 are displayed in Figure 1(a) and Figure 2(a), respectively. The embedded message is simulated using random bit stream with length 256×256 bits. Figure 1(b) and Figure 2(b) are the output stego-images by using EZ Stego method. Figure 1(c) and Figure 2(c) show the stego-images by using Fridrich's method. Figure 1(d) and Figure 2(d) show the stego-images by using the proposed method. The corresponding root-mean-square (RMS) errors between the original images and the stego-images are listed in TABLE 1. Figure 3(a) and Figure 3(b) show the graphs of benefit and cost functions for the images in Fig. 1(a) and Fig. 2(a) respectively. Fig. 4(a) and Fig. 4(b) show the graphs of the corresponding RMS errors with different iterations.

The obvious distortion distributed in Figure 1(b) and Figure 2(b) illustrates that the EZ Stego method may generate bad stego-images. The RMS errors in TABLE 1 shown 21.97 and 36.88 also support the bad quality results. Fridrich's method performs better than EZ Stego, but there is some false contouring happen (see the apple located in the image of Figure 1(c)). In addition, Fridrich's method may work badly for artificial images (such as cartoon pictures) since the color distance between palette entries are larger in artificial images than in the real images. Therefore, Fridrich's method may derive noises in the stego-images when it is employed in not real images.

4.2 Modification to Improve the Security

To achieve a higher steganography security, it is important to reduce the suspicion to the new created palette. The proposed method generates a very closed color entry pair with distance one after each iteration. If we execute too many iterations, it may cause a suspicious palette when someone look at the palette colors in the RGB color cube. Therefore, Eq. (9) could be modified to generate new color pairs with non-fixed distances. For an entry i of the palette with index color $C_i(r_i,g_i,b_i)$ and C_j is the first referenced color with different parity of C_i, where $j = R_{DP}^{first}(i)$. A new color entry color C_z could be created to be the new closest color for C_i with different parity and C_z is given as

$$r_z = r_i + \lfloor \alpha \times (r_j - r_i) \rfloor$$
$$g_z = g_i + \lfloor \alpha \times (g_j - g_i) \rfloor$$
$$b_z = b_i + \lfloor \alpha \times (b_j - b_i) \rfloor + \beta \quad (11)$$

where, α is a real number with value less than 0.5 and β is an adaptable integer with value 0 or 1 to keep the different parity rule. The benefit function of Eq. (10) is also modified as

$$Benefit(i) = \frac{1}{2} N(i) \times [(1-\alpha) \times d(i, j)] \quad (12)$$

The modified method with α=0.1 and α=0.3 are applied to the image in Fig. 1(a), the iterative procedure stops at 88 and 82 iterations with RMS values of 2.33 and 3.00 respectively. The results are also better than the Fredrich's method.

Fredrich and Rui[20] have improved the security of the original scheme[19] by carefully selecting the pixels that carry the secret information. They introduced the concept of optimal parity assignment and developed two adaptive steganographic methods to avoid embedding message bits into the areas of uniform color portions of the carrier image. The proposed iterative approach can be regarded as a preprocessing work to prepare a higher quality carrier image for message embedding. The security of the proposed scheme can also be further improved by using the similar concepts in [24].

4.3 A General Case Study

Not just for Fredrich's method, the proposed method can also be applied to other palette-based steganographic methods. A general case of removing a color entry of the proposed method can be described in Fig. 5. (a). Three cost terms are used and denoted as follows,
cost0 : the referenced error derived for the requirement of data embedding.
cost1: the replacement error of updating the color entry to the closest color.
cost2: the second referenced error derived when its first referenced color is removed in the palette.

In Fig. 5(a), each block stands for different color entry of the palette. Suppose that the central entry will be removed to spare an empty entry, all the image data pointed to this entry will redirect to the nearest color entry. The total cost can be derived from the following three types of cost,
Type 0: the cost caused by the original referenced error.
Type 1: the cost caused by redirecting to the new entry and the new referenced error
Type 2: the cost caused by redirecting references of some entries which originally referenced to the removed entry and now changed to their second references.
The total cost of removing an entry can be computed as the cost of Type1+Type2-Type0.

In Fig. 5(b), suppose that the central entry is selected to generating a new color entry. To simplify the procedure, we give a constrain that the new entry will satisfy the closest entry to the central entry and no other entries will redirecting to the new entry. The benefit of generating a new entry can be computed as the difference of two costs of Type 0.

To show the practice of the proposed method in a general case, we apply the iterative method to the EZ Stego method. First we can modify the EZ Stego method by using "near distance LSB" to replace the directly applying LSB of color index in Step 3 of Section 2.1. Since there are two choices for color entry with index from 1 to 254 in the sorting palette, the use of the near distance neighbor will greatly reduce the reference error. The RMS between the image of Fig. 1(a) and its stego-image generated by modified EZ Stego method will be reduced from 21.97 into 14.50. In addition, we apply the three types of errors in our iterative method to preprocessing before starting the modified EZ Stego method. The iterative method executes 117 iterations and the result stego-image will reduce the RMS value into 11.68. Although the result is not as good as just applying Fridrich's method, it exactly reduces the RMS value and improve the quality of the stego-image for EZ Stego method.

Fig. 1. (a)

Fig. 1. (b)

Fig. 1. (c)

Fig. 1. (d)

Fig. 1. An example to illustrate the steganography methods. (a) The original image "Fruit" of size 256×256 (b) The stego-image by using EZ Stego method (c) The stego-image by using Fridrich's method (d) The stego-image by using the proposed method with 89 iterations.

5 Conclusion

We have described a novel steganographic method for palette-based images that dynamically and iteratively modify the palette colors to minimize RMS error between the stego-image and the original image. The proposed method can be also applied for other steganographic methods to improve the quality of stego-images. Our experimental results reveal the practicability and superiority of the new technique.

Fig. 2. (a)

Fig. 2. (b)

Fig. 2. (c)

Fig. 2. (d)

Fig. 2. An example to illustrate the steganography methods. (a) The original image "Swimmer" of size 256×256 (b) The stego-image by using EZ Stego method (c) The stego-image by using Fridrich's method (d) The stego-image by using the proposed method with 116 iterations.

Table 1. The RMS errors between the original image and the stego-image by employing different steganographic methods.

	Fruit	Swimmer
EZ Stego	21.97	36.88
Fridrich's Method	7.78	20.41
The proposed method	2.22	0.38
The modified method with α=0.1	2.33	0.94
The modified method with α=0.3	3.00	3.14

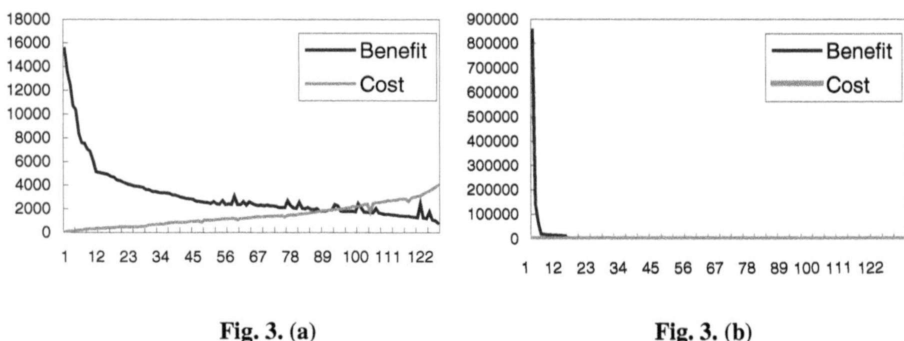

Fig. 3. (a) **Fig. 3. (b)**

Fig. 3. The graphs of the evaluated benefit and cost functions: (a) for the image in Fig. 1(a); . (b) for the image in Fig. 2(a).

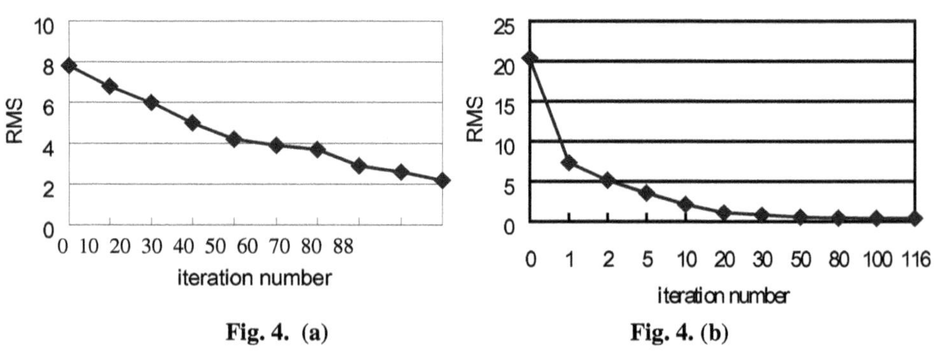

Fig. 4. (a) **Fig. 4. (b)**

Fig. 4. The RMS errors with different iterations by employing the proposed method: (a) for the image in Fig. 1(a) ; (b) for the image in Fig. 2(a), respectively.

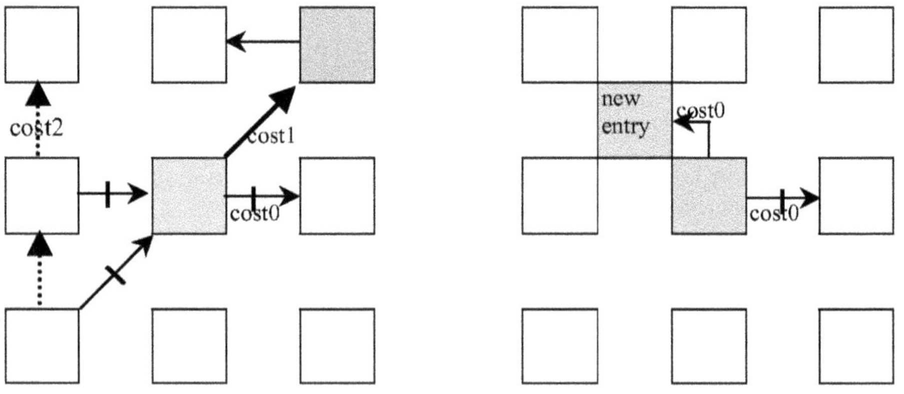

Fig. 5. (a) The process of removing an entry. **Fig. 5. (b)** The process of generating an entry.

Fig. 5. A diagram to display the process of removing and generating a color entry of the palette.

References

[1] J. Fridrich, "Applications of Data Hiding in Digital Images", Tutorial for The ISSPA'99, Brisbane, Australia, August,1999T.-S. Chen, C.-C. Chang, and M.-S. Hwang, "A Virtual Image Cryptosystem Based upon Vector Quantization", IEEE Trans. Image Processing, Vol. 7, No.10, pp. 1485–1488, 1998

[3] M. T. SandfordII, J. N. Bradley, and T. G Handel," The Data Embedding Method", SPIE Photonics East Conference ,1995

[4] W. Bender, D.Gruhl, N.Morimoto, and A. Lu, "Techniques for Data Hiding", IBM System Journal, Vol. 35, Nos 3&4, 1996, pp.313–336

[5] C.-T. Hsu and J.-L. Wu, "Hidden Signatures in Images", Proceedings of ICIP, 1996, pp. 223–226L. M Marvel, C.G Boncelet, and C.T.Retter, " Spread Spectrum Image Steganography", IEEE Trans. On Image Processing, Vol. 8, No. 8, 1999, pp. 1075–1083I.J. Cox, J. Kilian, F.T. Leighton, and T. Shamoon,"Secure Spread Spectrum Watermarking for Multimedia", IEEE Trans. On Image Processing, Vol. 6, 1997, pp.1673–1687

[8] V. Solachidis and I. Pitas,"Circularly Symmetric Watermark Embedding in 2-D DFT Domain", IEEE Trans. On Image Processing, Vol. 10, No. 11, 2001, pp.1741–1753

[9] H. Inoue, A.Miyazaki, A. Yamamoto, and T. Katsura, " A Digital Watermark Based on Wavelet Transform and Its Robustness on Image Processing", Proc. of ICIP, vol.2, 1998, pp.391–395

[10] P. Bas, J-M. Chassery, and F. Davoine,"Using the Fractal Code to Watermark Images", Proc. of ICIP, vol.1, 1998, pp.469–473

[11] V. Solachidis and F.M. Boland,"Phase Watermarking of Digital Images", Proc. of ICIP, vol.3, 1996, pp.239–242

[12] P. Bas, J.-M. Chassery, and B. Macq, "Geometrically Invariant Watermarking Using Feature Points", IEEE Trans. On Image Processing, Vol. 11, No. 9, 2002, pp.1014–1028

[13] I.J.Cox, M.L. Miller, and J.A. Bloom, Digital Watermarking, Morgran Kaufmann Publishers, San Francisco, 2002

[14] N. F. Johnson and S. Jajodia, "Exploring steganography: Seeing the Unseen", IEEE Computer, February,1998,pp.26–34

[15] Y.-K. Lee and L.-H. Chen,"High Capacity Image Steganographic Model", IEE Proceedings Vision, Image and Signal Processing, Vol. 147, Issue 3, 2000, pp. 288–294

[16] D.C. Wu and W.H. Tsai," A Steganographic Method for Images by Pixel-Value Differencing", Pattern Recognition Letters, Vol.24, 2003, 1613–1626

[17] Steganography software for Widows, http://www.jjtc.com/stegoarchive/stego/software.html

[18] R. Machado, EZ Stego, [http://www.stego.com]

[19] J. Fridrich," A New Steganographic Method for Palette-Based Images", IS&T PICS, Savannah, Georgia, April 25-28, 1999, pp. 285–289

[20] J. Fridrich and R. Du," Secure Steganographic Methods for Palette Images", Proc. The 3rd Information Hiding Workshop, LNCS vol. 1768, Springer-Verlag, New York, 2000, pp. 47–60

[21] A. Westfeld and A. Pfitzmann,"Attacks on Steganographic Systems", Proc. The 3rd Information Hiding Workshop, LNCS vol. 1768, Springer-Verlag, New York, 2000, pp. 61–75

[22] J. Fridrich, M. Goljan and D. Hogea, "Steganalysis of JPEG Images: Breaking the F5 Algorithm", 5th Information Hiding Workshop, Noordwijkerhout, The Netherlands, October 2002, pp. 310–323

[23] N. F. Johnson, Z. Duric, and S. Jajodia, Information Hiding: Steganography and Watermarking-Attacks and Countermeasures. Kluwer Academic Publishers, Boston, 2000

[24] N. F. Johnson and S. Jajodia," Steganalysis of Images Created Using Current Steganography Software", Proc. The Second Information Hiding Workshop, LNCS vol. 1525, Springer-Verlag, 1998, pp. 273–289

[25] N. Provos and P. Honeyman,"Detecting Steganographic Content on the Internet", CITI Technical Report 01–11, 2001. http://www.citi.umich.edu/techreports/reports/citi-tr-01-11.pdf

A Secure Steganographic Scheme against Statistical Analyses

Jeong Jae Yu[1], Jae Won Han[1], Kwang Su Lee[1], Seung Cheol O[1], Sangjin Lee[1], and Il Hwan Park[2]

[1] Center for Information and Security Technology, Korea University, Seoul, Korea
{shakehds,jaewon75,kslee,bangsil}@cist.korea.ac.kr, sangjin@korea.ac.kr
http://cist.korea.ac.kr
[2] NSRI, Daejeon, Korea
ilhpark@etri.re.kr

Abstract. Westfeld[1] analyzed a sequential LSB embedding steganography effectively through the χ^2–statistical test which measures the frequencies of PoVs(pairs of values). Fridrich[2] also proposed another statistical analysis, so-called RS steganalysis by which the embedding message rate can be estimated. This method is based on the partition of pixels as three groups ; Regular, Singular, Unusable groups. In this paper, we propose a new steganographic scheme which preserves the above two statistics. The proposed scheme embeds the secret message in the innocent image by randomly adding one to real pixel value or subtracting one from it, then adjusts the statistical measures to equal those of the original image.

1 Introduction

From old times, many methods were designed to send a secret information. For instance, one sent a random sequence which was generated by the promised table or an innocent-looking letter on which the secret message was written using salt water. Then receiver decoded the secret message from the table of random numbers or puts the letter over the fire until the secret writing appears. These methods are easily found in a detective story. The former is an example of cryptographic system, and the latter is that of steganographic system. Cryptographic security means informally that eavesdropper can not acquire any of the secret information nor forge the message. Steganographic security means that the watcher can not distinguish a message embedded object(stego–data) from a pure object(carrier). Cryptography is about protecting the content of messages and steganography is about concealing their very existence. The goals of each system are subtlely different, but these are closely related.

Today, we live in the highly developed digital community, but the security of the private information is not kept pace with the development of technology. If we can make the above two systems closely complemented, then our communication environment will be more secure one.

Since Simmons[3] first introduced an invisible communication as the "prisoners' problem", many steganographic systems have been proposed. However the

T. Kalker et al. (Eds.): IWDW 2003, LNCS 2939, pp. 497–507, 2004.
© Springer-Verlag Berlin Heidelberg 2004

majority of them are not secure because they can be detected by statistical analyses. Although these systems cannot detected by HVS(human visual system), they have made a distingushable distortion to a steged image during embedding procedure. Generally, they had a drawback which makes a difference between the original image and a steged one. In the steganalysis, this fact is used to determine whether the suspicious image embeds message or not.

Westfeld[1] performed the blind steganalysis on the basis of statistical analysis of PoVs(pairs of values). This method, so-called χ^2–statistical analysis, gave a successful result to a sequential LSB(least significant bit) embedding steganography. Provos[6] extended this method by re-sampling test interval and re-pairing values.

Fridrich[2] introduced a RS steganalysis which is based on the partition of an image' pixels as three groups ; Regular, Singular, Unusable groups. Fridrich could find that the RS ratio of a typical image should satisfy a certain rule through the large amount of experiments. Although this method needs some heuristic assumptions, Fridrich can estimate the possible embedded message length of the LSB steganography.

In this paper, we propose a new steganographic scheme which successfully evades these kinds of statistical attacks, we call this system SES(Steganography Evading Statistical analyses). SES embeds the secret message in the image by randomly adding one to real pixel value or subtracting one from it, after then, adjusts the statistical measures to equal those of the original image. So far, there has not been a steganographic scheme which considers and adjusts the RS statistic after message embedding. Perhaps, our proposal may be the first one that is designed to avoid the above two kinds of statistical attacks ; χ^2–statistical analysis and RS steganalysis. Moreover, SES has a sufficient embedding capacity comparing with F5[7] or OutGuess[6]; Maximum capacity of SES can be the same as that of the simple LSB embedding steganography and if we apply this embedding method to 2nd LSB, the message capacity can be increased more than that.

In the following section, we review the well-known statistical analyses, χ^2–test and RS steganalysis, then in section 3, present the details of SES. In section 4, we show the experimental results and conclude this paper with describing the future work in section 5.

2 Statistical Steganalyses

2.1 χ^2–Statistical Analysis

Westfeld[1] presented steganalysis method, so-called the χ^2–statistical test which is based on the statistical analysis into pairs of values(PoVs) in the LSB. For instance, the PoVs can be constituted of pixel values, quantized DCT coefficients, or palette indices that differ only in the LSB. In the general, the frequencies of the PoVs for the pure images are not distributed evenly, but in case of a LSB embedding steganography the frequencies of each PoVs would become equal–the assumption is that a cipher text should be embedded in the steganography. From this idea, Westfeld compared the occurrence of PoVs measured in a suspected image with the statistical random test[5]. The details of χ^2–statistical test are summarized as follows

1. Assume that there are k categories and that we have a random sample of observations. Each observation must fall in one and only one category. Without loss of generality, we concentrate on the odd values of the PoVs of the suspicious data.
2. The theoretically expected frequency in category i after embedding an equally distributed message is
$$n_i^* = \frac{|\{\text{color}|\text{sorted index of (color)} \in \{2i, 2i+1\}\}|}{2}$$
3. The measured frequency of occurrence in our random sample is
$$n_i = |\{\text{color}|\text{sorted index of (color)} = 2i\}|$$
4. The χ^2 statistic is given as $\chi^2_{k-1} = \sum_{i=1}^{k} \frac{(n_i - n_i^*)^2}{n_i^*}$ with $k-1$ degrees of freedom.
5. p is the message embedding probability under the condition that the distributions of n_i and n_i^* are equal. It is calculated by integration of the density function;
$$p = 1 - \frac{1}{2^{\frac{k-1}{2}} \Gamma\left(\frac{k-1}{2}\right)} \int_0^{\chi^2_{k-1}} e^{-\frac{x^2}{2}} x^{\frac{k-1}{2}-1} dx$$

Provos[6] extended the χ^2–test by re-sampling the test interval or re-pairing the pixel values; from the pixel pair between x and $(x+1)$, to x and $(x-1)$. Provos also proposed a steganography, called OutGuess, which embeds a secret message bit into a randomly selected LSB then equalizing the frequencies of PoVs to those of the original one with the part of unused LSBs. But OutGuess has a very limited embedding capacity and does not consider the RS statistical analysis.

On the contrary, as the proposed scheme SES changes the real pixel value by adding one to or subtract one from, the embedding procedure does not make the frequencies of PoVs equal. In addition, as though the same length of message as that of the simple LSB embedding steganography is embedded using SES, χ^2–test or extended χ^2–test could not detect at all in the 160 sample images–refer to Table 1.

2.2 RS Steganalysis

Fridrich[2] introduced the RS steganalysis which is based on the partition of an image's pixels as three disjoint groups; Regular, Singular and Unusable groups. Fridrich found that the RS ratio of a typical image should satisfy a certain rule through the large amount of experiments. To explain the details of RS steganalysis, we need to define some notations. Let C be the tested image which has $M \times N$ pixels and with pixel values from the set P. As an example, for an

8-bit grayscale image, $P = \{0, \ldots, 255\}$. Then divide C into disjoint groups G of n adjacent pixels

$$G = (x_1, \ldots, x_n) \in C.$$

The discrimination function is defined as follows;

$$f(x_1, x_2, \ldots, x_n) = \sum_{i=1}^{n-1} |x_{i+1} - x_i| \tag{1}$$

Generally, the noisier the group of pixels $G = (x_1, \ldots, x_n)$, the larger the value of the discrimination function becomes. The invertible operation F on x called *flipping* is also defined like that.

$$\begin{gathered} F_i(F_i(x)) = F_0(x) = x, \quad i \in \{-1, 1\} \\ F_1 : 0 \leftrightarrow 1, 2 \leftrightarrow 3, \ldots, 254 \leftrightarrow 255 \\ F_{-1} : -1 \leftrightarrow 0, 1 \leftrightarrow 2, \ldots, 253 \leftrightarrow 254, 255 \leftrightarrow 256 \end{gathered}$$

$$F_{-1}(x) = F_1(x+1) - 1 \quad \text{for all} \quad x \tag{2}$$

Then the group G is determined on one of three types of pixel groups.

$$\begin{gathered} \text{Regular groups} : G \in R \Leftrightarrow f(F(G)) > f(G) \\ \text{Singular groups} : G \in S \Leftrightarrow f(F(G)) < f(G) \\ \text{Unusable groups} : G \in U \Leftrightarrow f(F(G)) = f(G) \end{gathered}$$

For any mask M, $F_M(G) = (F_{M(1)}(x_1), \ldots, F_{M(n)}(x_n))$ is also determined on one of types in the R, S, U. Fridrich experimentally verified the following two statistical assumptions for a large database of images with unprocessed raw BMPs, JPEGs, and processed BMP images.

$$R_M + S_M \leq 1 \text{ and } R_{-M} + S_{-M} \leq 1$$

$$R_M \cong R_{-M} \text{ and } S_M \cong S_{-M} \tag{3}$$

$$R_M(1/2) = S_M(1/2) \tag{4}$$

where the mask M denotes $M = [F_0\ F_1; F_1\ F_0]$ and $-M$ denotes $[F_0\ F_{-1}; F_{-1}\ F_0]$ either. By an extensive experiments, Fridrich could get the estimation of RS–diagram in Fig 1. If a message with a length p%(in percent of pixels) is embedded in a steged image, without loss of generality, $(p/2)$%–assuming the message is a random bit stream–of a steged image pixels would be flipped with their corresponding values. Then the four points are acquired

$$R_M(p/2), \quad S_M(p/2), \quad R_{-M}(p/2), \quad S_{-M}(p/2)$$

By applying the flipping F_1 and the shift flipping F_{-1} to all pixels the next following four points are also calculated.

$$R_M(1-p/2), \quad S_M(1-p/2), \quad R_{-M}(1-p/2), \quad S_{-M}(1-p/2)$$

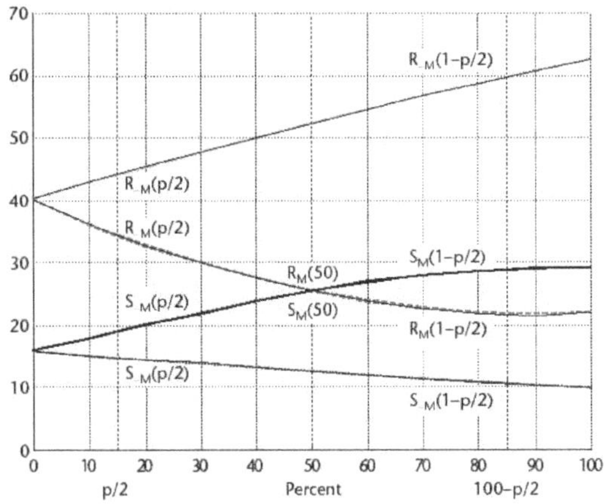

Fig. 1. RS–diagram of an image

The assumptions (3) and (4) make it possible to derive a simple equation (5) for the secret message length p

$$2(d_1 + d_0)x^2 + (d_{-0} - d_{-1} - d_1 - 3d_0)x + d_0 - d_{-0} = 0 \tag{5}$$

$$\begin{aligned} d_0 &= R_M(p/2) - S_M(p/2) \\ d_1 &= R_M(1 - p/2) - S_M(1 - p/2) \\ d_{-0} &= R_{-M}(p/2) - S_{-M}(p/2) \\ d_{-1} &= R_{-M}(1 - p/2) - S_{-M}(1 - p/2) \end{aligned}$$

The message length p is calculated from the root x whose absolute value is smaller by

$$p = x/(x - 1/2) \tag{6}$$

If a steged image satisfies that the constant coefficient of the equation (5) becomes zero i.e. $d_0 - d_{-0} = 0$–the assumption (3), then the possible message length p of that image is also estimated for zero.

Therefore, we designed SES to evade the RS steganalysis after a message embedding, by adjusting the $R_M(p/2)$'s and $R_{-M}(p/2)$'s rate. To do this effect, SES utilizes the unused embedding part of an image for adjusting RS statistic. Like the result Fridrich showed, as the general RS steganalysis brings some false-positive errors within 2% or more, we shall make a control the detection probability by RS steganalysis within this error bound after message embedding.

Because SES has an random effect on the real pixel value during the embedding process, the RS statistic is altered within a small amount of changes(10%) even if the maximum length of message is embedded ; Even though without adjusting RS statistic parts, as the random flipping make nearly same changes to both rates of $R_M(p/2)$ and $R_{-M}(p/2)$, the message embedded probability would be approximately zero. But to be sure the secure steganographic communication, we recommend that more than 50% of the image pixels should be used to adjust RS statistic.

3 The Proposed Scheme

3.1 SES(Steganography Evading Statistical Analyses)

Although SES is designed to preserve the known statistics of an innocent image as mentioned previous section, it can be easily implemented with a small complexity and relatively simple in comparison with F5[7] or OutGuess[6]. The detail parts of SES are as follows.

Fig. 2. Random permutation before message embedding

Step 1. Calculate the RS statistic of a carrier image and save it at the dummy memory.

Step 2. To spread the message embedding positions, scramble the image using the cryptographically secure random permutation which is generated from the shared key. Fig. 2 illustrates the scrambling and embedding procedure.

Step 3. Encrypt a secret message with a key and concatenate the message length l into the output ciphertext C. The message length l is concatenated in front of the ciphertext.

$$S = s_1||s_2||\dots||s_n = l||c_1||\dots||c_n. \quad l = n$$

Step 4. Compare the embedding message bit s_i with the LSB(least significant bit) of a scrambled carrier image's pixel value x_i. If the embedding message bit coincides with the LSB of a scrambled carrier image's pixel value, then apply F_0 operation to x_i. Otherwise, apply F_j operation to x_i, where j is randomly chosen from $\{-1, 1\}$.

$$x_i' = \begin{cases} x_i & \text{if} \quad s_i = LSB(x_i) \\ F_j(x_i) & \text{otherwise} \end{cases}$$

Step 5. Calculate the RS statistic of a steged image after **step 4** and compare this value with the RS statistic of an original carrier image. If the bias exceeds 2%, then adjust the RS statistic of a steged image utilizing the unused parts of the image for embedding.

Step 6. After applying the inverse permutation to the image, then send this image to the receiver. The message extracting is a reverse procedure of embedding.

3.2 Preservation of the Statistical Properties

The χ^2–statistical test is based on the analysis of the statistical measure, the occurrence of PoVs. Because SES alters the same pixel value x_i into $x_i + 1$ or $x_i - 1$ by random choice, after message embedding the frequency of pixel value y_i is not similar to that of $y_i + 1$ or $y_i - 1$. To prove this property more formally, let us assume we have two random variables X, Y for observed pixel values before and after SES embeds a message. $P(X = x)$ denotes the probability for the original cover image with a given pixel value x and $P(Y = y)$ denotes the probability for SES producing image with a given pixel value y. If the message bits are uniformly distributed, we can deduce $P(Y = n)$ as follows.

$$P(Y = n_i) = \frac{1}{2}P(X = n_i) + \frac{1}{4}P(X = n_{i-1}) + \frac{1}{4}P(X = n_{i+1}) \tag{7}$$

$$P(Y = n_{i+1}) = \frac{1}{2}P(X = n_{i+1}) + \frac{1}{4}P(X = n_i) + \frac{1}{4}P(X = n_{i+2}) \tag{8}$$

Without loss of generality, the followings are valid.

$$P(Y = n_i^*) = \frac{1}{2}\{P(Y = n_i) + P(Y = n_{i+1})\}$$

$$= \frac{3}{8}\{P(X = n_i) + P(X = n_{i+1})\} + \frac{1}{8}\{P(X = n_{i-1}) + P(X = n_{i+2})\}.$$

$$P(Y = n_i^*) \neq P(Y = n_i) \quad \text{nor} \quad P(Y = n_i^*) \neq P(Y = n_{i+1})$$

Therefore we can see that SES preserves the statistical property of PoVs after embedding. Notice that the extended χ^2–statistical test can not detect at all in the 160 sample tested images even though the same length(70kbytes per 570kbytes) of the message as the simple LSB embedding steganography is embedded–Table 1.

The proposed scheme, SES also adjust the RS statistic using the 2–cycle property of mask M or shift mask $-M$ after message embedding; $F_M(S_M) = R_M$. Since the random flipping make a nearly same masking effect or shift masking effect on the original image, after message embedding, the difference of R_M and R_{-M} or S_M and S_{-M} is likely to become small, hence only a few pixel groups need to be adjusted. Even the case applying F_1 and F_{-1} by turns instead of a random flipping operation, we can find the fact throughout 160 samples test that the detection probability did not exceed 10% without any RS statistical adjusting. Setting the error bound in **step 5** may be selective by the required security. To get the desirable security, we recommend that more than 50% of the image pixels should be used to adjust RS statistic.

4 Experimental Result

We implemented for a BMP format image and used AES[4] for an encryption and a random number generator. For our test, we collected the various kind(natural images, true color cartoon images and fractal images etc) of images which are acquired from a digital camera, scanner and internet. All of them are fitted to size as $512 \times 379 \times 24$ bits $\cong$ 570kbytes. We selected the 160 sample images whose detection probabilities are all zero by the χ^2–statistical test and the RS steganalysis, then embedded 10kbytes, 40kbytes and 70kbytes of ciphertext into the selected images respectively using the proposed scheme. Table 1 shows the

Table 1. Results of 160 sample images embedding 1bit per pixel

	10kbytes	40kbytes	70kbytes
χ^2–statistical test	0/160	0/160	0/160
RS steganalysis (4%)	0/160	0/160	4/160
RS steganalysis (2%)	0/160	3/160	9/160

result of the 160 sample images for the χ^2–statistical test, the RS steganalysis with the threshold 4%, and the RS steganalysis with the threshold 2%, respectively. As the result shows, the χ^2–statistical test can not detect at all regardless of the embedded message size and the RS steganalysis also can not detect the suspected image mostly. This fact shows that the larger parts of pixels are used to adjust the RS statistic, the fewer test images are detected.

Fig. 3. A steged image(40kbytes)

Table 2 shows the difference of the RS statistics between an original image and a steged image(40kbytes). Fig. 3's RS statistic satisfies equation (3) within

Fig. 4. A steged cartoon image(140kbytes)

Table 2. RS statistics of an innocent image, Fig. 3

	innocent image	stego-image(40kbytes)
number of R_M	59160	58100
number of S_M	26878	27919
number of R_{-M}	58952	58304
number of S_{-M}	26943	27850

an 2% error bound, therefore it can be hardly detected by the RS steganalysis in case of the blind detection. To increase the embedding capacity, the random flipping can be extended from -3 to $+3$ so that 2bits of message information should be embedded into one pixel value. Table 3 represents the results of 160 sample images embedding 2bits per pixel for 70kbytes, 100kbytes and 140kbytes of secret messages respectively. Fig. 5 with large random parts was determined to be highly suspicious by the RS steganalysis even though that image is really innocent. Surprisingly, after we embedded 70kbytes of ciphertext into Fig. 5 using SES, the steged image was determined to be innocent by RS steganalysis in a threshold 2%. Perhaps, it is expected that the random noise parts in the original image is decreased by the random flipping of SES. Table 4 shows the objective image quality distortion measure, SNR(signal to noise ratio) of Figs. 3, 4, 5 and 6.

Fig. 5. An image with large random parts(70kbytes)

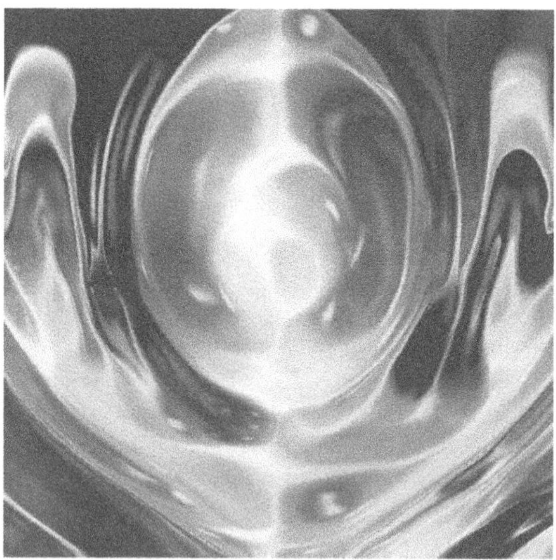

Fig. 6. A steged fractal image(140kbytes)

5 Conclusion and Future Work

In this paper, we proposed a new steganographic scheme evading the known statistical analyses. Since the proposed scheme preserves the statistical measures

Table 3. Results of 160 sample images embedding 2bits per pixel

	70kbytes	100kbytes	140kbytes
χ^2–statistical test	0/160	1/160	2/160
RS steganalysis (4%)	1/160	3/160	7/160
RS steganalysis (2%)	2/160	5/160	12/160

Table 4. S/N of Figures. 3, 4, 5 and 6

	S/N (dB)
shore018.bmp(Fig. 3)	52.537
"cartoon014.bmp(Fig. 4)"	44.345
goat.bmp(Fig. 5)	44.232
fractal02.bmp(Fig. 6)	44.706

which is mainly used to determine whether the secret message is embedded or not, it successfully evades these steganalyses. Moreover, SES can be easily implemented and has a large embedding capacity which is the same as or more than that of the simple LSB embedding steganography. If this scheme is carefully applied to the real society, it may be a good way to the secure communication or also used to the digital rights management system.

References

1. A. Westfeld, A. Pfitzmann, *"Attacks on Steganographic Systems," Information Hiding 1999*: pp.61–76.
2. J. Fridrich, M. Goljan, and R. Du, *"Detecting LSB steganography in color and gray-scale image,"* Magazine of IEEE Multimedia, 2001, pp. 22–28.
3. G.J. Simmons, , *"The Prisoner's Problem and the Subliminal Channel,"* in Advances in Cryptology, *Proceedings of CRYPTO'83*, Plenum Press, 1984, pp.51–67.
4. http://csrc.nist.gov/publications/fips/fips197/fips-197.pdf.
5. U. Maurer, *"A universal statistical test for random bit generators,"* in Advances in Crytology, *Proceedings of CRYPTO'90*,A. J. Menezes and S. A. Vanstone, eds., vol. 537 of Lecture Notes in Computer Science, Springer-Verlag, 1991, pp. 409–426.
6. N. Provos, *"Defending Against Statistical Steganalysis,"* in Proceedings of the 10th USENIX Security Symposium, 2001, pp.323–335.
7. A. Westfeld, *"F5–A Steganographic Algorithm,"* Information Hiding, 4th International Workshop, Pittsburgh, USA, April 2001, Proceedings, LNCS 2137, Springer-Verlag Berlin Heidelberg 2001, pp. 289–302

A Three-Dimensional Watermarking Algorithm Using the DCT Transform of Triangle Strips

Jeonghee Jeon, Sang-Kwang Lee, and Yo-Sung Ho

Kwangju Institute of Science and Technology (K-JIST)
1 Oryong-dong Puk-gu, Kwangju, 500-712, Korea
{jhjeon, sklee, hoyo}@kjist.ac.kr

Abstract. Since it is easy to design robust and imperceptible watermarking algorithms against malicious attacks, most watermarking techniques insert watermark signals in the frequency domain. However, three-dimensional (3-D) geometric models have difficulties in natural parameterization for frequency-based decomposition. In this paper, we propose a new scheme for 3-D model watermarking in the DCT domain. In order to insert and extract watermark signals in the frequency domain, we traverse the 3-D mesh model to generate triangle strips and transform their vertex coordinates in the spatial domain into frequency coefficients in the DCT domain. Watermarks are then inserted into the mid-frequency band of AC coefficients for robustness and imperceptibility. We show that the inserted watermarks survive various attacks, such as additive random noise, geometry compression by the MPEG-4 SNHC standard, affine transformation, and multiple watermarking.

1 Introduction

In recent years, digital multimedia data that are popularly exploited over the Web, provide a lot of advantages, such as complete duplication and ease distribution through the Web. However, owners of digital data are now being faced with unauthorized threaten of illegal users. In order to protect the ownership or copyright of digital media data, such as image, video, and audio, we try to employ data encryption and watermarking techniques. While data encryption techniques are mainly used to protect digital data during the transmission from the sender to the receiver, digital watermarking techniques are used for copyright protection, fingerprinting, broadcast monitoring, data authentication, indexing, medical safety, and data hiding [1][2].

Digital watermarking for three-dimensional (3-D) geometric models, such as surface model, solid model, or polygonal model, has received less attention from researchers because digital watermarking techniques for image, video and audio data cannot directly be applied to the work for 3-D data. The major reasons are that arbitrary surfaces of 3-D models lack natural parameterization for frequency-based decomposition and that simplification or other attacks may modify connectivity of the 3-D mesh model [3]. Most watermarking schemes for 1-D and 2-D data insert watermarks in the frequency domain because it is easier to design robust and

T. Kalker et al. (Eds.): IWDW 2003, LNCS 2939, pp. 508–517, 2004.
© Springer-Verlag Berlin Heidelberg 2004

imperceptible watermarking schemes in the frequency bands against possible malicious attacks.

Kanai et al. proposed a watermarking scheme for 3-D polygonal models based on the wavelet transform [4]. Their paper is the first one that applied a transformed-domain watermarking approach to 3-D meshes. Their watermarks are robust against affine transformation, partial resection, and random noise added to vertex coordinates. However, their scheme requires the mesh to have 1-to-4 subdivision connectivity. Praun et al. presented a robust watermarking scheme that is applicable to 3-D models of arbitrary vertex connectivity in the transform domain [3]. Their scheme modifies the shape of the mesh by a spatial kernel to insert watermarks in the low frequency band of the shape information. Yin et al. [5] reported a watermarking algorithm based on multiresolution decomposition of polygonal meshes by Guskov's signal processing method [6], which separates a mesh into detail and coarse feature sequences. They demonstrated that the algorithm is robust against vertex reordering, noise addition, simplification, filtering and enhancement, cropping, etc. Ohbuchi, et al. proposed a frequency-domain approach to watermarking 3-D shapes [7]. The algorithm employs mesh-spectral analysis to modify mesh shapes in their transform domain and it is robust against mesh simplification, and remeshing combined with resection, similarity transformation, and other attacks.

In this paper, we propose a new watermarking scheme for 3-D triangle meshes in the discrete cosine transform (DCT) domain. After we explain the concept of the proposed watermarking scheme, we describe watermark insertion and extraction operations in Section 2. Section 3 presents experimental results of the proposed scheme, and we conclude in Section 4.

2 A New Watermarking Scheme for 3-D Mesh Models

As shown in Fig. 1, our proposed watermarking scheme consists of three main function blocks: creating triangle strips, forward DCT and inverse DCT transform for vertex coordinates of each strip, and watermark generation.

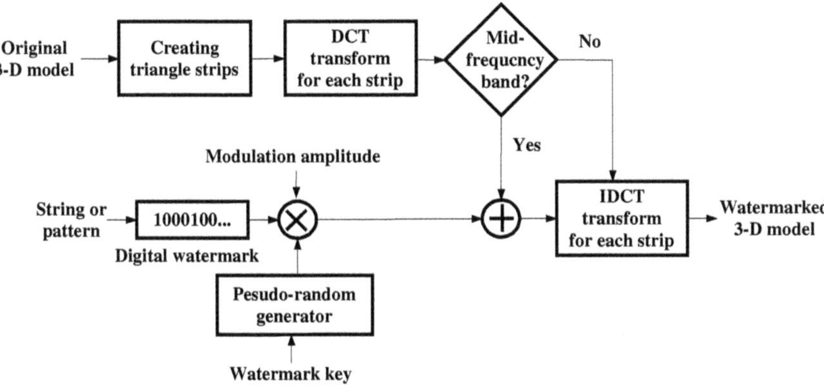

Fig. 1. Watermark insertion scheme

After the original 3-D model is represented by vertex coordinates and connectivity of VRML (virtual reality modeling language) file, we create triangle strips by traversing the model. We then transform the set of the vertex coordinates in the spatial domain into the DCT domain along the x-, y-, and z-coordinate, independently. Watermark signals are inserted into the mid-frequency band of AC coefficients, and then the watermarked 3-D model is represented after the inverse DCT transform.

2.1 Generation of Triangle Strips

Efficient rendering of triangle-based meshes often requires that we pack them into triangle strips. Strips provide interesting advantages: the mesh is stored in a more compact way because of wasting less memory space, and we can save bandwidth when we send it to our favorite rendering application program interface (API).

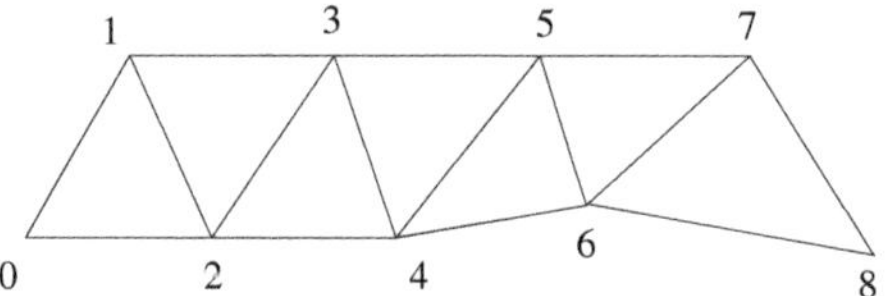

Fig. 2. A triangle strip

As shown in Fig. 2, the 3-D mesh model contains a list of connected triangles. Each triangle is made of three vertex references and two edges of them may be shared with one triangle or another. From this sharing, the list of indices forms a triangle strip. Thus, we can describe the triangulation using the strip {0,1,2,3,4,5,6,7,8} and assume the convention that the *i*-th triangle is described by *i*-th, (*i*+1)-th, and (*i*+2)-th vertices of the sequential strip. The sequential strip can reduce the cost to transmit *n* triangles from 3*n* to (*n*+2) vertices. In order to create triangle strips from a triangle mesh, we use the following algorithm [8].

Step 1. Choose a starting face for each strip.
Step 2. Choose a direction (i.e. an edge) in which we walk along the strip.
Step 3. Extend the strip in the chosen direction until there are no forward connections.
Step 4. Reverse the strip and extend it in the opposite direction.
Step 5. Go to *Step 1* until all faces have been visited.

Here, we note that the number of the triangle strips created by the algorithm can be different depending on mesh connectivity information. The number of vertices within each strip can also be different. Therefore, we can exploit these characteristics to design a new watermarking algorithm. First, the user who does not know the starting face for creating triangle strips cannot distinguish a watermark pattern because the starting face is determined by connectivity of the 3-D mesh. It is a very useful property for information hiding. Second, the triangle strips also have an attribution of mesh partition, such as a subset of the original mesh. Thus, if this attribution is used for 3-D model watermarking, we can improve robustness of watermarks from malicious attacks that try to remove watermarks. Finally, the multiple triangle strips can play an important role for strengthening robustness because watermarks can be repeatedly inserted into them. As a result, we can make use of these properties of triangle strips in designing a new watermarking scheme for 3-D triangle models.

2.2 DCT Transform of Triangle Strips

The discrete cosine transform (DCT) for 3-D geometric models is found in geometry compression of 3-D animation models [9]. They select one root triangle of the given 3-D model randomly and traverse neighboring vertices from the root triangle in the clockwise direction. The traversed edge is called the cutting edge since it cuts the given triangle along the edge. Once a triangle strip is obtained, we segment it by grouping vertices uniformly. Therefore, this segmentation algorithm produces several independent parts according to the topology of the 3-D model and the decomposition can group the similar vertices in the spatial domain. After the segmented blocks are transformed independently by 1-D DCT along the x-, y-, and z-coordinate, we encode the DCT coefficients. The definition of the 1-D forward DCT and inverse DCT are given by

$$\text{Forward DCT: } X(k) = \sqrt{\frac{2}{N}}\, C_k \sum_{n=0}^{N-1} x(n) \cos\left[\frac{(2n+1)k\pi}{2N}\right], \quad k = 0,1,\ldots,N-1 \tag{1}$$

$$\text{Inverse DCT: } x(n) = \sqrt{\frac{2}{N}} \sum_{k=0}^{N-1} C_k X(k) \cos\left[\frac{(2n+1)k\pi}{2N}\right], \quad n = 0,1,\ldots,N-1 \tag{2}$$

where $C_k = \begin{cases} 1/\sqrt{2} & k = 0 \\ 1 & k \neq 0 \end{cases}$.

In order to transform vertex coordinates of each strip, we employ the 1-D DCT transform. While the number of strips used in the algorithm is one, the number of triangle strips generated by the algorithm is not just one, but multiple. Note that the number of strips can be different depending on the connectivity information of the 3-D mesh. The size of the segmented block can be adjusted by padding the last AC coefficient, as shown in Fig. 3.

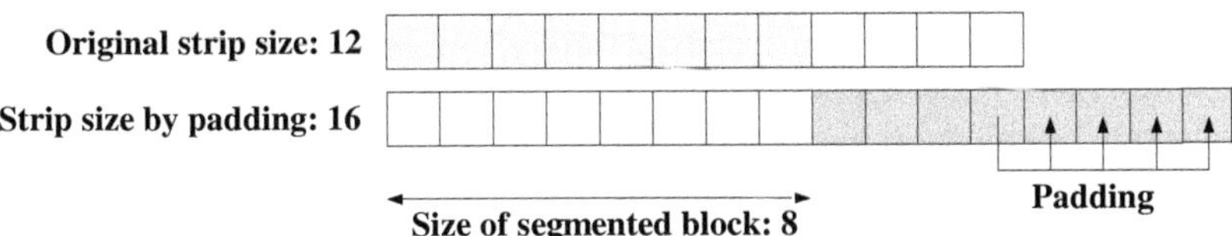

Fig. 3. Adjustment of segmented block size

2.3 Watermark Insertion

In the frequency domain, the low-frequency band represents the global shape and the high-frequency band describes local or detail contents. In various watermarking schemes, the frequency band is frequently used to insert watermark signals because it is not only imperceptible but also robust. In our scheme, we embed watermark signals into the mid-frequency band of AC coefficients in the DCT domain, as shown in Fig. 1, where the watermark insertion operation is similar to the spread-spectrum approach [10][11]. The watermark signal can be a company logo, some meaningful string, or random values. In this paper, a string of five characters is used as a watermark. The string provided by the user is converted into the ASCII code a as

$$a_j = (a_1, \cdots, a_m), \ a_j \in \{0,1\} \tag{3}$$

In order to spread the digit signal into a wide bandwidth, each bit a_j is duplicated by the chip rate c.

$$b_i = a_j, \quad j \cdot c \le i < (j+1) \cdot c \tag{4}$$

The chip rate c plays an important role of increment of robustness against an additive random noise. If b_i is zero, it is changed to the negative sign by

$$b_i' = 2b_i - 1 \tag{5}$$

Let us now consider the modulation operation of DCT coefficients in the x-coordinate only. As shown in Fig. 1, we insert the watermark signal into the mid-frequency band of AC coefficients. New DCT coefficients $\overline{W}_{x,j}$ are derived from the current DCT coefficients $W_{x,i}$ by

$$\overline{W}_{x,j} = W_{x,i} + b_i' \cdot p_i \cdot \alpha \tag{6}$$

where b_i' is the watermark signals, α is the modulation amplitude, and p_i is a pseudo-random number sequence generated by the watermark key. A bandwidth $MidFrequencyBand$ is determined by

$$MidFrequencyBand = (Min, Max] \tag{7}$$

$$\begin{cases} Min = (\dfrac{BlockSize}{2})/2 \\ Max = Min + (\dfrac{BlockSize}{2}) \end{cases}$$

where *BlockSize* is the size of the segmented block defined by the user. As a result, Eq. (6) produces modified coefficients. In order to insert watermark signals into the coefficients of y- and z-coordinates, we also apply the same operations. The watermarked 3-D model is easily represented by Eq. (2).

2.4 Watermark Extraction

Fig.4 shows the watermark extraction operation in the proposed private watermarking algorithm, which needs the original and the watermarked 3-D models. This operation can be expressed by

$$b_i' = (\overline{W}_{x,i} - W_{x,i}) \cdot p_i \tag{8}$$

The extracted b' is changed to b by Eq. (5) and b is converted to a by Eq. (4). After a is converted to a string by the ASCII code, we can assert the ownership by the extracted string.

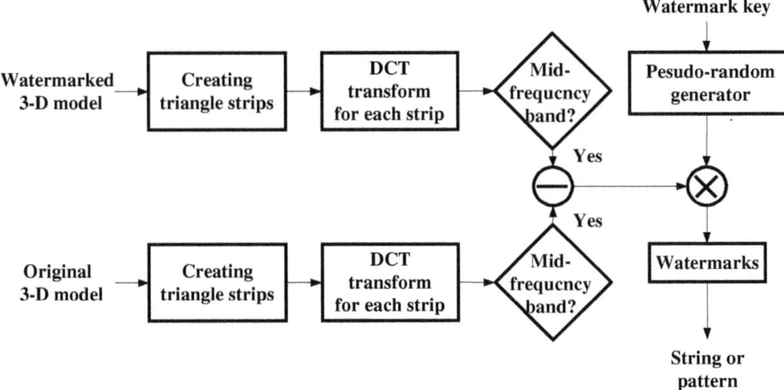

Fig. 4. Watermark extraction scheme

3 Experimental Results

An experimental system for 3-D watermark insertion and watermark extraction has been developed in MS VC++ 6.0. In order to evaluate the perceptual invisibility between the original and the watermarked models and resiliency against various attacks, such as additive random noise, mesh compression, affine transformation, and multiple watermarking, we perform computer simulations on 3-D mesh models: Beethoven model with 2521 vertices and 5030 faces, Horse model with 2620 vertices and 5200 faces, and Bunny model with 3116 vertices and 6100 faces, as shown in Fig. 5(a), Fig. 5(b), and Fig. 5(c), respectively.

3.1 Parameters for Digital Watermarking

Modulation amplitude. Basically, the modulation amplitude α is selected by the user in such a way that it is small enough to preserve appearance of the model while it is large enough to withstand from malicious attacks.

Perceptual invisibility. We employ the MESH (measuring error between surfaces using the Hausdorff distance) tool [13] to measure the distortion, which indicates the degree deformed by watermarks or attacks. The MESH tool evaluates on a variety of 3-D mesh models with the root-mean-square (RMS) distance as a function of the sampling step, which plays an important role in the precision of the measured distance. Among various methods to calculate RMS distances, we use one with the symmetric distance.

Watermark lengths, chip rate, and block size. In this paper, the watermark string, the chip rate, and the size of segmented block for DCT are "KJIST" with 35 bits, one, and eight, respectively. As we mentioned, even if the chip rate plays an important role for strengthening robustness of watermarks, we use one as the parameter value because watermarks are repeatedly inserted into the mid-frequency band of AC coefficients along the x-, y-, and z-coordinates of multiple triangle strips.

3.2 Perceptual Invisibility

In order to calculate distortions in 1-D signals or 2-D images, we employ various measures, such as the mean square error (MSE) and peak signal-to-noise ratio (PSNR). However, a measure for 3-D mesh models has rarely covered. Recently, Aspert et al. reported a method to estimate the distance between discrete 3-D surfaces [13]. We employ their method to measure the distortion of watermarked 3-D models.

Basically, the original data should be perceptually unchanged by embedding watermarks, but be imposed small modifications on it. In order to minimize a variety of the original 3-D model and withstand from some attacks, we inserted watermarks into the mid-frequency band. Simulation results for the RMS distance between the original and the watermarked models are shown in Fig. 5 and Table 1.

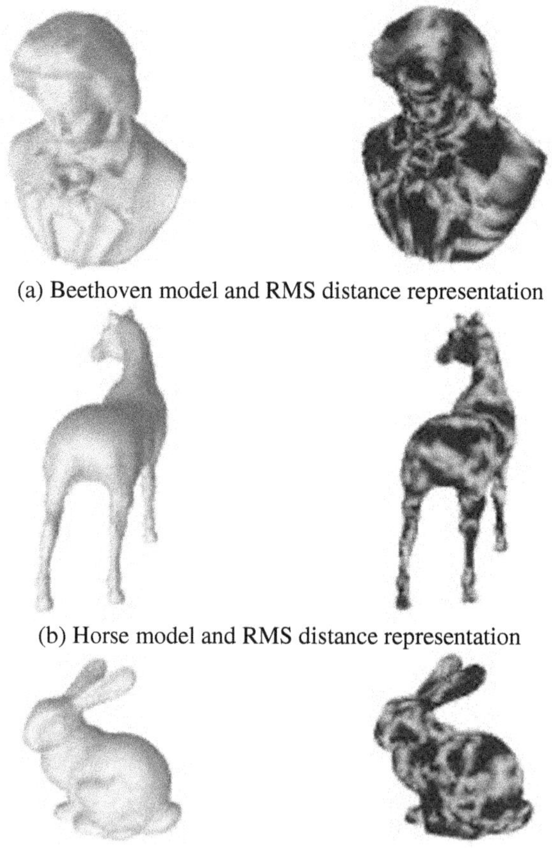

(a) Beethoven model and RMS distance representation

(b) Horse model and RMS distance representation

(c) Bunny model and RMS distance representation

Fig. 5. The original model and visual representation of RMS distance between the original and watermarked models

Fig. 5 shows that watermarks are located in the areas with the mid-frequency band, which is not fully smoothing and not roughly bumping. When the RMS distance of the watermarked model is increased, the surface color is dissolved. There is a trade-off between imperceptibility and robustness.

3.2 Resiliency against Various Attacks

Watermark detections for attacked Beethoven, Horse, and Bunny models are listed in Table 1, and some models are shown in Fig. 6. The models embedded with the modulation amplitude α in Table 1 are attacked by additive random noise, geometry compression by the MPEG-4 SNHC coding standard, affine transform, and multiple watermarking.

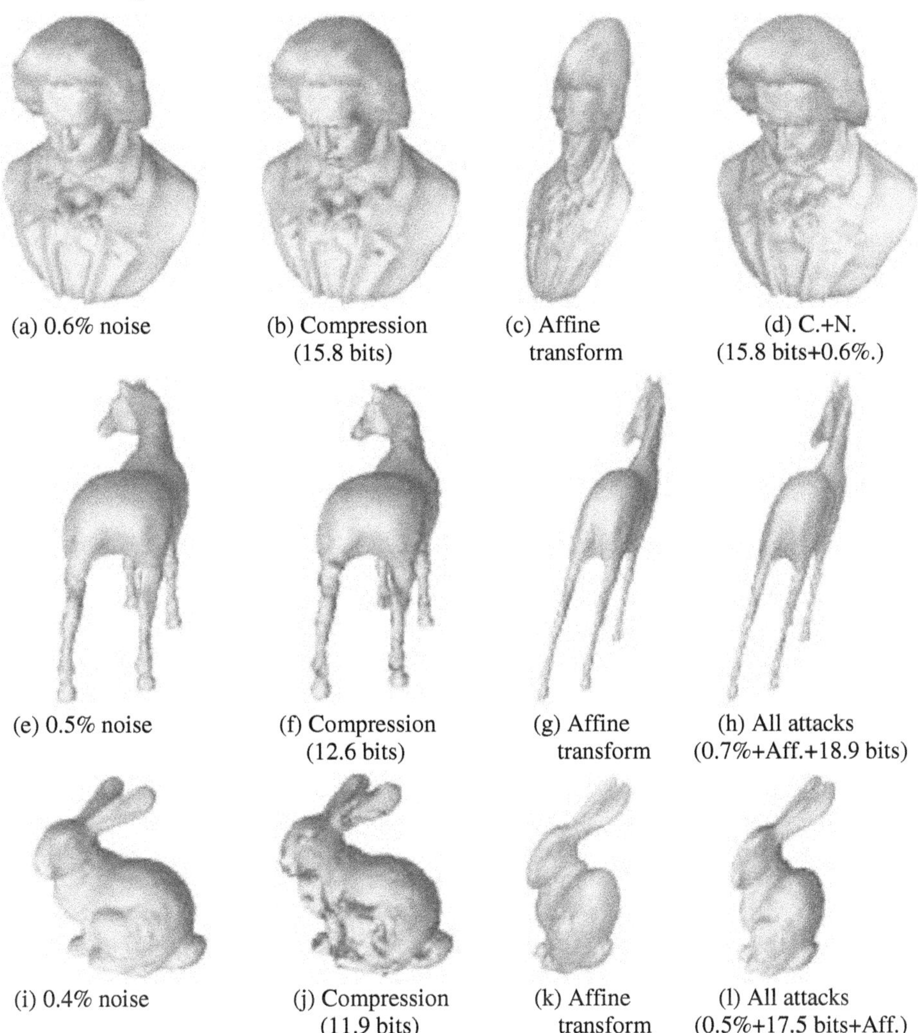

(a) 0.6% noise (b) Compression (15.8 bits) (c) Affine transform (d) C.+N. (15.8 bits+0.6%.)

(e) 0.5% noise (f) Compression (12.6 bits) (g) Affine transform (h) All attacks (0.7%+Aff.+18.9 bits)

(i) 0.4% noise (j) Compression (11.9 bits) (k) Affine transform (l) All attacks (0.5%+17.5 bits+Aff.)

Fig. 6. Attacked models

Table 1. Resiliency against attacks

Models (Number of inserted string)	α (Alpha)	RMS	Attacks								
			Additive Random Noise (%)			Geometry Compression (96 bits)			Aff.	Multiple Watermarking	
Beethoven (21)	3.05	0.075	0.6*	0.4	0.2	15.8*	18.8	21.8	7*	C+N*	All
			16	20	20	11	20	21		2	0
Horse (24)	0.0005	0.079	0.5*	0.4	0.2	12.3*	15.3	18.3	9*	N+A	All*
			18	20	23	1	15	23		7	6
Bunny (23)	0.0006	0.097	0.5	0.4*	0.2	11.9*	14.6	17.5	7*	N+C	All*
			19	19	21	0	2	19		12	7

(C: Geometry Compression, N: Additive Random Noise)
(Entries with asterisks are shown in Fig. 6)

As the additive random noise attack, we add noises to vertex coordinates of the watermarked model with a uniform random noise. In Fig. 6 and Table 1, the percentage of the additive random noise represents the ratio between the largest displacement and the largest side of the watermarked model [3]. As show in Table 1, for example, our algorithm extracts the full string "KJIST" of sixteen, twenty, and twenty numbers, respectively, when 0.6, 0.4, and 0.2 % random noises are uniformly added to the watermarked Beethoven model.

For the case of the compression attack, we also apply the geometry compression by the MPEG-4 SNHC standard [12]. Generally, the x-, y-, z-vertex coordinates of the 3-D polygonal model are stored by the floating-point variable of 32 bits per each coordinate. Thus, each of the first row elements in the compression attack is the bit number compressed by the MPEG-4 standard compression algorithm, and each of the second row elements represents the number of strings recovered completely.

For the affine transformation, we translate, scale, rotate, and shear the watermarked model. The multiple watermarking attacks have two different types. The first type is a consecutive attack to the first column of multiple watermarking in Table 1. For example, C+N attack of the Beethoven model adds random noise to the watermarked model after geometry compression. The second type is all attack, which applies the affine transformation to the Beethoven model after the first type attack.

In order to evaluate performance of the proposed algorithm, we do not use the bit error rate (BER), which is the ratio of the numbers of the inserted and extracted watermarks because the owner can clearly assert the ownership of the 3-D model through perfect reconstruction of the inserted watermark string. From Table 1 and Fig. 6, we notice that the inserted watermark survives various attacks, such as additive random noise, geometry compression by the MPEG-4 SNHC standard, affine transformation, and multiple watermarking. Especially, our watermarking scheme is very robust against signal processing operations, such as additive random noise; however, it is a little weak against geometry attacks.

4 Conclusions

In this paper, we have developed a 3-D watermarking algorithm for triangle strips in the DCT domain. The proposed watermark embedding operation inserted watermark signals into the mid-frequency band of AC coefficients of triangle strips because the mid-frequency band is less sensitive to the human eye than high- or low-frequency bands. Using the RMS distance measure, we have shown that our watermark insertion is effective for imperceptibility of the watermarked 3-D model and also demonstrated that the watermark embedded by the proposed algorithm has strong resiliency against typical attacks, such as additive random noise, 3-D geometry compression by the MPEG-4 standard, affine transformation, and multiple watermarking operations. Furthermore, the proposed scheme is robust to various signal processing attacks.

Acknowledgements. This work was supported in part by Kwangju Institute of Science and Technology (K-JIST), in part by the Ministry of Information and Communication (MIC) through the Realistic Broadcasting IT Research Center at K-JIST, and in part by the Ministry of Education (MOE) through the Brain Korea 21 (BK21) project.

References

1. Katzenbeisser, L. and Petitcolas, F. A. P.: Information Hiding Techniques for Steganography and Digital Watermarking, Artech House, (2000)
2. Langelaar, G. C., Setyawan, I., and Lagendijk, R. L.: Watermarking Digital Image and Video Data, IEEE Signal Processing Magazine, (2000) 20–46
3. Praun, E., Hoppe, H., and Finkelstein, A.: Robust Mesh Watermarking, SIGGRAPH Proceedings, (1999) 49–56
4. Kanai, S., Date, H., and Kishinami, T.: Digital Watermarking for 3D Polygons using Multiresolution Wavelets Decomposition, Proceedings Sixth IFIP WG 5.2 GEO-6, (1998) 296–307
5. Yin, K., Pan, Z., Shi, J., and Zhang, D.: Robust Mesh Watermarking Based on Multiresolution Processing, Computer and Graphics, Vol. 25, (2001) 409–420
6. Guskov, I., Sweldens, W., and Shröder, P.: Multiresolution Signal Processing for Meshes, SIGGRAPH Proceedings, (1999) 325–334
7. Obuchi, R., Mukaiyama, A., and Takahashi, S.: A Frequency-Domain Approach to Watermarking 3D Shapes, Computer Graphics Forum, Vol. 21, No. 3, (2002) 373–382
8. Terdiman, P's web site: http:// codercorner.com/Strips.htm
9. Ahn, J. H., Kim, C. S., Kuo, C. C., and Ho, Y. S.: Motion Compensated Compression of 3D Animation Models, SPIE Visual Communications and Image Processing, (2002) 593–602
10. Cox. I.J., Kilian, J., Leighton, T., and Shamoon, T.: Secure Spread Spectrum Watermarking for Multimedia, IEEE Transactions on Image Processing, Vol. 6, No. 12, (1997) 1673–1687
11. Hartung, F., Eisert, P., and Griod, B.: Digital Watermarking of MPEF-4 Facial Animation Parameters, Computer and Graphics, Vol. 22, No. 4, (1998) 425–435
12. ISO/IEC 14496-2, Coding of Audio-Visual Objects: Visual (MPEG-4 video), Committee Draft, (1997)
13. Aspert, N., Santa-Cruz, D., and Ebrahimi, T.: MESH: Measuring Errors between Surfaces using the Hausdroff Distance, Proceedings of the IEEE International Conference in Multimedia and Expo (ICME 2002), Vol. 1, (2002) 705–708

High Quality Perceptual Steganographic Techniques

Kisik Chang[1], Changho Jung[2], Sangjin Lee[2], and Wooil Yang[2]

[1] Service & Applications, Institute for Infocomm Research(I2R)
21 Heng Mui Keng Terrace 119613 Singapore
stusck@i2r.a-star.edu.sg

[2] Center for Information Security Technologies(CIST)
Korea University, Seoul, 136-701, Republic of KOREA
zangho@cist.korea.ac.kr, sangjin@korea.ac.kr,
doitnow@hananet.net

Abstract. Recently, several steganographic algorithms for two-color binary images have been proposed[16,1,14,2]. In this paper, we propose steganographic algorithms which embeds a secret message into bitmap images and palette-based images. To embed a message, the suggested algorithm divides a bitmap image into bit-plane images from *LSB*-plane to *MSB*-plane for each pixel, and considers each bit-plane image as a binary one. The algorithm splits each bit-plane image into $m \times n$ blocks, and embeds a r-bit($r = \lfloor \log_2(mn+1) \rfloor - 1$) message into the block. And our schemes embed a message to every bit-plane from LSB to MSB to maximize the amount of embedded message and to minimize the degradation. The schemes change at most two pixels in each block. Therefore, the maximal color changes of the new algorithm are much smaller than other bit-plane embedding schemes' such as the sequential substitution schemes[10,7,11].

1 Introduction

Techniques for steganography are getting sophisticated and have been used widely. The goal of steganography is to conceal the existence of secret communication between Sender and Receiver without being suspected by Warden. Therefore, it is important that steganography must have not only the property of indistinguishability between the cover-object and the stego-object, but also the function of inserting the secret message practically large enough into the cover-object. Even there are many proposals and published steganographic tools, it is hard to find anything that has the above-mentioned two properties simultaneously. If a steganographic algorithm is secure enough, it does not have enough capacity for the practical usage, and vice versa.

We propose steganographic algorithms which embed a secret message into a color images, such as a bitmap image and a palette-based image by extending Tseng and Pan's method[14]. Additionally, this algorithm also can be applied for other format files like audio and video clips. To embed a message, first our

T. Kalker et al. (Eds.): IWDW 2003, LNCS 2939, pp. 518–531, 2004.
© Springer-Verlag Berlin Heidelberg 2004

scheme splits the bitmap image into three color components and divides each color-plane into eight bit-planes from *LSB*-plane to *MSB*-plane. We are able to consider each bit-plane as a binary image and can adapt the TP's embedding method to each bit-plane.

The algorithm splits each bit-plane image into $m \times n$ blocks, and embeds a r-bit message into a block of each bit-plane, where $r = \lfloor \log_2(mn+1) \rfloor - 1$. This algorithm can embeds a message to every bit-plane from LSB to MSB to maximize the amount of embedded message. The maximum capacity is $\lfloor M/m \rfloor \times \lfloor N/n \rfloor \times r \times k \times 3$, where the parameters are the same as before. To minimize the degradation the scheme it changes at most two pixels in each block, and the upper bound of the number of modified pixels in a stego-image is $\lfloor M/m \rfloor \times \lfloor N/n \rfloor \times k \times 2 \times 3$, where the size of a cover-image is $M \times N$, the size of a block is $m \times n$, k is the number of used bit-planes, and 3 is the number of color-planes. So the maximal color change of the new algorithm is less smaller than that of the sequential substitution schemes[10,7,11], which changes almost pixels in a stego-image.

1.1 Related Works

Wu and Lee proposed an algorithm for two-color facsimile images[16], which embed a bit into a block of a cover-image. Since WL's scheme has a shortcoming in the capacity, Chen, Pan, and Tseng made up for CPT's by using a weight matrix[1]. But these two algorithms still have a fault for keeping the quality of a stego-image after embedding a message, because they select the location of pixels randomly in embedding process. Tseng and Pan remedied CPT's scheme to resolve the problem with a distance matrix[14]. Although TP's scheme keeps the quality of a stego-image, there might be still some skipped block, which we can not embed a message bits. Thus, Chang, Wu, and Hwang revised TP's scheme with concept of a distance matrix of an inverse block[2]. We describe Tseng and Pan's algorithm briefly in following sections.

Kawaguchi and Eason proposed a bit-plane based steganographic algorithm, BPCS for bitmap images[7]. BPCS algorithm has larger capacity than other steganographic algorithms for bitmap images, but driven by emphasizing the capacity, proponents did not consider the quality of stego-image after embedding a message. Recently Niimi, Eason, Noda, and Kawaguchi proposed a BPCS bit-plane based steganographic algorithm for palette-based images[11].

This paper has six sections. Section 2 describes the preliminaries for our works and Section 3 presents our schemes for color-images and we analysis them in Section 4. In Section 5, we present the result of experiment and Section 6 concludes the paper.

2 Preliminaries

In this section we define some terminology and symbols which are used over this paper. We will treat the image as the integer matrix. Given two matrices, B_1 and B_2 which are the same size, we define $B_1 \wedge B_2$ as *bit-wise AND* operation, and $B_1 \oplus B_2$ as *bit-wise eXclusive-OR* operation. Given a matrix B, we denote by $B_{j,k}$ the element of B at j-th row and k-th column, by $[B_i]_{j,k}$, the element of a i-th block and by $\mathsf{SUM}(B)$ the sum of all elements in the matrix B. Additional symbols are denoted as following:

- B : a binary cover-image
- K : a key matrix of size $m \times n$
- W : a weight matrix of size $m \times n$

A binary cover-image B will be partitioned into blocks of fixed size $m \times n$. For simplicity we assume that the size of cover image B is multiple of $m \times n$. Now we will illustrate the concept of TP's algorithm[14]. Tseng and Pan use the concept of a distance matrix and a weight matrix to reduce deterioration of the image and to preserve the quality. First, we assume that for a given binary cover-image B will be modified to two binary stego-images B_1 and B_2 as follows:

$$B = \begin{bmatrix} 1\,1\,0\,0\,0 \\ 1\,1\,0\,0\,0 \\ 1\,0\,0\,0\,0 \\ 1\,0\,0\,0\,0 \\ 1\,0\,0\,0\,0 \end{bmatrix}, \; B_1 = \begin{bmatrix} 1\,1\,0\,0\,0 \\ 1\,1\,0\,0\,0 \\ 1\,\mathbf{1}\,0\,0\,0 \\ 1\,0\,0\,0\,0 \\ 1\,0\,0\,0\,0 \end{bmatrix}, \; B_2 = \begin{bmatrix} 1\,1\,0\,0\,0 \\ 1\,1\,0\,0\,0 \\ 1\,0\,0\,0\,0 \\ 1\,0\,0\,\mathbf{1}\,0 \\ 1\,0\,0\,0\,0 \end{bmatrix} \tag{1}$$

Both B_1 and B_2 differ from B in one pixel. As shown above matrixes, we can grant that B_1 is more similar to B than B_2, because the position of a changed pixel in B_1 is next to the element whose value 1 in B. Thus the modified pixel in B_2 is more noticeable. Now we define a distance matrix as follows:

Definition 1. *An integer matrix, which has the same size as B, is called a* distance matrix *such that*

$$\mathsf{dist}([B]_{i,j}) = \min_{\forall x,y} \left\{ \sqrt{|i-x|^2 + |j-y|^2} \mid [B]_{i,j} \neq [B]_{x,y} \right\},$$

$\mathsf{dist}([B]_{i,j})$ *is distance from* $[B]_{i,j}$ *to the closest pixel* $[B]_{x,y}$ *such that the complement pixel of* $[B]_{i,j}$ *is equal to* $[B]_{x,y}$.

The distance matrix will be used to choose a pixel which will be modified in embedding process. For example, the distance matrix of previous block B in Eq.(1) is as follows:

$$\mathsf{dist}(B) = \begin{bmatrix} 2 & 1 & 1 & 2 & 3 \\ \sqrt{2} & 1 & 1 & 2 & 3 \\ 1 & 1 & \sqrt{2} & \sqrt{5} & \sqrt{10} \\ 1 & 1 & 2 & \sqrt{8} & \sqrt{13} \\ 1 & 1 & 2 & 3 & 4 \end{bmatrix} \tag{2}$$

TP's algorithm uses a revised weight matrix to improve the quality of the stego-image after embedding the message.

Definition 2. *An $m \times n$ matrix W is called a* revised weight matrix *if W is a weight matrix and for each 2×2 subblock of W, the block contains at least one odd element.*

For example, the following shows three possible ways to define a 6×6 revised weight matrix.

$$\begin{bmatrix} o\,o\,o\,o\,o\,o \\ e\,e\,e\,e\,e\,e \\ o\,o\,o\,o\,o\,o \\ e\,e\,e\,e\,e\,e \\ o\,o\,o\,o\,o\,o \\ e\,e\,e\,e\,e\,e \end{bmatrix}, \begin{bmatrix} o\,e\,o\,e\,o\,e \\ e\,o\,e\,o\,e\,o \\ o\,e\,o\,e\,o\,e \\ e\,o\,e\,o\,e\,o \\ o\,e\,o\,e\,o\,e \\ e\,o\,e\,o\,e\,o \end{bmatrix}, \begin{bmatrix} e\,o\,e\,o\,e\,o \\ o\,e\,o\,e\,o\,e \\ e\,o\,e\,o\,e\,o \\ o\,e\,o\,e\,o\,e \\ e\,o\,e\,o\,e\,o \\ o\,e\,o\,e\,o\,e \end{bmatrix}, \tag{3}$$

where 'o' and 'e' represent an odd and even number, respectively. The number of revised weight matrices is

$$\begin{aligned} &\left({}_{\frac{mn}{2}}C_{2^r-1} \times (2^r-1)! \times (2^r-1)^{\frac{mn}{2}-(2^r-1)}\right) \\ &\times \left({}_{\frac{mn}{2}}C_{2^r-1} \times (2^{r-1}-1)! \times (2^{r-1}-1)^{\frac{mn}{2}-(2^{r-1}-1)}\right). \end{aligned} \tag{4}$$

2.1 Embedding Process

TP's algorithm embeds r bits message into a block B_i of size $m \times n$ where

$$r \leqslant \lfloor \log_2(mn+1) \rfloor - 1. \tag{5}$$

To hide the r bits message, we should modify at most two pixels in a block. We will describe the embedding procedure roughly here.

For a given message $b_1 b_2 \ldots b_r$, embedding process is constructed to satisfy both condition Eq.(6) and Eq.(7), where B' is a stego-image

$$\begin{aligned} &\mathsf{SUM}((B_i' \oplus K) \otimes W) \equiv 0 \mod 2 \\ &\quad \Rightarrow \mathsf{SUM}((B_i' \oplus K) \otimes W)/2 \equiv b_1 b_2 \ldots b_r \mod 2^{r+1} \end{aligned} \tag{6}$$

$$\mathsf{SUM}((B_i' \oplus K) \otimes W) \equiv 1 \mod 2 \;\Rightarrow\; \text{there is no message in } B' \tag{7}$$

For each B_i, compute Eq.(8)

$$\mathsf{SUM}((B_i \oplus K) \otimes W). \tag{8}$$

And for each $B_i \oplus K$, and for $w = 1, 2, \ldots, 2^r - 1$ calculate the set Eq.(10),

$$S_w = \Big\{(j,k) | \Big[(([W]_{j,k} = w) \wedge ([B_i \oplus K]_{j,k} = 0) \wedge \Big(\mathsf{dist}\Big([B_i]_{j',k'}\Big) \leqslant \sqrt{2}\Big)\Big] \quad (9)$$
$$\vee \Big[(([W]_{j,k} = 2^{r+1} - w) \wedge ([B_i \oplus K]_{j,k} = 1) \wedge \Big(\mathsf{dist}\Big([B_i]_{j',k'}\Big) \leqslant \sqrt{2}\Big)\Big]\Big\},$$

where $\mathsf{dist}([B]_{j',k'})$ is an entry corresponding to the element of $\mathsf{dist}([B]_{j,k})$ in a block B_i. We define $S_w = S_{w'}$ for a $w \equiv w' \mod 2^{r+1}$.
Intuitively, we can handle the quality of the stego-image with the set, Eq.(10). Thus we are able to select a pixel which be flipped only when the complement of pixel is laid in a distance of $\sqrt{2}$. Finally calculate a weight difference as following Eq.(10) with modulus 2^{r+1}

$$d \equiv b_1 b_2 \ldots b_r || 0_{(2)} - \mathsf{SUM}((B_i \oplus K) \otimes W) \quad (10)$$

Now we must increase the SUM computed in Eq.(6) by d to satisfy Eq.(6) or Eq.(7). If $d = 0$, we keep B_i intact. Otherwise pick randomly an $h \in_R \{0, 1, \ldots, 2^r - 1\}$ such that $S_{hd} \neq \varnothing$ and $S_{-(h-1)d} \neq \varnothing$, and choose two pixels $[B_i]_{j,k}$ where $(j,k) \in_R S_{hd}$ and $[B_i]_{j',k'}$ where $(j',k') \in_R S_{-(h-1)d}$, and flip the two selected pixels. Then the SUM satisfies Eq.(6).

2.2 Extracting Process

Extracting the message is easy to compute relatively. Given the image B', the receiver partitions it into block B_i''s. For each B_i' they compute Eq.(11) to extract the message, only if B_i' is not completely black or white, and $\mathsf{SUM}((B_i' \oplus K) \otimes W)$ is even.

$$\frac{\mathsf{SUM}((B_i' \oplus K) \otimes W)}{2} \equiv b_1 b_2 \ldots b_r \mod 2^r \quad (11)$$

3 Proposed Schemes

We reviewed the steganographic schemes for binary two-color images in previous section. As the computer technologies and digital camera have been developed, the use of color images becomes more popular and the use of binary images is decreasing gradually. Many steganographic tools for color images are introduced in these days. In this section we propose two algorithms based on TP's scheme which try to embed a message into color images, bitmap and palette-based image.

3.1 A Scheme for Bitmap Images

As each pixel value in a bitmap image is composed of three component values that represent the relative intensities of red, green, and blue, we can consider a bitmap image as a RGB image, and a bitmap is composed of three color-plane. And each color is represented as 8 bits per pixel, so we can split a color-plane into eight bit-plane's, from *MSB*-plane to *LSB*-plane. Thus we can consider a bit-plane of cover image as a two-color image, and embed a message into each bit-plane of a color-plane because all pixels of a bit-plane have the value either 0 or 1.

Human Visual System(HVS) is very sensitive to changes in luminance than to changes in hue or saturation. Luminance Y is computed from RGB color by Eq.(12)[4]

$$Y = 0.299R + 0.587G + 0.114B. \tag{12}$$

Eq.(12) means that the green color component has the most effect on luminance, and the blue has the least effect in the sense of HVS. To avoid the changes in luminance, we have to embed a message into color-planes in less sensitive order; blue, red, and green.

Embedding Process

Given a bitmap image I, let us define a secret key K, a weight matrix W and the message M. A secret key is a mn bit sequence and also the key is regarded as a size $m \times n$ matrix. For a message sequence $b_1 b_2 \ldots b_r$, embedding process is constructed to satisfy both condition Eq.(13) and 14, where C' is a stego-image.

$$\begin{aligned} &\mathsf{SUM}((C'_i \oplus K) \otimes W) \equiv 0 \mod 2 && (13) \\ &\Rightarrow \mathsf{SUM}((C'_i \oplus K) \otimes W)/2 \equiv b_1 b_2 \ldots b_r \mod 2^{r+1} \\ &\mathsf{SUM}((C'_i \oplus K) \otimes W) \equiv 1 \mod 2 && (14) \\ &\Rightarrow \text{there is no message in } C' \end{aligned}$$

STEP 1. Separate a cover-image I into three color-planes, B, R, and G.

STEP 2. Select a proper color-plane C from three color-planes and separate a color-plane C into eight bit-planes, C^j, for $j = 0, \ldots, 7$. You should select a blue color-plane first to decrease changes in luminance after embedding. If a message is embedded on a blue color-plane, then select a red color-plane and embed a message into there continuously.

STEP 3. Select a proper bit-plane $C^j \in \{C^0, C^1, \ldots, C^7\}$ and partition C^j into blocks C_i^j of size $m \times n$. For simplicity, we will treat C_i as C_i^j. You should select a LSB-plane first which has the least effect on the luminance and quality of the stego-image. If a message is embedded on a LSB-plane, then select the 2nd LSB-plane and embed a message into there continuously.

STEP 4. For each block C_i, if a block is completely black or white, i.e., entries in C_i are all 0's or 1's, skip the following steps without embedding a message. Otherwise, execute the following steps.

STEP 5. For each C_i, compute Eq.(15)

$$\mathsf{SUM}((C_i \oplus K) \otimes W) \tag{15}$$
$$\tag{16}$$

STEP 6. For each $C_i \oplus K$ and for $w = 1, 2, \ldots, 2^r - 1$, calculate the set Eq.(17),

$$S_w = \Big\{(j,k) | \Big[(W_{j,k} = w) \wedge ([C_i \oplus K]_{j,k} = 0) \wedge \Big(\mathsf{dist}([C_i]_{j',k'}) \leqslant \sqrt{2}\Big)\Big] \tag{17}$$
$$\vee \Big[\Big(W_{j,k} = 2^{r+1} - w\Big) \wedge ([C_i \oplus K]_{j,k} = 1) \wedge \Big(\mathsf{dist}([C_i]_{j',k'}) \leqslant \sqrt{2}\Big)\Big]\Big\},$$

where $\mathsf{dist}([C_i]_{j',k'})$ is an entry corresponding to the element of $\mathsf{dist}([C_i]_{j,k})$ in a block C_i. We define $S_w = S_{w'}$ for a $w \equiv w' \mod 2^{r+1}$.

Intuitively, we can handle the quality of the stego-image in (STEP 6). We, therefore, are able to select a pixel which be flipped only when the complement of pixel is laid in a distance of $\sqrt{2}$.

STEP 7. Calculate a weight difference as Eq.(18) with modulus 2^{r+1}

$$d \equiv b_1 b_2 \ldots b_r || 0_{(2)} - \mathsf{SUM}((C_i \oplus K) \otimes W) \tag{18}$$

We must increase the SUM Eq.(15), which is computed in (STEP 5), by d to satisfy Eq.(13) or Eq.(14). If $d = 0$, we keep C_i intact; otherwise we execute the algorithm as shown in Fig.1. If there is some parts of a message not embedded, execute (STEP 3) again.

```
if (∃ h such that S_{hd} ≠ ∅ and S_{-(h-1)d} ≠ ∅)
then
   Randomly pick an h ∈_R {0, 1, ..., 2^r − 1} such that S_{hd} ≠ ∅ and S_{-(h-1)d} ≠ ∅;
   Randomly pick a (j, k) ∈_R S_{hd} and complement the bit [C_i]_{j,k};
   Randomly pick a (j', k') ∈_R S_{-(h-1)d} and complement the bit [C_i]_{j',k'};
else /* no data will be hidden */
   if SUM(C_i ∧ K) ≡ 1 mod 2 then
      Keep C_i intact;
   else
      Select a (j, k) such that [W]_{j,k} is odd and its dist([C]_{j',k'}) is smallest;
      Complement the bit [C_i]_{j,k};
   end if;
end if;
```

Fig. 1. Block changing algorithm of STEP 7 in embedding process

3.2 A Scheme for Palette-Based Images

A palette-base image consists of a palette of colors and an index image. A palette includes color vectors and a unique index. Color vectors are represented with 24-bit RGB color, and each index is done with 8-bit. Each pixel in an index image is corresponding to an index of color for the pixel. There are two categories to embed a message into a palette-based image: (i) permutation of color vectors in palette such as GIF Shuffle[8] and SteganoGifPaletteOrder[3], and (ii) modification of index value in an index image such as EzStego[9] and Optimal Parity Assignment[6].

Our approach is to change the index value like second category methods. To apply our method to palette-based images, we must consider two things: (1) how to treat a palette-based image as a binary image, and (2) how to keep the quality of the image after embedding a message.

First, let's look at how we can treat a palette-based image as a binary image. We can not apply our method to the color vectors in a palette like bitmap image, so we can not help using the indexed image in a palette-based image. Since the indexed image is represented with 8-bit value which indicate the color in the palette where 256 colors used in the image, we can split it into 8 bit-plane images and then consider each bit-plane as binary image. Thus we can embed a message into a palette-based image using the scheme like one used for bitmap images.

Second, it is clear that this embedding algorithm degrades the quality of image after embedding without handling a palette. Thus our algorithm needs to some operation for a palette to keep the quality. For this purpose, we should relocate indices of colors in the palette in a way that one color is next to a similar colors. The simplest sorting method is the used one in EzStego[9], in a way that the colors are sorted to follow a shortest path through the RGB cube.

Embedding process, therefore, consists of three stages, preprocessing for a palette, embedding a message, and postprocessing for a palette. For a given palette-based image, in preprocessing stage, we realign order of colors in the palette to avoid degrading the quality of image. In embedding process, we apply the embedding process used for bitmap images to the indexed image. In post-processing stage, we recover the order of colors to the original one not to be used for steganlysis as the signature of algorithm.

4 Analyses for Proposed Schemes

In this section, we introduce the capacity for a cover-image and the rate of alteration with bitmap images in the center after embedding.
Given a cover-image I, the maximum capacity is defined as:

$$\left\lfloor \frac{M}{m} \right\rfloor \times \left\lfloor \frac{N}{n} \right\rfloor \times r \times k \times 3,$$

where the size of I is $M \times N$, the size of a block is $m \times n$, $r = \lfloor \log_2(mn+1) \rfloor - 1$, k is the number of used bit-planes, and 3 is the number of color-planes. For example, let I is 512×512 size of an RGB image, a block size is 8×8, and assume that we embed a message into the 5th LSB-plane. Then the length of a message block is defined as:

$$r = 5 \leqslant \lfloor \log_2(8 \cdot 8 + 1) \rfloor - 1,$$

and is shown in Fig.2. Thus the maximum capacity is 307,200 bits(20.48%):

$$\begin{aligned} 307,200 \text{ (bits)} &\leqslant \left\lfloor \frac{512}{8} \right\rfloor \times \left\lfloor \frac{512}{8} \right\rfloor \times 5 \times 5 \times 3 \\ &= 64 \times 64 \times 5 \times 5 \times 3. \end{aligned}$$

Fig.2 shows that the rate, Eq.(19), of the length of a message embeddable into a $m \times n$ block.

$$\frac{\lfloor (\log_2 mn + 1) - 1 \rfloor}{mn} \tag{19}$$

Since two bits in a block are modified generally, the maximum number of changed pixels in the stego-image is,

$$\# \text{ of pixels } \leqslant \lfloor M/m \rfloor \times \lfloor N/n \rfloor \times k \times 2 \times 3,$$

where the size of I is $M \times N$, the size of a block is $m \times n$, k is the number of used bit-planes, and 3 is the number of color-planes. For example, let I is 512×512 size of an RGB image, a block size is 8×8, and assume that we embed a message into the 5th LSB-plane. Then, the maximum number of changed pixels in the stego-image is 98,304 pixels(37.5%),

$$\begin{aligned} 98,304 \text{ (pixels)} &\leqslant \left\lfloor \frac{512}{8} \right\rfloor \times \left\lfloor \frac{512}{8} \right\rfloor \times 5 \times 2 \times 3 \\ &= 64 \times 64 \times 5 \times 2 \times 3, \end{aligned}$$

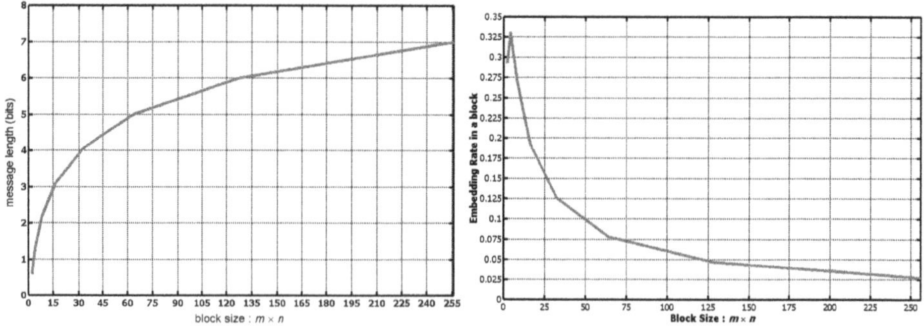

Fig. 2. The message length in a block of size $m \times n$ (left), and the message embedding rate in a block of size $m \times n$ (right).

and since the average number of changed pixels in a block is 1.5, the average number of changed pixels in the stego-image is 92,160 pixels(35.16%),

$$\begin{aligned} 92,160 \text{ (pixels)} &\leqslant \left\lfloor \frac{512}{8} \right\rfloor \times \left\lfloor \frac{512}{8} \right\rfloor \times 5 \times 1.5 \times 3 \\ &= 64 \times 64 \times 5 \times 1.5 \times 3. \end{aligned}$$

BPCS scheme embeds a message into bit-planes similar to our scheme, uses complexity measure to increase the capacity, and its purpose is to hide a message as much as possible[10,7]. As using BPCS algorithm, we can embed a message as the same size of a block, but it modifies bits approximately as much as a half of the block size. For example, let I is 512×512 size of an RGB image, a block size is 8×8, and assume that we embed a message into the 5th LSB-plane. Then, the maximum capacity is a 3,932,160 bits(62.5%),

$$\begin{aligned} 3,932,160 \text{ (bits)} &\leqslant \left\lfloor \frac{512}{8} \right\rfloor \times \left\lfloor \frac{512}{8} \right\rfloor \times 64 \times 5 \times 3 \\ &= 64 \times 64 \times 64 \times 5 \times 3. \end{aligned}$$

Since approximately a half size bits are modified in a block, the average number of changed pixels in a block of a color-plane is

$$\begin{aligned} \# \text{ of pixels } &\cong \left\lfloor \frac{mn}{2} \right\rfloor + \left\lfloor \frac{mn}{2^2} \right\rfloor + \cdots + \left\lfloor \frac{mn}{2^5} \right\rfloor \\ &= \left\lfloor \frac{31mn}{32} \right\rfloor, \end{aligned}$$

where the size of a block is $m \times n$ and a message is embedded to the 5th LSB-plane. For example, let I is 512×512 size of an RGB image, a block size is 8×8, and assume that we embed a message into the 5th LSB-plane. Then, the average number of changed pixels in a block is 62 pixels(96.88%),

$$\begin{aligned} 62 \text{ (pixels)} &\cong \left\lfloor \frac{64}{2} \right\rfloor + \left\lfloor \frac{64}{2^2} \right\rfloor + \cdots + \left\lfloor \frac{64}{2^5} \right\rfloor \\ &= \left\lfloor \frac{31mn}{32} \right\rfloor. \end{aligned}$$

Although the capacity of our scheme is smaller than BPCS, this scheme modifies almost all pixels, on the other hand, our scheme changes less smaller pixels relatively. Refer to the following ⟨Table 1⟩.

5 Experimental Results

We implemented our algorithm and performed some tests. For the experiments, 189 bitmap test images with sizes which varied from 448×336 to 1500×1124, and 153 palette-based images with size of 800×600. They are selected from digital camera community on Internet.

Table 1. Comparison between the proposed scheme and BPCS scheme.

k is the number of bit planes used in embedding process.

	Our Scheme	BPCS
Average Rate of changes (bits/block)	1.5	$mn/2$
Maximum Size of Capacity (bits/block)	$\lfloor \log_2(mn+1) - 1 \rfloor$	mn
Average # of Modified Pixels (pixels/block)	$4.5k$	$\sum_{i=1}^{k} \lfloor \frac{mn}{2^i} \rfloor$
Average # of Modified pixels in a Stego-Image	$4.5k \lfloor \frac{M}{m} \rfloor \lfloor \frac{N}{n} \rfloor$	$3 \sum_{i=1}^{k} \lfloor \frac{mn}{2^i} \rfloor$

In the following subsections, we show the maximum capacity of our algorithm, the quality of stego-images, the results of statistical analysis based on χ^2-test[15] as well as extended χ^2-test[12], and make a comparison between statistical analysis of our scheme and BPCS.

5.1 Capacity

To calculate a capacity of full length, we embedded a message into bitmap images and palette-based images using two block sizes, $4 \times 4 (m = n = 4,\ r = 3)$ and $8 \times 8 (m = n = 8,\ r = 5)$. ⟨Table 2⟩ and ⟨Table 3⟩ shows the capacities on bitmap images and palette-based images, where we embedded a message into each bit-plane with a capacity of full length.

As 8×8 block has four 4×4 subblocks, the capacity of the scheme based on 4×4 block is $3 \times 4/5 (= 2.4)$ times bigger than that of the scheme based on 8×8 block. As a matter of fact, we can see the similar result in our experiment, that is, the average capacity based on 4×4 block is about double compared to the one based on 8×8.

5.2 Quality of Stego-Images

To examine the changes of stego-image of quality, we embed a message into each bit plane of a test image using two difference block sizes, 4×4 and 8×8.

Under the observation for the test images, the quality of the bitmap stego-image starts to decrease gradually from the stego-image embedded to the 5th LSB-plane in 4×4 block case and to the 6th in 8×8 block case. And the quality of the palette-based images begins to degrade from the stego-image embedded

Table 2. Average capacity on 189 bitmap test images with the average size of 1, 089, 509 bytes based on 4×4 and 8×8 blocks

n-th bit plane	4×4 block		8×8 block	
	average capacity (bytes)	percentage (%)	average capacity (bytes)	percentage (%)
1	20,705.41	1.9379	9.627.14	0.9005
2	40,796.01	3.8186	19.121.79	1.7889
3	59,355.86	5.5571	28.174.91	2.6373
4	75,539.40	7.0755	36.414.28	3.4105
5	88,820.53	8.3258	43.531.58	4.0806
6	98,085.31	9.2725	49.252.93	4.6230
7	105,370.40	9.8980	53.388.35	5.0184
8	108,592.93	9.9671	55.608.58	5.2338

Table 3. Average capacity on 153 palette-based test images with size of 800×600 based on 4×4 and 8×8 blocks

n-th bit plane	4×4 block		8×8 block	
	average capacity (bytes)	percentage (%)	average capacity (bytes)	percentage (%)
1	8,989.31	1.8728	4,357.28	0.9078
2	17,509.12	3.6477	8,577.26	1.7869
3	25,342.06	5.2796	12,544.75	2.6156

to 4th indexed LSB-plane in 4×4 block case and to the 5th in 8×8 block case. This shows that the more a stego image has capacity, the more the quality deteriorates severely.

5.3 Statistical Analysis

In this subsection, we analyze our algorithm using two statistical tests, the χ^2-test introduced by Westfeld[15], and the extended χ^2-test by Provos[12]. ⟨Table 4⟩ shows the results of analysis on 189 bitmap test images and ⟨Table 5⟩ does on 153 palette-based images. To analyze the algorithm, we embedded a message into each bit-plane of a test image to capacity.

In this analysis, we give consideration to false positive error. We gathered hundreds test images and tested them with original χ^2 analysis and extended χ^2. And we selected test images within undetected images. The detection rate of the algorithm based on 4×4 block is more higher than the one based on 8×8 block because that changes much more pixels than this. Thus we should select the block size appropriately.

Table 4. The results of statistical analysis on 189 bitmap test images.

In the table, *Original* means the χ^2-test introduced by Westfeld[15], and *Extended* does the extended χ^2-test by Provos[12]. The first value indicate the number of detected images, and the value in parentheses does the percent of detection.

n-th bit plane	4 × 4 block				8 × 8 block			
	Original		Extended		Original		Extended	
1	11	5.82 %	31	16.40 %	0	0.00 %	5	2.65 %
2	15	7.94 %	45	23.81 %	0	0.00 %	7	3.70 %
3	21	11.11 %	55	29.10 %	0	0.00 %	7	3.70 %
4	26	13.76 %	75	39.68 %	2	1.06 %	9	4.76 %
5	38	20.11 %	77	40.74 %	3	1.59 %	9	4.76 %
6	42	22.22 %	102	53.97 %	4	2.12 %	11	5.82 %
7	51	26.98 %	102	53.97 %	5	2.65 %	13	6.88 %
8	49	25.93 %	103	54.50 %	6	3.17 %	20	10.58 %

Table 5. The results of statistical analysis on 153 palette-based test images.

In the table, *Original* means the χ^2-test, and *Extended* does the extended χ^2-test. The first value indicate the number of detected images, and the value in parentheses does the percent of detection.

n-th bit plane	4 × 4 block				8 × 8 block			
	Original		Extended		Original		Extended	
1	0	0.00 %	0	0.00 %	0	0.00 %	5	2.65 %
2	0	0.00 %	1	0.65 %	0	0.00 %	7	3.70 %
3	0	0.00 %	1	0.65 %	0	0.00 %	7	3.70 %

6 Conclusion

In this paper, we proposed steganographic algorithms for bitmap images and palette-based images, based on TP's algorithm, which has plenty of capacity and keeps the good quality. This algorithm can embed as many as $\lfloor \log_2(mn+1) - 1 \rfloor$ bits of data into each $m \times n$ block, and modifies averagely 1.5 bits in a $m \times n$ block. The quality of a stego-image is quite acceptable and the rate of detection is considerably reasonable against two statistical analyses.

Future research is to increase the capacity as well as to improve the deterioration of image quality when a message is embedded up to higher bit-plane, for example the 7th or the 8th bit-plane.

References

1. Y.Y. Chen, H.K. Pan, and T.C. Tseng, " A Secure Data Hiding Scheme for Two-Color Images," in *Proceedings of the Fifth IEEE Symposium on Computers and Communications*, 2000, pp.750–755.
2. C.C. Chang, M.N. Wu, and K.F. Hwang, "High Quality Perceptual Data Hiding Technique for Two-Color Images," in *Proceedings of Pacific Rim Workshop on Digital Steganography 2002*, Kitakyushu, Japan, July 11-13, 2002, pp.65–70.
3. David Glaude, "SteganoGifPaletteOrder," at `http://users.skynet.be/glu/sgpo.htm`
4. R.C. Gonzalez and R.E. Woods, *Digital Image Processing*, Addison-Wesley Publishing Company, Inc., 1992, pp.225–237.
5. J. Fridrich, "A New Steganographic Method for Palette Images," in *IS&T PICS*, Savannah, Georgia, April 25–28, 1999, pp.285–289.
6. J. Fridrich and Rui Du, "Secure Steganographic Methods for Palette Images," in *Information Hiding - Third International Workshop, IH'99*, vol.1768 of *Lecture Notes in Computer Science*, Springer-Verlag, pp.47–60.
7. E. Kawaguchi and R.O. Eason, "Principle and Applications of BPCS-Steganography," in *Proceedings of SPIE, Multimedia Systems and Applications*, Vol.3528, pp.464–473, 1998.
8. M. Kwan, "GIF Shuffle," at `http://www.darkside.com.au/gifshuffle/`.
9. R. Machado, "EzStego," at `http://www.stego.com/`
10. M. Niimi, H. Noda, and E. Kawaguchi, "An Image Embedding in Image by a Complexity Based Region Segmentation Method," in *International Conference on Image Processing (ICIP'97)* Vol.3, October 26–29, Washington, DC, 1997.
11. M. Niimi, R.O. Eason, H. Noda, and E. Kawaguchi, "A BPCS Steganographic Method for palette-Based Images using Luminance Quasi-Preserving Color Quantization," in *Proceedings of Pacific Rim Workshop on Digital Steganography 2002*, July, 2002, pp.84–91.
12. N. Provos, "Defending Against Statistical Steganalysis," in *Proceedings of the 10th USENIX Security Symposium*, August 2001, pp.323–335.
13. Test images are available on BPCS at `http://www.know.comp.kyutech.ac.jp/BPCSe/ BPCSe-testimages2.html`.
14. T.C. Tseng and H.K. Pan, "Secure and Invisible Data Hiding in 2-color Images," in *Proceedings of INFOCOM 2001*, IEEE, Vol.2, pp.887–896, 2001.
15. A. Westfeld and A. Pfitzmann, "Attacks on steganographic systems", in *Information Hiding - Third International Workshop, IH'99*, vol.1768 of *Lecture Notes in Computer Science*, Springer-Verlag, pp.61–76, 1999.
16. M.Y. Wu and J.H. Lee, "A Novel Data Embedding Method for Two-Color Facsimile Images," in *Proceedings of International Symposium on Multimedia Information Processing*, Chung-Li, Taiwan, R.O.C, December 1998.

A Watermarking Scheme Applicable for Fingerprinting Protocol

Minoru Kuribayashi and Hatsukazu Tanaka

Department of Electrical and Electronics Engineering
Faculty of Engineering, Kobe University
1-1 Rokkodai-cho, Nada-ku, Kobe, Japan 657-8501
{minoru,tanaka}@eedept.kobe-u.ac.jp

Abstract. Fingerprinting protocol applies a watermarking technique to embed a fingerprinting information in a digital content such as music, image, movie, etc.. The cryptographic protocol is studied by many researchers, but how to apply watermarking techniques is not remarked. In this paper, we study the problem to implement the watermarking techniques in the fingerprinting protocol, and then propose an ingenious method to embed a fingerprinting information in a digital image. The alteration of the embedded information is difficult for a hostile buyer in our scheme.

1 Introduction

Fingerprinting is one of cryptographic techniques to protect the copyright of a valuable content. The idea is to embed tiny signals in the insignificant parts in order to keep an ownership information. So if an illegal user redistributes the fingerprinted content which contains his identity, he will be traced from the content by extracting the ownership information. In order to embed such information in the contents such as music, image, movie, etc. watermarking techniques[1] can be applied.

Fingerprinting protocol is basically performed by two parties, a buyer and a merchant. A buyer makes a trade with a merchant to get his content and then the merchant wants to prevent him from redistributing the content. In the cradle of the research, a symmetric scheme has been proposed, in which a merchant embeds a buyer's identity in his content by himself and sends it to him. However, in this scheme the merchant may frame the legal buyer because the merchant can distribute the fingerprinted content by himself as he has it, and then may insist that the distributed content is the same one sold to the buyer. So in order to protect the buyer's right, asymmetric schemes[2],[3] have been proposed in which the fingerprinted contents can be obtained only by a buyer. The fingerprinting information is encrypted before it is sent to a merchant and the encrypted information is embedded in the encrypted content by the merchant. Because the ciphertext can be decrypted only by the buyer, nobody can obtain the fingerprinted content except the buyer. Further, the anonymity of the buyer can be achieved in [4],[5], and the enciphering rate has been improved in [6].

T. Kalker et al. (Eds.): IWDW 2003, LNCS 2939, pp. 532–543, 2004.
© Springer-Verlag Berlin Heidelberg 2004

In order to embed a fingerprinting information in a content, a watermarking technique should be applied. However, in previous scheme[7] it is not deeply considered how to embed an encrypted information in an encrypted content and how to make the system robust against attacks. We study both fingerprinting and watermarking techniques and find the following difficulty to implement. In watermarking techniques for digital image, it is desirable to embed an information in the frequency components for both robustness and perceptual quality. However, as the frequency components are real number, there is a difficult problem to apply cryptographic techniques directly because they are based on the algebraic property of an integer. In many watermarking schemes, an information bit is embedded in the frequency component by quantizing it to the nearest odd or even number depending on the information bit. However, it seems difficult to exploit the method without the knowledge of an information bit.

In this paper, we propose a new watermarking scheme to embed an encrypted information in an encrypted contents. In order to apply a public-key cryptosystem, all frequency components of an image are quantized to integer. In the operation, a fingerprinting information is embedded to the quantized value. Here the degradation of the image should be considered. From the perceptual property, the changes in low frequency components stand out compared with that of the other components and hence each component is quantized adaptively by a special quantization step size. As a quantization table used in the JPEG compression algorithm is designed considering human perceptual property, we modify the table so that it may be applicable for our embedding scheme. And in order to embed an information bit of which value is unknown, the frequency components in the embedding positions are quantized to a special number before embedding so that the value can be changed depending on the information bit.

2 Preliminaries

2.1 Fingerprinting

Fingerprinting technique enable an author to embed an information related to a buyer in his contents. If the buyer redistributes the copy, he is traced from the copy if the embedded information can be extracted correctly. Here, if the author can obtain the fingerprinted content in the embedding protocol, it occurs a problem as follows. A dishonest author might try to distribute by himself the fingerprinted content, and claim that the innocent buyer redistributes the copy. Therefore, if the author can obtain the fingerprinted content in the protocol, he cannot prove to a third party that an illegal buyer redistributes the copy. In order to solve the problem, cryptographic techniques are applied. If an author embeds an encrypted information in an encrypted content and only the buyer can decrypts the ciphertext, only the buyer can obtain the fingerprinted content. Hence the author can accuse the illegal buyer if he finds the illegal copy.

2.2 Homomorphic Property

In our proposed fingerprinting protocol[6], the additive homomorphic property of Okamoto-Uchiyama encryption scheme[8] is applied to embed an encrypted fingerprint in an encrypted content. In the cryptosystem, the parameters are only integers.

Let $E(m, r)$ be an encryption function of a message m and a random number r. The modulus of the cryptosystem is $N = p^2 q$, where p and q are large prime. If the function has the additive homomorphic property, the following equation can be satisfied.

$$E(m_1, r_1) \cdot E(m_2, r_2) = E(m_1 + m_2, r_1 + r_2) \pmod N \tag{1}$$

If we assume that a fingerprint is denoted by a number m_1 and a digital content is given by a number m_2, then a fingerprinted item becomes $m_1 + m_2$.

In public-key cryptosystems, several schemes retain a homomorphic property, but the above additive homomorphic property is for only a few schemes. In the schemes, Okamoto-Uchiyama scheme requires less computations and hence we adopt it. It can be replaced by Paillier cryptosystem[9] which enciphering rate is better because the structure is very similar to Okamoto-Uchiyama scheme except the modulus.

2.3 Fingerprinting Protocol

In the asymmetric scheme only a buyer can obtain the fingerprinted content after the fingerprinting protocol[2],[3]. In the protocol, first the buyer encrypts his identity information and sends it to the merchant. Then the merchant encrypts his content and embeds the buyer's identity information by multiplying the received ciphertext. Here, homomorphic property of the cryptosystem enable the merchant to embed the encrypted information into the encrypted content. Finally, the buyer receives the encrypted, fingerprinted ciphertext from the merchant and obtains the fingerprinted content by decryption using his secret key. This is illustrated in Fig.1. In detail, the asymmetric scheme has four protocols, key generation, fingerprinting, identification and dispute. The key generation protocol is a initial setting of the key parameters. And a merchant can identify the buyer from a illegal copy in the identification protocol and verify the fact in a dispute protocol. In the anonymous scheme, several protocols are added to the asymmetric scheme so as to guarantee the anonymity of the buyer. In the scheme a trusted third party ensures the registration of the buyer and hence the merchant can certify the anonymous buyer is a legal user of the system.

In [6] an anonymous fingerprinting protocol exploiting the additive homomorphic property of Okamoto-Uchiyama encryption scheme is proposed which improves the enciphering rate dramatically. So the scheme seems to be realistic model to implement. Here we review the protocol briefly.

The fingerprinting protocol is executed between a buyer $\mathcal{B}$ and a merchant $\mathcal{M}$. We assume that the bit length of $\mathcal{B}$'s identity information is ℓ and $\mathcal{M}$'s digital content is composed of L pieces of components(for example, pixel in an image). $\mathcal{B}$ encrypts each bits of his/her identity, $id = \sum w_j 2^j$, $(0 \le j \le \ell - 1)$ and sends them to $\mathcal{M}$, and $\mathcal{M}$ encrypts each components of his/her content $I = \{I_i \mid 0 \le i \le L - 1\}$ and multiplies each one to the received each ciphertext respectively. We assume that $\mathcal{B}$ has already registered at a center $\mathcal{RC}$ and sent the proof $E(id, 0)$ to $\mathcal{M}$. The fingerprinting protocol is given as follows.

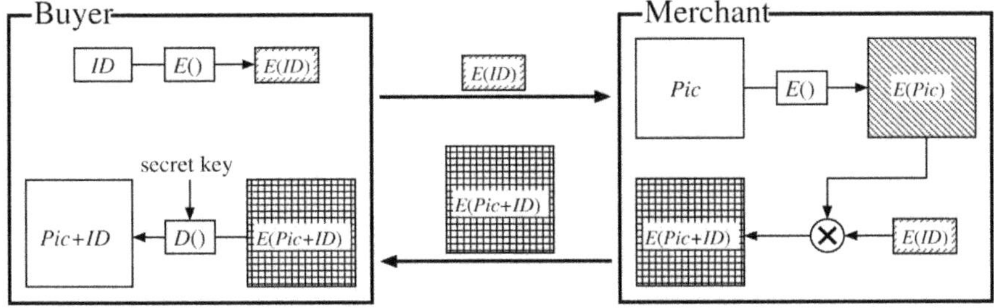

Fig. 1. Asymmetric fingerprinting protocol.

Step 1. $\mathcal{M}$ generates a random number $a(2^\ell < a < N)$ and sends it to $\mathcal{B}$.

Step 2. $\mathcal{B}$ decomposes a into ℓ random numbers a_j to satisfy the following equation.

$$a = \sum_{j=0}^{\ell-1} a_j 2^j \tag{2}$$

Each identify information bit w_j is encrypted using the a_j as a random number, and the ciphertexts $E(w_j, a_j)$ are sent to $\mathcal{M}$.

Step 3. $\mathcal{M}$ verifies the validity of the received ciphertexts using a and $E(id, 0)$ by the following congruence.

$$\prod_j E(w_j, a_j)^{2^j} \equiv E(id, 0) \cdot E(0, a) \pmod N \tag{3}$$

Step 4. $\mathcal{M}$ generates L random numbers $b_i \in (\mathbf{Z}/N\mathbf{Z})$ and embedding intensity T of even number. Then, in order to get the encrypted and fingerprinted content, $\mathcal{M}$ calculates

$$Y_i = \begin{cases} E(I_i - T/2, b_i) \cdot E(w_j, a_j)^T \pmod N & \text{embedding position} \\ E(I_i, b_i) \pmod N & \text{elsewhere,} \end{cases} \tag{4}$$

and sends it to $\mathcal{B}$

Step 5. Since the received Y_i is rewritten as

$$Y_i = \begin{cases} E(I_i + Tw_j - \frac{T}{2}, Ta_j + b_i) \pmod N & \text{embedding position} \\ E(I_i, b_i) \pmod N & \text{elsewhere,} \end{cases} \tag{5}$$

$\mathcal{B}$ can decrypt Y_i to get the plaintext.

$$\begin{cases} I_i + Tw_j - \frac{T}{2} \pmod p & \text{embedding position} \\ I_i \pmod p & \text{elsewhere} \end{cases}$$

On the deciphered message, if $w_j = 1$, then $T/2$ has been added to I_i, and if $w_j = 0$, then $T/2$ has been subtracted from I_i. As the characteristic is suitable for several watermarking schemes like [10], our scheme can be applied easily.

Remark 1. In Eq.(4) $E(w_j, a_j)^T$ can be shown by $E(Tw_j,\, Ta_j)$ because

$$\begin{aligned} E(w_j, a_j)^T &= E(w_j, a_j) \cdot E(w_j, a_j) \cdots E(w_j, a_j) \pmod N \\ &= E(\Sigma w_j, \Sigma a_j) \\ &= E(Tw_j, Ta_j). \end{aligned} \tag{6}$$

Therefore from the additive homomorphic property Y_i at the embedding position can be rewritten as

$$\begin{aligned} Y_i &= E(Tw_j,\, Ta_j) \cdot E(I_i - \tfrac{T}{2},\, b_i) \\ &= E(I_i + Tw_j - \tfrac{T}{2},\, Ta_j + b_i). \end{aligned} \tag{7}$$

2.4 Watermarking Technique

Watermarking is a technique to embed some information in digital contents without being perceived. The embedded information can be extracted from the watermarked contents using a secret key. There are two kinds of watermarking techniques to embed a watermark in an image. One exploits a spatial domain and the other a transformed domain using DCT, DFT, DWT, etc.. Generally a signal embedded in a transformed domain is robust against the signal processing which may be performed to remove the embedded signal[10].

"Requantization" is one of the popular techniques to embed a watermark in the transformed domain. First, an image is transformed to the frequency domain and then the components in the embedding position are quantized by a quantizing step size Q. The embedding procedure is given as follows(see Fig.2).

Step 1. An image is divided into smaller blocks, and each block is transformed to the frequency domain.

Step 2. A frequency component $f_{x,y}$ in the embedding position is quantized by a quantizing step size Q.

$$\hat{f}_{x,y} = int(f_{x,y}/Q) \tag{8}$$

Step 3. A watermarking information bit w_t is embedded by the following equation.

$$\hat{f}'_{x,y} = \begin{cases} \hat{f}_{x,y} + 1 & w_t \neq \hat{f}_{x,y} \bmod 2 \\ \hat{f}_{x,y} & \text{otherwise} \end{cases} \tag{9}$$

Step 4. $\hat{f}'_{x,y}$ is multiplied by Q, and the watermarked frequency domain is transformed inversely to obtain a watermarked image.

In the extraction procedure, Step.1 and Step.2 of the above procedure are executed. Then the watermarked information bit is determined being based on whether the value of a quantized frequency component is odd or even.

In the fingerprinting techniques, it is desirable that a lot of information can be embedded in a content. In the conventional schemes[2]-[4] the "patchwork" method[11] has been used. The scheme can be easily applied for the fingerprinting schemes, but the amount of embedded information is too small to use. So in our proposed scheme, the requantization scheme is applied in order to embed a lot of information in a image.

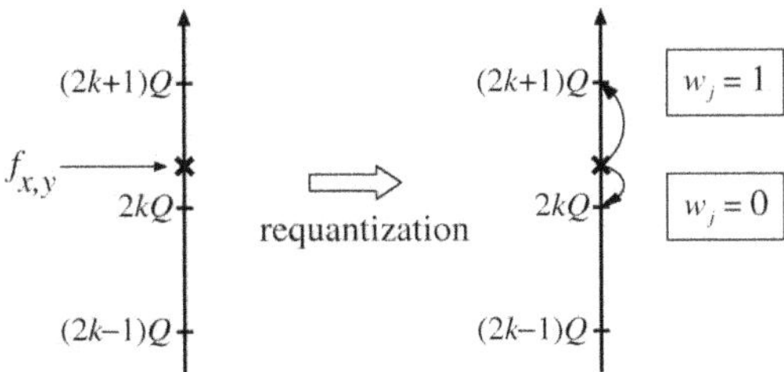

Fig. 2. Requantization procedure.

3 How to Embed an Encrypted Information

3.1 Basic Idea

In order to embed an encrypted fingerprinting information bit in an encrypted content, the additive homomorphic property of public-key cryptosystem is applied. In a fingerprinting protocol, the operation is performed by Eq.(4). However, such public-key cryptosystem cannot use real value. Hence watermarking schemes exploiting frequency domain cannot be applied in the protocol directly. The analog values of frequency components should be quantized to an integer so as to use cryptographic applications. Then the fingerprinting information bit is embedded using the watermarking technique explained in the previous section.

In the quantization process, if the frequency coefficients are quantized uniformly, it causes serious degradation of the image. So it should be quantized based on the human perceptual characteristic. And there is a serious problem in the embedding process. In the asymmetric and anonymous fingerprinting, a merchant $\mathcal{M}$ cannot get a buyer $\mathcal{B}$'s plain identity information unless $\mathcal{B}$ shows it because the identity information is encrypted and then embedded in $\mathcal{M}$'s contents by multiplying ciphertexts. In such a situation, it seems to be impossible that $\mathcal{M}$ embeds $\mathcal{B}$'s identity information bits in his/her content using the watermarking technique without knowing the plaintext itself. Because a coefficient is quantized to the nearest even number if the bit is zero, otherwise to the odd number. Without the knowledge of the embedding information bit, such procedure cannot performed. It is shown in Fig.3.

In order to embed an information bit w_j without knowing the plaintext, the frequency coefficients of the embedding positions is first quantized to the nearest even number in our scheme. After the frequency coefficients are quantized to the even number, the following equation is calculated to embed the information bit.

$$E(\hat{f}_{x,y}, b_i) \cdot E(w_j, a_j) = E(\hat{f}_{x,y} + w_j, b_i + a_j) \pmod{N} \tag{10}$$

In this case, the quantized frequency coefficient becomes odd number if $w_j = 1$, otherwise even number. So even if the plain information bit is kept secret using cryptographic technique, it can be embedded in the frequency coefficient of a content. Here, the original value $f_{x,y}$ of the frequency coefficient should be

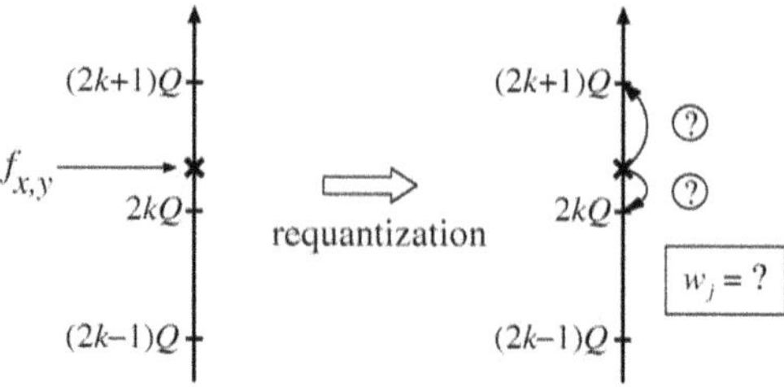

Fig. 3. Problem to embed an encrypted fingerprinting information.

considered as the following reason. If $f_{x,y}$ is less than the quantized coefficients, then $\hat{f}_{x,y} + w_j$ is not the nearest odd number and hence the degradation of the image is increased. Therefore Eq.(10) should be changed in such a case as follows.

$$E(\hat{f}_{x,y}, b_i) \cdot E(w_j, a_j)^{-1} = E(\hat{f}_{x,y} - w_j, b_i - a_j) \pmod{N} \tag{11}$$

Depending on $f_{x,y}$, one of the above two equation is selected to embed an encrypted and fingerprinting information bit.

3.2 Embedding Procedure

In a fingerprinting protocol, a buyer $\mathcal{B}$ encrypts his fingerprinting information bits w_j, and their ciphertexts $E(w_j, a_j)$ are sent to a merchant $\mathcal{M}$. First $\mathcal{M}$ performs DCT to the divided blocks of his content and then encrypts each quantized DCT coefficient. Finally the encrypted and fingerprinted content is calculated by multiplying the received $E(w_j, a_j)$ to the encrypted coefficients at the embedding positions. Here, the embedding positions are determined by $\mathcal{M}$'s secret key and hence intentional alteration of the embedded information bit is difficult for $\mathcal{B}$.

The embedding procedure of proposed method is summarized in the followings.

[Buyer:]
Each fingerprinting information bit w_j is encrypted and the ciphertext $E(w_j, a_j)$ is sent to $\mathcal{M}$.

[Merchant:]

Step 1. An image is partitioned into 16×16 blocks and each block is transformed by DCT.
Step 2. Each DCT coefficient $f_{x,y}$ of each block is quantized to the nearest integer using a quantizing step size $Q_{x,y}$. Here the coefficients in the embedding positions are quantized to the nearest even number.
Step 3. Each quantized coefficient $\hat{f}_{x,y}$ is encrypted using the $\mathcal{B}$'s public key.

Step 4. Using the $\mathcal{M}$'s secret key the embedding coefficients are specified, and each fingerprinting information bit is embedded by multiplying two ciphertexts as follows

- If $f_{x,y} > \hat{f}_{x,y}Q_{x,y}$, then $E(w_j, a_j)$ is multiplied to the ciphertext of $\hat{f}_{x,y}$, which can be calculated by Eq.(10).
- Else if $f_{x,y} \leq \hat{f}_{x,y}Q_{x,y}$, then $E(w_j, a_j)^{-1}$ is multiplied to the ciphertext of $\hat{f}_{x,y}$, which can be calculated by Eq.(11).

Step 4. The ciphertexts of fingerprinted content are sent to $\mathcal{B}$.

[**Buyer:**]

Step 1. The received ciphertexts are decrypted and the quantized DCT coefficients are recovered.

Step 2. Each quantizing step size $Q_{x,y}$ is multiplied to the corresponding quantized coefficient.

Step 3. By performing IDCT, the fingerprinted content can be obtained.

When $\mathcal{B}$ recovers the fingerprinted content, $Q_{x,y}$ used to quantize the original DCT coefficients is inevitable to recover the proper DCT coefficients. So we assume that they are shared previously between the buyer and the merchant.

In order to increase the robustness against attack, the embedding positions should not be selected from high frequency coefficients as such coefficients are very sensitive for general signal processing which may be performed by a hostile buyer. And if one information bit can be embedded being distributed in several coefficients, the robustness can be improved. Therefore, Step.3 of the merchant operation is repeatedly performed α times for different low frequency coefficients of several blocks.

3.3 Quantization Table

When a fingerprinting information is embedded in an image, perceptual degradation should be considered. In our scheme, an image is first transformed to the frequency domain and then the components should be quantized in order to apply cryptographic techniques which are based on the algebraic property of integer. Here, if the components quantized uniformly, the image quality must be degraded seriously. When a digital image is compressed by JPEG algorithm, a special quantization table shown in Table 1 is used. The table is designed to keep the perceptual quality as good as possible. So the table is suitable for quantization of an image. However, the table size is 8×8, and hence it is too small to keep the security of the information embedded in the block for the attack using the common signal processing. Therefore, we reconstruct a larger quantization table based on the original one.

Let the original table be $q_{x,y}, (0 \leq x, y \leq 7)$. First the table is expanded to horizontal direction, $b_{x,y}, (0 \leq x \leq 7, 0 \leq y \leq 15)$ as follows.

$$b_{x,y} = \begin{cases} q_{x,y/2} & (y{=}0,\ 2,\ 4,\ \ldots,\ 14) \\ (q_{x,y/2} + q_{x,y/2+1})/2 & (y{=}1,\ 3,\ 5,\ \ldots,\ 13) \\ q_{x,7} & (y{=}15) \end{cases} \tag{12}$$

Table 1. Quantization table of JPEG compression.

16	11	10	16	24	40	51	61
12	12	14	19	26	58	60	55
14	13	16	24	40	57	69	56
14	17	22	29	51	87	80	62
18	22	37	56	68	109	103	77
24	35	55	64	81	104	113	92
49	64	78	87	103	121	120	101
72	92	95	98	112	100	103	99

And then it is expanded to vertical direction and $Q_{x,y}, (0 \le x, y \le 15)$ is obtained.

$$Q_{x,y} = \begin{cases} b_{x/2,y} & (x{=}0,\ 2,\ 4,\ \ldots,\ 14) \\ (b_{x/2,y} + b_{x/2+1,y})/2 & (x{=}1,\ 3,\ 5,\ \ldots,\ 13) \\ b_{15,y} & (x{=}15) \end{cases} \tag{13}$$

Where the fraction value is rounded cutoff method.

When an image is compressed by JPEG algorithm, the quality can be determined by selecting a quality parameter q. Using the parameter, the quantizing step size can be calculated. Then we must change the above procedure so as to be applicable for our quantization table as follows.

$$Q'_{x,y} = \frac{(100 - q)}{50} Q_{x,y} \tag{14}$$

If the quality parameter q is decreased, the robustness against attack can be improved, but the image quality will be decreased. So it is necessary to consider the characteristic when the value of q is determined.

3.4 Extraction

Since the fingerprinting information is embedded by quantizing the DCT coefficients even/odd number, such information can be extracted easily if one has the secret key which is used to specify the embedding position. When $\mathcal{M}$ finds an illegal copy, the information is extracted as follows. First, it is transformed by DCT after partitioned into blocks. And then each coefficient in the embedding position is quantized using the corresponding $Q_{x,y}$. If the value is even, the information bit is regarded as 0, otherwise 1. When one information bit is extracted from several DCT coefficients, the amount of even and odd numbers are counted. Then the information bit can be determined by the sum of those amount. Here, the more accurate extraction method may be possible as the following reason. Generally, the quantized DCT coefficients will be changed slightly after embedding because of the round error when IDCT is performed. And the common signal processing such as JPEG compression, filtering, etc. will affect the frequency coefficients. However, the above changes will not be so large and hence the values of the DCT coefficients must contain the useful information to detect the the embedded information bit. Therefore, the analog information can be applied for the such extraction procedure.

4 Security

In this section, we consider the security of our proposed system. Here we assume the applied public-key cryptosystem is secure. Everyone can make a ciphertext of any message using the public key of a buyer, but no one can decrypt the ciphertext except the buyer who has the secret key. So the merchant cannot get the fingerprinting information from the received ciphertexts $E(w_j, a_j)$ directly. If the buyer redistributes a illegal copy and the embedded information is extracted from it, the merchant can obtain the fingerprinting information and hence trace the illegal buyer. The above discussion is described in [6].

Considering the robustness against common signal processing, one bit information bit is spread into α low frequency components. It seems to sacrifice the security as a hostile buyer may be able to find the embedding positions. However the above operation makes it more difficult for the following reasons. As the energy of the image is concentrated on the low DCT coefficients, such coefficients have large value, which distributes randomly. Such DCT coefficients in the embedding positions are quantized to the nearest even number and a information bit is embedded using Eqs.(10) or (11). So the quantized value of DCT coefficients can be regarded as a random value, which makes difficult to identify the embedding positions from the fingerprinted coefficients. If one information bit is embedded in only one coefficient, it may be changed by the attack such that a buyer changes the randomly selected coefficients. But the possibility can be decreased if several coefficients are used to embed one information bit because a buyer must change more than $\alpha/2$ coefficients without loss of the perceptual degradation. Further, as the number of DCT coefficients are much larger than that of information bits, there are a lot of candidates of the embedding positions for one information bit. And only the coefficients at the embedding positions are quantized even number, and such quantized coefficients are changed by the fingerprinting information, which makes the coefficients randomly distributed. Several buyers may collude to analyze the embedding position by taking the difference of each fingerprinted content. But such attack can be avoided using the collusion secure code[12]. As the consequence, our proposed scheme is secure against intentional alteration of a hostile buyer.

5 Simulation Results

In this section, we show several computer simulated results. Concerning to the fingerprinting protocol, the validity can be proved by the security of Okamoto-Uchiyama cryptosystem, and it has already proved in [6]. Therefore the perceptual quality of the embedded image and the robustness against several attacks are shown in this section. In our simulation we use a standard image "Lana" that has 256 level gray scale with size of 256×256. Considering the robustness against signal processing attack, the size of α should be large. However, if α is increased too much, an hostile user may be able to deter the embedding positions and change the values. Because the candidates for the embedding positions are decreased. Hence considering the trade-off, we set $\alpha = 75$ in the following simulations.

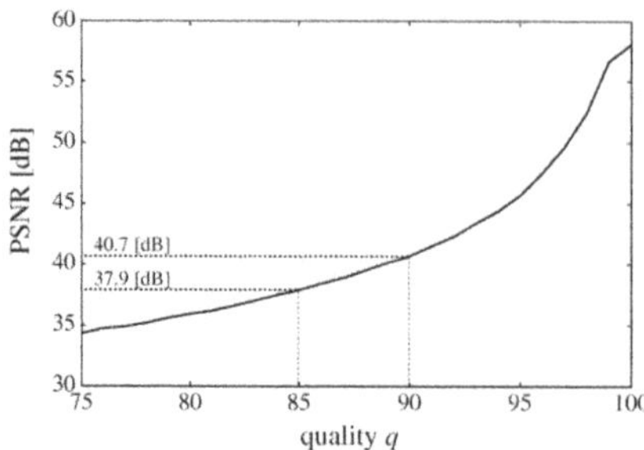

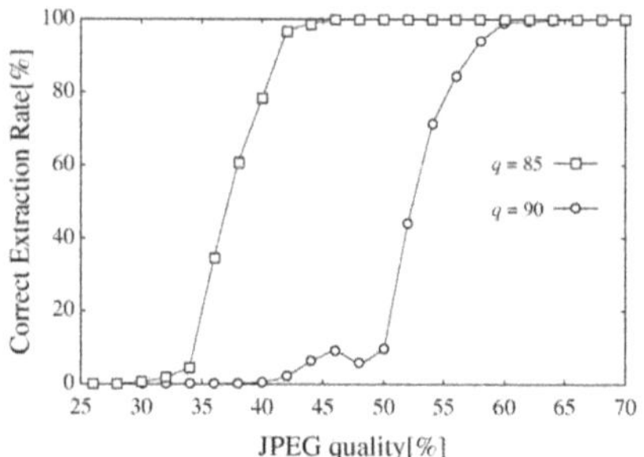

Fig. 4. PSNR versus quality q ($\alpha = 75$). **Fig. 5.** Tolerance for JPEG Compression.

If the quality factor q is decreased, the perceptual quality is decreased accordingly. Figure 4 shows the relation between q and PSNR. The robustness against attack can be increased if q is decreased, but the perceptual quality is decreased. Therefore there is a trade-off between the robustness and perceptual quality and it should be considered to apply our scheme. From our experiment, the value of q should is between 85 and 90.

The robustness against JPEG compression is examined and the results are shown in Fig. 5. From the results, the tolerance for JPEG compression is dependent on the value of q. Such value should be selected for the applied system. Concerning to the robustness against Gaussian filtering, the embedded information can be extracted without any errors.

6 Conclusion

We have proposed a watermarking scheme to embed an encrypted information in an encrypted content. In the conventional schemes, the protocol has been achieved by applying the additive homomorphic property, but their schemes do not mention how to use watermarking techniques. In this paper, we make clear how to embed an information keeping the true value secret, and how to use real value for a public-key cryptosystem using the quantization operation of DCT coefficients. Before embedding an information bit, all DCT coefficients are quantized. Then the coefficients in the embedding positions are quantized even number before embedding. Then to keep the image quality as good as possible, the quantization table of JPEG algorithm is modified to reconstruct a suitable table for our proposed scheme from a point of human perceptual property.

References

1. S. Katzenbeisser and F. A. P. Petitcolas, *Information hiding techniques for steganography and digital watermarking.* Artech house publishers, Jan. 2000.
2. B. Pfitzmann and M. Schunter, "Asymmetric fingerprinting," *Proc. of EUROCRYPT'96*, LNCS 1070, Springer-Verlag, pp.84-95, 1996.

3. B. Pfitzmann and M. Waidner, "Anonymous fingerprinting," *Proc. of EUROCRYPT'97*, LNCS 1233, Springer-Verlag, pp.88-102, 1997.
4. B. Pfitzmann and A. Sadeghi, "Coin-based anonymous fingerprinting," *Proc. of EUROCRYPT'99*, LNCS 1592, Springer-Verlag, pp.150-164, 1999.
5. B. Pfitzmann and A. Sadeghi, "Anonymous fingerprinting with direct non-repudiation," *Proc. of ASIACRYPT'2000*, LNCS 1976, Springer-Verlag, pp.401-414, 2000.
6. M. Kuribayashi and H. Tanaka, "A new anonymous fingerprinting with high enciphering rate," *Proc. of INDOCRYPT2001*, LNCS 2247, Springer-Verlag, pp.30-39, 2001.
7. N. Memon and P. W. Wong, "A buyer-seller watermarking protocol," *IEEE trans. on Image Process.*, vol. 10, no. 4, pp.643-649, 2001.
8. T. Okamoto and S. Uchiyama, "A new public-key cryptosystem as secure as factoring," *Proc. of EUROCRYPT'98*, LNCS 1403, Springer-Verlag, pp.308-318, 1998.
9. P. Paillier, "Public key cryptosystems based on degree residuosity classes," *Proc. of Eurocrypt'99*, LNCS 1592, Springer-Verlag, pp.223-238, 1999.
10. M. Kuribayashi and H. Tanaka, "A watermarking scheme based on the characteristic of addition among DCT coefficients," *Proc. of ISW2000*, LNCS 1975, Springer-Verlag, pp.1-14, 2000.
11. W. Bender, D. Gruhl and N. Morimoto, "Techniques for Data Hiding," *Proc. of SPIE*, pp.164-173, 1995.
12. D. Boneh and J. Shaw, "Collusion-secure fingerprinting for digital data," *IEEE* Trans. Inform. Theory, vol.44, no.5, pp.1897-1905, 1998.

A New Digital Watermarking for Architectural Design Drawing Using LINEs and ARCs Based on Vertex

Bong-Ju Jang[1], Kwang-Seok Moon[2], Young Huh[3], and Ki-Ryong Kwon[1]

[1]Department of Electronic and Computer Engineering, Pusan University of Foreign Studies, 55-1 Uam-dong, Nam-gu, Pusan 608-738, Republic of Korea,
krkwon@taejo.pufs.ac.kr, roachjbj@korea.com
[2]Division of Elec. and Telecomm. Eng., Pukyung National University, 55-9, Daeyun-dong, Nam-gu, Pusan, 608-810, KOREA
moonks@pknu.ac.kr
[3]Korea Electrotechnology Research Institute

Abstract. This paper proposed to digital watermarking technique for architectural design drawing using LINEs and ARCs based on vertex in CAD system to prevent infringement of copyright from unlawfulness reproductions and distribution. After extract LINEs and ARCs from designed drawing, we embed watermarks using adaptive algorithm in each characteristics. Watermarks robust to various attacks like as geometrical transformation as being embedded in LINE's length and ARC's angle information. Also, the proposed method satisfies enough transparency about watermarked drawing because have suitable embedding strength to each component. Because handlings that are regarded as attacks of watermarked drawing can consist in CAD program, it used AutoCAD 2002 that is common using as a CAD program for experiments. By experimental result, we confirmed robustness and invisibility of embedded watermarks in several conversions of architectural design drawing.

Keywords: architectural design drawing, CAD, digital watermarking, geometrical attack, copyright protection

1 Introduction

Today, multimedia society has many problems by unlawful reproduction or not admitted distribution from sudden increase of digital contents and multimedia data. To solve such problems, it is possible to hide data (information) within digital medium. The information is hidden in the sense that it is perceptually and statistically undetectable. With many schemes, the hidden information can still be recovered if the host signal is compressed, edited, or converted from digital to analog format and back. This can bear witness to ownership for the owner of the digital media from illegal application. Recently, the watermarking for video, speech and image are developing very actively, and specially, lots of researches for the image watermarking being reported. But, in fact, even so results of these progressed researches, many of them are not used in real world, moreover also studies about its other application are almost not achieved. As development of CAD systems, now almost architectural

T. Kalker et al. (Eds.): IWDW 2003, LNCS 2939, pp. 544–557, 2004.
© Springer-Verlag Berlin Heidelberg 2004

designs are completed on computer programs. Architectural drawing in CAD system is more detailer, exacter and easier to see. But likewise most of other computer files, CAD files are also easy to copy or circulation. So, sometimes they are exposed to embezzlement or illegal copy. Actually, we often see same modeling at another buildings, and have saw cases about appropriation of architectural design in TV news.

This paper is proposed for prevent from these embezzlements of such architectural design drawings and for stop shrinkage of architectural design techniques. We analysis architectural drawings made by CAD tool for architectural design, then we embed watermarks having transparency using a adaptive algorithm. And finally, develop a robust detection algorithm nevertheless various data handlings treating as attacks. Like as other almost watermarking algorithms, this method must consist in extents that satisfy transparency and toughness [1]. Embedded watermark in architecture design drawing must not be observed by users, and not be damaged or detected by other designers. And, even if it completed itself, because it is possible modifications and distortions without any limit as using CAD programs, it should be have specially robustness about attack on CAD programs. Swanson *et al.* [2] proposed watermarking method in the DCT domain using property of human perceptual system. This algorithm is used in the context of image compression using the perceptual based quantizers. Podilchuk *et al.* [3] developed a content adaptive scheme, where the embedding strength is adjusted for each DCT and wavelet coefficients. Ruanaidh *et al.* [4] have applied transfer modulation features of HVS in the transform domain to solve the problem of the compromise between the robustness and transparency. This method embeds the watermark into the Fourier coefficients in a middle frequency band with the same embedding strength assuming that the image spectra have isotropic characteristic. This assumption is caused by lead to some visible artifacts of images in the flat regions since it is an isotropic property of image spectra. Voloshynovskiy *et al.* [5] proposed adequate stochastic modeling for content adaptive digital image watermarking. By knowing stochastic models of the watermark and the host image, one can formulate the problem of watermark estimation/detection according to the classical MAP (maximum a posteriori probability) and stochastic models and also estimate the capacity issue of the image watermark scheme. The watermarking technique has perceptual characteristics about successive subband quantization and non-stationary Gaussian model in multiwavelet transform domain is proposed [6]. Ohbuchi *et al.* [7] presented method to insert watermark to each vertex there into after divide by rectangles that have vertices of fixed quantity using quadtree way in Vector Digital Map

2 Modeling for Digital Watermarking of CAD Data

2.1 Embedding Conditions

Various data transformations of DCT, DFT, DWT, LOG POLA Mapping etc. are available in case of raster based 2-D images. As based on raster, this is possible to transform in frequency domains as using variety characteristic with neighborhood pixels, therefore image processing in frequency domains is available. Most multimedia watermarking schemes are consisting in frequency domain, too. But, as almost CAD files have a characteristic of vector based image unlike general raster based image, transform to frequency domain is impossible because they have no relation with vertex information and neighborhood. The researches about wavelet transform of vertex data for 3D polygonal meshes are gone abuzz recently, but because CAD data is consisted of information of short piece that is not continued vertex information, this wavelet transform is impossible too. Therefore, processing by frequency domains or masks like as image watermarking is impossible, and processing in spatial domain is only applied. There is characteristic that method to embed watermark in CAD file is limited in spatial domain and have advantage that and may not consider attacks in frequency domain. Also, although already completed architectural design drawing, it is exposed in many attacks because handlings of the data using CAD tool are easy. This paper proposed necessary achievement process for simple and robust algorithm in CAD file that have such characteristics.

We analysis architectural drawings made by CAD tool for architectural design, then embed watermarks having transparency using the adaptive algorithm. And finally, we develop a robust detection algorithm nevertheless various data handlings treating as attacks. At first time, we acquire and classify components as LINEs and ARCs in the architectural drawing. Then, we embed watermarks adaptive to length and angle information of the components, because LINEs and ARCs are most basic components in CAD Data, therefore almost architectural drawings are designed on the basis of these two components, and they are indispensable elements of architectural drawings. The watermark having Gaussian random sequence, is embedded in the architectural drawing, and this algorithm has suitable embedding strength for transparency of the watermark. Fig.1 is simply displayed whole watermarking achievement process

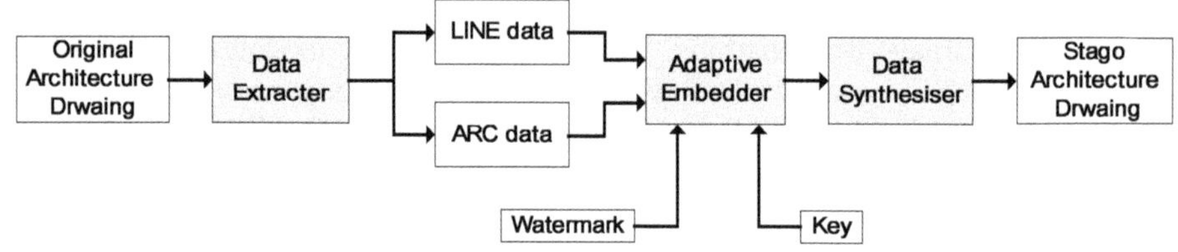

Fig. 1. The block diagram of proposed whole watermarking scheme.

Watermark is used with position key value to decide embedded position and sign. And, they are composed in original positions again after watermark was embedded. When detect watermarks, it can make to need not whole drawing of original but components that used only when watermark was embedded.

2.2 Conditions That Can Be Regarded as Attacks and Distortion

CAD data referred in 2.1 that transform to frequency domain is hard. In the meantime, including transformation of drawing that can consist in CAD tool, there is listed conditions that can be regarded as attack in watermarked architectural drawing.

- File format conversion: Watermarked drawings can change easily the format so that can use by other similar programs. For example, even if conversion of DWG and DWT, DWS, DXF etc. that is AutoCAD private file, watermark must be not damaged.
- Cropping: Watermark should be detected when inserted portion to attacker's drawing by cropping embedded whole design drawing, and regarded that would watermarked drawing or removed one part by attacker's necessity.
- Translation: Watermarks that are embedded to the ingredient must not be lost changes that movement of design drawing, or replacement of two ingredients in case is elements of same shape.
- Rotation: Attacker can rotate watermarked drawing by necessity. Watermark must not be broken in such cases.
- Scaling: Watermark should be available detection all in size change of whole drawing or only specification portion.
- Replacement and Resize: When after removed specification portion and inserted drawing such as it and after do Scaling again drawing to when did resizing similarly to original, watermarks must exist still.

It should be considered preferentially about attacks. This algorithm can be robustness in such attacks, and at the same time it makes user can't know existence of watermark.

In the meantime, architectural design drawing has no degradation of image quality like as other vertex based images even if magnify or reduce drawing extremely in software. Therefore, if distortions occur to design drawing by watermark, when he magnified drawing, the distortions can offend in user's eye. Therefore embedded watermark should be considered about the distortion rate about drawing, and these offenses should not be detected well if he magnified drawing extremely.

3 Proposed Watermarking Algorithm

3.1 LINE Watermarking

LINE Embedding Scheme. As one of components that are handled most in design drawing, LINE is consisted of beginning point coordinate (x_1, y_1) and end point coordinates (x_2, y_2). Actually, portion that watermark is embedded becomes coordinate of this vertex. There is performed as that do mapping to drawing embedded watermarks to extracted LINE components after extract LINE components from designed drawing.

Watermarks should be embedded in coordinates transparently by having distortion index α_L having size that users could not recognize for watermarks. Fig. 2 is embedding algorithm of watermarking about LINEs.

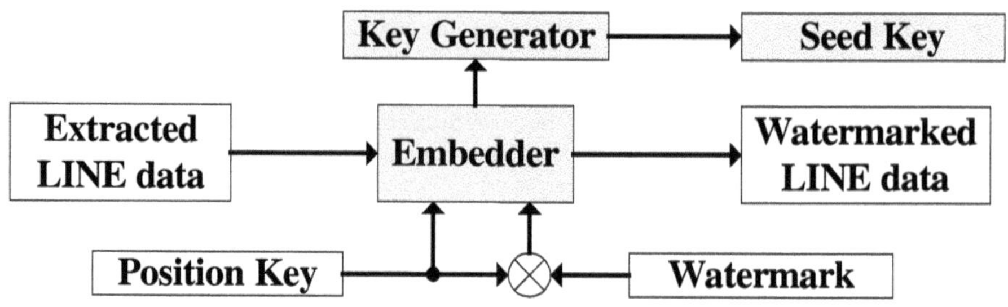

Fig. 2. LINE Embedding Algorithm.

We used random sequence of Gaussian distribution as watermark key including binary bit string as position key. This algorithm is to embed one watermark in all coordinates (x_1, y_1, x_2, y_2) to one LINE.

First, place be embedded in one LINE is decided by two position key bits k as (1).

$$P_n = \begin{cases} x_1 & \text{if } k_{n,n+1} = 00 \\ y_1 & \text{if } k_{n,n+1} = 01 \\ x_2 & \text{if } k_{n,n+1} = 10 \\ y_2 & \text{if } k_{n,n+1} = 11 \end{cases}, \quad k_{MAX} = w_{MAX+1} \tag{1}$$

And first key bit also uses to decide sign of original watermarks from (2).

$$s_n = \begin{cases} +1 & \text{if } k_n = 0 \\ -1 & \text{if } k_n = 1 \end{cases} \tag{2}$$

P_n is coordinate value that watermarks was embedded, and n means number of LINEs and watermarks. As doing this, embedded coordinates are concealed from users or attackers, also minimize visible artifacts, and can detect watermarks by using LINE's length or absolute value. And watermarks are embedded to LINE data by (3).

$$P_n^* = P_n + \alpha_L \cdot s_n \cdot w_n \tag{3}$$

There is distortion index α_L in relation of trade-off between robustness and transparency. Watermarked P_n^* is composed to original CAD data again. Then, compute the LINE's length including embedded coordinate points, finally, get difference value D_n of original LINE's length and watermarked LINE's length. Lastly, this difference $D_{0,1,\cdots,n-1}$ being values that are got as the *Seed Key*, and when detect, they are used to calculate similarity. If $k_{n,n+1} = 01$, numerical formula deciding difference value D_n is (4).

$$D_n = \left\{ \sqrt{(x_2 - x_1)^2 + (y_2 - P_n^*)^2} - \sqrt{(x_2 - x_1)^2 + (y_2 - y_1)^2} \right\} / \alpha_L \tag{4}$$

Seed Key value D_n has form of square and distortion index α_L is used as embedding strength. At last, Original CAD data and w_n used to embedding in LINEs, are not necessary in extracting process. It needs only extracted LINE from the original CAD data. Designer gets D_n as key. This method has robust algorithm as long as LINE's length does not change. And, we can get square term's Gaussian distribution similar to w_n as multiplying distortion index α_L to D_n.

This algorithm can have tenacious in attacks of rotation, translation, cropping, and so on as using length information of LINEs by watermark key,

Because only one watermark is embedded in 4-coordinate values, it can improve transparency. Also, by binary bit string, users cannot know whether watermark embedded in any coordinate point and as certain signs because decided concealment position. Furthermore, binary individual key used in concealment can do privily with key and signs value removing after watermark concealment because it is no necessity at detection algorithm.

Fig. 3 shows the distortion rate according to distortion index α_L of embedded watermarks by (3).

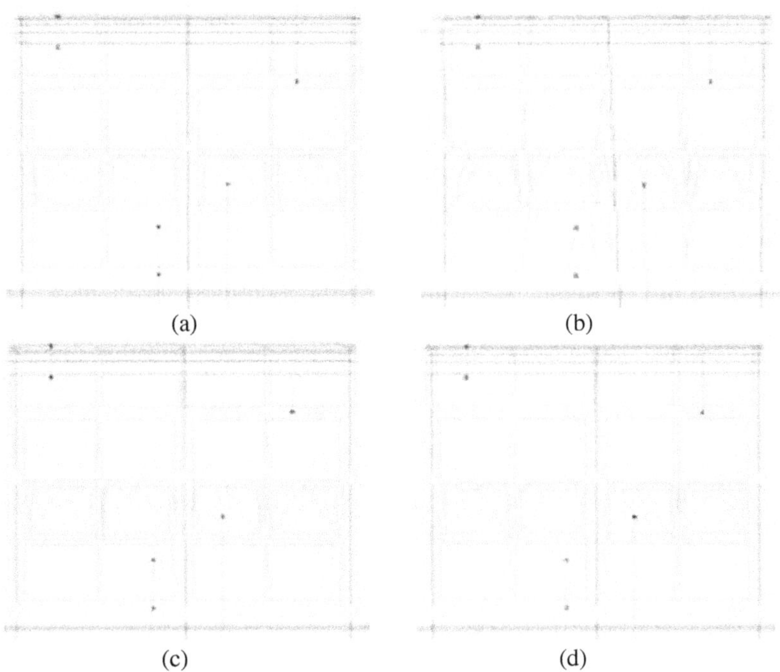

Fig. 3. Distortions of architectural design drawing by α_L factor. (a) Original CAD data, (b) $\alpha_L = 0.1$, (c) $\alpha_L = 0.01$, (d) $\alpha_L = 0.001$

Watermark Detection Scheme of LINE Data. Because we used length information of LINEs when we embedded watermarks to LINE, there is consist as detection process that calculate length of line for the first time. And original architectural drawing does not need in watermark detection process. Only, because watermark detection is possible if author has extracted LINE information in watermark embedding scheme, users cannot have any information about whole original architectural drawing. Watermark detection achieves as (5).

$$D_n^* = \left\{ \sqrt{(\bar{x}_2 - \bar{x}_1)^2 + (\bar{y}_1 - \bar{p}_n^*)^2} - \sqrt{(x_2 - x_1)^2 + (y_2 - y_1)^2} \right\} / \alpha_L \tag{5}$$

Similarity of detected watermarks is calculated as (6) comparing detected Seed Key D_n^* by (5) with original Seed Key D_n.

$$Sim(D_n, D_n^*) = \frac{D_n^* \cdot D_n}{\sqrt{D_n^* \cdot D_n^*}} \tag{6}$$

As α_L used in embedding algorithm is divided to D_n and D_n^*. When $-1 < D_n < 1$, original's difference D_n and detected D_n^* of similarity have cost smaller than w_n, because D_n and D_n^* have square term. In this reason, the similarity of (D_n, D_n^*) is smaller than the similarity of (w_n, w_n^*), but about other keys, similarity of (w_n, D_n^*) has very smaller value then similarity of (w_n, other keys). Therefore, difference of matched Seed Key's similarity and not matched is greaten extremely. It can help claim copyright more certainly by author.

3.2 ARC Watermarking

ARC Embedding Scheme. We could confirm robustness about most attacks by LINE watermarking, but because it has complexity of calculation and difficulty of correct abstraction that must calculate the scaling factor for detection similarity about scaling attack, and do resizing again, it has a weakness about scaling. This weakness is supplemented as embedding watermarks to ARC and LINE.

Fig. 4 shows ARC Layer's structure that is used in architectural design drawing.

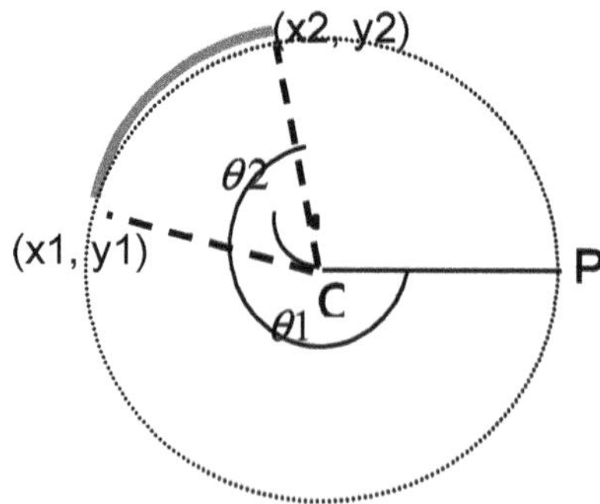

Fig. 4. Structure of ARC in architectural design drawing.

Where C is circle's emphasis that makes ARC, and R is radius from emphasis C to ARC, and P is reference axis of each angle $\theta 1$ and $\theta 2$ that appear to beginning point (x1, y1) and destination (x2, y2) of ARC. ARC consists as such each coordinate points and two angle, and, these angles are stable about geometrical transformation of rotation, scaling, and translation. We achieve watermark embedding that use ARC's angle $\theta 1$ and $\theta 2$ in ARC of fig. 4 in this method for robust watermarking algorithm. And because human's sight does not recognize delicate change of angle, we can embed watermark transparently.

To Embed watermark, after extract information of ARCs in original drawing and search for angle $\theta 1$ and $\theta 2$, we select one angle that watermark being embedded using (7), because we use technique to embed one watermark to one ARC.

```
IF θ1 <= 3 then,
        IF θ2 >= 357 then,
                watermark is embedded θ1
                  K = 1
        ELSE  watermark is embedded  θ2
                K = -1
ELSE  watermark is embedded θ1
        K = 1
```
(7)

Also to except cases that the angle values become negative or pass over 360 degree by embedded watermark, we used (7). After achieve (7), watermark is embedded by ARC's angle by (8).

$$\theta' = \theta + \alpha_A K w \tag{8}$$

Where θ' and θ are each watermarked angle and original angle, α_A is the distortion index of ARC watermarking, in this method, we decided $\alpha_A = 1$. And K is private key that is selected in (8), w is watermark. Because watermark is detected by difference of angle $\theta 1$ and $\theta 2$, private key K is decided as (7) and then acts to find sign of watermark automatically in watermark detection. After achieve this process, θ' is inserted in original position in architecture design drawing.

Fig. 5 compares original drawing and watermarked. We can know that cannot confirm distortion of drawing by embedded watermark visually through fig. 5.

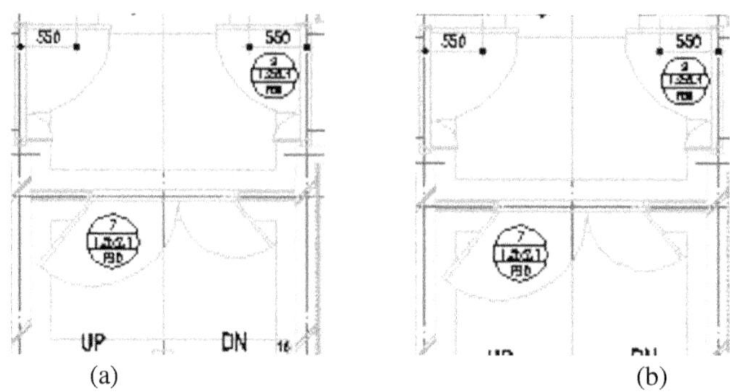

(a) (b)

Fig. 5. Transparency of ARC watermarking. (a) original drawing, (b) watermarked drawing

Watermark Detection Scheme of ARC Data. Watermark detection consists as extract ARC information again in watermarked drawing. Because watermark is embedded to angle information, detection is available as (9).

$$\omega = \{(\theta 2 - \theta 1) - (\theta 2^* - \theta 1^*)\} / \alpha_A \tag{9}$$

$(\theta 2 - \theta 1)$ and $(\theta 2^* - \theta 1^*)$ express each angles of original drawing and watermarked drawing. Finally, similarity of watermark is calculated by (10) comparing detected watermark ω by (9) with original watermark w.

$$sim(w, \omega) = \frac{\omega \cdot w}{\sqrt{\omega \cdot \omega}} \tag{10}$$

However, in certain special cases, the ARC's angles are influenced in case of design drawing received some processing or was embedded watermark. For example, if some ARC that have angle of 2 degree changes -3 degree by some subordinations, actuality the ARC's value is 359 degree. In this case, the ARC is except from watermark detection process. Even though these exceptions, because these happen in special cases, there is allowable in watermark detection. Finally, we calculate similarity about w and ω using (10) for ARC watermarking.

4 Experimental Results

This paper used drawings that are manufactured by 'AutoCAD 2002' tool for an experiment of proposed watermarking algorithm of architectural design drawing, and selected 'building external form drawing' and 'Stair section-detail drawing' drawings to main testing bench for an efficient experiment of proposed method that. After extracted each LINE and ARC, we embedded watermark. Key watermark used 20th seed of 1000 Gaussian random sequence and each A_L and A_C used 0.0001 and 1. We alternated already calculated D_n with the 20th key for the convenience in Line watermarking. And we embedded LINEs and ARCs apart each to two drawings for correct result of experiments. We embedded 916 watermarks to extracted 916 LINE in 'building external form drawing', and 1000 watermarks to extracted 2227 ARC in 'Stair section-detail drawing'.

Because there are no benchmarks about watermarking of architectural design drawing, we experiment robustness of LINE and ARC as attacks that describe to 2.2 and confirm the similarity.

Fig. 6 displayed watermarked images and similarities of detected watermarks to about original 'building external form drawing' and 'Stair section-detail drawing'. And Key was unlisted thing to seed in (e), but alternate by the 20th seed voluntarily for the convenience of an experiment. Because we used each different key values, forms of (e) and (f) are different.

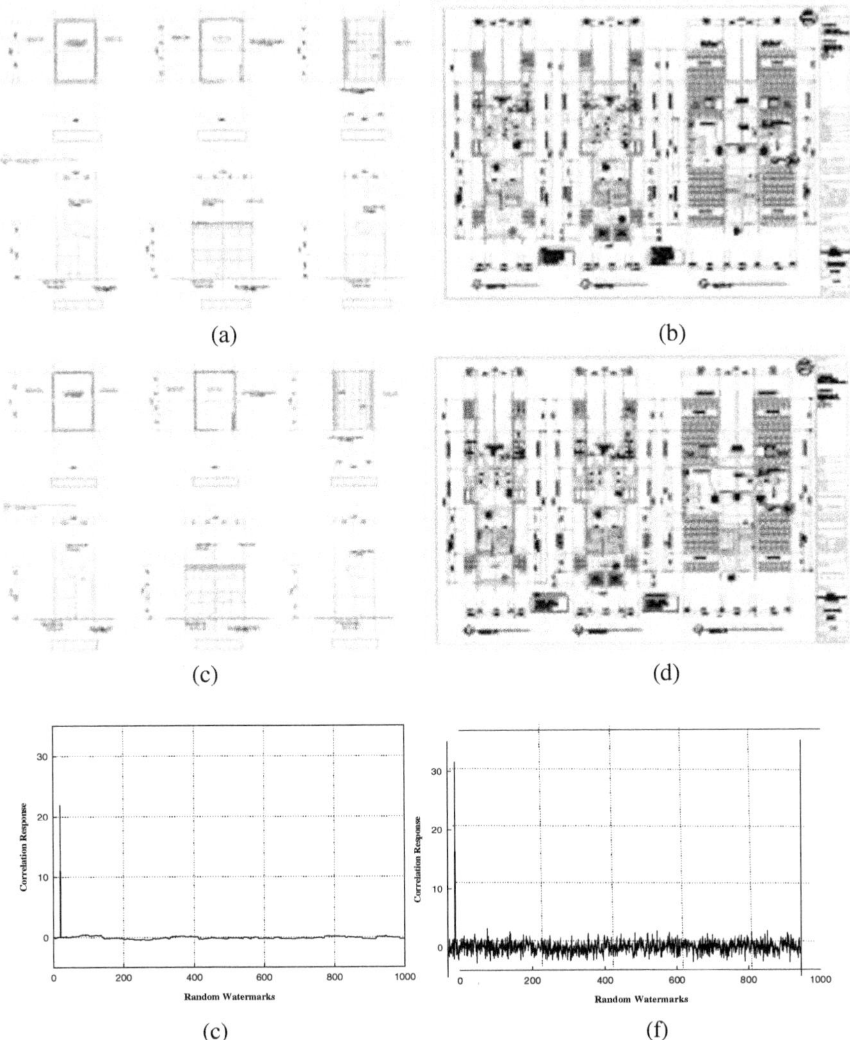

Fig. 6. Results of proposed watermarking in architectural design drawing. (a) and (b) are original drawings, (c) watermarked LINE of (a), (d) watermarked ARC of (b), (e) and (f) display each similarities of (c) and (d)

As can know in Fig. 6, watermarks were embedded transparently in architectural design drawings, and confirmed that also is detected with unique key value. When there was not attacked, LINE's similarity was 21.93, and ARC's similarity was 31.58.

Table 1 is result of an experiment of watermarks' similarities inspection, after changes embedded architectural design drawing in other formats-available to other similar software. We can know that there is no damage of all watermarks in LINEs and ARCs.

Table 1. Watermarks damage by file format conversion.

Format	DXF (2002)	DWG	DWT	DWS	DXF (early)
LINEs	21.93	21.93	21.93	21.93	21.93
ARCs	31.58	31.58	31.58	31.58	31.58

Fig. 7 is result that moves positions of each block from watermarked drawings, and displayed similarity to Fig. 8 after that attack.

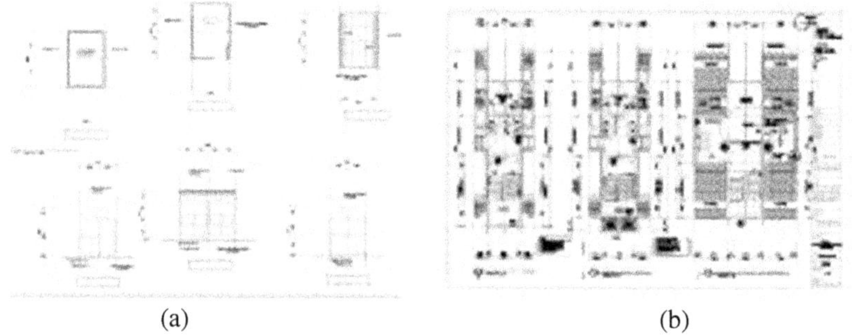

(a) (b)

Fig. 7. Translations of watermarked drawings as attack

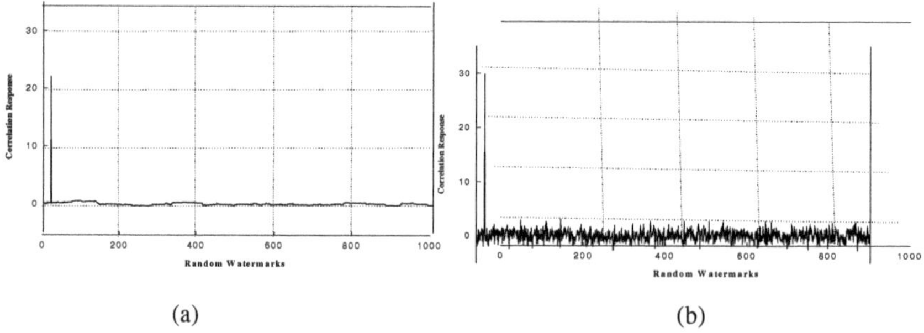

(a) (b)

Fig. 8. Similarities of watermark after translations attack in Fig. 7. (a) 21.93, (b) 29.89

In Fig. 8, regarding position translation as attack, after change positions of all blocks, watermark was not lost entirely. Fig. 9 and 10 displayed drawings after encounter different various attacks like as rotation, expansion and reduction. Fig. 11 and 12 display correlation response after doing such processes regarded as attacks.

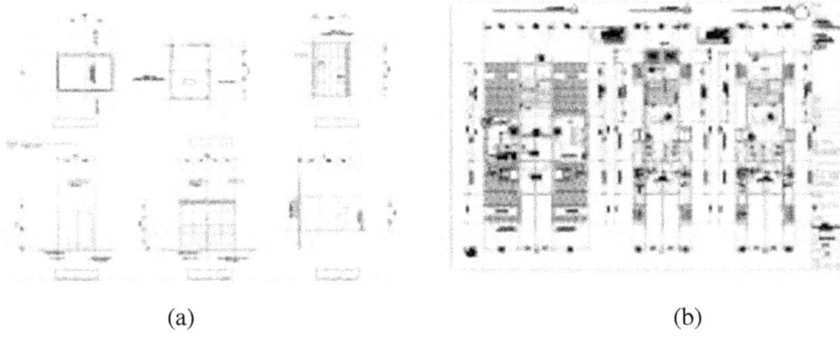

(a) (b)

Fig. 9. Rotations of watermarked architectural designed drawings as attack.

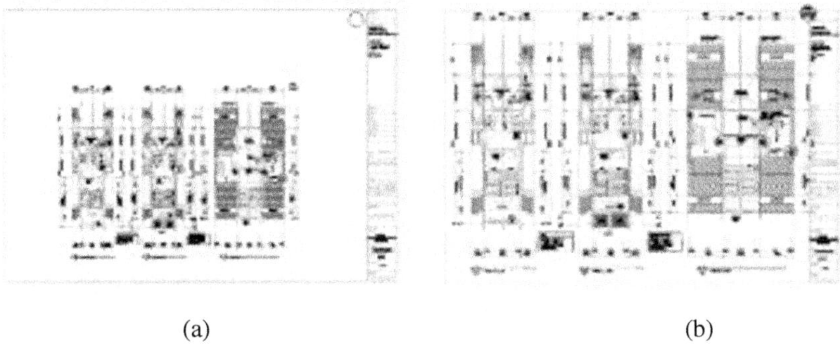

(a) (b)

Fig. 10. Scaling of watermarked architectural designed drawings. (a) and (b) are each expended and reduced drawings of ARC embedding.

As Fig. 11 displays correlation responses of Fig. 9, about rotation attack, we could know LINE and ARC's watermarks were not damaged. In Fig. 12, although watermark embedded in ARC was attacked with scaling, we could identify robustness of the embedded watermark.

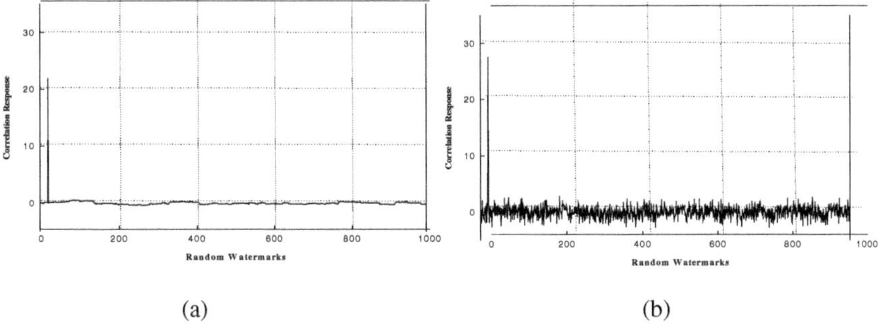

(a) (b)

Fig. 11. Similarities of watermark after rotation attack in Fig. 9. (a) 21.93, (b) 27.52

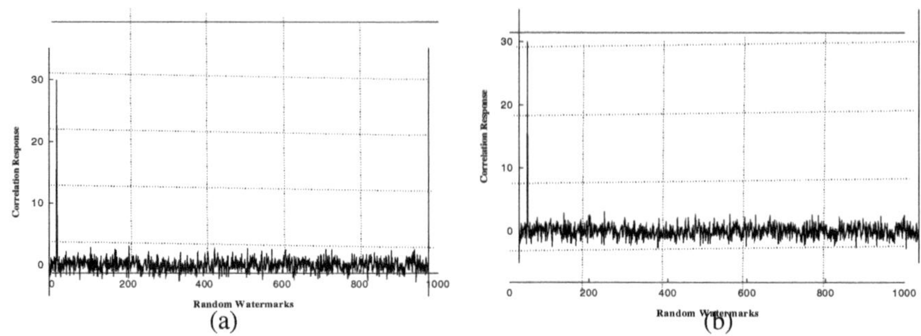

Fig. 12. Similarities of watermark in ARC after scaling attack in Fig. 10. (a) reduction(29.89), (b) expansion(29.89)

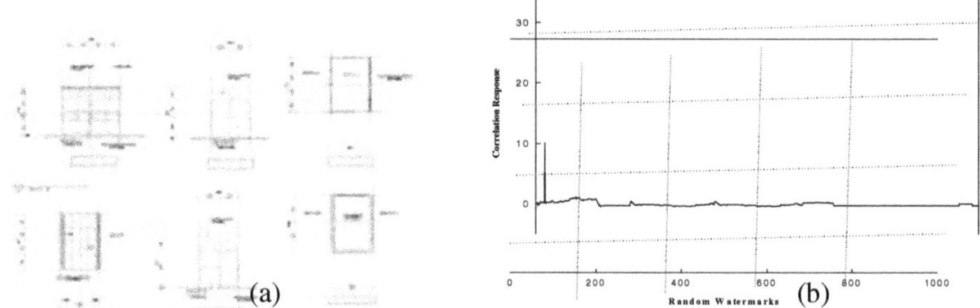

Fig. 13. Replacement and Resizing of LINE watermarking. (a) attacked drawing (b)correlati response of Fig. 13-(a)

Fig. 13-(a) shows attacked drawing in LINE watermarking about replaceme and resizing process Specially, about resizing, after changed positions of each bloc in drawing, then we changed size of blocks enlarger or smaller for experiment. A then we calculated scaling factors by comparing with original watermarked drawin and then we did resizing process again. We could know that watermark was damage in replacement and resizing attack. This problem occurred because resizing was n done perfectly after LINE's length was distorted by scaling process. In case expand reduce extremely the watermarked drawing as scaling attack, watermark that embedded in LINE is damaged, but we showed robustness to other attacks. Also v confirmed that watermarks that were embedded to ARC robust regardless of scali attack. Therefore, proposed method in this paper can display robust performance attacks more as using together these two watermarking algorithms.

Finally, we displayed result about cropping attack in Table 2, we could see th similarity decreases by cropping ratio, but confirmed many of them are exist. B cropping heightens the ratio, damage of watermark becomes a lot. This handles th escape a little in category of attack because it is damaged design drawing.

Table 2. Watermarks damage by cropping ratio in LINEs.

Similarity	Watermark number	Cropping ratio(%)
21.93	916	0
21.19	828	9.6
16.66	552	39.7
15.83	492	46.3
14.83	367	59.9
13.90	305	66.7

5 Conclusions

In this paper, we proposed a robust watermarking algorithm in geometrical attacks using LINEs and ARCs in architectural design drawing. In experiment result, perceptually artifact by watermarks embedded from proposed method did not recognize anyone, as confirmed before, we could know that watermark was showed robust characteristics under various kinds condition be regarded as geometrical or another attacks. These results can help to have copyright about building design technology is not protected by intellectual property entirely. As this, we expect that is going to ready minimum protection standard in copyright protection of exposed architectural design drawing shieldlessly. And we expect that may apply to watermarkings for more 2-D image based on vertex.

Acknowledgements. This work was supported by grant No.(R05-2003-000-10830-0) from Korea Science & Engineering Foundation.

References

1 I.Cox, J.Kilian, T.Leighton, and T.Shamoon.: Secure Spread Spectrum Watermarking for Multimedia. NEC Research Institute Tech Rep. 95–10, (1995)

2 M. Swanson, B. Zhu, and A. Twefik.: Transparent Robust Image Watermarking. IEEE International Conference on Image Processing ICIP96, Vol. 3. (1996) 211–214

3 C. Podilchuk and W.Zeng.: Image Adaptive Watermarking Using Visual Models. IEEE Journal on Selected Areas in Communication, Vol. 16, No. 4. (1998) 525–539

4 J. Ruanaidh and T. Pun.: Rotation, Scale and Translation Invariant Spread Spectrum Digital Image Watermarking. Journal of Signal Processing, Vol. 66, No.3. (1998) 303–317

5 Sviatoslav Voloshynovskiy, A. Herrigel, N. Baumgaertner, and T. Pun.: A Stochastic Approach to Content Adaptive Digital Image Watermarking. Proc. of Third Information Hiding Workshop. (1999)

6 K.R. Kwon and A.H. Tewfik.: Adaptive Watermarking Using Successive Subband Quantization and Perceptual Model Based on Multiwavelet Transform. SPIE, Vol. 4675–37. (2002)

7 R. Obuchi, H. Ueda, and S. Endoh.: Robust Watermarking of Vector Digital Maps. International Conference on Multimedia & Expo. (2002)

Public Watermark Detection Using Multiple Proxies and Secret Sharing

Qiming Li and Ee-Chien Chang

[1] Temasek Laboratories National University of Singapore tslliqm@nus.edu.sg
[2] Department of Computer Science National University of Singapore
changec@comp.nus.edu.sg

Abstract. A central issue in public watermarking schemes is the design of a detector that will not reveal sufficient information that leads to the erasure of embedded watermark, even if an adversary knows the detection algorithm and the public detection key (if any). Insofar, there is no such detector in "stand-alone" setting that achieves satisfactory security requirements. Recently, [1] gives a zero-knowledge detector that achieves security by introducing a server. We propose an alternative setting of public watermarking that involves multiple servers. In this setting, the *owner* keeps a secret watermark W. A *verifier*, given an image J (or any digital media), wants to detect whether J is watermarked. The detection is to be carried out by a group of independent *proxies*. The owner does not trust the verifier nor any individual proxy, thus wants to keep W hidden from them. On the other hand, the verifier does not trust the owner and any individual proxy either, and wants to protect himself against cheating. The proxies, as a group, are tasked to maintain the secrecy of the watermark, and protect the interest of the verifier. We propose a scheme based on secret sharing schemes which support arithmetic operations. The security is maintained if not too many individuals (including the proxies, the owner and the verifier) collude. The proposed scheme is efficient in terms of computation cost, and the number of rounds and bandwidth required in the communications. The scheme is arguably easy to implement.

1 Introduction

A central issue in public watermarking schemes [4] is the design of a detector that will not reveal the secret watermarks embedded into the media, even if an adversary knows the detection algorithm and the public detection key (if any).

A possible approach uses asymmetric watermarking schemes [10,8,7], where the key to embed watermarks is different from the key required during detection. However, the detection keys of known methods do reveal some crucial information, which leads to a number of successful attacks (for e.g., [7] listed a few attacks on specific schemes).

A simple approach achieves secrecy by introducing a trusted third party P. In which case the owner of the watermark gives his watermark W to P, and

T. Kalker et al. (Eds.): IWDW 2003, LNCS 2939, pp. 558–569, 2004.
© Springer-Verlag Berlin Heidelberg 2004

distributes images[1] with W embedded to the public. To check if an image is watermarked, a user sends it to P via the Internet, and the result is sent back from P. In this case both the secrecy of W and the interest of the users are protected assuming that P is honest.

It seems that the trusted third party is crucial to maintain security in the above simple approach. Recently, [1,6] gave interesting methods to remove the assumption of a trusted third party. The methods employ a *prover* (the owner) who proves the existence of the watermark in given images to *verifiers* (the users). The prover is prevented from cheating by the means of commitment schemes, and the secrecy of the watermark is maintained through zero-knowledge interactive proofs. Although these schemes are cryptographically secure, a main drawback is the large number of rounds and bandwidth required in the communications, and they are not easy to implement in practice. Furthermore, if the owner wishes to designate another party to perform the checking and proving, he has to reveal the secret key to this trusted party.

In this paper, we propose an alternative setting that can be viewed as a modification of the above approach. In this setting, we remove the expensive zero-knowledge interactive proofs without assuming the existence of a trusted third party. Instead, we replace the trusted third party P with a group of *proxies*. Security is maintained if the majority of the proxies are honest.

The individuals in our setting are an owner, a few proxies, and a verifier. At the beginning, the owner generates a secret watermark W and performs a *registration* with the proxies. During registration, the owner distributes some information about the watermark W to the proxies, so that they can carry out watermark detections on their own. After that, the owner embeds the watermark W into his images, which are then released to the public. (The owner could also request the proxies to perform the embedding, without revealing the watermark. We will not describe this operation in this paper.) On the other hand, when a verifier wants to determine if a given image is watermarked by W, he requests the proxies to perform a *detection*. During detection, the verifier sends information about the image to the proxies, who then perform some computations and return the results back to the verifier. Based on these results, the verifier would be able to decide whether the image is watermarked. The registration and detection processes are illustrated in Fig. 1 below.

Since we do not assume the existence of a trusted third party, no individual can be trusted. Therefore, during registration, the owner does not trust any individual proxy, so he cannot simply send W to each of them. Instead, he needs to distribute the watermark in such a way that it is information-theoretically impossible to compute W even if some of the proxies collude. During detection, the verifier does not trust all proxies because some of them might give wrong results, either intentionally or accidentally. Therefore, there has to be some mechanisms to allow the verifier to detect errors, or even correct them. Furthermore, the verifier does not trust the owner either. A dishonest owner might distribute a watermark that correlates with many images (for instance, in the well-known spread spectrum method [5], a watermark with very high energy would likely

[1] The "images" here can in fact be any digital contents in any media.

give a high correlation value with a randomly chosen image). The dishonest owner might also collude with a few proxies to mislead the verifier.

Note that in this setting, the role of the proxies (as a group) is similar to that of a trusted third party, who will not leak any information of the secret W, and will not cheat the verifier. The main difference is that, in this setting, we only require the integrity of the proxies as a group, which is a much weaker requirement than having a trusted third party. It is also noted that our setting relieves the owner from performing the detections. This is a secondary advantage of using proxies for detection.

The proposed setting naturally suggests the use of secret sharing schemes [15] as a basic building block. A secret sharing scheme breaks a secret z into *shares* and distributes each to a server. No individual server will know the secret unless a number of dishonest servers collude. There are many secret sharing schemes, satisfying various useful properties. For example, Shamir's scheme is also a threshold scheme, and with further modifications it can be verifiable [3,9] and proactive [11]. An important property required in our setting is that, both multiplications and additions can be supported on the shares. That is, if secrets z_1, z_2 and z_3 are integers and are shared among n severs, the shares of $z_1z_2 + z_3$ can be generated without revealing the values of z_1, z_2, z_3, and $z_1z_2 + z_3$.

We give a scheme based on secret sharing. This scheme achieves public watermarking as long as not too many individuals collude. This scheme is arguably easy to implement and is efficient in terms of computation and communication cost.

Outline. In Section 2.1, we describe the basic watermarking method (spread-spectrum method) used for discussion. Section 2.2 gives our proposed multiple proxies setting, and the security requirements. Section 3 gives a brief description of secret sharing schemes. Our scheme is described in Section 4, followed by the security analysis in Section 5. Some discussions on the error-correcting capability of the scheme will be given in Section 6.

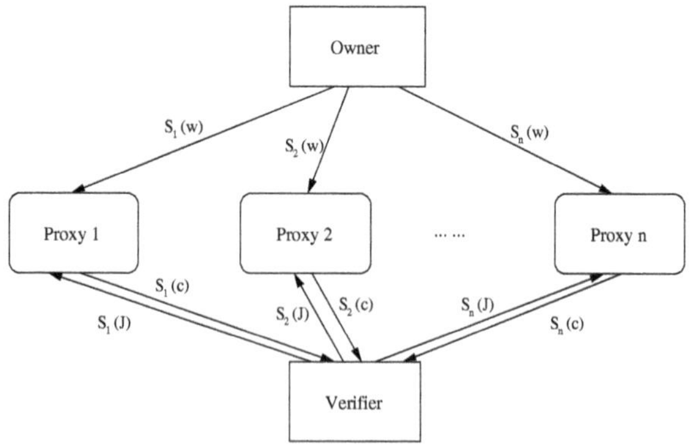

Fig. 1. The proposed setting.

2 Notations and Model

2.1 Watermarking Model

We employ a variant of the well-known spread spectrum method [5] to embed and detect watermarks. Other watermarking schemes can also be employed as long as the detection involves only multiplication and addition.

Our images and watermarks are "discretized". An image I is a vector $I = (x_1, x_2, \ldots, x_m)$ where each $x_i \in \{0, 1, 2, \ldots, d-1\}$ and d is some integer determined by the media/image representation. For example, d could be 256 if each x_i represents a pixel. The watermark W is also a vector $W = (w_1, w_2, \ldots, w_m)$ where each $w_i \in \mathbf{Z}$ is an integer. In addition, the energy of the watermark W is fixed, that is $W \cdot W = E$ where E is some predefined threshold, and $\cdot$ is the vector inner product. The constant E is made known to the public.

During embedding, given an image I and the watermark W, the watermarked image $\widetilde{I}$ is

$$\widetilde{I} = \text{trunc}(I + W),$$

where the function trunc() truncates/rounds the coefficients where values are not in the range $\{0, 1, 2, \ldots, d-1\}$.

During detection, given an image J, the correlation value $(J \cdot W)$ is computed. If the correlation value exceeds certain threshold, then J is declared to be watermarked.

Note that we omit the normalization of images in the embedding and detection. Normalization is not required in our discussion, but still can be incorporated if required. Thus, it is omitted for simplicity.

2.2 Owner, Proxies, and Verifier

The individuals in the proposed setting are an owner, n proxies $P_1, P_2, \ldots, P_n$, and verifiers. The number of verifiers is not important, so we assume that there is only one verifier.

During the *registration*, the owner generates a secret watermark W which satisfies $(W \cdot W) = E$, where E is a constant that every individual knows. The owner sends information of W to the n proxies. Let $S_i^{(0)}(W)$ be the data the owner sends to the proxy P_i. Let $S_i(W)$ be the data that P_i keeps and uses in subsequent computations. Note that it is not necessary that $S_i^{(0)}(W) = S_i(W)$. To guard against dishonest owner, the proxies might wish to transform the original $S_i^{(0)}(W)$'s distributed by the owner.

During the *detection*, a verifier wishes to know the correlation value $c = J \cdot W$ of a given image J with the secret watermark W. Firstly, the verifier splits J into n pieces, $S_i(J)$, $1 \le i \le n$, such that each of them contains partial information about J. Then it sends $S_i(J)$ to proxy P_i respectively. Next, each proxy P_i computes and sends the verifier partial information $S_i(c)$ of the correlation value c. After receiving data from all proxies, the verifier reconstructs the correlation value $(J \cdot W)$ (Fig. 1).

In our proposed scheme, the partial information communicated through the network, namely $S_i^{(0)}(W)$, $S_i(W)$, $S_i(J)$ and $S_i(c)$, corresponds to the "shares" in secret sharing schemes (see Section 3). Therefore, we will refer to those pieces of information as shares in the rest of this paper, even if some of them may be fraud sent by dishonest individuals.

2.3 Security Requirements

A parameter for the security requirement is the *security threshold* t where $t \leq n$. Vaguely, the scheme should tolerate at most $(t-1)$ dishonest individuals (including the proxies, the verifier and the owner). The security requirements can be roughly classified into (a) maintaining the secrecy of W, and (b) protecting the interest of the the verifier. In the following, the first requirement $S1$ belongs to the first class and the remaining belong to the second class.

S1. Secrecy of W. The owner generates and keeps the watermark W. Recall that the energy $(W \cdot W)$ is a predefined constant E, which is known by everyone. For any $(t-1)$ proxies, even if they collude, they should not know W. Specifically, to any group of $(t-1)$ proxies, any vector W' satisfying $(W' \cdot W') = E$ is a possible candidate for the secret watermark.

On the other hand, after detection, from the n sets of data $S_i(c)$'s obtained, the verifier should not know W. Specifically, to the verifier, any vector W' satisfying $(W' \cdot W') = E$ and $(J \cdot W') = c$ is a possible candidate for the secret watermark.

In general, any $(t-1)$ individuals, including the proxies and verifier, should not know W. That is, by combining all the data held by them, any vector W' satisfying $(W' \cdot W') = E$ and $(J \cdot W') = c$ is a possible candidate for the secret watermark.

S2. Dishonest owner during registration. During registration, instead of honestly sending $S_i(W)$ to the proxies, an owner may send other values so as to mislead the proxies to give high correlation value during detection. Here is an example of dishonest owner: the dishonest owner chooses a watermark w and embeds it into images according to the scheme, but registers with the proxies another watermark Aw where A is a very large constant. Thus, in the subsequent detections, whatever correlation value determined will be based on Aw, instead of w. Owe to the large value of A, the probability that a randomly chosen image is wrongly declared as watermarked is higher. Therefore, we require that, after registration, with at most $(t-1)$ dishonest proxies, any malicious behaviour of the owner can be detected. Specifically, the proxies can check that, indeed, $(W \cdot W) = E$.

S3. Dishonest proxies during detection. During detection, some of the proxies may collude so as to mislead the verifier. Thus, we require that, if at most $(t-1)$ proxies are dishonest, the verifier can detect that.

S4. Collusion among proxies and the owner during detection. A more interesting case is collusion among the owner and proxies. The owner may collude with a few proxies and mislead the verifier. The main difference of this case from the case in previous paragraph is that: here, the owner can reveal the watermark to the proxies. With this extra information, it is easier for the proxies to influence the detection. Thus, we require that, if the owner colludes with at most $(t-2)$ proxies (so the total number of dishonest individuals is at most $t-1$), the verifier should be able to detect that.

S5. Collusion among the owner, proxies and a verifier. It is interesting that we should consider collusion among dishonest owner and verifier. The owner may collude with the verifier and a few proxies, so as to obtain the $S_i(W)$ held by an honest proxy P_i. After obtaining the information, they can use it to influence subsequent detections. Thus we require that, by combining information from a verifier, $(t-3)$ proxies, and the owner, no sufficient information on data held by honest proxies can be derived.

Remarks. Note that currently we do not consider verifier/proxies who keep the history of communications. For example, a verifier who probes the proxies by sending in a series of images. This type of attacks is generally known as sensitivity attacks. We will address this in Section 7.

2.4 Requirement on Error-Correcting

A secondary requirement is error-correcting capability. More specifically, even if some proxies are dishonest or failed, detection can still be carried out. Note the difference between security and error-correcting capability. A scheme that immediately shuts down when malicious activities are detected is considered to be secure, but it is not capable of correcting errors. We say that the *error-correcting threshold* of a scheme is R, if all detection operations can be carried out when there are at least R honest proxies.

3 Backgrounds on Secret Sharing Schemes

A (t, n) secret sharing scheme splits a secret (for example, a binary file) into n pieces, which are referred to as *shares*. Then the shares are distributed to n servers respectively. The knowledge of any $t-1$ shares will not reveal the secret and the secret is reconstructible by putting together any t shares. When $t < n$, it is also known as a t out of n *threshold* scheme. Shamir gave such a scheme in 1979 [15]. For a secret $z \in \mathbf{Z}_p$, where p is a large enough prime known to everyone, the share for the i-th server is $f(i) \pmod p$ where $f(x)$ is a random polynomial of degree $(t-1)$ whose free coefficient $f(0) = z$. No individual server knows the coefficients of $f(x)$, thus any $t-1$ servers can not derive z from their shares. However, if t servers put their shares together, they can solve for the coefficients of $f(x)$ and thus reconstruct the secret z.

Shamir's scheme can be modified to achieve useful properties. For example, the schemes can be verifiable [3,9] and proactive [11]. It is also known that certain arithmetic operations of the secrets can be performed on their shares, such that the shares of the result can be obtained without revealing any of the secrets [2, 12]. In our scheme, we mainly make use of arithmetic operations on the shares. Proactive schemes can also be employed to enhance security.

3.1 Notations on Secret Sharing

A secret is an integer in $\mathbf{Z}_p$ where p is a prime. In this paper, all arithmetic operations (multiplications and additions) performed are followed by modulo p. Thus, for simplicity, we omit the notation (mod) when writing an arithmetic expression. For example, we simply write $z_1 + z_2 z_3 \pmod{p}$ as $z_1 + z_2 z_3$.

With respect to a secret sharing scheme, let $S_i(z)$ be the i-th share of z, the secret [2]. Let $S(V)$ be the i-th share of a vector $V = (v_1, v_2, \dots, v_m)$. Note that the "secret" in the secret sharing scheme is an integer, whereas the watermark W and image I are vectors. To compute $S(V)$, we treat each v_i as an independent secret. That is, $S_i(V) = (S_i(v_1), S_i(v_2), \dots, S_i(v_m))$. Since the shares are associated with the proxies, we also call $S_i(V)$ the share of V for the proxy P_i.

3.2 Arithmetic Operations on Shares

Consider two secrets α and β, which are encoded by $f(x)$ and $g(x)$ respectively as in Shamir's scheme, and the shares are distributed to $2t-1$ servers. Now, suppose the servers want to compute the shares of $\alpha+\beta$ without revealing the values of α, β or $\alpha+\beta$. This can be easily done by instructing each server to locally construct the new share by adding the two shares it holds.

The shares for $\alpha\beta$ can be computed similarly by computing $s_{i,1}s_{i,2}$, which is the share of $\alpha\beta$ encoded by $k(x) = f(x)g(x)$. However, the degree of $k(x)$ is raised to $2t-2$, thus $2t-1$ servers are required to reconstruct the secrets.

In our application, instead of general combinations of multiplications and additions, we require only inner products. That is, given the shares of $x_1, x_2, \dots, x_m$, and $v_1, v_2, \dots, v_m$, we want to compute the shares of the inner product $c = \sum_{i=1}^{m} x_i v_i$, without revealing the secrets $x_1, x_2, \dots x_m$, $v_1, v_2, \dots, v_m$, and the inner product c. For each server, its share of c can be easily computed locally by simply computing the summation of products on its shares of x_i, v_i's.

4 Public Watermark Detection Using Secret Sharing

The multiple proxies setting naturally suggests the use of secret sharing as a basic construction block.

Assume that there are n proxies. Suppose the security threshold we want to achieve is t, that is, if not more than $(t-1)$ individuals collude, the security is maintained. We also require that $(2t-1) \le n$.

[2] Note that the shares are computed based on some randomly chosen numbers. Thus to be more precise, we should write $S_i(R, z)$ for the share where R is the chosen sequence of random numbers. For simplicity, we omit R in the notation.

We choose a (t, n) secret sharing scheme where $(2t-1) \leq n$. Recall that n is the number of proxies, and $(t-1)$ is the number of dishonest individuals the system can tolerate.

The scheme consists of two parts: registration and detection.

REGISTRATION

§1. ***Distributing watermark.*** The owner, using the secret sharing scheme (with the notations defined in Section 2.2 and 3.1), computes $S_i^{(0)}(W)$, the share of W for each proxy P_i, $1 \leq i \leq n$. The owner then sends $S_i^{(0)}(W)$ to P_i secretly for all proxies.

§2. ***Refreshing the shares.*** After receiving the shares from the owner, the proxies refresh the shares of W using the mechanisms described in Section 3. At the end of this step, each proxy P_i has $S_i(W)$ as a new share of W, and old shares $S_i^{(0)}(W)$'s are discarded.

§3. ***Checking W is genuine.*** Each proxy P_i computes the value $(S_i(W) \cdot S_i(W))$, and broadcasts it to other proxies. Note that this value is also the share of the inner product $(W \cdot W)$ for each proxy. After receiving all data from other proxies, each proxy reconstructs $(W \cdot W)$ and confirms that indeed $(W \cdot W) = E$. If not, the registration fails.

The detection is initiated by a verifier. The verifier wants to know whether an image J is embedded with the watermark claimed by the owner.

DETECTION

§1. ***Distributing the image.*** The verifier computes the shares of J and sends the shares to the respective proxies.

§2. ***Computing the shares of the correlation value.*** Each proxy P_i computes the inner product $(S_i(J) \cdot S_i(W))$ and sends it back to the verifier.

§3. ***Reconstructing the correlation value.*** After receiving all the shares, the verifier reconstructs the correlation value $(J \cdot W)$. Recall that $(2t-1)$ shares are necessary and sufficient for reconstruction. Therefore, if $(2t-1) = n$, there is only one possible way to reconstruct such value. Otherwise, $(2t-1) < n$, and there are more than one group of $(2t-1)$ shares. For each group, the verifier reconstructs the value.

§4. ***Checking for corrupted data.*** Since the error-correcting threshold is $(2t-1)$, all proxies must be honest if $(2t-1) = n$. In this case, the only value the verifier reconstructed must be correct. Otherwise, the verifier checks whether there is any inconsistency among the values reconstructed from different groups of $(2t-1)$ shares. If so, it declares that some proxies are cheating.

To enhance security, the proxies can refresh their shares regularly. For example, after some number, say $m-1$ of detections have been carried out, the proxies can refresh the shares $S_i(W)$. This is to guard against sensitivity attacks. We will revisit these issues later.

5 Security Analysis

We want to show that the proposed scheme satisfies the requirements stated in Section 2.3. The requirements are generally in this form: if at most $(t-1)$ individuals collude, then either no extra information on W is revealed, or no sufficient information is revealed so that the colluders can manipulate the results.

In the following analysis, we treat each share as an equation, where the unknowns are the random numbers used to generate the share. To illustrate, consider a proxy P_i who is holding the share $S_i^{(0)}(W)$, and it wants to guess the watermark W. This share is generated by the owner using $(t-1)m$ random numbers (note that W is a vector of m coefficients). For example, let us consider only the first coefficient w_1, the proxy P_i can expresses what it has as the equation

$$S_i^{(0)}(w_1) = w_1 + r_1 i + r_2 i^2 + \ldots + r_{t-1} i^{t-1}$$

where $w_1, r_1, \ldots, r_{t-1}$ are the unknowns. If a proxy manages to gather t such equations or more, he would be able to solve for w_1. Otherwise, **any** value is a possible candidate for w_1.

Note that the security is achieved unconditionally. That is, even if the colluders have infinite computing power, they can not compute the secret. This is in contrast to schemes that are *computationally secure*, where the security is based on the assumption that certain problem is computationally difficult to solve. We will omit the details for security requirements ***S4*** and ***S5***.

S1. Secrecy of W. First, we investigate the case where all the $(t-1)$ colluders are proxies. Without loss of generality, let the colluders be the proxies $P_1, P_2, \ldots, P_{t-1}$. Note that each P_i has the shares $S_i(W)$ and $S_i^{(0)}(W)$, and all proxies know $S_j(E)$ for all j, and that $(W \cdot W) = E$. Now, we want to know whether combining the information from $(t-1)$ proxies will reveal additional information on W.

Let us consider only $S_i^{(0)}(W)$ first. For each coefficient w_i in vector W, $t-1$ random numbers are used to generate the shares. For w_i, there are t unkowns. On the other hand, the corresponding entry in each $S_i^{(0)}(W)$ proxy P_i possesses is equivalent to 1 equation. Therefore, for $t-1$ proxies, there are only $t-1$ equations, and any integer (in $\mathbf{Z}_d$) is a possible solution for w_i, as shown in [15]. This shows that these equations do not give the proxies any advantages in computing W. Furthermore, the new shares $S_i(W)$ are obtained after refreshing, and no information about W or $S_i^{(0)}(W)$ is exchanged among the proxies during this process. Therefore these values do not give any advantages in computing W either. Lastly, after computing $S_j(E) = S_i(W) \cdot S_i(W)$, information about the elements of $S_i(W)$ is hidden in the inner product, given that m is sufficiently large (which is true for most practical applications).

Next, suppose $(t-1)$ colluders are the verifier and $(t-2)$ proxies $P_1, \ldots, P_{t-2}$. The verifier knows the shares $S_i(c)$ for all i, where $S_i(c) = S_i(W) \cdot S_i(J)$. Similar to the above argument, given sufficiently large m, the information contained in the inner product is useless in attempts to obtain W.

S2. Dishonest owner during registration. The owner could be dishonest and try to mislead the proxies so that they give false results in the detection. For instance, he could give a false watermark with high energy, so that the correlation value of the watermark and any randomly chosen image would be large with high probability. This is prevented in the registration because the proxies compute the energy of the watermark and compare it to a known constant E (Step §3 in registration). If the energy is not E, the watermark would be rejected by the proxies, and the registration would fail.

S3. Dishonest proxies during detection. The proxies could also send false results of their inner products $S_i(W) \cdot S_i(J)$ to mislead the verifier. However, since we have more than $2t-1$ proxies in the system, we can perform reconstruction of $J \cdot W$ multiple times from different set of shares (Step §4 in detection). It is unlikely that the results are consistent if some proxies cheat. In this case, we can employ the method mentioned in Section 6 to both detect and correct the error.

6 Analysis on Error-Correcting

Besides the security requirement that no more than $t-1$ proxies collude, we also require that the verifier can detect errors from proxies and correct them if there are at least $(2t-1)$ honest proxies [3].

Here are two methods of error correction. The first method is to let the verifier compute a new image $J' = kJ$, where k is some integer chosen by the verifier. If the proxies are honest, the resulting correlation value $c' = J' \cdot W = k(J \cdot W)$ would have the integer k as its factor. If some proxies are dishonest, it is highly unlikely that the reconstructed correlation will still have k as its factor.

The other method let the verifier repeat the detection using the same image J, but using different random numbers to generate the shares of J. Thus, a group of $2t-1$ proxies would be able to give consistent results only if all of them are honest. By repeating the detections, the correct results can be obtained with arbitarily high probability. It is noted that the above two methods can be used together.

7 Sensitivity Attacks

A dishonest verifier might probe the proxies for the watermark. By designing the probes carefully, it may be able to get a good approximation of, or erase, the watermark, using small numbers of probes. This is generally known as sensitivity

[3] If an accidental error happens, say, during network transmission from a proxy to the verifier, we consider it as a dishonest behaviour (of the proxy).

attacks. Some general attacks are given in [4,13]. Practical attacks usually target at the image representation. For example, the well-know Stir-Mark provides a list of attacks [14].

We classify these attacks into two types. The first type is specific to our proposed scheme and not applicable to others schemes, for instance the zero-knowledge detector [1]. The second type of attacks are designed for general public watermarking schemes. For example, the attacks described in [4,14,13]. In this analysis, we focus on the first type. Further research is required to handle the second type of attacks.

Let us consider a dishonest verifier. The verifier may collude with $(t-2)$ proxies in attempt to get the secret watermark. Let $S = (s_1, s_2, \ldots, s_m)$ be the shares of W kept by an honest server. In each detection, the verifier knows the inner product of $S \cdot V$ where V is some vector chosen by the verifier. Although knowing $S \cdot V$ will not reveal any useful information of the watermark W, by sending in many different vectors, the verifier can determine S. If the verifier knows the inner product of $S \cdot V_i$ for $i = 1, \ldots, m$ and the V_i's are independent, then the verifier can solved for S. By knowing the shares in t proxies, the verifier can solve for W. Note that this attack is specific to our scheme. To prevent this, we can require the proxies to refresh their shares regularly, for example, after every $m-1$ detections.

8 Communication Cost

We measure the communication cost by the number of rounds of communication and the amount of data transmitted. The size of a coefficient is not more than $\lceil \log p \rceil$ bits, where p is the prime used in the secret sharing scheme. Note that we only require $p > n$ and p is larger than the range of the original image coefficient. Thus, it is not required to be very large. In contrast, for the zero-knowledge detector in [1], the size of one coefficient has to be large (for e.g., more than 200 bits), so that it is computationally infeasible to break the commitment scheme.

Let us assume that the size of each coefficient is 1 unit. Thus, the size of W and J is m. The size of each share is also m. During detection, the verifier sends the share $S_i(J)$ to each proxy P_i, and P_i returns the share $S_i(c)$ of the correlation value. Thus, only 1 round of communication is required. Since the size of each share $S_i(J)$ is m, and the size of each share $S_i(c)$ is 1, the total amount of data transmitted is $(mn + n)$. The zero-knowledge detector in [1] invokes an interactive proof protocol during detection. Due to the "probabilistic" nature of interactive proof, many rounds are required for high level of confidence.

Higher communication cost is required during registration. This is due to the communication required in refreshing. Fortunately, registration is only performed once for each watermark. During registration, refreshing without verification can be done in 1 round with mn^2 units of data. If verification is required, then the communication cost depends on the commitment schemes and the interactive proof protocol employed.

9 Conclusion

We propose a setting of public watermark detection using multiple proxies. The owner registers its watermark with a group of proxies, whereas the verifier contacts the proxies to check whether an image is watermarked. We give such a scheme based on secret sharing. As long as not too many individuals collude, the secrecy of the watermark can be maintained, and the verifier can be protected from cheating. In other words, public watermark detection is achieved by the integrity of the community. The scheme is efficient in terms of communication cost and is arguably easy to implement.

References

[1] A. Adelsbach and A. Sadeghi. Zero-knowledge watermark detection and proof of ownership. *4th Int. Workshop on Info. Hiding*, LNCS 2137:273–288, 2000.
[2] M. Ben-Or, S. Goldwasser, and A. Wigderson. Completeness theorems for non-cryptographic fault-tolerant distributed computation. In *STOC*, pages 1–10, 1988.
[3] B. Chor, S. Goldwasser, S. Micali, and B. Awerbuch. Verifiable secret sharing and achieving simultaneity in the presence of faults. In *FOCS*, pages 383–395, 1985.
[4] I.J. Cox and J-.P. Linmartz. Public watermarks and resistance to tampering. *IEEE Int. Conf. on Image Processing*, 3(0_3–0_6), 1997.
[5] I.J. Cox, M.L. Miller, and J.A. Bloom. *Digital Watermarking.* Morgan Kaufmann, 2002.
[6] S. Craver and S. Katzenbeisser. Copyright protection protocols based on asymmetric watermarking. In *CMS'01*, pages 159–170, 2001.
[7] J.J. Eggers, J.K Su, and B. Girod. Asymmetric watermarking schemes. *Sicherheit in Mediendaten*, September 2000.
[8] J.J. Eggers, J.K Su, and B. Girod. Public key watermarking by eigenvectors of linear transforms. *European Signal Processing Conference*, September 2000.
[9] P. Feldman. A practical scheme for non-interaive verifiable secret sharing. In *FOCS*, pages 427–437, 1987.
[10] T. Furon and P. Duhamel. An asymmetric public detection watermarking technique. *3rd Intl. Workshop on Information Hiding*, LNCS 1768:88–100, 2000.
[11] A. Herzberg, S. Jarecki, H. Krawczyk, and M. Yung. Proactive secret sharing or: How to cope with perpetual leakage. *CRYPTO'95*, LNCS 963:339–352, 1995.
[12] Martin Hirt, Ueli Maurer, and Bartosz Przydatek. Efficient secure multi-party computation. In *ASIACRYPT'00*, volume LNCS 1976, pages 143–161, 2000.
[13] Qiming Li and Ee-Chien Chang. Security of public watermarking schemes for binary sequences. *5th Int. Workshop on Info. Hiding*, pages 119–128, 2002.
[14] F.A.P. Petitcolas, R.J. Anderson, and M.G. Kuhn. Attacks on copyright marking systems. *2nd Intl. Workshop on Information Hiding*, LNCS 1525:219–239, 1998.
[15] Adi Shamir. How to share a secret. *Communications of the ACM*, 22(11):612–613, 1979.

Towards Generic Detection Scheme in Zero Knowledge Protocol for Blind Watermark Detection

Hang Hui Patrick Then and Yin Chai Wang

Faculty of Computer Science and Information Technology, University Malaysia of Sarawak, 94300 Kota Samarahan, Sarawak, Malaysia.
{tpatrick,ycwang}@fit.unimas.my

Abstract. A generic detection formula in zero-knowledge watermark detection protocol is proposed. This protocol is generic in term of its independence on the watermark detection formula. Regardless of the watermarking detection scheme, the prover, P, of an image sends watermark as commitment and other parameters to verifier, V. Prover is able to prove the existence of the watermark in an image without revealing any secret information about the watermark. In the proposed protocol, the verifier interacts with P and poses challenges as means to be convinced of the watermark presence in the image. Moreover, this protocol also eliminates the need for sub-protocols. As a minor contribution, this protocol does not need a trusted centre. However, situation permits, registration with trusted centre is easily workable with no modification on the protocol.

1 Introduction

Digital watermark has been commonly used in various applications such as proof of ownership, copy protection, authentication, fingerprinting, and steganography. For proof of ownership and some other applications, a highly robust watermark is useless without using an appropriate protocol to prove its existence. A prover will have to show his watermark to anyone who needs his proof of ownership. Dispute of ownership continue to propagate with all other images embedded with the same watermark. This seriously affects the practicality of digital watermarking scheme even though the watermark is very robust to all types of attacks.

In this paper, we are focusing on the protocol aspect on the proof of ownership particularly, for image. The ideal goal of the protocol is to prove the existence of a watermark in the image without revealing any information about the content of the watermark i.e. watermark location, number of bits, and its related correlation coefficient. Either an asymmetric watermarking scheme or zero knowledge protocol imposes a solution to this goal.

Asymmetric watermarking method has an obvious problem that its watermark detector is exposed to public. In turn, it is exposed to attacks too. Furthermore, their attacks are durable in the sense that the attacks can be carried out without any interaction with the prover or the owner of the secret key. Craver [2], and Craver and Katzenbeisser [12] had proposed two minimum knowledge protocols to prove the

T. Kalker et al. (Eds.): IWDW 2003, LNCS 2939, pp. 570–580, 2004.
© Springer-Verlag Berlin Heidelberg 2004

presence of watermark. Later, Adelsbach and Sadeghi [1] proposed zero-knowledge watermark detection protocols for proof of ownership.

Craver's methods are based on graph isomorphism and discrete logarithm. The methods are however not easy to be adapted with the state-of-the-art of digital watermarking schemes. Adelsbach and Sadeghi used commitment (discrete logarithm) as the core elements in the protocol run. Their experiments are based on Cox's spread spectrum watermarking that use Discrete Cosine Transform (DCT). The detection scheme of Cox's scheme is based on the correlation coefficient computed from the watermark and DCT-coefficients. This protocol is a zero-knowledge proof of knowledge because the watermark and all intermediary results involving watermark are perfectly hidden in the commitments.

Craver [2]'s detection protocol has to run in multi-rounds in order to yield negligible error probability 2^{-n} (where n is the rounds of protocol-run) to convince the verifier of the watermark presence. Protocol in [2] is further improved in [12] by concealing a genuine watermark by a series of fake ones. This protocol is also based on discrete logarithm and is again an interactive multi-round protocol as in [2]. Adelsbach and Sadeghi's protocol, however, has strong coherence to digital watermarking algorithm. This protocol depends on both the watermarking scheme and especially, its detection method. This dependency immediately indicates the amount of effort needed to modify the protocol if the correlation formula is different from [1]'s one. If watermarking schemes such as DCT coefficient ordering, salient-point modification, and fractal-based watermarking that are not correlation-based are used, extensive modification and adaptation have to be done. These drawbacks of works presented in [1], [2] and [12] have motivated our work. Firstly, we present and contrast the detection formulas of the state-of-the-art of digital watermarking schemes. Then, we point out the parts of protocols from [1], [2], and [12] that are necessary to improve in order to yield independence of the zero-knowledge protocol on detection formula of watermarking schemes. However, our work is still in preliminary stage. There are number of rooms for improvement which will be discussed in section 'Performance and Discussion.'

2 Diversified Detection Formula of the State-of-the-Art Watermarking Schemes

In this section, we present four state-of-the-art watermarking schemes, i.e. dirty paper coding, quantization, patchwork and frequency-domain-based [6, 7]. In each scheme, the detection formula is presented and their diversity is highlighted.

In dirty paper coding scheme, watermark detector works by searching the entire code to find the vector, w that is closest to a given received Cover data, c. The detector applies Viterbi algorithm using the entire trellis. The algorithm finds the path that produces the highest correlation with the received Cover data, c. The received message is decoded by looking at the bits represented by the arcs in that path. This post-process indicates extensive use of algorithm instead of straightforward correlation coefficient computation. Thus, it is not feasible to run under current zero-knowledge protocols.

In quantization based watermarking scheme, the detection is based on the correlation formula

$$c = \frac{1}{N}\sum_{n=1}^{N} y[n]w_k[n] \qquad (1)$$

where y is the pre-processed signal y=r-x, r=received signals, x=original signal [8].

Clearly, its detection formula (Equation 1) is different from Equation 3 as in Section 3. Moreover, quantization based watermarking scheme is a non-blind watermarking scheme since the detector needs the original image as input.

In patchwork, a special statistic is embedded into the image. Two patches are chosen pseudorandomly and then a small constant value d is added to the sample values of one patch A and same value d is subtracted from the sample values of another patch B. The detection scheme starts with subtraction of the sample values between two patches. Its detection scheme is based on hypothesis testing, $E[\overline{\alpha} - \overline{\beta}]$ i.e. the expected value of the differences of the sample means, where $\overline{\alpha}$ and $\overline{\beta}$ are sample means of the individual sample [9]. Thus, again the existing protocols have to be modified extensively to incorporate patchwork's detection formula.

Frequency domain based watermarking algorithms cover DCT, DFT, and DWT. Detection scheme of DWT is our focus in this paper since it is the most commonly used and efficient algorithm nowadays [10,14,15,16]. Though the embedding algorithms of different DWT scheme are similar, their detection formulas are different. In [10], the detection is formulated as to compute the detection response instead of computing correlation coefficient. In [15], wavelet packet decomposition is performed to extract the selected subband signals $B(i_k,j_k)$ based on the same rule of embedding. Elements are picked up from $B(i_k,j_k)$ to compute their mean $\overline{M}(i_k, j_k)$. This mean is later divided by a quantization step size, Q and rounded off. If the result is even number, the element contains no watermark and otherwise.

Based on the wide variety of detection formula used by different watermarking scheme, protocols that are depend on specific detection formula is clearly infeasible for generic use. Hence, the protocols should be modified so that they are independent of the detection formula.

3 Drawbacks of Existing Protocols

In this section, we present three protocols from Craver [2], Craver and Katzenbeisser [12], and Adelsbach and Sadeghi [1]. We highlight the drawbacks of [2] and [12] that lead to the much-improved protocol from [1]. From the steps of Adelsbach and Sadeghi's protocol-run, we highlight the needs for eliminating the protocol's dependency on watermark detection formula.

Craver's methods are based on secret permutation and discrete logarithm [2]. In secret permutation, the prover publishes scrambled version of watermarked object, $\tau(\overline{O})$ and watermark τ(WM). The ultimate goal of this protocol is to prove that $\tau(\overline{O})$

is the permuted version of $\overline{O}$ with the presence of watermark, WM. In each round, the prover chooses two permutations σ_i and ρ_i with the property that $\rho_i \circ \sigma_i = \tau$. The prover constructs an ownership ticket that contains commitments of both ρ_i and σ_i, hashes of permuted objects $\overline{O_i} = \rho_i(\overline{O})$ and $\overline{G_i} = \rho_i(\overline{G})$. The protocol involves the toss of coin by verifier and prover responses to the coin toss accordingly. The prover will open commitment containing σ_i or the commitment of ρ_I based on the coin toss result. In this protocol, the prover is able to cheat the verifier with probability 1/2 in each round. Thus, this protocol has to be run in multiple rounds to yield negligible probability in order to convince the verifier about the watermark presence to certain degree of certainty. Clearly, this protocol requires a lot of data to prove the existence of the watermark. There are lots of computations and data exchange between prover and verifier [13]. More importantly, giving the permuted version of watermark to the verifier exposes the coefficient of WM since it reveals the maximum or minimum threshold of the coefficient [11]. This protocol is also susceptible to oracle attacks and thus, is not a zero-knowledge protocol [11].

Re-computation of isomorphic graph is also essential in each round of the protocol. Prover has to re-produce unique hard Hamiltonian path problem in each round. This leads to the upper bound of the number of isomorphic graphs that is probably re-producible. As a result, generating public key is a difficult task. Besides uniqueness, there is no guarantee of hardness for the graph in each round according to the metric of likelihood of hardness. Though measure of closeness to the problem's phase transition can be used as the metric of likelihood of hardness, it is inadequate as proof of guarantee [13]. This indicates the need to increase the efficiency and effectiveness of the protocol in term of interactivity, distinct re-computations and hardness of graph problem.

In [12], prover computes a watermark $WM=a^h \bmod p$ from secret h. The security of this protocol is based on the intractability to compute h from W knowing a for large p. Based on ambiguity attack, k fake watermarks are embedded into the image. If a verifier wants to remove the correct watermark, he has to remove all watermarks and significantly degrade the quality of the image. This serves as the sole security measure of this protocol. The secrecy of the watermark is only increased linearly when the number of fake watermarks embedded into the image is increased [11]. Watermark generation based on discrete logarithm immediately imposes an incompatibility problem with existing watermarking schemes. Current watermarking schemes are not trivial to be incorporated into this protocol.

Adelsbach and Sadeghi had constructed a much improved protocol compared to [2] and [12]. Their protocol had successfully concealed the watermark in commitment [1]. The hiding property of the commitment scheme guarantees that no secret information about WM is revealed to verifier [11]. In order to prove the ownership of the watermark and/or the image, the prover has to prove to the verifier that the watermark contained in com(WM) is in the image. The prover has to prove to the verifier V that the value contained in com(C) is ≥ 0 (Equation 5), by running the protocol. This protocol was tested on the original Cox's spread spectrum DCT watermarking scheme. The correlation formula of the original detection scheme is computed as

$$corr = \frac{< DCT(\mathrm{I_w}, k), WM >}{\sqrt{< DCT(\mathrm{I_w}, k), DCT(\mathrm{I_w}, k) >}} \tag{2}$$

where $\mathrm{I_w}$ is the watermarked image, WM is watermark, and $\mathrm{DCT(I_w},k)$ are the DCT-coefficients. The detector tests whether corr $\geq \delta$, where δ is the predefined detection threshold.

For efficiency reasons, Adelsbach and Sadeghi modified the correlation formula to

$$C := \underbrace{(<\mathrm{DCT(I_w,k),WM}>)^2}_{A} - \underbrace{<\mathrm{DCT(I_w, k),DCT(I_w, k)}>* \delta^2}_{B} \tag{3}$$

If $C \geq 0$, the watermark is proven present.

The common inputs for prover and verifier are $\mathrm{par_{com}}$ (parameters for commitment that contains modulus n), $\mathrm{I_w}$, com(WM) and δ. Prover has his own secret input, $\mathrm{sk_{com}}$. The zero-knowledge detection protocol is shown in Figure 1.

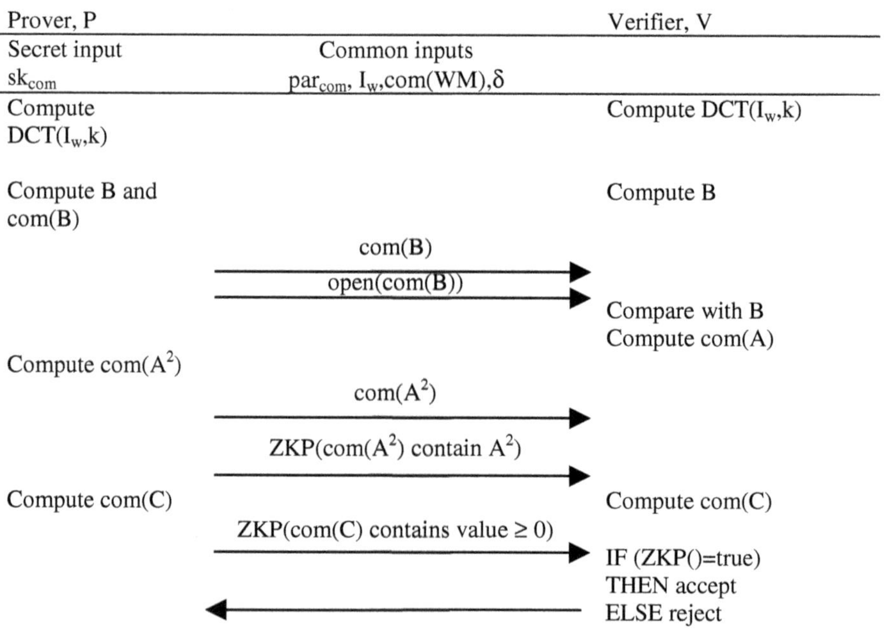

Fig. 1. Adelsbach and Sadeghi's Zero-knowledge Watermark Detection Protocol [1]

P and V compute the DCT of $\mathrm{I_w}$ then compute com(B). From Equation 2, $B=<\mathrm{DCT(I_w,k),DCT(I_w,k)}>* \delta^2$. P sends com(B) to V and opens it to V. V verifies that the opened commitment contains the same value B that he computed himself. After that, V computes the commitment com(A) according to Equation 4.

$$com(A) := \prod_{i=1}^{k} com(WM_i)^{DCT(I_w,k)_i} \bmod n \tag{4}$$

V uses the modulus n contained in the public commitment parameters par_{com}. P computes the value A^2 and commit to it. P then sends com(A^2) to V and proves to V that com(A^2) contains the square of the value contained in com(A) by running a sub-protocol, ZKP. After V is convinced that com(A^2) correctly contains the value A^2, P and V compute the commitment com(C) according to Equation 5.

$$com(C) := \frac{com(A^2)}{com(B)} \bmod n \tag{5}$$

Finally, P proves to V that the value contained in com(C) is ≥ 0 by running a sub-protocol, ZKP. If V accepts this proof then the watermark detection process ends with *true*, otherwise *false*.

This protocol is easily adaptable to any watermarking scheme that detects watermarks by computing a detection statistic, using operators +,*,-, and comparing the statistic to a threshold [11]. However, this protocol has two main drawbacks:

(i) Verifier has to be knowledgeable and computationally capable of computing the watermarking algorithm that is DCT in [1]'s case, as shown in Equation 4. The more obvious problem is that the verifier has to possess or obtain different formula when different watermarking schemes apart from DCT is used. However, there is no clear solution or need to eliminate the computational requirement for verifier since Equation 4 is essential to bind the watermark presence with the image.

(ii) Equation 5 shows the dependency of the protocol on the correlation coefficient formulation of digital watermarking schemes. As shown in section 2, the protocol has to adapt to different formula if the digital watermarking scheme uses different correlation or do not use correlation at all as its detection mechanism. Equation 5 has to be modified in order to adapt the change of the detection mechanism. This equation will somewhat become useless if the watermarking scheme does not use correlation coefficients in the detection formula. This drawback has already been highlighted in Section 2. To eliminate the protocol dependency on the detection formula is the main focus of this paper.

4 Generic Detection Scheme

In this paper, a generic protocol is proposed to minimize the dependency on watermarking schemes and eliminates its dependency on its detection formula, and to achieve the flexibility of running the protocol in sequence or parallel. Fiat and Shamir [3]'s work has motivated our ideas on this generic protocol. According to [13], a zero knowledge interactive proof can be transformed in a signature scheme. However, the zero knowledge property is lost. Our proposed protocol is more similar to [3]'s identification scheme in which the zero knowledge property is maintained. The final goal of this generic protocol remains the same as [1]: to prove the watermark contained in *com*(WM) exists in the Cover data without releasing any information about the watermark.

This protocol has a unique and yet practical feature. The verifier plays the initiator to start the protocol. This feature also eliminates the need for a trusted centre. The protocol-run starts as follows:

1. Prover, P, computes a large modulus n and chooses a pseudo random function f. Then, publish them to verifier, V. The modulus n is the product of two secret large primes. The function f should be indistinguishable from a truly random function by any polynomially bounded computation.
2. Prover performs the following steps:
   i. Compute the values $v_j = f(com(\mathrm{WM})^{A(Iw,par)}, j)$ for small values of j. A is the watermarking algorithm, *Iw* is the watermarked image, *par* is the parameters for the algorithm, WM is the watermark, and *com* is the commitment.
   ii. Choose k distinct values of j such that v_j is a modulus of n and compute the smallest square root s_j of v_i^{-1}.
   iii. Publish v_j and its indices to V.

3. P sends com(WM) and A(I_w,*par*) to V
4. V generates $v_j = f(com(\mathrm{WM})^{A(Iw,par)}, j)$ for $j=1,\ldots\ldots,k$

Repeat steps 5 to 8 for $i=1,\ldots\ldots,t$:

5. P picks a random $r_i \in [0,n)$ and sends $x_i = r_i^2 \bmod n$ to V
6. V sends a random binary vector $(e_{i1},\ldots\ldots,e_{ik})$ to P
7. P computes y_i and sends it to V
$$y_i = r_i \prod_{e_{ij}=1} s_j \bmod n$$
8. V checks that
$$x_i = y_i^2 \prod_{e_{ij}=1} v_j \bmod n$$

The verifier V accepts P's proof of ownership if and only if all the t checks are ended with true. If P cheats, this protocol has the error probability of 2^{-kt} [3]. The typical values for k and i are 6 and 5 respectively in order to achieve 2^{-30} level of security [3]. The values of k and i can be easily adjustable to yield higher level of security depending on specific requirement. By performing step 8, verifier is able to be convinced that the prover knows s_j. If prover knows s_j, this also means that the prover knows the watermark.

Step 4 is essential to prove that the watermark is embedded into the image. The prover could have used any watermark and prove its existence alone without proving its existence in the image. Step 4 allows verifier to compute the watermarking algorithm so that verifier could check whether the watermark contained in the commitment exists in the image, I_w.

This protocol is independent of the watermark detection formula. Watermarking schemes that either use correlation or no correlation at all for detection can be easily adapted to this proposed protocol. Step 7 and 8 are the crucial part of the protocol that contributes to this nature of generic.

5 Performance and Discussion

The performance of the proposed protocol is determined briefly in 5 aspects: completeness, soundness, choice of parameters, secrecy of input, and disclose of information during protocol-run. Further works will be done on the assessment of the protocol in terms of computation and communication complexity.

5.1 Completeness

Assuming both parties i.e. prover and verifier are honest, the protocol proves that Prover's inputs fulfill $x_i = y_i^2 \prod_{e_{ij}=1} v_j \bmod n$. It can be proven that the verifier always accepts the assertion by substituting x_i into the verification equation:

$$x_i = y_i^2 \prod_{e_{ij}=1} v_j = r_i^2 \prod_{e_{ij}=1} s_j^2 v_j = r_i^2 \pmod n$$

5.2 Soundness

If v is not a quadratic residue, then at most one of the values s and sv can be a quadratic residue. Hence, is at most one of them is an acceptable response x exists. Thus, the verifier will only accept with probability 1/2, and overall protocol with probability 2^{-t}.

5.3 Choice of Parameters

The proposed protocol requires that the modulus n and function f are computed by the verifier. It is crucial for verifier to compute n in order to impose higher security to the protocol. Prover's ability computing the square root of v_j does not imply that prover can factorize n since P was assisted by V who communicated with P who knew this square root of v_j. The coalition of the ability of real prover and arbitrary prover to factorize n only yields probability 1/2 [20].

Modulus n is the product of two large prime numbers, p_1 and p_2. These prime numbers, p_1 and p_2, are 3 mod 4 [18]. The random function f is proposed as random oracle model to ensure security of the proving process [19, 20].

Step 1 is still workable if a trusted centre performs it. The trusted centre will have to publish n and f to public, and s_j and its indices to P.

5.4 Secrecy of Input

Comparing works from [1], the proposed protocol yields equivalent level of secrecy. The verifier sees only commitments *com*(WM). Our protocol yields advantageous feature by eliminating dependence on detection formula of the watermarking scheme.

5.5 Disclosure of Information during Protocol-Run

The commitment that the verifier sees in each round of the protocol-run reveals no secret information about the watermark contents. The whole protocol is zero-knowledge due to its sequential composition [21].

5.6 Improvement

After discussion with researchers in this workshop, we have identified some aspects of the proposed protocol that need further modification and improvement [22,23,24].

5.6.1 Commitment Scheme

The commitment scheme, $com(\text{WM})^{A(Iw,par)}$, in Step 2(i) and 4 used the properties of correlation formula as its underlying elements. The com(WM) is raised to $A(I_w,par)$ has indeed based on the correlation formula [23].

5.6.2 Pseudo-Random Function

The pseudo-random function, *f*, used in $v_j = f(com(\text{WM})^{A(Iw,par)}, j)$ is redundant and unjustifiable. *com*(WM) is basically an instance of encryption. With the pseudo-random function, it means that the result of $\text{com(WM)}^{\text{A(Iw,par)}}$ is encrypted again. This immediately causes difficulty to justify the security of this double-encryption routine [22].

5.6.3 Binding Property

There is no binding property between the protocol and watermarked image [24]. The proposed protocol has eliminated the use of homomorphic property of commitment scheme in corresponding to the watermark detection formula [22]. This elimination poses a challenge to find a protocol that is independent to watermark detection formula. In order to realize such protocol, a binding property between the protocol and the existence of the watermark has to be discovered. It is doubtful that whether such binding property exists [22,23,24].

6 Conclusion

The proposed generic protocol has shown the challenge of eliminating dependency of existing protocol on the watermark detection formula. This further minimizes the protocol's dependency on the whole watermarking scheme. Without the needs for sub-protocol, this proposed protocol essentially maintains the efficiency and security level of previous protocols. Most importantly, this protocol has geared toward generic detection scheme in zero knowledge protocol for blind watermark detection. Though the protocol has been proposed on images, we believe this protocol can be applied to other format of digital data without the need of too much modification. Future evaluation of the protocol on computation and communication complexity is believed to yield positive results. A practical protocol will be workable after the issues highlighted in Section 5.6.6 are resolved.

References

1. Adelsbach,A. and Sadeghi,A-R.: Zero Knowledge Watermark Detection and Proof of Ownership. Information Hiding: Forth International Workshop, LNCS 2137, Springer-Verlag (2001) 273–288
2. Craver,S.: Zero Knowledge Watermark Detection. Information Hiding: Third International Workshop, LNCS 1768, Springer-Verlag (2000) 101–116
3. Fiat,A., Shamir,A.: How to Prove Yourself: Practical Solutions to Identification and Signature Problems, CRYPTO '86, LNCS 263, (1987) 186–194
4. Feige,U.,Fiat,A., Shamir, A.: Zero Knowledge Proof of Identity, ACM 1987, (1987) 210–216
5. Sakurai,K., Itoh, T.: On the Discrepancy between Serial and Parallel of Zero-Knowledge Protocols, Advances in Cryptology – CRYPT0 '92, LNCS 740, (1993) 246–259
6. Kim H.J.: Email communication, Dept. Control/Instrumentation Engineering, Kangwon National University, Korea, 3 May 2003
7. Miller,G.L., Doerr, G. J. and Cox, I. J. : Dirty-Paper trellis codes for Watermarking, IEEE Int. Conf. on Image Processing, Vol.2 (2002) 129–132
8. Eggers, J., and Girod, B.: Quantization Watermarking, Proceedings of SPIE, Security and Watermarking of Multimedia Contents II, Electronic Imaging 2000, Vol. 3971, (2000) 60–71
9. Yeo, I.K., Kim, H.J.: Modified Patchwork Algorithm: a novel audio watermarking scheme, Proceedings of International Conference on Information Technology: Coding and Computing, 2001. (2001) 237–242
10. Oh, S. H., Park, S.W., Kim, B.J.: DWT(discrete wavelet transform) based watermark system , International Conference on Consumer Electronics, 2002. ICCE. 2002 Digest of Technical Papers. (2002) 192–193
11. Adelsbach,A., Katzenbeisser,S, and Sadeghi, A-R.: Cryptography Meets Watermarking: Detecting Watermarks with Minimal or Zero Knowledge Disclosure, XI European Signal Processing Conference, vol.1, (2002) 446–449
12. Craver,S., Katzenbeisser,S.: Security Analysis of Public-Key Watermarking Schemes, Proc. SPIE vol. 4475, Mathematics of Data/Image Coding, Compression and Encryption IV, with Applications, (2001) 172–182
13. Hachez,G., and Quisquater, J-J.: Which directions for asymmetric watermarking?, XI European Signal Processing Conference, vol.1, (2002) #774
14. Wang,Y.,Doherty,J.,Van Dyck,R.E.: A Wavelet-Based Watermarking Algorithm for Ownership Verification of Digital Images, IEEE Trans on Image Processing, vol.11,no.2, (2002) 77–88.
15. Ejima, M.; Miyazaki, A.: A Wavelet-Based Watermarking for Digital Images and Video, International Conference on Image Processing, vol.3, (2000) 678–681

16. Barni,M.,Bartolini,F., Piva,A.: Improved Wavelet-Based Watermarking Through Pixel-Wise Masking, IEEE Transactions On Image Processing, Vol. 10, No. 5, (2001) 783–791
17. Reyzin,L.: Zero-Knowledge with Public Keys, PhD Thesis, Massachusetts Institute of Technology (2001)
18. Shoup,V.: On the Security of a Practical Identification Scheme, Journal of Cryptology, Volume 12, Number 4, (1999) 247–260
19. Micali,S. and Reyzin,L.: Improving the Exact Security of Digital Signature Schemes, Journal of Cryptology, Volume 15, Number 1, (2002)
20. Bellare,M. and Rogaway,P.: Random Oracles are Practical: A Paradigm for designing Efficient Protocols, Proceedings of the 1st ACM Conference on Computer and Communication Security, (1993) 62–73
21. Goldreich,O.: Foundations of Cryptography: Basic Tools,Cambridge University Press, (2001)
22. Kalker, T,. Discussion in IWDW03, 22 Oct 2003.
23. Katzenbeisser, S., Discussion in IWDW03, 21 Oct 2003.
24. Memon, N,. Discussion in IWDW03, 21 Oct 2003.

Lossless Watermarking Considering the Human Visual System

Mohammad Awrangjeb and Mohan S. Kankanhalli

Department of Computer Science
School of Computing
National University of Singapore, Singapore 117543
{mohammal, mohan}@comp.nus.edu.sg

Abstract. Due to quantization error, bit-replacement, or truncation, most data embedding techniques proposed so far lead to distortions in the original image. These distortions create problems in some areas such as medical, astronomical, and military imagery. Lossless watermarking is an exact restoration approach for recovering the original image from the watermarked image. In this paper we present a novel reversible watermarking technique with higher embedding capacity considering the *Human Visual System* (HVS). During embedding we detect the textured blocks, extract LSBs of the pixel-values from these textured blocks considering the HVS and concatenate the authentication information with the compressed bit-string. We then replace the LSBs of the textured blocks considering the HVS with this bit-string. Since we consider the HVS while extracting LSBs and embedding the payload, the distortions in the resulting watermarked image are completely reversible and imperceptible. We present experimental results to demonstrate the utility of our proposed algorithm.

1 Introduction

Content authentication of multimedia data like images is becoming more and more important in various fields such as law enforcement, medical imagery, astronomical research, etc. One of the most important requirements in this field is to have the original image during judgment to take the right decision. Cryptographic techniques based on either symmetric key or asymmetric key methods cannot give adequate security and integrity for content authentication. Chiefly, (i) people sharing the secret key can produce false links between the header and its corresponding image in the medical data base, (ii) public key infrastructure is essential, (iii) common image file-format is required, (iv) compression-decompression results in information loss, are problems with such techniques. Lossless watermarking, a type of fragile watermarking, is the process that allows exact recovery of the original image by extracting the embedding information from the watermarked image. If the watermarked image is deemed to be authentic, that means no single bit of the watermarked image is changed after embedding the payload to the original image. Some authors use distortion free, invertible, reversible, erasable watermarking interchangeably for lossless watermarking. This technique (lossless watermarking) embeds

T. Kalker et al. (Eds.): IWDW 2003, LNCS 2939, pp. 581–592, 2004.
© Springer-Verlag Berlin Heidelberg 2004

secret information with the image so that the embedded message is hidden, invisible and fragile. Any attempt to change the watermarked image will make the authentication fail.

Fridrich et al. [3] and Honsinger et al. [2] use the spread spectrum approach to add the information payload with the host signal. The methods are robust to a wide range of distortions, but due to use of modulo arithmetic salt-and-pepper noise are introduced and the embedding capacity is low. Celik et al. [1] propose a simple reversible data-hiding algorithm having high embedding capacity. It searches the whole image and finds out the lower L-levels of pixel-values (say for L = 4, pixel with values 0, 1, 2, 3) to obtain enough space after compression. The main problem with this method is that all images do not offer enough features (pixel-values) at low levels for lossless compression. So, as L becomes larger, distortions become higher and perceptually visible. The lossless compression and encryption of bit-plane method in [3] offers high embedding capacity with strength equivalent to the security offered by cryptographic methods. But noisy images and high payload force the embedding of the message in higher bit-planes and hence distortions become visible. The invertible authentication for JPEG images [3], [4], [10] is a fast algorithm offering high embedding capacity; but artifacts becomes visible for JPEG images with high quality factor. The RS-vector lossless data embedding method in [4], [7], [9] divides the image into disjoint groups (*R*egular, *S*ingular, and *U*nusable). The whole image is scanned and *R*egular-*S*ingular groups are checked whether there is a need to apply the flip operation while embedding information. Though this method involves low and invertible distortions, the capacity is not very high. Tian in [5], [17] proposes a high capacity watermarking algorithm based on difference expansion. This method involves no compression-decompression process of selected image features; but there is significant degradation of image quality due to bit-replacement. Macq et al. [12] proposed an original circular interpretation of bijective transformations as a solution to fulfill all quality and functionality requirements of lossless watermarking. In his first work [18] Macq proposes an additive method that is criticized by him in [19] for having 'salt-and-pepper' visual artifacts due to wrapped around pixels. In [19], [12] Macq et al. propose a modification that solves this problem. It essentially follows the idea of patchwork algorithm [20]. This method helps to convey embedded message from lossless environment to lossy environment and offers high capacity; but the visual quality of watermarked image is not good. Xuan et al. [13] propose a lossless algorithm based on integer wavelet transform. This method offers high embedding capacity but distortions are easily visible if multiple or higher bit-planes are used for embedding. Shi et al. [15] propose a high capacity distortion-free data hiding technique for palette image. They also propose a reversible data hiding technique [14] based on shifting of histogram. In this method though distortions are low the embedding capacity is limited by the frequency of most frequent pixel value in the image.

Celik et al. [1] classify the lossless watermarking techniques in two types. In the first type of algorithms [2], [3], during encoding a spread spectrum signal corresponding to the information payload is superimposed (added) on the host signal. During decoding the payload (watermark signal) is removed (subtracted) from the watermarked image in the restoration step. The advantage of these algorithms is the use of spread spectrum signal as payload increases robustness. But the disadvantages are they (i) create salt-and-pepper artifacts in watermarked image due to modulo arithmetic, and (ii) offer very limited capacity.

In the second type of algorithms [1], [4], [5], some features (portions) of the original image are replaced or overwritten with the watermark payload. The original portions of the image that will be replaced by watermark payload are compressed and passed as a part of the embedded payload during embedding. During the decoding process this compressed payload-part is extracted and decompressed. Thus the original image is recovered by replacing the modified portions with these decompressed original features. The advantage of second type of algorithms is they do not suffer from salt-and-pepper artifacts. The disadvantages are: (i) they are not as robust as the first type of algorithms, and (ii) the capacity found, though higher than the first type of algorithms offer, is still not good enough. However, algorithms of second type are better than first type for content authentication where fragility is more important than robustness.

This paper presents a novel reversible watermarking technique that considers the *Human Visual System* (HVS) [6]. The proposed method offers completely distortion-invisible watermarked image with higher embedding capacity. We find out textured blocks from the original image and embed information in these textured blocks considering the HVS. We keep a pixel of a textured block as is if the corresponding *Just Noticeable Distortion* (JND) value of the pixel does not allow to change the pixel value by the required amount. Finally when we complete the embedding we do not leave any pixel distorted out of a certain limit determined by its JND value. Hence, the distortions in the watermarked image become completely invisible. However we can get higher capacity to pass the authentication information as well as the side information (helps during decoding) by compressing the bit-string of LSBs using a simple lossless compression algorithm, such as arithmetic coding [8]. Extra capacity can be used to embed necessary information as required. Our implementation and experimental results show that the proposed algorithm fulfills the requirements (invisible distortions and higher capacity) of lossless watermarking technique and is better than other existing algorithms in the literature.

The rest of the paper goes as follows: section 2 represents the general principle of lossless or reversible data embedding technique, and the *Human Visual System* (HVS), section 3 presents our proposed algorithm, section 4 presents experimental results we have found and decision by comparing the proposed algorithm with other methods published so far, and finally section 5 concludes with advantages and disadvantages of proposed algorithm.

2 The General Principle of Reversible Data Hiding and HVS

First we present the general principle [7] of reversible data hiding technique in section 2.1. Then we describe the *Human Visual System* [6] (in section 2.2) that we use in the proposed algorithm.

2.1 The General Principle of Reversible Data Hiding

The general principle of reversible data hiding is that for a digital object (say a JPEG image file) I, a subset J of I ($J \subset I$) is chosen. J has the structural property that it can be easily randomized without changing the essential property of I, and it offers lossless compression itself to have enough space (at least 128 bits) to embed the authentication message (say hash of I). During embedding J is replaced by the authentication message concatenated with compressed J. If J is highly compressible only a subset of J can be used. During the decoding process authentication information together with compressed J is extracted. This extracted J (compressed) is decompressed to replace the modified features in the watermarked image; hence the exact copy of the original image is found.

However when we do embedding for reversible watermarking we have the following points to consider: (i) embedding method should find enough capacity to embed sufficient amount of message, (ii) there should be no expansion of image size due to embedding, (iii) embedded message should be useful, (iv) distortions in original image are kept as low as possible, so artifacts are imperceptible, (v) watermarked image should be fragile to attempt to any kind of change, (vi) encryption with a secret key can increase security and integrity of image data.

2.2 The Human Visual System

The most important requirement of lossless watermarking is that any difference (distortion) between the original image and the watermarked image should be perceptually invisible. The *Human Visual System* (HVS) is the factor that can be exploited to achieve this requirement. But until now there is no lossless watermarking method proposed has utilized the properties of HVS. HVS essentially results in the fact that each pixel value of an image can be changed only by a certain amount without making any perceptible difference to the image quality. This limit is called the *just noticeable distortion* or JND level. If we keep the distortion to a pixel not out of the limit defined by its JND level the degradation of the pixel is imperceptible in the watermarked image [6].

We divide the original image into 8×8 blocks, and then take the *Discrete Cosine Transfer* (DCT) of each 8×8 block. In a block with abrupt changes between adjacent pixels, the signal energy tends to be concentrated in the AC coefficients. The equation (1) gives the energy, E_{AC}, in the AC coefficients, and the equation (2) gives the maximum energy, E_{max}. The maximum energy is found when the adjacent pixels have maximum and minimum permissible gray values. By using E_{max} as the normalization factor we measure the roughness level R_b for block b (equation 3).

$$E_{AC} = \log \sum (x_{i,j}^2 - x_{0,0}^2),\ 0 \le i, j < 8\ . \tag{1}$$

$$E_{\max} = \log(\frac{G}{2})^2\ . \tag{2}$$

$$R_b = \frac{E_{AC}}{E_{\max}} \ . \tag{3}$$

Where x_{ij} is the (i,j) DCT coefficient of a block, G is the maximum permissible gray value (for 8-bit image it is 255), and we use log for range compression. The range of R_b is uniformly divided into 8 subgroups and depending on the value of R_b each block is given a block distortion index I_b, $I_b \in \{1, 2, \ldots, 8\}$. The fluctuation of energy at position (i,j) of each block (where the pixel value is $P_{i,j}$) is given by its gradient $\nabla P_{i,j}$ (equation 4). In textured image $\nabla P_{i,j}$ would be large at a large number of locations. A gradient-threshold λ is taken to decide whether the gradient is larger than a certain limit and a count-threshold C is taken to decide whether the block has an edge or is highly textured. All the blocks satisfying the constraint $I_b \in \{6, 7, 8\}$ are subjected to the test: a block is highly textured if it satisfies the equation (5).

$$\nabla P_{i,j} = abs(p_{i+1,j} - p_{i,j}) + abs(p_{i,j+1} - p_{i,j}) \ . \tag{4}$$

$$\left\| \left\{ P_{i,j} \middle| P_{i,j} \text{ is a pixel and } \nabla P_{i,j} > \lambda \right\} \right\| > C \ . \tag{5}$$

$$J(i,j,b) = \hat{J}_b + \left\lfloor \frac{(\frac{G}{2} - P_{i,j,b})^2}{\alpha} \right\rfloor . \tag{6}$$

Where $\| \ldots \|$ is the cardinality of the set, α is predetermined constant, and $P_{i,j,b}$ is the pixel value at position (i,j) of block b. Each block based on its corresponding I_b is mapped to a JND value $\hat{J}_b$, $\hat{J}_b \in \{3, 4, \ldots, 10\}$ while $I_b \in \{1, 2, \ldots, 8\}$. We do one to one mapping for simplicity. We also consider pixel-luminance to have the final *Just Noticeable Distortion* (JND), $J(i,j,b)$, at any pixel position (i,j) in each textured block b (equation 6). It is actually incorporating the effect of luminance into JND value, since the distortion in an image is more noticeable in the mid-gray region and sensitivity changes parabolically as the gray value fluctuates on the both sides of mid-gray level. Note that (i,j) means the element at row number (i+1) and column number (j+1) in a two dimensional array.

3 The Proposed Lossless Watermarking Algorithm

During the embedding process we find out the textured blocks in the original image I, then considering the HVS we extract the LSBs of the pixels in these textured blocks. The extracted LSBs are stored in a bit-string that is compressed losslessly to have

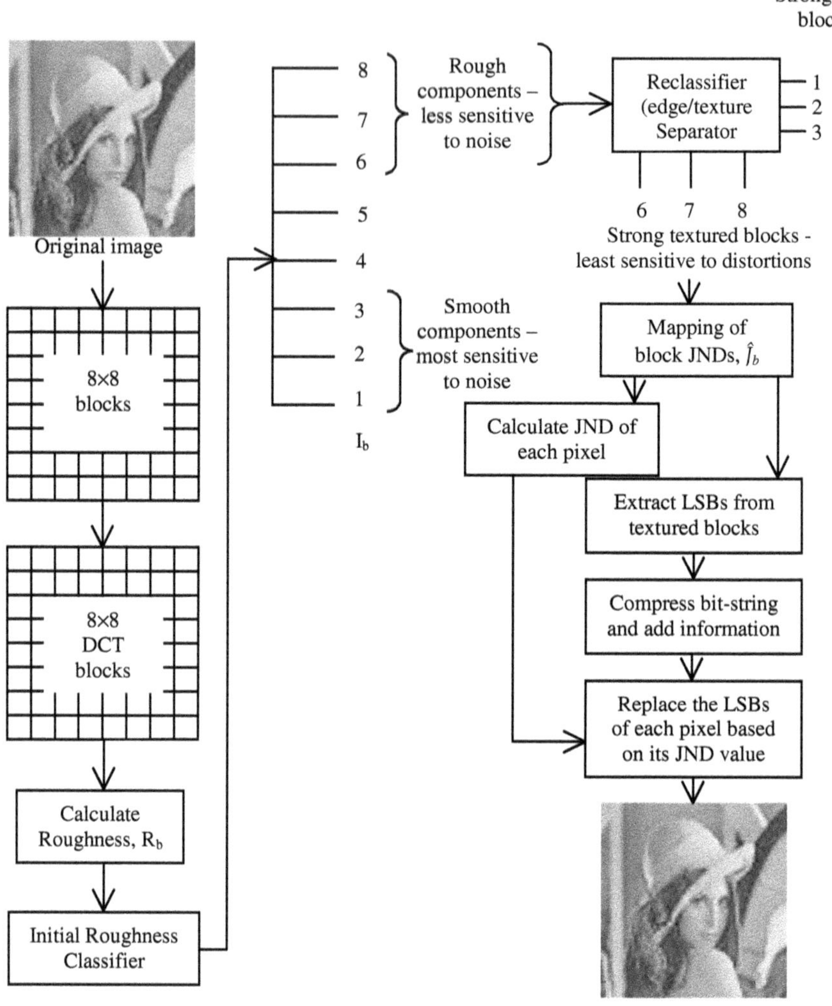

Fig. 1. Embedding process

enough space to concatenate the authentication information, say the hash of the original image. We use arithmetic coding [8] for lossless compression. The resultant bit-string is called the watermark to be embedded into the original image. While embedding watermark we again consider the HVS to replace the LSBs of the pixels in the textured blocks. While extracting the LSBs of the pixels of textured blocks we try to minimize the amount of side information required. We find out the maximum JND value ($J_{max,b}$) for each block b and calculate the number of bits required to represent the $J_{max,b}$ by $bit_b = \log_2(J_{max,b})$. So we extract bit_b bits of LSBs per pixel of the textured block b. For making the decoding process easy we need to add some side information (unchanged pixel-indexes) with the watermark. Also we replace some LSBs (original LSBs are added to the watermark before compression) of first few blocks (say 10) to pass the initial side information (textured block-numbers, number of LSBs extracted per pixel of each block, watermark-length) to initiate the decoding process. In words the embedding process (Fig.1) includes the following steps:

- Divide the original image into 8×8 blocks
- Calculate the DCT of each 8×8 block
- Calculate the roughness of each block
- By using initial classifier separate the rough components (blocks) that are less sensitive to noise
- Reclassify the rough components to separate the high textured blocks from the strong edge blocks
- Map the block JNDs, $\hat{J}_b$
- Calculate the JND of each pixel in textured blocks
- Calculate the number of LSBs, $bit_b = \log_2(J_{max,b})$, to be extracted from each block b
- Extract the bit_b LSBs per pixel of textured block b and store in a bit-string
- Compress the bit-string losslessly
- Calculate the hash of the original image and concatenate it (together with other information as required) with the compressed bit-string
- While replacing bit_b bits of LSBs per pixel of block b with bit_b bits of watermark: let x_1 = decimal value of bit_b LSBs of a pixel value at position (i,j); x_2 = decimal value of bit_b bits of watermark to be embedded, $J(i,j,b)$ = JND value of pixel at position (i,j). If $(abs(x_2 - x_1) \leq J(i,j,b))$ then replace the bit_b LSBs of this pixel with bit_b bits of watermark, else keep the pixel unchanged.

Note that we do replacement of the LSBs of pixels (of textured blocks) instead of adding the watermark data. This leaves only a few or no pixels without embedding data. That is why the amount of side information of indexes of pixels without embedding is very low.

During decoding we extract the payload using the side information. After separating the authentication information we decompress the compressed bit-string of LSBs. Finally we replace the LSBs of the pixels of the textured blocks using the side information to get the exact copy of the original image. We calculate the hash of the reconstructed image and compare the calculated hash to the extracted hash.

4 Experimental Results and Discussion

We first present here our experimental results and then compare the results with other algorithms proposed so far.

4.1 Experimental Results

We have implemented our algorithm and applied to several images of different types: medical, astronomical, and general images used in the literature. We have used

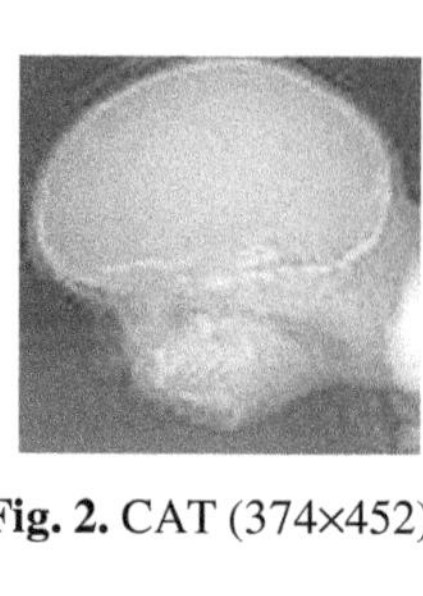

Fig. 2. CAT (374×452)

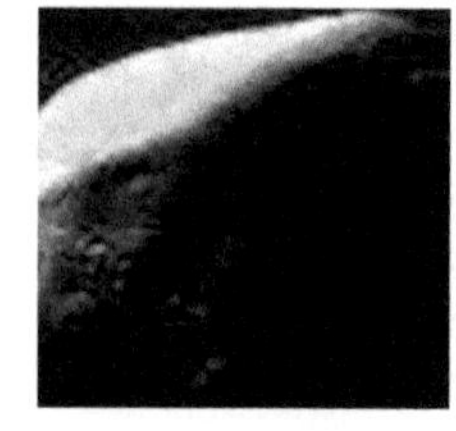

Fig. 3. Mars Moon (683×1000)

Fig. 4. Tank (512×512)

Fig. 5. Man (256×256)

Fig. 6. Lena (300×300)

Fig. 7. Lena (512×512)

Fig. 8. Airplane (512×512)

Fig. 9. Boat (512×512)

Fig. 10. Elaine (512×512)

Fig. 11. Tiffany (512×512)

Fig. 12. House (512×512)

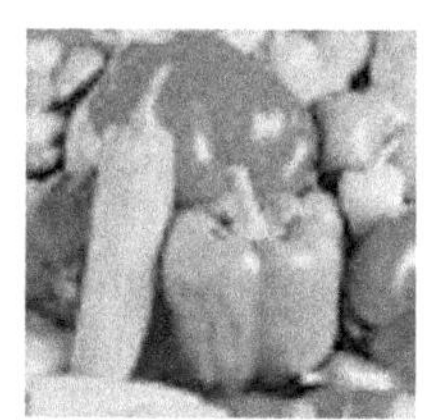

Fig. 13. Peppers (512×512)

Fig. 14. Sailboat (512×512)

Fig. 15. Bridge (512×512)

Fig. 16. Jet (512×512)

arithmetic coding for compression [8]. Table 1 shows the experimental results we have found for our proposed algorithm. All images are 8-bit grayscale. These results show that the proposed algorithm offers reversible data hiding with higher capacity and imperceptible artifacts.

4.2 Comparison with Other Algorithms

First we reveal limitations of the recent proposed lossless watermarking algorithms. Lossless compression and encryption of bit plane method by Fridrich et al. [3] has the limitations: (i) capacity is not very high, and (ii) higher payload forces the method to embed watermark at higher bit-planes and hence the artifacts are easily visible. Other watermarking methods proposed by Fridrich et al. in [4], [7], [9], [10] either offer limited capacity or create artifacts that are easily visible. Another problem is that these algorithms do not offer enough capacity after lossless compression for images of smaller sizes. Reversible data hiding method by Celik et al. [1] gives high capacity.

Table 1. Experimental results of the proposed algorithm

no	Image (width×height)	PSNR (dB)	Capacity (byte)
1	CAT (374×452)	44.46	5521
2	Mars moon (683×1000)	41.90	1078
3	Tank (512×512)	37.93	379
4	Man (256×256)	37.49	775
5	Lena (300×300)	37.72	594
6	Lena (512×512)	38.98	1901
7	Airplane (512×512)	39.38	3656
8	Boat (512×512)	40.69	1939
9	Elane (512×512)	42.79	2140
10	Tiffany (512×512)	36.38	5087
11	House (512×512)	37.72	3981
12	Peeper (512×512)	38.70	3218
13	Sailboat (512×512)	36.56	1261
14	Bridge (512×512)	39.80	676
15	Jet (512×512)	44.86	5238
--	Average	39.69	2496

But the fundamental limitation with this method is: images that do not give enough data for losslessly compression, the embedding level becomes larger and the artifacts are too much visible. For example this method does not give enough capacity (at least 128 bits) for images 1, 7, 9, 10, 13 in table 1 while we use compression algorithms like LZW [11], JBIG [21] or arithmetic coding [8] even if we increase the embedding level up to 50. Celik et al. suggest to use CALIC [16] lossless algorithm. But if we increase the embedding level up to 50 for image Tiffany we get only 256 bytes of data. It is impossible to compress such small amount of data to have enough space (at least 16 bytes) for embedding information. Moreover, amount of distortion is at most 50, so artifacts are easily visible. Methods proposed in [5], [12], [13] though offer high capacity, artifacts are visible. These algorithms also offer limited capacities for images of smaller sizes.

Recently, two lossless watermarking algorithms have been proposed [14], [15]. The method in [15] is especially for palette images. In [14] the capacity is limited by the frequency of the most frequent gray-level in the image. We provide some data to compare [14] with our proposed algorithm (Table 2).

Table 2. Comparing capacity and PSNR offered by [14] and the proposed algorithm

no	Image (512×512)	Capacity (byte)		PSNR (dB)	
		[14]	Proposed	[14]	Proposed
1	Airplane	2022	3656	48.3	39.38
2	Lena	683	1901	48.2	38.98
3	Tiffany	1098	5087	48.2	36.38
4	Jet	7498	5238	48.7	44.86
5	Pepper	681	3218	48.2	38.7
6	Sailboat	913	1261	48.2	36.56
7	House	1789	3981	48.3	37.72
-	Average	2098	3478	48.3	38.94

The method in [14] offers a fixed PSNR 48.13 for all images because of its embedding criteria (shifting of histogram). We found that the claimed embedding of 60k bits of data by [14] was not always guaranteed. It was possible for the image Jet, which is a special case due to the flat nature of the image. If we exclude the Jet image, table 2 indicates that [14] offers an average of 9.5k bits of embedding capacity with a average (constant) PSNR 48.23dB, whereas our proposed method gives average embedding capacity 25.5k bits with average PSNR 37.95dB. Including the image Jet the proposed algorithm offers higher average capacity (28k bits) than [14] (17k bits). The average values including the Jet image are shown in Table 2, where the capacities are in bytes. We try to exclude the smooth images (like the image Jet) into account here because they always offer enough embedding capacity.

The lossless compression and encryption of bit-plane(s) by Fridrich et al. [3] offers low capacity for two reasons: (i) since bits at LSB positions are truly random, they do not offer a good compression ratio, and (ii) the amount of data to be compressed is very low; for a 512×512 8-bit image we get only 4kB data if only 1 key bit-plane is selected. The RS-vector method [4] divides pixels into *R, S, U* groups. *U* groups are unusable, however it embeds only 1 bit per group. If each group contains 4 pixels and there is no *U* group at all, a 512×512 8-bit image can embed maximum 8kB data. On the other hand, our proposed method selects 8×8 blocks based on image nature and embeds 256 bits data per block on the average. To have the same capacity like RS-vector method mentioned above we need only 256 blocks on the average out of 4096 blocks for a 512×512 8-bit image.

Hence, the experimental results prove that our proposed algorithm is better, since it gives higher capacity for almost all images and better PSNR compared to other methods proposed so far. The most important aspect of our proposed algorithm is the consideration of the HVS during embedding, and hence the artifacts are completely imperceptible. Thus the proposed algorithm fulfills the requirements (invisible distortions and higher capacity) of lossless watermarking technique and is better than other existing algorithms in the literature.

5 Conclusions

We present here a lossless watermarking technique with a higher embedding capacity. By considering the *Human Visual System* (HVS) we leave no pixel into the watermarked image with a distortion greater than the limit determined by the JND value of that pixel. Hence, there is no visible distortion at all in the watermarked image by our proposed algorithm. The experimental results prove that the proposed algorithm is better than any other algorithm proposed so far in the lossless watermarking literature. Additional security against active attacks can be obtained by encrypting the watermark bit-string with a secret key K before embedding. The proposed method can also be used for color images. It works on both smooth and textured images. It also works on small images as well as large images. The proposed method is simpler, gives higher average capacity with no perceptual distortion. Hence, we believe that the proposed method will be useful lossless watermarking applications concerning medical, astronomical, and military imagery.

References

1. Celik, M.U., Sharma, G., Tekalp, M.A., Saber, E.: Reversible Data Hiding. In Proceedings of International Conference on Image Processing, vol. 2. Rochester, NY, USA (24 Sep 2002) 157 –160
2. Honsinger, C.W., Jones, P.W., Rabbani, M., Stoffel, J.C.: Lossless Recovery of an Original Image Containing Embedded Data. US Patent # 6,278,791 (Aug 2001)
3. Fridrich, J., Goljan, M., Du, R.: Invertible Authentication. In Proc. of SPIE Photonics West, Security and Watermarking of Multimedia Contents III, vol. 3971. San Jose, California, USA (Jan 2001) 197-208
4. Fridrich, J., Goljan, M., Du, R.: Lossless Data Embedding – New Paradigm in Digital Watermarking. Special Issue on Emerging Applications of Multimedia Data Hiding, vol. 2. (Feb 2002) 185–196
5. Tian, J.: Wavelet-based reversible watermarking for authentication. In Proc. Security and Watermarking of Multimedia Contents IV, Electronic Imaging 2002, vol. 4675. (20-25 Jan 2002) 679–690
6. Kankanhalli, M.S., Rajmohan, Ramakrishnan, K.R.: Content-based Watermarking of Images. In Proceedings of 6th ACM International Multimedia Conference. Bristol, UK (Sep1998) 61–70
7. Fridrich, J., Goljan, M., Du, R.: Lossless Data Embedding for all Image Formats. In Proc. SPIE Photonics West, Electronic Imaging, Security and Watermarking of Multimedia Contents, vol. 4675. San Jose, California, USA, (Jan 2002) 572–583

8. Sayood, K.: Introduction to Data Compression. 2nd edn. Morgan Kaufmann (2000) 77-104
9. Goljan, M., Fridrich, J., Du, R.: Distortion-free Data Embedding. In 4th Information Hiding Workshop, LNCS, vol. 2137. Springer-Verlag, New York, USA (2001) 27–41
10. Fridrich, J., Goljan, M., Du, R.: Invertible Authentication Watermark for JPEG Images. In Proc. of Information Technology: Coding and Computing. Las Vegas, Nevada, USA, (2–4 Apr 2001) 223–227
11. Gonzalez, R.C., Woods, R.E.: Digital Image Processing. 2nd edn. Pearson Education International, Prentice Hall (2002) 446–448
12. Vleeschouwer, C.D., Delaigle, J.F., Macq, B.: Circular Interpretation of Histogram for Reversible Watermarking. In IEEE 4th Workshop Multimedia Signal Processing. (2001) 345–350
13. Xuan, G., Chen, J., Zhu, J., Shi, Y.Q., Ni, Z., Su, W.: Lossless Data hiding based on Integer Wavelet Transform. In IEEE International Workshop on Multimedia Signal Processing. Marriott Beach Resort St. Thomas, US Virgin Islands (9-11 Dec 2002)
14. Ni, Z., Shi, Y.Q., Ansari, N., Su, W.: Reversible Data Hiding. In: Proceedings of International Symposium on Circuits and Systems (ISCAS 2003), vol. 2. Bangkok, Thailand (25-28 May 2003) 912–915
15. Hongmei, L., Zhefeng, Z., Jiwu, H., Xialing, H., Shi, Y.Q.: A High Capacity Distortion-free Data Hiding Algorithm for Palette Image. In: Proceedings of International Symposium on Circuits and Systems (ISCAS 2003), vol. 2. Bangkok, Thailand (25-28 May 2003) 916–919
16. WU, X.: Lossless Compression of Continuous-Tone Images via Context Selection, quantization, and modeling. In: IEEE Transactions on Image Processing, vol. 6, no. 5. (May 1997) 656–664
17. Tian, J.: Reversible Watermarking by Difference Expansion. In Proceedings of Workshop on Multimedia and Security, ACM, Juan-les-Pins, France (Dec 2002) 19–22
18. MACQ, B.: Lossless Multiresolution Transform for Image Authenticating Watermarking. In Proceedings of EUSIPCO, Tempere, Finland, (Sep 2000)
19. Vleeschouwer, C.D., Delaigle, J.F., Macq, B.: Circular Interpretation of Bijective Transformations in Lossless Watermarking for Media Asset Management. In IEEE Transaction on Multimedia, (Mar 2003)
20. Bender, W., Gruhl, D., Morimoto, N., LU, A.: Techniques for Data Hiding. In IBM Systems Journal, vol. 35, no. 3-4. (1996) 313–336
21. Sayood, K.: Introduction to Data Compression. 2nd edn. Morgan Kaufmann (2000) 106–114

Data-Hiding Capacity Improvement for Text Watermarking Using Space Coding Method

Hyon-Gon Choo and Whoi-Yul Kim

Division of Electrical and Computer Engineering, Hanyang University, Seoul, Korea
gon@vision.hanyang.ac.kr, wykim@hanyang.ac.kr
http://vision.hanyang.ac.kr

Abstract. Text watermarking using text lines has a limited capacity problem in hiding data. In this paper, a method to increase the data-hiding capacity of text watermarking using Space coding is proposed. Using the orthogonal property between different sine waves, two or more messages can be embedded at once. Experimental results show that the proposed method keeps the detection rate of the original method the same while increasing the data capacity

1 Introduction

The improvement of printing and scanning technology requires complementary methods to protect against the forgery of text documents. Text watermarking is a method to embed invisible information in the text for various applications: to prevent illegal modification of the text, to protect copyright, etc. Due to the binary nature of text documents, however, text watermarking is more difficult than applying watermarking to other applications such as audio, video or image formats.

A few different approaches have been proposed for text watermarking. Brassil et al. proposed *Line-shift coding* and *Word-shift coding* [1-5]. In Line-shift coding the location information of text lines is used for encryption, whereas in Word-shift coding the location information of words in the text lines is used. These two methods, however, require the original text to detect the watermark and require reference information such as control lines and control blocks. For these reasons, several feature-based text watermarking methods have been proposed utilizing certain text features such as font, line width and pixel size [1], [4], [6], [7]. These methods are sensitive to noise and limited to applications where no size variations are allowed, however.

To overcome these limitations, Huang and Yan proposed a watermarking method using the interword space variation, called *Space coding* [8]. In the method, the average space between words within a text line is modified based on the information represented in a form of the sine wave to embed. Since the average spaces are modified to have the characteristics of a sine wave, information can be embedded invisibly and the embedded information can be detected without the original text image. However, the data hiding capacity is still limited and at least three lines are required to embed even a simple message.

T. Kalker et al. (Eds.): IWDW 2003, LNCS 2939, pp. 593–599, 2004.
© Springer-Verlag Berlin Heidelberg 2004

In this paper, we present a method to deal with the limited capacity problem of the Space coding method. A mixed sequence with two sine waves of different frequency is embedded into the lines of text to generate the modified space. The orthogonality of sine sequences guarantees their detection, which is the basis for the increase in data-hiding capacity.

In Section II, the Space coding method is briefly reviewed. In Section III, we explain how to increase the data capacity in Space coding. In Section IV, an analysis of the proposed method is provided with the results from the experiment. In the last section, we conclude this paper.

2 Space Coding

Space coding is a text watermarking method that modifies interword spaces in text lines so that the average values of interword spaces along each line have the periodic characteristics of a sine wave [8]. To analyze the advantages and disadvantages of Space coding, it is necessary to review Huang's Space coding procedure.

2.1 Embedding Procedure

To embed the watermark using Space coding, the average interword space is calculated first. To get the average space between words, the words and lines are segmented from a binary text image using vertical and horizontal projection profiles. From the profiles, the space information between words is also obtained. From the space information, the average interword space of each line is then calculated. For a line that contains d words, the average interword space is as follows:

$$S_a = \frac{S_t}{d-1} \quad ,d \neq 1 \tag{1}$$

where S_t is the total interword space in the line.

Next, we calculate the watermark components for text lines. To determine the intensity of a watermark, the group mean of the average interword spaces is obtained. For the group mean, only text lines that have words of more than a key value are selected for a group, which we call workspace in this paper. Then, the group mean of the average interword spaces in the workspace is calculated as follows:

$$a = \frac{\sum_{n}^{N} S_a(n)}{N} \quad ,N > 1 \tag{2}$$

where S_a (n) is the average interword space of the nth line, and N is the number of lines in a workspace.

Then, for each line, a watermark component is determined as follows:

$$W(n) = Ca\sin(\omega(n-\phi)), \ \mathrm{C:constant} \tag{3}$$

where *W(n)* is the modifying watermark component for the nth line, ω is the radian frequency of a sine wave, and ϕ is a lag to indicate the phase angle. ω and ϕ are provided by user: ω acts as the key and ϕ for the message.

Next, using *W(n)*, a new average space between words is calculated. Depending on the type of detection, blind or non-blind, the new space is determined as follows:

$$S'_a(n) = \begin{cases} S_a(n) + W(n), & nonblind \\ a + W(n) \quad , & blind \end{cases} \tag{4}$$

Finally, the word length in the text is modified according to the new average space. For each word, the difference becomes proportional to its length. That is, a longer word has a larger change. This makes the modification of word length in a line imperceptible.

In order for the text line not to be affected by the change of word length, the modification of word length at both ends of a line will be limited, i.e., the total length of a line will not be affected. In our implementation, we treated words at both ends of a line as connected to form a ring. Then, the total space of the connected word is modified, and the connected word is divided into two words at both ends. Thus, the total line length is not changed by the changes of word length.

2.2 Detection Procedure

To detect the embedded watermark, the watermark component *W(n)* can be obtained by calculating S_a. In non-blind mode, *W(n)* is simply obtained by the difference of the average space between the original and the watermarked image. In blind mode, *W(n)* can be obtained by the difference between the average space S_a and the mean of average space of the workspace. Next, the cross-correlation between *W(n)* and a the detecting sine wave is calculated to detect the marked phase information:

$$r(j) = \frac{1}{T}\sum_{n}^{T-1} W(n)\sin(\omega_d(n-j)) \tag{5}$$

where T is the total number of lines in a workspace, ω_d is the frequency of the detecting sine wave and j is the lag of the sine wave. The original phase information can be estimated from j when $r(j)$ has the maximum correlation value.

3 Multiple Message Encoding

In Space coding, the characteristics of space in a text document are expressed as a random variable by the average space, and the watermark component is added to the random variable. Therefore, the watermark is embedded in a vertical direction or between lines and each variation in a line is spread to the horizontal direction, which makes it robust against interference. However, the capacity of the information to hide using Huang's method is very low. To embed the message of a bit in a sine-waved form, at least 3 lines are required.

To overcome this limited capacity of Space coding, we use its characteristics of sine-formed watermark component.

3.1 Orthogonal Property of Sinusoidal Waves

Using the orthogonal property of the sinusoidal wave, various messages can be embedded using Space coding. For example, a signal generated by the addition of two sine waves with different frequencies can be represented as follows:

$$f(x) = a_1 \sin(m_1 x) + a_2 \sin(m_2 x) \tag{6}$$

Two sine waves of different frequencies are orthogonal to each other.

$$\frac{2}{T}\int_T \sin(m_1 x)\sin(m_2 x)dx = \begin{cases} 1 & m_1 = m_2 \\ 0 & otherwise \end{cases} \tag{7}$$

From (7), we can get a sine component from $f(x)$ as follows:

$$\frac{2}{T}\int_T f(x)\sin(m_1 x)dx = a_1 \tag{8}$$

Another component can be extracted in a similar manner.

This is a basis for a Fourier analysis and is used for communication as FM. In this paper, we apply this concept to increase the data capacity of Space coding.

3.2 Multiple Messages Embedding and Detecting in Space Coding

The proposed method to increase data capacity is explained in Fig 1. From two different messages, two sine sequences with different frequencies are generated. Next, the two sequences are added onto one composite sequence:

$$W(n) = a \times (C_1 \sin(\omega_1 (n - \phi_1)) + C_2 \sin(\omega_2 (n - \phi_2))) \tag{9}$$

where a is the group mean of the average line spaces, ω is the radian frequency of a sine wave, ϕ is a lag to indicate the phase angle and C is a constant. Each lag is determined by each message, and the radian frequency is determined by the user's key number or by the size of the workspace. Then, the words in the workspace are modified according to the sequence, $W(n)$.

In the detection procedure, the extraction of the watermark component $W(n)$ is the same as Space coding method. We can get both messages by repeating (5).

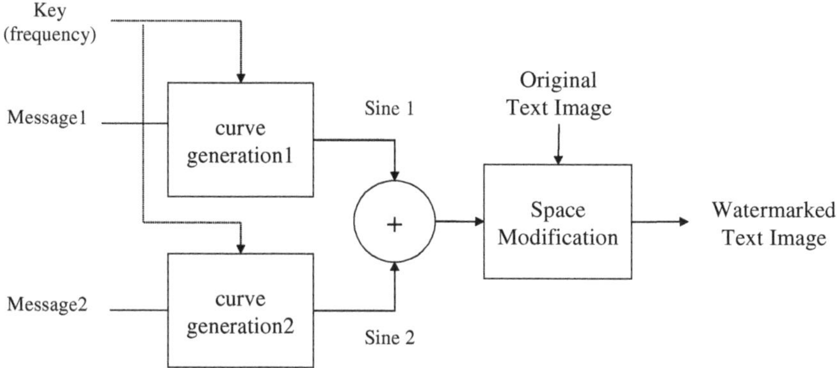

Fig. 1. Multiple messages embedding in Space coding

Although the data capacity increases using our method, the detection rate may decrease. To make up for the lower detection rate in our implementation, the frequency of a sine wave is selected as twice that of the other one, and the amplitude C in (9), is chosen as half of the other. That is, C_1 is twice C_2 while ω_1 is a half of ω_2. As a result, the period of the composite sequence remains the same as that of a sine wave and the maximum amplitude of the composite sequence does not exceed one and half times the bigger amplitude. In the detection stage, we first calculate C_1 and ω_1 using (5). Then, we reconstruct a sine wave sequence using C_1 and ω_1, and subtract the sine sequence from $W(n)$ as follows

$$W'(n) = W(n) - C_1 a \sin(\omega_1 (n - \phi_1)) \tag{10}$$

Next, for the remaining component $W'(n)$, we divide it into two parts. If the period of $W'(n)$ is N, the size of each part becomes $N/2$. Then two parts are added to make a new sequence. Finally using the correlation of (5), we can retrieve the remaining message.

In terms of data capacity, three or more different messages can be embedded at once. However, since less change is desired in terms of the invisibility of watermarking, only two different sine waves were used in our implementation.

4 Experimental Results

To show the efficiency of our method, we compared the detection rate and data capacity with Huang's Space coding method. Twenty images of text were tested: ten images were captured from "pdf" documents and the other images were scanned using an UMAX scanner (UMAX S-12) at 300 dpi. Images acquired from scanner were corrected to have no rotational distortions. Only blind detection in Huang's and our method was compared and the key frequency was assumed to be known to the detector. In the experiment, the larger period of sine wave was set to 8 while the smaller one to 4.

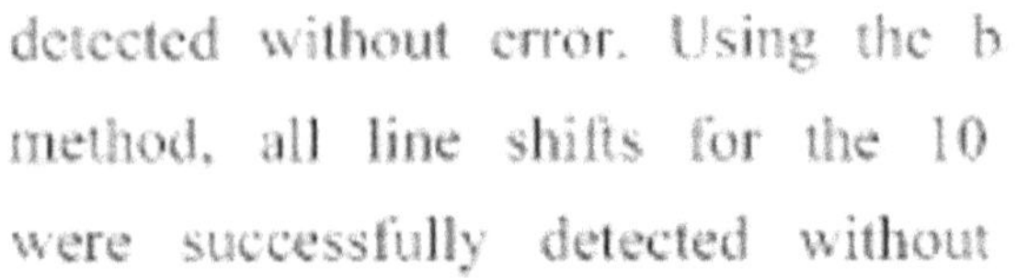

detected without error. Using the b
method, all line shifts for the 10
were successfully detected without

(a)

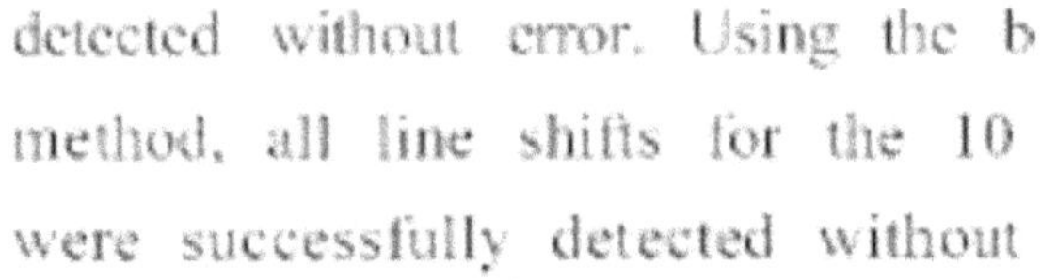

detected without error. Using the b
method, all line shifts for the 10
were successfully detected without

(b)

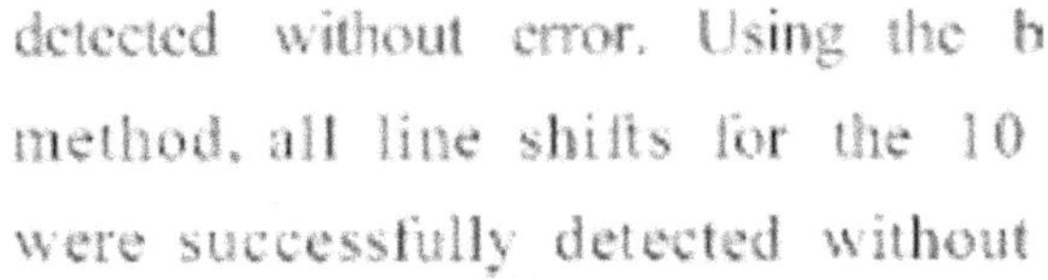

detected without error. Using the b
method, all line shifts for the 10
were successfully detected without

(c)

Fig. 2. Results of watermarking. (a) Original image, (b) Result image using Huang's method and (c) Result image using the proposed method.

Fig. 2 shows examples of the watermarking results by Huang's and the proposed method. The results for detection rate and data capacity are summarized in Table 1.

Table 1 shows that the data capacity of Space coding is increased by the proposed method while the detection rate remains the same. For a workspace in a text, when the workspace has 8 lines, 2 bit or 67% more than Huang's method can be embedded.

Table 2 shows the robustness of Space coding in coping and scanning experiments. Twenty text images printed by a laser printer at 600 dpi were scanned at 300 dpi. Results in Table 2 shows that both methods can be used in printing and scanning, common processes with text documents.

Table 1. Comparison of detection rate and data capacity

	Detection rate	Data capacity in a period
Huang's method	100 %	3 bits
Proposed method	100 %	5 bits

Table 2. Comparison of detection rate and data capacity in coping and scanning experiments

Detection rate	Print and Scan	1st Copy and Scan
Huang's method	100 %	100 %
Proposed method	100 %	100 %

5 Conclusions

Space coding is a text watermarking method embedding watermark information by modifying the average inter-word spaces in text lines. Embedding is performed on both horizontal and vertical directions to be robust against interference. However, it has the drawback of limited data capacity. In this paper, a method to overcome the capacity limitation problem has been considered. Instead of a sine wave, a combined wave mixed with sine waves of different frequencies is utilized to carry two different messages at once. Experimental results have shown that the proposed method keeps the detection rate of the original method the same while increasing the data capacity.

The proposed method can be applied to other watermarking methods. As long as the message can be converted to a form with orthogonal properties, our method can be effective for video, audio, and image watermarking. In addition, the proposed method can be utilized to allow different levels of right to access using different keys. For example, one key and message are used to examine the existence of watermarking while the other key and message are used to validate the integrity of the watermark.

References

1. J. Brassil, S. Low, N. Maxemchuk, and L. O'Gorman, "Electronicmarking and identification techniques to discourage document copying," *IEEE J. Select. Areas Commun.*, vol. 13, pp. 1495–1504, Oct. 1995.
2. J. Brassil, S. Low, N. Maxemchuk, L. O'Gorman, "Hiding Information in Document Images, " *Proceedings of the 29th Annual Conference on Information Sciences and Systems*, Johns Hopkins University, March 1995 Page(s): 482–489.
3. A. Choudhury, N. Maxemchuk, S. Paul, and H. Schulzrinne, "Electronic Document Distribution," *IEEE Network*, Volume: 9 Issue: 3, May-June 1995 pp. 12–20.
4. S. Low and N. Maxemchuk, "Performance Comparison of Two Text Marking Methods," *IEEE J. Select Areas Commun.*, vol. 16, pp. 561–572, May, 1998.
5. S. Low, N. Maxemchuk and A. Lapone, "Document identification for copyright protection using centroid detection," *IEEE Trans. Communications*, vol. 46, pp. 372–383, Mar. 1998.
6. M. Wu, E. Tang and B. Liu, "Data Hiding in Digital Binary Image," *IEEE Inter. Conf. on Multimedia & Expo (ICME'00)*, New York City, 2000.
7. A. Bhattacharjya and H. Ancin, "Data embedding in text for a copier system," *Proceedings of ICIP*, Vol. 2, pp. 245–249, 1999.
8. D. Huang and H. Yan, "Interword distance changes represented by sine waves for watermarking text images," *IEEE Trans. Circuits and Systems for Video Technology*, vol. 11, no. 12, pp. 1237–1245, Dec. 2001.
9. M. Kutter, "Performance Improvement of Spread Spectrum Based Image Watermarking Schemes Through M-ary Modulation," in Andreas Pfitzmann (Ed.), *Proc. of Information Hiding'99*, Vol. LNCS 1768, pp. 237–252,September 1999.
10. A. Oppenheim, *Discrete-Time Signal Processing*, Prentice Hall, 1989.
11. I. Cox, M.Miller and J. Bloom, *Digital Watermarking*, Morgan Kaufmann Press, 2001.
12. R. Gonzalez and R. Woods, *Digital Image Processing*, 2nd, Prentice Hall, 2001.

Author Index

GPSR Compliance
The European Union's (EU) General Product Safety Regulation (GPSR) is a set of rules that requires consumer products to be safe and our obligations to ensure this.

If you have any concerns about our products, you can contact us on

ProductSafety@springernature.com

In case Publisher is established outside the EU, the EU authorized representative is:

Springer Nature Customer Service Center GmbH
Europaplatz 3
69115 Heidelberg, Germany

www.ingramcontent.com/pod-product-compliance
Ingram Content Group UK Ltd.
Pitfield, Milton Keynes, MK11 3LW, UK
UKHW021902190726
13853UKWH00003B/1381

* 9 7 8 3 6 6 2 1 8 1 3 8 6 *